Student Assessment and Learning Guide

for use with

Understanding Business

Eighth Edition

William G. Nickels
University of Maryland

James M. McHugh
St. Louis Community College at Forest Park

Susan M. McHugh
Applied Learning Systems

Prepared by
Barbara Barrett
St. Louis Community College-Meramec

Boston   Burr Ridge, IL   Dubuque, IA   Madison, WI   New York   San Francisco   St. Louis
Bangkok   Bogotá   Caracas   Kuala Lumpur   Lisbon   London   Madrid   Mexico City
Milan   Montreal   New Delhi   Santiago   Seoul   Singapore   Sydney   Taipei   Toronto

Student Assessment and Learning Guide for use with
UNDERSTANDING BUSINESS
William G. Nickels, James M. McHugh, Susan M. McHugh

Published by McGraw-Hill/Irwin, an imprint of The McGraw-Hill Companies, Inc., 1221 Avenue of the Americas, New York, NY 10020. Copyright © 2008 by The McGraw-Hill Companies, Inc. All rights reserved.

1 2 3 4 5 6 7 8 9 0 QPD/QPD 0 9 8 7 6

ISBN 978-0-07-310604-5
MHID 0-07-310604-6

www.mhhe.com

TO OUR STUDENTS

This study guide is designed to give you, the Introduction to Business student, every advantage in mastering the concepts presented in *Understanding Business,* eighth edition, by Bill Nickels, Jim McHugh and Susan McHugh.

Using this study guide will give you an edge; you will go beyond just memorizing terms, to developing and using the critical thinking and creative problem solving skills that are so important in today's dynamic business environment.

Using The Study Guide

There are many different ways to learn, so I can only make suggestions about how to use this guide more effectively. You may find a different way, which suits you better.

First, this study guide is not designed to replace reading the text! In fact, reading the text is an integral part of using this study guide. You can use the guide to help point out places where you need more work, or need to review. The guide is very detailed, and requires you not only to remember facts, but also to apply concepts in a way that will help you to develop a better understanding of today's business environment.

You will find that there is a lot of writing in completing these exercises. Writing the answers to the questions, rather than just choosing a number or matching a term with a letter, will help to reinforce the material. You will also be better prepared to answer essay or short answer questions when you have studied by writing out answers in your own words.

Finally, to make effective use of this study guide, I suggest that you:

- Read the text before each class period, and outline important concepts. You will probably have a syllabus that outlines the reading assignments for each class.
- Attend class and take good, detailed notes. Ask questions in class; get involved!
- Do the exercises in the study guide *after* you have completed the first two steps. . I would suggest that you do the exercises in stages, and not try to do the whole chapter at one sitting. For example, if there are 6 learning goals, do the exercises pertaining to the first three learning goals on one day, and then complete the remaining exercises the next day. Or, do the factual based exercises one day, the critical thinking exercises the next, and so on.
- Do *all* the exercises in the guide, not just the ones that take less time!
- Review your answers, and mark the questions you had problems answering. Then, reread the section of the text that deals with those areas.
- Before a test, review your class notes, the text and the study guide material.
- Remember, your instructor may add material in class that is not in the text, and the study guide won't cover that material. That takes us back to the first suggestions: read the book before class, attend every class, take notes, and get involved!

Design Of This Study Guide

Each chapter in this guide contains the following sections to help you be successful in this Introduction to Business course.

- *Learning goals:* Each learning goal is listed in the order in which it appears in the text. This is to help you focus on what is important throughout the chapter. The appropriate learning goal for each exercise is also noted in the side margin as you go through the chapter.

- *Learning the Language:* This section identifies the key terms and definitions from the chapter. This is a matching section, in which you read the definition then choose the appropriate term. Many of the definitions will be direct quotes from the chapter, or a slight variation.

- *Assessment Check:* These exercises help you to learn the facts of the material from the text. You will be writing answers to factually based questions from the chapter, organized by learning goals. This section is designed to develop your knowledge of the text material. I suggest you keep the book nearby while doing these exercises, but do as much as you can without opening the book. This will help you to determine the areas where you need to review.

- *Critical Thinking Exercises:* Business people need a variety of skills. Among the most important skills you can bring to a job is the ability to think for yourself, analyze problems, develop solutions based upon your analysis, and present the solutions in written form. There are many opportunities to hone these skills with this text. In this section of the study guide, the questions will require you to think and apply the material from the chapter to come up with a solution to the situation presented. These application questions are designed to provide you with the opportunity to enhance your decision-making skills and understanding of the material. In some cases, there are no definitive answers, only suggested answers.

- *Practice Test:* In all likelihood, you will be required to take some objective exams. The practice test is divided into two sections, multiple choice, and true false. Keep in mind this is only a sample of the types of questions you could see on an exam, and these are not the actual questions you will see on a classroom test! The practice exam will give you the chance to find out what areas of the chapters you need to take some extra time with before your classroom exam.

- *You Can Find It On The Net:* Business research is an integral part of being a successful businessperson. These Internet exercises provide an opportunity to practice your research skills on the Internet. The web addresses listed are only an entry to the information available; there is so much to explore on the Internet! Use your imagination to see where you can "travel"! The web sites were valid at the time of this writing. Please understand that the Internet changes daily, and not all the web sites may be available when you are completing the exercise.

- *Answers:* The answers to all the Retention Check, Critical Thinking Exercises and Practice Tests are at the end of each chapter.

There is no substitute for just plain hard work. To be successful in tomorrow's work world, you will need to work hard today to develop the skills employers are looking for. The text, *Understanding Business,* and this study guide are designed to help you to be successful by starting you on the road to developing those skills. The rest is up to you. Good Luck!

Acknowledgments

Many thanks are due, and I will be brief. First, thanks to Bill Nickels, Susan McHugh and Jim McHugh, and to McGraw-Hill/Irwin for allowing me to continue my involvement with this wonderful text. To Ryan and Chad, thank you for your support, understanding, and computer consultation! And to all my colleagues at the Meramec campus of St. Louis Community College, thanks for your support and encouragement.

Barbara Barrett

CONTENTS

CHAPTER 1 – MANAGING WITHIN THE DYNAMIC BUSINESS ENVIRONMENT: TAKING RISKS AND MAKING PROFITS

LEARNING GOALS

After you have read and studied this chapter, you should be able to:

1. Describe the relationship of businesses' profit to risk assumption and discuss how businesses and nonprofit organizations add to the standard of living and quality of life for all.
2. Explain the importance of entrepreneurship to the wealth of an economy.
3. Examine how the economic environment and taxes affect businesses.
4. Illustrate how the technological environment has affected businesses.
5. Identify various ways that businesses can meet and beat competition.
6. Demonstrate how the social environment has changed and tell what the reaction of the business community has been.
7. Analyze what businesses must do to meet the global challenge, which includes war terrorism.
8. Review how trends from the past are being repeated in the present and what such trends will mean for tomorrow's college graduate.

LEARNING THE LANGUAGE

Listed below are important terms found in the chapter. Choose the correct term for each definition and write it in the space provided.

Business	Goods	Revenue
Business environment	Identity theft	Risk
Database	Loss	Services
Demography	Nonprofit organization	Stakeholders
E-commerce	Outsourcing	Standard of living
Empowerment	Productivity	Technology
Entrepreneur	Profit	
Factors of production	Quality of life	

1. The resources businesses use to create wealth are called _factors of production_ and include land, labor, capital, entrepreneurship and knowledge.

2. Buying and selling products and services over the Internet is known as _e-commerce_.

3. _Quality of life_ refers to the general well-being of a society in terms of freedom, a clean natural environment, education, health care, safety, free time, and everything else that leads to satisfaction and joy.

4. An _entrepreneur_ is the person who risks time and money to start and manage a business.

5. Products that are intangible, such as education, heath care, insurance, recreation and travel and tourism are known as _services_.

6. A _business_ is any activity which seeks to provide goods and services to others while operating at a profit.

7. When a business's expenses are more than its revenues a _loss_ has occurred.

8. Entrepreneurs take a _risk_ when they take the chance that they will lose time and money on a business that may not prove to be profitable.

9. A society's _standard of living_ is the amount of goods and services people can buy with the money they have.

10. A _nonprofit organization_ is an organization whose goals do not include making a personal profit for its owners or organizers.

11. An electronic storage file where information is kept is known a(n) _database_ and can be used to store vast amounts of information about consumers.

12. When we study _demography_ we are looking at a statistical study of the human population with regard to its size, density and other characteristics such as age, race, gender and income.

13. Known as _empowerment_ this means giving frontline workers the responsibility, authority, and freedom to respond quickly to customer requests.

14. Computers, food, clothing, cars, and appliances are tangible products known as _goods_.

15. _Profit_ is the amount of money a business earns above and beyond what it spends for salaries and other expenses.

16. A business's _stakeholders_ are all the people who stand to gain or lose by its policies and activities.

17. The total amount of money a business takes in during a given period by selling goods and services is called _revenue_.

18. _Technology_ is considered to be everything that makes business processes more efficient and productive, such as phones, copiers, computers, medical imaging devices, personal digital assistants and various software programs.

19. The surrounding factors of the _business environ._ either help or hinder the development of businesses.

20. The amount of output you generate given the amount of input such as hours worked is called _productivity_.

21. Assigning various functions, such as accounting, production, security, maintenance, and legal work to outside organizations is known as _outsourcing_.

22. _Identity theft_ is obtaining private information about a person, such as Social Security number and credit card numbers, and using that information for illegal purposes.

ASSESSMENT CHECK

Learning goal 1
Business and Entrepreneurship: Revenues Profits and Losses

1.   What are two things businesses provide for entrepreneurs and for people in general?

   a.   _____

   b.   _____

2.   Describe the difference between revenue and profit.

3.   When does a company experience a loss? Over time, what will likely result from business losses?

4.   What is the relationship between risk and profit?

5.   How do the federal government and local communities use the taxes that are paid by employees and businesses?

6.   Why might the same product, such as a container of milk or a bottle of beer, cost more in one country than in another?

7.   Describe the challenges businesses of the 21st century will face with regard to stakeholders and profitability.

8.   What is "insourcing" and what are the benefits?

9.   How do nonprofits use financial gains?

Entrepreneurship Versus Working for Others

10.   What are two ways to succeed in business, according to the text? What are the advantages of each way?

11.   How have individuals from other countries, members of minority groups, and women business owners in the United States participated in entrepreneurship?

12.   List the 5 factors of production.

      a. _____   d. _____

      b. _____   e. _____

      c. _____

13.   What combination of the factors of production distinguishes rich countries from poor countries?

Learning Goal 3
The Business Environment

14.   What are the 5 elements in the business environment?

      a. _____   d. _____

      b. _____   e. _____

      c. _____

15.   What are the results of a healthy business environment? What are the results of poor business environmental conditions?

The Economic and Legal Environment

16.   What are six ways governments can reduce the risk of starting businesses and thus increase entrepreneurship?

   a. _____

   b. _____

   c. _____

   d. _____

   e. _____

   f. _____

Learning goal 4
The Technological Environment

17.   Describe the difference between "effectiveness" and "efficiency".

18.   What are the two major types of e-commerce?

   a. _____

   b. _____

19.   How do businesses make use of bar codes?

20.   Once the information from the bar code is in a database, how do companies use the information?

Learning Goal 5
The Competitive Environment

21.   What must companies offer in order to stay competitive in today's world markets?

22.   What is meant by the phrase: "Competing by Exceeding Customer Expectations"?

23.   Describe the concept of Competing by Restructuring and Empowerment.

Learning Goal 6
The Social Environment

24.   What are four general ways in which the social environment is changing?

a. _____

b. _____

c. _____

d. _____

25.   How has the meaning of diversity changed?

26.   How have companies and local governments responded to a more diverse customer base?

27.   What kinds of business opportunities are presented by the increase in the number of older Americans?

28.   What will be the impact of an increasing population of older Americans on Social Security and what are the options for fixing the problem?

29.   There has been dramatic growth in the number of two income families and of single parent families in the United States. These families have different needs than workers of the past. What kinds of programs have companies implemented to respond to those needs?

Learning Goal 7
The Global Environment

30. Two important global environmental changes have been:

    a. _____

    b. _____

31. Improvements in what two areas have lead to more trade?

    a. _____

    b. _____

32. Describe the effects of war and terrorism on business.

33. How will these global changes affect you?

Learning Goal 8
The Evolution of American Business

34. How has the agricultural industry and farm employment changed in the last century?

35. What has been the consequence of increased productivity in the manufacturing sector regarding jobs? Where have workers found jobs as a result?

36. How important is the services industry to our economy and to job creation?

CRITICAL THINKING EXERCISES

Learning Goal 1

1.   Monika lives in Germany, works for the Mercedes plant in her hometown and makes the equivalent of $55/hour American. Her cousin Joe lives in the United States and works for the Chrysler plant in his hometown. When Monika visits Joe she is amazed at how big his house is compared to where she lives, his sound system and how well he seems to live. "Boy" says Monika, "I sure can't live like this at home. Why not?"

Learning Goals 1, 2

2.   Revelle Industries is a small company located in an area of the country where unemployment has been very high for the last 5 years. In 2005, Revelle was struggling. There were only 20 employees, and profits were low. With new management things began to turn around, and now Revelle employs almost 75 people. This year they sold 120,000 units of their only product line, a component part used in the manufacture of automobiles. The price of their product is $20/unit. The cost of salaries, expenses and other items was $2,050,000. Sales forecasts look good for the next several years, as Revelle has customer's world wide and will be expanding their product line in the next 18 months.

a.   What are Revelle's revenues?

b.   What are Revelle's profits?

c.   How has the company generated wealth and created a higher standard of living?

Learning Goal 3

3.   Eastern Europe experienced dramatic changes during the 1990's, with changes in both government and economic policies. The newly formed countries have struggled for the last decade with questions about how to be successful in the 21st century. What will be the key to developing the economies of these countries?

Learning Goal 4

4. Schnucks is a large grocery retailer located in the St. Louis, Missouri area. The company is expanding, and continually improving the technology in their stores. How can a database help Schnucks better serve its customers? How do you think a grocery store such as Schnucks will compete in the area of e-commerce?

Learning Goal 5

5. Consider your college or university, or, if you are employed, consider the company for which you work:

    a. Who are its competitors?

    b. How does the organization meet and (hopefully) exceed their customers' expectations?

    c. Who are the organization's stakeholders? Does it meet the needs of the stakeholders? Why or why not?

    d. How has the organization restructured to empower its workers?

Learning Goals 4,5,6,7

6. Consider a company with which you are familiar. For example, evaluate the company where you or someone in your family is currently employed.

    a. How are various technologies implemented in the business? Does the company sell their products on a website? Evaluate the website. Is it customer friendly?

    b. What kinds of programs has the company implemented to meet the needs of two career families and other employees?

    c. Does the company appear to be competing in the manner described by your text, by meeting the needs of its employees and its customers?

    d. How diverse is the company's workforce?

    e. How important is the global marketplace to this business?

7.   How do the changes and programs companies have implemented to meet the needs of two career families and single parent families help these companies to be more competitive?

Learning Goal 7

8.   How can increased global competition benefit the United States and U.S. workers?

Learning Goal 8

9.   How are the changes we are experiencing in manufacturing and services similar to the changes in the farming industry we saw in previous centuries?

PRACTICE TEST

MULTIPLE CHOICE - Circle the best answer.

Learning Goal 1

1.   A loss occurs when a company
   a.   has revenues greater than expenses.
   b.   hires too many new workers.
   c.   has expenses greater than revenues.
   d.   has taken a risk.

2.   In general, the _____ the risk, the _____ the profit.
   a.   higher/higher
   b.   lower/higher
   c.   higher/lower
   d.   faster/quicker

3.   Taxes would not be used to support which of the following activities?
   a.   Build a new school
   b.   Support people in need
   c.   Keep a clean environment
   d.   Help run a privately owned day care center

4.   A clean environment, safety, free time and health care are elements which contribute to our:
   a.   standard of living.
   b.   quality of life.
   c.   economic environment.
   d.   factors of production.

5.   A list of stakeholders of an organization would include:
   a.   customers.
   b.   employees.
   c.   stockholders.
   d.   all of the above are stakeholders.

6. Insourcing is:
   a.   contracting with other companies to do some or all of the functions of a firm.
   b.   keeping all essential functions within the firm.
   c.   when a foreign company sets up design and production facilities in the United States.
   d.   providing in-house consulting services for employees.

Learning Goal 2
7.   The number of businesses owned by immigrants, minority groups, and women has _____ in recent years.
   a.   declined
   b.   stabilized
   c.   grown
   d.   been dramatically reduced

8.   Which of the following is (are) not considered a factor of production?
   a.   Information
   b.   Capital
   c.   Labor
   d.   Taxes

9.   The two factors of production that contribute most to making countries rich are:
   a.   land and labor.
   b.   capital and land.
   c.   entrepreneurship and use of knowledge.
   d.   use of knowledge and taxes.

Learning Goal 3
10.   In today's environment, businesses have found they must do all but which of the following in order to remain competitive?
   a.   Meet the needs of all stakeholders of the business.
   b.   Meet the needs of employees by supervising them more closely.
   c.   Serve customers by exceeding their expectations.
   d.   Provide good quality products at reasonable prices as quickly as possible.

11.   To foster entrepreneurial growth governments must
   a.   pass laws that enable business people to write contracts that are enforceable in court.
   b.   establish a high tax rate to support loans for small businesses.
   c.   take over ownership of small businesses when they are first getting started.
   d.   reduce the value of their currency to encourage foreign investment.

12.   One of the most serious negative results of the increased use of databases by companies has been:
    a. an decrease in the amount of "junk mail" received by consumers.
    b. an increase in identity theft.
    c. increased failure rates by Internet companies.
    d. changes in the organizational structures of companies leading to loss of jobs.

13.   Efficiency means
    a. producing items using the least amount of resources.
    b. the amount of output you generate in a given amount of time.
    c. using high tech equipment to do a job.
    d. producing as much as you can as fast as you can, regardless of cost.

Learning Goal 5

14.   What must companies do to be competitive in today's market?
    a. offer high quality products and outstanding service at competitive prices.
    b. create innovative and high quality marketing programs.
    c. create alliances with competitors.
    d. focus on those activities that will create the most profit.

Learning Goal 6

15.   The trend toward two-income families has led to:
    a. businesses paying lower wages and hiring fewer workers.
    b. policies allowing only one family member to work for the same company.
    c. programs such as flexible work schedules, pregnancy benefits, and elder care programs.
    d. fewer opportunities in the area of human resource management.

16.   Increased diversity of the population of the United States has
    a. led to companies with more diverse workforces.
    b. much narrower definition of the meaning of diversity.
    c. fewer conflicts between groups at work as they learn to work with one another.
    d. fewer diversity management programs as companies don't see the need to recruit minorities.

Learning Goal 7

17.   Among the changes resulting from increased global trade are:
    a. less need for efficient distribution systems.
    b. less global competition as companies set up manufacturing systems in foreign countries.
    c. less need for employees to update skills as workers conform to U.S. standards.
    d. improved living standards around the world.

18.   The impact of war and terrorism on U.S. business is that:
    a. fewer jobs will be created in the United States.
    b. companies have grown more slowly as money has been diverted to the war effort in Iraq.
    c. there is less global trade.
    d. lower organizational costs for security personnel and equipment as firms are depending upon the government to provide those items.

Learning Goal 8

19.   Since the mid-1980s, the _____ has generated most of the increases in employment in the United States.
        a.   manufacturing sector
        b.   agricultural sector
        c.   service sector
        d.   goods producing sector

20.   The making of steel and machine tools are a part of the _____ .
        a.   goods producing sector.
        b.   services sector.
        c.   agricultural sector.
        d.   intangible services sector.

TRUE-FALSE

Learning Goal 1

1. _____   An entrepreneur is an individual who has worked for a nonprofit organization for their entire career.

2. _____   As a potential business owner, you may want to invest your money in a company with a lot of risk, in order to earn a lot of money quickly.

3. _____   Profit refers to the difference between revenue and cost.

4. _____   Mariko, who lives in Tokyo, makes the equivalent of approximately $35,000 per year, while Donada, living in the United States makes only $25,000. From this you can assume Mariko has a higher standard of living than Donada.

5. _____   Business skills are useful and necessary in non-profit institutions.

Learning Goal 2

6. _____   In analyzing factors of production that make a country "rich" it has been observed that some relatively poor countries often have plenty of land and natural resources.

7. _____   Workers in high tech industries are sometimes called knowledge workers.

Learning Goal 3

8. _____   Governments can reduce the risk of starting businesses and increasing entrepreneurship by keeping taxes and regulations to a minimum.

9. _____   Corrupt and illegal activities in one company rarely have an effect on other companies.

Learning Goal 4

10. _____   Few technological changes have had a greater impact on business than the emergence of information technology, such as computers, modems and cell phones.

11. _____   Most new Internet companies have succeeded since e-commerce has become so important to our economy.

Learning Goal 5

12. _____   Successful organizations must listen to the needs of consumers and adjust products, policies and practices to meet customer needs.

13. _____   One of the ways a company can compete is to empower frontline workers.

Learning Goal 6

14. _____   The Bureau of the Census predicts that the U.S. population will remain essentially the same throughout the next century, in terms of diversity.

15. _____   Social Security has become a major issue as older Americans drain the system.

Learning Goal 7

16. _____   Improvements in transportation and in communication have led to more global trade.

17. _____   Threats of war and terrorism have had little impact on businesses either in the U.S. or anywhere in the world.

Learning Goal 8

18. _____   When workers in the industrial sector were laid off, many of them went back to work in the agricultural sector.

You Can Find It On The Net

This is an additional exercise for your own exploration and information. The answers for this section aren't provided.

The purpose of this exercise is to gather data regarding trends in occupations and in the population and the social environment and to analyze how these changes affect Americans and American businesses. To answer these questions, begin with the Census Bureau homepage on the Internet at www.census.gov

Select the population Clock from the Census bureau's homepage. Record the time and population of the United States. Try to find the population of the world. What proportion of the world's population is represented by the United States?

What is the fastest growing occupation? What could contribute to the increase in this profession? The Bureau of Labor Statistics is a good place to search for occupational growth stats.

What is the population of your home state? What percentages of the population of your home state are from minority groups?

What are the average salaries for individuals with high school degrees, college degrees, master's degrees, and professional degrees? What is the trend, and what does that indicate about incomes in the United States for the future?

Return to the Census Bureau's homepage. What is the population of the country now? If you come back to the homepage for three consecutive days, you will see how quickly the population is growing. How can businesses use this information?

ANSWERS

LEARNING THE LANGUAGE

1. Factors of production	9. Standard of living	17. Revenue
2. E-commerce	10. Nonprofit organization	18. Technology
3. Quality of life	11. Database	19. Business environment
4. Entrepreneur	12. Demography	20. Productivity
5. Services	13. Empowerment	21. Outsourcing
6. Business	14. Goods	22. Identity theft
7. Loss	15. Profit	
8. Risk	16. Stakeholders	

ASSESSMENT CHECK

Learning Goal 1
Business and Entrepreneurship: Revenues, Profits and Losses

1.   a.   Businesses provide people with the opportunity to become wealthy
   b. and with necessities such as food, clothing, housing, medical care, and transportation.

2.   Revenue is money generated by selling goods, while profit is the money left over after a business has paid its expenses.

3.   A company will have a loss when expenses of doing business are greater than the revenues generated. If a business loses money over time, it will likely have to close, putting people out of work.

4.   In general, the companies that take the most risk can make the most profit. According to the text, the more risk you take the higher the rewards may be.

5.   Taxes are used by the federal government and local communities to build hospitals, schools, libraries, playgrounds and other facilities. Taxes are also used to keep the environment clean and to support people in need.

6.   The reason the same goods may cost more in other countries is due to higher taxes and higher government regulations.

7.   The challenge for the 21st century will be for organizations to remain profitable while trying to maintain a balance between the needs and wants of all stakeholders. For example, the need for a business to make a profit may be balanced against the needs of employees for sufficient income. The need to stay competitive may require businesses to outsource jobs to other countries which could do great harm to a community from the loss of jobs.

8.   Insourcing refers to the fact that some foreign companies are setting up design and production facilities here in the United States. This creates many new jobs and helps to offset the loss of jobs created by outsourcing.

9.   Nonprofit organizations use financial gains to benefit the stated social or educational goals of the organization rather than profit.

Entrepreneurship Versus Working for Others

10.   The two main ways to succeed in business according to the text are to rise up through the ranks of a business, and to start your own business.
        The advantage of working for others is that someone else assumes the risk and provides you with benefits. The advantage of starting your own business is that you can reap the profits. The down side of owning your own business is that many small businesses fail each year, and you don't receive any benefits. You have to provide them for yourself.

11.   Many groups in the United States have benefited tremendously from opportunities in entrepreneurship. The number of Hispanic-owned businesses has increased considerably, as have the number of businesses owned by members of other groups such as Asians, American Indians, Pacific Islanders, Alaskan Natives and African Americans. The number of businesses owned by women has also increased dramatically in the last 20 years.

12.   The five factors of production are:
        a.   land and other natural resources
        b.   labor
        c.   capital, such as, machines tools, and buildings. It does NOT include money.
        d.   entrepreneurship
        e.   knowledge

13.   If you were to analyze rich countries versus poor countries the factors of production that makes countries rich today is a combination of entrepreneurship and effective use of knowledge. A lack of entrepreneurship and the absence of knowledge among workers, along with a lack of freedom contribute to keeping poor countries poor.

Learning Goal 3
The Business Environment

14.   The five elements in the business environment are:
        a.   the economic and legal environment
        b.   the technological environment
        c.   the competitive environment
        d.   the social environment
        e.   the global business environment

15.   A healthy business environment helps businesses to grow and prosper. Job growth and wealth make it possible to have a high standard of living and a high quality of life. The results of poor environmental conditions lead to job loss, business failures, and a low standard of living and quality of life.

The Economic and Legal Environment

16.   Governments can increase entrepreneurship by:
        a.   keeping taxes and regulations to a minimum.
        b.   allowing private ownership of businesses.
        c.   minimizing interference with the free exchange of goods and services.
        d.   passing laws that enable business people to write contracts that are enforceable in court.
        e.   establishing a currency that is tradable on world markets.
        f.   minimizing corruption.

Learning goal 4
The Technological Environment

17.   Effectiveness means producing the desired result. Efficiency means producing goods and services using the least amount of resources.

18.   The two major types of e-commerce are:
a.   business-to-consumer (B2C)
b.   business-to-business (B2B).

19.   Bar codes identify the product being purchased and can be used by retailers to tell what size you have purchased, in what color, and at what price. The scanner at the checkout counter reads that information and puts it into a database.

20.   Once information from bar codes is in a database, companies can send you catalogs and other direct mail that offers the kind of products you might want, as indicated by past purchases. The use of the database enables stores to carry the merchandise that the local population wants.

Learning Goal 5

The Competitive Environment

21.   To be competitive in today's world markets, a company must offer quality products and outstanding service at competitive prices.

22.   This phrase means that businesses today must be customer driven, and that customer's wants and needs must come first. Successful organizations must listen more closely to their customers and adjust the firm's products, policies, and practices to meet the needs of their customers.

23.   In order to meet the needs of customers front line workers such as office clerks, front-desk people, salespeople, for example must be empowered. This means giving those workers the responsibility, authority, freedom, training, and equipment they need to respond quickly to customer requests and to make decisions essential to providing high quality goods and services. This can require restructuring an organization so that managers are willing to give up authority and employees are willing to assume more responsibility.

Learning Goal 6
The Social Environment

24.   The social environment is changing through:
a.   increased diversity
b.   an increase in the number of older Americans
c.   more two income families
d.   more single parent families

25.   Diversity has come to mean more than minorities and women. Many groups are now included in diversity efforts, including seniors, the disabled, homosexuals, extroverts, introverts, married, singles, atheists, and the devout.

26. Companies have responded to an increasingly diverse customer base by hiring a more diverse work force, adding diversity officers to their management team, and taking diversity management seriously. Local governments have adapted to a diverse population by changing signs, brochures, and forms to other languages.

27. The increase in the number of older Americans will provide many business opportunities in travel, medicine, nursing homes, assisted-living facilities, adult day care, home health care, recreation, and others.

28. Since 1985 Social Security tax revenues have exceeded benefit payments. But the government has been spending that money on other items rather than leaving it in the Social Security system. By the year 2018 less money will be going into Social Security that going out, and the government will have to do something about the shortfall. The options to fix the problem are not popular: raise taxes, cut benefits, reduce spending elsewhere or borrow.

29. A number of programs have been implemented to help two income families. Pregnancy benefits, parental leave programs, flexible work schedules, and eldercare programs are some examples, as well as referral services that provide counseling to families needing child care or elder care.

Learning Goal 7
The Global Environment

30. Two important global environmental changes have been:
    a. the growth of international competition
    b. the increase of free trade among nations

31. Improvements in:
    a. transportation
    b. communication have lead to more trade.
    These changes include more efficient distribution systems and communication advances such as the Internet.

32. The war in Iraq has drawn billions of dollars out of the American economy. Some companies have benefited but most have not, and have grown more slowly as money has been diverted to the war effort. The threat of terrorism adds to organizational costs including the cost of security personnel and equipment and insurance. The government has experienced huge cost increases from domestic security issues.

33. Global changes will affect you in a number of ways. New jobs will be created as businesses expand to serve global markets. These jobs will be created both in the United States and globally. Students must be prepared to compete in a rapidly changing world-wide environment that necessitates continuous learning to stay competitive.

Learning Goal 8
The Evolution of American Business

34. The farming industry became so efficient through the use of technology that the number of farmers had dropped considerably over the last century. The millions of small farms that used to exist have been replaced by huge farms resulting in a loss of farm jobs. Most of these farm workers went to work in manufacturing. However, agriculture is still a major industry in the U.S. and U.S. agricultural workers are the most productive in the world.

35.   The manufacturing industry, like the farming industry, has used technology to become more productive. As a consequence, many jobs were eliminated. Many of these workers found jobs in the service sector.

36.   Today, the leading firms in the U.S. are in services, which make up more than one-half of today's economy. Since the mid-1980s the service industry has generated almost all of the U.S. economy's increases in employment.

CRITICAL THINKING EXERCISES

Learning Goal 1

1.   Monika is surprised at the standard of living Joe seems to have attained compared to hers, while working at a similar job. While Monika makes more per hour (equivalent U.S. dollars) than Joe, the cost of food, housing and other services is probably much higher for her. Therefore she can't buy as much with her money as Joe can - it simply costs too much. A similar situation exists in the United States when you compare one region to another. Compare average housing prices for example in San Francisco, California to those in St. Louis, Missouri. When you compare per capita income for those areas, you will also find a difference.

Learning Goals 1,2

2.   a. $2,400,000 in revenue
      b. Profit is $350,000 after taking expenses of $2,050,000.
      c. Companies like Revelle generate wealth and create a higher standard of living in many ways. Workers pay taxes that federal and local governments use to build hospitals, schools, roads and playgrounds. Tax money is also used to keep the environment clean. Businesses also pay taxes to the federal government and the local community. Standards of living go up because people can buy goods and services with the money they earn from being employed. When businesses start, grow and prosper, and generate wealth, our quality of life improves as the taxes the workers and the business pay provide for good schools, good health care, a clean environment and so on.

Learning Goal 3

3.   In the analysis of the factors of production, the most important factor is not capital, natural resources or labor. Countries in Eastern Europe have land and labor, but they are still poor countries. The key to developing an economy is entrepreneurship and the effective use of information and knowledge. In many of these countries businesses have been owned by the government, and there has been little incentive to work hard or create profit.

A government interested in developing its economy must encourage business and entrepreneurship and provide the information necessary to help people to move ahead.

Many of these countries do not have laws that enable companies to write enforceable contracts, necessary to do business. This makes the risk of starting a business much higher. Further, these countries are still attempting to stabilize the value of their currency. The governments are corrupt in many cases, making it impossible to get permits without expensive bribes. Lastly taxes in many developing countries are high, minimizing a businesses' return on investment.

Learning Goal 4

4.　　The new retailing technology allows a retailer to determine what kind of products customers purchase, in what amount, in what size and at what price. That information, plus information such as the name, address and family information about a customer will go into a database.

With that information Schnucks can send direct mail pieces to customers offering exactly what they want. It will allow Schnucks to carry inventory specifically for a customer base in different areas around the city. For example, if there is an area with a large Italian population, the Schnucks store in that area will carry more of the type of products those customers might buy. If there is a large Jewish population in another area of the city, the store serving that area may carry fewer of the Italian products, and more for the dietary needs of the Jewish customer, and so on. These stores will also be able to replace the items quickly through contact with the suppliers, who also have the bar code information. If Schnucks is interested in developing direct mail pieces or other types of services, this technology will help decision makers to know exactly what to feature, and mailing lists will be readily available.

Learning Goal

5.　　a.　　Competitors for some schools will be the other colleges and universities in the local community. For others it may be other schools in the region or the nation.

　　　b.　　A college or university may please its customers (students) by offering classes at convenient times (many schools offer weekend college programs for example), in convenient locations (off site locations), encouraging faculty to be accessible to student through designated office hours or mentoring programs, offering a variety of programs, offering Internet or other technology based courses, establishing a format for easy access to faculty and assignments through the Internet, and, of course, having winning sports teams!

　　　c.　　The stakeholders are students, parents of students, employees, taxpayers, the community in which the school is located and alumni for example. How schools meet the needs of its stakeholders may be through a variety of course offerings, tuition and rate of tuition increases, level of community involvement by the school's administrators, responsiveness to student organizations, cooperation with alumni groups, and so on.

　　　d.　　Students may have difficulty answering how the school meets the needs of employees. You may find out if there is a structure for faculty and staff to communicate openly with their manager, for example, or how employees view the administration and the school's policies.

Learning Goals 4,5,6,7

6.　　Answers to this question will vary. Most companies have computerized everything from inventory management to payroll to customer checkout. Students will find that companies are using technology in hundreds of different ways. Most companies will have a Web site. Some offer their products for sale, others will direct customers to local retailers that carry their products. Many companies today are offering benefits such as time off to work as a volunteer, on-site day care centers and more. Most will also find that the company is involved in some way in the international area, even if it is just selling or buying a few products imported from overseas. Many of these companies will have a diverse workforce, and employ a variety of international workers at all levels.

7.   By developing programs such as those mentioned in the text, companies better meet employee needs. This can make a company more competitive by fostering a positive environment with satisfied workers who may then be more productive. Further, these programs can be used to attract the kinds of skilled workers companies will need in the future to remain competitive.

Learning Goal 7
8.   If U.S. firms want to be competitive in today's global environment, they must continue to focus on quality issues in the same way that countries like China and India have done. U.S. firms have begun to serve the growing global markets with the highest quality products and services at the lowest possible prices. This has provided U.S. workers with jobs by expanding our global marketplace.

Learning Goal 8
9.   As the agricultural industry became more productive through advances in technology, fewer people were needed to produce the same or greater volume. Agricultural workers had to find jobs elsewhere, in other industries, and learn new skills. Many of these people went to work in manufacturing, helping to make the United States a world manufacturing power in the first half of this century.

The same trend has occurred today in the industrial or manufacturing sector. As factories have been able to improve productivity through technology, fewer workers are needed to produce the same or greater volume of high quality products. Factory workers today have found new employment in the service industries, which have generated almost all of the employment growth increases since the mid-1980s.

PRACTICE TEST

MULTIPLE CHOICE

TRUE FALSE

LG 1	#1-6		LG 1	# 1-5
LG 2	# 7-9		LG 2	# 6-7
LG 3	# 10-11		LG 3	# 8-9
LG 4	# 12-13		LG 4	# 10-11
LG 5	# 14		LG 5	# 12-13
LG 6	#15-16		LG 6	# 14-15
LG 7	#17-18		LG 7	#16-17
LG 8	# 19-20		LG 8	# 18

1.	c		11.	a		1.	F	10. T
2.	a		12.	b		2.	F	11. F
3.	d		13.	a		3.	T	12. T
4.	b		14.	a		4.	F	13. T
5.	d		15.	c		5.	T	14. F
6.	c		16.	a		6.	T	15. T
7.	c		17.	d		7.	T	16. T
8.	d		18.	b		8.	T	17. F
9.	c		19.	c		9.	F	18. F
10.	b		20.	a				

CHAPTER 2 – HOW ECONOMICS AFFECTS BUSINESS: THE CREATION AND DISTRIBUTION OF WEALTH

LEARNING GOALS

After you have read and studied this chapter you should be able to:

1. Compare and contrast the economics of despair with the economics of growth.
2. Explain the nature of capitalism and how free markets work.
3. Discuss the major differences between socialism and communism.
4. Explain the trend toward mixed economies.
5. Discuss the economic system of the United States including the significance of key economic indicators, productivity, and the business cycle.
6. Define fiscal policy and monetary policy and explain how each affects the economy.

LEARNING THE LANGUAGE

Listed below are important terms found in this chapter. Choose the correct term for each definition
below and write it in the space provided.

Brain Drain	Fiscal policy	Monopoly
Business cycles	Free market economies	National debt
Capitalism	Gross domestic product	Oligopoly
Command economies	Inflation	Perfect competition
Communism	Invisible hand	Producer price index
Consumer price index	Macroeconomics	Recession
Deflation	Market price	Resource development
Demand	Microeconomics	Socialism
Depression	Mixed economies	Supply
Disinflation	Monetary policy	Unemployment rate
Economics	Monopolistic competition	

1. The quantity of products that manufacturers or owners are willing to sell at different prices at a specific time is known as _____.

2. The part of economic study that looks at the behavior of people and organizations in particular markets is called_____.

3. The country is in a _____when GDP has declined for two consecutive quarters.

4. The economic system known as _____ is one in which all or most of the factors of production and distribution are privately owned and operated for profit.

5. _____ is the quantity of products that people are willing to buy at different prices at a specific time.

6. We define the _____ as the number of civilians at least 16 years old who are unemployed and tried to find a job within the prior four weeks.

7. In economic systems considered _____ the market largely determines what goods and services get produced, who gets them, and how the economy grows.

8. The _____ consists of monthly statistics that measure the pace of inflation or deflation.

9. The sum of government deficits over time is called the _____.

10. A course in _____ will teach us how society chooses to employ resources to produce goods and services and to distribute them for consumption among various competing groups and individuals.

11. Government economists keep a close watch on _____, which is the general rise in the price level of goods and services over time.

12. One key economic indicator is _____, the total value of goods and services in a country in a given year.

13. Some countries operate under _____, economic systems in which the government largely decides what goods and services will be produced, who will get them, and how the economy will grow.

14. In developing _____ the government is managing the money supply and interest rates.

15. _____ is a situation in which price increases are slowing.

16. A severe recession is known as a(n)_____.

17. _____ is an economic system based on the premise that some, if not most basic businesses should be owned by the government so that profits can be evenly distributed among the people.

18. When the federal government makes an effort to keep the economy stable, it may use _____, by increasing or decreasing taxes or government spending.

19. _____are economic systems where some allocation of resources is made by the market and some by the government.

20. The economy is experiencing _____ when prices are actually declining.

21. A _____ is a market in which there is only one seller for a product or service.

22. The market situation known as _____ is where there are many sellers in a market and no seller is large enough to dictate the price of the product.

23. Adam Smith coined the term _____ to describe the process that turns self-directed gain into social and economic benefits for all.

24. A form of competition where the market is dominated by just a few sellers is called a(n)_____.

25. The part of economic study called _____ looks at the operation of a nation's economy as a whole.

26. The study of _____ focuses on how to increase resources and to create the conditions that will make better use of those resources.

27. The _____ is the price determined by supply and demand.

28. _____ is the market situation in which there are a large number of sellers that produce similar products, but the products are perceived by buyers as different.

29. The economic and political system called _____ is one in which the state (the government) makes all economic decisions and owns almost all the major forms of production.

30. The index that measures prices at the wholesale level is the _____.

31. _____ describe the periodic rises and falls that occur in all economies over time.

32. The loss of the best and brightest people to other countries is called the _____.

ASSESSMENT CHECK

Learning Goal 1
How Economic Conditions Affect Businesses

1. How is macroeconomics different from microeconomics?

2. How can businesses contribute to business through resource development?

3. What do followers of Thomas Malthus (neo Malthuasians) believe? How do their views differ from other economists?

4. What did Adam smith believe was vital to the survival of any economy?

5.   Describe Adam Smith's theory of the invisible hand and how wealth would be created.

Learning Goal 2
Understanding Free-Market Capitalism

6.   In a capitalist system, who/what owns the businesses and decides what to produce, how much to produce, how much to pay workers and how much to charge for goods?

7.   The foundation of the U.S. economic system is: _____

8.   What are the four basic rights of a free market (capitalist) system?

        a._____   c._____

        b._____   d._____

9.   Describe how decisions about what to produce, and in what quantities are made in a free market system.

10.   What is "supply" in economic terms, and what happens to quantity supplied as price goes up?

11.   What is "demand" in economic terms and what happens to demand as price goes up?

12.   The key factor in determining quantity supplied and quantity demanded is:

        _____.

13. Label the graph

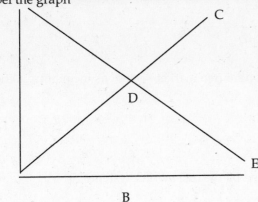

14. What is the equilibrium point and what is its relationship to price?

15. Describe what proponents of a free market system say about government involvement in a free market system.

16. What happens in countries where there is no mechanism, such as a free market, for businesses to determine what and how much to produce?

17. Describe:
a. perfect competition: _____

_____

b. monopolistic competition: _____

_____

c. oligopoly: _____

_____

d. monopoly: _____

_____

18. What has been the benefit of the free market system for industrialized countries?

19. The text describes the limitation of the free market system as inequality. What does that mean?

20. How have ethics been compromised by the free market system?

Learning Goal 3
Understanding Socialism

21. What are the basic characteristics of socialism?

22. Describe the major benefits of socialism.

23. What are the negative consequences of socialism?

Understanding Communism

24. In a communist system, how are economic decisions made?

25. What are two problems associated with communism, and what have been the results?

Learning Goal 4
The Trend Toward Mixed Economies

26.   What is the major principle of each of the two major economic systems in the world?

a. Free market economies: _____

_____

b. Command economies: _____

_____

27.   Experience has shown that neither capitalism nor socialism has had optimal results in terms of the economy. What are the problems with:

a.   A free market system (Capitalism) _____

_____

b.   Socialism/communism: _____

_____

c.   As a result of those problems, the trends in free market economies and in socialist and communist countries has been: _____

_____

28.   What kind of economic system do we have in the United States? Why is it considered to be this type of system?

Learning Goal 5
Understanding the Economic System of the United States

29.   What are three major indicators of economic health?

a. _____

b. _____

c. _____

30.   Is the production output for foreign companies, such as Honda, included in GDP figures?

31.   What is one major influence on the growth of GDP?

32.   Describe the four types of unemployment.

       a. _____

       b. _____

       c. _____

       d. _____

33.   What is the difference between inflation and disinflation?

34.   What is the difference between inflation and deflation?

35.   What is happening during a period of stagflation?

36.   List two measures of price changes over time.

       a. _____   b. _____

37.   The CPI is an important figure because: _____

       _____

38.   Why are business people eager to increase productivity?

39.   What is a problem with regard to measuring productivity in the service sector?

40. The four phases of long-term business cycles are:

a. _____   c. _____

b. _____   d. _____

41. What is the difference between a "boom" and a recovery?

42. What three things happen when a recession occurs?

a. _____

b. _____

c. _____

43. Identify three negative consequences of a recession.

a. _____

b. _____

c. _____

Learning goal 6
Stabilizing the Economy Through Fiscal Policy

44. What 2 areas are addressed with fiscal policy?

a. _____   b. _____

45. Theoretically, high tax rates could: _____

_____

46. What is meant by the term "national deficit"? How is the national deficit related to the national debt?

47. What is one way to reduce annual deficits?

48.   What is the Federal Reserve Bank (The Fed)?

49.   What are two areas managed by monetary policy?

      a.   _____

      b.   _____

50.   What action does the Fed take when the economy is booming? What happens in the economy as a result?

51.   What happens when the Fed lowers interest rates?

CRITICAL THINKING EXERCISES

Learning Goal 1

1.   They're everywhere! McDonald's hamburgers can be purchased in cities and suburbs, on riverfronts, in college football stadiums and in discount stores. There are fast food restaurants at most major road intersections, and billions of dollars are spent annually to advertise everything from fast food frozen yogurt to kid's meals. Grocery stores have even gotten into the act with their own versions of fast food restaurants.
        Families with sick children can stay in Ronald McDonald houses located close to the hospital where the children are receiving treatment, and businesses routinely come to the aid of disaster victims.

        How does the founding and growth of entrepreneurial ventures like McDonald's and the resulting growth in other, similar businesses illustrate Adam Smith's invisible hand theory?

Learning Goal 2

2.   There are four basic rights under the capitalist economic system;

Private property   Competition
Profit   Freedom of choice

Read the situations below and determine which of these is being demonstrated.

a. _____ The owners of Pro Performance, Inc. make a profit for the owners for the first time in their history and decide to pay themselves a dividend.

b. _____ The owners of Pro Performance, Inc. bought a piece of land for investment purposes.

c. _____ Proctor and Gamble spends almost $4 billion a year on advertising.

d. _____ Tom Oswalt decided to take a job as manager of an insurance agency after he graduated from college.

e. _____ Arthur Tower receives a patent for a new method he devised to make metal springs

f. _____ Alfred Rockwood, after he retired, decided to move to northern Michigan and start his own fly-tying business.

g. _____ Microsoft introduces a new, upgraded version of its popular video game, X-Box 360, in order to grab a larger share of the toy market.

h. _____ The Andersens, a young, dual income couple, draw up a will, making their children their beneficiaries of their home, property and other assets.

3.   Plot a supply curve using the information below:

Unit price (dollars)	Amount supplied (units)
$125	500
100	400
75	300
50	200
25	100

On the same graph, plot the demand curve using the information listed below.

Unit Price (dollars)	Amount Demanded (units)
$125	100
100	200
75	300
50	400
25	500

a. What is the equilibrium price? _____

b. How many units will be supplied and purchased at that price? _____

4. Indicate whether the market price of a product will most likely go up or down in the following situations:

a. _____   There is a drought in the Midwest (bushel of wheat)

b. _____   Strawberries are in season with a bumper crop.

c. _____   It's the ski season (price of motel rooms in ski areas).

d. _____   A nutrition study indicates that red meat should be eaten only in moderation, if at all. (price of red meat)

e. _____   A major corporation announces that it has to borrow money from the government in order to stay in business. (price of its stock)

5. There are four degrees of competition:

perfect competition   oligopoly
monopolistic competition   monopoly

Match the type of competition to the situation described below

a. _____   Murray Barnard takes his soybean crop to the grain elevator in Decatur Illinois. He found that because of government price supports he would make a nice profit this year.

b. _____   Because it is the only provider of electrical service in the area, AmerenUE is carefully regulated by the Missouri Public Service Commission.

c. _____   Cheer cleans in all temperatures. Ivory Snow is gentle enough to launder a baby's clothes and Tide cleans the dirtiest clothes. Procter and Gamble makes these brands, as well as several others, which all appear to be different. Procter and Gamble competes with many other manufacturers and retains control over advertising, branding and packaging.

d. _____   The purchasing agent for a steel specialty products company says that he buys the steel the company uses to make their sign posts primarily on the basis of the best delivery date and the highest quality, rather than price, since all of his suppliers charge the same dollar amount per ton. The company has very few competitors.

6. Julie Marshall's first cousin, Jean-Paul, lives and works in Belgium. They have had long "discussions" via e-mail about the benefits and drawbacks of living in the U.S., a capitalist system, vs. living in Belgium a socialist economic system. Both Julie and Jean-Paul defend their country's system. What do you think Julie would say about the benefits of living in the U.S. and the drawbacks of living in Belgium, and how would Jean-Paul respond?

7. Think back to Chapter 1 and the discussion about the ways governments foster entrepreneurship. What impact could the high tax rates found in socialist countries have on entrepreneurship?

Learning Goals 2, 3, 4

8. Four basic economic systems are:

Capitalism	Socialism
Mixed Economy	Communism

Read the following examples and using the table on p. 45 as well as other material in the text determine which system is MOST likely being described:

a. _____ John works for a large business in a major industry which is owned by the government (public ownership) of the country in which he lives. He is considered to be a government employee, but his brother owns his own small printing business.

b. _____ Because the market is "ruled " by supply and demand with little government involvement, Maria has a wide variety of goods and services available for purchase where she lives and there are rarely shortages of goods and services.

c. _____ Many of the products Maria purchases have been made or assembled outside her country. These products are available because the government of her country does not control or interfere with trade with other countries.

d. _____ Although he disagrees with many of his government's policies, Ahmo cannot protest any of the government actions, and he is unable to buy the home he would like for his family.

e. _____ Hong's uncle works for a large corporation where promotions and raises are given to those who work hard and do a good job. The only problem is, the tax rate is so high there is little incentive for anyone to work that hard. Hong is a teacher in a public school, and the government controls his wages.

f. _____ Sam is a farmer in his country, and is being paid government subsidies to so that over supply of the crops he grows is controlled.

g. _____ Ramon works hard at his job because where he lives and works, profits are kept by the owners of the company, and he is one of the owners. The government controls the pricing in his company because he works in an industry that is a monopoly.

h. _____ Enrique has a cousin in another country who tries to supply him with blue jeans and other products which are in very short supply in his country. Enrique often finds that some basic things, such as some food and clothing products are in short supply.

Learning Goal 5
9. Discuss the relationship between productivity and price levels. What is the relationship between productivity and Gross Domestic Product?

10. There are four types of unemployment:
frictional   cyclical
structural   seasonal

Match the situation being described to the type of unemployment

a. _____ As sales of new homes decline, the constructions industry lays off thousands of workers.

b. _____ A migrant worker, finished with his job in the potato fields in Idaho, travels to Michigan to look for a job harvesting fruit.

c. _____ A middle manager is laid off. His job has been eliminated with the installation of high tech information processing equipment.

d. _____ A businessman quits his job over a major disagreement with company policy.

Learning Goal 6

11.   Determine whether fiscal policy or monetary policy is being discussed:

a. _____   Congress debates a major income tax revision.

b. _____   The Federal Reserve raises interest rates to combat inflation.

c. _____   A candidate for major political office promises to cut spending for social programs to reduce the national debt.

d. _____   Major government programs lose federal funding.

e. _____   In an attempt to ease unemployment, the Fed increases the money supply.

f. _____   A proposal is made to cut defense spending, but to raise taxes to fund defense spending.

g. _____   American taxpayers express concern over tax loopholes for the rich.

h. _____   A debate centers on whether to lower the national debt through an increase in the tax rate, less spending, or both.

12.   Political campaigns often revolve around the issue of taxes and how an increase or a decrease will affect government spending and revenues. Since government revenues come from collecting taxes, discuss how a tax *decrease* <u>could</u> have the effect of *raising* government revenues. (Some of this answer will come from what you learned in Chapter 1)

PRACTICE TEST

MULTIPLE CHOICE- Circle the best answer

Learning Goal 1

1.   _____ is the study of how to increase resources and to create conditions that will make better use of those resources.
    a. Economics
    b. Macroeconomics
    c. Microeconomics
    d. Resource development

2.   The foundation of the U.S. economic system is considered to be:
    a. capitalism.
    b. socialism.
    c. a command economy.
    d. a mixed economy

3. Adam Smith's theory of the "invisible hand" means that
    a. people should work in order to provide funding for charitable causes.
    b. through working for their own prosperity, people will actually help the economy grow and prosper.
    c. governments should own major businesses so that resources are equally distributed.
    d. the government manages the economy through monitoring government taxes and government spending.

Learning Goal 2
4. One of the problems with_____ is that it naturally leads to unequal distribution of wealth.
    a. communism
    b. socialism
    c. a command economy
    d. capitalism

5. Which of the following is not one of the four basic rights of a capitalist system?
    a. The right to have a job.
    b. The right to private property
    c. The right to compete
    d. The right to freedom of choice

6. Typically, the quantity of products that manufacturers are willing to supply will _____ when prices _____.
    a. increase/increase
    b. decrease/increase
    c. stay the same/increase
    d. increase/stay the same

7. One holiday season a few years ago, there was a toy called Tickle My Elbow that was all the rage. Demand for this toy was so high, that stores couldn't keep them on the shelf! There was quite a shortage of Tickle My Elbow that year. When a shortage such as this exists, what generally happens?
    a. the price goes up
    b. the price stays the same, and mothers everywhere fight for the last toy
    c. the government intervenes, and forces the manufacturer to make more of the toy
    a. when customers realize they can't get the toy, they give up, and the price goes down

8. A(n)_____shows the amount people are willing to buy at the prices at which sellers are willing to sell.
    a. supply curve
    b. demand curve
    c. marginal revenue point
    d. equilibrium point

9. What's going on here? As soon as Dewey Cheatum and Howe Motors increases the prices on their sport utility vehicle, then so does their only competitor, You Betcha Motors! Their prices are basically the same for similar vehicles, although their advertising says their products are really very different. What kind competition exists here?
    a. perfect competition
    b. monopoly
    c. oligopoly
    d. monopolistic competition

Learning Goal 3

10. Citizens of socialist nations can rely on the government to provide all of the following except:
    a. education.
    b. health care.
    c. unemployment and retirement benefits.
    d. money to start a business.

Learning Goal 3

11. Socialist systems tend to:
    a. encourage innovation.
    b. keep up with countries like the U.S. in the areas of job and wealth creation.
    c. discourage the best from working as hard as they can.
    d. have relatively low tax rates.

12. What kind of a system exists when the government largely determines what goods and services get produced, who gets them and how the economy grows?
    a. Capitalist economy
    b. Socialist economy
    c. Free market economy
    d. Communist economy

Learning Goal 4

13. The country of Amerensk has, for the last several years, been moving from a communist country to a more mixed economic system. Which of the following most likely would NOT occur in Amerensk ?
    a. An increase in the level of government involvement in trade.
    b. Private ownership of business.
    c. An increase in the rate at which jobs are created.
    d. More incentives for workers to work harder.

Learning Goal 5

14. Which of the following would not be considered a key economic indicator?
    a. GDP
    b. The unemployment rate
    c. The tax rate
    d. The price indexes

15. Juan Valdez was laid off from his job at the coffee factory, because the demand for coffee has weakened. The kind of unemployment Juan is experiencing would be:
    a. frictional.
    b. seasonal.
    c. structural.
    d. cyclical.

16. When the economy in the United States began to slow, price increases, while still measurable, began to slow. This situation is known as:
    a. inflation.
    b. disinflation.
    c. deflation.
    d. fiscal policy.

17. Measures to increase productivity:
    a. are failing in manufacturing, as productivity is slowly decreasing.
    b. can improve quality of service providers, but not always improve worker output.
    c. are always successful in manufacturing and services industries.
    d. are becoming unimportant in today's competitive market.

18. Which of the following won't occur during a recession?
    a. high unemployment
    b. increase in business failures
    c. drop in the standard of living
    d. increase in interest rates

Learning Goal 6
19. Fiscal policy is at issue when:
    a. The Federal Reserve raises interest rates to its member banks.
    b. The Federal Reserve debates combating inflation by cutting the money supply.
    c. Congress debates a proposal to cut defense spending, and raising taxes to support spending for education.
    d. Unemployment goes up as the country slides into a recession.

20. Which of the following is not a part of the business cycles that occur in economics over time?
    a. Economic boom.
    b. Depression.
    c. Structural unemployment.
    d. Recovery.

21. The sum of all the federal deficits over time is known as the:
    a. national debt.
    b. gross national debt.
    c. fiscal policy.
    d. aggregate demand for money.

TRUE-FALSE

Learning Goal 1

1. _____ The world's population is growing more slowly than expected, and there are some industrial countries in which growth may be so slow that there will be too many old people and too few young people to support them.

2. _____ Today many U.S. businesspeople are becoming more concerned about social issues and their obligation to return to society.

Learning Goal 2

3. _____ In a free market system, price is determined through negotiation between buyers and sellers.

4. _____ When there is a surplus of products, manufacturers will tend to raise the price so that they will make a profit from those products they are able to sell.

5. _____ Monopolistic competition exists when just a few sellers dominate a market.

6. _____ As capitalist systems have evolved in the United States and other parts of the world, wealth has become more equally distributed.

Learning Goal 3

7. _____ One of the consequences of a socialist system is a high tax rate on those who do work, in order to pay for services for those that don't, or can't, work.

8. _____ A negative consequence of socialism has been brain drain.

9. _____ Socialism and communism are popular terms used to describe free market economies.

10. _____ A communist system is based upon the premise that the government owns all major forms of production and all economic decisions are made by the government

Learning Goal 4

11. _____ The United States is a purely free market economy.

12. _____ Mixed economies exist where some allocation of resources is made by the marketplace, and some by the government.

Learning Goal 5

13. _____ Production from a foreign company located in the U.S., like Honda, is not included in calculating GDP.

14. _____ Betty Bixler worked for Chrysler for 20 years before being laid off when her job was eliminated because updated technology made her job obsolete. Betty is structurally unemployed.

15. _____ The PPI is important because some government benefits, wages and salaries, rents and leases, tax brackets, and interest rates are all based upon this figure.

16. _____ It has become relatively easy to measure productivity in the service sector due to the influx of machinery.

17. _____ An increase in productivity means the same worker produces more in the same amount of time.

18. _____ During a recession, we could experience an overall drop in our standard of living, high unemployment, and increased business failures.

19. _____ During a period of disinflation, prices are actually going down.

Learning Goal 6

20. _____ When a political candidate indicates that the only way to cut the deficit is to cut spending and raise taxes, the candidate is addressing fiscal policy.

21. _____ High tax rates are encouraged by small business owners, because the increase in government revenues from higher taxes will be used by the government for small business loans.

You Can Find It on The Net

Many economic statistics can be found on government sites. Visit the Bureau of Labor Statistics at www.bls.gov .

What is the most recent change in the Consumer Price Index?

Use the inflation calculator to determine the cost of tuition at your school in 10 years. What would tuition have been 10 years ago?

What is the most recent unemployment rate for the United States?

Go to the International Statistics link. How do the unemployment rate and the changes in the Consumer Price Index in the United States compare to other major countries such as Canada, Japan and parts of Europe?

Click on the map of the United States on your state. What is the unemployment rate in your state?

What is the trend over 6 months, indicated on this web page?

ANSWERS

LEARNING THE LANGUAGE

1. Supply	12. Gross Domestic Product	23. Invisible hand
2. Microeconomics	13. Command economies	24. Oligopoly
3. Recession	14. Monetary policy	25. Macroeconomics
4. Capitalism	15. Disinflation	26. Resource development
5. Demand	16. Depression	27. Market price
6. Unemployment rate	17. Socialism	28. Monopolistic competition
7. Free market economies	18. Fiscal policy	29. Communism
8. Consumer price index	19. Mixed economies	30 Producer Price Index
9. National debt	20. Deflation	31. Business cycles
10. Economics	21. Monopoly	32. Brain drain
11. Inflation	22. Perfect competition	

ASSESSMENT CHECK

Learning Goal 1
How Economic Conditions Affect Business

1. Macroeconomics looks at the operation of a nation's economy as a whole, and microeconomics looks at the behavior of people[and organization sin particular markets. For example while macroeconomics looks at how many jobs exist in the whole economy, microeconomics examines how many people will be hired in a particular industry or in a certain region of the country.

2. Businesses contribute to an economic system and resource development by inventing products that increase available resources. Businesses may discover new energy sources or new ways of growing food.

3. Followers of Thomas Malthus believe that there are too many people in the world and that the solution to poverty is birth control. However, statistics show that populations in some countries are growing so slowly that there may be too many old people and too few young people to care for them.
   These views differ from other economists because there are macroeconomists who believe that a large population can be a valuable resource, especially if the people are educated. They believe that one of the keys to economic growth in the world is to educate people better.

4. Adam Smith believed that freedom was vital to the survival of any economy, especially the freedom to own land or property and the freedom to keep the profits from working the land or running a business. He believed people will work hard if they have the incentive to do so. People have a desire to improve their "condition in life", and as long as workers can see economic reward for their efforts they will work long hours and work hard. As a result of those efforts the economy would prosper.

5. The "invisible hand" is how Smith believed an economy grows and prospers, through the production of needed goods and services. The idea is that people working for their own benefit will provide goods and services, which are needed by others. To become wealthy business owners have to hire workers to produce those goods and services. As a consequence, an area has plenty of goods and services, and many people have jobs.

43

Learning Goal 2
Understanding Free-Market Capitalism

6. In a capitalist system, all or most of the factors of production and distribution are privately owned, (not owned by the government) and are operated for profit. So, in a capitalist system, business people decide what to produce, how much to pay workers, how much to charge for goods and services, whether to produce certain goods domestically, import them, or contract to have them made in other countries, and so on.

7. The foundation of the U.S. economic system is capitalism

8. The four basic rights of a free market (capitalist) system are:
   a. The right to private property
   b. The right to own a business and keep the profits
   c. The right to freedom of competition
   d. The right to freedom of choice

9. In a free market system decisions about what to produce and in what quantities are made by the market. Consumers in a free market economy send signals to producers that tell the producers what and how much to make by choosing to buy, or not to buy, products and services, at the price we are charged in the store. As long as we are willing to pay the price, the supplier will continue to make that supply available. As a consequence there is rarely a long-term shortage of goods in the United States. If something is wanted but isn't available, the price tends to go up until someone begins making more of the product, sells what's on hand, or makes a substitute.

10. Supply refers to the quantity of products that manufacturers or owners are willing to sell at different prices at a specific time. In general, as price goes up, the quantity supplied will go up because sellers can make more money with a higher price.

11. Demand refers to the quantity of products that people are willing to buy at different prices at a specific time. In general, as price goes up, quantity demanded will go down.

12. The key factor in determining the quantity supplied and the quantity demanded is price.

13. A. Price   E. Demand curve
    B. Quantity   D. Equilibrium point
    C. Supply curve

14. The equilibrium point, or equilibrium price, is the point on a graph where the quantity supplied is equal to the quantity demanded. In the long run, that price becomes the market price.

15. Proponents of a free market system argue that there is no need for government involvement or government planning, because if surpluses develop, when quantity supplied exceeds quantity demanded, a signal is sent to sellers to lower the price. If shortages develop, when quantity demanded exceeds quantity supplied, a signal is sent to sellers to increase the price. Eventually supply and demand will again be equal, if nothing interferes with the market forces.

16. In countries where there is no mechanism for businesses to determine what and how much to produce there are often shortages or surpluses. In these countries the government decides what to produce and in what quantities, but the government has no way of knowing proper quantities.

17.   a.   Perfect competition exists when there are many sellers in a market and no one producer is big enough to dictate the price of a product. Sellers produce products that appear to be identical. An example would be agricultural products.

       b.   Monopolistic competition exists when a large number of sellers produce products that appear similar, but are perceived as being different by the buyers. Product differentiation is the key to success in this type of competitive situation.

       c.   In an oligopoly, just a few sellers dominate the market, as is the case in the cereal and soft drink markets for example. The initial investment to enter an oligopoly is very high, and prices are similar. Product differentiation is usually the main factor in market success.

       d.   A monopoly exists where there is only one seller for a product or service. One seller controls supply, and so could raise prices dramatically. For this reason laws in the United States prohibit monopolies, except for approved monopolies such as utility service.

18.   The benefit of the free market system for industrialized countries is that it was a major factor in creating the wealth these countries now enjoy. Capitalism encourages businesses to be more efficient so they can successfully compete on price and quality.

19.   Even as the free market system has brought prosperity to the United States and many other parts of the world, it has brought inequality at the same time. A free market economy leads to inequality of wealth because business owners and managers will make more money and have more wealth than workers. Further, there will be people who are unable or unwilling to work or start a business. Others may not have the talent or drive to do so.

20.   One of the dangers of a free market system is that business people may let greed dictate how they act in order to increase personal assets. To overcome this limitation of capitalism some countries have adopted socialism.

Learning Goal 3
Understanding Socialism

21.   The basic premise of a socialist system is that most basic businesses, such as steel mills, coal mines, and utilities, should be owned by the government so that profits can be evenly distributed among the people. In a socialist system the government is expected to provide education, health care retirement benefits, unemployment benefits and other social services. Entrepreneurs often own and run small businesses, but private businesses and individuals are taxed steeply to pay for social programs.

22.   The major benefit of socialism is social equality, because income is taken from the wealthier people through taxes and redistributed to the poorer members of the population. Other benefits are free education through college, free health care, free childcare, longer vacations, shorter workweeks, and more generous employee benefits.

23.   One of the negative consequences of socialism is brain drain. Brain drain is the term used to describe the trend for professionals like doctors and lawyers, and business people and others with high incomes, to leave socialist countries for more capitalistic countries with lower tax rates. Socialism also results in fewer inventions and less innovation because those who come up with the ideas usually don't receive as much reward as they would in a capitalist system.

Understanding Communism

24. In a communist system all economic decisions are made by the government and the government owns all the major factors of production.

25. One problem with a communist system is that a government doesn't always know the right amount to produce because prices don't reflect supply and demand. As a result, there can be shortages of many goods, even basics such as food. Another problem with communism is that it doesn't inspire businesspeople to work hard because the government takes most of their earnings. Therefore communism is slowly disappearing as an economic form. Communist countries today are suffering severe economic depression and some people are starving.

Learning Goal 4
The Trend Toward Mixed Economies

26. a. Free market economies exist when the marketplace largely determines what goods and services get produced, who gets them and how the economy grows. The popular term for this system is capitalism.
    b. Command economies exist when the government largely decides what goods and services to produce, who will get them and how the economy will grow. Socialism and communism are terms used to describe this type of system.

27. a. Many believe that a free market system is not responsive enough to the needs of the old, the disabled, the elderly and the environment.
    b. Socialism and communism have not created enough jobs or wealth to keep economies growing fast enough.
    c. The results of these problems have been a trend for free market economies, such as the United States, to adopt many social and environmental programs. Communist governments are disappearing and socialist countries are cutting back on social programs and lowering taxes.

28. The United States is a mixed economy because of government involvement in the economy. The government is now the largest employer in the United States.

Learning Goal 5
Understanding the Economic System of the United States

29. Three major indicators of economic health are:
    a.   the gross domestic product
    b.   the unemployment rate
    c.   the price indexes

30. Production values from foreign manufacturers are included in the U.S. GDP as long as the company is located within the country's boundaries.

31. A major influence on the growth of GDP is the productivity of the workforce.

32.   a. *frictional unemployment* refers to those people who have quit work, and who haven't yet found a new job.
   b. *Structural unemployment* refers to unemployment caused by the restructuring of firms or by a mismatch between the skills or location of job seekers and the requirements or location of available jobs.
   c. *Cyclical unemployment* refers to unemployment caused because of a recession or similar downturn in the business cycle.
   d. *Seasonal unemployment* occurs where demand for labor varies over the year.

33.   Inflation is a rise in prices, and disinflation is a condition where the rise in prices is slowing, or in other words, the inflation rate is declining.

34.   Inflation is a rise in prices of goods and services over time, and deflation is a situation where prices are actually declining.

35.   During a period of stagflation, the economy is slowing, but prices are still going up.

36.   Two measures of prices changes over time are:
   a.   consumer price index
   b.   producer price index

37.   The CPI is an important figure because some government benefits, wages and salaries, rents and leases, tax brackets, and interest rates are all based on the CPI.

38.   Business people are eager to increase productivity because an increase in productivity means that a worker can produce more goods and services than before. Higher productivity means lower costs in producing goods and services and lower prices. This can help to make a firm more competitive.

39.   Measuring productivity is a problem in the service industry because technology may add to the *quality* of the service provided, but not to the *output per worker*, which is defined as productivity.

40.   The four phases of long-term business cycles are:
   a.   boom
   b.   recession
   c.   depression
   d.   recovery

41.   A boom is a time when businesses are doing well. When we are in a recovery, we are coming out of a recession, and the economy is stabilizing and starting to grow. This will eventually lead to a boom, starting the cycle over again.

42.   When a recession occurs
   a.   prices fall
   b.   people purchase fewer products
   c.   more businesses fail

43.   Three negative consequences of a recession are:
   a.   high unemployment
   b.   increased business failures
   c.   overall drop in living standards

Learning goal 6
Stabilizing the Economy Through Fiscal Policy

44. Two areas addressed by fiscal policy are:
    a. taxes   b. government spending

45. Theoretically, high tax rates could slow the economy because they draw money away from the private sector and put it into the government. High tax rates also may discourage small-business ownership.

46. The national deficit is the amount of money that the federal government spends over and above the amount it gathers in taxes. The national debt is the sum of the deficits over time.

47. One way to reduce annual deficits is to cut government spending.

Using Monetary Policy to Keep the Economy Growing

48. The Federal Reserve Bank, or the Fed, is a semi-private organization that is not under the direct control of the government, but its head is appointed by the President.

49. Two areas managed by monetary policy are:
    a. money supply
    b. interest rates

50. When the economy is booming, the Fed tends to raise interest rates. This makes money more expensive to borrow. Businesses borrow less, and the economy slows. Businesspeople spend less money on everything they need to grow, including labor and machinery.

51. In theory when the Fed lowers interest rates businesses tend to borrow more and the economy takes off.

CRITICAL THINKING EXERCISES

Learning Goal 1
1. Adam Smith believed that an economy would prosper when people were allowed to produce needed goods and services and keep the profit in an attempt to improve their own standard of living. When people saw the potential gain from working hard and hiring others to help work, Smith argued that new businesses would be created, fueled by a desire for wealth. The invisible hand turned individual gain into social and economic benefits. Ray Kroc, the founder of McDonald's saw a need for fast food in the marketplace. He took an idea and developed it into a multibillion-dollar corporation. He became a self-made millionaire, and spawned several companies along the way.
   These companies have provided jobs for thousands of people, from high school kids working the counter after school to the franchisee who owns twenty restaurants to the advertising executive in charge of the McDonald's account. The companies benefiting from McDonalds' success provide a service U.S. consumers need and want, make a living providing goods and services and give people jobs. McDonald's also goes beyond jobs and other tangible economic benefits, with Ronald McDonald Houses providing a social benefit beyond economic measure.

Learning Goal 2

2.   a. Profit   e. Private property
      b. Private property   f. Freedom of choice
      c. Competition   g. Competition
      d. Freedom of choice   h. Private property

3.

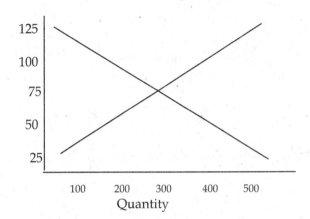

    a.   The equilibrium price is $75.
    b.   300 units will be supplied at that price.

4.   a. up   d. down
      b. down   e. down
      c. up

5.   a. perfect competition   c. monopolistic competition
      b. monopoly   d. oligopoly

Learning Goals 2,3

6.   In her discussions with Jean-Paul, Julie might defend capitalism by saying that one benefit of the free-market system is that it allows open competition among companies. Businesses must provide customers with quality goods and services at fair prices with good service or they will lose customers to other companies that do just that. She might also say that in the U.S. there is a benefit to working hard because we have the incentive of being able to keep the rewards of our work – i.e. profits.

    Julie might say further that the drawback of living in a socialist system is that the tax rate is so high that there is little incentive to work hard, be innovative and create new products because the government takes away so much of what you earn. Consequently, there are fewer inventions and less innovation because those who come up with new ideas usually don't receive as much reward as they would in a capitalist system.

    Jean-Paul may respond that a major limitation of capitalism is the inequality of wealth distribution in a capitalist system. Business owners make more money than the workers, and some people who are old, disabled or don't have the talent to run a business can't create wealth for themselves. A major benefit of socialism is social equality. There is more equality because income is taken from the richer people in the form of taxes and redistributed to the poorer members of the population through various government programs such as free education, free health care, and free child care. Workers in these countries get longer vacations and tend to work fewer hours per week and have more employee benefits than workers in capitalist countries.

7. In Chapter One we learned that one of the ways governments can foster entrepreneurship is to keep tax rates reasonable. High tax rates tend to discourage entrepreneurship because small businesses, particularly, can't afford to pay those taxes. Since socialist nations traditionally have high tax rates, the potential is that entrepreneurship could be adversely affected, and some people who would ordinarily start a business don' t do so because they would not be able to afford the tax rates imposed on them by a socialist system.

Learning Goals 2,3,4
8.   a. Socialism   f. Mixed economy
        b. Capitalism   g. Could be either capitalism or mixed economy
        c. Capitalism   h. Communism
        d. Communism
        e. Socialism

Learning Goal 5
9. Increases in productivity mean that the same amount of labor is able to produce a greater output. Costs are thus lower in producing goods and services, and so prices can be lower. So, efficiency in both manufacturing and the service sector can help to hold down inflation. If productivity slows, GDP growth could also slow. This would have a negative effect on the economy.

10.   a. cyclical   c. structural
       b. seasonal   d. frictional

Learning Goal 6
11.   a. Fiscal policy   e. Monetary policy
       b. Monetary policy   f. Fiscal policy
       c. Fiscal policy   g. Fiscal policy
       d. Fiscal policy   h. Fiscal policy

12. Small business owners, who create many of the jobs and much of the wealth for the economy, are often severely affected by changes in the tax rates. In theory, these business owners may add jobs and hire more people when they know their tax liability will be lower as a result of a tax reduction. Consequently, while tax rates may be lower, a greater number of people will be paying in to the system, and this could have the effect of increasing government tax revenues.

PRACTICE TEST

MULTIPLE CHOICE
LG 1 # 1-3
LG 2 #4-10
LG 3 #11-13
LG 4 #14
LG 5 #15-18
LG 6 #19-21

TRUE-FALSE
LG 1 #1-2
LG 2 # 3-6
LG 3 #7-10
LG 4 # 11-12
LG 5 #13-19
LG 6 #20-21

1. d	12. d	1. T	12.T
2. a	13. a	2. T	13. F
3. b	14. c	3. T	14. T
4. d	15. c	4. F	15. F
5. a	16. b	5. F	16. F
6. a	17. b	6. F	17. T
7. a	18. d	7. T	18. T
8. d	19. c	8. T	19. F
9. c	20. c	9. F	20. T
10. d	21. a	10.T	21. F
11. c		11. F	

CHAPTER 3 – COMPETING IN GLOBAL MARKETS

LEARNING GOALS

After you have read and studied this chapter, you should be able to:

1. Discuss the growing importance of the global market and the roles of comparative advantage and absolute advantage in global trade.
2. Explain the importance of importing and exporting, and understand key terms used in global business.
3. Illustrate the strategies used in reaching global markets and explain the role of multinational corporations in global markets.
4. Evaluate the forces that affect trading in global markets.
5. Debate the advantages and disadvantages of trade protectionism.
6. Discuss the changing landscape of the global market and the issue of offshore outsourcing.

LEARNING THE LANGUAGE

Listed below are important terms found in this chapter. Choose the correct term for each definition and write it in the space provided.

Absolute advantage	4	Embargo	6	Joint venture	12
Balance of payments	5	Exchange rate	10	Licensing	13
Balance of trade	9	Exporting	15	Multinational corporation	16
Common market	14	Foreign direct investment	23	North American Free Trade Agreement (NAFTA)	26
Comparative advantage theory	17	Foreign subsidiary	24	Strategic alliance	1
Contract manufacturing	18	Free trade	20	Tariff	2
Countertrading	22	General Agreement on Tariffs and Trade (GATT)	27	Trade deficit	8
Devaluation	19	Import quota	7	Trade protectionism	21
Dumping	3	Importing	11	World Trade Organization (WTO)	25

1. A long-term partnership between two or more companies, a _____ is established to help each company build competitive market advantages.

2. A tax known as a _____ is imposed on imports.

3. The practice of selling products in foreign countries at lower prices than you charge for the same products in the producing country is known as _____.

4. A country has a(n) _____ when it has a monopoly on the production of a specific product or is able to produce it more efficiently than all other countries.

5. The difference between money coming into a country and money leaving the country plus money-flows from other factors such as tourism, foreign aid, military expenditures and foreign investment is the _____.

6. A(n) _____ is a complete ban on the import or export of a certain product or when all trade with a particular country has been stopped.

7. When there is a limit on the number of products in certain categories that can be imported, a(n) _____ has been established.

8. An unfavorable balance of trade, or _____ occurs when the value of a country's imports exceeds that of its exports.

9. A nation's _____ is its ratio of exports to imports.

10. The _____ is the value of one currency relative to the currencies of other countries.

11. A country is involved in _____ when it is buying products from another country.

12. In a _____ a partnership has been formed in which two or more companies, often from different countries, have joined to undertake a major project.

13. A global strategy known as _____ is one in which a firm allows a foreign company to produce its product in exchange for a fee.

14. The European Union is an example of a _____, a regional group of countries that have no internal tariffs, a common external tariff and a coordination of laws to facilitate exchange between countries. It is also known as a trading bloc.

15. A company is involved in _____ when it is selling products to another country.

16. An organization that manufactures and markets products in many different countries and has multinational stock ownership and multinational management is a(n) _____.

17. The theory of _____ asserts that a country should sell to other countries those products that it produces most effectively and efficiently, and buy from those other countries those products that it cannot produce as effectively and efficiently

18. Also known as outsourcing, _____ occurs when a foreign country produces private-label goods to which a domestic company then attaches its brand name or trademark.

19. Lowering the value of a nation's currency relative to other currencies is known as _____.

20. There is _____ when the movement of goods and services among nations occurs without political or economic obstruction.

21. The use of government regulations to limit the import of goods and services is considered to be _____, which advocates believe will allow domestic producers to survive and grow, producing more jobs.

22. A complex form of bartering known as _____ occurs when several countries each trade goods for goods or services for services.

23. Many countries today are involved in _____, which is the buying of permanent property and businesses in foreign nations.

24. A _____ is a company that is owned in a foreign country by another company called the parent company.

25. This organization, known as the _____, replaced the GATT agreement and was assigned the duty to mediate trade disputes among nations.

26. The agreement known as the _____ created a free trade agreement between the United States, Canada, and Mexico.

27. The agreement signed in 1948 called the _____ established an international forum for negotiating mutual reductions in trade restrictions.

ASSESSMENT CHECK

Learning Goal 1
The Dynamic Global Market

1. What are some facts that indicate the importance of international business for U.S. firms?

a._____

b._____

c._____

d._____

e._____

2. What are three reasons why countries trade with each other?

a. _____

b. _____

c. _____

3. What are the pros and cons of free trade?

Pros   Cons

a. _____   a. _____

b. _____   b. _____

c. _____   c. _____

d. _____   d. _____

e. _____   e. _____

55

4. How does the comparative advantage theory benefit the United States and its trading partners?

Learning Goal 2
Getting Involved in Global Trade

5. Where is the greatest job potential for working in global markets?

6. Explain how many individuals and entrepreneurs have become involved in the global marketplace through importing and exporting.

7. How would you describe the impact exporting has had on the U.S. economy?

Measuring Global Trade

8. What is the difference between a favorable balance of trade and an unfavorable balance of trade?

9. Why do countries prefer to have a favorable balance of trade?

10. Explain the difference between the balance of trade and the balance of payments. What is the goal regarding the balance of payments?

11. Does the United States have a favorable or unfavorable balance of trade?

12. How can we explain that while the U.S. has an unfavorable balance of trade (trade deficit) the U.S. is still one of the world's largest exporters?

13. Why do countries use the tactic of dumping?

Learning Goal 3
Strategies for Reaching Global Markets

14. List seven strategies for reaching global markets

    a._____   d._____

    b._____   e._____

    c._____   f._____

15. What are the advantages and disadvantages of licensing?

    Advantages: a. _____

                     b. _____

                     c. _____

    Disadvantages: a. _____

                     b. _____

                     c._____

16. What is an Export Assistance Center? What are export-trading companies?

17. When they go global, franchisers must be careful to:

18. Describe the benefits of contract manufacturing.

19. What are the reasons companies enter into international joint ventures?

20. What are the benefits and drawbacks of international joint ventures?

Benefits   Drawbacks

a. _____   a. _____

b. _____   b. _____

c. _____   c. _____

21. What do strategic alliances provide for participating companies? How is a strategic alliance different from a joint venture?

22. How does a foreign subsidiary operate? What are the advantages? Disadvantages?

23. In what way is a multinational corporation different from a company that is simply doing business globally?

Learning goal 4
Forces Affecting Trading in Global Markets

24. Four forces affecting trading in global markets are:

a. _____

b._____

c._____

d._____

25. What elements are included in a description of the term "culture"?

26. How have American business people adapted to global marketing compared to business people from other nations?

27. Identify the components of culture that have significant impact on business operations, according to the text.

28. A sound philosophy to adopt in global markets is

_____

29. Discuss how economic conditions will affect consumption of goods that might seem to have great global opportunity.

30. What is meant by a "high value of the dollar"? What impact does a "high value of the dollar" have on U.S. businesses?

31. What is meant by a "low value of the dollar"? What impact does this have on U.S. businesses?

32. What is a floating exchange rate"? How is supply and demand for currencies created?

33. Why would a country devalue it s currency?

34. When a country has an especially weak currency the only possibility of trade is often through *bartering*, which is: _____

35. The understanding of what three things is vital to a company's success in the global market?

  a. _____ b. _____ c. _____

36. What characteristics of legal and regulatory forces make conducting global business so difficult?

37. What does the Foreign Corrupt Practices Act prohibit? What is the impact on American firms?

38. With regard to legal and regulatory forces, what must businesses do to increase their chances of success in foreign markets?

39. Give some examples in the area of technology that pose challenges for doing business in global markets.

Learning Goal 5
Trade Protectionism

40. According to the text, advocates believe trade protectionism allows_____.

    Countries often use trade protectionism measures to_____.

41. Describe the economic philosophy that led governments to impose tariffs.

42. List five forms of trade protectionism

    a. _____   d. _____

    b. _____   e. _____

    c. _____

43. Distinguish between a revenue tariff and a protective tariff.

44. What are non-tariff barriers? Provide examples of non-tariff barriers.

45. What was the purpose of the GATT? What two areas are covered by the Uruguay round of the GATT, passed in 1994?

46. How was the World Trade Organization created, and what is the primary task of the WTO?

47. What are some of the continuing problems and challenges faced by the WTO?

48. What is the EU?

49. The euro is: _____

50. What countries are a part of the Mercosur? How successful has the Mercosur been in reaching its goals?

51. What does NAFTA stand for? What three countries are a part of the NAFTA agreement?

52. The objectives of NAFTA were:

a. _____

b. _____

c. _____

d. _____

e. _____

f. _____

53. The opponents of NAFTA warned _____

The supporters of NAFTA predicted _____

54. Has NAFTA been successful?

55. What is CAFTA? What are the issues surrounding this agreement?

Learning Goal 6
The Future of Global Trade

56. How has the Internet changed global trade?

57. Describe the importance of the Chinese market in today's global trade environment.

58. What are some concerns about entering the Chinese market?

59. What is the potential for markets in India and Russia and other parts of Asia? What are the concerns?

60. What is meant by the term "offshore outsourcing"? How is the "second wave" of offshore outsourcing changing this practice?

61. What two countries are at the center of the offshore outsourcing controversy, and in what areas are these countries focusing?

CRITICAL THINKING EXERCISES

Learning Goal 1
1. How does the theory of comparative advantage relate to the development of free trade agreements around the world, such as NAFTA and the EU?

Learning Goal 2

2. Re-read the example of the ice factory in Africa, and the other examples of opportunities found in international markets. How do they illustrate the importance of entrepreneurship, capitalism and Adam Smith's "invisible hand" theory in the international market? How can you take advantage of the opportunities?

3. There are several terms used in global trade:
    a. Balance of trade
    b. Trade deficit
    c. Balance of payments
    d. Dumping

    Match the term with the description below:

    _____ An un favorable one means that there is more money flowing into the country than flowing out of the country

    _____ Japan, Brazil, Russia and Canada have all been accused of this in the U.S. market.

    _____ A favorable one occurs when the value of the country's exports exceeds the value of the country's imports.

    _____ Another name for this is an unfavorable balance of trade.

Learning Goals 2, 3

4. There are several ways to reach global markets:

    Licensing   Contract manufacturing
    Exporting   International Joint ventures
    Franchising   Foreign Direct Investment

    Match the term with the situations below:

    a. _____ This partnership with a Japanese food concern gave Campbell Soup a chance to increase its low market share in Japan's soup market, which is very difficult to enter.

    b. _____ In this kind of agreement, also known as outsourcing, Nike gives it's name to shoes manufactured overseas and distributed in the United States.

    c. _____ McDonald's, Holiday Inn, and Dunkin Donuts have agreements to operate in foreign markets using this form of arrangement, after allowing the local operators to change their product to suit local tastes.

d. _____ In the early 2000s Anheuser Busch acquired the Harbin Brewery Group in Harbin China, and currently operates a total of 14 breweries in that country.

e. _____ GE has a number of bilingual workers with advanced degrees in its trading department to help the corporation with this kind of international trade, selling their product to foreign markets.

f. _____ Coke and Pepsi often enter foreign markets by allowing a foreign manufacturer to use its trademark and pay them (Coke and Pepsi) a royalty for that right.

Learning Goal 4
5. Discuss the issues of the value of the dollar relative to other currencies. What is the impact of a lower value of the dollar? How would American businesses be affected if the dollar were devalued, as the Mexican peso was a few years ago?

6. The everyday difficulties of doing business at home are compounded by a variety of differences between U.S. and foreign markets. Difficulties can stem from cultural and social differences, economic problems, legal and political regulations and physical and environmental forces such as technology. Keep those ideas in mind in completing the following.

    You have a successful ice cream/frozen yogurt business in the United States, and are especially interested in opening a store in South America, probably Argentina or Chile. You market your product thorough free- standing buildings in the U.S., but are unsure of how to start up in South America. You have begun to seriously think about the possibility, but are concerned about some of the problems you may encounter. What are forces affecting trade in global markets will you need to consider before going ahead with your plan?

7. Governments have developed a number of ways to protect their domestic industries from what they would consider the potentially negative impact of foreign trade:

Protective tariffs   Embargoes

Revenue tariffs   Non-tariff barriers

Import quotas

Match the correct type of trade protectionism to each of the following:

_____   a. The amount of Argentine beef brought into the United States is limited by this form of agreement

_____   b. Mexico has several of this type of tariff, designed to raise money for its government.

_____   c. The U.S. imposed this type of "restriction" on Chinese textiles, in retaliation for the pirating of U.S. made products by Chinese manufacturers. The effect of this "restriction" was an increase in the cost of Chinese textiles sold in the United States.

_____   d. The U.S. has refused to allow the products of Cuba and some other countries to be sold in the U.S. under one of these programs.

_____   e. Denmark requires margarine to be sold in cubes, cutting off those companies that manufacture margarine in tubs.

Learning Goals 4, 6
8. Look at the website for Coca-Cola (www.coke.com). How has today's technology enabled this company to reach a much larger marketplace? What has this company done to address the issues involved in taking an "American" company global?

Learning goal 6
9. Using the Google search engine, search the term "Chinese market." Click on any of the first few websites that appear. What information appears? How does this reinforce the examples in the text about the growing importance of the Chinese market worldwide?

PRACTICE TEST

MULTIPLE CHOICE – Circle the best answer

Learning Goal 1

1. Selling products to another country is known as:
    a. importing.
    b. trade protectionism.
    c. comparative advantage
    d. exporting.

2. All of the following are reasons for countries to participate in foreign trade except
    a. it is just as easy to start a business overseas as it is in the U.S.
    b. no nation can produce all of the products its people want and need.
    c. even if a country were self-sufficient, other nations would seek to trade with that country in order to meet the needs of its own people
    d. some nations have resources, but not technological know-how; while others have know-how, but lack resources.

3. The idea that countries should produce and sell goods that they produce most effectively and efficiently, and buy goods that other countries produce most effectively and efficiently is known as:
    a. absolute advantage.
    b. free trade.
    c. international marketing.
    d. comparative advantage theory.

Learning Goal 2

4. When the value of exports from a country exceeds the value of imports into that country, there is a:
    a. trade deficit.
    b. balance of payments.
    c. favorable balance of trade.
    d. unfavorable balance of trade.

5. The difference between money coming into a country from exports and money leaving a country due to imports, plus money flows from other factors, is known as the:
    a. balance of trade
    b. free trade.
    c. balance of payments.
    d. trade deficit.

6. The United States exports:
    a. less volume, but a greater percentage of our products than other countries.
    b. greater volume than other countries, and a greater percentage of our products.
    c. about the same volume as other countries , but a lower percentage of our products.
    d. a greater volume than other countries, but a lower percentage of our products.

7. In global trade, the term "dumping" refers to:
    a. a situation that exists when a country exports more than it imports.
    b. the buying of permanent property and businesses in foreign nations.
    c. the practice of selling products in a foreign country at lower prices than those charged in the producing country.
    d. A foreign company's production of private-label goods to which a domestic company attaches its own brand name.

8. In recent years the Nestle Company has acquired several U.S. firms, such as Carnation. Carnation now operates in the U.S. as a(n):
    a. exporter.
    b. subsidiary.
    c. licensing agent.
    d. franchise.

9. Coke and Pepsi often enter foreign markets by allowing a foreign manufacturer to use their trademark and pay them (Coke or Pepsi) a royalty for that right. This is an example of
    a. a joint venture.
    b. exporting.
    c. licensing.
    d. a strategic alliance.

10. In franchising to foreign markets, companies such McDonald's and KFC have had to:
    a. be careful to adapt to the countries they are attempting to enter.
    b. find franchisees with money they can afford to lose if the franchise fails.
    c. be sure not to alter their products for the foreign countries, so that consumers know exactly what they are getting.
    d. find opportunities for joint ventures, as franchising doesn't seem to work in foreign markets.

11. Multinational corporations :
    a. are typically extremely large corporations.
    b. are companies that simply export everything they produce.
    c. do not necessarily have manufacturing capacity in other nations.
    d. are predominantly small companies that export their products to many different countries.

12. Americans are often been accused of ethnocentricity. This means that:
    a. Americans feel their culture is superior to others.
    b. Americans welcome diversity in their workforce.
    c. U.S. firms are actively seeking international markets.
    d. U.S. businesses are pursuing a policy of multiculturalism.

13. Guillermo Martinez was concerned that his new boss, Donald Darr didn't know his job very well. Donald is continually asking Guillermo and the other workers in the company's plant in Mexico City to give him their opinions before he makes a final decision. Guillermo's concern stems from _____differences between Donald and him.
    a. economic
    b. cultural
    c. language
    d. regulatory

14. The makers of Whirlpool washers and other electrical appliance manufacturers need to be concerned about the kind and availability of electricity in the global marketplace. If there were a compatibility problem, it would be the result of a _____difference.
    a. cultural
    b. technological
    c. economic
    d. societal

15. The law that specifically prohibits "questionable" or "dubious" payments to foreign officials in an effort to secure business contracts is called the:
    a. North American Free Trade Agreement
    b. General Agreement on Tariffs and Trade
    c. Securities and Exchange Act
    d. Foreign Corrupt Practices Act

16. A low value of the dollar would mean
    a. your American dollar is worth more when purchasing a foreign made good.
    b. a dollar could be traded for less foreign currency than normal.
    c. you could trade in your money for gold.
    d. costs of foreign manufacturing would be higher.

17. When Mexico devalued the peso, the peso became _____ valuable relative to other currencies.
    a. more
    b. less
    c. equally
    d. significantly more

Learning Goal 5
18. Using government regulations to limit the import of goods and services is called:
    a. mercantilism.
    b. regulating the balance of trade.
    c. global marketing.
    d. trade protectionism.

19. When the Vietnamese government imposes a tax on imported electronics products to help their relatively young electronics industry compete in the global marketplace, a(n) _____ is being levied.
    a. protective tariff
    b. import quota
    c. embargo
    d. revenue tariff

20. The EU is an example of a trading bloc, or a _____, which has a common external tariff, no internal tariffs and the coordination of laws to facilitate trade between member countries.
    a. strategic alliance
    b. common market
    c. joint venture
    d. multinational export assistance center

21. The _____ was created 1995, and is assigned the task of mediating trade disputes.
    a. WTO
    b. EU
    c. GATT
    d. NAFTA

22. NAFTA has:
    a. been totally successful, with no difficulties.
    b. decreased exports from the U.S. to its NAFTA partners by 25%.
    c. greatly increased trade flows for Mexico.
    d. reduced concerns about illegal immigration.

23. There are those who hope that the _____ is a precursor to the creation of a Free Trade Area of the Americas. The agreement is between the United States and several Central American countries.
    a. NAFTA
    b. EU
    c. Mercosur
    d. CAFTA

24. Which of the following is not considered to be a concern when evaluating trade with China?
    a. The one-party political system
    b. Human rights policies
    c. A shrinking market
    d. A growing trade imbalance

25. The term "China price" means
    a. the price that would be charged in China for a good sold there.
    b. the price that China charges it's U.S. manufacturers.
    c. the price that companies think customers will want to pay.
    d. the lowest price possible.

TRUE-FALSE

Learning Goal 1
1. _____ It is expected that the amount of international trade will level off or decline in the next millennium.

2. _____ An example of exporting is the Meridian Group, based in the United States, selling sand from the U.S. to customers in the Middle East.

Learning Goal 2
3. _____ When the country of Monrovia is buying less from the United States than it is selling to the United States, a favorable balance of trade exists for Monrovia.

4. _____ Even today, most large businesses are not involved in global trade.

5. _____ In general, it is better to have a favorable balance of trade.

Learning Goal 3
6. _____ An example of contract manufacturing is when Dell contracts with a computer company to manufacture PCs, on which Dell puts the Dell name.

7. _____ One disadvantage of licensing is the cost to the company of licensing its product or trademark (the licensor) to the foreign firm (the licensee).

8. _____ Export Assistance Centers serve the role of matching buyers and sellers from different countries and of providing other services to ease the process of exporting.

Learning Goal 4
9. _____ Religion is an important element of a society's culture and should be considered in making many business decisions.

10. _____ Economic differences between countries can affect purchasing patterns, such as quantity purchased at a given time.

11. _____ A sound global philosophy is "always assume that what works in one country will work in another".

12. _____ It is not necessary to contact local businesspeople in the host country, as they will discourage your attempts to enter their markets for fear of too much competition.

Learning Goal 5

13. _____ Trade protectionism is based upon the idea that barriers will help domestic producers grow and create more jobs.

14. _____ Non-tariff barriers can be just as detrimental to free trade as tariffs.

15. _____ The WTO totally eliminated the internal national laws that impeded global trade expansion.

16. _____ The official monetary unit of the EU is the euro.

Learning Goal 6

17. _____ Investment in China is still considered to be too risky to invest a great deal of money.

18. _____ India and Russia are considered to be potentially lucrative markets for the future.

You Can Find It On The Net

Find the most recent trade statistics for
  a. The United States   Exports / Imports / Balance of Trade (deficit) (surplus)

  b. Your state   Exports/ Imports/ Balance of Trade

What are the top ten countries with which your state trades? What is the largest category of foreign sales? How does this affect businesses and jobs, in your area?

These statistics can be found on the Internet with just a bit of looking around. A good place to start for the information regarding the U.S Trade Statistics is www.census.gov.

For the state data, use a search engine with the key words "exports" and the name of your state. Several websites should appear, including your state's department of economic development.

ANSWERS

LEARNING THE LANGUAGE

1. Strategic alliance	10. Exchange rate	19. Devaluation
2. Tariff	11. Importing	20. Free trade
3. Dumping	12. Joint venture	21. Trade protectionism
4. Absolute advantage	13. Licensing	22. Countertrading
5. Balance of payments	14. Common market	23. Foreign direct investment
6. Embargo	15. Exporting	24. Foreign subsidiary
7. Import quota	16. Multinational corporation (MNC)	25. World Trade Organization (WTO)
8. Trade deficit	17. Comparative advantage theory	26. North American Free Trade Agreement (NAFTA)
9. Balance of trade	18. Contract manufacturing	27. General Agreement on Tariffs and Trade (GATT)

ASSESSMENT CHECK

Learning Goal 1
The Dynamic Global Market
1. a. There are over 6 billion people in the world, and most of them live outside the U.S.
    b. Approximately 75% of the world's population lives in developing areas.
    c. Americans buy billions of dollars' worth of goods from countries such as China and Japan.
    d. The United States is the largest exporting nation in the world.
    e. The United States is the largest importing nation in the world.

2. a. No nation can produce all of the products its people need and want
    b. Even if a given country were self-sufficient, other nations would want to trade with that country to meet the needs of its people
    c. Some nations have many natural resources but limited technological know how, while other countries have sophisticated technology but few resources. Trade allows nations to produce what they are capable of producing and to buy from other nations what they need.

3. Pros
    a. Global market has over 6 billion customers
    b. Productivity grows with comparative advantage
    c. Global competition and lower-cost imports keep prices down
    d. Free trade encourages innovation
    e. Interest rates lower due to uninterrupted flow of capital

    Cons
    a. Domestic workers in manufacturing could lose jobs
    b. Workers face pay-cut demands from employers
    c. Competitive pressure makes some jobs vulnerable to operations moving overseas
    d. Domestic companies can lose comparative advantage when competitors build operations in low wage countries

4. The theory of comparative advantage states that a country should produce and sell to other countries those products that it produces most effectively and efficiently, and should buy from other countries those products it cannot produce as effectively or efficiently. The United States has a comparative advantage in producing goods and services such as software

and engineering services. But we lack a comparative advantage in other areas such as growing coffee, so we import those goods. Through specializing in certain areas, the U.S. and its trading partners can realize mutually beneficial exchanges.

Learning Goal 2
Getting Involved in Global Trade

5. The greatest job potential in global markets may be with small businesses. Today in the U.S. small businesses generate about half of the private-sector commerce, but account for only 30 percent of exports.

6. Exporting and importing products have created a number of opportunities for individuals and entrepreneurs. Foreign students have noticed that some products widely available in their countries are not available in the U.S. Some people see a lack in the U.S. of a particularly appealing product from elsewhere, such as that which Howard Schultz of Starbucks saw in Italy.

   Also, just about any good or service that is used in the U.S. can be used in other countries as well, and the competition abroad is often not nearly as intense for most providers of these products as it is at home.

7. Exporting has been a terrific boost to the U.S. economy. The Institute for International Economics estimates that every $1 billion in U.S. exports generates 25,000 jobs at home.

Measuring Global Trade

8. A favorable balance of trade exists when the value of exports exceeds the value of imports. An unfavorable balance of trade occurs when the value of the country's imports exceeds that of its exports.

9. Countries prefer to export more than they import, or have a favorable balance of trade, because the country will retain more of its money to buy other goods and services. As the example in the text illustrates, if I sell you $200 worth of goods, and only buy $100, I have an extra $100 available to buy other things.

10. The balance of trade is a nation's relationship of exports to imports. The balance of payments is the difference between money coming into a country from exports and money leaving a country for imports, plus money flows from other factors. The goal is always to have more money flowing into the country than flowing out of the country; in other words, a favorable balance of payments.

11. The United States has bought more goods from other nations than it has sold to other nations every year since 1975. So, the U.S. has an unfavorable balance of trade.

12. Even though the U.S. exports the largest volume of goods globally, it exports a much lower percentage of its products than other countries do. In the past, as few as 10% of U.S. firms exported products.

13. Dumping is sometimes used to reduce surplus products in foreign markets or to gain a foothold in a new market by offering products for lower prices than domestic competitors.

Strategies for Reaching Global markets

14. a. Licensing
    b. Exporting
    c. Franchising

    d. Contract manufacturing
    e. International joint ventures and strategic alliances
    g. Foreign direct investment

15. <u>Advantages of licensing are</u>:
   a. Additional revenue from a product that would not have generated domestic revenues
   b. Start-up supplies, materials and consulting services must be purchased from the licensing firm, which generates even more revenue and reduces costs of entering a foreign market.
   c. Licensors spend little or no money to produce and market their products. Most costs are borne by the licensee.

   <u>Disadvantages with licensing include</u>:
   a. A firm often must grant licensing rights to its product for as long as 20 years. Revenue from an especially successful product would then go to the licensee.
   b. If a foreign licensee learns the technology, it could break its agreement and begin to produce the product on its own. The licensing company loses trade secrets and royalties.

16. An Export Assistance Center (EAC) provides hands-on exporting assistance and trade finance support for small and medium sized businesses that choose to export. Export trading companies are specialists in matching buyers and sellers from different countries and providing services to ease the process of entering foreign markets.

17. When going global, franchisers must be careful to adapt the customs of the countries they serve. They must consider customs, tastes, and other social factors in developing markets for their products.

18. Through contract manufacturing a company can experiment in a new market without heavy start-up costs, which reduces risk. A firm can also use contract manufacturing temporarily to meet an unexpected increase in orders.

19. Sometimes joint ventures are mandated by governments as a condition of doing business in their country. There are business reasons that joint ventures are developed, such as the opportunity to expand low market share in participating countries.

20. Benefits of international joint ventures include:
   a. Shared technology and risk.
   b. Shared marketing and management expertise.
   c. Entry into markets where foreign companies are not allowed unless their goods are produced locally.
   Drawbacks are:
   a. One partner can learn the other's technology and go off on its own as a competitor.
   b. Over time, technology may become obsolete
   c. Joint venture may become too large to be flexible.

21. These alliances can provide access to markets, capital and technical expertise, but unlike joint ventures, they do not involve sharing costs, risk, management or profits. Strategic alliances can be flexible and they can effectively link firms of different sizes.

22. A foreign subsidiary operates much like a domestic firm, with production, distribution, promotion, pricing, and other business functions under the control of the foreign subsidiary's management. The primary advantage of a subsidiary is that the company maintains complete control over any technology or other expertise it may possess.

    The major disadvantage of creating a subsidiary is that the parent company is committing a large amount of funds and technology within foreign boundaries. If relations with the host country take a downturn, the firm's assets could be taken over by the foreign government. That kind of takeover is called an expropriation.

23. Multinational corporations are typically extremely large corporations. They are different from a company that is simply doing business globally because an MNC has manufacturing capacity or some other physical presence in different nations. A business that is exporting everything it produces and derives 100 percent of its sales and profits globally would not be considered multinational.

Learning Goal 4
Forces Affecting Trading in Global Markets

24. Four forces affecting trading in global markets are:
    a. Socio-cultural
    b. Economic and financial
    c. Legal and regulatory
    d. Physical and environmental

25. Culture refers to the set of values, beliefs, rules, and institutions held by a specific group of people. Primary components of a culture can include social structure, religion, manners and customs, values and attitudes, language, and personal communication.

26. Many American businesspeople have been accused of ethnocentricity, the feeling that one's own culture is superior to all others. By contrast, foreign business people are very good at adapting to U.S. culture.

27. Some of the socio-cultural elements of which it is important to be aware when working with individuals from other cultures are religion and religious customs, and management of employees.

28. A sound philosophy to adopt in global markets is "Never assume that what works in one country will work in another."

29. The text cites examples such as in Haiti, where customers can only buy small quantities of gum, for example because of their low incomes. Cultural conditions as well as economic conditions affect companies like Hershey's, Skippy peanut butter and Coca-Cola. Indians only consume three soft drinks per person because they drink tea, and most people can't afford chocolate or peanut butter.

30. A high value of the dollar means that the dollar can be traded for more foreign currency than previously. When the dollar is high the products of foreign producers become cheaper, because it takes fewer dollars to buy them. The cost of U.S.-produced goods, on the other hand, becomes more expensive to foreign buyers, because of the dollar's high value.

31. A low value of the dollar means that the dollar will buy or can be traded for less foreign currency than normal. Therefore, foreign goods become more expensive in the U.S. because it takes more dollars to buy them; but American goods become cheaper to foreign buyers because it takes less foreign currency to buy American goods.

32. The floating exchange rate is a system in which currencies "float" according to the supply and demand in the market for the currency. The supply and demand for currencies is created by global currency traders, who create a market for a nation's currency based on the perceived trade and investment potential of the country.

33. A country may devalue its currency in order to increase the export potential of its products.

34. Bartering is the exchange of merchandise for merchandise or service for service with no money involved.

35. To be successful in global markets it is important to understand:
    a. economic conditions   b. currency fluctuations   c. countertrade opportunities

36. Some of the legal and regulatory difficulties in the global market stem from the fact that in global markets no central system of law exists, so different systems of laws and regulations may apply. Businesspeople find laws and regulations in global markets that are often inconsistent. Important legal questions related to antitrust rules, labor relations, patents, copyrights, trade practices, taxes, product liability, child labor, prison labor, and other issues are written and interpreted differently country by country.

37. The Foreign Corrupt Practices Act specifically prohibits "questionable" or "dubious" payments to foreign officials to secure business contracts. This type of legislation can create hardships for American businesses in competing with foreign competitors, because in some countries actions such as corporate bribery are acceptable, and sometimes the only way to secure a lucrative contract.

38. To be successful in global markets it is often important to contact local businesspeople and gain their cooperation and sponsorship. Local contacts can help a company penetrate the market and deal with bureaucratic barriers.

39. Technological constraints may make it difficult to conduct business in developing countries. Some developing countries have primitive transportation and storage systems that make international distribution ineffective. Technological differences also affect the nature of exportable products, such as electrical appliances. Computer and Internet usage in many developing countries is also a concern, because it can be spotty or even non-existent in some countries. This would make doing business and conducting e-commerce difficult.

Trade Protectionism

40. Advocates of trade protectionism believe it allows domestic producers to survive and grow, producing more jobs.

    Countries often use protectionist measures to guard against such practices as dumping. Many countries are wary of foreign competition in general.

41. Tariffs basically came out of the economic belief called mercantilism. The primary idea behind mercantilism is for a nation to sell more goods to other nations than it bought from them, or, to have a favorable balance of trade. This should result in a flow of money to the country that sells the most globally.

42. Forms of trade protectionism are:
    a. Protective tariffs
    b. Revenue tariffs
    c. Import quotas
    d. Embargoes
    e. Non-tariff barriers

43. A protective tariff is designed to raise the retail price of an imported good so the domestic product will be more competitive. The revenue tariff is designed to raise money for the government and to help infant industries compete in global markets.

44. Nontariff barriers take a variety of forms. They are not as specific as other forms of protectionism but can be as detrimental to free trade. Countries have imposed restrictive standards that detail exactly how a product must be sold in a country, such as Denmark, which requires companies to sell butter in cubes. Japan for many years used the keiretsu as a way to keep out foreign manufacturers. The Japanese tradition of keiretsu was one in which corporate families forged semi-permanent ties with suppliers, customers, and distributors with the support of the government.

45. The GATT established an international forum for negotiating mutual reductions in trade restrictions. Countries agreed to negotiate to create monetary and trade agreements that might facilitate the exchange of goods, services, ideas, and cultural programs.

   The Uruguay round of the GATT lowered tariffs by 38 percent worldwide and extended GATT rules to new areas such as agriculture, services and the protection of patents.

46. The World Trade Organization (WTO) was created by the Uruguay round of the GATT to assume the task of mediating trade disputes. The WTO acts as an independent entity that oversees key cross-border trade issues and global business practices.

47. One area that affects the WTO are the legal and regulatory problems which impede trade expansion. Also, a wide divide exists between developing nations, which are a majority of WTO membership, and industrialized nations such as the United States, in areas of protection of manufactured goods, subsidies on agricultural products and continuing protectionist measures that impede global trade.

48. The EU is a group of nations in Europe that united economically and formed a common market. EU nations make Europe the world's second largest economy and a strong competitor in global commerce.

49. The euro is the currency commonly used in most member countries of the EU.

50. The Mercosur consists of the countries of Brazil, Argentina, Paraguay, Uruguay and associate members Chile and Bolivia. Its goals are economic in nature, and include a single currency. The Mercosur trade bloc has not advanced its goals.

51. NAFTA stands for the North American Free Trade Agreement. The three countries that are part of NAFTA are the United States, Canada and Mexico.

52. The objectives of NAFTA were to:
    a. eliminate trade barriers and facilitate cross-border movement of goods and services between the three member countries.
    b. promote conditions of fair competition in the free trade area.
    c. increase investment opportunities in the territories of the three nations.
    d. provide effective protection and enforcement of intellectual property rights.
    e. establish a framework for further regional trade cooperation.
    f. improve working conditions in North America.

53. Opponents of NAFTA warned of serious economic consequences. Their concerns focused on the loss of U.S. jobs and the amount of capital leaving the U.S. Supporters predicted that NAFTA would open a vast new market for U.S. exports that would create jobs and market opportunities in the long term.

54. NAFTA has had positive and negative consequences. The value of U.S. exports to NAFTA partners, and trade have increased significantly since the agreement was signed.
    On the down side, it is estimated that the U.S. has lost between 500,000 and 1 million jobs. Per capita income in Mexico still lags behind the U.S. causing illegal immigration to be a continuing problem.

55. CAFTA is an agreement which created a free trade zone with the U.S. and several Central American nations - Costa Rica, the Dominican Republic, El Salvador, Guatemala, Honduras, and Nicaragua.
    Supporters claim that the agreement will open new markets, lower tariffs, and ease regulations. Critics argue that the agreement will cost American jobs in textiles and sugar industries.

Learning Goal 6
The Future of Global Trade

56. The growth of the Internet and advances in e-commerce have enabled companies worldwide to bypass normally required distribution channels to reach a large market.

57. China's economy has grown since it changed from a central planning economy to free markets and the country has now surpassed Japan to become the world's third largest exporter. U.S. foreign direct investment in China is the primary means by which U.S. companies deliver goods to China, and China attracts more foreign investment than the United States. Companies such as General Motors and Wal-Mart have invested heavily in the Chinese market.

58. Concerns remain about China's one-party political system, its human rights policies, the growing trade imbalance, and difficulties in China's financial markets. Product piracy and counterfeiting are also significant problems, and China's underground economy actively counterfeits everything from Callaway Golf clubs to Kiwi shoe polish and Louis Vuitton bags. Economists warn that profits will take a long time to materialize for companies doing business in China.

59 India and Russia represent enormous opportunities because of their large populations. The concerns stem from poverty, difficult trade laws, political, currency and social problems.

    Developing nations of Indonesia, Thailand, Singapore, the Philippines, Korea, Malaysia and Vietnam also offer potential for U.S. businesses.

60. Offshore outsourcing refers to the shift in outsourcing manufacturing and services from domestic businesses to countries with much lower wage rates. The "second wave" of offshore outsourcing involves large numbers of skilled, well-educated, middle-income workers in service sector jobs such as accounting, law, financial and risk management, health care, and information technology that were thought to be safe from foreign market competition.

61. China and India are the countries where many jobs are moving. China is concentrating on low technology manufacturing, but is intent on developing advanced manufacturing technology. India is focusing currently on areas such as call centers, telemarketing, data entry, billing and low-end software development. However the country has a large number of scientists, software engineers, chemists, accountants, lawyers, and physicians.

CRITICAL THINKING EXERCISES

Learning Goal 1
1. The theory of comparative advantage states that a country should sell to other countries those products that it produces most effectively and efficiently, and buy from other countries those products it cannot produce as effectively or efficiently. The development of free trade agreements such as NAFTA and the EU can enable trading partners not only to reduce prices of traded products within those countries, but enables these trading blocs to use comparative advantage to their benefit to realize mutually beneficial exchanges for all members by focusing their efforts on those products and services in which each member has a comparative advantage. The trading blocs have an economic advantage that can make them a strong competitor in the global market, better able to take advantage of the theory of comparative advantage.

Learning Goal 2
2. It was stated in chapter 2 that developing countries must allow entrepreneurship to flourish if their economies are to develop and become active participants in the global market. The same can be said for any part of the world. Adam Smith's idea of the invisible hand was simply that when an individual is allowed the incentive to work hard by being allowed to keep the profits from his business, society will benefit by getting needed goods or services. The story of the ice factory illustrates the invisible hand theory - the entrepreneur started the factory and gained a considerable return on his idea, the people in the country have a needed product and more jobs.

The way to take advantage of these ideas is by doing research, traveling, finding a need either in the United States for a product that can be imported, or overseas for a product that can be exported. The key is to <u>be creative</u>.

3. c – Balance of payments
   d - dumping
   a – balance of trade
   b – trade deficit

Learning Goals 2,3
4. a. International Joint venture.
    b. Contract Manufacturing
    c. Franchising

    d. Foreign direct investment
    e Exporting
    f. Licensing

Learning Goal 4
5. A lower value of the dollar means that a dollar is traded for less foreign currency than normal. Foreign goods would become more expensive because it would take more dollars to buy them. It also makes American goods cheaper to foreign buyers because it would take less foreign currency to buy them. In the long run, this could benefit U.S. firms in foreign markets. Devaluing a currency means lowering the value of a nation's currency relative to other currencies. This can cause problems with changes in labor costs, material costs and financing.
American businesses would find their products less expensive in foreign countries, which could be beneficial for sales, but their cost of doing business in foreign countries could be negatively affected by devaluation.

6. One of the first things that should be considered is how the South Americans feel about ice cream/frozen yogurt as a product. How it's eaten, their views on dairy products (some religions have different views on dairy products and how they should be handled), where it

can be marketed (do they have the same kind of grocery stores? do you open a free standing store?), even their familiarity with the product are all issues that must be addressed. There is a possibility that this may be a totally new product concept and you as a seller of the product will need to be aware of how to convince the South American people that this is a viable and acceptable product.

Social and economic differences from the American market must also be considered. In the U.S. frozen yogurt and ice cream may be purchased on a trip to the grocery store, and stored at home in the refrigerator. Is that a similar life style to the South Americans? Is the type of equipment available which is needed to store the product before it is purchased? Does a typical South American home have the type of storage needed, i.e. a freezer? American families may go to an ice cream or frozen yogurt stand as a family outing. Would that be true of a typical South American family? We eat ice cream or frozen yogurt as a dessert or sometimes as a snack. How would the South American population view the product? When might they choose to eat it?

Although Argentina, for example, as a nation may be wealthy, does the average Argentinean have the money to buy a nonessential item like this?

Further questions to be answered revolve around legal and regulatory differences. The way of doing business in South America is quite different from that of the U.S. Laws and regulations will vary, and practices will be different there than at home. The manner of entering business in South America will be different from the U.S.

Additionally, will it be economically feasible to invest in South America? How is the American dollar against the currency of the country you choose? That may affect the ability and willingness of the South Americans to try your product should you simply decide to export your product to the country. Should you decide to attempt to produce and sell your product in South America, the value of the U.S. dollar will take on even more significance in light of the greater investment?

Learning Goal 5
7. a. Import quotas   d. Embargoes
    b. Revenue tariffs   e. Non-tariff barriers
    c. Protective tariffs

Learning Goals 4,6
8. Coca-Cola has been able to reach their international markets conveniently through their website. A website allows them to "advertise", or promote, their product internationally because it is easily accessible to anyone with access to the Internet. It also allows Americans to see how their counterpart soft drink fans are slightly different. The website has geared its various sites to local markets by using the native language and modifying the content of the page for the "local" international market. Each page is different as they have modified each country's page to fit to individual cultures.

Learning Goal 6
9. The article "Luxury Brands Upbeat on Chinese Market" from Bloomberg News showed up on a Google search as this book was being written. The article says that such Italian luxury brands as Prada, Valentino, and Bulgari have entered the Chinese market and are planning to expand the number of stores in that country. The article goes on to state that the market is growing at a pace of 50%-60% a year.

This illustrates the information in the text that the market in China is vast and growing quickly. While the text states that Wal-Mart is expanding in China, this article clearly indicates that it is no only the budget end of the market that has potential, but that the luxury market for high end goods is also expanding.

PRACTICE TEST

MULTIPLE CHOICE

LG 1   #1-3
LG 2   # 4-7
LG 3   # 8-11
LG 4   # 12-17
LG 5   #18-23
LG 6   #24-25

1.	d	13.	b
2.	a	14.	b
3.	d	15.	d
4.	c	16.	b
5.	c	17.	b
6.	d	18.	d
7.	c	19.	a
8.	b	20.	b
9.	c	21.	a
10.	a	22.	c
11.	a	23.	d
12.	a	24.	c
		25.	d

TRUE-FALSE

LG 1   # 1-2
LG 2   # 3-5
LG 3   # 6-8
LG 4   # 9-12
LG 5   # 13-16
LG 6   # 17-18

1.	F	10.	T
2.	T	11.	F
3.	T	12.	F
4.	F	13.	T
5.	T	14.	T
6.	T	15.	F
7.	F	16.	T
8.	F	17.	F
9.	T	18.	T

CHAPTER 4 – DEMONSTRATING ETHICAL BEHAVIOR AND SOCIAL RESPONSIBILTIY

LEARNING GOALS

After you have read and studied this chapter, you should be able to:

1. Explain why legality is only the first step in behaving ethically.
2. Ask the three questions one should answer when faced with a potentially unethical action.
3. Describe management's role in setting ethical standards.
4. Distinguish between compliance-based and integrity-based ethics codes, and list the six steps in setting up a corporate ethics code.
5. Define social responsibility and examine corporate responsibility to various stakeholders.
6. Analyze the role of American businesses in influencing ethical behavior and social responsibility in global markets.

LEARNING THE LANGUAGE

Listed here are important terms found in this chapter. Choose the correct term for each definition and write it in the space provided.

Compliance-based ethics codes	1	Ethics	4
Corporate philanthropy	6	Insider trading	9
Corporate policy	3	Integrity-based ethics codes	5
Corporate responsibility	8	Social audit	2
Corporate social initiatives	11	Whistleblowers	10
Corporate social responsibility	7		

1. Known as _____, these ethical standards emphasize preventing unlawful behavior by increasing control and by penalizing wrongdoers.

2. When a corporation performs a _____ it is conducting a systematic evaluation of an organization's progress toward implementing programs that are socially responsible and responsive.

3. _____ is the dimension of social responsibility that refers to the position a firm takes on social and political issues.

4. Standards of moral behavior, or _____, is behavior that is accepted by society as right or wrong.

5. _____ are ethical standards that define the organization's guiding values, create an environment that supports ethically sound behavior, and stress a shared accountability among employees.

6. The dimension of social responsibility that includes charitable donations to nonprofit groups is called _____.

7. When a business shows concern for the welfare of a society as a whole, it is demonstrating _____.

8.	A dimension of social responsibility known as _____ includes everything from minority hiring practices to making safe products.

9.	An unethical activity called _____ occurs when insiders use private company information to further their own fortunes or those of their family and friends.

10.	People who report illegal or unethical behavior are known as _____.

11.	This form of corporate philanthropy differs from the traditional in that it is directly related to the company's competencies; the efforts are known as _____.

ASSESMENT CHECK

Learning Goal 1
Ethics Is More Than Legality

1.	What are some things that could be done to restore trust in the free market system and in corporate leaders?

2.	According to the text, what kind of thinking has led to the recent scandals in business and government in the United States?

3.	What is the difference between being "ethical" and being "legal"?

4.	How "socially minded" are Americans in general? What information does the text cite to support that claim?

5.	Ethical behavior begins with _____.

	We cannot expect society to become more moral and ethical unless _____.

6.	Describe an "ethical dilemma".

7.   What are three questions to ask yourself when faced with an ethical dilemma?

    a. _____

    b. _____

    c. _____

Managing Businesses Ethically and Responsibly

8.   Organizational ethics begin at _____

    People learn their standards and values from _____

9.   What are the reasons to manage ethically?

    a. _____

    b. _____

    c. _____

    d. _____

    e. _____

    f. _____

    g. _____

    h. _____

10.   Identify the difference between a compliance-based ethics code and an integrity-based ethics code.

11. What are six steps to follow for a long-term improvement of America's business ethics?

a._____

b._____

c._____

d._____

e._____

f._____

12. What is the most important factor to the success of enforcing an ethics code? What makes that person effective?

Learning Goal 5
Corporate Social Responsibility

13. Describe the important characteristics of corporate social responsibility.

14. Identify the four dimensions of corporate social responsibility.

a. _____

b. _____

c. _____

d. _____

15. What examples of socially responsible behavior demonstrated by some U.S. businesses and individuals can you provide?

16. What are four groups that comprise the stakeholders to whom businesses are responsible?

a. _____   c. _____

b. _____   d. _____

17. One responsibility of business toward customers is: _____.

One of the surest ways of failing to please customers is_____.

18. What could be the payoff for socially conscious behavior for a business?

19. How does socially responsible behavior affect shareholders? How do many potential investors view companies which are socially responsible?

20. What is required by Regulation FD, adopted by the SEC in the early 2000s?

21. What responsibilities do businesses have toward employees?

a. _____

b. _____

c. _____

22. When employees feel they have been treated unfairly, they could:

a. _____

b. _____

c. _____

d. _____

e. _____

f. _____

g. _____

23.   What are four areas of business responsibility to society?

        a. _____

        b. _____

        c. _____

        d. _____

24.   What kinds of social contributions have companies made in their effort to build a community?

25.   A major problem of conducting a social audit is _____

        _____

26.   What are some examples of socially responsible business activities?

        a._____

        b._____

        c._____

        d._____

        e._____

27.   How is a "net social contribution" calculated?

28.   Describe the four types of "watch-dog" groups that monitor how well companies enforce ethical and social responsibility policies.

        a. _____

        b. _____

        c. _____

        d. _____

International Ethics and Social Responsibility

29.   Are ethical problems unique to the United States? What is new about the ethical standards used to judge government leaders?

30.   What are many American businesses demanding from their international suppliers in terms of social responsibility?

31.   Describe the Joint Initiative on Corporate Accountability and Workers' Rights.

32.   What questions surround the issue of American ethical standards and international suppliers?

33.   Is it likely that there will be a single set of international rules governing multinational corporations? Why or why not?

CRITICAL THINKING EXERCISES

Learning Goal 1
1.   You are a buyer for a major manufacturer of automotive parts and have control over multi-million dollar contracts. You were recently talking with one of your suppliers and mentioned that you were planning a pleasure trip to Los Angeles with your family, and weren't sure yet where you would be staying. "It's so expensive in L.A. I'm afraid we won't find a decent place to stay." The supplier said that he has contacts in L.A. in the hotel industry, and that he would not only make the reservation for you, but would pay for the hotel stay for you and your family.

Your company's policy regarding "gifts" from suppliers is not entirely clear. Tangible gifts with a value over $50 are not to be accepted. Other things such as dinners, and other intangibles, are to be evaluated on a case-by-case basis, and acceptance is left up to the discretion of the employee. Any employee who violates the policy could face severe penalties, including dismissal.

Is this an ethical dilemma? Why or why not? What ethical issues are involved? Is there a question of "legal versus ethical"? What would you do?

2.   Refer to the ethics check questions in your text and determine how you would handle the following situation.

Daryl, the general supervisor of a marketing department of a mid-sized Midwestern corporation, is an ambitious young man. He is writing a book that he hopes will make a name for himself in the business community. Because the typing for the actual text is very time-consuming, Daryl is using the secretary he shares with 2 other managers, as well as some of his market research interns to both do research and to type the book while they're at work. Because they are often busy doing his book, people from the other departments are finding they can't get their work-related business done. The secretary and interns feel they have to do what Daryl says because he is their direct supervisor.

You are Daryl's peer in another department and you also have outside work you need to have typed. You're annoyed at Daryl's actions, but would rather not inform your boss, (who is also Daryl's boss) about what's going on because you want to maintain a friendly working relationship with Daryl. Besides, you never know how "the boss" is going to react. Sometimes you begin to think that if Daryl can get away with using company equipment, personnel, and time for his personal projects, why can't you? Discuss what you believe are the ethical issues in this situation, and determine how you would handle this situation.

3.   You work for a major car manufacturer as a district manager, calling on car dealerships as a representative of the manufacturer. It is three days before the end of a sales incentive contest, and one of your dealers is close to winning a trip to Hawaii. If your dealer wins the contest for your area, you get a lot of recognition and a good chance for a promotion, which will enable you to stop traveling so much during the week. The dealer wants you to report as "sold" eight cars that he has not yet sold but will have deals on next week, several days after the end of the contest. Those eight cars will put him over the top and enable him to win the contest. You just received a directive from the corporate headquarters on this practice of pre-reporting sales, indicating that the company would take strong action against anyone discovered taking such steps. Your boss and his superior have taken you aside and encouraged you to take whatever action is necessary to win the contest. You think you could get by with it and not get caught. An added problem is that the customer warranty starts the day the car is reported sold, so whoever purchases the car would lose several days of warranty service. What is your manager's role in this situation? What would you do?

Learning Goal 4

4. Ethics codes can be classified into two major categories:
   Compliance-based   Integrity-based

   Read the following examples of corporate behavior, and determine which kind of ethical code the company may be using.

   a. _____ At Mary's Flowers employees are encouraged to be active in community affairs, and to be aware of their obligation to society. The company stresses honesty, provides seminars on making ethical choices, and has a commitment to hire an ethnically diverse workforce.

   b. _____ At Pro-Tec, management has developed and distributed a code of ethics for employees. It defines what is acceptable behavior, and states that "behavior deemed to be unethical will not be tolerated." The policy does not define behavior that would be considered unethical, but does say that if there is a question a manager should be consulted.

5. You have just been hired as Pro-Tech's first Ethics officer. You feel that your first project should be to set up the company's corporate code of ethical conduct. How would you start, and what steps would you take?

Learning Goal 5

6. "...corporate social responsibility is the concern businesses have for the welfare of society." Read the situation described below and answer the questions that follow:

   MUMC is a successful medium-sized firm that supplies parts for electric motors.
   Dan Furlong, the president, was being interviewed by the business features writer of the local newspaper. The reporter asked Dan his views on social responsibility, and how MUMC reflected a socially responsive position. Dan replied that although he had never done a so-called social audit (as the textbooks call it) he did figure that the firm was a good corporate citizen. He said, "We pay our employees a good salary, and the guys in the shop are getting paid above hourly wages for this area. We make a profit, and give everyone a bonus at the holidays. We take a lot or precautions in the shop, and no one has had an accident to speak of in several years. A few cuts or bruises, but that's part of that kind of job. Whenever we have customer complaints, I make sure someone handles them right away. We charge what I think is a fair price for our product, which I think is higher quality than most of my competitors. I pay my bills on time and don't cheat on my taxes. I guess you could say that we are a pretty socially responsible company."

   a. In keeping with the idea of social audits and socially responsible business activities, is Mr. Furlong running the business in a socially responsible manner?

b. Who are Mr. Furlong's stakeholders?

c. What suggestions can you make to improve MUMC's social responsibility position?

7.   Who are four stakeholders to whom businesses are responsible?   What does "being responsible" to each of these groups require?

Learning Goal 6
8.   How does the increasingly global nature of U.S. business impact the issue of social responsibility and ethics?

PRACTICE TEST

MULTIPLE CHOICE – Circle the best answer

Learning Goal 1
1.   What would not be included in a list of actions needed to restore the trust of the American public in the free market system?
    a.   Pass new accounting laws.
    b.   Punish those who have broken the law.
    c.   Define the concept of ethics more narrowly, and make the definition closer to the definition of legality.
    d.   Pass new laws making business, religious and government leaders more accountable for their actions.

2.   The difference between ethics and legality is that:
    a.   Legality reflects how people should treat each other, while ethics is more limiting.
    b.   Ethics refers to ways available to us to protect ourselves from theft, violence, and fraud.
    c.   Legality is narrower than ethics and refers to laws written to protect ourselves.
    d.   Ethics refers to a narrower range of behavior than legality.

3.   A survey revealed that
    a.   many Americans decide what's ethical behavior based upon the situation in which they find themselves.
    b.   most Americans give a considerable amount of time to their communities.
    c.   employees rarely violate safety standards or "goof off" at work.
    d.   most Americans have an absolute sense of what is moral.

4.   According to the text, ethical behavior begins with:
    a.   Corporate leaders.
    b.   Government leaders.
    c.   Religious leaders.
    d.   You and me.

5.   Sometimes an obvious choice from an ethical standpoint has personal or professional drawbacks. An example might be when a supervisor asks you to do something unethical, and you face negative consequences if you refuse. When you are in such a situation you are faced with:
    a.   two lousy choices.
    b.   an ethical dilemma.
    c.   deciding the legality of your choice.
    d.   a social responsibility issue.

6.   Which of the following is not included as one of the questions we must ask when faced with an ethical dilemma?
    a.   Is it legal?
    b.   Is it balanced?
    c.   How will it make me feel about myself?
    d.   Is it okay if everyone else is doing it?

7.   The most basic step in an ethics based management system is asking the question:
    a.   Is it legal?
    b.   Who will know?
    c.   Is it balanced?
    d.   Has it been done before?

Learning Goal 3
8.   Which of the following is the best reason for a business to be managed ethically?
    a.   Business leaders don't want to get caught behaving unethically.
    b.   An ethically managed business can reduce employee turnover.
    c.   If the company is engaged in a lawsuit, it can use the ethics code as a legal defense.
    d.   So that new customers will not be able to complain about the ethical behavior of the company.

9.   Organizational ethics begin
    a.   at the top levels of management.
    b.   only with employees.
    c.   with the unions.
    d.   with mid level managers.

Learning Goal 4
10.   Which of the following is not a part of an integrity-based ethics code?
    a.   stresses shared accountability
    b.   emphasizes penalizing of wrong-doers
    c.   supports ethically sound behavior
    d.   defines an organization's guiding principles

11. In establishing an effective ethics program, which of the following steps would not be taken?
    a. Managers must be trained to consider ethical implications of all decisions.
    b. Outsiders such as suppliers, distributors, and customers must be told about the program.
    c. Employees must understand that they must set their own ethical standards and communicate that standard to management.
    d. An ethics office must be set up.

Learning Goal 5

12. When UPS and FedEx shopped emergency relief supplies for free to victims of the Asian tsunami disaster, these companies were demonstrating which element of corporate social responsibility?
    a. corporate philanthropy
    b. corporate social initiatives
    c. corporate policy
    d. corporate responsibility

13. Business has a responsibility to:
    a. Investors.
    b. Customers.
    c. Employees.
    d. All of the above

14. Being energy conscious, ensuring that employees have a safe working environment, and monitoring corporate hiring policies to prevent discrimination is part of:
    a. corporate responsibility.
    b. corporate philanthropy.
    c. corporate policy.
    d. corporate legal standards.

15. In terms of social responsibility, many people believe that
    a. it does not make good financial sense for companies to be "up front" about potential product problems.
    b. it makes financial and moral sense to invest in companies whose goods and services benefit the community and the environment.
    c. businesses have no responsibility to create jobs.
    d. businesses have no responsibility to social causes.

16. In terms of social responsibility, the "contented cow" idea states that
    a. it is important to provide cafeteria style benefits to employees.
    b. corporations have a responsibility to provide aid to struggling American farmers.
    c. companies that treat employees with respect will make a difference in the bottom line, and have outgrown their corporate counterparts.
    d. corporations owe a responsibility to the environment and to make the physical environment so good that it would create "contented cows."

17. Which of the following areas would not be included in a social audit?
    a. Support for higher education, the arts, and nonprofit social agencies
    b. Community related activities such as fund raising.
    c. Employee-related activities
    d. Ability to compete with other major firms

18. Which of the following is not one of the watchdog groups that evaluate how well companies enforce their ethical and social responsibility policies?
    a. Socially conscious investors and consumers
    b. Environmentalists
    c. Union officials
    d. Employees

Learning Goal 6
19. Government and business leaders are being held to:
    a. lower ethical standards than in the past.
    b. ethical standards in the United States, but foreign leaders are not being subjected to ethical scrutiny.
    c. higher ethical standards than in the past.
    d. ethical standards that cannot be met by most leaders.

20. American businesses are
    a. demanding socially responsible behavior from international suppliers, particularly in the areas of environmental standards and human rights issues.
    b. holding international suppliers to different standards than American companies must adhere to in the United States.
    c. not concerned with the ethical or socially responsible behavior of their international suppliers.
    d. are demanding that international suppliers adhere to higher standards than their American counterparts.

TRUE-FALSE

Learning Goal 1
1. _____ One danger in writing new laws to correct behavior is that people may begin to think that any behavior that is within the law is also ethically acceptable.

2. _____ Ethics and legality are basically the same thing.

Learning Goal 2
3. _____ Solutions to ethical problems are usually easily determined.

4. _____ In an organization, ethics begin at the top.

Learning Goal 3
5. _____ One of the reasons for ethical management is to avoid lawsuits.

Learning Goal 4
6. _____ Compliance-based ethics codes define an organization's guiding values, create an environment that supports ethical behavior and stresses shared accountability.

7. _____ An important factor to the success of enforcing an ethics code is the selection of an ethics officer.

8. _____ The best way to communicate to all employees that an ethics code is serious and cannot be broken is to back the program with timely action if rules are broken.

9. _____ Whistleblowers are individuals who report unethical or illegal behavior in an organization.

10. _____ Corporate social responsibility is the concern businesses have for their profitability.

11. _____ In reality, it appears that even people who want to be socially responsible can't define what being socially responsible means.

12. _____ One of the best ways to please customers is to hide product defects from them.

13. _____ Insider trading involves employees buying and selling the stock of the company by which they are employed.

14. _____ Businesses have a responsibility to employees to create jobs.

15. _____ Regulation FD requires that companies that release any information share the information with everyone, not just a few select people.

Learning Goal 6

16. _____ Ethical problems and issues of social responsibility are unique to the United States.

You Can Find It On the Net

Go to the Ben and Jerry's website www.benjerry.com and find the company's mission statement.

What three areas are included in their mission statement?

What is Ben and Jerry's social mission?

What campaigns and causes does Ben and Jerry's support?

What is the purpose of the Ben and Jerry's Foundation?

Check out the most recent Social Audit. In this document the company reports their activities in a number of areas, regarding their social responsibility behavior. What has Ben and Jerry's been up to?

ANSWERS

LEARNING THE LANGUAGE

1. Compliance based ethics codes	7. Corporate social responsibility
2. Social audit	8. Corporate responsibility
3. Corporate policy	9. Insider trading
4. Ethics	10. Whistleblowers
5. Integrity based ethics codes	11. Corporate social initiatives
6. Corporate philanthropy	

ASSESSMENT CHECK

Learning Goal 1
Ethics Is More Than Legality

1. In order to restore trust in the free market system and in corporate leaders, we need to punish those who have broken the law. No one should be above those laws. In addition, new laws making accounting records easier to read and understand, and passing more laws making business people and others more accountable may also help.

2. According to the text, many Americans have no moral absolutes. Many decide according to the situation whether it's all right to steal, lie, or drink and drive. It appears that these people think that what is right is whatever works best for the individual, and that each person works out for him or herself the difference between right and wrong.

3. Ethics and legality are very different things. Being legal means following the laws written to protect ourselves from fraud, theft and violent acts. Ethical behavior requires more than simply following the law and looks at behavior in terms of people's relations with one another.

4. A recent study revealed that a majority of the American population reported never giving any time to their community. One third reported never giving to a charity. Business managers and workers cited low managerial ethics as a major cause of competitive woes for American businesses. Employees report violating safety standards and many students report cheating on exams. In other words, Americans are not especially "socially minded." The text cites examples from college classrooms and from corporate leaders' behavior as examples.

5. Ethical behavior begins with you and me.

   We cannot expect society to become more moral and ethical unless individuals commit to becoming more moral and ethical.

6. An ethical dilemma is a situation in which there may be no desirable alternative. You must choose between equally unsatisfactory alternatives when making a decision.

Learning Goal 2
7. Three questions to ask are:
   a. Is it legal? (Am I violating any law or company policy?)
   b. Is it balanced? (Am I acting fairly?)
   c. How will it make me feel about myself? (Would I feel proud if my family learned of my decision?)

Managing Businesses Ethically and Responsibly
8.   Organizational ethics begin at the top.

People learn their standards and values from observing what others do.

9.   Reasons to manage ethically are:
    a.   to maintain a good reputation
    b.   to keep existing customers
    c.   to attract new customers
    d.   to avoid lawsuits
    e.   to reduce employee turnover
    f.   to avoid government intervention
    g.   to please customers, employees, and society
    h.   it's the right thing to do

10.   *Compliance based* ethics codes emphasize preventing unlawful behavior by increasing control and by penalizing wrongdoers. This type of ethics code is based on avoiding legal punishment. *Integrity based* ethics codes define the organization's guiding values, create an environment that supports ethically sound behavior, and stress a shared accountability among employees.

11.   a.   Top management must adopt and support an explicit code of conduct.
    b.   Employees must understand that top management expects ethical behavior.
    c.   Managers and employees must be trained to consider ethical implications of business decisions.
    d.   Companies must set up an ethics office for employees to inquire about ethical matters.
    d.   Outsiders must be told about the ethics program.
    e.   The ethics code must be enforced.

12.   An important factor to the success of enforcing an ethics code is to select an ethics officer. The effective ethics officer will set a positive tone, communicate effectively, and relate well with employees at every level.   It is important the ethics officers have strong communications skills.

Learning Goal 5
Corporate Social Responsibility

13.   Corporate social responsibility is based on a company's concern for the welfare of all its stakeholders, not just owners. It is based on a commitment to the principles of integrity, fairness, and respect.

14.   a.   *Corporate philanthropy* includes charitable donations to nonprofit groups.
    b.   *Corporate social initiatives* include enhanced forms of traditional philanthropy. These initiatives differ from traditional philanthropy in that they are directly related to the company's competencies.
    c.   *Corporate responsibility* includes responsibility in all business decisions, such as hiring, pollution control, product decisions, responsible use of energy, and providing a safe work environment.
    d.   *Corporate policy* refers to the position taken on social and political issues

15. There are a number of examples of socially responsible behavior from organizations. Xerox has a program which allows employees to leave for up to a year and work for a nonprofit organization. IBM and Wells-Fargo Bank have similar programs. The Citizen Corps is a new program designed to strengthen homeland security efforts through volunteers who donate professional health skills and train others in disaster response and emergency preparedness. There are several other similar volunteer organizations.

16. Four stakeholder groups are:
    a. Customers
    b. Investors
    c. Employees
    d. Society and the environment

17. One responsibility of business is to satisfy customers by offering them goods and services that have a real value to the customer.

    One of the surest ways of failing to please customers is not being totally honest with them.

18. The payoff for socially conscious behavior could result in new business as customers switch from rival companies simply because they admire a company's social efforts. This can become a powerful competitive edge because customers prefer to do business with companies they trust.

19. Ethical and socially responsible behavior is good for shareholder wealth and adds to the bottom line. Many people believe it makes financial as well as moral sense to invest in companies that are planning ahead to create a better environment. By choosing to put their money into companies whose goods and services benefit the community and the environment, investors can improve their own financial health while improving society's health.

20. Regulation FD (for fair disclosure) requires that companies which release any information share it with everyone, not just a few select people. If companies tell anyone, they must tell everyone, at the same time.

21. Business' responsibility to employees includes:
    a. a responsibility to create jobs.
    b. an obligation to fairly reward hard work and talent.
    c. treating employees with respect.

22. When employees feel they have been treated unfairly they will strike back, and get even in such ways as:
    a. blaming mistakes on others
    b. not accepting responsibility for decision making
    c. manipulating budgets and expenses
    d. making commitments they intend to ignore
    e. hoarding resources
    f. doing the minimum needed to get by
    g. making results look better than they are.

23 Four areas of responsibility to society are:
    a. to create wealth
    b. to promote social justice
    c. to play a role in building a community that goes beyond giving back
    d. to make a contribution toward making the environment a better place

24. When companies play a role in building a community, their contributions can include cleaning up the environment, providing computer lessons, supporting the elderly and children from low-income families, and building community facilities.

25. A major problem of conducting a social audit is establishing procedures for measuring a firm's activities and their effects on society. The question is: what should be measured?

26. Examples of socially responsible business activities include:
    a. Community related activities such as fund raising for local causes.
    b. Programs designed to benefit employees such as flextime, improved benefits, equal opportunity programs, and others.
    c. Taking a stand on such political issues as gun control, pollution control, and nuclear safety.
    d. Support of higher education, the arts, and non-profit agencies.
    e. Consumer education programs, honest advertising, prompt complaint handling, and honest pricing policies.

27. A "net social contribution" is calculated by adding all positive social actions, and then subtracting negative effects such as layoffs and pollution.

28. Four watchdog groups are:
    a. Socially conscious investors, who insist that companies extend the company's high standards to all their suppliers.
    b. Environmentalists, who apply pressure by naming companies that don't abide by environmentalists' standards.
    c. Union officials, who force companies to comply with standards to avoid negative publicity.
    d. Customers who take their business elsewhere if a company demonstrates unethical and socially irresponsible practices.

Learning Goal 6
International Ethics and Social Responsibility

29. No, ethical problems are not unique to the U.S. What is new about the moral and ethical standards by which government leaders are being judged is that the standards are much stricter now. In other words, government leaders are now being held to a higher standard than in the past.

30. Many American businesses are demanding socially responsible behavior from their international suppliers by making sure their suppliers do not violate U.S. human rights and environmental standards.

31. The Joint Initiative on Corporate Accountability and Workers' Rights is a project that is designed to create a single set of labor standards with a common factory inspection system. The goal is to replace the current system of multiple approaches with something that is easier and cheaper to use.

   If it works, one of the outcomes is that the common guidelines will keep companies from undercutting one another on labor standards. A major issue is what constitutes a living wage in different areas of the world.

32.   Examples of the questions surrounding the issues of international ethics are:
Is it always ethical for American companies to demand compliance with our moral standards? What about countries where child labor is an accepted part of society? What about foreign companies doing business in the U.S.? Should foreign companies expect American companies to comply with their ethical standards? To what country's standards should multinational companies adhere?

33.   It is unlikely that there will be a single set of international rules governing multinational corporations in the near future. There are too many differing opinions about what is ethical and socially responsible. Most standards set by various international bodies are advisory only.

CRITICAL THINKING EXERCISES

Learning Goal 1
1.   In many people's opinion, this situation would be an ethical dilemma because you are deciding between essentially violating company policy and not having a nice place for you and your family to stay in L.A. Both of these are unsatisfactory options. At issue are the ethical dilemma of violation of company policy, and the "ethics questions" checklist. The sense of "legal" versus "ethical" comes from company policy, which isn't very well defined.

Learning Goals 1, 2
2.   a) This is a difficult problem, but ethically it's not really too hard to figure out what to do. The decision about going to the boss is an individual one, but using the secretary and the interns for personal business, particularly to the extent that Daryl is using, is probably unethical. To answer the ethics questions: a) Is it legal? Daryl's actions are most likely violating some company policy.
b) Is it balanced? This seems to be a win-lose situation, because while Daryl is getting what he needs, the typing, others in the company are not able to get their work done because of Daryl's actions. c) How will it make me feel about myself? This is a personal question that only the individual can answer.

Learning Goals 2, 3
3.   There is no "correct" answer to this question although there is probably a "most appropriate" mode of behavior. In this era of customer service and quality products in a competitive marketplace, these kinds of decisions are likely to come up frequently. Now is the time to think about how you would act. A helpful guide would be to ask yourself the questions the text proposes: a. Is it legal? b. Is it balanced? Would I want to be treated this way? Do I win at the expense of someone else? c. How will it make me feel about myself?

Learning Goal 4
4.   a. Integrity-based ethics code
b. Compliance-based ethics code

5.   As a company's Ethics Officer, the first step you would probably take is to set up a meeting with the company's top executives to ensure their support of any actions you want to take regarding setting up a code of conduct. The unconditional support of top management is vital to the success of a corporate ethics code. The next step most likely is to develop a set of standards of acceptable behavior, and to make sure that employees understand the expectations of those standards. Employees must be trained to consider the ethical implications of their decisions, so there must be explicit standards and guidelines to follow.

Further, as the Ethics Officer, your office must set up a system so that employees can report and discuss ethical issues anonymously, and whistleblowers must feel protected. Your office must also inform outsiders such as suppliers, subcontractors, distributors, and customers of the ethics code. This can be done easily on your company's web site.

Lastly, the ethics code must be enforced by taking timely action when a violation has occurred.

Learning Goal 5

6.   a.   Social responsibility includes providing a safer work environment, good benefits, a safe, high quality product line, prompt complaint handling, and honest pricing policies. The result of a social audit would indicate that Mr. Furlong is running his business in a socially responsible manner, as far as he goes.

   b.   Mr. Furlong's stakeholders would be his boss, the stockholders, employees, customers, competitors, suppliers and the general public.

   c.   Although he would get fairly high scores from his employees in the area of social responsibility, Mr. Furlong doesn't appear to have any involvement with the community in which he operates. Of the four dimensions of corporate social performance, he addresses only the corporate responsibility issue; those of corporate philanthropy, corporate social initiatives and corporate policy appear to be ignored. He could improve community relations (and even increase his customer base) by encouraging his employees to get involved in community related projects, donating time and/or money to local charities, developing a stand on local issues, improving employee-related benefits with job enrichment and employee development, and making opportunities for members of ethnic and minority groups.

7.   Businesses are responsible to four general stakeholder groups: customers, investors, employees, and society in general. Being responsible to *customers* means offering them goods and services of real value. This includes being honest with customers about problems with products, and committing resources to solve the problems.

   Responsibility to *investors* means making money for stockholders. This includes financial ethical behavior. Many believe that it makes financial as well as moral sense to invest in companies that are planning ahead to create a better environment.

   Responsibility to *employees* means creating jobs, making sure that hard work and talent are fairly rewarded, and demonstrating respect for employees by treating them fairly. This includes giving employees salaries and benefits that help them reach their personal financial goals.

   Responsibility to *society* means creating wealth, promoting social justice, giving back to communities, and helping to make the environment a better place.

Learning Goal 6

8.   In the past, officials of foreign firms have been judged by standards that were less harsh than those used in the United States. More recently, it seems that top leaders in some parts of the world are being judged by stricter standards. This could stem from the fact that American businesses have begun to demand more socially responsible behavior from international suppliers. As the business sector becomes increasingly globalized, international suppliers will be expected to conform to U.S. standards concerning ethics, human rights codes and the environment.

   The justness of requiring international suppliers to adhere to American ethical standards is not clear-cut. There are questions such as: Is it always ethical for companies to demand compliance with the standards of their own countries? What about countries where child labor is an accepted part of the society and families depend on the children's earnings for survival? Should foreign companies doing business in the United States expect American companies to comply with their ethical standards? To which society's standards should multinational companies conform? None of these questions have easy answers, but demonstrate the complexity of social responsibility issues in international markets.

PRACTICE TEST

MULTIPLE CHOICE

LG 1   #1-3
LG 2   #4-7
LG 3   # 8-9
LG 4   #10-11
LG 5   #12-17
LG 6   #18

TRUE-FALSE

LG 1   #1-2
LG 2   # 3-4
LG 3   # 5
LG 4   # 6-7
LG 5   # 8-15
LG 6   # 16

1.	c	11.	c
2.	c	12.	b
3.	a	13.	d
4.	d	14.	a
5.	b	15.	b
6.	d	16.	c
7.	a	17.	d
8.	b	18.	d
9.	a	19.	c
10.	b	20.	a

1.	T	9.	T
2.	F	10.	F
3.	F	11.	T
4.	T	12.	F
5.	T	13.	F
6.	T	14.	T
7.	T	15.	T
8.	T	16.	F

CHAPTER 5 – CHOOSING A FORM OF BUSINESS OWNERSHIP

LEARNING GOALS

After you have read and studied this chapter, you should be able to:

1. Compare the advantages and disadvantages of sole proprietorships
2. Describe the differences between general and limited partnerships and compare the advantages and disadvantages of partnerships.
3. Compare the advantages and disadvantages of corporations and summarize the differences between C corporations, S corporations and limited liability companies.
4. Define and give examples of three types of corporate mergers and explain the role of leveraged buyouts and taking a firm private.
5. Outline the advantages and disadvantages of franchises and discuss the opportunities for diversity in franchising and the challenges of global franchising.
6. Explain the role of cooperatives.

LEARNING THE LANGUAGE

Listed below are important terms found in this chapter. Choose the correct term for each definition and write it in the space provided.

Acquisition	General partner	Limited partnership
Conglomerate merger	General partnership	Master limited partnership
Conventional corporation (C)	Horizontal merger	Merger
Cooperative	Leveraged buyout (LBO)	Partnership
Corporation	Limited liability	S Corporation
Franchise	Limited Liability company (LLC)	Sole proprietorship
Franchise agreement	Limited Liability partnership (LLP)	Unlimited liability
Franchisee	Limited partner	Vertical merger
Franchisor		

1. A _____ joins two firms in the same industry.

2. A legal form of business with two or more owners is a _____.

3. A _____ is an arrangement whereby someone with a good idea for a business sells the rights to use the business name and to sell a product or service to others in a given territory.

4. In a(n) _____ one company purchases the property and obligations of another company.

5. Limited partners and shareholders have _____ because they are only responsible for the losses of a business up to the amount they invest.

6 This unique government creation called a(n) _____ looks like a corporation but is taxed like sole proprietorships and partnerships.

7. A _____ is a company that develops a product concept and sells others the rights to make and sell the products.

8. A business proposition that joins firms in completely unrelated industries is called a(n) _____.

9. An agreement such as a(n) _____ is a partnership with one or more general partners and one or more limited partners.

10. A (n)_____ looks much like a corporation in that it acts like a corporation and is traded on a stock exchange but is taxed like a partnership and thus avoids corporate income tax.

11. A legal entity with authority to act, a(n) _____ has liability separate from its owners.

12. The result of two firms forming one company is a _____.

13. A _____ is a person who buys a franchise.

14. A partner is called a _____ when she has invested money in a business but does not have any management responsibility or liability for losses beyond the investment.

15. A company that is similar to an S corporation, but without the special eligibility requirement is called a (n) _____.

16. A partner who has unlimited liability is called a _____ and is active in managing the firm.

17. A _____ is a business that is owned and controlled by the people who use it: producers, consumers or workers with similar needs who pool their resources for mutual gain.

18. A partnership is called a(n) _____ when all owners share in operating the business and in assuming liability for the business's debts.

19. An attempt by employees, management, or a group of investors to purchase an organization primarily through borrowing is called a(n) _____.

20. A _____ is the right to use a business name and to sell a product or service in a given territory.

21. In the business venture known as a(n) _____, two companies which are involved in different stages of related businesses join together.

22. A business that is owned, and usually managed, by one person is a _____.

23. The concept of _____ means that business owners are responsible for all of the debts of a business.

24. A _____ is one that limits partners' risk of losing their personal assets to only their own acts and omissions and to the acts and omissions of people under their supervision.

25. A state-chartered legal entity with authority to act and have liability separate from its owners is a _____.

ASSESSMENT CHECK

Learning Goal 1
Basic Forms of Business Ownership

1. What are three general forms of business ownership? Which is the most common form of business ownership?

   a._____

   b. _____

   c._____

2. Which form of ownership is separate from its owners?

3. What are the advantages of a sole proprietorship?

   a. _____

   b. _____

   c. _____

   d. _____

   e. _____

   f. _____

4. What do you have to do to start a sole proprietorship?

5. How are profits taxed in a sole proprietorship?

6. The disadvantages of sole proprietorships are:

   a. _____

   b. _____

   c. _____

   d. _____

   e. _____

   f. _____

   g. _____

7. How are the debts of a sole proprietorship handled?

8. The forms of ownership that have a greater probability of obtaining needed financial backing are: _____

Learning Goal 2
Partnerships

9. What are the forms of partnerships?

   a. _____

   b. _____

   c. _____

   d. _____

10. What is the difference between a general partnership and a limited partnership? What is the minimum number of general partners required?

11. What is the difference between a general partner and a limited partner?

12. Describe the characteristics of a limited liability partnership (LLP).

13. The Uniform Partnership Act (UPA) identifies what three key elements of a general partnership?

   a. _____

   b. _____

   c. _____

14. What are the advantages of a partnership?

   a. _____

   b. _____

   c. _____

   d. _____

15. What are the disadvantages of a partnership?

   a. _____

   b. _____

   c. _____

   d. _____

16. In a partnership, who is responsible for the debts of the firm and has unlimited liability?

17. Because of potential conflict between partners, all terms of the partnership should:

   _____

Learning Goal 3
Corporations

18. Explain the following statement. "A corporation is separate from its owners". What is another name for the owners of a corporation?

19. What are the advantages of conventional "C" corporations?

a._____

b._____

c._____

d._____

e._____

f._____

g._____

20. What are three ways a corporation can raise money?

a. _____

b. _____

c. _____

21. What is the benefit of the size of a large corporation? Does a company have to be large to be a corporation?

22. How do the owners of a corporation (stockholders) influence how a business is managed?

23. What are the disadvantages of conventional "C" corporations?

a._____

b._____

c._____

d._____

e._____

f._____

g._____

24. What is meant by two tax returns and "double taxation"?

25. How can size be a disadvantage of a large corporation?

26. Illustrate the basic structure of a corporation

27. What are the advantages for individuals when they incorporate?

28. In order to qualify as an "S" corporation a company must:

   a._____

   b._____

   c._____

   d._____

29. Compare and contrast S corporations with conventional C corporations.

30. What are the types of corporations, other than an "S"?

   a._____   f._____

   b._____   g._____

   c._____   h._____

   d._____   i. _____

   e._____

31. What are the advantages of limited liability companies?

a. _____

b. _____

c. _____

d. _____

e. _____

32. List the disadvantages of an LLC

a. _____

b. _____

c. _____

d. _____

e. _____

33. How is ownership transferred in an LLC?

34. What could happen to an LLC in the event of a member's death?

Learning goal 4
Corporate Expansion: Mergers and Acquisitions

35. What is the difference between a merger and an acquisition?

36. Describe:
a. vertical mergers: _____

_____

b. horizontal mergers: _____

_____

c. conglomerate mergers: _____

_____

37. What is involved in "taking a firm private"?

38. How are the funds in a leveraged buyout (LBO) used? Who become the owners of the firm?

Learning Goal 5
Special Forms of Ownership

39. Describe the difference between a franchisor and a franchisee.

40. The most popular businesses for franchising are _____.

41. List the advantages of owning a franchise

   a._____   d._____

   b._____   e._____

   c._____

42. What are the reasons that a franchisee has a greater chance of succeeding in business?

43. List the disadvantages of owning a franchise.

   a._____   d._____

   b._____   e._____

   c._____   f. _____

44. What is a recent change in franchising regarding management regulation of franchisees?

45. Describe the coattail effect.

46. How have women been involved in franchising?

47. How has minority involvement in franchising changed?

48. What government agency provides training for minorities in franchising?

49. Identify four advantages of home franchising.

    a. _____   c. _____

    b. _____   d. _____

50. What are the ways in which e-commerce is affecting franchising?

51. What is at issue concerning franchisee-sponsored websites?

52. How are franchisors using technology?

53. What areas of the world are popular targets for international franchising?

54. The characteristics that make franchising successful in international markets are _____

    _____

55. What must foreign franchisors do in order to be successful in foreign markets?

Learning Goal 6
Cooperatives

56. Describe the two kinds of cooperatives mentioned in the text.

a. _____

_____

b. _____

_____

57. Give some examples of successful cooperatives in the United States.

CRITICAL THINKING EXERCISES

Learning Goal 1
1. Jeff Baker has his own business as the owner of a tanning salon in his hometown. He is talking with a good friend, Bill Jacobs, who is interested in going into business for himself. "After I had purchased the necessary equipment, all I had to do was fill out a form for the county and open my doors, easy as that," Jeff mentioned, over lunch one day. "The only problem is, now I owe a lot of money for this tanning equipment. I'll be in rough shape if we go under!" "You know", said Bill "I have company- paid life and health insurance where I work now. I'm a little concerned about losing that." "Yeah, that's a concern," replied Jeff," but I can try things with this business that my old bosses would never have let me try. I can be really creative. I think we earned enough this year to open a second facility after we pay off the loans we have now. We're at our limit at the bank. But at least I can do what I want to with the money and not share it with anyone else." "What about the amount of time you spend at work? Any problem?" asked Bill. "Well... I usually get to the salon at 8 a.m. and don't leave until 10 or 11 p.m., if that's what you're asking," answered Jeff, "but you know, I don't mind, because this business is all mine, and it has been worth the hard work. Right now, though, I am having some problem finding a good person to help me out." "Listen", he continued," I have to go. I've got an appointment with the accountant in 20 minutes. He saved me a lot of money last year, and I didn't owe anything on my taxes. Great guy! My lawyer needs some information from him, too. I 'm making a will to make sure the kids will get the business if anything happens to me. Hey Bill, good luck!"

Identify the advantages and disadvantages Jeff mentioned regarding a sole proprietorship.

Learning Goal 2

2. There are four basic types of partnerships

General partnership   Master limited partnership
Limited partnership   Limited liability partnership

Using the information below, distinguish between each type of partnership

a. _____   Sunoco Logistics is a type of partnership that is traded on a stock exchange.

b. _____   Joe Allen invested in his friend Jose's business, but he doesn't have any management responsibilities.

c. _____   Dave Pardo and his partner Bettina Gregory both stand to lose a lot of money if their business goes under, as they are both responsible for the debt the business has undertaken.

d. _____   Even though any of us could buy stock in Perkins Family Restaurant, the company is taxed like a partnership.

e. _____   When Terry Esser invested in Dave and Bettina's company, she figured it was a minimal risk, because she (Terry) isn't active in the business and would only stand to lose what she invested if the company didn't make it.

f. _____   Randy Ford and Marty Dietrich have agreed to spend all their time managing the business they have just started.

g._____   Partners in the now defunct Arthur Andersen who were not involved in the Enron scandal could expect to be exempt from losses incurred by guilty partners because Arthur Andersen is this type of partnership.

3. After some consideration, Bill Jacobs decided he would ask Jeff Baker if he could become a partner in Jeff's business. "After all," Bill said to himself, "I've got some money, and Jeff does want to expand, and he's looking for someone to work for him. I'll just work with him, give him some free time. I'm a little nervous about taking on the debt, but the statistics say we're more likely to stay in business than a sole proprietorship is, so it shouldn't be too bad."
Bill went to Jeff and began to discuss becoming a partner in the business.
"Whoa..wait a minute" interrupted Jeff when he heard Bill's offer." I have to think about this. I like making my own decisions, and I like keeping my profits! How do I know you'll work as hard as I do? Who will work when? What happens when I want to borrow money for some new equipment and you don't want to?" Bill had to admit these were things he hadn't thought of. "Well...if it doesn't work out, we can just split up, can't we? " said Bill. "It's just not that simple, Bill..."

What advantages and disadvantages of partnerships did Bill and Jeff discuss? How could Bill and Jeff overcome some of the disadvantages?

Learning Goal 3

4.   Bill and Jeff eventually did form a partnership. Business has been very good. They have expanded their facility, rented some space to several hair stylists, and added several product lines that compliment the tanning and hair salon area. They now have a total of three facilities and are wondering if they should incorporate their business, as they would like to expand even further, perhaps one day franchising their idea. What can you tell them about the advantages and disadvantages of incorporation, and what would you suggest for them?

5.   What benefit does a corporation have over partnerships and sole proprietorships, for a small business owner?

6.   There are several terms used to describe different types of corporations

      alien   quasi-public
      domestic   professional
      foreign   nonprofit
      closed (private)   multinational
      open (public)

Match the type of corporation to each of the following:

a. _____   The stock of Maritz, Inc. is held by a small number of people and is not listed on a stock exchange.

b. _____   Procter and Gamble has sold more than 200 million shares of stock.

c. _____   General Motors is incorporated in Delaware, but has its headquarters in Detroit, Michigan.

d. _____   You can have a Big Mac and fries in Three Rivers, Michigan, Paris, France, Sydney, Australia and Moscow, and expect the same quality.

e. _____   Toyota is incorporated in Japan, but has corporate offices located in the United States

f. _____   Mainini Home Improvement is incorporated in Missouri, has its headquarters in Ellisville, Missouri and only does business in Missouri.

g. _____   The Red Cross sponsors a classic car show and auction every year to raise funds for disaster relief.

h. _____   Ameren U.E., an electrical service provider, must apply to a government agency when it wants to raise rates to its customers.

i. _____   Dr Kory and Dr Schoenwalder have incorporated their practice of internal medicine in order to benefit from the advantages of incorporation, however their stock won't be traded on a exchange.

7. Two forms of business ownership have received some attention recently:

"S" corporations   Limited liability companies.

Which one is being described in the following?

a. _____   This offers flexible ownership rules and personal asset protection.

b. _____   This type can tell the IRS how it wants to be taxed.

c. _____   Looks like a corporation but is taxed like sole proprietorships and partnerships.

d. _____   If the company loses its status as this type of company, it can't reelect this status for five years.

e. _____   This business may have no more than 100 shareholders.

f. _____   With this form of ownership, there are fewer incentives available, and since there is no stock, stock options can't be used as an employee incentive.

Learning Goal 4
8. There are several types of corporate mergers and buyouts. Match the situation being described to the correct term:

Acquisition   Conglomerate merger
Vertical merger   Leveraged buyout
Horizontal merger   Taking a firm private

a. _____   Tommy Hilfilger bought its Canadian distributor and its American licensee, Pepe Jeans USA, in order to own manufacturing and distribution rights.

b. _____   When KKR bought Toys R Us, they borrowed billions of dollars.

c. _____   The Boeing Company bought McDonnell Douglas. Subsequently, the McDonnell–Douglas Corporation ceased to exist.

d. _____   Two drug companies, Glaxo Wellcome PLC and SmithKline Beecham PLC began talks to merge their companies.

e. _____   Berkshire-Hathaway, which owns Dexter Shoe Company and International Dairy Queen, bought Helzberg Diamonds, a jewelry store chain in the Midwest.

f. _____   JLM founder John Macdonald and shareholder Philip Sassower, paid $1.40 per share for each of the roughly 5.3 million shares owned by other JLM investors and are now the sole owners of the business.

Learning Goal 5

9. KFC is a nationwide fast-food franchise. All prospective KFC franchise owners must go through an evaluation process, during which they must submit an application and site proposal for approval and submit to a personal interview in Louisville, KY, KFC's headquarters. Upon approval, KFC offers the franchisee a training program covering management functions such as accounting, sales, advertising and purchasing. KFC pays a portion of this training program. KFC makes an advertising, and promotion kit available to the franchisee as well as opening assistance, equipment layout plans, and a choice of interior decor from a list they provide. In addition to standard menu items, a franchisee may offer other items upon approval from KFC management. KFC outlines the estimated cash requirements for opening for such things as equipment, insurance payments, utility down payments, as well as for the facility itself to give franchisees an idea of their cash needs. The franchise fee and the costs of the building and land are the responsibility of the franchisee. There is a royalty rate based on a percentage of gross sales, which is paid on a regular basis to KFC for continuing franchises.

    KFC advertises on nationwide television on behalf of its franchisees, so local owners do not have to develop their own television advertising. The local owners do pay a percentage of their gross sales to KFC as a national advertising fee, and each franchisee is required to spend an additional percentage for local advertising.

    Based on this description, identify some of the benefits and drawbacks of owning a franchise.

Learning Goals 1, 2, 3

10. There are many choices for business ownership. What would be the best choices for the following types of businesses? Why?

    a.   Landscape/lawn care service

    b.   Small manufacturer of a component part for automobiles

    c.   Fast food restaurant

    d.   Construction/Remodeling firm

Learning Goal 6

11. Visit www.oceanspray.com and click on the "about us" link. What kind of cooperative is Ocean Spray, based on the description in the text?

PRACTICE TEST

MULTIPLE CHOICE – Circle the best answer

Learning Goal 1
1. Which form of ownership is the most common?
    a. Corporations
    b. Master limited partnerships
    c. General partnerships
    d. Sole proprietorships

2. One of the problems with a _____ is that there is no one with whom to share the burden of management.
    a. sole proprietorship
    b. limited partnership
    c. S corporation
    d. limited liability company

3. If you are interested in starting your own business, you want to minimize the hassle and you don't want to have anyone tell you what to do, you should organize your business as a (n):
    a. S corporation.
    b. limited partnership.
    c. sole proprietorship.
    d. closed corporation.

Learning Goal 2
4. At Sound Off!, a store that buys and sells used c.d.'s, there is only one owner, Sonia. She spends all her time running the business, and makes all the decisions. Sonia's mother and brother put up money for her to buy the store, but they work full time at other jobs and have no management say in the running of Sound Off! This is an example of a:
    a. general partnership.
    b. master limited partnership.
    c. S corporation.
    d. limited partnership.

5. When going into a partnership, you should always:
    a. put all terms of the partnership into writing, in a partnership agreement.
    b. make sure that you have limited liability while you are in charge.
    c. make sure all the profits are reinvested into the company.
    d. divide the profits equally.

118

6. A new form of business ownership looks like a corporation in that it is traded on the stock exchanges like a corporation, but it is taxed like a partnership and avoids the corporate income tax. This is known as a:
   a. sole proprietorship.
   b. master limited partnership.
   c. "S" corporation.
   d. general partnership.

7. One of the benefits a general partnership has over a sole proprietorship is:
   a. limited liability.
   b. more financial resources.
   c. easy to start.
   d. a board of directors to help with decisions.

8. Which form of partnership limits your liability to only your actions, or those of your subordinates, so that you can operate without fear that one of your partners might commit an action of malpractice that could cause you to lose your personal assets?
   a. General partnership
   b. Limited partnership
   c. Master Limited Partnership
   d. Limited Liability Partnership

Learning Goal 3
9. The owners of a corporation are called:
   a. general partners.
   b. stockholders.
   c. limited partners.
   d. proprietors.

10. A _____ is one whose stock is not available to the general public through a stock exchange.
    a. alien corporation
    b. domestic corporation
    c. public corporation
    d. closed corporation

11. All of the following are advantages of a corporation except:
    a. unlimited liability.
    b. the amount of money for investment.
    c. the ease of changing ownership.
    d. ability to raise money from investors without getting them involved in management.

12. A form of ownership which can have only 100 shareholders, who must be permanent residents of the United States, is called a:
    a. conventional C corporation.
    b. closed corporation.
    c. limited liability partnership.
    d. S corporation.

13. _____ can be both an advantage and a disadvantage of a conventional corporation, as they have the ability to raise large amounts of money and hire experts, but can become inflexible and tied down in red tape.
   a. Size
   b. Tax returns
   c. Termination
   d. Limited liability

14. Which of the following is not considered an advantage of a limited liability company?
   a. limited number of shareholders
   b. personal asset protection
   c. choice of how to be taxed
   d. flexible ownership rules

15. When Jeanne-Marie Delacourt was born, her American grandmother bought her 10 shares of Disney stock. As Jeanne-Marie grows, so will her investment. However, if Disney should happen to go out of business:
   a. Jean-Marie will be responsible for some of the debt of Disney.
   b. Jean-Marie will have to go to court to show she has no involvement in the firm.
   c. Jean-Marie will only lose the value of her shares.
   d. Jean-Marie will have to borrow money from her grandmother to pay for the value of her shares.

16. In a corporation, the Board of Directors:
   a. consists of a group of major shareholders who want a say in running the business.
   b. is elected by the owners/stockholders.
   c. is made up of lenders to the corporation.
   d. have unlimited liability.

Learning Goal 4
17. When the Federated Department Stores, which owns several department store chains, bought the May Company, another department store chain, so Federated could expand their product offerings, it was a:
   a. vertical merger.
   b. horizontal merger.
   c. conglomerate merger.
   d. cooperative merger.

18. The main reason for a conglomerate merger is that:
   a. the investors want more for their money.
   b. it ensures a constant supply of materials needed by other companies.
   c. it allows for a firm to offer a variety of related products.
   d. the business can diversify its business operations and investments.

19. When a major national bakery bought out a smaller more regional bakery in the east, it took over all their assets and their debt and the smaller bakery ceased to exist. This is an example of a(n):
   a. acquisition.
   b. merger.
   c. nationalization.
   d. appropriation.

20. In order to avoid a hostile takeover by a Kollmorgaen, managers at Pacific Scientific considered making a bid for all the company's stock themselves and taking it off the open market. The term to describe this action is:
    a. a leveraged buyout.
    b. a conglomerate merger.
    c. taking the firm private.
    d. forming a master limited partnership.

Learning Goal 5
21. When Pat Sloane bought a Tidy Maid franchise, she became a:
    a. franchisor.
    b. stockholder.
    c. venture capitalist.
    d. franchisee.

22. One of the advantages of a franchise is:
    a. receiving management and marketing expertise from the franchisor.
    b. fewer restrictions on selling than in other forms of businesses.
    c. lower start up costs than other businesses.
    d. you get to keep all the profits of your business after taxes.

23. When your profitable franchise fails simply because other franchisees have failed, this is known as the:
    a. royalty rate.
    b. coattail effect.
    c. failure rate.
    d. green ceiling.

24. International franchising is:
    a. a successful area for both small and large franchises.
    b. costs about the same as domestic franchising.
    c. becoming increasingly difficult, and so is not growing.
    d. easy, because you really do not have to adapt your product at all.

Learning Goal 6
25. In a _____, members democratically control the business by electing a board of directors that hires professional management.
    a. corporation
    b. cooperative
    c. franchise
    d. master limited partnership

TRUE-FALSE

Learning goal 1
1. _____ One of the benefits of a sole proprietorship is that you have easy availability of funds from a variety of sources.

2. _____ It is relatively easy to get in and out of business when you are a sole proprietor.

3. _____ A common complaint among sole proprietors is that good workers are hard to find because they can't afford to pay competitive salaries and fringe benefits.

4. _____   It is best to form a limited partnership because then there is no one individual who takes on the unlimited liability.

5. _____   In a partnership, one of the major disadvantages is the potential for disagreements among the partners.

6. _____   A master limited partnership is much like a corporation because its stock is traded on a stock exchange.

Learning Goal 3

7. _____   Individuals are not permitted to incorporate.

8. _____   The owner of a corporation is called a director.

9. _____   One advantage of a corporation is the limited liability of the owners.

10. _____   An S corporation avoids the double taxation of a conventional C corporation.

11. _____   A disadvantage of incorporation is the possibility of conflict between the officers of the corporation and the stockholders and/or the board of directors.

12. _____   A limited liability company can choose to be taxed either as a corporation or as a partnership.

Learning Goal 4

13. _____   An example of a vertical merger was the merger between Daimler, a German automaker, and Chrysler, an American automotive manufacturer.

14. _____   In a leveraged buyout the managers of a company buy all of the stock of a firm and take it off the open market.

Learning Goal 5

15. _____   A franchise can be formed as a sole proprietorship, a partnership, or a corporation.

16. _____   As a franchisee, you are entitled to financial advice and assistance from the franchisor.

17. _____   One of the disadvantages of a franchise is that if you want to sell, the franchisor must approve the new owner.

18. _____   Female participation in franchising grows as the cost of the franchise increases.

19. _____   One of the advantages that a home based franchisee has over a business owner based at home is that the franchisee feels less isolated.

Learning Goal 6

20. _____   One common element of a cooperative is for members to work a few hours a month as part of their duties.

You Can Find It On the Net

INC Magazine is dedicated to helping small businesses get off the ground. Visit their website at www.inc.com

What special hints are available to small business owners?

What kinds of advice does INC make available to entrepreneurs and small business owners?

Link into the Businesses for Sale page. What kinds of opportunities are available?

What kinds of resources are offered to buyers and sellers?

Go back to the home page. What information is offered about franchising?

If you are interested in obtaining a specific franchise, you can click onto the Buying a Franchise page and download the franchise evaluation form provided by this site. Use it to evaluate your potential business.

Now, visit www.betheboss.com

What are the most popular franchises listed?

Click on the Resources link, then on the Introduction to Franchising.

What are the four types of franchises?

What are the 5 steps of franchising, according to this site?

There are also a number of helpful guides on this site to determine the financial requirements of a franchise you might be interested in acquiring.

ANSWERS

LEARNING THE LANGUAGE

1. Horizontal merger	10. Master limited partnership (MLP)	18. General partnership
2. Partnership	11. Corporation	19. Leveraged buyout (LBO)
3. Franchise agreement	12. Merger	20. Franchise
4. Acquisition	13. Franchisee	21. Vertical merger
5. Limited liability	14. Limited partner	22. Sole proprietorship
6. S Corporation	15. Limited liability company	23. Unlimited liability
7. Franchisor	16. General partner	24. Limited liability partnership
8. Conglomerate merger	17. Cooperative	25. Conventional corporation
9. Limited partnership		

ASSESSMENT CHECK
Learning Goal 1
Basic Forms of Business Ownership

1. a. sole proprietorship
   b. partnership
   c. corporation

   The sole proprietorship is the most common form of business ownership

2. A corporation is the only form of ownership where the business is separate from the owners.

3. a. Ease of starting and ending business
   b. Being your own boss
   c. Pride of ownership
   d. Leaving a legacy
   e. Retention of company profit
   f. No special taxes

4. All you have to do to start a sole proprietorship is buy or lease the needed equipment and put up some announcements indicating that you are in business. You may have to get a permit or license from the local government.

5. Profits of a sole proprietorship are taxed as the personal income of the owner.

6. a. Unlimited liability and the risk of losses
   b. Limited financial resources
   c. Management difficulties
   d. Overwhelming time commitment
   e. Few fringe benefits
   f. Limited growth
   g. Limited life span

7. With a sole proprietorship, the debts or damages incurred by the business are your debts and you must pay them, even if it means selling your personal assets.

8. The forms of ownership that have a greater probability of obtaining the needed financial backing are partnerships and corporations.

Learning Goal 2
Partnerships

9. Four forms of partnerships agreements are:
   a. general partnership   c. master limited partnership
   b. limited partnership   d. limited liability partnership

10. In a general partnership agreement, the partners agree to share in the operation of the business and assume unlimited liability for the company's debts. In a limited partnership, the limited partners do not have an active role in managing the business, and have liability only up to the amount invested in the firm. That is called limited liability. There must be at least one general partner in any partnership.

11. A general partner is active in managing the firm and has unlimited liability. A limited partner invests money in the business, but doesn't have any management responsibilities.

12. An LLP limits partners' risk of losing their personal assets to only their own acts and to the acts of the people under their supervision. Thus, an LLP allows you to operate without the fear that one of your partners might commit an act of malpractice that would result in a judgment that takes away your assets. This protection may not extend to liabilities such as bank loans and other financial obligations.

13. The Uniform Partnership Act identifies these elements as key to a general partnership
   a. Common ownership
   b. Shared profits and losses
   c. The right to participate in managing the operations of the business

14. Advantages of partnerships include:
   a. More financial resources
   b. Shared management/pooled skills and knowledge
   c. Longer survival
   d. No special taxes

15. Disadvantages of partnerships include:
   a. Unlimited liability
   b. Division of profits
   c. Disagreements among partners
   d. Difficult to terminate

16. In a partnership each general partner is liable for the debts of the firm, no matter who was responsible for causing the debts. You, as a partner, are responsible for your partner's mistakes as well as your own.

17. Because of potential conflict between partners, all the terms of the partnership should be spelled out in writing in a partnership agreement.

18. The fact that a corporation is separate from its owners means that the owners are not liable for the debts or any other problems of the corporation beyond the money they invest. Another name for the owners of a corporation is a stockholder, or shareholder.

19. The advantages of a "C" corporation include:
    a.   Limited liability
    b.   More money for investment
    c.   Size
    d.   Perpetual life
    e.   Ease of ownership change
    f.   Ease of drawing talented employees
    g.   Separation of ownership from management

20. A corporation can raise money by:
    a.   selling stock, or ownership, to anyone who is interested
    b.   borrowing money from individual investors through issuing bonds
    c.   obtaining loans from financial institutions

21. Because large corporations have the ability to raise large amounts of money to work with, corporations can build modern factories or software development firms with the latest equipment. They can hire experts or specialists, and buy other corporations to diversify their risk. In other words, they have the size and resources to take advantage of opportunities anywhere in the world. However, a company does not have to be large to be a corporation. Individuals and small companies can also incorporate.

22. The owners have an influence on how a business is managed by electing the board of directors. The directors hire the officers of the corporation and oversee major policy issues. The owners/stockholders thus have some say in who runs the corporation but they have no control over the daily operations.

23. The disadvantages of a "C" corporation include:
    a. Paperwork
    b. Double taxation
    c. Two tax returns
    d. Size
    e. Difficulty of termination
    f. Possible conflict with stockholders and board of directors
    g. Initial cost

24. If an individual incorporates, he or she must file a corporate return and an individual tax return. Corporate income is taxed twice, because the corporation pays tax on income before it can distribute any to stockholders, then the stockholder pays tax on the income they receive from the corporation.

25. Size can be a disadvantage because large corporations sometimes become too inflexible and too tied down in red tape to respond quickly to market changes.

26. The structure of a corporation looks like this:

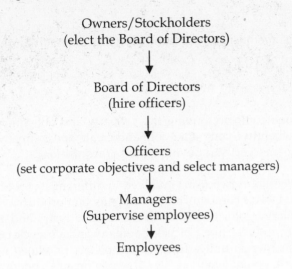

Owners/Stockholders
(elect the Board of Directors)

↓

Board of Directors
(hire officers)

↓

Officers
(set corporate objectives and select managers)

↓

Managers
(Supervise employees)

↓

Employees

27. The major advantages to individuals incorporating are limited liability and possible tax benefits.

28. a. Have no more than 100 shareholders.
     b. Have shareholders that are individuals or estates and are citizens or permanent residents of the United States
     c. Have only one class of outstanding stock
     d. Not have more than 25% of income derived from passive sources such as rents, royalties, interest etc.

29. The paperwork and some details of the S corporation are similar to those of conventional C corporations. S corporations have shareholders, directors, and employees and have the benefit of limited liability.
     However, S corporations are taxed as the personal income of the shareholders so the owners avoid double taxation.

30. The types of corporations other than "S" include:
     a. Alien   f. Quasi-public
     b. Domestic   g. Professional
     c. Foreign   h. Nonprofit
     d. Closed (private)   i. Multinational
     e. Open (public)

31. The advantages of limited liability companies are:
     a. Limited liability
     b. Choice of taxation
     c. Flexible ownership rules
     d. Flexible distribution of profit and losses
     e. Operating flexibility

32. The disadvantages of an LLC include
     a. No stock
     b. Limited life span
     c. Fewer incentives
     d. Taxes
     e. Paperwork

33. LLC ownership is not transferable. LLC members need the approval of other members in order to sell their interests.

34. The death of an LLC member can cause the company to dissolve automatically.

Learning Goal 4
Corporate Expansion: Mergers and Acquisitions

35. An acquisition is one company buying the property and obligations of another company, while a merger is when two companies join and create one company. It's like the difference between a marriage (merger) and buying a house (acquisition).

36. a. A vertical merger joins two firms involved in different stages of related businesses, like a merger between a bicycle company and a company that produces bike wheels.
   b. A horizontal merger joins two firms in the same industry and allows them to diversify or expand their products, like a bicycle company and a tricycle company.
   c. A conglomerate merger unites firms in completely unrelated industries. The primary purpose of a conglomerate merger is to diversify business operations and investments.

37. When taking a firm private, a group of stockholders or management obtains all a firm's stock for themselves.

38. A leveraged buyout is an attempt by employees, management, or a group of investors to purchase an organization primarily through borrowing. The funds borrowed are used to buy out the stockholders in the company. The employees, managers, or investors now become the owners of the firm.

Learning Goal 5
Special Forms of Business Ownership

39. A *franchisor* is someone with a good idea for a business who sells the right to use the business name to someone else, the *franchisee.*

40. The most popular businesses for franchising are restaurants, retail stores, hotels and motels, and automotive parts and service centers.

41. The advantages of a franchise are:
   a. Management and marketing assistance
   b. Personal ownership
   c. Nationally recognized name
   d. Financial assistance
   e. Lower failure rate

42. A franchisee has a greater chance of succeeding because he or she has an established product, help with choosing a location, help with promotion, and assistance in all phases of operation.

43. The disadvantages of franchising are:
   a. High start up costs
   b. Shared profit
   c. Management regulation
   d. Coattail effects
   e. Restrictions on selling
   f. Fraudulent franchisors

44. One of the biggest changes in franchising in recent years is the banding together of many franchisees to resolve their grievances with franchisors rather than fighting their battles alone.

45. The coattail effect is a term used to describe the fact that if other franchisees fail, you could be forced out of business even if your particular franchise has been profitable.

46. Studies show that as the cost of a franchise increases, female ownership decreases and women receive little venture capital money. As a result, women are becoming franchisors as well as franchisees when they have trouble obtaining financing to expand their business.

47. Minority owned businesses are increasing in number, and franchisors are becoming focused on recruiting minority franchisees.

48. The U.S. Commerce Department's Federal Minority Business Development Agency provides minorities with training in how to run a franchise.

49. Four advantages of home franchising are:
   a.   Relief from the time and stress of commuting
   b.   Extra time for family activities
   c.   low overhead expenses
   d.   home based franchisees feel less isolated than other home based business owners.

50. Many franchisees with existing brick-and-mortar stores are expanding their businesses online. Franchisees that started with a limited territory are branching out to customers throughout the world.

51. Many franchisors prohibit franchisee-sponsored websites. Conflicts between franchisors and franchisees can erupt if the franchisor then creates its own website. The franchisees may be concerned that the site will pull sales from their brick and mortar locations.

52. Franchisors are using technology to meet the needs of both their customers and their franchisees. Technology can streamline communication, give immediate access to subjects involving the franchise operation, including forms to complete. Franchisees can be kept up to date on company news via e-mail.

53. Some areas of the world which are popular for international franchising include Canada, South Africa, the Philippines, the Caribbean, the Middle East Malaysia, Indonesia, Singapore, Japan, Venezuela, and Thailand. The United States has become a popular market for foreign franchisors.

54. The characteristics that make franchising successful in international markets are convenience and a predictable level of service and quality.

55. In order to be successful in foreign markets, foreign franchisors, including U.S. franchisors in overseas markets, as well as foreign franchisors in the U.S. must adapt products and services to the region into which the franchisor wants to expand.

Learning Goal 6
Cooperatives

56. Two kinds of cooperatives can be described as:
    a. A cooperative in which members/customers work at the cooperative for a number of hours a month as part of their duties. Members control these businesses by electing a board of directors that hires professional management.
    b. Another kind of cooperative is formed to give members more economic power as a group than they would have as individuals. These are often farm cooperatives, which now buy and sell fertilizer, farm equipment, seed, and other products needed on the farm. These cooperatives now own many manufacturing facilities. Farm cooperatives do not pay the same kind of taxes as corporations and so have an advantage in the marketplace.

57. Some successful cooperatives include Land O Lakes, Sunkist, Ocean Spray, Blue Diamond, Associated Press, Ace Hardware, True Value Hardware, Riceland Foods and Welch's.

CRITICAL THINKING EXERCISES

Learning Goal 1
1. Jeff and Bill covered most of the advantages and disadvantages of owning a sole proprietorship. Jeff mentioned the ease of starting the business, the fact that you are your own boss and how proud he seemed to be of what he had accomplished with his hard work. He also mentioned that his tax liability was reasonable (in other words, he didn't have to pay any special taxes), and that he was making a profit that was his to keep and do with as he pleased. Some of the disadvantages Jeff mentioned were that he worked long hours, and had some difficulty in finding financial sources beyond the bank. He was nervous about the unlimited financial liability, and agreed that few fringe benefits was a concern. He also noted that he's having a problem finding a good person to work for him as is common with sole proprietorships. Lastly, he noted one final disadvantage of sole proprietorship, the limited life span. He is making arrangements for his children to inherit the business and continue with it if something happens to him.

Learning Goal 2
2. a. Master Limited Partnership (MLP)
   b. Limited partnership
   c. General partnership
   d. MLP
   e. Limited partnership
   f. General partnership
   g. Limited Liability partnership

3. It appears that Bill thought of most of the advantages and Jeff could only find disadvantages! Bill realized that he could give Jeff the financial resources he needed, and could relieve Bill of the long hours he was spending at the business. He also recognized that statistics indicate that partnerships have a longer survival rate than sole proprietorships. The one disadvantage Bill mentioned was the unlimited liability taken on by a general partner. Jeff was quick to point out the disadvantages of shared profits, potential disagreements and the difficulty of terminating a partnership.

One way that Bill and Jeff could overcome some of these problems is to put all of the conditions of the partnership in writing, in the form of a partnership agreement.

4.   There are a number of things to consider before Bill and Jeff decide to incorporate. If they are interested in expanding even further, incorporating would give them a wider source of funds for investment, because they could sell stock and keep the investors out of management for the most part. However, their business is small, and there is a question of how "marketable" their stock would be. A major advantage for them both is the aspect of limited liability. Expansion may require going into debt, and if they incorporate, Bill and Jeff would not be liable should something happen to the business. Another advantage for both of the partners is the perpetual life of a corporation. If something should happen to either Bill or Jeff, the remaining owners could still continue with the business. Further, if one of them decided to get out of the business, it is relatively easy, as they would simply have to sell their stock to the remaining owners.

One major disadvantage of incorporating is the initial cost, which can be very high. It also requires a lot of additional paperwork, particularly regarding the accounting records. Bill and Jeff would have to file more tax returns, and they would be taxed twice, once on their earned income and additionally on the income they received from dividends.

It appears that Bill and Jeff should incorporate, as it looks like the advantages may outweigh the disadvantages. Because they are a small company, they will become a closed corporation. That will eliminate the problem of having a market for their stock. They may also want to consider becoming an "S" corporation.

5.   One of the primary advantages of a corporation over proprietorships and partnerships is unlimited liability for the owners. There are additional sources of revenue for a corporation and many times it is easier to attract talented employees because a corporation may be able to offer better benefits. Some corporations are very large, and so size becomes a distinct advantage in terms of facilities and the ability to hire specialties. For a small business owner, the primary advantages would seem to be the unlimited liability, perpetual life, and ease of ownership change.

6. a. Closed   f. Domestic
    b. Open   g. Nonprofit
    c. Foreign   h. Quasi public
    d. Multinational   i. Professional
    e. Alien

7. a. Limited liability   d. "S" corporation
    b. Limited liability   e. "S" corporation
    c. "S" corporation   f. Limited liability

8. a. vertical merger   d. horizontal merger
    b. leveraged buyout   e. conglomerate merger
    c. acquisition   f. taking a firm private

9. This description identifies several of the benefits of owning a franchise. One of the first in this case is the fact that KFC is a nationally recognized name, which almost guarantees an established customer base. That helps to reduce the risk of failing. KFC provides management training and pays for part of it. They offer advice with opening the store, for such things as advertising, for such things as layout and interior decor. They offer financial advice also and give the franchisee a feel for what the initial costs are going to be. The franchisee can take advantage of a national advertising campaign, while still advertising on a local basis so they are able to meet local needs.

The drawbacks stem from the franchise fee, which could be relatively high for a nationally recognized franchise, and adds to the initial cost of opening. Further, a royalty rate must be paid on a regular basis to KFC, which takes away part of your profits, and the franchisee must contribute to a national advertising fund. Your menu items are limited to what the franchisor tells you, and you must get permission to offer anything different, so you are closely regulated in terms of the menu, as well as interior decor.

Learning Goals 1, 2, 3

10. a. The landscape/lawn care firm could start out as a sole proprietorship or partnership. There may be no great need for capital to start out with, so there would be no need to incorporate. A partnership may be an advantage because of the amount of labor involved, in order to build the business and do more than one job in a day. Another possibility would be to be a sole proprietor and hire workers to help.
    b. A small manufacturer of component parts would likely do best as a corporation, primarily due to the capital investment required and the need for a variety of skills such as marketing, manufacturing, engineering and so on. There is also the potential for liability in a manufacturing setting, and a corporate structure would protect the owners. This may initially be a closed corporation or even an "S" corporation.
    c. If you want to get into the fast food business, one of the easiest ways would be to investigate owning a franchise. Some fast food franchises are among the fastest growing franchises in the country, and the industry is very competitive. A "guaranteed" market would be a definite plus! The drawback is the initial expense, but if you can come up with the money a franchise may be the best way to go.
    d. The construction/remodeling business again could be a sole proprietorship or partnership. There is a definite need for several people to be working, so you could either hire workers to work for you, or find a partner who can help in the business. The investment in tools may be substantial which may be another indication of the need for a partner.

Learning Goal 6

11. Based upon the description in the text it appears that Ocean Spray is the kind of cooperative set up to give members more economic power as a group than they would have as individuals. The members of the cooperative are cranberry growers who initially formed in order to expand their market, and the cooperative has grown since its inception to a large organization with many different products, while remaining a cooperative.

PRACTICE TEST

MULTIPLE CHOICE

LG 1 # 1-3
LG 2 #4-8
LG 3 #9-16
LG 4 # 17-20
LG 5 # 21-24
LG 6 # 25

1.	d	14.	a
2.	a	15.	c
3.	c	16.	b
4.	d	17.	b
5.	a	18.	d
6.	b	19.	a
7.	b	20.	c
8.	d	21.	d
9.	b	22.	a
10.	d	23.	b
11.	a	24.	a
12.	d	25.	b
13.	a		

TRUE-FALSE

LG 1 # 1-3
LG 2 # 4-6
LG 3 # 7-12
LG 4 # 13-14
LG 5 #15-19
LG 6 #20

1.	F	11.	T
2.	T	12.	T
3.	T	13.	F
4.	F	14.	F
5.	T	15.	T
6.	T	16.	T
7.	F	17.	T
8.	F	18.	F
9.	T	19.	T
10.	T	20.	T

CHAPTER 6 – ENTREPRENEURSHIP AND STARTING A SMALL BUSINESS

LEARNING GOALS

After you have read and studied this chapter, you should be able to:

1. Explain why people are willing to take the risks of entrepreneurship, list the attributes of successful entrepreneurs, describe the benefits of entrepreneurial teams and intrapreneurs, and explain the growth of home-based and Web-based businesses.
2. Discuss the importance of small business to the American economy and summarize the major causes of small-business failures.
3. Summarize ways to learn about how small businesses operate.
4. Analyze what it takes to start and run a small business.
5. Outline the advantages and disadvantages small businesses have in entering global markets.

LEARNING THE LANGUAGE

Listed here are important terms found in this chapter. Choose the correct term for each definition and write it in the space provided.

Business plan	Micropreneurs
Enterprise zones	Service Corps of Retired Executives (SCORE)
Entrepreneurial team	Small business
Entrepreneurship	Small Business Administration (SBA)
Incubators	Small-business investment company program (SBIC)
Intrapreneurs	Venture capitalists
Market	

1. A _____ consists of people with unsatisfied wants and needs who have both the resources and willingness to buy.

2. Governments try to attract private business investment to specific geographic areas known as _____ by offering lower taxes and other government support.

3. A group of experienced people from different areas of business who join together as an _____ form a managerial team with the skills needed to develop, make, and market a new product.

4. A _____ is independently owned and operated, not dominant in its field of operation, and meets certain standards of size in terms of employees or annual receipts.

5. Individuals or companies known as _____ invest in new businesses in exchange for partial ownership of those businesses.

6. Centers called _____ offer new businesses low-cost offices with basic business services.

7. The SBA office known as the _____ has volunteers from industry, trade associations, and education who counsel services for small businesses at no cost, except for expenses.

8. _____ is accepting the risk of starting and running a business.

9. Creative people known as _____ work as entrepreneurs within corporations.

10. A _____ is a detailed written statement that describes the nature of the business, the target market, the advantages the business will have in relation to competition, and the resources and qualifications of the owners.

11. The program through which private investment companies are licensed by the Small Business Administration to lend money to small businesses is called the _____.

12. _____ are entrepreneurs willing to accept the risk of starting and managing the type of business that remains small, lets them do the kind of work they want to do, and offers them a balanced lifestyle.

13. The U.S. government agency called the _____ advises and assists small businesses by providing management training and financial advice and loans.

ASSESSMENT CHECK

Learning Goal 1
Why People Take the Entrepreneurial Challenge

1. What are four reasons why people become entrepreneurs?

   a. _____

   b. _____

   c. _____

   d. _____

2. Five desirable attributes for entrepreneurs are:

   a. _____

   b. _____

   c. _____

   d. _____

   e. _____

3.   Why might entrepreneurial teams be better than an individual entrepreneur?

4.   Describe a micropreneur and how he or she differs from an entrepreneur.

5.   Describe the reasons for the growth of home-based businesses

        a.   _____

        b.   _____

        c.   _____

        d.   _____

6.   Identify 5 challenges faced by the owners of home-based businesses.

        a.   _____

        b.   _____

        c.   _____

        d.   _____

        e.   _____

7.   If you are interested in getting into a home office, you should focus on:

        a.   _____ instead of _____

        b.   _____ instead of _____

        c.   _____ instead of _____

        d.   _____ instead of _____

        e.   _____ instead of _____

8.   How "big" are Web based businesses?

9. What must Web-based businesses do to be successful?

10. What are some Internet sites that help entrepreneurs in setting up online stores?

a._____   d. _____

b. _____   e. _____

c. _____

11. What is the difference between an entrepreneur and an intrapreneur? What is the idea behind intrapreneurs?

12. What was part of the intention of the Immigration Act of 1990? What are investor visas?

13. The government could have a significant effect on entrepreneurship by _____

_____

14. What kinds of services are offered by incubators? How do they help businesses survive?

Learning Goal 2
Getting Started In Small Business

15. What are three criteria used by the SBA to classify a business as "small"?

a._____

b._____

c._____

16. What is meant by "small is relative"?

17. What are some statistics that illustrate the impact of small business on the American economy?

18. The number of women owning small businesses _____

    _____

    Minority owned businesses are_____

    _____

19. What are two advantages small business owners believe they have over big business?

20. What is the failure rate of small business? Why are the statistics misleading?

21. a. If you want to be both independent and rich, you need to go after: _____

    b. In general the easiest businesses to start are:_____

    c. In general the easiest businesses to keep alive are: _____

    d. In general the businesses that can make you rich are: _____

Learning Goal 3
Learning About Small-Business Operations

22. What are three ways to learn about small business?

    a._____

    b._____

    c._____

23. What will other small business owners tell you when you talk to them about running your own business?

24.   What is the "rule of thumb" about getting experience in small business?

25.   Where do many new entrepreneurs come from? Why?

26.   Three factors used to determine the value of a business are:

        a._____

        b._____

        c._____

Learning Goal 4
Managing a Small Business

27.   What two management functions are of primary concern when you are first starting your business? What three functions are of concern after the start-up, when managing the business?

28.   List the tips for small business owners who want to borrow money from a bank.

        a. _____

        b. _____

        c. _____

        d. _____

        e. _____

        f. _____

        g. _____

29. List the information that generally should be included in a business plan.

a. _____

b. _____

c. _____

d. _____

e. _____

f. _____

g. _____

h. _____

i. _____

j. _____

30. List several sources of small business funding.

a. _____

b. _____

c. _____

d. _____

e. _____

f. _____

g. _____

h. _____

i. _____

31. Other than personal savings, the primary sources of capital for entrepreneurs are

_____

32. Describe an angel investor.

33.   What is one potential drawback with using venture capital?

34.   If you're a very small company, which funding source are you more likely to use, venture capital or an angel investor? Why?

35.   What are six types of financial assistance provided by the Small Business Administration?

        a. _____

        b. _____

        c. _____

        d. _____

        e. _____

        f. _____

36.   What are microloans and what criteria are used to award microloans?

37.   A Small Business Investment Company can help small businesses from defaulting on loans by

        _____

        _____

38.   Describe a Small Business Development Center, and how they help small businesses.

39. Three important factors for success in your small business are:

a. _____

b. _____

c. _____

40. Once you have identified your market and its needs, you must:

_____

41. What is one of the greatest advantages small businesses have over larger businesses?

42. What three criteria are critical for a small business owner with regard to managing employees?

a. _____

b. _____

c. _____

43. How do employees of small businesses often feel about their jobs? Why?

44. Describe some of the important questions and issues surrounding managing employees in small businesses.

45. Most small business owners feel they need assistance the most in the area of _____

_____

46. How can an accountant help in managing a small business?

47. What are five areas in which you may need assistance as a small business owner?

a. _____   d. _____

b. _____   e. _____

c. _____

48. In what ways can a lawyer help a small business owner?

49. In what areas will a marketing research study help a small business owner?

50. How would a small business owner benefit from the advice of a commercial loan officer and an insurance agent?

51. Describe some important sources of information for small business owners.

Learning Goal 5
Going International: Small-Business Prospects

52. In general, what is the level of small businesses involvement in the global market place?

53. What are four hurdles small businesses face in the international market?

a. _____

b. _____

c. _____

d. _____

54.   Good reasons for going international are:

a. _____

b. _____

c. _____

d. _____

e. _____

55.   Small businesses have advantages over large business in the international market because:

a. _____

b. _____

c. _____

d. _____

CRITICAL THINKING EXERCISES

Learning Goal 1
1.   You have read in earlier chapters that many parts of Eastern Europe and developing countries in other parts of the world are trying to move to a free market system. How can these developing countries encourage entrepreneurship, and why is it important that entrepreneurship be supported and encouraged?

2.   Eric is a young man with a vision. He sees himself as heading up a large corporation someday, a company that he has started and helped to grow. He has basically supported himself since he was fifteen, and has, at the age of 20, already started and sold 2 successful small businesses. Right now he is going to college full time because he feels that getting an education will be beneficial to him in the long run. He is supporting himself partially with the money he received from the sale of his last business. He intends to start yet another business as soon as he graduates.

Eric's most recent business was in a fairly competitive market in the area in which he lives. He says that while he received some encouragement from a few friends, for the most part they all said he was crazy to work as hard as he was working. But Eric says he just felt that he "had to do things my own way" and built his business to become the second largest of its type in the area.

How does Eric portray the entrepreneurial attributes your text identifies?

Learning Goals 2,3
3.   Eric seems to have beaten the odds already. What do you think Eric would tell you about success (or failure) and how to learn to be a successful small business owner?

4.   Eric has graduated from school, and is ready to start his new business. He has never applied for a bank loan, and has come to you for advice on how to beat the odds. What will you tell him?

5.   Maria Ruiz has a degree in business, but at this point in her business career has decided to stay home with her small children. Maria would like to start a small home-based business helping other small business owners write business plans, and contracting with other, larger business, in writing grant proposals. What would you tell Maria about home-based businesses and the challenges she will face?

Learning Goals 3,4
6.   After planning and financing, the functions necessary to be successful in running your small business include:

Knowing your market	Keeping efficient records
Managing employees	Looking for help

Read the following situation, keeping in mind what you have learned about operating successful small businesses. Do you think this small business will "beat the odds?"

Dave and Kevin worked together as sales representatives for a clothing manufacturer in Michigan. They were successful, but were interested in working on their own, and developed a plan for a partnership as manufacturer's representatives selling clothing and hats to their current customers, using a supplier network they would develop. While they were working full time, Dave and Kevin spent 6 months finding backers and lining up suppliers, and got a feel for which of their current customers they could count on later. They casually consulted with an accountant and a lawyer.

Finally they decided they were ready, and opened up under the name of Premium Incentives, Inc. Here is the situation on the day Premium Incentives opened:

* They each worked at home.

* They had promises, but no written contract from two suppliers to lend them a total of $100,000 over a one year period in return for all their business.

* They decided not to do a business plan, as they already had financing.

* Dave's wife agreed to do the bookkeeping as a favor. She had a degree in business, but not in accounting. However she had a full time job and a three-year-old child and was expecting another child in 5 months.

* They hired sales representatives to help with sales outside their home state, and planned to pay them on commission.

* They set up a price schedule designed to under-cut their competitors by a significant amount.

After two months in business, Dave and Kevin were still hopeful, but disappointed. They had made $5000 in sales, but hadn't yet been paid, as the product hadn't been delivered to the customers, and they had over $3,000 in start-up expenses. This would not have been a problem had the suppliers come through on their promises to finance Premium Incentives. However, one of the suppliers, after reconsidering, decided not to lend them any money, and the second dropped his offer down to $5000 a month for six months, with repayment beginning in the seventh month. Since Premium Incentives, Inc. did not have a written contract, they had no legal recourse. Dave and Kevin didn't worry too much about repaying the loan, as they figured they still had four months to build up the business. The problem was, their customers weren't buying as much as Dave and Kevin had anticipated, and they weren't sure what to do to find new customers.

Dave's wife was having problems keeping up with the books, so Dave began spending several days a week working on that, in addition to trying to sell. His wife suggested they develop some way of billing a customer, then re-billing if they hadn't paid within 15 days. Dave and Kevin disagreed about what to do, and eventually did nothing. They did finally hire a bookkeeper after several months of doing the books themselves. They continued to struggle with not knowing when a customer was going to pay, and therefore had no idea how much income they were going to have each month.

What do you think? What did Dave and Kevin do right? What did they do wrong? What are their chances of success?

7.   A. Draw up a list of the types of consultants whose services you may need in starting
          and managing your small business.

a. _____   e. _____

b. _____   f. _____

c. _____   g. _____

d. _____

B. What other sources of information are available?

a. _____   d. _____

b. _____   e. _____

c. _____   f. _____

Learning Goal 5

8.   Chad Lane is the owner of a small software business based in California. Chad is
         interested in growing his business, but he has seen that the market in the U.S. has
         become very competitive, and the technology market as a whole has slowed
         considerably. He is considering the possibilities of "going global" with his small
         business, and would like to explore some international opportunities. What would you
         tell him as his advisor?

PRACTICE TEST

MULTIPLE CHOICE – Circle the best answer

1.   Entrepreneurs take the risk of starting a business for all of the following reasons except:
     a.   they want independence.
     b.   they like the challenge and the risk.
     c.   they want to make money for themselves.
     d.   they want to work less.

2.   Steve Jacobie is an entrepreneur to the max. Steve has started three businesses, two of which he sold for a great deal of money. He is now involved in running his third business, with plans to sell it shortly and start yet another one. When commenting on his success as an entrepreneur, he says that once an idea comes to him, he just can't wait to start working on it and bring it to reality, and that is what he focuses on. Which of the traits of successful entrepreneurs does this suggest is characteristic of Steve?
     a.   Action-oriented
     b.   Self nurturing
     c.   Self-directed
     d.   Tolerant of uncertainty

3.   An entrepreneurial team is:
     a.   a group of people who work within a corporation to launch new products.
     b.   a group of experienced people who join together to develop and market a new product.
     c.   a group from the Small Business Administration which consults with small business owners.
     d.   a group of managers who get together to find creative solutions to problems.

4.   Federico Romero is a business owner who works from home as a freelance video producer. He really enjoys his work, but isn't looking to "set the world on fire" with his company. He just wants to make a good living and spend time with his family when he can. Federico would be classified as a(n)
     a.   entrepreneur.
     b.   intrapreneur.
     c.   micropreneur.
     d.   venture capitalist.

5.   An incubator is:
     a.   A U.S. government agency that advises and assists small businesses.
     b.   A program through which private investment companies licensed by the S.B.A. lend money to small businesses.
     c.   A center that offers new businesses low-cost offices with basic business services.
     d.   A specific geographic area to which governments try to attract private businesses by a variety of means.

6.   Which of the following is among the challenges faced by those with home based businesses?
     a.   Computer technology
     b.   Managing time
     c.   Changes in social attitudes
     d.   New tax laws

7. Which of the following is a false statement about small business?
    a. The number of women owning small businesses is increasing.
    b. The vast majority of non-farm businesses in the U.S. are considered small.
    c. The first job for most Americans will probably not be in a small business.
    d. The majority of the country's new jobs are in small business.

8. A small business:
    a. must have fewer than 100 employees to be considered small.
    b. is considered small relative to other businesses in its industry.
    c. cannot be a corporation.
    d. should be an S corporation.

9. In general
    a. the easier to start the business, the more likely it is to succeed.
    b. businesses that are more difficult to start are most likely to fail.
    c. the easier a businesses is to start the higher the growth rate.
    d. businesses that are difficult to start are the easiest ones to keep going.

10. Miriam Njunge wants to start a small business importing some products from her native Kenya. Before she starts, some good advice to Miriam would be:
    a. talk to others who have been or are in the import business.
    b. get a loan right away.
    c. find a business to buy as soon as possible.
    d. incorporate immediately.

11. In measuring the value of a small firm, which of the following would not be included?
    a. What the business owns.
    b. What the business earns.
    c. What makes the business unique.
    d. What products the business sells globally.

Learning Goal 3

12. The primary concerns when first starting your business are:
    a. marketing and accounting.
    b. planning and human resources.
    c. financing and planning.
    d. financing and marketing.

13. A business plan for a new business does not need to include:
    a. a marketing plan.
    b. a discussion of the purpose of the business.
    c. a description of the company background.
    d. the name of the lending bank.

14. What are the primary sources of funding for entrepreneurs?
    a. personal savings and individual investors
    b. finance companies and banks
    c. the Small Business Administration and banks
    d. former employers and the Economic Development Authority

15. For a market to exist there must be potential buyers:
   a. and a product that is safe and inexpensive.
   b. who have a willingness and the resources to buy.
   c. and stores which are willing to carry the product.
   d. who are looking for a bargain.

16. According to the text, one of the drawbacks of using venture capital is that:
   a. venture capital firms won't give the small business owner any advice.
   b. they don't know your customers.
   c. venture capital firms may ask for a stake in your business.
   d. the venture capital firm asks for very high interest rates.

Learning Goal 4
17. Small business owners often say that the most important assistance they need is in
   a. marketing.
   b. accounting.
   c. planning .
   d. manufacturing.

18. SCORE is:
   a. A U.S. government agency that advises and assists small business by providing management training and financing.
   b. A program through which private investment companies lend money to small businesses.
   c. An SBA service with 13,000 volunteers who provide counseling services for small businesses free, except for expenses.
   d. A group of individuals or companies that invest in new businesses in exchange for partial ownership of those businesses.

Learning Goal 5
19. Small businesses have an advantage over large business in international trade in all these ways except:
   a. They can begin shipping faster.
   b. Their prices are usually lower.
   c. Overseas buyers like dealing with individuals rather than large bureaucracies.
   d. They can provide a wide variety of services.

20. There are many reasons why small business owners don't go international. Which of the following is not one of those reasons?
   a. They don't know how to get started.
   b. Financing is often difficult to find.
   c. Paperwork is often overwhelming.
   d. The market doesn't have great potential.

TRUE-FALSE

Learning Goal 1
1. _____ It is important for an entrepreneur to be self-directed and self-nurturing.

2. _____ Entrepreneurs will sometimes look for opportunities by determining what customers <u>don't</u> need.

3. _____ A Web-based business will be more successful if it offers the same products available in local stores at better prices.

Learning Goal 2
4. _____ The Immigration Act of 1990 created investor visas which allow 10,000 people to come to the U.S. if they invest $1 million in an enterprise that creates 10 jobs.

5. _____ The majority of new jobs in the United States are created by big business.

6. _____ Many of the businesses with the lowest failure rates require advanced training to start.

7. _____ Small business owners report that their greatest advantages over big companies are their more personalized customer service and the ability to respond quickly to opportunities.

8. _____ The Small Business Administration reports that a vast majority of small business failures are the result of poor management.

Learning Goal 3

9. _____ An effective business plan should catch the reader's interest right away.

10. _____ The most important source of funds for a small business owner is bank loans.

11. _____ Angel investors will ask for a stake in your business in exchange for the cash to start up.

12. _____ The SBA offers a lot of advice, but no financial assistance to small business owners.

13. _____ Small business owners could consider borrowing from a potential supplier to the business.

14. _____ A market is basically anyone who wants to buy your product.

Learning Goal 4
15. _____ Employees of small businesses are often more satisfied with their jobs than counterparts in big business.

16. _____ Most small businesses can't afford to hire experts as employees, so they need to turn to outside assistance for help.

17. _____ It is best to stay away from other small business owners for counsel, as they are likely to use your ideas before you can get started.

18. _____ It is not necessary to obtain legal advice when operating a small business, as it is unlikely that your business will be involved in legal matters.

Learning Goal 5
19. _____ The growth potential for small businesses internationally is minimal.

20. _____ One of the major hurdles for a small business in going international is cultural differences.

You Can Find It on the Net

If you are interested in starting your own small business, the Small Business Administration can help. Go the to Small Business Administration Web site (www.sbaonline.sba.gov) Find the following information about the SBA services available in your area.

1. In what areas does the S.B.A. offer assistance, in general?

2. What is the address and phone number of the SBA office nearest you?

3. Are there any SBA sponsored special events scheduled in your area? If so, what are they?

4. Is there a Small Business Development Center in your area? Where?

5. What are your local financing resources?

6. What kind of financing resources are available in your state?

7. What types of training programs are offered by the S.B.A. in your state?

8. Find the home page for your state. What types of incentives, services and help are offered to businesses in your state? (To find your state's home page, use a search engine and type in the name of your state with the words "home page". For example," State of New Mexico home page".)

ANSWERS

LEARNING THE LANGUAGE

1. Market	8. Entrepreneurship
2. Enterprise zones	9. Intrapreneurs
3. Entrepreneurial team	10. Business plan
4. Small business	11. Small Business Investment Company program (SBIC)
5. Venture capitalists	12. Micropreneurs
6. Incubators	13. Small Business Administration (SBA)
7. Service Corps of Retired Executives (SCORE)	

ASSESSMENT CHECK

Learning Goal 1
Why People Take the Entrepreneurial Challenge

1. Four reasons people become entrepreneurs are:
    a. Opportunity   c. Independence
    b. Profit   d. Challenge

2. Five desirable attributes for entrepreneurs are:
    a. Self-directed   d. Highly energetic
    b. Self-nurturing   e. Tolerant of uncertainty
    c. Action-oriented

3. An entrepreneurial team may be better than an individual entrepreneur because a team can combine creative skills with areas such as marketing and production skills from the beginning. A team can ensure better cooperation and coordination between functions of a business.

4. Many micropreneurs are home-based business owners who are interested in simply enjoying a balanced lifestyle while doing the kind of work they want to do. While micropreneurs can be happy if their companies remain small, an entrepreneur may be committed to growing his or her business.

5. The reasons for the growth of home-based businesses are:
    a. Computer technology allows home based-businesses to look and act like their corporate competitors.
    b. Corporate downsizing has made workers aware that job security is not a sure thing.
    c. Social attitudes have changed.
    d. New tax laws have loosened restrictions regarding deductions for home offices.

6. Challenges for home-based businesses include:
    a. Getting new customers
    b. Managing time
    c. Keeping work and family tasks separate
    d. Abiding by city ordinances
    e. Managing risk

7. Home-based business owners should focus on:
   a. finding opportunity instead of security.
   b. getting results instead of following a routine.
   c. earning a profit instead of a paycheck.
   d. trying new ideas instead of avoiding mistakes.
   e. long-term vision instead of a short-term payoff.

8. Web based businesses have experienced a great deal of growth. By 2010 the online channel is expected to account for 13 percent of retail sales.

9. Web-based businesses have to do more than offer the same merchandise customers can buy at local stores. They must offer unique products and services.

10. Internet sites for entrepreneurs include:
    a. DistributorMatch.com
    b. Hypermart.com
    c. Sitecritique.net

11. While entrepreneurs are risk takers who have started their own businesses, intrapreneurs are creative people who work as entrepreneurs within corporations. The idea is to use existing human, financial and physical resources to launch new products and generate new profits.

12. Part of the intention of the Immigration Act of 1990 was to encourage more entrepreneurs to come to the United States. The act created a category of "investor visas" that allows 10,000 people to come to the U.S. each year if they invest money in an enterprise that creates or preserves 10 jobs.

13. The government could have a significant effect on entrepreneurship by offering investment tax breaks to businesses that make the kind of investments that would create jobs.

14. Incubators are centers that offer new businesses low cost offices with basic business services such as accounting, legal advice, and secretarial help. Incubators help companies survive because they provide assistance in the early stage of a businesses' development.

Learning Goal 2
Getting Started in Small Business

15. A small business is one that is:
    a. independently owned and operated.
    b. not dominant in its field of operation.
    c. meets certain standards of size in terms of employees or annual receipts.

16. A small business is considered small relative to the industry it is in. If it still meets the criteria listed above, a $22 million business would still be considered small. In manufacturing a company can have 1,500 employees and still be considered small.

17. Small business is very "big". There are about 20 million full and part-time home-based businesses in the United States. Nearly 750,000 tax paying, employee hiring businesses are started every year, and of all non-farm businesses in the U.S., almost 97 percent are considered small. Small businesses produce 75% of new jobs, account for over 50% of GDP, and employ more than the combined populations of Australia and Canada. About 80 percent of Americans find their first jobs in small businesses.

18.   The number of small businesses owned by women has grown to nearly 6 million. That's more than one-third of all small businesses.

   Minority owned businesses are one of the fastest-growing segments of the U.S. economy. This includes businesses owned by Asians, Hispanics and African Americans.

19.   Small businesses owners believe their advantages over large businesses are: more personal customer service and their ability to respond quickly to opportunities.

20.   The SBA reports a failure rate of 60 percent within 6 years. A study by an economist indicates that the failure rate is only 18 percent over the first 8 years. However, the statistics can be misleading because when small business owners went out of business to start new and different businesses, they were included in the business failure statistics. Also, when a business changes its form of ownership from a partnership, for example, to a corporation, it was included in the statistics, as were retirements.

21.   a. If you want to be both independent and rich, you need to go after growth.

   b. In general the easiest businesses to start are the ones that tend to have the least growth and the greatest failure rate.

   c. In general the easiest businesses to keep alive are the difficult ones to get started.

   d. In general the businesses that can make you rich are the ones that are both hard to start and hard to keep going.

Learning Goal 3
Learning About Small Business Operations

22.   Three ways to learn about small business are:
   a. learn from others
   b. get some experience
   c. take over a successful firm

23.   When you talk to others about starting a small business, they will tell you that location is critical, not to start without enough money, and warn you about the problems of finding and retaining good workers. They will also suggest that you hire a lawyer and an accountant.

24.   The rule of thumb is: have three years' experience in a comparable business.

25.   Many new entrepreneurs come from corporate management. They are tired of the big business life or have been laid off due to corporate downsizing.

26.   Three factors used to determine the value of business are:
   a. what the business owns
   b. what it earns
   c. what makes it unique

27. The two management functions of primary concern are planning and financing. The three important functions after the startup are knowing your customers (Marketing), managing your employees (Human resource development), and keeping records (Accounting).

28. Tips for small business owners wanting to borrow money are:
    a. pick a bank that serves small businesses
    b. have a good accountant prepare a complete set of financial statements and personal balance sheet
    c. make an appointment before going to the bank
    d. demonstrate good character
    e. ask for all the money you need
    f. be specific
    g. be prepared to personally guarantee the loan

29. The information that should generally be included in a business plan includes:
    a. Cover letter
    b. Executive Summary of proposed venture
    c. Company background
    d. Management team
    e. Financial plan
    f. Capital required
    g. Marketing plan
    h. Location analysis
    i. Manufacturing plan
    j. Appendix which includes marketing research and other information about the product

30. Sources of small business funding include:
    a. Personal savings
    b. Relatives
    c. Former employers
    d. Banks
    e. Finance companies
    f. Venture capitalists
    g. Small Business Administration
    h. Farmers Home Administration
    i. Economic Development Authority

31. Other than personal savings the primary source of capital for most entrepreneurs are individual investors.

32. Angel investors are private individuals who invest their own money in potentially hot companies before they go public.

33. The potential drawback with venture capital is that these companies will often ask for as much as 60% ownership in your business.

34. If you're a very small company you don't have a very good chance of getting venture capital. Since the burst of the dot.com bubble, venture capitalists have tightened the purse strings on how much they are willing to invest in a business and how much they expect back. You will stand a better chance of finding an angel investor.

35. The types of financial assistance from the Small Business Administration are:
     a   Guaranteed loans
     b. Microloans
     c. Export Express
     d. Community Adjustment and Investment program
     e. Pollution Control Loans
     f. 504 Certified Development Company loans

36. The microloan program provides very small loans and technical assistance to small business owners. These loans are awarded on the basis of belief in the borrowers' integrity and the soundness of their business ideas.

37. A Small Business Investment Company can help small businesses from defaulting on loans by identifying a business's trouble spots early, giving entrepreneurs advice, and rescheduling payments.

38. Small Business Development Centers are funded jointly by the federal government and individual states and are usually associated with state universities. SBDCs can help a small business owner evaluate the feasibility of their idea, develop the business plan and complete the funding application, all of which is free of charge.

39. Three important factors for success in your small business are:
     a. knowing your customers
     b. managing your employees
     c. keeping efficient records

40. Once you have identified your market and its needs, you must fill those needs by offering top quality at a fair price with great service.

41. One of the greatest advantages that small businesses have over larger ones is the ability to know their customers better and to adapt quickly to their changing needs.

42. Three criteria critical for small business owners regarding managing employees are:
     a. hiring
     b. training
     c. motivating employees

43. Employees of small companies are often more satisfied with their jobs than their counterparts in big business. Often they find their jobs more challenging, their ideas more accepted, and their bosses more respectful.

44. It is not easy to find good, qualified help when as a small business you are able to offer less money, fewer benefits, and less room for advancement than larger firms. Often entrepreneurs find it difficult to delegate authority to others, causing questions about to whom to delegate, and how much to delegate. Entrepreneurs who have built their companies often feel compelled to promote employees who have been with them from the start, even when those employees aren't qualified as managers.

45. Most small business owners say they need the most assistance in accounting.

46. A good accountant can help in setting up computer systems for record keeping such as inventory control, customer records, and payroll. He/She can also help make decisions such as whether to buy or lease equipment and whether to own or rent a building. Further, an accountant can help with tax planning, financial forecasting, choosing sources of financing, and writing requests for funds.

47. Small business owners have learned they need help with
   a. legal advice
   b. tax advice
   c. accounting advice
   d. marketing
   e. finance

48. Lawyers can help with such areas as partnership agreements, leases, contracts, and protection against liabilities.

49. Marketing research can help you determine where to locate, whom to select as your target market, and what would be an effective strategy for reaching those people.

50. A commercial loan officer can help a small business owner design an acceptable business plan, offer financial advice and lend money when necessary. An insurance agent will explain all the risks associated with a small business and how to cover them most efficiently with insurance and other means.

51. Important sources of information is the Service Corps of Retired Executives (SCORE), local colleges which may have business professors who will advise small businesses, other small-business owners, local chambers of commerce, the Better Business Bureau, national and local trade associations, the business reference section of the library, and many small-business related sites on the Internet.

Learning Goal 5
Going International: Small Business Prospects

52. In general, most small businesses still do not think internationally. Only a small percentage of small businesses export even though the number of small businesses that export has tripled in the last decade.

53. Four hurdles in the international market are:
   a. Financing is difficult to find
   b. Many would-be exporters don't know how to get started
   c. Potential global business people do not understand cultural differences
   d. The bureaucratic paperwork can be overwhelming

54. Good reasons for going international are:
   a. most of the world's markets lie outside the U.S.
   b. exporting can absorb excess inventory
   c. exporting softens downturns in the domestic market
   d. exporting extends product lives
   e. exporting can spice up dull routines

55. Small businesses have advantages over big businesses, such as:
    a. Overseas buyers enjoy dealing with individuals rather than large corporate bureaucracies
    b. Small companies can begin shipping faster
    c. Small companies provide a wide variety of suppliers
    d. Small companies can give more personal service and more undivided attention

CRITICAL THINKING EXERCISES

Learning Goal 1

1. Developing (and developed) countries have several options available to support entrepreneurship. Creating a system that makes it easy for investors to come into the country is an important step. The United States, for example, passed the Immigration Act of 1990, which created a special category of visa designed to lure entrepreneurs to the U.S.

   Many developing countries do not have the infrastructure to support a rapidly growing economy. Governments need to prioritize building the kind of infrastructure businesses need. Providing tax credits and tax breaks to businesses is another way to encourage entrepreneurship.

   Entrepreneurship creates jobs, and when people are working, and spending, that creates more jobs, and so the economy grows. Developing countries need the kind of programs that will encourage investments, which create jobs. Encouraging and supporting entrepreneurship is one way these countries can help their economies to grow, become self-sufficient and to be participants in the emerging global economy.

2. The text mentions that desirable entrepreneurial attributes include being self-directed, self-nurturing, action-oriented, highly energetic, and tolerant of uncertainty. Eric demonstrates these characteristics in several ways. He is self-directed in that he had the discipline not only to build 2 businesses, but to leave those businesses when he decided that he wanted to go on to college. He has been self-supporting for a number of years, and so most likely is quite tolerant of uncertainty, and probably felt quite comfortable with that element of risk in starting his own businesses. He continued to work while his friends told him he was "crazy for working that hard" so it seems that he doesn't depend on other people's approval i.e. he's self-nurturing, and appears to be pretty energetic. He must be action oriented, able to build his "dream into a reality" by taking an idea and creating a successful business.

Learning Goals 2,3

3. Eric seems to lend validity to the questionable failure statistics the text refers to. He has beaten the odds twice, and it would seem that the odds of failure may have been lower than traditionally reported.

   Eric may tell you that you need to talk to people who have already started their own businesses and get their advice. They can give you valuable information about the importance of location, finding good workers, and having enough capital to keep you going.

   He may also suggest that you work for a successful entrepreneur and get some experience in the fields in which you're interested.

Another idea is to take over a firm that has already been successful. (That's what the <u>buyers</u> of Eric's most recent firm decided to do!) A strategy may be to work for the owner for a few years, then offer to buy the business through profit sharing or an outright purchase.

4.   I would tell Eric to be prepared. First, have a well-written business plan already prepared. Pick a bank that serves small businesses, have an accountant prepare complete financial statements, including a personal balance sheet and take all the financial information with you to the bank, along with the business plan. Make an appointment with the loan officer, and ask for exactly what you need. Be prepared to personally guarantee the loan.

Eric could also work with the Small Business Administration to determine if he qualifies for some of their loan programs. Small Business Investment Companies also lend money to small businesses meeting their criteria. Further options include Small Business Development Centers and angel investors.

5.   Maria could be considered a micropreneur, interested in balancing her family life with her work life. Home-based businesses have experienced a great deal of growth in recent years as access to computer technology has expanded and social attitudes have changed.

Maria will face challenges as a home-based business owner. Finding new customers could be more difficult, and she will have to become a great time manager while balancing work and caring for her small children. One idea for Maria will be to develop a web site for her business to be better able to compete with larger businesses and to get the word out to potential customers. Maria will also need to create a network of contacts through family, friends and community connections to encourage referrals.

Learning Goals 3, 4

6.   Dave and Kevin followed one of the suggestions in the text for successfully starting a business - they worked for someone else in the same field before starting out on their own. They knew their customers, and by all indications the market was there with the resources to buy what Dave and Kevin were selling. Other than Dave's wife, they had no employees to manage because they were using independent sales representatives. As is typical in some small business partnerships, Dave and Kevin couldn't agree on some issues.

Keeping efficient records seems to be a real weakness. Dave's wife didn't really have the skill or time to do the books. Hiring a bookkeeper was a good idea. Perhaps the bookkeeper can suggest an effective billing method.

Although Dave and Kevin had funding, it appears to have been very "casual", and not very well thought out. They made no plan to repay the supplier's loan, which was to come due in 4 months. They didn't look for any help, and so ran the risk of running into legal as well as financial problems. Since they decided not to do a business plan, they don't seem to have been very well organized. They had no marketing plan, and no effective strategy for reaching customers other than those they started out with. They appear to have made many of the mistakes the text mentions being causes for small business failure, i.e. poor planning and inadequate financial management.

(**Ed. not**e: The company "limped along" for about three years before Dave and Kevin began to disagree on how to proceed. They were sued by the supplier for non payment of the loan, and eventually the business dissolved. Each partner went out on their own. Neither is still in business.)

7.   A. There are a number of outside consultants that a small business owner can go to for help in starting and managing their businesses, for example:

a. Accountant
b. Lawyer
c. Marketing research service
d. Commercial loan officer
e. Insurance agent
f. Other business owners
g. Business professors

B. Other sources of information include:

a. Chambers of Commerce
b. Better Business Bureau
c. National and local trade associations
d. Library business sections
e. The Internet
f. Computer bulletin boards

Learning Goal 5

8.   The international market provides a lot of growth potential for a small business and Chad is in a good field for that market according to Figure 6-8. The global market may especially be a good idea for Chad if he sees a softening in the domestic market. As a small business owner he has several advantages over larger businesses because he can deal with his customers personally and he can start providing his product immediately.

There are several hurdles to overcome in the international market, especially if Chad is inexperienced. Cultural differences for the product may not be a problem, but sales techniques will vary from those in the United States. In addition, the paperwork in developing an international market can be overwhelming. There are several places available to Chad to find information, including the SBA, the Commerce Department, export management companies, and export trading companies.

PRACTICE TEST

MULTIPLE CHOICE

LG 1   # 1-6
LG 2   # 8-11
LG 3   # 12-16
LG 4   # 17-18
LG 5   #19-20

TRUE-FALSE

LG 1   # 1-3
LG 2   # 9-14
LG 3   # 9-14
LG 4   # 15-18
LG 5   #19-20

MULTIPLE CHOICE				TRUE-FALSE			
1.	d	11.	d	1.	T	11.	F
2.	a	12.	c	2.	T	12.	F
3.	b	13.	d	3.	F	13.	T
4.	c	14.	a	4.	T	14.	F
5.	c	15.	b	5.	F	15.	T
6.	b	16.	c	6.	T	16.	T
7.	c	17.	b	7.	T	17.	F
8.	b	18.	c	8.	T	18.	F
9.	d	19.	b	9.	T	19.	F
10.	a	20.	d	10.	F	20.	T

CHAPTER 7 – MANAGEMENT, LEADERSHIP, AND EMPLOYEE EMPOWERMENT

LEARNING GOALS

After you have read and studied this chapter, you should be able to:

1. Explain how the changes that are occurring in the business environment are affecting the management function.
2. Describe the four functions of management.
3. Relate the planning process and decision making to the accomplishment of company goals.
4. Describe the organizing function of management.
5. Explain the differences between leaders and managers, and describe the various leadership styles.
6. Summarize the five steps of the control function of management.

LEARNING THE LANGUAGE

Listed below are important terms found in the chapter. Choose the correct term for the definition and write it in the space provided.

Autocratic leadership	Internal customers	Planning
Brainstorming	Knowledge management	PMI
Conceptual skills	Leading	Problem solving
Contingency planning	Management	Staffing
Controlling	Middle management	Strategic planning
Decision making	Mission statement	Supervisory management
Enabling	Objectives	SWOT analysis
External customers	Operational planning	Tactical planning
Free-rein leadership	Organization chart	Technical skills
Goals	Organizing	Top management
Human relations skills	Participative (democratic) leadership	Vision

1. A _____ is a planning tool used to analyze an organization's strengths, weaknesses, opportunities, and threats.

2. Individuals and units within the firm called _____ receive services from other individuals or units.

3. _____ are specific short- term statements detailing how to achieve the organization's goals.

4. The process of _____ involves developing detailed, short-term statements about what is to be done, who is to do it, and how it is to be done.

5. Finding the right information, keeping the information in a readily accessible place, and making the information known to everyone in the firm is known as _____.

6. The level of management that includes general managers, division managers, and branch and plant managers who are responsible for tactical planning and controlling is called _____.

7. The process of _____ means choosing among two or more alternatives.

8. An individual who uses _____ makes managerial decisions without consulting others.

9. The management function of _____ includes designing the structure of the organization, and creating conditions and systems in which everyone and everything work together to achieve the organization's goals and objectives.

10. A _____ is an encompassing explanation of why the organization exists and where it's trying to head.

11. When an individual uses _____, managers and employees work together to make decisions.

12. _____ is the process of determining the major goals of the organization and the policies and strategies for obtaining and using resources to achieve those goals.

13. The management function of _____ includes hiring, motivating, and retaining the best people available to accomplish the company's objectives.

14. Skills that involve the ability to perform tasks in a specific discipline or department are considered _____.

15. The leadership style known as _____ involves managers setting objectives and employees being relatively free to do whatever it takes to accomplish those objectives.

16. The management function of _____ involves anticipating trends and determining the best strategies and tactics to achieve organizational goals and objectives.

17. The highest level of management, consisting of the president and other key company executives who develop strategic plans is called _____.

18. When a manager does _____, he or she is in the process of preparing alternative courses of action that may be used if the primary plans don't achieve the objectives of the organization.

19. A(n) _____ is a visual device that shows relationships among people and divides the organization's work: it shows who is accountable for the completion of specific work and who reports to whom.

20. _____ is the process used to accomplish organizational goals through planning organizing, leading, and controlling people and other organizational resources.

21. _____ involve the ability to picture the organization as a whole and the relationship among its various parts.

22. The management function of _____ involves establishing clear standards to determine whether or not an organization is progressing toward its goals and objectives, rewarding people for doing a good job, and taking corrective action if they are not.

23. Creating a vision for the organization, and guiding, training, coaching, and motivating others to work effectively to achieve the organization's goals and objectives is called _____.

24. The level of management known as _____ includes managers who are directly responsible for supervising workers and evaluating their daily performance.

25. Broad, long-term statements known as _____ are accomplishments an organization wishes to attain.

26. _____ means giving workers the education they need to make decisions.

27. When a manager is doing _____ he or she is setting work standards and schedules necessary to implement the company's tactical objectives.

28. Dealers, who buy to sell to others, and ultimate customers, or end users, who buy products for their own personal use are called _____.

29. The _____ is an outline of the fundamental purposes of the organization.

30. Skills that involve communication and motivation, called _____, enable managers to work through and with people.

31. In a _____, all the pluses for a solution are listed in one column, all the minuses in another and the interesting implications in a third column.

32. When individuals are involved in _____, they are coming up with as many solutions to a problem as possible in a short period of time with no censoring of ideas.

33. _____ is the process of solving the everyday problems that occur: it is less formal than the decision-making process and usually calls for quicker action.

ASSESSMENT CHECK

Learning goal 1
Manager's Roles are Evolving

1. Describe how today's managers have changed.

Functions of Management

2.   Identify some of the activities involved in a manager's job.

3.   The four functions of the management process are:

          a. _____   c. _____

          b. _____   d. _____

4.   Identify the activities performed in each of the management functions.

<u>Function</u>   <u>Activities</u>

a._____   a._____

                                       b._____

                                       c._____

                                       d._____

b._____   a._____

                                       b._____

                                       c._____

                                       d._____

c._____   a._____

                                       b._____

                                       c._____

                                       d._____

                                       e._____

d._____   a._____

                                       b._____

                                       c._____

                                     d. _____

5. The trend today in planning is _____

    _____

6. In organizing, many of today's organizations are: _____

7. What must organizations do in order to please the customer at a profit?

8. In leading, the trend today is: _____

    _____

Learning Goal 3
Planning: Creating a Vision Based On Values

9. Distinguish between a "vision" and a goal.

10. List the areas a meaningful mission statement should address:

    a. _____

    b. _____

    c. _____

    d. _____

    e. _____

    f. _____

11. A mission statement becomes _____

    _____

12. What is the difference between goals and objectives?

13. What questions are answered as a part of the SWOT analysis?

14. Describe the process of performing a SWOT analysis.

15. What are four forms of planning?

    a. _____   c. _____

    b. _____   d. _____

16. At the strategic planning stage, the company decides _____

    _____

17. Why is strategic planning becoming more difficult? What are some companies doing in response?

18. What activities are included in tactical planning? At what level of management is tactical planning usually done, compared to strategic planning?

19. How is operational planning different from strategic planning? At what level of management is operational planning done?

20. Why is it wise to make contingency plans?

21. a. Planning is a key management function because _____.

    b. The idea is to stay _____.

22. What are the 7 D's of the decision making process?

a. _____

b. _____

c. _____

d. _____

e. _____

f. _____

g. _____

23. Describe two problem-solving techniques that companies use.

Learning Goal 4
Organizing: Creating a Unified System

24. What are the three levels of management?

a._____ b._____ c._____

25. What are the responsibilities of a

CEO: _____

COO: _____

CFO: _____

CIO/CKO: _____

26. List examples of positions found in middle management. What has happened to some middle management positions?

27. What is another name for supervisory management?

28. Describe the three categories of skills managers should have.

a. _____

b. _____

c. _____

29. How do the various levels of management differ in the skills needed?

30. What has been the dominating question regarding organizing in recent years? How are large organizations responding?

31. According to the text, companies are organizing so that _____have the greatest influence.

32. The organizing task is more complex today because _____

_____.

33. What makes staffing so critical today?

Learning Goal 5
Leading: Providing Continuous Vision and Values

34. Describe the difference between management and leadership.

35. In terms of leadership, how is the workplace changing?

36.   What are four things leaders must do?

        a. _____

        b. _____

        c. _____

        d. _____

37.   Describe the important aspects of:

        Autocratic leadership: _____

        _____

        Participative leadership: _____

        _____

        Free rein leadership: _____

        _____

38.   Which leadership style is best?

39.   How do traditional leaders differ from progressive leaders? How is a manager's role
        changing as a result?

40.   What is the difference between empowerment and enabling? How is enabling the key to
        the success of empowerment?

41.   What are the two steps in developing a knowledge management system? What is the key
        to a successful knowledge management system?

42.   List the five steps in the control process

      a._____

      b._____

      c._____

      d._____

      e._____

43.   Which of the five steps in the control process ties the planning function to the control function and why are clear standards important?

44.   Standards must be:

      a. _____ b. _____ c. _____

45.   The criterion for measuring success in a customer-oriented firm is: _____

_____

46.   Other than your answer to the above question, identify other criteria for measuring organizational effectiveness.

CRITICAL THINKING EXERCISES

Learning Goal 1

1.   Re read the first section of this chapter, "Managers' Roles are Evolving". If you have a job or an internship, (or if you used to have a job) evaluate your manager's actions using the description of management behavior in this section. For example, does your manager tell you what to do, or does he or she place more emphasis on training you to make decisions on the job? Does management emphasize teamwork and cooperation? Has this manager been with the company for a long time, or has he or she moved around from one company to another? Is your manager a skilled communicator, team player, planner, coordinator, organizer?

Learning Goal 2

2. There are four functions of management:

Planning   Leading
Organizing   Controlling

Read the following examples and identify which leadership function the manager is performing.

a. _____ Grant Wimmer is concerned about his newest employee, Peter Wong. In looking over his sales reports, Grant sees that Peter hasn't been performing well and has only met his sales goals once in the past 6 months. Grant is thinking about ways to help Peter improve his sales performance

b. _____ John Bradford is a manager for a firm in the technology industry. John feels it is vital for him to monitor the changes in the industry and look for opportunities presented by those changes. If he sees a major trend emerging, John sets an objective to learn more about it and to determine ways for his company to participate in the trend.

c. _____ Elvira Mihalek is a manager who spends a lot of time with her employees helping them to attain their goals. She looks for ways to motivate them, makes sure they are trained well, and gives them a great deal of freedom to do their jobs in the best way for them, while still working to achieve the goals of the organization.

d. _____ Phil Ardmore is focused on how his company can better serve their customers. He is constantly looking for ways he can design jobs and his department in the best way to be as flexible as possible to meet the needs of their customers.

Learning Goal 3

3. Below are examples that illustrate the planning function for an automotive manufacturer. Match the statement with the proper term:

Mission statement   Objectives
Goals   Vision

a. _____ To assemble and distribute automotive products worldwide and achieve market share leadership.

b. _____ Introduce a hybrid version of a current model within the next three years to U.S., Canadian, and European markets.

c. _____ To be the premier auto company in North America in the world by 2015. The purpose of this company is to build cars and trucks that people will buy, will enjoy driving, and will want to buy again.

d. _____ Our vision is to be the world leader in transportation products and related services. In order to achieve this vision, we recognize that many issues must be addressed and many goals attained. It is imperative that economic, environmental and social objectives be integrated into our daily business objectives and future planning activities so that we can become a more sustainable company.

4. Strategic and Tactical planning provide the framework for the planning process. Contingency planning provides alternative plans of action.

Eric Benoit wants to start his own business making a product he has invented for the automotive industry. It's a windshield design that automatically darkens when the car is in the sun, then lightens when the car is in the shade, or as it gets later in the day. The technology is the same as that used in some eyeglass lenses. The windshield can be installed in the factory, but can also be installed by dealers, or by windshield repair/replacement companies, at any time after the manufacture of the car. The product's brand name and the name of Eric's company is"Sun-2-Shade".

Complete the following for Eric's new company:

Mission Statement:

a. Strategic plan

b. Tactical plan

c. Contingency plan

5. Using the information in your text and in the Spotlight on Small Business, do a brief SWOT analysis for Sun-2-Shade. In other words, what do you believe may be the strengths, weaknesses, opportunities and threats for this company in the coming years?

Learning Goal 4

6. Identify two individuals at your college or university, or at your place of employment at each level of management. Can you draw a simple organization chart? With some research, you may be able to find an organizational chart for your school or your company.

a. Top   _____

        _____

b. Middle   _____

        _____

c. Supervisory   _____

        _____

7. We have read about changes occurring in business and in the marketplace in previous chapters. In this chapter we read about the changes in the <u>structure</u> of business, which is becoming customer-oriented. Businesses are forming partnerships with firms and creating systems of companies working together. Given what you know from previous chapters, why do you think this type of organizational structure has begun to evolve?

8. There are many specific skills needed by various levels of management:

    Technical skills   Managing diversity
    Human relations skills   Decision-making
    Conceptual skills

    For each of the following situations, indicate the management level and the skills being used or described.

    A. Alice Burling is concerned about Bob Mailing's sales performance. In their meeting, Alice and Bob agree there's a problem. Alice listens carefully to Bob while he explains the situation in his territory, and after asking some questions, Alice shows Bob how to handle things differently. After the meeting, Alice completes a schedule assigning new accounts to various salesmen in her department. Later, with one of the sales people, Alice makes a sales call to a particularly important customer.

        a. Management level _____

        b. Skills _____

    B. In a typical week in her office, Maria works on a long range forecast for a new product the company is considering, and decides to implement a new program to encourage communication and idea exchange between division heads. She appoints several division heads to formulate a plan for implementation. She schedules most meetings, but leaves time open for interruptions and unplanned meetings with subordinates.

        a. Management level _____

        b. Skills _____

    C. In reviewing weekly production reports, Joel Hodes notices a drop in overall production from last month. He works for several days on an incentive plan he thinks will push production back up to the company's objectives and still maintain high morale. He then calls a meeting with the line supervisors. After getting their responses and suggestions, Joel revises and implements the plan in his plant.

        a. Management level_____

        b. Skills_____

9.   You have been hired to be a supervisor in the Sun-2-Shade plant where they are going to make the self-darkening windshields, referred to in a previous exercise. Your workers are well educated and highly skilled. How do you intend to lead and organize these employees? How will your leading (or directing) differ from Eric's, the top manager?

10.   Effective leadership styles range along a continuum based upon the amount of employee involvement in setting objectives and making decisions. The three leadership styles are called:

Autocratic   *Participative (Democratic)*   *Free rein*

Which of those styles are being illustrated in the following situations?

A. Production workers complain about having to punch a time clock each day.

        a. _____   "Too bad, I'm not getting rid of it!"

        b. _____   "Let's get a committee together and see if we can come up with some alternatives to using the time clock."

B. A university sees a need for some action to be taken to reverse declining enrollment trends.

        a. _____   "Let's form a committee of faculty and administrators to study the problem and give recommendations on how to solve the problem."

        b. _____   "The objective for each division is to increase enrollment by 10% for the next school year. Each division is free to take whatever action is appropriate for their area in order to reach the objective."

C. A manager notices that an employee consistently turns in work past the deadline.

        a. _____   "Bob, your work has been late three times this month. This is a problem. How can we work together to solve it?"

        b. _____   "Bob, your work has been late three times this month. One more time and you will be disciplined. Two times and you're fired. Got it?"

11. Sun-2-Shade, the company that makes self-darkening windshields for the automotive industry, has been in business for several months and you have just been assigned to re-organize the production department. Eric Benoit, the CEO, knows that he will need inventory if things go as planned. Production is very slow right now but there are some orders to fill. Money, however, is tight. All the production workers are peers (none are supervisors), but there is one member of the group who appears to be the informal leader. The workers are paid by the hour, and they are well paid by normal standards.

You have some ideas about how to increase production without increasing costs. One idea, for example, is to change the method of paying workers from hourly to by how much they produce. The way you have it figured, the workers would have to produce more to make the same income. Another way is to set up individual workstations to cut down on the amount of socializing you have seen going on.

While you are confident these ideas, and others you have thought of, are the best solutions, you aren't sure how to implement the changes. You do know that this will be a test of your management and leadership skills.

a. How would you go about developing alternatives and implementing changes you believe are necessary to increase productivity and save money?

b. What leadership style do you think you used in developing your solution? Why?

12. You have been in your supervisory position for several months, and have found your boss to be a great person to work with. She speaks often about the kind of division she wants to create, where all the employees feel a sense of loyalty to a team. She stresses customer service, high product quality, and fair treatment of her employees. If she makes a mistake, she is always up front about it. She insists on honesty from her employees, and you notice that all her employees are treated fairly and with respect. She expects a lot from you and her other subordinates, but is sure to let you make your own decisions (as well as your own mistakes!). She encourages employee problem solving and is quick to implement changes, which will make the division more effective and efficient. How does your boss differ from the old style "manager", and demonstrate the leadership of today?

13.   "The control system's weakest link tends to be the setting of standards." Standards must be : specific, attainable, and measurable.

Improve the way the following vague standards are written:

a. "Increase sales" _____

b. "Get a degree" _____

c. "Be a better manager" _____

PRACTICE TEST

MULTIPLE CHOICE – Circle the best answer

Learning Goal 1
1.   Managers today:
       a. closely supervise highly skilled workers who would like to "do their own thing."
       b. emphasize teamwork and cooperation, and act as coaches, rather than "bosses."
       c. have to become specialists in one or two functional areas.
       d. have to function as intermediaries between workers and unions.

Learning Goal 2
2.   Which of the following would not be included in a discussion of the four functions of management?
       a. producing
       b. organizing
       c. leading
       d. controlling

3.   "We believe in creating loyal customers by providing a superior experience at a great value. We are committed to direct relationships, providing the best products and services based on standards-based technology, and outperforming the competition with value and superior customer experience." This statement is a part of Dell's:
       a. objectives
       b. strategy
       c. mission statement
       d. goal

Learning Goal 3
4.   H. Ameneggs is working on a project to determine his company's strengths and weaknesses by looking at the economy, technology, the competition, social, and other changes that are affecting his firm. He is looking to identify some opportunities his company can take advantage of in the new economy. H. is also concerned about some things he has identified that inhibit his company's growth. H. is working on
       a. Setting objectives
       b. A mission statement
       c. A SWOT analysis
       d. Contingency planning

5.   A(n) _____ is a specific short-term statement detailing how to achieve _____.
        a.   mission statement/ goals
        b.   goal/ objectives
        c.   goal/the mission statement
        d.   objective/goal

6.   Maria Mainini is in the middle of setting her plan for the next year. She knows the company has the goal of increasing market share in the Northeast, so she has developed a plan for expanding the advertising budget for the next year and adding at least one more sales person to cover the larger territories. Maria is involved in:
        a.   Contingency planning
        b.   Operational planning
        c.   Strategic planning
        d.   Tactical planning

7.   Which of the following employees of the local hardware store, Hammerhead, would most likely be involved in strategic planning?
        a.   Joe Hartley – department head
        b.   Annelise Oswalt – advertising manager
        c.   Elliot Nessy – President and CEO
        d.   Manny Martinez – chief accountant

8.   Which of the following is not part of the seven Ds of decision making?
        a.   Define the situation
        b.   Develop alternatives
        c.   Determine if the alternatives are possible.
        d.   Decide which alternative is best.

9.   In the process of problem solving, managers sometimes use the technique of _____, which involves listing all the minuses of a solution in one column, all the plusses in another, and the implications in a third.
        a.   PMI
        b.   brainstorming
        c.   strategic planning
        d.   SWOT analysis

Learning Goal 4
10.   General managers, division managers, plant managers and college deans are all a part of
        a.   supervisory management
        b.   middle management
        c.   top management
        d.   first-line management

11.   The three basic categories of skills managers must have include all of the following except:
        a.   technical skills
        b.   mechanical skills
        c.   human relations skills
        d.   conceptual skills

12. The level of management most likely to need the ability to picture the organization as a whole is
    a. supervisory
    b. first –line
    c. middle
    d. top

13. Which of the following is a false statement?
    a. Companies are looking at the best way to organize to respond to the needs of customers.
    b. General consensus is that larger companies are more responsive to customer needs than smaller companies.
    c. Many large firms are being restructured into smaller, customer-focused units.
    d. Companies are organizing so that customers have more influence, not managers.

14. The management function of _____ includes hiring, motivating and retaining the best people to accomplish the company's objectives.
    a. planning
    b. staffing
    c. controlling
    d. leading

Learning goal 5
15. Which of the following is not characteristic of a leader?
    a. A leader has a vision and rallies others around the vision.
    b. A leader will establish corporate values.
    c. A leader will emphasize corporate ethics.
    d. A leader will always attempt to keep things from changing.

16. When a manager uses democratic leadership, he or she will
    a. work with employees to make decisions together.
    b. set objectives and allow employees to be relatively free to do what it takes to accomplish them.
    c. give employees direction, and be sure that they are doing their job the way the manager wants them to.
    d. make managerial decisions without consulting employees.

17. At Schwinn, the bicycle manufacturer, managers of the various new departments were told, " Go out and shape the department the way you want. You have total freedom." That is an example of:
    a. effective delegating
    b. free rein leadership
    c. decision making
    d. technical skills

18. The first step in developing a knowledge management system is:
    a. find answers to questions from the SWOT analysis
    b. determine what knowledge is most important
    c. setting goals and developing action plans
    d. establishing performance standards

19.   Measuring performance relative to objectives and standards is part of _____
         a.   decision making
         b.   using technical skills
         c.   directing
         d.   controlling

20.   Which step in the control process is considered to be the weakest?
         a.   Setting clear standards
         b.   Monitoring and recording results
         c.   Communicating results to employees
         d.   Taking corrective action

21.   Which of the following statements is stated most effectively as a control standard?
         a.   Cut the number of finished product rejects.
         b.   Empower employees to make more decisions next year.
         c.   Praise employees more often this month.
         d.   Increase sales of our top end product from 2000 in the first quarter to 3000 during the
              same period by the year 2008.

True-False

Learning Goal 1
1. _____   Today progressive managers are being educated to tell people what to do and to
              watch over the new type of workers.

2. _____   Because employees tend to stay at the same company for most of their careers,
              managers don't have a need to earn the trust of their employees.

Learning Goal 2
3. _____   Planning in businesses today could include planning teams, which help monitor the
              environment, find opportunities and watch for challenges.

4. _____   Organizing involves giving workers assignments and motivating employees to
              work to meet organizational objectives.

Learning Goal 3
5. _____   A mission statement outlines a company's fundamental purpose.

6. _____   Operational planning answers the questions "What is the situation now?" and"
              Where do we want to go?"

7. _____   A SWOT analysis begins with an analysis of the company's profitability.

8. _____   The first step in decision making is to describe and collect the kind of information
              needed to make the decision.

Learning Goal 4
9. _____   Today staffing is a critical part of organizational success.

10. _____   The difference between managers and leaders is that a leader creates the vision, the
              manager carries it out.

11. ____ Top managers will spend their time developing tactical level plans.

12. ____ The skills needed by managers are different at different levels of management.

Learning Goal 5
13. ____ Enabling means giving employees the authority (the right) to make decisions on their own.

14. ____ Generally, there is one best leadership style to which all leaders should adhere.

15. ____ Autocratic leadership will be effective in emergencies or when absolute followership is needed.

16. ____ Progressive leaders are less likely than traditional leaders to give specific instructions to employees.

17. ____ Knowledge management tries to keep people from "re-inventing the wheel", or duplicating the work of gathering information, every time a decision needs to be made.

Learning Goal 5
18. ____ The first step in the control process is to monitor and record performance results.

19. ____ The criteria for measuring success in a customer-oriented firm is customer satisfaction of both internal and external customers.

20. ____ External customers include the ultimate customer, also known as the "end user".

You Can Find It On the Net

Visit www.businessweek.com or www.inc.com and search for leadership related articles. What topics are new in the leadership area? Topics will change over time. How do the topics covered in the articles reinforce the material related in our text?

Click on http://www.impactfactory.com/ and then click on leadership. Scroll down to "leadership quiz". Do you have what it takes to be a good leader?

Alternatively click on http://crs.uvm.edu/gopher/nerl/personal/Assess/b.html
And take the quiz Assessment of leadership qualities and skills.

Do a Google search of "management skills". What kinds of skills can you find mentioned?

ANSWERS

LEARNING THE LANGUAGE

1. SWOT analysis	13. Staffing	25. Goals
2. Internal customers	14. Technical skills	26. Enabling
3. Objectives	15. Free rein leadership	27. Operational planning
4. Tactical planning	16. Planning	28. External customers
5. Knowledge management	17. Top management	29. Mission statement
6. Middle management	18. Contingency planning	30. Human relations skills
7. Decision making	19. Organization chart	31. PMI
8. Autocratic leadership	20 Management	32. Brainstorming
9. Organizing	21. Conceptual skills	33. Problem solving
10. Vision	22. Controlling	
11. Participative (democratic) leadership	23. Leading	
12. Strategic planning	24. Supervisory management	

ASSESSMENT CHECK

Learning goal 1
Manager's Roles are Evolving

1. Traditional managers were called "bosses", and their job was to tell people what to do and watch over them to be sure the employees did what they were told. Today's managers are being educated to guide, train, support, motivate, and coach employees rather than to tell them what to do. Modern managers will emphasize teamwork and cooperation rather than discipline and order giving. In general, management is experiencing a revolution.

    Today's managers are also younger, more are female, and fewer were educated at elite universities. They tend to move from one company to another more than in the past.

Learning Goal 2
Functions of Management

2. Some of the activities managers today must perform include giving direction to their organizations, providing leadership and deciding how to use organizational resources to accomplish goals. In addition, mangers today must deal with conflict resolution, create trust in an atmosphere where trust has been shaken, help create balance between work lives and family lives, and effectively and efficiently use organizational resources.

3. The four functions of the management process are:
    a. planning   c. leading
    b. organizing   d. controlling

4.   Function   Activities
        a. Planning   a. Set goals
                                        b. Develop strategies to reach goals
                                        c. Determine resources needed
                                        d. Set standards

        b. Organizing   a. Allocate resources, assign tasks, establish procedures
                                        b. Create structure
                                        c. Recruit, select, train, develop employees
                                        d. Effective placement of employees

        c. Leading   a. Guiding and motivating employees to work effectively
                                        b. Give assignments
                                        c. Explain routines
                                        d. Clarify policies
                                        e. Provide performance feedback

        d. Controlling   a. Measure results against objectives
                                        b. Monitor performance relative to standards
                                        c. Reward outstanding performance
                                        d. Take corrective action

5.   The trend today in planning is to have <u>planning teams</u> to help monitor the environment, find business opportunities, and watch for challenges.

6.   In organizing, many of today's organizations are being designed around the customer. The idea is to design the firms so that everyone is working to please the customer at a profit.

7.   In order to please the customer at a profit, the organization must remain flexible and adaptable because customer needs change and organizations must either change also, or risk losing their business.

8.   In leading, the trend today is to empower employees, giving them as much freedom as possible to become self-directed and self-motivated. In smaller firms the role of managers is often telling employees exactly what to do. In most large modern firms, however, managers no longer tell people exactly what to do because often knowledge workers and others know how to do their jobs better than the manager.

Learning Goal 3
Planning: Creating a Vision Based On Values

9.   Goals are broad, long-term accomplishments that an organization wants to reach. A vision is greater than a goal; it's the larger explanation of why the organization exists and where it's trying to head.

10.   A meaningful mission statement should address:
        a.   The organization's self concept
        b.   Company philosophy/ Goals
        c.   Long-term survival
        d.   Customer needs
        e.   Social responsibility
        f.   Nature of product or service

11. A mission statement becomes the foundation for setting goals and selecting and motivating employees.

12. Goals are the broad, long-term accomplishments an organization wishes to obtain. Objectives are specific, short-term statements detailing how to achieve the goals that have been set.

13. The questions answered by a SWOT include: What is the situation now? What is the state of the environment? What opportunities exist? What products and customers are most profitable? Why do people buy our products? Who are our major competitors? What threats are there to our business? Where do we want to go? How much growth do we want? What is our profit goal? What are our social objectives? What are our personal development objectives?
The last question is the most important part of planning: How can we get there from here?

14. The process of performing a SWOT analysis begins with an analysis of the organization's environment in general. Then it identifies strengths and weaknesses. Finally as a result of the environmental analysis, it identifies opportunities and threats.

15. Four forms of planning are:
   a. Strategic   c. Operational
   b. Tactical   d. Contingency

16. At the strategic planning stage, the company decides which customers to serve, what products or services to sell, and the geographic areas in which the firm will compete.

17. Strategic planning is becoming more difficult because changes are occurring so fast that plans set for even months in the future may quickly become obsolete. Therefore, some companies are making shorter-term plans that allow for quick responses to the market.

18. Tactical planning is the process of developing detailed, short-term strategies about what has to be done, who will do it and how it is to be done. This type of planning involves setting annual budgets and deciding on other details and activities necessary to meet the strategic objectives. Managers or teams of managers at lower levels of the organization do this type of planning, whereas strategic planning is done at top levels of management.

19. Whereas strategic planning looks at the organization as a whole, operational planning focuses on specific supervisors, department managers, and individual employees. The operational plan is the department manager's tool for daily and weekly operations. Operational planning is done by the department manager, and his/her tool for daily and weekly operations.

20. It is wise to have alternative plans of action because the environment changes so rapidly. Contingency plans are needed in anticipation of those changes.

21. a. Planning is a key management function because the other management functions depend on having good plans.

   b. The idea is to stay flexible, listen to customers, and seize opportunities when they come, whether they are planned or not.

22. The 7 D's of the decision making process are:
    a. Define the situation
    b. Describe and collect needed information
    c. Develop alternatives
    d. Develop agreement among those involved
    e. Decide which alternative is best
    f. Do what is indicated (implement solution)
    g. Determine whether the decision was a good one and follow up

23. Two problem solving techniques companies use are brainstorming and PMI. Brainstorming means coming up with as many solutions as possible in a short period of time with no censoring of ideas. PMI is listing all pluses for a solution in one column, all the minuses in another and the implications in a third column.

Learning Goal 4
Organizing: Creating a Unified System

24. The three levels of management are:
    a. supervisory or first-line
    b. middle
    c. top

25. CEOs are responsible for introducing change into an organization.

    The COO is responsible for putting those changes into effect. His or her tasks include structuring, controlling, and rewarding to ensure that people carry out the leader's vision.

    The CFO is responsible for obtaining funds, budgeting, collecting funds, and other financial matters.

    The CIO/CKO is responsible for getting the right information to other managers.

26. Middle management positions include general managers, divisional mangers, branch managers, plant managers and at a college, deans. Many firms have eliminated some middle managers through downsizing.

27. Supervisory managers are also known as first-line managers because they're the first level above workers.

28. Three skills managers must have are:
    a. technical skills involve the ability to perform tasks in a specific discipline.
    b. human relations skills involve communication and motivation, and those associated with leadership, coaching, morale building, delegating, training and development, and help and support.
    c. conceptual skills are needed in planning, organizing, controlling systems development, problem analysis, decision making, coordinating, and delegating.

29. First line managers need to be skilled in all three areas, but most of their time is spent on technical and human relations tasks. They spend little time on conceptual tasks. Top managers need to use few technical skills. Almost all of their time is devoted to human relations and conceptual tasks. Middle managers reduce their use of technical skills. Their human relations skills also change considerably.

30. The dominating question of organizing in recent years has been how to best organize the firm to respond to the needs of customers and other stakeholders. The general consensus is that smaller organizations are more responsive than larger organizations; so many larger organizations are being restructured into smaller more customer-focused units.

31. According to the text, companies are organizing so that <u>customers</u> have the greatest influence.

32. The organizing task is more complex today because firms are forming partnerships and joint ventures, so the job becomes an effort to organize the whole system, not just one firm.

33. Staffing is critical because recruiting good employees is an important part of organizational success. It is especially important today in the Internet and high-tech areas. Firms with the most innovative and creative workers can go from start-up to major competitor with leading companies in a very short time.

Learning Goal 5
Leading: Providing Continuous Vision and Values

34. One difference between managers and leaders is that managers strive to create order and stability while leaders embrace and manage change. Leadership is creating a vision for others to follow, establishing corporate values and ethics, and transforming the way the organization does business. Good leaders motivate workers and create the environment for workers to motivate themselves, while management is the carrying out of the vision.

35. In terms of leadership the workplace is changing from a place where a few dictate the rules to others to a place where all employees work together to accomplish common goals.

36. Four things leaders must do are:
   a. Communicate a vision and rally others around the vision.
   b. Establish corporate values.
   c. Promote corporate ethics.
   d. Embrace change.

37. a. Autocratic leadership involves making managerial decisions without consulting others. Such a style is effective in emergencies and when absolute followership is important.

   b. Participative or Democratic leadership consists of managers and employees working together to make decisions. This type of leadership usually increases job satisfaction.

   c. Free rein leadership involves managers setting objectives and employees being relatively free to do what it takes to accomplish those objectives. More and more firms are adopting this style of leadership with some employees. The traits needed by managers in such organizations include warmth, friendliness, and understanding.

38. Research indicates that successful leadership depends on what the goals and values of the firm are, who is being led and in what situation. Different leadership styles may be successful depending on the people and the situation and a leader may use different styles with different employees. There is no such thing as a leadership trait that is effective in all organizations.

39. Traditional leaders give explicit instructions to workers, telling them what to do to meet the goals and objectives of the organization. This is called directing. Progressive leaders are less likely than traditional leaders to give specific instructions to employees. They are more likely to empower employees to make decisions on their own. In cooperation with employees, managers will set up teams that will work together to accomplish goals. The manager's role is becoming less that of a boss and director and more that of a coach, assistant, counselor, or team member.

40. Empowerment means giving employees the authority and responsibility to respond quickly to customer requests. Enabling is the term used to describe giving workers the education and tools they need to assume their new decision-making powers.

41. The two steps to developing a knowledge management system include determining what knowledge is most important, and then setting out to find answers to those questions. The key to success is learning how to process information effectively and turn it into knowledge that everyone can use to improve processes and procedures.

Learning Goal 6
Controlling

42. The five steps in the control process are:
    a. Establish clear performance standards
    b. Monitoring and recording actual performance
    c. Comparing results against plans and standards
    d. Communicating results and deviations to the employees involved
    e. Taking corrective action when needed

43. Setting clear performance standards ties the planning function to the control function. Without clear standards, control is impossible.

44. Standards must be:
    a. specific
    b. attainable
    c. measurable

45. The criterion for measuring success in customer-oriented firms is customer satisfaction of both internal and external customers.

46. Other criteria of organizational effectiveness may include the firm's contribution to society and its environmental responsibility. Traditional measures of success are usually financial. These are still important, but they're not the whole purpose of the firm. The purpose of the firm today is to please, employees, customers, and other stakeholders.

CRITICAL THINKING EXERCISES

Learning Goal 1
1. Your answer will of course be determined by your own experience. The key is to look at how your manager fits into the new style of management, or if he or she is more traditional. If you work for a small firm, it may be that your manager acts in a more traditional manner, for example. But, if the company you work for is a larger organization, management styles may be different.

Learning Goal 2

2.   a.   Controlling   c.   Leading
      b.   Planning   d.   Organizing

3.   a.   Goals   c.   Mission statement
      b.   Objectives   d.   Vision

4.   Eric has a big job ahead of him. There are many possible responses to this question, but an example might be:

Mission statement: Sun-2-Shade's mission is to make and develop products for the automotive industry. We are committed to helping our employees develop their potential and encourage their creativity and energy. We intend to continually create value for our customers by forming long lasting partnerships with our customers and suppliers, and to exceed our customer's expectations.

   a. Strategic plan – Become the supplier of self-darkening windshields for automobiles within the next 5 years, with a 25% market share. Become the major supplier for self-darkening windshields to the automotive aftermarket.

   b. Tactical plan - Contact the production and/or engineering managers of the major automobile manufacturers and sell them on the product within the next 12 months. Develop a sales program to present to automotive aftermarket dealers, such as windshield repair companies.

   c. Contingency plan - If the automakers are not interested right now, begin focusing on the automotive after-market, to sell the product as an add-on.

5.   A suggested SWOT analysis for Sun-2-Shade could contain:

Strengths: Young, creative workforce
               Energetic CEO

Weaknesses: New company
               Finding financing sources

Opportunities: Increasing interest in "luxury" options for automobiles
               Increasing household incomes
               Increased interest in products that make life more pleasant

Threats: Competition from other companies utilizing this technology

These are only suggestions. You may have come up with additional ideas!

6.　There are many variations for answering this question, depending upon your school or company. Some possibilities for a school are:

   a. Top Managers - Chancellor, President, Provost
   b. Middle - Dean of Instruction, Executive Dean, Associate Dean
   c. Supervisory - Lab supervisor, Department chair, Business manager

   The organization chart may look like this:

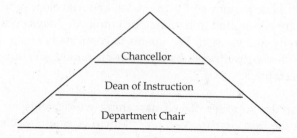

7.　In earlier chapters we have learned about the changing nature of U.S. business, increasing global competition and about the continuing push for quality and increased productivity. These new structures are reflective of the need to focus on productivity, quality and the needs of the consumer in an increasingly competitive marketplace. For example, to be more productive we must cut costs, which inter-firm relationships help to make possible. Further, to be more competitive, we must respond to customer demands by creating a "Customer-Oriented organization" with smaller, more customer-focused units.

8.　　A.　a. Supervisory level
   　　　 b. Human relations, technical skills

   　　B.　a. Top management
   　　　 b. Decision making, conceptual skills

   　　C.　a. Middle management
   　　　 b. Human relations skills, technical skills, decision making, conceptual skills

9.　As a manager of educated and skilled workers you are less likely to be giving specific instructions to your employees. Instead, you may give them the authority to make decisions, which will allow them to respond quickly to any customer requests. In all likelihood, you will set up a team approach for the plant, using self-managed work teams if possible. Your job will be more that of a coach and team member, allowing for more participation in decision-making and more flexibility for the workers.

Eric, as the top manager of the company, will be concerned with a broader view of where he wants the company to go. As a first line manager, your job will be more specific, and your goals and objectives more specific than those Eric has outlined for the entire company. So your directions to subordinates, to the extent you will give them direction, will be more specific.

10. A. a. Autocratic
         b. Participative
     B. a. Participative
         b. Free rein
     C. a. Participative
         b. Autocratic

11. Your answers will vary, as each of you will have your own individual style. However, review the material in this section of the chapter. Would a team-based approach be appropriate for this group? Could you use a participative management style? Did you consider getting opinions from the workers about what they see as a method to increase production without raising costs? Did you ask for advice? Are you making an effort to both empower and enable your employees?

12. Your boss appears to see the importance of customer service and high quality products in today's competitive marketplace. She has a vision of how she wants the division to operate, which is a characteristic of a good leader. She trusts employees to make their own decisions, thus empowering them with control over their jobs. This helps to create a sense of loyalty and job satisfaction for workers. She believes in a democratic or participative leadership approach which is important for effectively managing today's new style of worker. It seems that she is very different from the old style manager who directed employees' activities and used a more autocratic approach to leadership.

13. a. Increase sales of Product X by 10% in the next 6 months.
     b. Get a Bachelor's Degree in Business in 4 years.
     c. Spend 3 hours a week reading management articles or books. Praise employees twice a week. Ask for employee input or suggestions monthly.

PRACTICE TEST

MULTIPLE CHOICE   **TRUE - FALSE**

LG 1	# 1
LG 2	#2-3
LG 3	# 4-9
LG 4	#10-14
LG 5	#15-18
LG 6	# 19-21

LG 1	# 1-2
LG 2	# 3-4
LG 3	# 5-8
LG 4	# 9-12
LG 5	# 13-17
LG 6	# 19-21

1. b	12. d	1. F	11. F
2. a	13. b	2. F	12. T
3. c	14. b	3. T	13. F
4. c	15. d	4. F	14. F
5. d	16. a	5. T	15. T
6. d	17. b	6. F	16. T
7. c	18. b	7. F	17. T
8. c	19. d	8. F	18. F
9. a	20. a	9. T	19. T
10. b	21. d	10. T	20. T
11. b			

CHAPTER 8 – ADAPTING ORGANIZATIONS TO TODAY'S MARKETS

LEARNING GOALS

After you have read and studied this chapter, you should be able to:

1. Explain the historical organizational theories of Fayol and Weber.
2. Explain the various issues involved in structuring organizations.
3. Describe and differentiate between the various organizational models.
4. Discuss the concepts involved in inter-firm cooperation and coordination.
5. Explain how restructuring, organizational culture, and informal organizations can help businesses adapt to change.

LEARNING THE LANGUAGE

Listed below are important terms found in the chapter. Choose the correct term for each definition and write it in the space provided.

Benchmarking	14	Flat organization structure	16	Organizational (or corporate) culture	5
Bureaucracy	8	Formal organization	18	Real time	24
Centralized authority	9	Hierarchy	2	Restructuring	4
Chain of command	12	Informal organization	6	Span of control	11
Core competencies	7	Inverted organization	10	Staff personnel	20
Cross-functional self managed teams	1	Line organization	23	Tall organization structure	22
Decentralized authority	15	Line personnel	13	Transparency	25
Departmentalization	17	Matrix organization	19	Virtual corporation	26
Economies of scale	21	Networking	3		

1. Groups of employees from different departments who work together on a long- term basis are called _____.

2. A _____ is a system in which one person is at the top of the organization and there is a ranked or sequential ordering from the top down of managers who are responsible to that person.

3. Using communications technology and other means to link organizations, or _____, allows them to work together on common objectives.

4. Redesigning an organization so that it can more effectively and efficiently serve its customers is known as _____.

5. Widely shared values within an organization, or the _____, provide unity and cooperation to achieve common goals.

6. The _____ is the system of relationships and lines of authority that develop spontaneously as employees meet and form power centers; that is, the human side of the organization that does not appear on any organization chart.

7.   Those functions that the organization can do as well as or better than any other organization in the world are called _____.

8.   A _____ is an organization with many layers of managers who set rules and regulations and oversee all decisions.

9.   An organization in which decision-making authority is maintained at the top level of management at the company's headquarters utilizes _____.

10. In a(n) _____ contact people are at the top and the chief executive officer is at the bottom of the organization chart.

11. The _____ refers to the optimum number of subordinates a manager supervises or should supervise.

12. The line of authority that moves from the top of the hierarchy to the lowest level is called the _____.

13. Employees known as _____ are part of the chain of command that is responsible for achieving organizational goals.

14. When a company is using _____, it is comparing its practices, processes, and products against the world's best.

15. When decision-making authority is delegated to lower-level managers more familiar with local conditions than headquarters' management could be, a company is said to have _____.

16. A _____ has few layers of management and a broad span of control.

17. Dividing organizational functions into separate units is called _____.

18. The _____, is the structure that details lines of responsibility, authority, and position and is shown on the organizational chart.

19. A _____ is one in which specialists from different parts of the organization are brought together to work on specific projects but still remain part of a traditional line and staff structure.

20. Employees known as _____ advise and assist line personnel in meeting their goals.

21. The concept of _____ describes a situation in which companies can reduce their production costs if they can purchase raw materials in bulk, so the average cost of goods goes down as production levels increase.

22. An organizational structure in which the pyramidal organization chart would be quite tall because of the various levels of management would be called a _____.

23. A _____ is one that has direct two-way lines of responsibility, authority, and communication running from the top to the bottom of the organization, with all people reporting to only one supervisor.

24. The present moment or the actual time in which something takes place is called _____.

25. When companies are so open to other companies working with them that the once-solid barriers between them have become "see through" and electronic information is shared as if the companies are one, there is a situation called _____.

26. A _____ is a temporary, networked organization made up of replaceable firms that join the network and leave it as needed.

ASSESSMENT CHECK

Learning Goal 1
Building an Organization from the Bottom Up

1. Describe:

   a.   Division of labor: _____

   b.   Job specialization: _____

2. Structuring an organization consists of:

   a.   _____

   b.   _____

   c.   _____

   d.   _____

   e.   _____

   f.   _____

3. What are the reasons organizations have changed so much?

4.   Identify and briefly describe 10 of Fayol's "principles" of organizing

     a._____

     b._____

     c._____

     d._____

     e._____

     f._____

     g._____

     h._____

     i_____

     j._____

5.   What was the result of organizational design using Fayol's principles?

6.   Identify four characteristics of Max Weber's bureaucracy.

     a._____

     b._____

     c._____

     d._____

7.   How do workers today differ from those during the time that Weber was writing, and how did that affect management?

8.   In a company with many layers of management, what is the process for an employee to introduce a work change? What did Weber mean by the term "bureaucrat"?

9. According to the text, what happens when employees have to ask their manager for permission to make a change?

10. How are companies reorganizing to make customers happy?

Learning Goal 2
Issues Involved in Structuring Organizations

11. When would a company use centralized or decentralized authority?

12. What is the trend in today's organizations regarding span of control?

13. How is span of control different in tall and flat organizational structures?

14. Describe how flat structures differ from tall structures in terms of response to customer demands.

15. What is meant by the term "the traditional functional structure"?

16. What are the advantages and disadvantages of the traditional functional structure?

Advantages   Disadvantages

a. _____   a. _____

b. _____   b. _____

c. _____   c. _____

d. _____   e. _____

17.   What are five methods of grouping, or departmentalizing, workers?

   a._____   d._____

   b._____   e._____

   c._____

18.   The decision about which way to departmentalize depends on _____

   _____

19.   A hybrid form of departmentalization is being used when _____

   _____

20.   How has the Internet affected ways for reaching customers?

Learning Goal 3
Organization Models

21.   Name four types of organizational structures.

   a._____   c._____

   b._____   d._____

22.   What are the disadvantages of a line organization, for a larger organization?

23.   Identify the areas of a business that are considered staff. What is the difference between line and staff personnel and the kind of authority each has?

24.   What disadvantage is common to both line and line and staff organizations? What benefits do both forms of organization have in common?

25.   In a matrix system, a product manager can: _____

_____

This is important in industries in which the emphasis is on _____

_____

26.   What are the advantages and disadvantages of a matrix structure?
       Advantages:

       a. _____

       b. _____

       c. _____

       d. _____

       Disadvantages:

       a. _____

       b. _____

       c. _____

       d. _____

27.   A potential problem with the teams created by matrix management is _____

_____

An answer to the disadvantage of the teams created by matrix management is: _____

_____

28.   Describe the characteristics of cross-functional teams.

29.   Who should be included on cross-functional teams?

Managing the Interactions among Firms

30.   How have the Internet, real time and the concept of transparency, changed the way information is shared between organizations, and what is the result on organizational design and structure?

31.   How does benchmarking lead to outsourcing, and ultimately to a firm's core competencies?

Learning Goal 5
Adapting to Change

32.   Why is introducing change in an organization difficult?

33.   Illustrate and describe an inverted organization.

34.   How does the inverted organization support front line personnel? How does this change the requirements for front-line personnel?

35.   How is the culture of an organization reflected?

36.   Describe the kind of organizational cultures that the best organizations have, including the key to a productive culture.

37.   What are two organizational systems that all companies have?

a. _____   b. _____

38.   What is a drawback of the formal organization? What is a benefit of the formal organization?

39.   What is the drawback of the informal organization? What is the benefit?

40.   What is the nerve center of the informal organization?

41.   How have managers' views toward the informal organization changed in the new more open organizations?

CRITICAL THINKING EXERCISES

Learning Goal 1

1.   Many organizations today have been organized around principles developed by <u>Henri Fayol</u> and <u>Max Weber</u>. Read the following and determine whose ideas are being described.

a. _____   Introduced several "principles" of organizing.

b. _____   Believed workers should think of themselves as coordinated teams, and that the goal of the team is more important than individual goals.

c. _____   Promoted a bureaucratic organization.

d. _____   Believed that large organizations demanded clearly established rules and guidelines, which were to be precisely followed.

e. _____   Wrote that each worker should report to only one boss.

f. _____   Said that managers should treat employees and peers with respect

g. _____   Wrote that functions are to be divided into areas of specialization such as production, marketing and so on.

h. _____   Believed in written rules, decision guidelines and detailed records.

i. _____   Said that staffing and promotions should be based solely on qualifications.

j. _____   Proposed that an organization should consist of three layers of authority: top managers, middle managers, and supervisors.

k. _____   Believed the less decision-making employees had to do, the better.

l. _____   Believed that managers have the right to give orders and expect obedience.

Learning Goal 2

2.   You are a manager for Sun-2-Shade, a company that makes a self-darkening windshield for automobiles using the same technology that is used for prescription eyeglasses. Sun-2-Shade is a small company right now, with just a few workers. Eric is the CEO and founder of the company. You are the plant manager. The customers for Sun-2-Shade for right now are automobile manufacturers. Do you think a centralized or decentralized authority structure would be most effective? Why?

3.   As companies are moving away from traditional methods of organizing, and taking different perspectives regarding span of control, how are companies changing in the area of centralization versus decentralization, and tall versus flat organizational structures?

4.   There are a number of ways companies have tried to departmentalize to better serve customers:

Product   Customer group   Process
Function   Geographic location

The hybrid structure is an organization that has used several forms of departmentalization.

Match each of the following to the correct form:

a. _____   General Motors has the Saturn, Chevrolet and Pontiac divisions, and the Buick, and Cadillac divisions, each employing separate staffs for design, engineering, product development and so on.

b. _____   At the highest corporate levels, G.E. has a corporate strategic planning staff, production staff, human resources staff, technical resources staff and finance staff.

c. _____ Apple Computer, in manufacturing the Macintosh Computer System, begins with an assembly line that makes the logic board; another line makes the analog board. Once assembled, the boards go through diagnostic tests before being assembled into a computer unit.

d. _____ When Wendy's made the decision to expand into the European market, the company created a separate European division.

e. _____ Most banks have commercial loan officers who deal only with business customers and consumer loan specialists for personal loans.

5. Re-read the advantages and disadvantages of the traditional functional method of departmentalizing organizations. Apply what you know about changes in the global marketplace and in businesses to explain why companies are redesigning their structures, away from the traditional methods.

Learning Goal 3
6. There are 4 types of organizational structures:

Line   Matrix
Line and Staff   Cross-functional self-managed teams

Read below brief descriptions of several companies and decide which form of organizational structure would be most suitable for each.

a. _____ A small company, Dynalink, is in the biotechnology industry. Competition is fierce, and new product development is of highest importance. The field is changing and growing so rapidly that new product ideas must come fast and furious. The firm employs highly skilled, very creative people.

b. _____ Another small firm is Cleanem Up, a dry cleaning establishment, with one owner and one store. They are located in a suburban area and have a loyal clientele. The store is known for its quality and courteous service.

c. _____ Wells Industries is a medium sized firm employing about 1500 people. Wells makes a variety of business- related products such as stationary, forms, and so forth. They have a good sales force, which knows the product very well. While this is a fairly competitive industry, new product development happens as the need arises, such as when firms went from sophisticated word processing machines to even more sophisticated computerized office management.

d. _____ Mitsubishi wants to develop a new luxury car to compete with Lexus, Infiniti, and others. Time is important, as they want to enter the market within 18 months.

Learning goals 3,4
7. How will cross functional self managed teams impact organizational designs of the future?

8. Why do you think Gallo Winery, known for its wines, chooses <u>not</u> to grow grapes?

Learning goal 5
9. How does the inverted organizational structure relate to the other kinds of changes we have read about in this chapter, such as wider spans of control, decentralization, cross functional teams, outsourcing, benchmarking, and so on?

10. What is the relationship between leadership style, the organizational structure (such as tall vs flat organizations, span of control, delegation, teams) and the creation of an organizational culture?

11. How does the informal organization help to create the corporate culture?

12.   Think about the organizational design of the school you are attending, or an organization
       with which you are familiar, such as where you work. Can you identify the "hierarchy"?
       Identify how many layers of management come between the front-line workers and the
       highest level of management. Are there separate departments for various functions
       (instruction, bookstore, and so on)? Are there rules and regulations that seem to keep
       workers organized and are meant to make the organization run efficiently? (Hint -
       perhaps your instructor will have a copy of the organizational chart for your school, or
       your manager may have one for the company for which you work.)

13.   Sun-2-Shade is in a growth state and Eric, the CEO and founder, wants to be sure to
       build on a good foundation. The product is a windshield that darkens automatically
       when your car goes into a sunny area, much like the sunglasses. This is a small
       company, with educated and well trained workers, and Eric is very concerned about
       customer service. What suggestions can you give Eric about organizational design,
       knowing what you already know about the company and its employees?

PRACTICE TEST

MULTIPLE CHOICE – Circle the best answer

Learning Goal 1

1.   Division of labor is a term that means:
      a.   dividing up tasks among a group of workers.
      b.   dividing tasks into smaller jobs.
      c.   delegating decision making to lower level managers.
      d.   grouping workers into departments based on similar skills, expertise, or resource
            use.

2.   In general, organizations today are:
      a.   eliminating managers and giving power to lower-level employees.
      b.   getting bigger, more international, and so are adding management layers.
      c.   becoming more bureaucratic.
      d.   managing employees more closely as they reduce the layers of management.

3.   Which of the following does not fit in when describing a bureaucratic organization?
      a.   many rules and regulations that everyone is expected to follow.
      b.   people tend to be generalists, and function in many different areas of the business
      c.   procedures, regulations, and policies are consistent.
      d.   the organization is set up by function, with separate departments for marketing,
            engineering and so on.

4.   The principle of _____ means that each person should know to whom they report, and that managers should have the right to give orders and expect others to follow.
      a.   unity of command
      b.   division of labor
      c.   order
      d.   hierarchy of authority

5.   Robin Banks is in a supervisor for a large, bureaucratic organization on the West Coast. According to the views of a bureaucratic organization, this means that Robin should:
      a.   be included on decision making when decisions affect her workers.
      b.   do her work and let middle and upper level managers do the decision making.
      c.   try to get her workers organized into cross-functional teams.
      d.   have a wide span of control.

Learning Goal 2
6.   A manager's span of control :
      a.   can narrow as subordinates need less supervision.
      b.   will narrow as the manager gets to higher levels in the organization and work becomes less standardized.
      c.   will decrease as employees become more professional.
      d.   is generally the same in most organizations.

7.   Who Dunnit is a new firm that makes murder mystery games for sale in retail stores and through catalogs. The company has very few management positions, and most everybody pitches in when they need to, to get the job done. It is really a "team" effort, with very few layers of management. Who Dunnit is an example of a:
      a.   tall organization
      b.   bureaucratic organization
      c.   centralized organization
      d.   flat organization

8.   Dewey, Cheatum and Howe is a car company that makes four models, a sport utility, a sports car, a four door sedan, and a compact car. Workers at Dewey basically work on only one type of vehicle, and separate marketing and product development processes are designed for each type of vehicle, to better serve the customers for each type of vehicle. Dewey Cheatum and Howe is departmentalized by:
      a.   product
      b.   function
      c.   process
      d.   customer

9.   In order to more quickly respond to customer needs, Hewlett Packard is changing it's organizational structure to give more authority and responsibility to field managers located across the country. These managers spend time with customers and know what the customers need right away. It appears that H-P is moving toward a _____ structure.
      a.   more decentralized
      b.   more centralized
      c.   more bureaucratic
      d.   more traditional

10.   The form of organizational structure that is most flexible, and allows the organization to take on new projects without adding to the organizational structure is the:
    a.   Line
    b.   Line and staff
    c.   Matrix
    d.   Cross-functional self managed team

11.   An answer to the temporary teams created by matrix organizations is the use of:
    a.   the line and staff form organization.
    b.   the line organization.
    c.   cross functional teams.
    d.   traditional functional organizations.

12.   Banana Computers is restructuring, and intends to implement cross-functional teams. All of the following *are likely to* serve on a cross-functional team except:
    a.   a Banana engineer.
    b.   an employee of Peelit, Inc. one of Banana's competitors.
    c.   an employee of Monkeyshine, one of Banana's suppliers.
    d.   a Banana salesperson.

13.   One of the advantages of the matrix organization is:
    a.   It is less costly.
    b.   It can result in creative solutions to problems.
    c.   There is less need for interpersonal skills because there is constant communication.
    d.   It is a long term solution to problems.

Learning Goal 4

14.   When a firm is rating its processes and products against the best in the world, the firm is practicing:
    a.   total quality management
    b.   outsourcing
    c.   their core competencies
    d.   benchmarking

15.   The Daimler-Chrysler plant in suburban St. Louis is "connected" to its seat supplier in a way that the seat supplier has the information it needs to schedule its production to coordinate with the production of vans at the plant. The seat supplier knows, for example, that B. Goode's cherry red van with tan leather interior is scheduled for production, so that it can make sure that the correct seats are in the process when the van is made. This type of system is known as:
    a.   a cross functional team
    b.   a virtual corporation
    c.   Transparency
    d.   Benchmarking

16.   In an inverted organization, the managers' job is to:
        a.   maintain direct contact with customers.
        b.   direct and closely monitor employee performance.
        c.   look for the best ways to outsource functions.
        d.   assist and support sales personnel and other employees who work directly with customers.

17.   When IBM changed its organizational design, the company gave more authority to lower level employees, to become more flexible in responding to customer needs. The company broke down barriers between functions, and ended top-down management. This process is known as:
        a.   creating an informal organization
        b.   changing span of control
        c.   restructuring
        d.   becoming more bureaucratic

18.   Which of the following would not be used to describe a company with a positive corporate culture?
        a.   Emphasizes service to others, especially customers.
        b.   People enjoy working together to provide good products at reasonable prices.
        c.   Less need for policy manuals, formal rules and procedures.
        d.   Closer supervision of employees.

19.   The corporate structure shown on the organizational chart, which details lines of responsibility is known as the:
        a.   informal structure
        b.   bureaucratic structure
        c.   formal structure
        d.   grapevine

20.   Mr. Bilko is the one to see in the company when there is something you need. He will obtain what you need quickly, and can avoid the red tape that often delays action. Mr. Bilko is the one to see if you need advice or help. Mr. Bilko is an important member of the firm's:
        a.   purchasing deportment
        b.   informal structure
        c.   formal structure
        d.   bureaucratic structure

TRUE-FALSE

Learning Goal 1

1. _____   Job specialization refers to dividing tasks into smaller jobs.

2. _____   Structuring an organization consists of devising a divison of labor, setting up teams or departments to do specific tasks and assigning responsibility and authority to people.

3. _____   A bureaucratic organizational system is a good when workers are relatively well educated and trained to make decisions.

4. _____ A hierarchy is a system in which one person is at the top of the organization and there is a ranked order from the top to the bottom of the organization of managers and others who are responsible to that person.

5. _____ To make customers happier, some companies are reorganizing to give upper management the primary power to make more decisions and to have strict rules and regulations.

Learning Goal 2

6. _____ A company that must focus on regional or global differences in customer tastes should use decentralized authority.

7. _____ Today's rapidly changing markets tend to favor centralization of authority, so decisions can be made quickly.

8. _____ The trend today is to expand the span of control as organizations reduce the number of middle managers.

9. _____ An organization with many layers of management, such as the U.S. Army or a large corporation, is a good example of a flat organization.

10. _____ The decision about which way to departmentalize depends greatly on the nature of the product and the customers served.

11. _____ Firms should not use more than one form of departmentalization.

Learning Goal 3

12. _____ Safety, quality control, and human resource management are examples of staff positions in a manufacturing firm.

13. _____ Companies that create cross-functional self-managed teams empower the teams to make decisions on their own without seeking the approval of management.

Learning Goal 4

14. _____ When a company can't perform a certain function as well as the best, the company may outsource that function, in order to concentrate on the functions at which they are the best.

15. _____ Most organizations today are not self sufficient, and are part of a larger network of global businesses that work closely together.

Learning Goal 5

16. _____ In general, an organizational culture cannot be negative.

17. _____ The informal organization in most organizations is not particularly powerful.

You Can Find It on the Net

Visit the website http://www.organizedchange.com/index.htm

Click on Teams and Facilitation

What is meant by "facilitation" and what must facilitation do?

What kinds of groups are defined?

What types of seminars and training does this company provide that corresponds to the material related in this and previous chapters?

ANSWERS

LEARNING THE LANGUAGE

1. Cross-functional self managed teams	10. Inverted organization	19. Matrix organization
2. Hierarchy	11. Span of control	20. Staff personnel
3. Networking	12. Chain of command	21. Economies of scale
4. Restructuring	13. Line personnel	22. Tall organization structure
5. Organizational (or corporate) culture	14. Benchmarking	23. Line organization
6. Informal organization	15. Decentralized authority	24. Real time
7. Core competencies	16. Flat organization structure	25. Transparency
8. Bureaucracy	17. Departmentalization	26. Virtual corporation
9. Centralized authority	18. Formal organization	

ASSESSMENT CHECK

Learning Goal 1
Building an Organization from the Bottom Up

1.   a.   Division of labor refers to dividing up tasks among workers
        b.   Job specialization is dividing tasks into smaller jobs

2.   Structuring an organization consists of:
        a.   devising a division of labor
        b.   setting up teams or departments to do specific tasks
        c.   assigning responsibility and authority to people
        d.   allocating resources
        e.   assigning specific tasks
        f.   establishing procedures for accomplishing organizational objectives

3.   Much of the change in organizations today is due to the changing business environment – more global competition and faster technological change. Consumer expectations have also changed, and consumers expect the highest quality products and fast, friendly service at a reasonable cost.

4.   a.   Unity of command – reporting to only one boss
        b.   Hierarchy of authority – workers should know to whom they report
        c.   Division of labor – functions are divided into areas of specialization
        d.   Subordination of individual interests to the general interest – team work
        e.   Authority – managers have the right to give orders and power to enforce obedience
        f.   Degree of centralization – The amount of decision making power given to top management
        g.   Clear communication channels – workers should be able to easily contact each other
        h.   Order – people and materials should be in the proper location
        i.   Equity – managers should treat employees with respect and justice
        j.   Esprit de corps – a spirit of pride and loyalty should be created

5.	These principles tended to become rules and procedures as organizations became larger. This led to rigid organizations that didn't always respond quickly to consumer requests.

6.	Four characteristics of Weber's bureaucracy are:
	a.	Job descriptions
	b.	Written rules, decision guidelines and detailed records
	c.	Consistent procedures, regulations and policies
	d.	Staffing and promotions based on qualifications

7.	Workers during Weber's time were much less educated and trained than today's workers. Weber felt that a firm would do well if employees would do what managers told them to do. The less decision making employees had to do, the better.

8.	In a company with many layers of management, if employees want to introduce work changes, they ask a supervisor, who asks a manager, who asks a manager at the next level up, and so on. Eventually a decision is made and passed down from manager to manager until it reaches the employee. Decisions can take weeks or months to be made. Weber used the term bureaucrat to describe a middle manager whose function it was to implement top management's orders.

9.	When employees have to ask their manager for permission to make a change, the process may take so long that customers become annoyed. This can happen in both large and small organizations. Since customers want efficient, quick service, slow service is not acceptable.

10.	To make customers happy, organizations are giving employees more power to make decisions on their own. They don't have to follow strict rules and regulations. Rather, they are encouraged to please the customer no matter what.

Learning Goal 2
Issues Involved in Structuring Organizations

11.	A company might use centralized authority when they need greater management control to make radical changes, a simpler distribution system, or the company wants a strong brand or corporate image.
	A company may use decentralized authority when customers may differ from one market to another and faster decision making is needed.

12.	The trend is to expand the span of control by reducing the number of middle managers and hiring more educated and talented lower level employees. This is included in the idea of empowerment. . This is possible as employees become more professional, and as information technology makes it possible for managers to handle more information and as employees take on more responsibility for self-management.

13.	In a tall organization there are many levels of management, and span of control is small. In a flat organization, there are fewer layers of management, and the span of control gets broader.

14.	A flat organization structure is one where there are few layers of management. Such structures are usually much more responsive to customer demands than tall organizations because authority and responsibility to make decisions may be given to lower-level employees (empowerment) and managers don't have to make so many day to day decisions. This is unlike a tall structure where there are several layers of management, and decision-making stays with managers.

15. The traditional functional structure refers to grouping workers into departments based on similar skills, expertise, or resource use.

16. The advantages and disadvantages of the traditional functional structure are:

   Advantages
   a. Skills can be developed in depth and employees can progress as skills are developed.
   b. Economies of scale develop because resources can be centralized.
   c. Coordination with the function.

   Disadvantages
   a. Lack of communication among departments.
   b. Employees identify with the department and not with the corporation as a whole.
   c. Response to change is slow.
   d. People trained too narrowly.
   e. People in the same department tend to think alike – groupthink.

17. Five methods of grouping, or departmentalizing, workers are:
   a. Product   d. Geographic location
   b. Function   e. Process
   c. Customer group

18. The decision about which way to departmentalize depends upon the nature of the product and the customers served.

19. A hybrid form of departmentalization is being used when companies use a combination of departmentalization techniques.

20. The development of the Internet has created new opportunities for selling to customers directly. The company can interact with customers, ask them questions and provide them with any information they want.

Learning Goal 3
Organization Models

21. Four organizational structures are:
   a. Line organizations   c. Matrix-style organizations
   b. Line and staff organizations d. Cross-functional self-managed teams

22. In a large business, a line organization may have the disadvantages of being too inflexible, having too few specialists, having long lines of communication, and being unable to handle complex decisions necessary in a large organization.

23. Areas of a business that would be considered staff are marketing research, legal advising, information technology, and human resource management.

   The difference between line and staff personnel is authority. Line personnel have formal authority to make policy decisions. Staff personnel have the authority to advise the line personnel and make suggestions, but they can't make policy changes themselves. Staff positions strengthen the line positions and are not inferior or lower paid. It is like having well-paid consultants on the organization's payroll.

24. Both line and line and staff structures have a certain amount of inflexibility, which is a disadvantage.

However, both types of organizations have established lines of authority and communication and both work well in companies with a relatively unchanging environment and slow product development.

25. In a matrix system a product manager can borrow people from different departments to help design and market new product ideas.

This is important in industries where competition is stiff, and the life cycle of new ideas is short, and where the emphasis is on new product development, creativity, special projects, rapid communication, and interdepartmental teamwork.

26. The advantages and disadvantages of a matrix structure are:

Advantages
a. Flexibility in assigning people to projects.
b. Encourages cooperation among departments.
c. Can produce creative solutions to problems.
d. Allows for efficient use of resources.

Disadvantages
a. Costly and complex.
b. Can cause confusion among employees as to where their loyalty belongs.
c. Requires good interpersonal skills and cooperative managers and employees.
d. Temporary solution to long term problem.

27. A potential problem with teams created by matrix management is that the project teams are not permanent. After a problem is solved or a product developed, the team breaks up, so there is little opportunity for cross-functional training.

An answer to the disadvantage of the temporary teams created by matrix management is to develop permanent teams and to empower them to work closely with suppliers, customers, and others to quickly and efficiently bring out new, high-quality products while giving great service.

28. Cross- functional teams consist of groups of employees from different departments who work together on a semi permanent basis. Usually the teams are empowered to make decisions without having to seek the approval of management. Barriers between functions fall when these interdepartmental teams are created.

29 Cross- functional teams work best with customer input. Suppliers and distributors should also be included on the team

Learning Goal 4
Managing the Interactions among Firms

30.   Organizations are so closely linked by the Internet that each organization knows what the others are doing, in real time. Since data is so readily available to organizational partners, companies are so open to one another that the solid walls between them have become transparent. Because of this integration, two companies can now work together so closely that they operate as two departments within one company.

Most organizations are no longer self-sufficient or self-contained. Many modern organizations are part of a vast network of global businesses. An organizational chart showing what people do within any one organization may not be complete because the company is actually part of a larger system of firms.

Organizational structures tend to be flexible and changing. Experts from one company may work for one company one year, and another the next year. Organizations deal with each other on a temporary basis and the ties between organizations are no longer permanent. These are often called virtual corporations because they are made up of replaceable firms that join the network and leave it as needed. This is called a virtual corporation.

31.   Benchmarking demands that organizations compare each function against the best in the world. If an organization can't do as well as the best in a particular area, it often will try to outsource the function to an organization that is the best. Outsourcing is assigning various functions to outside organizations. When a firm has completed the outsourcing process, the remaining functions are the firm's core competencies, which are functions that the organization can do as well as, or better than, any other organization in the world.

Learning Goal 5
Adapting To Change

32.   Introducing change in an organization is difficult because managers and employees may have a tendency to "get stuck" in their old ways, and resist the efforts to change.

33.

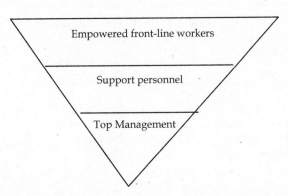

An inverted organization has contact people at the top and the chief executive officer at the bottom. There are few layers of management, and the manger's job is to assist and support front-line people, not boss them around.

34. Companies based upon an inverted organization structure support front-line personnel with internal and external databases, advance communication systems and professional assistance.

This means that front line personnel have to be better educated, better trained and better paid than in the past

35. The culture of an organization is reflected in stories, traditions, and myths.

36. The best organizations have cultures that emphasize service to others, especially customers. The atmosphere is one of friendly, concerned, caring people who enjoy working together to provide a good product at a reasonable price. Those companies have less need for close supervision of employees, policy manuals, organization charts and formal rules, procedures and controls. These companies stress high moral and ethical values such as honesty, reliability, fairness, environmental protection, and social involvement. The key to a productive culture is mutual trust.

37. All companies have a(n)
   a.   formal organization   b.   informal organization

38. The drawback of the formal organization is that it is often too slow and bureaucratic to enable an organization to adapt quickly. The benefit of a formal organization is that it provides helpful guidelines and lines of authority to follow in routine situations.

39. The drawback of the informal organization is that it is often too unstructured and emotional to allow careful, reasoned decision-making on critical matters. But the informal organization is very effective in generating creative solutions to short-term problems and providing a feeling of camaraderie and teamwork among employees.

40. The nerve center of the informal organization is the grapevine, the system through which unofficial information flows between employees and managers.

41. In more traditional organizations, managers and employees were often at odds, and the informal structure often hindered management. In the new, more open organizations, managers and employees work together and the informal structure is viewed as an asset that promotes harmony among workers and establishes a positive corporate culture.

CRITICAL THINKING

Learning Goal 1

1.
a.	Fayol	e.	Fayol	i.	Weber
b.	Fayol	f.	Fayol	j.	Weber
c.	Weber	g.	Fayol	k.	Weber
d.	Weber	h.	Weber	l.	Fayol

2.   Sun-2-Shade is very small with a customer base where most of the needs are similar. In other words, there is no need to customize products to meet different regional needs, only shapes and sizes for different automobile brands. This company could use centralized authority because it is small and decision-making can still be made quickly. Employees probably have easy access to Eric, the founder and CEO of the company, who may want to retain control over his new company for the time being.

3.   Changes in the areas we have been discussing are closely related to the changes we are seeing in the area of decision making.   As spans of control widen and non-traditional ways of grouping workers emerge, decision-making is being delegated to lower levels of management, or even to non-management levels. Cross functional Self-managed teams, which are at the "lowest levels" of the organization, for example, are being given decision-making authority.   Today's rapidly changing markets and differences in consumer tastes are favoring a more decentralized structure, flatter organizational structures, with wider spans of control and a team based structure.

4.   a.   Product and function (hybrid)   d.   Geographic location
      b.   Function   e.   Customer group
      c.   Process

5.   In previous chapters we have learned about the global nature of our economy and of the business sector in particular. We have also read about the focus on productivity, and the search for ways to make firms in the United States more efficient and customer oriented. With globalization comes competition from companies that have been focusing on those productivity and customer service issues for quite some time. The disadvantages of the more traditional methods of departmentalization (the functional structure in particular) are lack of communication, slow response times to external changes, and narrowly focused training. These can serve to hinder efforts to become more competitive in the global market through increasing productivity and better serving a demanding customer base.

6.   a.   The <u>best</u> answer is most likely a matrix system.
      b.   Line
      c.   Line and staff
      d.   Cross-functional self-managed teams

7.   Cross functional self managed teams will have a major impact on organizational designs of the future.   Companies will be linked with customers, suppliers, and distributors through these teams, often through virtual corporations, creating an integrated system of firms working together to create products and services designed to quickly and exactly meet customers needs. Firms designed in such a manner will have a real competitive edge over corporations that are more traditional in their organizational structure.

8.   Gallo's vision is **"To become the most innovative global marketer and distributor of wines"** Gallo Winery chooses to stick to what it does best, which is the production and marketing of wine products, and the company outsources other functions to companies that perform those functions more effectively and efficiently than Gallo. Gallo knows its core competencies, and has the most up-to-date information and distribution systems to help them be the best at serving the wine market, without growing grapes.

9. These organizational changes are focused on designing the organization with meeting the needs of the customer as the most important objective. Inverted organizations empower front-line workers, who deal directly with the customers, and provide them with the information and support to satisfy customers. There is a focus on customer service and an emphasis on the firm's core competencies, outsourcing the functions at which the company is less proficient. Those functions that are not outsourced are benchmarked against the best in the world. The Internet makes it possible for firms to link with suppliers and customers to bring the "voice of the customer into the organization. The common theme is customer service.

10. The best organizations have positive corporate cultures that emphasize service to customers, have a relaxed atmosphere and concerned employees who enjoy working together to provide the best product at the best price. Companies that have good organizational cultures have less need for close supervision of employees, organization charts and formal rules, procedures and controls. That would indicate broad spans of control, empowered employees, flatter organizations, and a participative leadership style. Employees who need minimal supervision will flourish in self-managed teams, and there is mutual trust between workers and management.

11. The informal organization is the human side of a company that does not show up on the organization chart. It is the system of relationships that develop over time in a company. At the center of the informal organization is the grapevine, the unofficial flow of information. In a company with a positive culture, the informal organization can help to create a spirit of cooperation between managers and employees. It can strongly reinforce a feeling of teamwork and cooperation and can be an invaluable asset that promotes harmony among workers.

   On the other hand, the informal organization can also be disruptive and negative, and powerful in influencing employees to resist management directives. Consequently, it is important for managers to do whatever they can to create a positive work environment and a culture in which employees work together to reach the company's goals.

12. There will obviously be many different answers to this question. A typical hierarchy in a community college for example may be President, Dean of Instruction, Associate Deans, Department Chairs, and faculty for instruction. For non-instruction areas, there may be Associate Deans, Directors, and non-management positions. There are often many layers of management between the lowest levels and the higher levels, and functional areas are well defined. There will be similar kinds of structures in a company.

13. How you would design the organization is up to you. Many of the ideas presented in the chapter will be helpful. This is a small company, so a line organization might be appropriate. We noted earlier that the workers are well educated and trained and don't need a lot of supervision, so close monitoring could prove to be counter-productive. There doesn't seem to be an immediate need for new product development, so a matrix structure wouldn't be necessary. The emphasis on customer service has been apparent throughout the chapter, so however you design the company, the focus should be on whatever design will most effectively help the company to meet customer needs using such tools as the Internet, to develop strong ties with both customers and suppliers.

PRACTICE TEST

MULTIPLE CHOICE

LG 1   # 1-5
LG 2   # 6-9
LG 3   #10-13
LG 4   #14-15
LG 5   #16-20

1.	a	11.	c
2.	a	12.	b
3.	b	13.	b
4.	a	14.	d
5.	b	15.	c
6.	b	16.	d
7.	d	17.	c
8.	a	18.	d
9.	a	19.	c
10.	c	20.	b

TRUE-FALSE

LG 1   # 1-5
LG 2   # 6-11
L G 3   # 12-13
LG 4   #14-15
LG 5   #16-17

1.	T	10.	T
2.	T	11.	F
3.	F	12.	T
4.	T	13.	T
5.	F	14.	T
6.	T	15.	T
7.	F	16.	F
8.	T	17.	F
9.	F		

CHAPTER 9 – PRODUCING WORLD-CLASS GOODS AND SERVICES

LEARNING GOALS

After you have read and studied this chapter, you should be able to:

1. Describe the evolution of production in the United States.
2. Define operations management.
3. Distinguish between the various production processes and describe several of the production techniques that have improved the productivity of U.S. companies, including, computer aided design and manufacturing, flexible manufacturing, lean manufacturing, and mass customization.
4. Describe the operations management planning issues involved in both the manufacturing and the service sectors, including facility location, facility layout, materials requirement planning, purchasing, just-in-time inventory control and quality control.
5. Explain the use of PERT and Gantt charts to control manufacturing processes.

LEARNING THE LANGUAGE

Listed below are important terms found in the chapter. Choose the correct term for each definition and write it in the space provided.

Assembly process	Form utility	Production
	Gantt chart	Production management
Computer-aided design (CAD)	Intermittent process	Program evaluation and review technique (PERT)
Computer- aided manufacturing (CAM)	ISO 9000	Purchasing
Computer integrated manufacturing (CIM)	ISO 14000	Quality
Continuous process	Just-in-time (JIT) inventory control	
Critical path	Lean manufacturing	Six Sigma quality
Enterprise resource planning (ERP)	Mass customization	Statistical process control (SPC)
Facility layout	Materials requirement planning (MRP)	Statistical quality control (SQC)
Facility location	Operations management	
Flexible manufacturing	Process manufacturing	

1. A bar graph showing production managers what projects are being worked on and what stage they are in at any given time is called a _____.

2. A quality measure known as _____allows only 3.4 defects per million opportunities.

3. A computer application called _____enables multiple firms to manage all of their operations on the basis of a single, integrated set of corporate data.

4. A production process called the _____ puts together components into a finished product.

5. The term_____ is used to describe all the activities managers do to help their firms create goods.

6. Some managers use the process known as _____ to continually monitor all phases of the production process to assure that quality is being built into the product from the beginning.

7. The use of computers in the design of products is called _____.

8. A concept known as _____means tailoring products to meet the needs of individual customers.

9. A specialized area in management called _____converts or transforms resources into goods and services.

10. The function in a firm that searches for quality material resources, finds the best suppliers and negotiates the best price for goods and services is known as _____.

11. The term _____ refers to the physical arrangement of resources in the production process.

12. The use of computers in the manufacturing of products is known as _____.

13. Consistently producing what the customer wants while reducing errors before and after delivery to the customer is known as _____.

14. The value added by the creation of finished goods and services, or _____, refers to the value added, for example, by taking silicon and making computer chips or putting services together to create a vacation package.

15. The production process known as _____physically or chemically changes materials.

16. Designing machines to do multiple tasks so that they can produce a variety of products is called _____.

17. _____ is the production of goods using less of everything compared to mass production.

18. In a PERT network, the _____ is the sequence of tasks that takes the longest time to complete.

19. A computer based production management program called _____ uses sales forecasts to make sure that needed parts and materials are available at the right time and place.

20. Uniting computer-aided design with computer- aided manufacturing is called _____.

21. Production processes known as _____ have long production runs that turn out finished goods over time.

22. The common name given to quality management and assurance standards is _____.

23. The process of _____ consists of taking statistical samples of product components at each stage of the production process and plotting those results on a graph. Any variances from quality standards are recognized and can be corrected if beyond the set standards.

24. When a minimum of inventory is kept on the premises, and parts, supplies and other needs are delivered just in time to go on the assembly line, the company is using _____

25. The process of _____ is selecting a geographic location for a company's operations.

26. A method called _____ means analyzing the tasks involved in completing a given project, estimating the time needed to complete each task, and identifying the minimum time needed to complete the total project.

27. _____ is the creation of finished goods and services using the factors of production: land, labor, capital, entrepreneurship and knowledge.

28. A(n) _____ is a production process in which the production run is short and the machines are changed frequently to make different products.

29. A collection called _____ identifies the best practices for managing an organization's impact on the environment

ASSESSMENT CHECK

Learning Goal 1
U.S. Manufacturing in Perspective

1. Has U.S. manufacturing output risen or declined in recent years? By how much?

2. What are 7 areas American manufacturers have emphasized to regain a competitive edge in the world marketplace?

a._____

b._____

c._____

d._____

e._____

f._____

g._____

Learning Goal 2
From Production to Operations Management

3. What is the difference between production management and operations management?

4. Describe some of the activities involved in operations management.

5. What is the focus of operations management in the service sector?

6. What has become the quality standard in the services industry?

Learning Goal 3
Production Processes

7. What are the three basic requirements of production, according to Andrew Grove?

a._____

b._____

c._____

8.   What is the difference between process manufacturing and assembly process?

9.   What is the difference between a continuous production process and an intermittent process, in manufacturing?

10.   Why do most manufacturers today use intermittent processes?

11.   What four major developments have radically changed the production process in the United States?

a. _____   c. _____

b. _____   d. _____

12.   What is made possible with the use of CAD/CAM?

13.   What is CIM and what is the benefit?

14.   How can flexible manufacturing reduce labor costs?

15.   How does a company become "lean"?

16.   What are some examples of how companies have used mass customization?

17. What are the issues included in operations management planning?

   a. _____   d. _____

   b. _____   e. _____

   c. _____   f. _____

18. One strategy in selecting a facility location is to find a location that _____

   _____

19. What do brick and mortar stores have to do to compete with services offered over the Internet?

20. List the major issues that affect site selection for manufacturers.

   a. _____

   b. _____

   c. _____

   d. _____

   e. _____

   f. _____

   g. _____

   h. _____

   i. _____

21. What is the key reason why firms move their plants?

22. Other key reasons that firms move their production facilities include:

   a. _____

   b. _____

23. In reducing time to market, what do manufacturers need?

24. What is the benefit, for companies, of locating close to their suppliers?

25. Why do businesses build factories in foreign countries? What do U.S. firms consider in choosing a site in a foreign country?

26. Identify the quality of life questions that firms consider in the facilities location process.

27. How is the Internet changing the area of operations management?

28. What actions might state and local governments take to provide incentives for companies looking to locate in their area?

29. What is the idea of facility layout, and upon what does facility layout depend?

30. What is important in terms of facilities layout, for services?

31. In manufacturing, what kind of layout is replacing the assembly line?

32.   Describe:

        a. A process layout:

        b. A fixed position layout:

33.   How is ERP different from MRP?

34.   What is the result from using ERP?

35.   How has the purchasing function in companies changed?

36.   What is required in order for a JIT (just-in-time inventory) program to work effectively?

37.   What problems can result from JIT?

38.   How does a JIT program work?

39.   JIT systems make sure that _____

_____

40.   How was quality control done in the past? What problems were associated with that process?

41.   a: Six sigma quality detects _____

        b. Statistical quality control is the process used to_____

        _____

        c. Statistical process control eliminates _____

        _____

42.   Who ultimately determines what the standard for quality should be.

43.   What are the seven key areas in which a company must show quality in order to qualify
        for the Baldrige Awards?

        a. _____   e. _____

        b. _____   f. _____

        c. _____   g. _____

        d. _____

44.   Name the two major criteria for earning the Baldrige Awards.

        a. _____

        b. _____

45.   What is the International Organization for Standardization?

46.   What do the new ISO 9004: 2000 standards require?

47.   Why is ISO certification so important for U.S. firms?

48.   What is the difference between ISO 9000 and ISO 14000?

49.   What are the requirements for ISO 14000 certification?

Learning Goal 5
Control Procedures: PERT and Gantt charts

50.   List the four steps in designing a PERT chart

        a._____

        b._____

        c._____

        d._____

51.   Why is it "critical" to identify the critical path?

52.   What is the difference between a Gantt Chart and a PERT Chart?

53.   How can a manager use a Gantt Chart?

CRITICAL THINKING EXERCISES

Learning Goal 1
1.   We have been reading throughout the text of the move toward a global marketplace, and
        the need for U.S. firms to make changes to be competitive. How are production
        processes and productivity fundamental to the process?

2.   Why has the term "production management" been changed to "operations management"? What are some examples of operations management?

Learning goal 3

3.   In manufacturing, two types of manufacturing processes are:

a) process manufacturing , which is changing materials
b) assembly process which is putting together components

In addition, production processes are either: continuous or intermittent

Match the correct type of production process to each of the following, according to the description:

a. _____   The steel industry never shuts down its ovens.

b. _____   In the furniture industry, a store will sell custom designed furniture and pass the order on to the manufacturer, who then custom makes each piece.

c. _____   The Macintosh computer is assembled piece by piece along an assembly   line.

d. _____   In the steel industry, ore is melted down, poured into forms, and then cooled.

4.   How do flexible manufacturing systems, lean manufacturing, and mass customization reflect the customer orientation we have discussed in earlier chapters?

5.   How does CAD/CAM relate to mass customization?

6. You have learned in earlier chapters that one advantage small businesses often have over larger, less flexible companies is the ability to move quickly to serve the needs of their markets and provide more customized service. As increasing numbers of large businesses implement the modern production techniques discussed in this chapter, what potential impact could this have on small businesses?

7. Five radically different production techniques have emerged in recent years:

    Just-in-time inventory control   Mass customization
    Flexible manufacturing   Lean manufacturing

    Distinguish the differences between each technique in the following:

    a. _____   The Daimler-Chrysler plant in Fenton, Missouri receives shipments about every four hours from its seat supplier, (located in a neighboring town), and literally hundreds of other parts continually. There is virtually no storage space in the plant.

    b. _____   Volvo uses modular construction in their plants, where workers are grouped into autonomous teams working on mobile assembly platforms that carry the cars to the workers. Each worker has been trained to do a whole cluster of tasks. This system enabled Volvo to build quality cars with fewer workers in more space efficient plants, and has reduced the number of hours need to assemble a car.

    c. _____   Levi's markets a service that enables any customer to order a custom-made pair of jeans from any retailer at any time. The jeans cost $10 more than an "off-the-rack" pair.

    d. _____   At Dynalink Industries, 15 machines are used to make, test and package component parts for stereo and quadraphonic sound systems. The parts are never touched by human hands.

Learning goal 4

8. Businesses may choose to locate close to where the buying power for their product is located, where labor is inexpensive and/or skilled, where land and other resources are inexpensive and readily available, close to their markets or where quality of life is high.

    Evaluate the area in which you live based on the site-selection criteria discussed in the text. Does your area have an advantage in the variables considered for site selection? If so, which ones? Are you located close to markets? What could you say to convince a producer or service business to locate in your area? In some areas there will be an organization that addresses these very issues. In St. Louis, Missouri, for example, the Regional Chamber and Growth Association (www.stlrcga.org) addresses many of the site selection factors for the St. Louis region.

9.   How does the concept of facility layout help companies become more "customer focused" and more competitive?

10.   How has increased global competition forced U.S. firms to "rethink" quality?

Learning Goals 3,4

11.   Sun-2-Shade, a company that makes self-darkening windshields for automobiles, is beginning to gear up for production. It has 2 main product lines: a windshield that is designed to be installed during the automotive assembly process, and an "after-market" product, to be sold in auto parts stores, which can be installed by companies that repair and install windshields after manufacture. These windshields are made from a lightweight, specially formulated plastic. Sun-2-Shade buys the raw material from a plastic supplier. The plastic is melted down and poured into molds, which are then allowed to cool. The windshields are then transformed into the self-darkening type windshield using proprietary processes. For added durability the last stage of manufacturing applies a scratch resistant hard coat to all windshields. The process is similar for both product lines, with some alterations needed for the retail version. What type of production process is Sun-2-Shade likely to be using? How can the company ensure their product is available when the assembly plant needs it, and when the retailer wants to sell it?

Learning Goal 5

12.   PERT, Critical Path and Gantt charts are control measures used to ensure that products are manufactured and delivered on time.

Draw a PERT Chart for cooking and serving a breakfast of 3-minute eggs, buttered toast and coffee and identify the critical path.

PRACTICE TEST

MULTIPLE CHOICE – Circle the best answer

Learning Goal 1

1.   What statement does <u>not</u> fit in when describing the trend in manufacturing in the United States?
    a.   Operations management has replaced "production" management.
    b.   New manufacturing techniques have replaced more traditional forms.
    c.   Rebuilding America's manufacturing base will be a major business issue in the future.
    d.   Foreign competition has not affected U.S. manufacturers.

2.   When looking at how American manufacturers have regained a competitive edge, which of the following would <u>not</u> be included?
    a.   Reducing product quality to keep costs low.
    b.   Relying on the Internet to unite companies.
    c.   Practicing continuous improvement.
    d.   Focusing on customers.

3.   New production techniques have:
    a.   been difficult and costly to implement, and so have been largely ignored.
    b.   made it possible to custom-make products for individual buyers.
    c.   have been implemented primarily by foreign manufacturers.
    d.   have not been shown to be effective in making U.S. manufacturers competitive.

Learning Goal 2

4. _____ is a specialized area in management that converts or transforms resources into goods and services and includes the areas of inventory management, quality control, production scheduling, follow-up services and more.
   a. Lean manufacturing
   b. CAD/CAM
   c. Flexible manufacturing
   d. Operations management

Learning Goal 3

5. Paul Klabber designs and makes custom wood furniture. The process Paul uses in his business is an example of a(n):
   a. assembly process.
   b. intermittent process.
   c. analytic system.
   d. continuous process.

6. Which of the following is <u>not</u> included in a list of major developments that have changed the production process in the United States?
   a. Assembly line processes
   b. Flexible manufacturing
   c. Mass customization
   d. Lean manufacturing

7. Quon Ho believes that there must be a way to cut down on the amount of resources his company uses in the production process. Quon feels that the company uses more space, tools and time to make their product than is necessary. Quon should examine the benefits of:
   a. lean manufacturing.
   b. CAD/CAM.
   c. mass customization.
   d. facilities layout.

8. _____ makes it possible to custom-design products to meet the needs of small markets with very little increase in cost.
   a. CAD/CAM
   b. Site selection
   c. Production management
   d. Process manufacturing

Learning Goal 4

9. Which of the following is <u>not</u> considered a strong reason for companies to move production facilities from one area to another?
   a. availability of cheap labor
   b. cheaper natural resources
   c. the level of unemployment in a geographic area
   d. reducing the time it takes to deliver products to the market

10. Sun-2-Shade is beginning to see some competition for their self-darkening windshield. In order to remain competitive, Sun-2-Shade must be sure to:
    a. replace all workers with automated equipment.
    b. move all manufacturing to foreign countries.
    c. train all salesmen in aggressive selling techniques.
    d. keep the costs of manufacturing down.

11. For brick and mortar stores to beat competition from Internet businesses, they must:
    a. undercut prices found on the Internet.
    b. advertise more, especially on the Internet.
    c. choose good locations and offer outstanding service.
    d. develop different products from what is available on the Internet.

12. The idea of facility layout is to:
    a. make it easy for workers to find their work stations.
    b. have offices, machines, and storage areas in the best position to enable workers to produce goods and services for their customers.
    c. ensure that the building meets all building codes for the area in which they are located.
    d. facilitate the assembly line process.

13. The U.S. award that recognizes firms that meet customer needs, produce high quality products and have high quality internal operations, is known as:
    a. ISO 9000 standards.
    b. The Customer Excellence Award.
    c. The Malcolm Baldrige National Quality Award.
    d. ISO 14000 standards.

14. One reason ISO 9000 standards are so important is that:
    a. they must be met in order to win any quality awards.
    b. most free trade agreements require that these standards be met.
    c. meeting these standards will automatically increase worker productivity.
    d. companies that want to do business with the EU must be certified by ISO standards.

15. Many companies are moving from a(n) _____, in which workers do only a few tasks at a time to a _____, in which teams of workers combine to produce more complex units of the final product.
    a. modular layout; assembly line layout
    b. intermittent process; continuous process
    c. assembly line layout; modular layout
    d. continuous process; process manufacturing

16. Tony Ruggali is in the process of opening a new restaurant. Tony wants to be sure that his new place The Fresh Place, always has the freshest ingredients, and will always be known for being the "freshest place in town." He also wants to devote most of the space in the restaurant to tables for diners, not for storing products. Tony could make use of:
    a. analytic production.
    b. Gantt charts.
    c. Just in time inventory control.
    d. mass production.

17. Sun-2-Shade wants to link its resource planning and manufacturing with its suppliers in order to develop a more integrated system. Sun-2-Shade could use:
    a.   enterprise resource planning.
    b.   continuous process manufacturing.
    c.   PERT charts.
    d.   total quality control.

18. _____ is the process managers use to continually monitor al phases of the production process to ensure that quality is being built into the product from the beginning.
    a.   Six sigma quality
    b.   Statistical process control (SPC)
    c.   Statistical quality control (SQC)
    d.   Process manufacturing

Learning Goal 5
19. A _____ is a bar graph that shows which projects are being worked on and how much has been completed.
    a.   PERT chart
    b.   flexible manufacturing system
    c.   Gantt chart
    d.   CAD/CAM system

20. Hector Lopez is a production supervisor at the local cucumber processing plant. Hector is looking at a chart that illustrates for him the sequence of tasks involved in processing the cukes. He is especially interested in the sequence of tasks that take the longest time to complete. Hector is interested in the:
    a.   Gantt chart.
    b.   total quality management process.
    c.   critical path.
    d.   lean manufacturing process.

TRUE-FALSE

Learning Goal 1
1. _____   One thing American manufacturers have done to regain a competitive edge has been to incorporate more rigid management styles.

2. _____   The United States now has what is called a service economy – that is one that is dominated by the service sector.

3. _____   The production picture in the United States is better than many people think, and overall production is expected to rise in coming years.

4. _____   Global competition has had little effect on American manufacturers

Learning Goal 2
5. _____   Operations management is a specialized area in management that converts resources into goods and services.

6. _____ Operations management is becoming an interfirm process where companies work together to design, produce, and ship products to customers.

7. _____ Delighting customers by anticipating their needs has become the quality standard for most service businesses.

Learning Goal 3
8. _____ Form utility is the value added by placing goods and services in areas easily accessible to your customers.

9. _____ The ultimate goal of manufacturing and process management is to provide high-quality goods and services instantaneously in response to customer demand

10. _____ Computer integrated manufacturing (CIM) unites computer aided design machines with computer aided manufacturing machines

11. _____ Flexible manufacturing systems are so flexible that a special order, even a single item can be produced without slowing down the manufacturing process.

12. _____ Mass customization is a means of manufacturing small batch products using mass production techniques.

Learning Goal 4
13. _____ Quality of life issues are generally not important when firms are considering site locations.

14. _____ Enterprise Resource Planning is a way of integrating functions within a single firm.

15. _____ Operations managers today have to adjust from a one-firm system to an interfirm environment.

16. _____ Facility layout is not an important factor in the services industry.

17. _____ The Internet has transformed the purchasing function.

18. _____ Six Sigma quality control standards allow for no defects whatsoever

Learning Goal 5
19. _____ A Gantt computer program will allow a manager to trace the production process minute by minute to determine which tasks are on time and which are behind.

20. _____ The critical path in a PERT network is the group of activities that must be completed in order for the project to be successful.

You Can Find It on the Net

We have studied some of the ideas of lean manufacturing in this chapter. To learn more, visit www.leanstrategies.com

What are the key strategies of "lean" companies?

What are "lean customer relationships"? How do you create them?

What are the areas to consider in lean order fulfillment?

What do lean supply chains do, and what areas are important?

What must a company do to have lean product development?

ANSWERS

LEARNING THE LANGUAGE

1. Gantt chart	11. Facility layout	21. Continuous process
2. Six Sigma quality	12. Computer aided manufacturing (CAM)	22. ISO 9000
3. Enterprise resource planning (ERP)	13. Quality	23. Statistical process control (SPC)
4. Assembly process	14. Form utility	24. Just in time inventory control (JIT)
5. Production management	15. Process manufacturing	25. Facility location
6. Statistical quality control (SQC)	16. Flexible manufacturing	26. Program evaluation and review technique (PERT)
7. Computer aided design (CAD)	17. Lean manufacturing	27. Production
8. Mass customization	18. Critical path	28. Intermittent process
9. Operations management	19. Materials Requirement Planning (MRP)	29. ISO 14000
10. Purchasing	20. Computer integrated manufacturing (CIM)	

ASSESSMENT CHECK

Learning Goal 1
U.S. Manufacturing in Perspective

1. U. S. manufacturing output has risen in the last two decades.   It rose by 3.7 percent per year from 1990 to 1995, and it rose by 5.7 percent each year from 1995 to 2001. More than 60% of manufacturers planned on hiring new workers in 2006

2. Manufacturers today have emphasized:
    a. Focusing on customers
    b. Maintaining close relationships with suppliers and other companies to satisfy customer needs
    c. Practicing continuous improvement
    d. Focusing on quality
    e. Saving on costs through site selection
    f. Relying on the Internet to unite companies
    g. Adopting new manufacturing techniques

Learning Goal 2
From Production to Operations Management

3. Production management is the term used to describe all the activities managers do to help their firms create goods. To reflect the change of importance from manufacturing to services, the term *production* is often replaced by *operations* to reflect both goods and services. Operations management is a specialized area in management that converts or transforms resources into goods and services.

4. Operations management includes inventory management, quality control, production scheduling, follow-up services and more. In an automobile plant operations management transforms raw materials, human resources, parts, supplies, paints, tools, and other resources into automobiles, for example.

5. Operations management in the service sector is all about creating a good experience for those who use the service.

6. The quality standard in the services industry has become delighting the customers by anticipating their needs.

Learning Goal 3
Production Processes

7. According to Andrew Grove, the three basic requirements of production are:
   a. Build and deliver products in response to demands of a customer at a scheduled delivery time
   b. Provide an acceptable quality level
   c. Provide everything at the lowest possible cost

8. Process manufacturing physically or chemically changes materials, such as the process used to change sand into glass. Assembly process puts components together, such as in the assembly of an automobile.

9. A continuous process is one in which long production runs turn out finished goods over time, as in the chemical industry. An intermittent process is an operation where the production run is short and the machines changed frequently to product different products, as in custom made furniture.

10. Most new manufacturers use intermittent processes because the use of computers, robots, and flexible manufacturing processes make it possible to make custom-made goods almost as fast as mass-produced goods were once made.

11. Four major developments that have changed the production process in the United States are:
    a. Computer aided design and manufacturing
    b. flexible manufacturing
    c. lean manufacturing
    d. mass customization

12. CAD/CAM has made it possible to custom-design products to meet the needs of small markets with very little increase in cost. A manufacturer can program the computer to make a simple design change, and that change can be incorporated directly into the production line.

13. Computer integrated manufacturing, CIM, is software that unites CAD with CAM. It can reduce the amount of time needed to program machines by as much as 80% and thus reduces the cost of manufacturing.

14. Flexible manufacturing allows manufacturers to design machines to do multiple tasks so that they can produce a variety of products. Products and changes are made without any labor, thus reducing labor costs.

15. A company becomes lean by continuously increasing the capacity to produce high quality goods while decreasing its need for resources.

16. Companies in both the manufacturing and the service sector are using mass customization. GNC stores for example feature machines that allow shoppers to custom design several products. Other companies provide custom made books, custom greeting cards and custom fitted shoes and clothes. In the service sector there are customized insurance policies, fitness programs, and vacation packages.

Learning goal 4
Operations Management Planning

17. The issues in operations management planning include:
   a. facility location   d. purchasing
   b. facility layout   e. inventory control
   c. materials requirement planning   f. quality control

18. One strategy in selecting a facility location is to find a location that makes it easy for customers to access your service and to maintain a dialogue about their needs.

19. In order for bricks and mortar stores to compete with Internet shopping they have to choose good locations and offer outstanding service to those who come to the store.

20. The major issues that affect site selection for manufacturers are:
   a.   labor costs
   b.   availability of resources, including labor
   c.   access to transportation that can reduce time to market
   d.   proximity to suppliers
   e.   proximity to customers
   f.   low crime rates
   g.   quality of life for employees
   h.   cost of living
   i.   the ability to train or retrain the local workforce

21. A key reason why producers move their plants is the availability of inexpensive labor, or the right kind of labor.

22. Other key reasons for moving production facilities include:
   a.   inexpensive resources
   b.   to reduce the time-to-market

23. In reducing time to market, manufacturers need sites that allow products to move through the system quickly, at the lowest costs, so they can be delivered rapidly to customers. Access to transportation is critical, and information technology is important, so companies look for areas with the most advanced information systems.

24. The benefit of locating close to suppliers is that it cuts the cost of distribution and makes communication easier.

25. Companies choose to locate in foreign counties in order to get closer to international customers. U. S. firms consider whether they are near to transportation facilities so that raw materials and finished goods can be moved quickly and easily in global markets.

26. Quality of life questions include: Are there good schools nearby? Is the weather nice? Does the local community welcome new businesses? Do the chief executive and other key managers want to live there?

27. Companies are creating new relationships with suppliers over the Internet so that operations management is becoming an "interfirm" process, where companies work together to design, produce, and ship products to customers. Many manufacturing companies are developing new Internet-focused strategies that will enable them and others to compete more effectively. The changes are having a dramatic effect on operations managers who have to adjust from a one-firm system to an interfirm environment.

28. State and local governments may compete with one another by giving tax reductions and other support such as zoning changes and financial aid, so that businesses will locate there.

29. The idea of facilities layout is to have offices, machines, storage areas, and other items in the best possible position to enable workers to produce goods and provide services for their customers. Facilities layout depends on the processes that are to be performed.

30. For services, the layout is designed to help the consumer find and buy what they need. Often this means helping consumers to find and buy things on the Internet. Some stores have added kiosks that enable customers to search for goods on the Internet and place the order from the store.

31. In manufacturing, many companies are moving from an assembly line layout to a modular layout, where teams of workers combine to produce more complex units of the final product.

32. a. A process layout is one in which similar equipment and functions are grouped together. The order in which the product visits a function depends on the design of the item.
    b. A fixed position layout allows workers to congregate around the product to be completed.

33. MRP allows manufacturers to make sure that needed parts and materials are available at the right place and the right time. ERP is the newest variation of MRP. Enterprise resource planning is a computer-based production and operations system that enables multiple firms to manage all of their operations on the basis of a single, integrated set of corporate data.

34. The result of using ERP is shorter time between orders and payment, less staff to do ordering and order processing, reduced inventories, and better customer service for all firms involved.

35. In the past, manufacturers tended to deal with many different suppliers. Today manufacturers are relying more heavily on one or two suppliers because so much information is shared that firms don't want to have so many companies knowing their business. Thus, the relationship between suppliers and manufacturers is much closer than ever before. The Internet has significantly reduced the cost of purchasing items.

36. To work effectively, the JIT process requires excellent coordination with carefully selected suppliers.

37. JIT runs into problems when suppliers are located at some distance from their customers. Weather may delay shipments for example.

38. In a JIT program, a manufacturer sets a production schedule using enterprise resource planning or a similar system, and determines what parts and supplies will be needed. Suppliers are connected electronically so they know immediately what will be needed and when. The supplier delivers the goods just in time to go on the assembly line.

39. JIT systems make sure the right materials are at the right place at the right time at the cheapest cost to meet customer needs and production needs.

40. In the past quality control was often done at the end of the production line in the quality control department. The problems that resulted were:
    a. There was a need to inspect other people's work. This took extra people and resources.
    b. If errors were found, someone would have to correct the mistake or scrap the product. This is costly.
    c. A customer who found the mistake could be dissatisfied and buy from someone else.

41. a. Six sigma quality detects potential problems before they occur.
    b. Statistical quality control is the process used to continually monitor all processes in the production process to assure that quality is being built into the product from the beginning.
    c. Statistical process control eliminates or minimizes the need for having a quality control inspection at the end of a production line. Any mistakes would have been caught much earlier in the production process.

42. The customer is ultimately the one who determines what the standard for quality must be.

43. To qualify for a Baldrige Award, a firm must show quality in:
    a. leadership   e. human resources focus
    b. strategic planning   f. process management
    c. customer and market focus   g. business results
    d. information and analysis

44. The two major criteria for earning the Baldrige Awards are
    a. whether customer wants and needs are met
    b. customer satisfaction ratings are better than the competition

45. The International Organization for Standardization is a worldwide federation of national standards bodies from more than 140 countries that set the global measures for the quality of individual products.

46. ISO 9004: 2000 standards require that a company must determine what customer needs are, including regulatory and legal requirements. There must also be communication arrangements to handle issues like complaints. Other standards involve process control, product testing, storage, and delivery.

47.   ISO certification is important for U.S. firms because the European Union is demanding that companies that want to do business with the EU be certified by ISO standards.

48.   ISO 9000 is the name given to quality management and assurance standards. ISO 14000 is a collection of the best practices for managing an organization's impact on the environment. It does not prescribe a performance level like ISO 9000 does.

49.   The requirements for ISO 14000 include having an environmental policy, having specific improvement targets, conducting audits of environmental programs, and maintaining top management review of the processes.

Learning Goal 5
Control Procedures: PERT and Gantt charts

50.   The four steps involved in developing a PERT chart include:
       a.   Analyze and sequence tasks that need to be done
       b.   Estimate the time needed to complete each task
       c.   Draw a PERT network illustrating the 2 previous steps
       d.   Identify the critical path

51.   The critical path in a PERT chart identifies the sequence of tasks that takes the longest time to complete. It is critical because a delay in the time needed to complete this path would cause the project or production run to be late.

52.   A PERT chart analyzes the tasks involved in completing a given project, estimating the time needed to complete each task, and identifying the minimum time needed to complete the total project. It is done by computer. A Gantt chart is used to measure production progress using a bar chart that shows what projects are being worked on and how much has been completed at any given time.

53.   With a Gantt chart, a manager can trace the production process minute by minute to determine which tasks are on time, and which are behind so that adjustments can be made to stay on schedule.

CRITICAL THINKING EXERCISES

Learning Goal 1
1.   Production is the creation of goods and services using the factors of production, while productivity measures how efficiently the goods and services have been created. To be competitive in world markets, manufacturers must keep the cost of production low while production must be relatively high. The fundamental question is: How does a producer keep costs low and still produce high quality products that satisfy customer needs? In other words, how do manufacturers increase productivity?

      U.S. manufacturers have emphasized areas such as: focusing on customers, maintaining close relationships with suppliers and other companies, focusing on quality, saving on costs through site selection, relying on the Internet to unite companies, and adopting new manufacturing techniques to increase productivity and regain a competitive edge in the global marketplace.

2.   The term production has changed to operations to reflect the fact that the United States has become a service-based economy, and the term "operations" reflects both goods and services production. Operations management is a specialized area of management, and includes inventory management, quality control, production scheduling and more. An example of operations management in goods manufacturing is an automotive plant, where operations management transforms raw materials, human resources, parts, supplies, and other resources into automobiles. In a college, operations management takes inputs such as information, professors, supplies, buildings and so on and creates a process of education.

Learning goal 3
3.   a. continuous   c. assembly process
         b. intermittent assembly process   d. process manufacturing

4.   Flexible manufacturing systems, lean manufacturing and mass customization are all ways companies have available to put customer needs first. Manufacturers can custom-make goods at a very low cost very quickly, which is exactly what consumers want!

5.   CAD/CAM is the integration of computers into the design and manufacture of products. This process has enabled manufacturers to tailor products to meet the needs of individual consumers at very little or no extra cost. A simple design change can be incorporated directly into the production line. It is what has enabled Nike to offer "custom made" athletic footwear at very little additional cost. CAD/CAM systems have revolutionized the production process and have essentially <u>created </u>and allowed for the concept of mass customization.

6.   As bigger businesses increase the use of sophisticated manufacturing technology, they will be able to meet the changing needs of their markets much more quickly. This weakens one advantage small businesses have had, which has been the ability to adapt quickly to changing customer markets. Additionally, big businesses are now able to customize their product, enabling them to meet the needs of smaller target markets, traditionally a stronghold for smaller businesses.

7.   a. Just-in-time inventory control   c. Mass customization
         b. Lean manufacturing   d. Flexible-manufacturing system

Learning goal 4
8.   The area in which you live may meet a number of important criteria. Look for a population that may be willing to work hard for less pay, such as new immigrants. What kind of skilled labor is available in your area? Is your state a "right to work" state or a heavily unionized state? That affects labor costs. Are you in a rural, suburban or urban area? That affects the availability and costs of land.

         If you live in a large urban area, such as Chicago, New York, or Los Angeles, businesses may be attracted because that's where their customers are. However land is more expensive, so a large production facility may not be built there. There may be lots of opportunity for a service-based business to locate in that area. Government support will vary from one area to another, in the form of tax incentives and zoning laws.

9. Most of the decisions about facilities layout revolve around finding the most benefit for the customer. In services, facilities layout is usually designed to help the consumer find and buy things. In manufacturing, plants have been redesigned to reduce cost, increase productivity, simplify the production process and speed things up. That benefits the consumer in the form of lower prices, and lower time to market. Both of these aspects of facilities layout make companies more competitive, as they serve customer needs more effectively.

10. If U.S. firms want to remain competitive in today's global environment, they must focus on quality issues the same way that European and Asian countries have done. As we have read in earlier chapters these countries are often able to produce high quality goods at low prices. Further ISO standards have provided a common denominator of business quality around the world. U.S. firms have begun to realize that in order to be competitive; they must not only compete with, but also cooperate with, international firms to continue to serve global markets with the highest quality products and services at the lowest possible prices.

U.S. firms have adopted programs such as Six Sigma, SQC and SPC to both reduce costs and ensure high quality products for their customers

Learning Goals 3,4
11. It sounds like Sun-2-Shade uses the process manufacturing system to create the product, as they mold the plastic used for the windshields into a product to meet their needs. This would most likely be an intermittent process, as the machines or molds may need to be changed depending upon the style of automobile for which they are making the windshield. This can be done entirely by using a flexible manufacturing system.

Sun-2-Shade needs to keep track of its own inventory, as well as that of the auto assembly plants and their retail customers. Enterprise resource planning is a sophisticated computer-based operations system that would link Sun-2-Shade with their suppliers, as well as with their customers. With this system, Sun-2-Shade could track the availability of the plastic they need from their supplier. They could monitor their own inventory to ensure adequate stock at crucial times, and be sure that their customers have what they need when they need it to keep production flowing smoothly, and sales at the retail level from slacking off.

Sun-2-Shade must also consider locating their plant(s) near the plants assembling the cars installed with their windshield. This is especially important for any automotive assembly plant using JIT systems.

12.   To cook a breakfast of 3-minute eggs, buttered toast and coffee, a PERT chart may look like this:

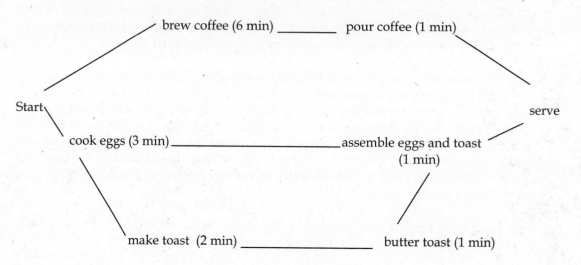

The critical path is the brewing and pouring of the coffee, as it takes the longest time to complete.

PRACTICE TEST

MULTIPLE CHOICE

LG 1   *# 1-3*
LG 2   *#4*
LG 3   *#5-8*
LG 4   *# 9-18*
LG 5   *# 19-20*

1.	d	11.	c
2.	a	12.	b
3.	b	13.	c
4.	d	14.	d
5.	b	15.	c
6.	a	16.	c
7.	a	17.	a
8.	a	18.	c
9.	c	19.	c
10.	d	20.	c

TRUE-FALSE

LG 1   *# 1-4*
LG 2   *# 5-7*
LG 3   *# 8-12*
LG 4   *# 13-18*
LG 5   *#19-20*

1.	F	11.	T
2.	T	12.	F
3.	T	13.	F
4.	F	14.	T
5.	T	15.	T
6.	F	16.	F
7.	T	17.	T
8.	F	18.	F
9.	T	19.	T
10.	T	20.	F

CHAPTER 10 – MOTIVATING EMPLOYEES AND BUILDING SELF-MANAGED TEAMS

LEARNING GOALS

After you have read and studied this chapter, you should be able to:

1. Explain Taylor's scientific management.
2. Describe the Hawthorne studies and relate their significance to management.
3. Identify the levels of Maslow's hierarchy of needs and relate their importance to employee motivation.
4. Distinguish between motivators and hygiene factors identified by Herzberg.
5. Explain how job enrichment affects employee motivation and performance.
6. Differentiate among Theory X, Theory Y and Theory Z.
7. Explain goal setting theory and how management by objectives (MBO) exemplifies the theory.
8. Describe the key principles of expectancy, reinforcement, and equity theories.
9. Explain how open communication builds teamwork, and describe how managers are likely to motivate teams in the future.

LEARNING THE LANGUAGE

Listed below are important terms found in the chapter. Choose the correct term for each definition and write it in the space provided.

Equity theory	Intrinsic reward	Motivators
Expectancy theory	Job enlargement	Principle of motion economy
Extrinsic reward	Job enrichment	Reinforcement theory
Goal-setting theory	Job rotation	Scientific management
Hawthorne effect	Management by objectives (MBO)	Time-motion studies
Hygiene factors	Maslow's hierarchy of needs	

1. Herzberg's theory of motivating factors called _____, cause dissatisfaction if missing, but do not motivate employees if increased.

2. The theory that positive and negative reinforcers motivate a person to behave a certain way is called _____.

3. Begun by Frederick Taylor, _____ are studies of which tasks must be performed to complete a job and the time needed to do each task.

4. A(n) _____ is the personal satisfaction you feel when you perform well and complete goals.

5. A system of goal setting and implementation known as _____ involves a cycle of discussion, review, and evaluation of objectives among top and middle-level managers, supervisors, and employees.

6. A job enrichment strategy known as _____ involves combining a series of tasks into one assignment that is challenging and interesting.

7. A(n) _____ is something given to you by someone else as recognition for good work, including pay increases, praise and promotions.

8. A motivational strategy that emphasizes motivating the workers through the job itself is called_____.

9. Herzberg's theory of motivating factors known as _____cause employees to be productive and give them satisfaction.

10. _____ is the idea that setting ambitious but attainable goals can motivate workers and improve performance if the goals are accepted, accompanied by feedback and facilitated by organizational conditions.

11. The _____refers to the tendency for people to behave differently when they know they are being studied.

12. Known as _____this is a job enrichment strategy involving moving employees from one job to another.

13. Victor Vroom's _____ indicates that the amount of effort employees exert on a specific task depends on their expectations of the outcome.

14. The study of workers to find the most efficient way of doing things and then teaching people those techniques is known as _____.

15. _____is the idea that employees try to maintain equity between inputs and outputs compared to others in similar positions.

16. Frank and Lillian Gilbreth developed the _____ which is the theory that every job can be broken down into a series of elementary motions.

17. The theory of motivation called _____ is based on unmet human needs from basic physiological needs to safety, social, and esteem needs to self-actualization needs.

ASSESSMENT CHECK

Learning Goal 1
The Importance of Motivation

1. Who is known as the Father of Scientific Management? What was his goal?

2.   What did Taylor believe were the ways to improve productivity?

      a. _____

      b. _____

      c. _____

3.   What three elements were basic to Scientific Management?

      a._____

      b._____

      c._____

4.   What is Gantt known for?

5.   What contribution did Frank and Lillian Gilbreth make to the field of Scientific Management?

6.   How did proponents of scientific management view workers?

7.   How are the ideas of Scientific Management being used today?

Learning Goal 2
Elton Mayo and the Hawthorne Studies

8.   What did the Hawthorne Experiments originally intend to test and what problem was revealed during the initial experiments?

9. Why did the experimenters believe the Hawthorne Experiments were a failure after the second series of experiments?

10. Describe three conclusions drawn from the Hawthorne Experiments

a. _____

b. _____

c. _____

11. Describe the Hawthorne effect.

12. How did research, and assumptions about employees, change after the Hawthorne Experiments?

Learning goal 3
Motivation and Maslow's Hierarchy of Needs

13. According to Maslow, people are motivated to satisfy _____

_____

14. Describe the five need levels on Maslow's Hierarchy

a._____

b._____

c._____

d. _____

e. _____

15.   According to Maslow, what happens when a need is satisfied?

16.   How does the application of Mazlow's theory differ between less developed countries and developed countries, such as the United States?

Learning Goal 4
Herzberg's Motivating Factors

17.   What did Herzberg's research find were the most important factors that motivate workers?

a._____   h. _____

b. _____   i. _____

c. _____   j. _____

d. _____   k. _____

e. _____   l._____

f. _____   m. _____

g. _____   n. _____

18.   Based upon this list, what did Herzberg note about workers with regard to what motivates them and what doesn't motivate them?

19.   What is the difference between Herzberg's motivators and hygiene factors?

20. Identify Herzberg's motivators.

a._____

b._____

c._____

d._____

e._____

21. List Herzberg's hygiene factors.

a._____

b._____

c._____

d._____

e._____

22. According to these factors, what is the best way to motivate employees?

23. Is money the number one motivator for most people? Why or why not?

Learning Goal 5
Job Enrichment

24. In a job enrichment motivational strategy, work is assigned: _____

_____

The motivational effect of job enrichment can come from: _____

_____

25. Describe the five characteristics of work important in affecting individual motivation and performance.

a._____

b._____

c._____

d._____

e._____

26. What is job simplification?

27. What is the difference between job enlargement and job rotation?

Learning Goal 6
McGregor's Theory X and Theory Y

28. Identify the assumptions of a Theory X manager.

a._____

b._____

c._____

d._____

29. What are the consequences of a Theory X manager's attitudes?

30. What are the assumptions of a Theory Y manager?

a. _____

b. _____

c. _____

d. _____

e. _____

f. _____

g. _____

31. How do the Theory Y manager's attitudes affect behavior toward employees?

32. Empowerment gives employees _____

_____

33. What steps should management follow in order to use empowerment as a motivator?

a. _____

b. _____

c. _____

34. What is the management trend in today's companies, in terms of Theory X, Theory Y? Why?

35. According to William Ouchi, the American management approach, or Type A involves:

a. _____   e. _____

b. _____   f. _____

c. _____   g. _____

d. _____

258

36. List the major elements of Ouchi's "Type J" management approach, based on Japanese culture.

a. _____   e. _____

b. _____   f. _____

c. _____   g. _____

d. _____

37. Describe Theory Z, and its major elements.

38. How is the Japanese management system changing and why?

39. According to the text, what is the appropriate management style?

Learning Goal 7
Goal-Setting Theory and Management By Objectives

40. Goals can motivate workers and improve performance if the goals are:

a. _____

b. _____

c. _____

41. The four things a manager does in an MBO program are:

a. _____

b. _____

c. _____

d. _____

42. When is MBO most effective?

43.　　What is the central idea behind MBO programs, and when do problems arise?

Learning Goal 8
Meeting Employee Expectations: Expectancy Theory

44.　　According to expectancy theory, what are three questions employees ask before exerting maximum effort to a task?

a. _____

b. _____

c. _____

45.　　What are the steps to improving employee performance, according to expectancy theory?

a. _____

b. _____

c. _____

d. _____

e. _____

Reinforcing Employee Performance: Reinforcement Theory

46.　　In the words of reinforcement theory, motivation is the result of _____

_____

47.　　Positive reinforcements are _____

Negative reinforcement includes _____

48.　　What is meant by the term "extinction", in reinforcement theory?

Treating Employees Fairly: Equity Theory

49.　　What are the basic principles of Equity theory?

50.   What do people do when they perceive an inequity?

51.   Equity judgments are based on _____

        Workers are going to feel rewards are inequitable when: _____

        _____

        Organizations deal with this by:_____

        The best remedy is: _____

Learning Goal 9
Building Teamwork through Open Communication

52.   How do open communication and self managed teams benefit companies?

53.   Procedures for encouraging open communication include:

        a. _____

        b. _____

        c. _____

        d. _____

54.   How can managers "re-invent work"?

55.   How will managers of tomorrow motivate workers?

56.   What makes motivating workers today more complicated?

57. How will generational differences between baby boomers and Generation X affect motivation?

58. According to the text, what type of management will Gen X managers provide?

59. Generation Yers tend to share the following characteristics:

   a. _____

   b. _____

   c. _____

   d. _____

   e. _____

60. These talents and tendencies dominate the Generation Yers:

   a. _____

   b. _____

   c. _____

   d. _____

   e. _____

   f. _____

   g. _____

CRITICAL THINKING EXERCISES

Learning Goal 1

1. Extrinsic and intrinsic rewards are important aspects of motivation for workers, as well as for students! Think about the job you currently hold, or a job you would like to have in the future, or alternatively, about your "job" as a student. Identify some of the extrinsic rewards that are specific to your job or to you as a student. What intrinsic rewards do you find in those jobs?

2.   Early management studies were conducted by:

Frederick Taylor - Scientific Management
Frank and Lillian Gilbreth - Motion economy
Elton Mayo – Hawthorne Experiments

Read the following and indicate which ideas are being described.

a. _____   Conducted a series of experiments designed to measure the effect of working conditions on worker productivity

b. _____   These studies became the basis for human-based management.

c. _____   Created time-motion studies to measure output over time.

d. _____   Discovered that worker productivity could increase despite adverse conditions.

e. _____   Believed the way to improve productivity was to scientifically study the most efficient ways to perform each task, determine the one "best way" to do things, then teach people those methods.

f. _____   The principle of motion economy was based on his theory.

g. _____   Developed the principle of scientific management.

h. _____   Discovered that when workers are involved in planning and decision-making, the workers are more motivated.

i. _____   Found that workers were motivated in an informal atmosphere where they could interact with supervisors.

j. _____   Believed people would be motivated primarily by money.

k. _____   Identified the tendency for people to behave differently when they know they are being studied.

l. _____   Developed the idea that every job could be broken down into a series of elementary motions, which could then be analyzed to make it more efficient.

m. _____   His findings lead to new assumptions about employees, including the idea that pay is not the only motivator for workers.

3.   How did Taylor and other proponents of Scientific Management view workers? How does that compare to Mayo's Hawthorne Studies?

Learning Goal 3

4.   The principle behind Maslow's ideas is that only unmet needs are motivators, and that needs could be arranged in a hierarchy. Complete the illustration shown below, and give two examples for each need level, where appropriate.

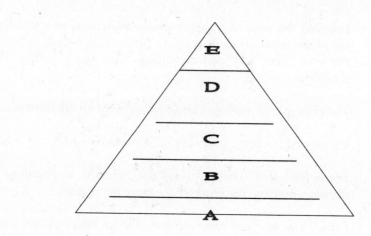

A._____   D._____

   1._____   1._____

   2._____   2._____

B._____   E._____

   1._____   1._____

   2._____   2._____

C._____

   1._____

   2._____

5. Read the following statements, and determine which need on Maslow's Hierarchy is being described.

a. _____ Ryan Raley gets home from school and immediately raids the refrigerator.

b. _____ Jan Stahl joins as many campus organizations as she can fit into her schedule.

c. _____ Bill Cook wins "Zone Manager of the Month" in his sales office, in recognition of his outstanding performance.

d. _____ Wendy Armstrong, a 33 year old student with severe cerebral palsy, receives her bachelor's degree, a lifelong dream.

e. _____ A union contract negotiator makes sure that layoffs will be made on the basis of seniority.

6. In developed countries, people seek to fill social, self-esteem, and self-actualization needs at work. Give two actions that a company or a manager could take to fill each of these higher level needs. What would motivate you?

a. Social

b. Self-esteem

c. Self-actualization

Learning Goal 4
7. Workers at Universal Industries are among the best paid in the industry. Their factories are clean and workers seem to get along well with one another. "The bosses are okay" one worker is quoted as saying, "but they sure do hang around us a lot". The union has made sure that everyone has a secure position. Management at Universal is aware that their competitive position is in jeopardy, as several foreign firms have been making inroads into their market. Management is also aware that while it doesn't seem that there are problems with the workers, they don't seem to be motivated. Using Herzberg's theory of motivators and hygiene factors, discuss what the problem may be and what could be done to solve it.

8.   Make your own personal ranking of the 14 job related factors listed in the text. Relate them to a job you have had, or currently have, to explain why you were or were not motivated!

1._____   8._____

2._____   9._____

3._____   10._____

4._____   11._____

5._____   12._____

6._____   13._____

7._____   14._____

Learning Goal 5
9.   Four job design strategies are:

            job enrichment   job enlargement
            job simplification   job rotation

Which of the following is being illustrated in each of the following examples?

a.   Employees at Published Image, a financial newsletter, are combined into a team so that one team has the entire responsibility of selling, writing, proofing, editing and distributing the newsletter to their own group of clients. While each member will specialize in a certain area, each member of the team knows enough about all the jobs to get the product out. _____

b.   New zone managers at Ford Motor Company move from one job to another during their training program, to familiarize themselves with the operations of the district sales office. _____

c.   At the Pasta House Company restaurant, you are either an expediter, a host, a busser or a server. The job lines don't cross, and are distinct from one another.
_____

d.   At the Hosin Manufacturing Company, production is such that each worker makes an entire motor, instead of working only on separate parts.
_____

10.   Keeping in mind the five characteristics of work important in affecting motivation and performance, design an "enriched" job for publishing campus newsletters or for another area with which you are familiar.

11.   McGregor observed that managers had two different attitudes toward workers, which led to different management styles. He called these styles Theory X and Theory Y.

        Which type of manager would make each of the following statements?

        a. _____   "Joe is pretty good at solving these kinds of problems. Let's get his input on this."

        b. _____   "Ann, I know you'd like that promotion. Keep up the good work and I think you'll be the next new product manager."

        c. _____   "Tell that secretary that if she values her job, she'll keep those coffee breaks down to 15 minutes!"

        d. _____   "I think that secretary takes long coffee breaks because she gets her work done so quickly and then doesn't have much to do. She's been asking about working on the new product project. I'll talk to her about it and see what she thinks."

        e. _____   "Ann, new product managers have to work a lot of weekends and evenings. If you think you want that job, you'll have to prove to me you're willing to work those extra hours."

        f. _____   "Joe you need to do exactly what I tell you to fix the problem in your department. This needs to be done my way!"

12.   Think back to Chapter 7, in which leadership styles are discussed. What kind of leadership style would a Theory X manager use most often? Theory Y? Why?

13.   Using the outline below, illustrate the relationship between Maslow, Herzberg and where McGregor's X and Y managers would fall.

        MASLOW   HERZBERG   MCGREGOR

14.   Things have really been happening at Sun-2-Shade, a company that manufactures self-darkening windshields. Lots of changes have been made and it would seem like things ought to be going smoothly. However, there are problems with the workers, and you just can't figure out what's wrong. People don't seem to be motivated, although they are being paid well. You have been in charge, made the decisions you thought were best for the company and the workers, and have even pitched in and shown people how you want things done from time to time. Everybody has their own job, and they know exactly how it's supposed to be done. You have heard some people complain that their job is boring, but you know that the way you have shown them is the best way to get things done. People come in late, and sometimes seem to actually resent your help! You would really like the employees of this company to feel like they are a team. How will you solve this problem?

Re-read your answer - Are you a Theory X or a Theory Y manager?

Learning Goal 7
15.   Review MBO programs described in the text. How do you think an MBO program fits into the ideas of Maslow and Herzberg? What are some potential problems with MBO?

Learning Goal 8
16.   Think about expectancy theory and how it works for you. What is something you really want? How likely is it that you can reach the goal? Will the hard work be worth the effort? For example:

What kind of job do you want as a career? (or, go back and review the exercise you completed in Chapter 7 on planning, when you were asked to write out some long range and short range goals for yourself)

What do you need to do to get that kind of job? Is it possible to get that job if you exert the effort?

What intrinsic and extrinsic benefits will you get from this kind of job?

17. You are a manager of entry-level workers in an office of about 15 people. You have an employee who is consistently late for work, as often as 2 times per week. This is a problem because this individual is responsible for answering phones from both internal and external customers, and he has often missed important phone calls. Using reinforcement theory, how would you try to solve the problem with this employee, whose work is excellent, when he is there? You don't want to fire this person, because it would be costly and difficult to replace him.

18. Hal Yard is in marketing with a major manufacturer of sailboats. He has been happy with his job since he started there 3 years ago. He has received several raises, and has always gotten very good reviews. He is in line for a good promotion, which he should know about soon. Hal recently went to lunch with a new co-worker, Donna Telli. Donna just got her degree at night school, and this is her first "real" job. During the course of their conversation, Donna mentioned her starting salary, which is only $50 per month lower than Hal's!

How would you feel if you were Hal? Why? What would you do? What theories of motivation may come into play here?

Learning Goal 9
19. If you are currently working, think about the ways that your company encourages, or discourages, open communication, particularly using the techniques described in the text. How does this affect the motivation of the employees? If you aren't working, ask the same questions of someone you know who is working.

PRACTICE TEST

MULTIPLE CHOICE – Circle the best answer

Learning Goal 1

1.   Time and motion studies, methods of work and rules of work were all part of the ideas of
_____.
        a.   Maslow's hierarchy of needs.
        b.   Herzberg's two-factor theory.
        c.   Taylor's scientific management.
        d.   The Hawthorne Experiments.

2.   Scientific Management viewed people largely as_____.
        a.   Machines that needed to be programmed.
        b.   Individuals who had specific needs that were filled at work.
        c.   Workers in groups who needed to be self managed.
        d.   Important contributors to management decision-making.

3.   Frederick Taylor believed the best way to improve worker productivity was to:
        a.   scientifically determine the most efficient way to perform a task and then teach people.
        b.   design jobs to be interesting and challenging.
        c.   determine people's needs at work and find ways to meet those needs.
        d.   give people the authority to make decisions.

Learning Goal 2

4.   Which of the following was not determined as part of the Hawthorne Experiments?
        a.   Workers enjoyed the atmosphere of their special room.
        b.   The workers thought of themselves as a social group.
        c.   It was not important to involve workers in the planning of the experiment.
        d.   Workers felt their ideas were respected.

5.   The tendency for people to behave differently when they know they're being studied is referred to as:
        a.   Maslow's Hierarchy
        b.   The Hawthorne effect
        c.   Motivating factors
        d.   Theory X

Learning Goal 3

6.   Which of the following is not included as one of Maslow's needs?
        a.   self-actualization
        b.   social
        c.   esteem
        d.   physical

7.   Harry Leggins has worked for Shavem Industries for a number of years. He has just been passed over for promotion, again, and is considering leaving his employer because it seems that his managers don't appreciate his abilities. The only problem is that he really likes his co-workers, and they have an undefeated softball team. Harry is concerned with filling:
       a.   esteem needs
       b.   social needs
       c.   self-actualization needs.
       d.   safety needs

8.   According to Maslow's theory, when a need is satisfied:
       a.   the need disappears, and will not re-appear.
       b.   another, higher level need emerges and motivates a person to satisfy that need.
       c.   it will continue to motivate a person, but not as strongly.
       d.   we are content, and will continue to work, but will only be motivated by more money.

Learning Goal 4
9.   According to Herzberg, workers felt that good pay and job security
       a.   are the most important motivators for most workers.
       b.   were important for participative management.
       c.   provided a sense of satisfaction, but did not motivate them.
       d.   were the best way to keep jobs interesting and to help them achieve their objectives.

10.   Herzberg's hygiene factors include:
       a.   achievement
       b.   salary
       c.   work itself
       d.   recognition

11.   Surveys conducted to test Herzberg's theories have supported his findings that:
       a.   money is the number one motivator.
       b.   motivation comes primarily from good working conditions.
       c.   the absence of good working conditions has little to no effect on job satisfaction.
       d.   the number one motivators are a sense of achievement and recognition for a job well done.

Learning Goal 5
12.   The strategy of making work interesting and motivating employees by moving them from one job to another is called:
       a.   job enlargement
       b.   job simplification
       c.   job rotation
       d.   job enrichment

13.   The degree to which a job has a substantial impact on the work of others in the company is called:
       a.   skill variety
       b.   task identity
       c.   autonomy
       d.   task significance

14. At the NOVA car manufacturing company, workers are grouped into self- managed teams, which are responsible for completing a significant portion of the automobile. Unlike the typical assembly plant, the car stops along the way, and the team completes their portion of the car before the vehicle moves on. The team is given the freedom to decide who does which job, and they receive constant feedback from the company. NOVA is using a job strategy of:
   a.   job rotation
   b.   job enlargement
   c.   job enrichment
   d.   job simplification

Learning Goal 6
15. At Flo Valley Manufacturing workers are encouraged to find their own solutions to problems, and to implement their solutions when practical. They work with little supervision because management feels they are committed workers, and that the workers are pretty creative. Flo Valley reflects a(n) _____ attitude about workers.
   a.   Theory X
   b.   autocratic
   c.   scientific
   d.   Theory Y

16. _____emphasizes life time employment, collective decision making and individual responsibility for the outcome of decisions.
   a.   Theory Z
   b.   Theory X
   c.   Theory Y
   d.   Theory M

17. Douglas McGregor believed that managers with a Theory X attitude believed:
   a.   workers prefer to be directed.
   b.   people seek responsibility.
   c.   people will use imagination in problem solving.
   d.   workers like work.

Learning Goal 7
18. According to the text, setting ambitious but attainable goals can motivate workers and improve performance if:
   a.   people know what is expected of them.
   b.   the goals are not too ambitious.
   c.   the goals are accepted.
   d.   there is a definite time frame for completing the goals.

19. The central idea of MBO is that:
   a.   managers need to set realistic goals for employees.
   b.   employees need to motivate themselves.
   c.   job satisfaction comes from the ability to learn new skills
   d.   employees must be closely supervised, and giving them goals will help to achieve that.

20. Which of the following is not one of the questions employees will ask themselves before committing a maximum effort toward a task?
    a. Can I accomplish this task?
    b. Is the reward worth the effort?
    c. Will the task include negative feedback?
    d. If I do accomplish the task, what is the reward?

21. Reinforcement theory is based on the idea that:
    a. positive and negative reinforcers motivate a person to behave a certain way.
    b. perceptions of fairness and how those perceptions affect employees' willingness to perform.
    c. the way managers go about motivating people at work depends on their attitudes toward workers.
    d. attainable goals will lead to high levels of motivation under certain conditions.

22. According to equity theory, when workers perceive an inequity, they will
    a. try to reestablish an equitable feeling in a number of ways.
    b. always reduce their efforts in the future.
    c. always increase their effort in the future.
    d. generally be mistaken in their perceptions.

Learning Goal 9
23. According to the text, companies with highly motivated workers usually have
    a. high pay scales and good benefits.
    b. good managers who tell employees exactly what to do and how to do it.
    c. open communication systems and self-managed teams.
    d. autocratic leadership and bureaucratic structures.

24. To create an atmosphere of "us working together" and encourage open communication, managers should do everything but:
    a. provide feedback.
    b. eliminate separate facilities for managers.
    c. develop precise job descriptions so that everyone knows what to do.
    d. reward all upward communication, even if the discussion is negative.

25. Generation X managers:
    a. may tend to focus more on results than on hours in the workplace.
    b. will tend to be inflexible
    c. will have narrower viewpoints than their predecessors
    d. will most likely closely supervise their workers, especially the Generation Y workers.

TRUE-FALSE

Learning Goal 1
1. _____ The satisfaction you feel when you have finished a term paper and done a good job is an example of an extrinsic reward.

2. _____ Frank and Lillian Gilbreth developed the principle of motion economy and therbligs.

3. _____ The ideas of Frederick Taylor and Scientific Management were good for their time, but are no longer being implemented in today's workplace.

Learning Goal 2
4. _____ The problem with the initial experiments of the Hawthorne Study was that the productivity of the experimental group actually decreased when lighting was changed.

5. _____ The Hawthorne Experiments led to new assumptions about workers, including that pay was not the only motivator.

6. _____ One of the conclusions of the Hawthorne Experiments was that workers were more motivated because the felt their ideas were respected and that they were involved in decision making.

Learning Goal 3
7. _____ According to Maslow, satisfied needs will continue to motivate most individuals.

8. _____ Self-actualization needs on Maslow's Hierarchy refer to the need for recognition, acknowledgement and self respect.

Learning Goal 4
9. _____ Herzberg's research results showed that the most important factors that motivate workers were a sense of achievement and earned recognition

10. _____ Pay is included in the list of Herzberg's motivators.

Learning Goal 5
11. _____ Job enrichment strategy is one in which work is assigned to individuals so that they have the opportunity to complete an identifiable task from beginning to end.

12. _____ A type of job enrichment is job enlargement, which combines a series of tasks into one challenging and interesting assignment.

Learning Goal 6
13. _____ A Theory Y manager believes that employees should be involved in both defining problems and in designing the solutions.

14. _____ Today, fierce competition is forcing Japanese companies to move away from their traditional ways of conducting business.

Learning Goal 7
15. _____ Goal-setting theory is based on the notion that workers will be more motivated if they know they have a goal in terms of the amount of money they will earn if they do a certain amount of work.

16. _____ The best way to implement MBO programs is to make sure that managers set goals in cooperation with everyone in the organization.

Learning Goal 8
17. _____ In reinforcement theory positive reinforcements are rewards such as praise, recognition, or a pay raise.

18. ____ The basic principle of expectancy theory is that workers try to maintain equity when they compare what they expect to gain to people in similar situations.

Learning Goal 9
19. ____ The concept of re-inventing work involves respecting workers, rewarding good work, developing worker skills and decentralizing authority.

20. ____ One procedure for encouraging open communication in an organization is to create a culture that rewards listening.

You Can Find It On the Net

Visit the web site www.accel-team.com/motivation   What motivation theories that have been discussed in this chapter can you identify from these pages?

How does what is noted compare to what is discussed in your text?

What is the "take" on money as a motivator?

How does the article indicate job design can be used to motivate?

What is meant by the "self-fulfilling prophecy"? Can you give any personal examples of how this has been in effect in your work life?

Sometimes we wonder what companies can do to create a motivated workforce in the "real world". Go to the Fortune Magazine web site www.fortune.com . Link to the magazine's list of America's Most Admired Companies, the top 100 companies to work for in the United States and look through the articles that you are able to link to. What do you think makes the companies listed good places to work?
(If you are unable to access this link at home, you may go to your school or public library, and they should have the proper passwords or subscriber access).

ANSWERS

LEARNING THE LANGUAGE

1. Hygiene factors	7. Extrinsic reward	13. Expectancy theory
2. Reinforcement theory	8. Job enrichment	14. Scientific management
3. Time-motion studies	9. Motivators	15. Equity theory
4. Intrinsic reward	10. Goal setting theory	16. Principle of motion economy
5. Management by objectives (MBO)	11. Hawthorne effect	17. Maslow's hierarchy of needs
6. Job enlargement	12. Job rotation	

ASSESSMENT CHECK

Learning Goal 1
The Importance of Motivation

1. Frederick Taylor is known as the Father of Scientific Management. His goal was to increase worker productivity so that both the firm and the worker could benefit from higher earnings.

2. The way to improve productivity according to Taylor was to
   a.   scientifically study the most efficient way to do things
   b.   determine the one best way
   c.   teach people those methods

3. Three elements basic to Taylor's approach are:
   a. time   b. methods   c. rules of work

4. Gantt is known for charts which managers use to plot the work of employees a day in advance down to the smallest detail.

5. Frank and Lillian Gilbreth used Taylor's ideas to develop the principle of motion economy, which showed that every job could be broken down into a series of elementary motions called a therblig.

6. Scientific management viewed people largely as machines that needed to be programmed. There was little concern for psychological or human aspects of work.

7. Today, some of Taylor's ideas are still being implemented. Some companies still place more emphasis on conformity to work rules than on creativity, flexibility, and responsiveness. UPS is a modern example of Scientific Management at work today.

Learning Goal 2
Elton Mayo and The Hawthorne Studies

8. Elton Mayo and his colleagues wanted to test the degree of lighting associated with optimum productivity, a traditional scientific management study.

The problem with the initial experiments was that productivity of the experimental group compared to other workers doing the same job went up regardless of whether the lighting was bright or dim.

9.   The second series of experiments added a number of other environmental factors to the experiment, such as temperature and humidity. Productivity went up with each experiment. No matter what the experimenters did, productivity went up thus proving the initial ideas were invalid.

10.   Three conclusions drawn from the Hawthorne Experiments are:
       a.   People in work groups think of themselves as a social group.
       b.   Involving employees in decision-making motivates them.
       c.   Job satisfaction increases with a friendly atmosphere and additional compensation.

11.   The Hawthorne Effect refers to the tendency of people to behave differently when they know they're being studied.

12.   After the Hawthorne Experiments, the emphasis of research shifted away from Taylor's scientific management to a new human-based management. Mayo's findings led to new assumptions about employees, and found that money was a relatively ineffective motivator. That change led to many theories about the human side of management.

Learning goal 3
Motivation and Maslow's Hierarchy of Needs

13.   According to Maslow, people are motivated to satisfy unmet needs. Needs that have been satisfied no longer provide motivation. Needs are placed in order of importance, a hierarchy.

14.   The five need levels on Maslow's Hierarchy are:
       a. Physiological - basic survival needs, such as the need for food, water and shelter
       b. Safety – the need to feel secure at work and at home
       c. Social – the need to feel loved, accepted and part of a group
       d. Esteem - the need for recognition and acknowledgement from others, self respect and
                  sense of status or importance
       e. Self-actualization - the need to develop one's fullest potential

15.   Maslow believed that people are motivated to satisfy unmet needs. When one need is satisfied another, higher level need emerges, and a person will attempt to satisfy that need. Needs that have been satisfied do not provide motivation

16.   In many parts of the world, workers struggle to meet the basic needs, such as the physiological and safety needs. In countries such as the United States, lower level needs do not dominate, and workers seek to satisfy higher level needs such as social, esteem and self actualization.

       To compete successfully, U.S. firms must create a work environment that motivates the best and brightest workers. This means establishing a work environment that includes goals such as social contribution, honesty, reliability, service, quality, dependability, and unity.

17.   Herzberg's research found that the most important factors that motivated workers are:

    a. sense of achievement   h. pay
    b. earned recognition   i. supervisor's fairness
    c. interest in the work   j. company policies and rules
    d. opportunity for growth   k. status
    e. opportunity for advancement   l. job security
    f. importance of responsibility   m. supervisor's friendliness
    g. peer and group relationships   n. working conditions

18.   Herzberg noted that the factors that motivated workers clustered around job content. Workers like to feel that they contribute. They want to earn recognition and feel their jobs are important. They want responsibility and want recognition for that responsibility by having a chance for growth and advancement. They also want their jobs to be interesting.

Herzberg also noted that factors having to do with job environment were not considered motivators by workers. This includes pay, which workers feel gives them a sense of satisfaction, but does not motivate.

19.   Herzberg's motivators had to do with job content, and caused employees to be productive and gave them satisfaction. Hygiene factors (or maintenance factors) had to do with job environment, and could cause dissatisfaction if missing, but would not motivate employees if these factors were increased.

20.   Herzberg's motivators are:
    a. The work itself
    b. Achievement
    c. Recognition
    d. Responsibility
    e. Growth and advancement

21.   Hygiene factors are:
    a. Company policy and administration
    b. Supervision
    c. Working conditions
    d. Interpersonal relations
    e. Salary

22.   The best way to motivate employees is to make the job interesting, help them to achieve their objectives, and recognize that achievement through advancement and added responsibility.

23.   Surveys have supported Herzberg's finding that the number one motivator is not money but a sense of achievement and recognition for a job well done.

The reason for this may be that organizations review an employee's performance only once a year and give raises at that time. To motivate employees, their accomplishments must be recognized more often than once a year.

Learning Goal 5
Job Enrichment

24.   In a job enrichment strategy, work is assigned to individuals so that they have the opportunity to complete an identifiable task from beginning to end. They are held responsible for successful completion of the task.

        The motivational effect of job enrichment can come from the opportunities for personal achievement, challenge, and recognition.

25.   The characteristics of work important in affecting individual motivation and performance are:
        a. Skill variety -   The extent to which a job demands different skills
        b. Task identity -   The degree to which the job requires doing a task with a visible outcome from beginning to end.
        c. Task significance -   The degree to which the job has a substantial impact on the lives or work of others in the company
        d. Autonomy -   The degree of freedom, independence, and discretion in scheduling work and determining procedures.
        e. Feedback -   The amount of direct and clear information that is received about job performance

26.   Job simplification produces task efficiency by breaking down a job into simple steps and assigning people to each of those steps.

27.   Job enlargement combines a series of tasks into one assignment that is more challenging, interesting, and motivating. Job rotation also makes work more interesting, but does so by moving employees from one job to another.

Learning Goal 6
McGregor's Theory X and Theory Y

28.   The assumptions of a Theory X manager are:
        a.   The average person dislikes work and will avoid it if possible.
        b.   The average person must be forced, controlled, directed or threatened with punishment to make them work.
        c.   The average worker prefers to be directed, wants to avoid responsibility, has little ambition and wants security.
        d.   Primary motivators are money and fear.

29.   As a result of his or her attitudes, a Theory X manager will watch people closely, telling them what to do and how to do it. Motivation will take the form of punishment for bad work, rather than reward for good work. Workers are given little responsibility, authority, or flexibility.

30.   The assumptions of a Theory Y manager are:
        a.   The average person likes work, and feels it is as natural as play or rest.
        b.   The average person naturally works toward goals to which they are committed.
        c.   How committed a person is to goals depends on the rewards for achieving them.
        d.   Under certain conditions, the average person accepts and seeks responsibility.
        e.   People are capable of creativity, cleverness, and imagination.
        f.   The average person's intellectual potential is only partially used in industry.
        g.   People are motivated by a variety of rewards, unique to each worker.

31.   A Theory Y manager will emphasize a relaxed atmosphere, in which workers are free to set objectives, be creative, be flexible, and go beyond the goals set by management. A key factor in this environment is empowerment.

32.   Empowerment gives employees the ability to make decisions and the tools to implement the decisions they make.

33.   For empowerment to be a motivator, management should:
      a.   Find out what problems people think are in the organization.
      b.   Let them design the solutions
      c.   Get out of the way and let them put the solutions into action

34.   The trend today is toward a Theory Y management style. One reason for this is that many service industries are finding Theory Y is better for dealing with on the spot customer problems.

      Another reason for companies to adopt a more flexible managerial style is to meet competition from foreign firms.

35.   The American management approach, or Type A involves:
      a.   short term employment   e.   explicit control mechanisms
      b.   individual decision making   f.   specialized career paths
      c.   individual responsibility   g.   segmented concern for
      d.   rapid evaluation and promotion   employees

36.   The elements of Type J management include:
      a.   life-time employment   e.   informal control mechanisms
      b.   consensus decision making   f.   nonspecialized career paths
      c.   collective responsibility   g.   holistic concern for employees
      d.   slow evaluation and promotion

37.   Theory Z blends the characteristics of Type J and Type A. This approach involves long-term employment, collective decision-making, individual responsibility for the outcome of decisions, slow evaluation and promotion, moderately specialized career paths, and a holistic concern for the employee, including the family. Theory Z emphasizes participative decision-making and views the organization as a family that fosters cooperation and organizational values.

38.   Economic decline, demographic and social changes, and fierce global competition are forcing Japanese managers to reevaluate the way they conduct business. Japanese managers and firms need more dynamic ways to become more efficient in order to compete more effectively in today's changing global economy. Many managers think that too much conformity has hurt Japanese business.

39.   According to the text, the appropriate management style is one that fits the culture, the situation, and the specific needs of the organization.

Goal-Setting Theory and Management by Objectives

40.   Goals can motivate workers and improve performance if the goals are:
    a.   accepted
    b.   accompanied by feedback
    c.   facilitated by organizational conditions.

41.   The four things a manager does in an MBO program are:
    a.   Set goals in cooperation with everyone in the organization
    b.   Commit employees to the goals
    c.   Monitor results
    d.   Reward accomplishments

42.   MBO is most effective in relatively stable situations where long-range plans can be made and implemented with little need for major changes

43.   The central idea behind MBO programs is that employees need to motivate themselves. Problems arise when management uses MBO to force managers and workers to commit to goals that are not mutually agreed upon, but are instead set by top management.

Learning Goal 8
Meeting Employee Expectations: Expectancy Theory

44.   Before exerting maximum effort employees will ask:
    a.   Can I accomplish the task?
    b.   If I do accomplish it, what's my reward?
    c.   Is the reward worth the effort?

45.   To improve employee performance, managers should:
    a.   Determine what rewards are valued by employees
    b.   Determine the employee's desired performance standard
    c.   Ensure performance standards are attainable
    d.   Guarantee rewards are tied to performance
    e.   Be certain rewards are considered adequate

Reinforcing Employee Performance: Reinforcement Theory

46.   In the words of reinforcement theory, motivation is the result of the carrot-and-stick approach, reward and punishment. Individuals act to receive rewards and avoid punishment.

47.   Positive reinforcements are rewards such as praise, recognition, or a pay raise.

    Negative reinforcement includes reprimands, reduced pay, layoff or firing.

48.   Extinction is what happens when a manager tries to stop undesirable behavior by not responding to it. The hope is that the unwanted behavior will eventually become extinct.

Treating Employees Fairly: Equity Theory

49.   Equity theory has to do with perceptions of fairness and how those perceptions affect employees' willingness to perform. The basic principle is that workers try to maintain equity between inputs and outputs compared to people in similar positions. It is based on the perceptions of fairness and how those perceptions affect employees' willingness to perform.

50.   When workers perceive an inequity, they will try to make the situation more equitable. They may change their behavior or rationalize the situation in some way.

51.   Equity judgments are based on perceptions.

Workers are going to feel rewards are inequitable when they overestimate their own contributions, as happens often. So they will feel that any rewards given out for performance are inequitable.
Organizations try to deal with this by keeping salaries secret, but that can make things worse.

The best remedy is clear and frequent communication.

Learning Goal 9
Building Teamwork through Open Communication

52.   Companies which have established open communication and self-managed teams have highly motivated work forces. Open communication helps mangers and team members understand objectives and work to achieve them. Teams create an environment in which learning happens at the peer level, which is the level at which people have an interest in helping each other along. Empowerment works when people share knowledge.

53.   Procedures for encouraging open communication include:
   a.   Create an organizational culture that rewards listening by creating places for employees to talk, and by providing feedback, adopting employee suggestions and rewarding upward communication.
   b.   Train supervisors and managers to listen
   c.   Remove barriers to open communication such as separate facilities for management.
   d.   Take efforts to facilitate open communication, with large tables in lunch areas, conference rooms, picnics, company athletic teams and so on.

54.   Re-inventing work means companies must focus on respecting workers, providing interesting work, rewarding good work, developing workers' skills, allowing autonomy, decentralizing authority and behaving ethically toward all employees.

55.   The managers of tomorrow will not be able to use any one formula for all employees. Instead, they will have to get to know each worker personally and tailor the motivational effort to the individual. This is true because different employees respond to different managerial and motivational styles.

56.   Motivating workers is made more complicated by the increase in global business and the fact that managers now work with employees from many different cultures and from different generations. Different cultures and members of different generations experience motivational approaches differently.

57. Baby boomer managers will need to learn to be flexible with their Generation X employees, or risk losing them. Generation X employees will need to use their enthusiasm for change and streamlining to their advantage.

58. Gen X managers will understand that there is more to life than work, and they may tend to focus more on results than on hours in the workplace. They will be flexible and good at collaboration and consensus building. They will have a broader perspective than earlier generations because they have been exposed to many different kinds of problems through the media. They may tend to have a great impact on team members because they will likely give the people working for them the goals and the parameters of the project and then leave them alone to do their work. Their best asset might be their ability to give their employees positive feedback.

59. Generation Yers tend to share the following characteristics:
    a. impatient
    b. skeptical
    c. blunt and expressive
    d. image driven
    e. inexperienced

60. These talents and tendencies dominate the Generation Yers.
    a. adaptable
    b. tech savvy
    c. able to grasp new concepts
    d. multi-taskers
    e. efficient
    f. tolerant
    g. have a sense of commitment

CRITICAL THINKING EXERCISES

Learning Goal 1
1. Of course your answer will be specific to your personality. Some extrinsic rewards for you could be pay, but other others might be, for example, a chance to play on a softball team with a group of co-workers you enjoy.

Learning Goals 1,2

2.				
a.	Elton Mayo - Hawthorne experiments	h.	Hawthorne experiments
b.	Hawthorne studies	i.	Hawthorne experiments
c.	Taylor	j.	Taylor
d.	Hawthorne studies	k.	Hawthorne experiments
e.	Taylor	l.	Gilbreth
f.	Gilbreth	m.	Hawthorne experiments
g.	Taylor		

3. Taylor and the other proponents of scientific management viewed people largely as machines which, properly programmed, could perform at a high level of effectiveness. Time and motion specialists studied every move a worker made, and standardized every motion. The most important tools were a stopwatch and observation.

Although the Hawthorne studies grew out of Taylor's research, they came to a very different conclusion. Mayo began by studying environmental effects on worker productivity, with the idea of determining the degree of lighting associated with optimum productivity. When productivity increased regardless of the amount of illumination, a second series of experiments was conducted. When those experiments had similar results, Mayo guessed that some human or psychological factor was involved. When workers were interviewed about their feelings Mayo recognized that people were motivated at work by a relaxed atmosphere, being involved in decision-making, and by being in a social group as well as by additional compensation.

The Hawthorne Studies, then, recognized the human and psychological factors that impact worker productivity. This was different from scientific management, which ignored the human aspect of work.

The intrinsic rewards you could get as a student, for example could he satisfaction from completing a paper, or the sense of camaraderie from playing on your school's softball team.

Learning Goal 3

4. A. Physiological
        1. Food
        2. Rest
    B. Safety
        1. Locks on your doors
        2. Job security
    C. Social
        1. Belonging to a club
        2. Family life

    D. Self-esteem
        1. Winning an award
        2. Getting a desired promotion
    E. Self-actualization
        1. Accomplishing a goal
        2. Getting an "A" in a difficult class

5. a. Physiological
    b. Social
    c. Self-esteem

    d. Self-actualization
    e. Safety

6. a. To fill social needs companies could sponsor baseball teams, hold picnics, and implement self-managed work teams
    b. Esteem needs can be met by recognition programs, recognizing an employee's achievement in a company newsletter, allowing employees to participate in decision-making
    c. To help fill self-actualization needs, companies could offer tuition assistance programs, provide job training, allow people to set their own goals, implement self-managed work teams, provide appropriate rewards for accomplishing objectives.

Learning Goal 4

7. From Herzberg's perspective, it looks like management and the union both have been concentrating on hygiene factors, while ignoring those factors that would motivate workers to greater productivity. The workers are apparently satisfied, as there are no problems, according to management. This means that the workers are content with pay, supervision, working conditions and interpersonal relations, as is indicated throughout the story. If management wants motivated workers, they should continue what they are doing now, but also find ways to give workers a sense of achievement, make the work more interesting, give workers more responsibility, a chance for growth and advancement. According to Herzberg, these are factors which will motivate workers.

8. The way you have ranked the 14 job-related factors Herzberg researched will be unique to you. Look, however, to see which type of things you ranked near the top, and near the bottom. Are motivators more important to you? or, did you focus on those factors Herzberg listed as hygiene factors? If the motivators ranked highest, you may want to look at firms that are using the "new" approach to management. If hygiene factors ranked highest, you may be happier in a more traditional organizational setting.

Learning Goal 5

9. a. job enrichment   c. job simplification
    b. job rotation   d. job enlargement

10. An "enriched" job would include skill variety, task identity, task significance, autonomy and feedback. For publishing a newsletter, you could create self-managed teams, with each team member trained to do all the jobs necessary to get the newsletter out on deadline: editing, proofing, research, layout, selling advertising, fielding questions. The team members will be responsible for deciding which member will do what job, what the deadline needs to be, how to coordinate with the other teams, and will evaluate their own performance. This meets all the criteria identified

Learning Goal 6

11. a. Y   d. Y
    b. Y   e. Y
    c. X   f. X

12. A Theory X manager would most likely use an autocratic style of leadership. When a manager believes that workers prefer to be told what to do, and do not want to assume responsibility, they are not likely to involve workers in decision making. A Theory X manager will make decisions, then announce the decision to his/her workers.

    A Theory Y manager is more likely to use a more democratic or participative leadership style. Employee input will be important to a Y manager, who believes that people are creative and seek responsibility. In essence Theory Y empowers employees to reach their potential. A Theory Y manager may also lean toward a laissez-faire leadership style.

13. Comparing Maslow, Herzberg and McGregor

MASLOW	HERZBERG	MCGREGOR
	Motivators	
self-actualization	challenge	Theory Y
	work itself	Participative management
self-esteem	achievement	style
	recognition	
	responsibility	
	growth	
	Hygiene	
social	interpersonal relations	
safety	company policy	Theory X
	supervision	Autocratic management
	working conditions	style
physiological	salary	

14. How you would solve these problems is really up to you. It's a matter of personal style. However, there are some suggestions. You may want to sit down with these people and find out exactly what <u>they</u> think the problem is, or even if they recognize that there is a problem. It will help to listen to them, ask for their suggestions about how to solve the problems and implement those suggestions.

It sounds like you have been making most of the decisions yourself, and not generally trusting these workers to be responsible. In other words, sounds like you have used a Theory X approach focusing on Herzberg's hygiene factors as a way to increase productivity. This may be appropriate in some instances, but you recall from previous chapters that these are the "new breed" of workers, who may prefer less direction and "bossing" and more "coaching". You can act as a resource, teaching, guiding and recommending, but not actively participating in doing work. Allow them to decide the most appropriate way of designing their jobs. Programs such as job enlargement may be appropriate, or job rotation. You may also consider self-managed teams. Many of the programs and theories described in this chapter may provide the solution to your problems.

Learning Goal 7

15. MBO programs could fill upper level needs on Maslow's hierarchy and serve as motivators in Herzberg's terms, by giving workers responsibility, a chance for growth and helping them to meet their own personal goals. Involvement of employees in setting goals is a key because it focuses on the participative management aspects of MBO, which is the type of leadership or management style these theories support. This motivates employees by making them feel part of the team.

Potential problems with MBO programs often stem from the way the programs are implemented. The important element of employee involvement is lost when management uses MBO as a strategy for forcing managers and workers to commit to goals that are not mutually agreed on, but set by top management

Learning Goal 8

16. The answer to this question will depend on what your goals are, and how hard you are willing to work to reach them. The level of motivation you feel will be determined, according to expectancy theory, by how strongly you value what you say your goals are, and whether or not you feel like you can "make the grade", or get the kind of job you want. And lastly, in the end, your level of motivation will be determined by whether or not you feel that the effort would actually be worth it.

17. In reinforcement theory you have a number of options available to solve the problem with this employee. You could reprimand the employee for being late and threaten pay reduction if he continues to be late. That would be "punishment". You could publicly praise him when he shows up on time, which is using positive reinforcement, and withhold the praise when he is late, a form of extinction. The strategy you use will depend on your style.

18. If you were Hal, you may feel like there is an inequity in your level of compensation compared to Donna's. This is equity theory at work! After all, she is new, and you have been a good employee for three years. What you would do will depend upon your own view of how big the inequity is. You may choose to talk to your boss, work harder to get promoted and recognized, work a little less for a while, rationalize the inequity in some way, or take the afternoon off! This could involve Maslow's Hierarchy, and Herzberg's theories in addition to equity theory.

286

19.   In the end, it is really the individual that motivates him or herself. The manager's job is to understand that all workers are different and respond to different motivational styles. Managers will have to get to know each worker as an individual and fit the "reward" to each individual. Rewards will come from the job itself, rather than from external rewards. Managers need to give workers what they need to do a good job: the right tools, the right information and the right amount of cooperation.

PRACTICE TEST

MULTIPLE CHOICE

LG 1	#1-3	
LG 2	#4-5	
LG 3	#6-8	
LG 4	#9-11	
LG 5	#12-14	
LG 6	#15-17	
LG 7	#18-19	
LG 8	#20-22	
LG 9	#23-25	

1.	c	14.	b
2.	a	15.	d
3.	a	16.	a
4.	c	17.	a
5.	b	18.	c
6.	d	19.	b
7.	a	20.	c
8.	b	21.	a
9.	c	22.	a
10.	b	23.	c
11.	d	24.	c
12.	c	25.	a
13.	d		

TRUE-FALSE

LG 1	#1-3	
LG 2	# 4-6	
LG 3	#7-8	
LG 4	#9-10	
LG 5	#11-12	
LG 6	# 13-14	
LG 7	# 15-16	
LG 8	#17-18	
LG 9	#19-20	

1.	F	11.	T
2.	T	12.	T
3.	F	13.	T
4.	F	14.	T
5.	T	15.	F
6.	T	16.	T
7.	F	17.	T
8.	F	18.	F
9.	T	19.	T
10.	F	20.	T

CHAPTER 11 – HUMAN RESOURCE MANAGEMENT: FINDING AND KEEPING THE BEST EMPLOYEES

LEARNING GOALS

After you have read and studied this chapter, you should be able to:

1. Explain the importance of human resource management and describe current issues in managing human resources.
2. Summarize the five steps in planning human resources
3. Describe methods companies use to recruit new employees and explain some of the issues that make recruitment challenging
4. Outline the six steps in selecting employees.
5. Illustrate the use of various types of employee training and development methods.
6. Trace the six steps in appraising employee performance.
7. Summarize the objectives of employee compensation programs and describe various pay systems and fringe benefits.
8. Explain scheduling plans managers use to adjust to workers' needs.
9. Describe the ways employees can move through a company: promotion, reassignment, termination, and retirement.
10. Illustrate the effects of legislation on human resource management.

LEARNING THE LANGUAGE

Listed below are important terms found in the chapter. Choose the correct term for the definition and write it in the space provided.

Affirmative action	Human resource management	Off-the-job training
Apprentice programs	Job analysis	On-the-job training
Cafeteria-style fringe benefits	Job description	Online training
Compressed workweek	Job sharing	Performance appraisal
Contingent workers	Job simulation	Recruitment
Core time	Job specifications	Reverse discrimination
Employee orientation	Management development	Selection
Flextime plan	Mentor	Training and development
Fringe benefits	Networking	Vestibule training

1. The set of activities called _____ are used to obtain a sufficient number of the right people at the right time.

2. The written summary of the minimum qualifications required of a worker to do a particular job is called the _____.

3. A work schedule known as _____ gives employees some freedom to choose when to work, as long as they work the required number of hours.

4. Employment activities designed to "right past wrongs "by increasing opportunities for minorities and women are known as _____.

5.   Training programs known as _____ involve a period during which a learner works alongside an experienced employee to master the skills and procedures of a craft.

6.   The process of _____ is the training and educating of employees to become good managers and then monitoring the progress of their managerial skills over time.

7.   Known as _____ these include sick-leave pay, vacation pay, pension plans, and health plans that represent additional compensation to employees beyond base wages.

8.   Discrimination against whites or males in hiring or promoting is called _____.

9.   An experienced employee known as a(n) _____ is one who supervises, coaches and guides lower-level employees by introducing them to the right people and generally acts as their organizational sponsor.

10.   The process of determining human resource needs is called _____, and involves recruiting, selecting, developing, motivating, evaluating, compensating, and scheduling employees to achieve organizational goals.

11.   A _____ is a work schedule that allows an employee to work a full number of hours per week but in fewer days.

12.   A _____ is a study of what is done by employees who hold various job titles.

13.   The process of _____ involves establishing and maintaining contacts with key managers in one's own organization and other organizations and using those contacts to weave strong relationships that serve as informal development systems.

14.   The process of gathering information and deciding whom should be hired, under legal guidelines, for the best interests of the individual and the organization is known as _____.

15.   A training program known as _____ occurs away from the workplace and consists of internal and external programs to develop a variety of skills or to foster personal development.

16.   A _____ is a summary of the objectives of a job, the type of work to be done, the responsibilities and duties, the working conditions and the relationship of the job to other functions.

17.   The _____ refers to the period when all employees are expected to be at their job stations.

18.   An arrangement known as _____ is one whereby two part-time employees share one full-time job.

19.   The program known as _____ is one where the employee immediately begins his or her tasks and learns by doing, or watches others for a while and them imitates them, all right at the workplace.

20.	_____ includes all attempts to improve employee performance by increasing an employee's ability to perform. It focuses on short term skills.

21.	The activity known as _____ introduces new employees to the organization; to fellow employees; to their immediate supervisors; and to the policies, practices and objectives of the firm.

22.	A _____ is an evaluation in which the performance level of employees is measured against established standards to make decisions about promotions, compensation, additional training or firing.

23.	A type of training known as _____ is done in schools where employees are taught on equipment similar to that used on the job.

24.	A program called _____ is a fringe benefits plan that allows employees to choose the benefits they want up to a certain dollar amount.

25.	A training method that uses equipment that duplicates job conditions and tasks so that trainees can learn skills before attempting them on the job is _____.

26.	Workers known as _____ do not have the expectation of regular, full-time employment.

27.	_____ is a program in which employees "attend' classes via the Internet.

ASSESSMENT CHECK

Learning Goal 1
Working with People is Just the Beginning

1.	Identify the functions of human resource management.

a. _____	e. _____

b. _____	f. _____

c. _____	g. _____

d. _____	h. _____

2.	Why has human resource management received increased attention in recent years, and how has it changed?

3.   What challenges are facing the human resources area?

        a._____

        b._____

        c._____

        d._____

        e._____

        f._____

        g._____

        h._____

        i._____

        j._____

        k._____

        l._____

Learning Goal 2
Determining Your Human Resources Needs

4.   List the steps in human resource planning

        a._____   d._____

        b._____   e._____

        c._____

5.   What information is included in a human resources inventory?

6.   What's the difference between a job description and job specifications?

7.   What affects future demand for employees?

8.   How will future supply of employees change?

9.   What information must be addressed in a human resources strategic plan?

Learning Goal 3
Recruiting Employees from a Diverse Population

10.   What has made recruiting more difficult?

a. _____

b. _____

c. _____

11.   Five methods of internal recruiting include:

a. _____

b. _____

c. _____

d. _____

e. _____

12.   What are the benefits of recruiting from within?

a. _____

b. _____

13. Your text lists 21 sources of external recruiting. What are seven of them?

a._____

b._____

c._____

d._____

e._____

f._____

g._____

14. Newer tools for recruiting employees include _____

Learning Goal 4
Selecting Employees Who Will Be Productive

15. List the six steps in selecting employees

a._____

b._____

c._____

d._____

e._____

f._____

16. How do legal guidelines affect the application form and process?

17. Describe "Smart Assessment". What benefits does it provide?

18. What do employment tests measure? What is the important element of employment tests?

19. What is the importance of a background check?

20. How do states vary in their requirements regarding employment or preemployment physical exams?

21. What is the benefit to the firm of a trial, or probationary, period?

22. What are the reasons that firms hire contingent workers?

23. What are the positives and negatives of being a contingent worker?

Learning Goal 5
Training and Developing Employees for Optimum Performance

24. What is the difference between training and development?

25. What are three steps taken in the process of creating training and development programs?

    a._____

    b._____

    c._____

26. Describe an employee orientation program.

27. When is on-the- job training effective? How have intranets affected on-the-job training programs?

28. What types of jobs would you train for in an apprenticeship? What job classification comes after apprenticeship? How will apprenticeship programs change?

29. Off-the-job training is expanding to include what other types of training?

30. What are the benefits of online, or distance training?

31. How does job simulation differ from vestibule training and when would this type of training be used?

32. Describe these types of management development programs:

    On-the-job coaching:

    Understudy positions:

    Job rotation:

    Off-the-job courses and training:

33.   What are three reasons for companies to develop mentoring and networking programs for women and minorities in the workplace?

a. _____

b. _____

c. _____

Learning Goal 6
Appraising Employee Performance to get Optimum Results

34.   What kinds of decisions are based upon a performance appraisal?

35.   What are the steps followed in a performance appraisal?

a. _____

b. _____

c. _____

d. _____

e. _____

f. _____

36.   Performance standards must be:

a. _____

b. _____

c. _____

37.   Describe the 360-degree review type of performance appraisal.

Learning Goal 7
Compensating Employees: Attracting and Keeping the Best

38.   Why are compensation and benefit packages being given special attention today?

39. What objectives can be accomplished by a well-managed compensation and benefit program?

   a._____

   b._____

   c._____

   d._____

   e._____

40. Describe the various types of pay systems

   a._____

   b._____

   c._____

   d._____

   e._____

   f._____

   g._____

   h._____

41. In looking at team compensation, what is the problem when pay is based strictly on individual performance?

42. Describe a skill based pay system for teams, including the drawbacks.

43. Describe a gain sharing system of compensation for teams.

44. Where does individual compensation fit into these team-based plans?

45. What are some of the benefits included in fringe benefits packages? How big a part of companies' compensation plans are fringe benefits?

46. Describe "soft benefits".

47. Why have companies implemented cafeteria-style benefits packages? What is the key to offering these types of plans?

48. The cost of administering benefits programs has become so great that a number of companies

_____

Learning Goal 8
Scheduling Employees to Meet Organizational and Employee Needs

49. Flextime plans are designed to _____

_____

50. What are the disadvantages of flextime?

51. What is a disadvantage of a compressed work week?

52. What are the benefits to working at home for workers, and for employers?

53. The benefits to job sharing include:

a. _____

b. _____

c. _____

d. _____

e. _____

54.   What are some disadvantages to job sharing for employers?

Learning Goal 9
Moving Employees Up, Over, and Out

55.   Four ways of moving employees through the organization are:

a._____   c._____

b._____   d._____

56.   What are the benefits of promotion from within a company?

57.   Why is it more common now for employees to move over to a new position, rather than move up?

58.   What is the doctrine of "employment at will"? How has the "employment at will" doctrine changed?

59.   What is a "golden handshake"?

60.   What are two advantages of early retirement programs, over laying off employees?

61.   Why would an organization want to learn about an employee's reason for leaving, and how can the organization get the information?

Learning Goal 10
Laws Affecting Human Resource Management

62.   What is prohibited by Title VII of the Civil Rights Act of 1964?

63.   What is the EEOC and what powers does the EEOC have?

64.   How did affirmative action programs result in charges of reverse discrimination?

65.   The Civil Rights Act of 1991 _____

        _____

66.   Who does the Vocational and Rehabilitation Act of 1973 protect?

67.   What is required by the ADA?

68.   "Accommodation "means: _____

        Accommodations include: _____

        _____

69.   The Age Discrimination in Employment Act:

70. Identify four important aspects of the impact of legislation on human resource management.

a._____

b._____

c._____

d._____

CRITICAL THINKING EXERCISES

Learning Goal 1

1. Six functions of human resource management are:

Human resource planning   Training and development
Recruitment   Evaluation
Selection   Compensation

You have read in previous chapters of the changing structure of American business and about population trends occurring in the United States. In this chapter, we read about the challenges in human resource management.

For each of the following, identify at least one area of human resource management that could be affected, and how companies are affected or how companies could respond to the change.

	AREA AFFECTED	COMPANY RESPONSE
a. Shortages of trained workers	_____	_____
		_____
		_____
b. An aging workforce	_____	_____
		_____
		_____
c. Increases in single parent and two-income families	_____	_____
		_____
		_____
		_____
d. Changing attitudes toward work	_____	_____
		_____
		_____
e. Complex laws	_____	_____
		_____
		_____
f. Concern over work environment and equality	_____	_____
		_____
		_____

Learning Goal 2

2.　　　Five steps in human resource planning are:

Prepare a human resource inventory
Prepare a job analysis
Assess future human resource demand
Assess future supply
Establish a strategic plan

Match the correct step to each of the following:

a. _____　　　A large West Coast two-year college recently required its clerical staff to identify all the tasks involved in their jobs and to show how each job related to the other areas of their department.

b. _____　　　Ford periodically requests employees to update information in their personnel file, for such things as recent courses taken, recent training programs and other employee information.

c. _____　　　General Motors anticipates that its plant managers will need to develop updated skills in new management techniques as technology changes.

d. _____　　　Daimler-Chrysler makes arrangements with a local college for on-site training for its plant managers, and arranges to retrain workers at state-sponsored retraining programs.

e. _____　　　The human resource manager of a large East Coast firm gets statistics on the educational background of the graduating MBA classes of several East Coast colleges, including two schools with a large minority enrollment and two high tech schools.

Learning Goal 3

3.　　　Be observant! Look around you and observe how many different methods that firms are using to recruit employees. Newspapers, radio, signs in windows, college placement office, job fairs, offering internships? What ways would you use to look for a job, and "be recruited "to apply? How many Internet recruiting sites can you find?

Talk to a person in charge of recruiting for the company where you work. What methods does the company use? What challenges has your manager found in finding qualified personnel?

4.   A typical selection process may involve six steps

         Complete application   Background investigations
         Initial and follow-up interviews   Physical exams
         Employment tests   Trial periods

Match each of the following to the correct step in the selection process:

a. _____   Contributes to the high cost of turnover but enables a firm to fire
                     incompetent employees after a certain period of time.

b. _____   Helps a firm to determine the information about an employee that is
                     pertinent to the requirements of the job. Legal guidelines limit what
                     companies can ask.

c. _____   An investigation of pervious work records and school records, and
                     follow-up on recommendations.

d. _____   These have been criticized because of charges of cultural
                     discrimination. They are most often used to measure specific job skills.

e. _____   Used to screen applicants after the application form has been reviewed.
                     Gives the company an opportunity to assess communication skills.

f. _____   A major controversy in this step is pre-employment drug testing to
                     detect drug or alcohol abuse, and AIDS screening.

Learning Goals 1,2,3,4
5.   Sun-2-Shade is a company that makes self-darkening windshields for the automobile
         industry. The company needs the human resources manager to begin developing some job
         descriptions, identify the various skills needed to perform the different jobs in the company
         and to start to develop a recruitment and selection process. Select at least one job that will be
         a part of Sun-2-Shade's organization, write a job description, job specifications, and develop
         a plan for recruiting and selecting job candidates.

6. Firms have several types of training programs available:

    Employee orientation   Vestibule training
    On-the-job training   Job simulation
    Apprentice programs   Management development
    Off-the-job training

    Match the correct type of training program to each situation described:

    a. _____   Before Tom Hershberger went to work for a construction firm, he had a lot of training on how to use the heavy equipment he was assigned to.

    b. _____   Bill Martin is a plumber. Before he became a journeyman, he had to work for several years alongside another plumber to learn the skills and procedures for the job.

    c. _____   Maria Alvarez went on a sales call her second day on the job. She basically "learned by doing."

    d. _____   Scott Toblin is learning to fly the newest, and largest, commercial aircraft, a 797. Before he takes it up in the air, he will work the control panel, and "land" on the runways of virtually every airport in the United States, all while staying right on the ground.

    e. _____   Bernie Breen spent three weeks at a seminar learning effective communications and human relations skills for his job as a middle manager in a major corporation.

    f. _____   In his first day on the job, Hong Nyu was introduced to several department managers, studied a corporate brochure describing all the company's products and saw a video of the history of his company. He was even assigned a mentor.

7. The text discusses networking and its importance in business. How could networking become even more important in the future, and how can you start <u>now</u> to develop a "network"?

8. You are the newly appointed sales manager for Sun-2-Shade, and your job is to develop a new appraisal system that is effective and objective. This is the first real test of your skills as a manager. What, specifically, do you think you should do? In other words, what kinds of things will you include on an appraisal form, and then what will you do after that's completed?

9. Right now at Sun-2-Shade, you have a salesman who doesn't seem to be performing the way she should. You know something must be done. This is the second real test of your management skills. How will you handle this situation?

Learning Goal 7

10. Basic pay systems include:

Salary systems	Bonus plans
Hourly wage	Profit-sharing
Piecework	Gain sharing
Commission plans	Stock options

Give a suggested pay system for each situation described below. Your suggestion can be a combination of systems:

a. _____ A sales job that includes a variety of non selling functions such as advising, keeping records and setting up displays.

b. _____ An assembly line operation in which each worker completes several tasks before the product moves to the next station.

c. _____ An office manager just starting out with new office equipment designed to increase productivity.

d. _____ The president of a small firm that makes computer chips.

e. _____ A worker in a garment factory, making shirts.

f. _____ A manager with specific goals to meet in his department, and who has been with the company for several years.

11. How can a company ensure that their benefits programs meet the needs of a changing workforce? Why is that important?

12.   Changing workforces mean changing schedules for many companies and their employees. Some alternative work schedules are:

Job sharing   Compressed work weeks
Flextime plans   In-home work

What kind of program is being described:

a. _____   This type of program can give an employee a break, and lets them sleep in once in a while!

b. _____   At Renovation Capital, employees work 35 hours in 4 days for each week in May, giving everyone a three day weekend.

c. _____   At St. Lukes Hospital, Julie Andersen works as an accountant every morning, and Mary Krull takes over each afternoon.

d. _____   Felicia Hill has a fax, modem, and a computer that she carries with her wherever she goes, but she doesn't have an office!

e. _____   Some of the benefits of this schedule include a reduction in absenteeism and tardiness, because people can handle their other duties in off hours.

f. _____   With this program, Juan and Elena Morena can schedule their days so that one of them is home to see their children off in the morning, and the other is home when the children come home from school.

g. _____   One of the disadvantages of this program is the need to hire, train and supervise twice as many people.

h. _____   Gil Pfaff likes this schedule, because it allows him to avoid the heavy morning traffic during his commute to work.

i. _____   Manager David Whitsell likes this program because he has found workers who take advantage of it are often more productive and its easier for him to schedule people into peak demand periods for his department.

j. _____   Debbie Rhodes schedules doctor's appointments on days when she comes in early and leaves early.

13.   How have the changes in the workforce and in the workplace, discussed in this and other chapters, affected the ways companies move employees around?

14.   How have changes in the "make-up" of the workforce - more immigrants, more minorities, more women, and so on, affected corporations from a legal perspective?

PRACTICE TEST

MULTIPLE CHOICE – Circle the best answer

Learning Goal 1
1.   Human resources management does not include:
        a.   leading
        b.   evaluation
        c.   recruitment
        d.   selection

2.   Among the challenges faced by human resource managers are:
        a.   An oversupply of people trained to work in growth areas.
        b.   Fewer laws to direct the actions of human resources managers.
        c.   Continued downsizing that is taking a toll on employee morale, and increased demand for temporary workers.
        d.   Fewer older workers, and too many of them want to retire, making it difficult to fill their jobs.

Learning Goal 2
3.   A job analysis will provide information about:
        a.   what is done by various employees who fill different job titles.
        b.   whether or not the labor force is paid adequately.
        c.   the strategic plan for recruiting, selecting training and development.
        d.   education, capabilities, training and specialized skills to determine if the company's labor force is technically up-to-date.

4.   "Clerical worker, with responsibilities for answering phones, greeting clients, filing for human resources department. Some weekends required." This is an example of a:
        a.   job analysis
        b.   job specification
        c.   job description
        d.   human resource inventory

5.	Which of the following is <u>not</u> included in a list of reasons why recruiting has become difficult?
	a.	Sometimes people with necessary skills aren't available.
	b.	The number of available recruiting tools has begun to shrink.
	c.	The emphasis on participative management makes it important to hire people who fit in with the corporate culture.
	d.	Some companies have policies that make it difficult to recruit.

6.	According to the text, the greatest advantage of hiring from within is:
	a.	it is quick.
	b.	it requires less training.
	c.	it helps maintain employee morale.
	d.	it keeps the firm from having an oversupply of workers trained in certain areas.

Learning Goal 4
7.	What is the first step in the selection process?
	a.	Obtaining a completed application form.
	b.	Contacting an employment agency.
	c.	Background investigation.
	d.	Interviews.

8.	Background investigations:
	a.	are no longer legal.
	b.	help identify which candidates are most likely to succeed.
	c.	include an investigation of skills.
	d.	are not good predictors of who will be successful.

9.	Employment tests must:
	a.	be directly related to the job.
	b.	measure only specific skills.
	c.	be conducted in the initial job interview.
	d.	in general be avoided, because of legal issues.

Learning Goal 5
10.	Internal and external programs to develop a variety of skills and to foster personal development away from the job is called:
	a.	off-the-job training.
	b.	vestibule training.
	c.	an apprentice program.
	d.	employee orientation.

11.	_____is a type of management development that exposes managers to different functions of the organization by giving them assignments in a variety of departments.
	a.	Understudy positions
	b.	On-the-job coaching
	c.	Job enlargement
	d.	Job rotation

12. In developing a performance appraisal, standards should have all of the following characteristics <u>except</u>:
    a. they should be specific.
    b. they should be subject to measurement.
    c. they should be easily attainable.
    d. they should be reasonable.

13. Decisions about promotions, compensation, additional training, or firing are all based on:
    a. going through the appropriate training program.
    b. having the right selection process in place.
    c. performance evaluations.
    d. legal considerations.

14. Henry Aguerra is interested in making a lot of money. He is a very good salesperson. People tell him he could sell sand to Saudi Arabia! He is a very hard worker, and is willing to work a lot of hours to make the kind of money he wants. Henry should most likely look for the kind of job that is paid:
    a. on salary with overtime.
    b. by commission.
    c. with profit sharing.
    d. in a situation with team based compensation.

15. Studies of compensation for teams have shown that:
    a. it is recommended that pay should be based on team performance.
    b. team based pay programs are pretty well developed and need not be changed.
    c. team members should be compensated as individuals.
    d. skill based pay programs are relatively easy to apply.

16. Fringe benefits:
    a. include pay, as well as items such as executive dining rooms and country club memberships.
    b. are usually set, and won't change over time.
    c. Is relatively easy for a company to administer, once benefits have been determined.
    d. are expensive for companies, and account for as much as 30 percent of payroll today.

17. A program that gives employees freedom to adjust when they work, as long as they work the required number of hours is called:
    a. job sharing
    b. flextime
    c. a compressed workweek
    d. home based work

18. Among the disadvantages, or challenges, of telecommuting, or home based work is:
    a. reduced productivity for the organization.
    b. makes job performance appraisal more difficult.
    c. reduces the amount of time available for work for the employee.
    d. increases the amount of office politics as workers who have to come in are jealous of those who work at home.

19.   The effect of downsizing and the resulting flatter corporate structures is that:
        a.   fewer layers of management make it more difficult for employees to be promoted to higher levels of management.
        b.   companies are now scrambling to re-hire those workers who were laid off.
        c.   a decrease occurs in the level of complexity of managing human resources.
        d.   less need to adhere to employment law.

20.   Employment at will is:
        a.   the right for an employee to choose any job they would like.
        b.   rigorously enforced in most states today.
        c.   is a financial incentive used to encourage early retirement for long term employees.
        d.   the right of employers to fire workers.

21.   Title VII of the Civil Rights Act:
        a.   requires that disabled applicants be given the same consideration for employment as people without disabilities.
        b.   prevents businesses from discrimination against people with disabilities on the basis their physical or mental handicap.
        c.   prohibits discrimination in hiring, firing, and other areas on the basis of race, religion, creed, sex or national origin.
        d.   gives the victims of discrimination the right to a jury trail and punitive damages

22.   The law that requires employers to give disabled applicants the same consideration for employment as people without disabilities is the:
        a.   Age Discrimination in Employment Act.
        b.   Equal Employment Opportunity Act.
        c.   Americans with Disabilities Act.
        d.   Civil Rights Act.

TRUE-FALSE

1. _____   Qualified labor is more scarce today, which makes recruiting and selecting more difficult.

2. _____   Human resource management has become so important that it is no longer a function of just one department, but a function of all managers.

3. _____   Because technology changes so rapidly, training programs should not be started too long before the skills are needed, in case the skills become outdated.

4. _____   New tools used to recruit employees include Internet online services.

5. _____   Recruiting qualified workers may be difficult for small businesses because they may not be able to offer the sort of compensation that attracts qualified workers.

6. _____   In recruiting, it is important to look for individuals who are skilled, but less important that they fit in with the culture, as skilled workers will quickly learn how to fit in.

Learning Goal 4

7. _____ The application form and the initial interview are good ways for a company to find out about an applicant's family and religious backgrounds.

8. _____ Employment physical exams are always illegal.

Learning Goal 5

9. _____ Training focuses on short-term skills, whereas development focuses on long-term abilities.

10. _____ It is important for companies to take the initiative to develop female and minority managers because it is a key to long-term profitability.

11. _____ In a mentoring program, an older, more experienced worker will coach and guide a selected lower-level manager by introducing him or her to the right people and groups.

Learning Goal 6

12. _____ Discussing the results of a performance evaluation with the employee should be avoided because it's important to let an employee "sink or swim" in a job.

13. _____ A 360 degree performance review includes employees, peers, subordinates, and managers.

Learning Goal 7

14. _____ While compensation and benefits packages are important to keep employees, these programs play little role in attracting qualified employees.

15. _____ Soft benefits include things such as on-site haircuts and shoe repair and free breakfasts.

Learning Goal 8

16. _____ One benefit of job sharing has been reduced absenteeism and tardiness.

17. _____ Some companies have found that telecommuting has helped the company to save money.

Learning Goal 9

18. _____ While early retirement programs are a more expensive strategy of downsizing than laying off employees, it can increase the morale of remaining employees.

19. _____ Learning why an employee leaves a company is not especially valuable information for a company to determine.

Learning Goal 10

20. _____ Legislation and legal decisions have had little effect on human resource management.

21. _____ The EEOC is charged with enforcing affirmative action programs.

22. _____ A key concept of Title VII of the Civil Rights Act of 1964 is accommodation in the workplace.

You Can Find It On the Net

The Web site www.workforceonline.com is a comprehensive Human Resources site that provides a considerable amount of information about a wide variety of topics. These topics will vary over time.

What "Features" topics did you find? How do they relate to what we have learned in this chapter?

What topics were in the "News" portion? What additional information is provided beyond what has been discussed in this chapter?

What topics are listed under the following areas:
Compensation and Benefits
HR Management
Recruiting and Staffing
Training and Development

ANSWERS

LEARNING THE LANGUAGE

1. Recruitment	10. Human resource management	19. On-the-job training
2. Job specifications	11. Compressed work week	20. Training and development
3. Flextime plans	12. Job analysis	21. Employee orientation
4. Affirmative action	13. Networking	22. Performance appraisal
5. Apprenticeship programs	14. Selection	23. Vestibule training
6. Management development	15. Off-the-job training	24. Cafeteria-style benefits
7. Fringe benefits	16. Job description	25. Job simulation
8. Reverse discrimination	17. Core time	26. Contingent workers
9. Mentor	18. Job sharing	27. Online training

ASSESSMENT CHECK

Learning Goal 1
Working With People Is Just the Beginning

1.   The functions of human resource management include:
a. Determining human resource needs
b. Recruiting
c. Selecting
d. Developing
e. Motivating
f. Evaluating
g. Compensating
h. Scheduling

2.   Human resource management has received greater attention recently because the U.S. economy has experienced a major shift from manufacturing to service industries and high tech industries that require highly technical job skills. Qualified employees are scarcer today which makes recruiting more difficult.

In the past, most firms assigned the human resources functions to various departments, and the personnel department was responsible for clerical functions.

In the future, human resource management will be responsible for dealing with all aspects of a firm's personnel. It is no longer a function of one department, but a function of all managers.

3.   Challenges facing the human resources area are:
a.   Shortages of people trained to work in growth areas.
b.   A large population of skilled and unskilled workers from declining industries who are unemployed or underemployed and need retraining.
c.   A growing percentage of new workers who are undereducated and unprepared for jobs in the contemporary business environment.
d.   A shift in the age composition of the work force, including older workers and aging baby boomers who are deferring retirement.
e.   Complex laws in human resource management.
f.   Increasing numbers of single parent and two-income families who need programs like day care, job sharing and family leave.
g.   Changing employee attitudes toward work with leisure having a greater priority.
h.   Downsizing, its effect on morale and need for contingency workers.
i.   Challenges from an overseas labor pool who will accept lower wages.
j.   Increased demand for benefits tailored to the individual.
k.   Growing concern for issues such as health care, elder care and employment for people with disabilities.
l.   A decreased sense of employee loyalty resulting in higher turnover and increased costs.

Learning Goal 2
Determining Your Human Resources Needs

4.   a.   Prepare a human resource inventory of the organization's employees.
b.   Prepare job analyses, job descriptions, and job specifications.
c.   Assess future demand.
d.   Assess future supply.
e.   Establish a strategic plan.

5.   A human resources inventory includes ages, names, education, capabilities, training, specialized skills and other information pertinent to the organization, such as languages spoken. This information reveals whether or not the labor force is technically up to date and thoroughly trained.

6.   In brief, the job description is about the job, and job specifications are about the person who does the job.

7.   The demand for employees will be affected by changing technology, and often training programs must be started long before the need is apparent.

8.   There are likely to be increased shortages of some skills in the future, and an oversupply of other types of skills.

9.   A human resources strategic plan must address recruiting, selecting, training and developing, appraising, compensating, and scheduling the labor force.

Recruiting Employees from a Diverse Population

10.   Recruiting has become difficult because:
   a.   Some organizations' have policies that demand promotions from within, or other policies that make recruiting and keeping employees difficult or subject to restrictions.
   b.   The emphasis on culture, teamwork, and participative management makes it important to hire the right kind of people.
   c.   Sometimes people with the necessary skills are not available, and so workers must be hired and trained internally.

11.   Five methods of internal recruiting include:
   a.   Transfers
   b.   Promotions
   c.   Employee recommendations
   d.   Retrained employees
   e.   Department reorganizations

12.   The benefits of recruiting from within include:
   a.   It is less expensive.
   b.   It helps maintain employee morale.

13.   The list can include:
   a.   Public and private employment agencies
   b.   personal applications
   c.   College placement bureaus
   d.   Management consultants
   e.   New graduates
   f.   Former employees
   g.   Part-time applicants

   The complete list is in Figure 11-3 in your text.

14.   Some of the new tools used to recruit employees are Internet online services, such as CareerBuilder.com and Monster.com

Learning Goal 4
Selecting Employees Who Will Be Productive

15.   a.   Obtaining a complete application form   d.   Background investigations
      b.   Initial and follow-up interviews   e.   Physical exams
      c.   Employment tests   f.   Establishing trial periods

16.   Legal guidelines limit the kinds of questions one can ask on an application or in an interview.

17.   "Smart Assessment" is an artificial intelligence program used to make the application process more effective and efficient. An applicant sits down at a computer and spends a half hour answering questions about job experience, time available and personality related statements. A report e-mailed to the hiring manager indicates whether or not to interview the applicant.

Smart Assessment can significantly cut the amount of time needed to replace employees and provide for a better fit between employees and their jobs. This can raise productivity.

18. Employment tests measure basic competencies in specific job skills, and help evaluate applicants' personalities and interests. It is important that the employment test be related to the job.

19. Background checks are important because it is so costly to hire, train, and motivate people. These checks help to identify which candidates are most likely to succeed in a given position.

20. In some states, physical exams can be given only after an offer of employment has been accepted. Other states allow pre-employment physical exams, but they must be given to everyone applying for the same position.

21. During a trial period, a person can prove his or her worth to the firm. After the trial period, a firm has the right to discharge an employee based upon performance evaluations, so it is easier to fire inefficient or problem employees.

22. A varying need for employees is the most common reason for hiring contingent workers. Other reasons include situations when full time employees are on leave, there is a peak demand for labor, or quick service to customers is a priority. Companies in areas where there are qualified contingent workers available and in which jobs require minimum training are most likely to consider contingency workers.

23. Contingent workers are often offered full-time positions, and because they are told there is a possibility of full time employment they are often more productive than permanent workers.

   As contingent workers they receive few health, vacation and pension benefits. They also tend to earn less than permanent workers.

Learning Goal 5
Training and Developing Employees for Optimum Performance

24. Training is short-term skills oriented, while development is long-term career oriented.

25. Three steps in the process of creating training and development programs are:
   a. Assessing the needs of the organization and the skills of the employees to determine training needs.
   b. Designing the training activities to meet the needs.
   c. Evaluating the effectiveness of the training.

26. During an employee orientation program, new employees will be introduced to fellow employees and to their immediate supervisors, and learn about the policies, practices and objectives of the firm. Orientation programs included everything from informal talks to formal activities that last a day or more and include visits to various departments and required reading of handbooks.

27. On- the-job training is the easiest kind of training to implement when the job is relatively simple, such as clerking in a store, or repetitive, such as cleaning carpets. Intranets are leading to cost-effective forms of on-the-job training programs that are available 24 hours a day, all year long. These online training programs can monitor output and give instructions.

28. As an apprentice, you would train for a craft, such as a bricklaying or plumbing. Workers who successfully complete an apprenticeship earn the classification of journeyman. In the future, there are likely to be more but shorter apprenticeships programs to prepare people for skilled jobs in changing industries.

29. Off-the-job training is expanding to include further formal education, such as a Ph.D. and personal development in areas such as time management, stress management, health and wellness and other areas.

30. The benefit of online training or distance learning is that it gives employers the ability to provide consistent content tailored to specific training needs. It also allows training to occur at convenient times and can be administered to large numbers of employees.

31. Job simulation is the use of equipment that duplicates job conditions and tasks so trainees can learn skills before attempting them on the job. It differs from vestibule training in that simulation attempts to duplicate the *exact* conditions that occur on the job.

32. a. On-the-job coaching - means that a senior manager will assist a lower-level manager by teaching them the needed skills and providing direction, advice, and feedback.

   b. Understudy positions – are a successful way of developing managers. Selected employees work as assistants to higher-level managers and participate in planning and other managerial functions until they are ready to assume such positions themselves.

   c. Job rotation - is used so that managers can learn about different functions of the organization. Managers are given assignments in a variety of departments to get a broad picture of the organization, which is necessary to their success.

   d. Off-the-job courses and training - occurs when managers periodically go to schools or seminars for a week or more to more fully develop technical and human relations skills. In these courses they learn the latest concepts and create a sense of camaraderie as they live, eat, and work together in a college-type atmosphere.

33. Companies taking the initiative to develop female and minority managers understand that:
   a. grooming women and minorities for management positions is a key to long term profitability
   b. the best women and minorities will become harder to attract and retain in the future
   c. more women and minorities at all levels means that businesses can better serve female and minority customers.

Learning Goal 6
Appraising Employee Performance to get Optimum Results

34. Decisions about promotions, compensation, additional training or firing are all based on performance appraisals.

35. a   Establish performance standards
   b. Communicate the standards
   c. Evaluate performance
   d. Discuss results with employees
   e. Take corrective action
   f. Use the results to make decisions

36. Performance standards must be:
   a. understandable
   b. subject to measurement
   c. reasonable

37. The 360-degree review calls for feedback from superiors, subordinates and peers. The goal is to get an accurate and comprehensive idea of the worker's abilities.

Learning Goal 7
Compensating Employees: Attracting and Keeping the Best

38. Compensation and benefits packages have become a main marketing tool used to attract qualified employees. At the same time, employee compensation is one of the largest operating costs for many organizations, and the firm's long-term survival may depend on how well it can control employee costs, and optimize employee efficiency.

39. A well managed compensation and benefit program can meet objectives such as:
   a. Attracting the kind of people the organization needs.
   b. Providing employees with incentives
   c. Keeping valued employees from leaving
   d. Maintaining a competitive position in the marketplace
   e. Assuring employees a sense of financial security through insurance and retirement benefits

40. a. Salary systems – fixed compensation computed on weekly, biweekly, or monthly pay periods.
   b. Hourly wage or daywork – wage based on the number of hours or days worked, used for most blue-collar and clerical workers.
   c. Piecework - wage based on the number of items produced rather than by the hour or day.
   d. Commission plans – pay based on some percentage of sales, often used to compensate sales personnel.
   e. Bonus plans – extra pay for accomplishing or surpassing certain objectives. Two forms of bonuses are monetary and cashless.
   f. Profit sharing plans – share of the company's profits over and above normal pay.
   g. Gain-sharing plans – annual bonuses paid based on achieving specific goals such as quality or customer service measures, and production targets.
   h. Stock Option plans – the right to purchase stock in the company at a specific price over a specific period of time.

41. The problem with paying members of a team based on individual performance is that it erodes team cohesiveness and makes it less likely that the team will meet its goals as a collaborative effort.

42. Skill-based pay is related to the growth of the individual and of the team. Base pay is raised when team members learn and apply new skills. The drawbacks of the skill-based pay system are that the system is complex and that it is difficult to correlate skill acquisition and bottom-line gains.

43. In a gain sharing system bonuses are based on improvements over a previous performance baseline.

44. Outstanding team players that go beyond what is required and make an outstanding individual contribution to the firm should be separately recognized for their additional contribution. A way to avoid alienating recipients who feel team participation was uneven is to let the team decide which members get what type of individual award.

45. Fringe benefits include sick-leave pay, vacation pay, pension plans, and health plans. They can also include recreation facilities, company cars, country club memberships, discounted massages, special home-mortgage rates, paid and unpaid sabbaticals, day care services and executive dining rooms, dental care, eye care, elder care, legal counseling, mental health care and shorter work weeks. Fringe benefits account for approximately 30 percent of payrolls today.

46. "Soft benefits" include such things as on-site haircuts and shoe repair, concierge services and free breakfasts that help workers maintain the balance between work and family life.

47. Firms offer cafeteria-style benefits to counter the growing demand for different kinds of benefits. Today employees are more varied and need different kinds of benefits.

   The key to cafeteria-style benefits is choice, where individual needs can be met.

48. The cost of administering benefits programs has become so great that a number of companies hire outside companies to run their employee benefits plans. This saves money and helps companies avoid the growing complexity and technical requirements of the plans.

Learning Goal 8
Scheduling Employees to Meet Organizational and Employee Needs

49. Flextime plans are designed to allow employees to adjust to demands on their time, and to have freedom to adjust when they work, as long as they work the required number of hours.

50. One disadvantage of flextime is that it doesn't work in assembly-line processes where everyone must work at the same time, or for shift work. In addition, managers often have to work longer days to be able to assist and supervise employees. Flextime can make communication more difficult, as certain employees may not be at work when you need to talk to them. Further, some employees could abuse the system, and that could cause resentment.

51. A disadvantage to a compressed workweek is that some employees get tired working such long hours, and productivity could decline.

52. Workers who work at home can choose their own hours, interrupt work for childcare and other tasks, and take time out for personal reasons.

   Telecommuting can be a cost saver for employers, can increase productivity and can broaden the available talent pool.

   A full list of benefits and challenges of home based work can be found in Figure 11-7

53. Benefits to job sharing include:
   a. employment opportunities to those who cannot or prefer not to work full-time.
   b. a high level of enthusiasm and productivity.
   c. reduced absenteeism and tardiness.
   d. ability to schedule people into peak demand periods.
   e. retention of experienced employees who might have left otherwise.

54. The disadvantages to job sharing include having to hire, train, motivate and supervise twice as many people and to prorate some fringe benefits.

Learning Goal 9
Moving Employees Up, Over and Out

55. Four ways of moving employees through an organization are:
    a. Promotions   c. Reassignment
    b. Terminations   d. Retirement

56. Many companies find that promotion from within the company improves employee morale. Promotions are also cost-effective because the promoted employees are already familiar with the corporate culture and procedures.

57. Because of flatter corporate structures it is more common for workers to move over to a new position than to move up to a new position. Such transfers allow employees to develop and display new skills and to learn more about the company overall.

58. "Employment at will" is an old doctrine that meant that managers had as much freedom to fire workers as workers had to leave voluntarily. Most states now have written employment laws that limit the "at will" doctrine to protect employees from wrongful firing. Companies can no longer fire someone who has exposed a company's illegal actions (whistleblowers), refused to violate a law. This has restricted management's ability to terminate employees as it has increased workers' rights to their jobs.

59. Golden handshakes are financial incentives such as one-time cash payments, used to entice older and more expensive workers to retire.

60. Two advantages of early retirement programs are increased morale of surviving employees and greater promotion opportunities for younger employees.

61. Learning about an employee's reasons for leaving can help to prevent the loss of other good employees. One way to learn the reasons why people leave a company is to have a third party conduct an exit interview.

Learning Goal 10
Laws Affecting Human Resource Management

62. Title VII of the Civil Rights Act of 1964 prohibits discrimination in hiring, firing, compensation, apprenticeships, training, terms, conditions, or privileges of employment based on race, religion, creed, sex, national origin or age.

63. The EEOC, the Equal Employment Opportunity Commission is a regulatory agency created by the Civil Rights Act in 1964 and strengthened by the Equal Opportunity Act of 1972. . Specifically, the EEOC has the power to issue guidelines for acceptable employer conduct in administering equal employment opportunity, enforce mandatory record-keeping procedures and insure that mandates are carried out.

64. Charges of reverse discrimination primarily resulted from the interpretation of affirmative action laws. Reverse discrimination charges have occurred when companies have been perceived as unfairly giving preference to women or minority groups in hiring and promoting, when following affirmative action guidelines.

65. The Civil Rights Act of 1991 expanded the remedies available to victims of discrimination. Now victims have the right to a jury trial and punitive damages.

66. The Vocational Rehabilitation Act of 1973 extended protection from discrimination, in all areas of human resource management, to people with disabilities.

67. The Americans with Disabilities Act of 1990 requires that disabled applicants be given the same consideration for employment as people without disabilities. Companies must make "reasonable accommodations" to people with disabilities.

68. Accommodation means treating people according to their specific needs.

    Accommodations include putting up barriers to isolate people readily distracted by noise, reassigning workers to new tasks, and making changes in supervisors' management styles.

69. The Age Discrimination in Employment Act pretests individuals who are 40 hears of age or older from employment discrimination based on age. Additionally, the law outlawed mandatory retirement in most organizations; unless evidence shows the ability to perform a particular job diminishes with age or poses a danger to society.

70. Four important aspects of the impact of legislation on human resource management are:
    a. Employers must know and act in accordance with the legal rights of all groups in the workplace.
    b. Legislation affects all areas of human resource management.
    c. It is clear that it is sometimes legal to go beyond providing equal rights for minorities and women to provide special employment and training to correct past discrimination.
    d. New court cases and legislation change human resource management almost daily which makes it important to keep current.

CRITICAL THINKING EXERCISES
Learning Goal 1

1.

	AREA	COMPANY RESPONSE
a. Shortages of trained workers	Training Recruitment	Training programs, aggressive recruiting programs
b. Aging work force	Compensation Planning	Demand for good retirement programs will change benefits packages. Companies will also need to plan for replacement of workers in the future. Also family leave programs needed for workers to care for older parents
c. Increases in single-parent and two income families	Compensation	Companies will need to look at income; offering day care; continuing to offer cafeteria style benefits will be especially important as companies experience shortages of trained workers.
d. Changing attitudes about work	Planning	Need to look at flextime and compressed work weeks to meet needs of future workers.
e. Complex laws	Selection Recruitment Compensation	These laws will require companies to look at their policies regarding hiring, promotion and termination.
f. Concern over work environment and equality	Planning Compensation	Companies will begin to offer programs to help employees deal with issues regarding eldercare; and to assess the work place as to accessibility for disabled workers

Learning Goal 2

2.
    a. Job analysis   d. Establish a plan
    b. Human resource inventory   e. Assess future supply
    c. Assess future human resource demand

3.   You will probably notice a number of ways that companies are trying to recruit new employees. One good reason to develop a "network" is that employers often use current employees to find new hires. The newspaper, especially on Sundays, may have several pages of employment opportunities. On your college campus, there may be signs in windows, ads in the college newspaper, ads on electronic bulletin boards among a myriad of other ways that companies are using to look for qualified employees. You may also visit a web site such as Monster.com and investigate the methods used on this recruiting website. Additionally, your college may have an Employer Recruitment site, on which students can post resumes to be screened by potential employers.

Managers will describe many challenges in finding qualified personnel. A common theme will probably be finding people willing to work for the pay the company can afford to offer.

Learning Goal 4

4.
    a. Trial periods
    b. Complete application
    c. Background investigations

    d. Employment tests
    e. Initial and follow up interviews
    f. Physical exams

5.   Your answer will depend upon what kind of job you have chosen. There are many different jobs which will be a part of Sun-2-Shade: Sales, production, marketing, accounting, and clerical, to name a few.

For a sales job, a job description may be:

"Sales for a small manufacturing company, calling on automotive manufacturers and/or automotive after market dealers. Sales territory will be primarily based on geographic location. Duties will include sales calls; follow up reports, working directly with production manager, direct input into marketing program development. Compensation will be salary plus commission.

Skills required include familiarity with electronic communication equipment, teamwork skills, good oral and written communications skills, presentation skills, and a Bachelor's degree, preferably in marketing or a related area."

You may make use of any of the recruiting tools listed in the text. Good sources may include current employees, local colleges, a local professional marketing organization, or using an Internet recruiting tool. The selection process should include several interviews, in particular with the people with whom the sales person will work, such as the production manager, other marketing people, and other members of the team he/she will work with.

Learning Goal 5

6.
    a. Vestibule training
    b. Apprenticeship
    c. On-the-job training

    d. Job simulation
    e. Management development
    f. Employee orientation

7.   As corporations downsize, and layers of management "thin out" your network of co-workers, friends and professional associations could become especially important. To get the kind of job that meets your needs, you may have to do a lot of searching. To "move up the ladder" in the face of declining numbers of management positions, you may have to find the right mentor.

In college, you can begin to develop a network in a number of ways. If there are student chapters of professional business organizations, such as The American Marketing Association or The American Management Association for example, you could take advantage of student membership rates and attend monthly meetings and meet people already working in the field. Your professors may have contacts in the area you are interested in, also. Further, you could begin a series of "informational interviews". Make appointments with managers in corporations you may have an interest in working for in the future, and find out exactly what kind of skills they are looking for, what kinds of jobs they think will be available in the future and a little bit about the company. Lastly, network with your fellow students. You never know who may be the future CEO of the company you're dying to work for!

8.   The first thing you need to do in developing this appraisal system is decide exactly what elements of the salespersons' jobs will be included in the system. For example, you will probably include: sales volume, number of sales calls, number of sales compared to number of sales calls (called the closing ratio), dollar amount per sale, number of units per sale, sales expenses, average dollar volume per customer, and so on. You will also have to determine what time frame will be used for evaluations, for example, six months or a year. After that, you will want to decide what is an acceptable and reasonable standard for each of those areas - i.e. how many sales calls per month is enough? What's an acceptable dollar amount per sale? What is an acceptable sales volume in the given period?

        Lastly, these standards must be communicated to each salesperson, explained clearly and precisely. Each individual must know exactly what is expected of him or her.

9.   How you would deal with an employee who is not performing well is a matter of individual style. However there are a number of suggestions to make the process more effective. The most important thing to do first is to discuss the problem with the employee and determine what is causing the problem. There may be a problem in her territory, family problems that took her away from work or inadequate support from the company. Figure 11-4 gives you some specific suggestions about conducting an effective appraisal. It will be important to get agreement from the employee that there is a problem, and suggestions from her about how to take corrective action. It may be a good idea to give her a period of time to improve, and then re-evaluate.

Learning Goal 7

10.   These are some <u>suggested</u> answers:
        a. Salary or salary plus commission, gain sharing
        b. Hourly wages plus profit sharing
        c. Salary plus bonus for meeting objectives, gain sharing
        d. Salary plus profit sharing, or bonus for meeting profit objective
        e. Piecework, plus profit sharing
        g. Salary, plus gain sharing or stock options

11.   To counter growing demands for more individualized benefits, companies have begun to offer cafeteria-style benefits. The key to this type of program is providing enough choices so that employees can meet their varied needs, while still maintaining cost effectiveness. These types of programs are particularly important in light of the predicted difficulty in finding skilled employees. These programs are also important to retain good quality workers.

Learning Goal 8

12.   a. Flextime   f. Flextime
        b. Compressed work week   g. Job sharing
        c. Job sharing   h. Flextime
        d. In home work   i. Job sharing
        e. Job sharing   j. Flextime

13. As downsizing has created flatter organizational structures, there are fewer opportunities for employees to be promoted. To keep morale from sagging, and to keep employees productive, it is common today for companies to reassign workers rather than move them up. This kind of transfer allows employees to develop and display new skills. Downsizing has also forced companies to struggle with layoffs and terminations. Many companies are reluctant to rehire permanent workers because of the high cost involved. Legislation has also made firing more difficult, in light of wrongful discharge lawsuits, and some companies find it more cost effective to use contingent workers to replace permanent workers when the need arises.

As an alternative to layoffs, companies have offered early retirement to entice older employees to resign, and allow younger workers to move up. As the workforce gets older, these programs will enable companies to reduce the number of older, more expensive workers. However, if skilled workers are in short supply, companies may need experienced workers, and could reconsider offering early retirement plans.

14. As the workforce becomes more culturally diverse, laws protecting minorities from discrimination will be carefully monitored. These areas have become very complex, and a diverse workforce makes enforcement even more complex. However, as more women and minorities with the necessary skills enter the workforce, compliance with these laws may actually become less an issue than in the past.

A major issue has been providing equal opportunity for people with disabilities. Companies are finding that making structural accommodations is less difficult than understanding the difference between the need to be accommodating and the need to be fair to all employees. As the workforce ages, age discrimination may become an issue.

PRACTICE TEST

MULTIPLE CHOICE

LG 1	# 1-2
LG 2	# 3-4
LG 3	# 5-6
LG 4	# 7-9
LG 5	# 10-11
LG 6	# 12-13
LG 7	# 14-16
LG 8	# 17-18
LG 9	# 19-20
LG 10	# 21-22

TRUE-FALSE

LG 1	# 1-2
LG 2	# 3-4
LG 3	# 5-6
LG 4	# 7-8
LG 5	# 9-11
LG 6	# 12-13
LG 7	# 14-15
LG 8	# 16-17
LG 9	# 18-19
LG 10	# 20-22

MULTIPLE CHOICE		TRUE-FALSE	
1. a	12. c	1. T	12. F
2. c	13. c	2. T	13. T
3. a	14. b	3. F	14. F
4. c	15. a	4. T	15. T
5. b	16. d	5. T	16. T
6. c	17. b	6. F	17. T
7. a	18. b	7. F	18. T
8. b	19. a	8. F	19. F
9. a	20. d	9. T	20. F
10. a	21. c	10. T	21. T
11. d	22. c	11. T	22. F

CHAPTER 12 – DEALING WITH EMPLOYEE-MANAGEMENT ISSUES AND RELATIONSHIPS

LEARNING GOALS

After you have read and studied this chapter, you should be able to:

1. Trace the history of organized labor in the United States.
2. Discuss the major legislation affecting labor unions.
3. Outline the objectives of labor unions.
4. Describe the tactics used by labor and management during conflicts and discuss the role of unions in the future.
5. Explain some of the controversial employee-management issues such as executive compensation, pay equity, child care and elder care, drug testing, and violence in the workplace.

LEARNING THE LANGUAGE

Listed below are important terms found in the chapter. Choose the correct term for the definition and write it in the space provided.

Agency shop agreement	Givebacks	Right-to-work laws
American Federation of Labor	Grievance	Secondary boycott
Arbitration	Industrial unions	Sexual harassment
Bargaining zone	Injunction	Shop stewards
Certification	Knights of Labor	Strike
Closed shop agreement	Lockout	Strikebreakers
Collective bargaining	Mediation	Union
Congress of Industrial Organizations	Negotiated labor-management agreement (labor contract)	Union security clause
Cooling-off period	Open shop agreement	Union shop agreement
Craft union	Primary boycott	Yellow-dog contract
Decertification		

1. The _____ is the range of options between the initial and final offer that each party will consider before negotiations dissolve or reach an impasse.

2. A time known as the _____ is a period when workers in a critical industry return to their jobs while the union and management continue negotiations.

3. The process known as _____ is one by which workers take away a union's right to represent them.

4. A charge by employees that management is not abiding by the terms of the negotiated labor-management agreement is called a _____.

5. This tactic, known as a _____, is an attempt by management to put pressure on unions by closing the business.

6. A tactic called a _____ occurs when the union encourages both its members and the general public not to buy the products of a firm involved in a labor dispute.

7. An employee organization known as _____ has the main goal of representing members in employee-management bargaining about job-related issues.

8. A clause in a labor-management agreement that says employers may hire nonunion workers who are not required to join the union but must pay a union fee is called an _____.

9. Under _____ a third party, called a mediator, encourages both sides to continue negotiating and often makes suggestions for resolving the dispute.

10. Known as _____ this includes unwelcome sexual advances, requests for sexual favors and other conduct of a sexual nature that creates a hostile work environment.

11. A _____ was a type of contract that required employees to agree as a condition of employment not to join a union; prohibited by the Norris-LaGuardia Act in 1932.

12. _____ are union officials who work permanently in an organization and represent employee interests on a daily basis.

13. A provision in a negotiated labor-management agreement known as a _____ stipulates that employees who benefit from a union must either officially join or at least pay dues to the union.

14. An organization known as the _____ consisted of craft unions that championed fundamental labor issues; founded in 1886

15. Concessions made by union members to management or gains from labor negotiations given back to management to help employers remain competitive and thereby save jobs are called _____.

16. Under this type of agreement, known as a(n) _____ workers in right to work states have the option to join or not join the union, if one exists in their workplace.

17. Workers who are hired to do the jobs of striking employees until the labor dispute is resolved are called _____.

18. The formal process of a union becoming recognized by the NLRB as the bargaining agent for a group of employees is called _____.

19. Labor organizations called _____ consist of unskilled and semi-skilled workers in mass production industries such as automobiles and mining.

20. This clause in a labor-management agreement called a _____, indicates that workers do not have to be members of a union to be hired, but must agree to join the union within a prescribed period.

21. The process known as _____ is where union representatives, and management form a labor-management agreement, or contract, for workers.

22. The first national labor union was the _____, which was formed in 1869.

23. A _____ is an attempt by labor to convince others to stop doing business with a firm that is the subject of a primary boycott; prohibited by the Taft-Hartley Act.

24. The agreement to bring in an impartial third party to render a binding decision in a labor dispute is called _____.

25. The clause in a labor-management agreement known as a _____ specified that workers had to be members of a union before being hired.

26. A _____ is an agreement that sets the tone and clarifies the terms under which management and labor agree to function over a period of time.

27. Legislation that gives workers the right, under an open shop, to join or not join a union if it is present is called _____.

28. A union strategy known as a _____ means that workers refuse to go to work; the purpose is to further workers' objectives after an impasse in collective bargaining.

29. The _____ is the union organization of unskilled workers that broke away from the AFL in 1935 and rejoined it in 1955.

30. An organization of skilled specialists in a particular craft or trade is a _____.

31. A(n) _____ is a court order directing someone to do something or to refrain from doing something.

ASSESSMENT CHECK

Learning Goal 1
Employee-Management Issues

1. Why did workers originally form unions?

2. Why has union strength declined in the last 2 decades?

3. What impact did the Industrial Revolution have on the economic structure of the U.S. and the rise of unions?

4.   The first national labor organization was the: _____

       Its intention was to: _____

5.   What was the AFL and why did the AFL limit membership?

6.   Why was the CIO formed?

7.   How did the AFL-CIO form?

Learning Goal 2
Labor Legislation and Collective Bargaining

8.   Five major pieces of labor-management legislation are:

       a._____

       b._____

       c._____

       d._____

       e._____

9.   The major elements of the Norris LaGuardia Act are that it:

       a.   _____

       b.   _____

       c.   _____

10.   What are the major provisions of the Wagner Act (National Labor Relations Act)?

11.   The NLRB provides _____

       _____

12. What did the Fair Labor Standards Act do for workers?

13. What act did the Taft-Hartley Act amend, and what does Taft-Hartley permit and prohibit?

14. What are the major elements of the Landrum-Griffin Act?

Learning Goal 3
Objectives of Organized Labor

15 How are the objectives of organized labor today different from those in the 1970s and 1980s?

16. List the general topics covered in labor-management agreements.

a. _____   g. _____

b. _____   h. _____

c. _____   i. _____

d. _____   j. _____

e. _____   k. _____

f. _____

17. Distinguish between:

Union security clause:

Union shop agreement:

Agency shop agreement:

Closed shop agreement:

Open shop agreement:

18. What areas will be the focus of union negotiations in the future?

Resolving Labor-Management Disagreements
19. What are generally the sources of grievances?

a. _____   d. _____

b. _____   e. _____

c. _____

20. What are three methods used to resolve labor-management disputes?

a. _____   c. _____

b. _____

21. When does mediation become necessary? What is the job of a mediator?

22. How does arbitration differ from mediation?

Tactics Used in Labor-Management Conflicts

23.   What are the tactics used by <u>labor</u> (unions) in labor-management disputes?

        a. _____   c. _____

        b. _____   d. _____

24.   What are the effects of a strike?

25.   What is picketing and what is the purpose of picketing?

26.   What is the difference between a primary boycott and a secondary boycott?

27.   What are the tactics available to management in labor-management disputes?

        a._____   c. _____

        b._____

28.   When does management seek an injunction?

29.   For a court to issue an injunction management must: _____

_____

30.   What is the state of union membership today?

31.   How will unions have to change in order to grow in the future?

32.   How are unions assisting management today?

Learning Goal 5
Controversial Employee-Management Issues

33.   What are the central issues regarding executive compensation today? What is the controversy surrounding using stock options as a form of compensation for CEOs?

34.   What did management consultant Peter Drucker say regarding the level of executive compensation?

35.   How does the pay of U.S. executives compare to executive pay in other countries? What may be an explanation for the difference?

36.   Describe the issue of pay equity.

37.   What explains the disparity between women's pay and men's pay, and how is the disparity changing?

38.   In evaluating sexual harassment, a person's conduct on the job could be considered illegal if:

        a. _____

        b. _____

39.   What is the difference between "quid pro quo" sexual harassment and "hostile environment" harassment?

40. What is a problem with implementing harassment policies? What should companies do to ensure compliance with EEOC requirements?

41. Child care issues raise the concerns of employers for two key reasons:

a. _____

b. _____

42 What controversial questions surround child care in the public and private sector?

a. _____

b. _____

c. _____

43. List five kinds of programs companies are providing to help with child care concerns.

a. _____

b. _____

c. _____

d. _____

e. _____

44. What statistics illustrate why the issue of elder care has become important in today's workplace?

45. What programs can businesses offer to employees dealing with elder care responsibilities?

46. What is the future of the elder care issue in the United States?

47.   What is the loss to business due to substance abuse? What have companies done in response?

48.   Describe the impact of workplace violence in the workplace.

49.   What actions have firms taken to deal with the growing threat of workplace violence?

CRITICAL THINKING EXERCISES

Learning Goal 1

1.   What were the issues that concerned the early crafts unions before and during the Industrial Revolution? How do those issues compare with modern day work issues?

Learning Goal 2

2.   Five major pieces of legislation which have had an impact on the development of labor unions are:

Norris-LaGuardia Act 1932
National Labor Relations Act (Wagner Act) 1935
Fair Labor Standards Act 1938
Labor-Management Relations Act (Taft-Hartley Act) 1947
Labor-Management Reporting and Disclosure Act (Landrum-Griffin Act) 1959

Identify which act is being discussed in each of the following:

a. _____   Texas, Florida, Georgia, Iowa, Kansas and 17 other states have passed right-to-work laws under this act.

b. _____   The AFL-CIO and Teamsters file financial reports every year with the U.S. Department of Labor.

c. _____   Union members picketed the Price Chopper grocery stores to protest the stores' use of non-union labor.

d. _____ A retail store in Michigan is prevented from getting an injunction against a worker who is trying to organize a union.

e. _____ Workers at a General Motors plant in Ohio went on strike, forcing closings at another plant that needed parts supplied by the striking plant.

f. _____ A grocery store in Illinois carries products produced by a company the AFL-CIO is striking. Under this law, the AFL-CIO cannot call for a boycott of the grocery store.

g. _____ Voter fraud was alleged in the election of a UAW union official, and is being investigated.

h. _____ In an attempt to avoid a strike, union and management officials in the automotive industry begin negotiating a year in advance of the end of the current contract.

i. _____ In the mid-1990s Congress raised the minimum wage to $5.15 per hour and has debated raising the minimum wage to over $6.00

Learning Goal 3

3.　There are four types of union agreements:
　　closed shop　　　　　　union shop
　　agency shop　　　　　　open shop

　　Identify each of the following:

a. _____ When Tom Oswalt worked in an automotive factory for the summer in Michigan, he chose not to join the local union. However, he was still required to pay a fee to the union under a union-security clause.

b. _____ After the Wagner Act was passed, unions sought security with this type of agreement. With passage of the Taft-Hartley Act in 1947, however, these types of shops were made illegal.

c. _____ When Peter Tobler went to work at Tyson Foods in Springdale, Arkansas, he was not required to join the union, and did not have to pay any fees to the union.

d. _____ Gary Reese took a job with the Saint Louis plant of Anheuser-Busch in August. He had until October to join the union.

Learning Goals 2, 3

4.　　　Several years ago, the National and American League baseball players went on strike, and ended the baseball season for the year without playoffs or the World Series. While player representatives continued to negotiate with team owners, (sporadically) the strike was still not resolved by the opening of the season in the spring of the following year. Even then- President Bill Clinton could not convince the owners and players to come to the bargaining table and talk to one another. What options are available to labor and management for resolving agreements, which could have been used before the players went on strike, or while they were on strike?

Learning Goal 4

5.　　　When the collective bargaining process breaks down, both management and labor have specific tactics available to them to reach their objectives.

Management	**Labor**
Injunction	Strike
Lockout	Picketing
Strikebreakers	Primary boycotts
	Secondary boycotts

3

Match the tactic being used in each of the following descriptions;

a. _____　　In the past, members of various unions have mounted campaigns to persuade consumers not to buy Coors Beer, because Coors does not use union labor.

b. _____　　When contract negotiations broke down, the owners of the national hockey clubs refused to allow players to play, and delayed the start of the season by several weeks.

c. _____　　While the hockey players were being prevented from working, the baseball players were refusing to work!

d. _____　　In order to start a season anyway, the baseball club owners hired replacement players, bringing many up from the minor leagues.

e. _____　　During a strike against producers members of the American Federation of Musicians of the United States and Canada attempted to raise public awareness and sympathy for their cause by gathering outside Broadway theaters in New York City carrying signs outlining their grievances.

f. _____　　To prevent a sympathy strike by its machinists, United Airlines obtained a court order making it illegal for the machinists to strike during a strike by the flight attendants.

g. _____　　Although it is illegal, the employees of an airline threatened this action against the railways in sympathy with the railroad strikers.

6. What might be the unions' role in the concepts we have discussed in previous chapters, such as self-managed teams, continuous improvement, and so on?

Learning Goal 5

7. What justifications can you state for the high level of executive pay in the United States?

8. What are the negative aspects of the high level of executive pay in the United States?

9. The issue of pay equity centers on comparing the value of jobs traditionally held by women with the value of jobs traditionally held by men. What do comparisons of "men's jobs" with "women's jobs" show? How are things changing?

10. As more women have entered the workforce, the issue of sexual harassment has become increasingly visible. What are the problems surrounding this issue, and what are companies doing about it?

11.   What are the issues surrounding:

Child care:

Eldercare:

Drug testing:

Violence in the workplace:

PRACTICE TEST

MULTIPLE CHOICE – Circle the best answer

Learning Goal 1
1.   Workers originally formed unions:
    a.   as social organizations.
    b.   to protect themselves from intolerable work conditions and unfair treatment.
    c.   as a way to increase job security.
    d.   to have the rights to strike and to picket.

2.   Most historians agree that today's union movement is an outgrowth of:
    a.   the Great Depression.
    b.   the Civil War.
    c.   the Industrial Revolution.
    d.   the Revolutionary War.

Learning Goal 2
3.   The minimum wage and maximum hours for workers were established by the:
    a.   Norris-LaGuardia Act.
    b.   Taft-Hartley Act.
    c.   Landrum-Griffin Act.
    d.   Fair Labor Standards Act.

4. When Joe Kerr began working at his local bakery, he felt there was a need for the workers to sit down with management and talk about some of the problems facing the workers at their job. Joe found out there was a union representing the bakery workers, but that management didn't take them seriously, and refused to sit down with the union and negotiate. After some research Joe found out that under the _____, workers had the right to expect management to negotiate with them.
    a.   Norris-LaGuardia Act
    b.   Wagner Act
    c.   Fair Labor Standards Act
    d.   Taft-Hartley Act

5. A yellow-dog contract:
    a.   requires employees to agree not to join a union as a condition of employment.
    b.   requires management to negotiate with labor.
    c.   requires that employees join a union as a condition of employment.
    d.   requires labor to collectively bargain with management

Learning Goal 3
6. When Dave Sutton went to work for a printing shop, he thought he was going to have to join the union representing the shop. However on his first day of work he was told that while there was a union representing the workers, he was not *required* to join, and he didn't have to pay any dues to the union if he chose not to join. Dave works in a(n) _____ shop.
    a.   union
    b.   agency
    c.   closed
    d.   open

7. The sources of grievances are generally
    a.   overtime rules, promotions and layoffs.
    b.   money and company policies.
    c.   hours worked, other employees and contract negotiations.
    d.   items to be included in contract negotiations.

8. A bargaining zone is:
    a.   the location in which negotiations take place.
    b.   a type of legislation that gives workers the right to join or not join a union.
    c.   a contract that requires employees to agree not to join a union as a condition of employment.
    d.   the range of options between the initial and final offer that each party will consider before negotiations dissolve.

9. When baseball players went on strike, an individual was brought in to help resolve the dispute between management and players. This third party was involved to make suggestions, but legally could not make any decisions about how the players dispute should be settled. This is an example of:
    a.   arbitration
    b.   grievance
    c.   mediation
    d.   a bargaining zone

10. When organized labor encourages its members not to buy products made by a firm in a labor dispute, it is encouraging a:
    a. strike.
    b. primary boycott.
    c. secondary boycott.
    d. injunction.

11. Which of the following is a tactic used by management in a labor dispute?
    a. picketing
    b. strikes
    c. boycotts
    d. injunction

12. Union membership has:
    a. continued to grow as companies face worker discontent with overseas outsourcing.
    b. been steady in the last decades, and is expected to grow very slowly in the next 10 years.
    c. been steadily declining for many years.
    d. has declined to near zero, and unions most likely will disappear in the next 10 years.

13. For unions to grow in the future, they will have to:
    a. continue to grant givebacks to management.
    b. begin to organize foreign workers in overseas markets.
    c. adapt to a more culturally diverse, white collar workforce.
    d. take up the fight against continuous improvement and employee involvement.

Learning Goal 5

14. When compared to their European and Japanese counterparts, U.S. corporate executives:
    a. are making considerably more than executives in other countries.
    b. are being paid much less that their counterparts, considering how much more they work.
    c. are compensated better when times are good, but worse when the company isn't doing as well.
    d. are at about the same level in terms of compensation.

15. The issue of pay equity deals with:
    a. paying equal wages to men and women who do the same job.
    b. equal pay for different jobs that require similar levels of training and education or skills.
    c. assuring that men and women have equal opportunity in the job market.
    d. ensuring that executive pay is not more than 20 times the pay of the lowest paid worker.

16. Which of the following is <u>not</u> included in a discussion of behavior that would be considered sexually harassing?
    a. An employee must submit to a certain behavior as a condition of employment.
    b. Submission or rejection of a behavior is used as a basis for employment decisions.
    c. A behavior interferes with job performance or creates a hostile working environment.
    d. Reporting of a behavior results in job dismissal.

17. Which of the following is true regarding the issue of child-care for workers?
    a. Federal child-care assistance has declined considerably.
    b. A major question is who should pay for child-care services.
    c. A majority of major companies provide some kind of child- care services.
    d. Parents have made it clear they will compromise on the issue of child- care.

18. Companies have responded to requests for assistance in child-care with all of the following <u>except</u>:
    a. discount arrangements with national child care chains.
    b. vouchers that offer payment toward the kind of child care the employee prefer.
    c. on-site child-care centers.
    d. increases in the number of allowable sick leave days for employees to use when a child is ill.

19. Elder care issues in the United States:
    a. will continue to grow and become more costly as higher executives and managers begin to deal with the care of elderly parents and relatives .
    b. has become less important as many women stay at home and can take on the care of elderly parents and relatives.
    c. is becoming easier for companies to address.
    d. have been addressed by many companies in the form of elder care programs and benefits.

20. Which of the following is <u>not</u> included as a major issue which companies will have to address in the coming years?
    a. elder care issues
    b. union growth and power
    c. child care
    d. violence in the workplace

TRUE-FALSE

Learning Goal 1

1. _____ Labor unions were largely responsible for the establishment of minimum-wage laws, overtime rules, worker's compensation, severance pay, and more.

2. _____ The CIO, Congress of Industrial Organizations, grew out of the Knights of Labor.

3. _____ In the early part of the last century (the 1900s), it was common for workers to have an 80 hour work week.

4. _____   Yellow dog contracts, preventing workers from joining a union as a condition of employment, were outlawed by the Fair Labor Standards Act.

5. _____   The minimum wage was established by the Fair Labor Standards Act.

6. _____   Under the Wagner Act, labor was granted the right to collectively bargain, but was expected to bargain in good faith.

7. _____   In a decertification campaign, workers take away a union's right to represent them.

Learning Goal 3

8. _____   A union security clause stipulates that union workers with seniority will be the last workers to be laid off.

9. _____   Under an agreement called an agency shop, companies can hire nonunion workers, who are not required to join the union, but who must pay a special union fee.

10. _____   In right to work states, workers may choose not to join a union, even if one exists to represent them in their work place.

11. _____   In the process of arbitration, an impartial third party will make a binding decision in a labor dispute.

Learning Goal 4

12. _____   Many states prohibit strikes by people in jobs such as police officers or fire fighters.

13. _____   "Just cause" must be shown when a union wants to go on strike.

14. _____   Unions have begun to assist management in training workers, redesigning jobs and helping to recruit and train workers who need special help to adapt to the job requirements of the new economy.

15. _____   A "cooling off" period requires that management must allow 30 days after a contract dispute before requiring that labor go back to the bargaining table.

Learning Goal 5

16. _____   In the past, the primary explanation for the disparity between men and women's pay has been that women often aren't as educated as men.

17. _____   "Quid pro quo" harassment exists when the employees submission to such conduct is made either explicitly or implicitly a term or condition of employment.

18. _____   The issue of elder care is expected to decline in importance in coming years.

19. _____   A key reason that child-care issues are important to companies today is that absences related to child care cost them billions of dollars annually.

20. ____ Individuals who use illegal drugs are more likely to be involved in workplace accidents and to file a worker's compensation claim.

You Can Find It on the Net

Let's take a look at the issues unions are considering in the 21st century. Visit the AFL-CIO website at **www.aflcio.org**

What are some of the issues featured the Hot Features section? How do those issues reflect what you have read in this chapter?

Find out what the AFL-CIO has to say about equal pay for women. Click on Issues link, then on the Working Women link, and follow the subsequent links. What are the important issues addressed?

Click on the "Corporate Watch" link, then on "Executive Paywatch" and scroll down to the CEO and You link. This link will show you how much your pay would be if you were a CEO. How much would you be making today if you were the CEO? Pick a company and find out what the CEO of that company made.

Enter one of the blogs and give your opinion about the topics that interest you on this page. (At the time of this writing, there was a "Bad Boss" contest being run!)

Go to www.uaw.org
What issues that we have discussed are included in this website?

ANSWERS

LEARNING THE LANGUAGE

1. Bargaining zone	12. Shop stewards	22. Knights of Labor
2. Cooling off period	13. Union security clause	23. Secondary boycott
3. Decertification	14. American Federation of Labor (AFL)	24. Arbitration
4. Grievance	15. Givebacks	25. Closed shop agreement
5. Lockout	16. Open shop agreement	26. Negotiated labor management agreement
6. Primary boycott	17. Strikebreakers	27. Right-to-work laws
7. Unions	18. Certification	28. Strike
8. Agency shop agreement	19. Industrial unions	29. Congress of Industrial Organizations (CIO)
9. Mediation	20. Union shop agreement	30. Craft union
10. Sexual harassment	21. Collective bargaining	31. Injunction
11. Yellow dog contract		

ASSESSMENT CHECK

Employee-Management Issues
Learning Goal 1

1. Workers originally formed unions to protect themselves from intolerable work conditions and unfair treatment from owners and managers. They also wanted to secure some say in the operations of their jobs.

2. It is suggested that the reasons for the decline in union strength/membership are global competition, shifts from manufacturing to service and high-tech industries, growth in part-time work, and changes in management philosophies. Others believe that the membership decline is related to labor's success in seeing the issues it has promoted become law.

3. Most historians agree that today's unions are an outgrowth of the economic transition caused by the Industrial Revolution. The workers who worked in the fields became dependent upon factories for their living. Over time, workers learned that strength through unions could lead to improved job conditions, job security and better wages.

   The Industrial Revolution changed the economic structure of the United States. Productivity increases from mass production and job specialization made the U.S. a world economic power.

   This growth brought problems for workers in terms of expectations, hours of work, wages and unemployment. Workers who failed to produce lost their jobs. People had to go work when they were ill or had family problems. Hours of work were expanded, and an 80-hour work week was not uncommon. Wages were low, and the use of child labor was widespread.

4. The first national labor union was the Knights of Labor. The intention of the Knights of Labor was to gain significant political power and eventually restructure the entire U.S. economy.

5. The American Federation of Labor, AFL, was an organization of craft unions that championed fundamental labor issues.

   The AFL limited membership to skilled workers assuming they would have better bargaining power in getting concessions from employers.

6. The Congress of Industrial Organizations broke away from the AFL, and was formed to organize both craftspeople and unskilled workers.

7. The AFL and the CIO merged in 1955 after each organization struggled for leadership for several years.

Learning Goal 2
Labor Legislation and Collective Bargaining

8.   a.   Norris-LaGuardia Act 1932
       b.   National Labor Relations Act (Wagner Act) 1935
       c.   Fair Labor Standards Act 1938
       d.   Labor Management Relations Act (Taft-Hartley Act) 1947
       e.   Labor Management Reporting and Disclosure Act (Landrum-Griffin Act) 1959

9.   The major elements of the Norris-LaGuardia Act are that it
       a.   Prohibited courts from issuing injunctions against nonviolent union activities
       b.   Outlawed contracts forbidding union activities
       c.   Outlawed yellow dog contracts.

10.   The Wagner Act (National Labor Relations Act) gave employees the right to form or join labor organizations, and the right to collectively bargain in good faith with employers who were obligated to meet at reasonable times. It also gave workers the right to engage in strikes, picketing, and boycotts. The act prohibited certain unfair labor practices by management, and established the National Labor Relations Board. It also provided workers with a clear process to remove a union as its workplace representative.

11.   The NLRB provides guidelines and offers legal protection to workers that seek to vote on organizing a union to represent them in the workplace. This process is called certification.

12.   The Fair Labor Standards Act set a minimum wage and maximum basic hours for workers.

13.   The Taft-Hartley Act amended the Wagner Act. It permitted states to pass right to work laws, and set up methods to deal with strikes affecting national health and safety. The act also prohibits secondary boycotts, closed- shop agreements, and featherbedding.

14.   The Landrum-Griffin Act amended the Taft-Hartley Act and the Wagner Act. It guaranteed individual rights of union members in dealing with their union, and required annual financial reports to be filed with the U.S. Department of Labor. One goal of this act was to clean up union corruption.

Learning Goal 3
Objectives of Organized Labor

15.   The primary objectives of labor unions in the 1970s were additional pay and additional benefits. In the 1980s the focus shifted to issues related to job security and union recognition. In the 1990s and early 2000s, the focus was still on job security but global competition and its effects became the central concern.

16. The general topics covered in labor-management agreements are:

a. Management rights

g. Hours of work and time-off policies

b. Union recognition

h. Job rights and seniority principles

c. Union security clause

i. Discharge and discipline

d. Strikes and lockouts

j. Grievance procedures

e. Union activities and responsibilities

k. Employee benefits, health and welfare

f. Wages

17. <u>Union security clause</u>: Stipulates that employees who reap benefits from a union must either officially join or at least pay dues to the union.

<u>Union shop agreement</u>: Workers do not have to be members of a union to be hired for a job, but must agree to join the union within a prescribed period of time.

<u>Agency shop agreement</u>: Employers may hire nonunion workers, who are not required to join the union, but must pay a special union fee or pay regular union dues.

<u>Closed shop agreement</u>: Specified that that workers had to be members of a union in order to be hired. This practice was outlawed by the Taft-Hartley Act.

<u>Open shop agreement</u>: Gives workers the option to join or not join a union when one is present in the workplace.

18. In the future unions will focus on child and elder care, worker retraining, two-tiered wage plans, offshore outsourcing, employee empowerment and integrity and honesty testing.

Resolving Labor-Management Disagreements

19. Sources of grievances are:

a. overtime rules

d. transfers

b. promotions

e. job assignments

c. layoffs

20. a. Grievance

c. Arbitration

b. Mediation

21. Mediation becomes necessary if labor-management negotiators aren't able to agree on alternatives within the bargaining zone. The mediator evaluates facts in a dispute and makes suggestions for resolving the dispute.

22. In arbitration, an impartial third party will render a binding decision in the labor dispute. A mediator can only make a suggestion.

Tactics Used in Labor-Management Conflicts

23   Tactics used by labor in labor-management disputes are:
    a.   Strikes   c.   Primary boycotts
    b.   Picketing   d.   Secondary boycotts

24.   A strike attracts public attention to a labor dispute and at times causes operations in a company to slow down or totally shut down. Strikes can lead to a resolution of a dispute, but have also led to violence and extended bitterness. Few labor disputes lead to a strike today.

25.   When strikers picket, they walk around the outside of the organization carrying signs and talking with the public and the media about the issues in a labor dispute. Unions also use picketing as an informational tool before going on strike.

       The purpose is to alert the public about an issue that is stirring labor unrest even though no strike has been voted.

26.   A primary boycott is when labor encourages its membership not to buy the product of a firm involved in a labor dispute. A secondary boycott is an attempt to convince others to stop doing business with a firm that is the subject of a primary boycott.

27.   Tactics available to management in labor-management disputes include:
    a.   Lockouts   c.   Use of strikebreakers
    b.   Injunctions

28.   Management seeks injunctions to order striking workers back to work, to limit the number of pickets that can be used during a strike, or deal with actions that could be detrimental to the public welfare.

29.   For a court to issue an injunction management must show "just cause", such as the possibility of violence or the destruction of property.

30.   Membership in unions has declined from a peak of almost 36% in 1945 to just 12.5% today, and only 8% of workers in the private sector are unionized. Union membership varies by state. The largest union today is the National Education Association.

31.   For unions to grow, they will have to adapt to a work force that is increasingly culturally diverse, white collar, female, and foreign born.

32.   Unions are helping management in training workers, redesigning jobs, and assimilating the new workforce. They are helping to recruit and train foreign workers, unskilled workers, and others who may need special help in adapting to the job requirements of the new economy.

Controversial Employee-Management Issues

33.   The central issue regarding executive compensation seems to be the level of executive pay. The average CEO of a major company makes 160 times the amount of the average hourly worker. Stock options account for a major portion of executive pay, and a

problem arises when executives are compensated with stock options even when the company doesn't meet expectations.

34. Management consultant Peter Drucker suggested that CEOs should not earn much more than 20 times as much as the company's lowest paid employee.

35. American CEOs typically earn two to three times as much as executives in Europe and Canada.

One explanation for the difference between the pay of American CEOs and that of European chief executives is that European companies often have workers who sit on the board of directors. Since boards set executive pay, this could be a reason why the imbalance between starting pay and top pay is less for European executives.

36. Pay equity goes beyond the concept of equal pay for equal work. Pay equity is the concept that people in jobs that require similar levels of education, training, or skills should receive equal pay. It centers on comparing jobs that have traditionally been held by women with those that have traditionally been held by men.

37. In the past the primary explanation for the pay disparity between men and women was that women only worked a portion of their available years once they left school, whereas men worked all of those years. This explanation no longer applies. Now the explanation is that many working women devote more time to their families and so opt for lower paying jobs.

Studies have found that earnings of women with a college degree earn today close to what men earn, and in some fields women out earn men.

38. Conduct can be considered sexually harassing if:
   a. an employee's submission to such conduct is made either explicitly or implicitly a term of employment or is the basis for employment decisions.
   b. the conduct interferes with a worker's job performance or creates an intimidating, hostile or offensive work environment.

39. "Quid pro quo" harassment could be a threat such as "go out with me or you are fired", for example. This explicitly creates a term or condition of employment.

A "hostile environment" is created when an individual's conduct interferes with a worker's job performance or creates an intimidating or offensive work environment. A key term is "unwelcome", which refers to behavior that would offend a reasonable person.

40. A major problem with implementing harassment policies is that workers and managers often know that a policy exists but have no idea what it says.

It is suggested that companies offer management training, and require sexual harassment workshops for all employees, which can be done on the Internet.

41. Child- care issues are important to employers today because:
   a. It is estimated that child care related absences already cost American businesses billions of dollars each year
   b. They raise the question of who should pay for child care services.

42. The questions surrounding child care today concern:
    a. responsibilities for child- care subsidies
    b child care programs
    c. parental leave

43. Companies have responded to the need for safe, affordable day care by providing:
    a. Discount arrangements with national child care chains.
    b. Vouchers that offer payments toward whatever child care the employee chooses.
    c. Referral services that help identify quality child care facilities.
    d. On-site child care centers.
    e. Sick-child care centers.

44. The issue has become important because the workforce in the U.S. is aging, and many workers are going to confront the problem of how to care for older parents. The number of households with at least one adult providing elder care has dramatically increased in the last two decades and is expected to continue to grow.

    Current estimates suggest that companies are presently losing $11 billion a year in reduced productivity, absenteeism, and turnover from employees who have responsibilities with aging parents.

45. Companies can allow employees to move to flextime, telecommuting, part-time employment or job sharing. Certain companies offer employees employee assistance programs or elder care management services. However, few companies offer any type of elder care benefits programs.

46. It is expected that costs to companies will rise as more experience and high ranking employees become involved in caring for older parents and relatives. Estimates are that costs could go as high as $25 billion annually. Companies already realize that transfers and promotions are often out of the question for employees whose parents need ongoing care. The problem will continue to exist well into the 21st century.

47. Individuals who use drugs are three and a half times more likely to be involved in workplace accidents and five times as likely to file a worker's compensation claim. Illegal drug use costs U.S. companies $81 billion in lost productivity annually, according to the U.S. Department of Labor. The National Institute of Health estimates that each drug abuser costs an employer approximately $11,000 a year.

    In response, over 70% of major companies now test workers and job applicants for substance abuse.

48. There is a growing trend toward violence in the workplace. The U.S. Department of Labor cites homicide as the second leading cause of job-related fatalities. Workplace homicides account for 16 percent of all workplace deaths.

49. Many firms have begun to hold focus groups for employee input, have hired managers with strong interpersonal skills, and employed skilled consultants to deal with the growing employee/management issue of workplace violence.

CRITICAL THINKING EXERCISES

1. The development of crafts unions, beginning in 1792 came about to discuss work issues such as pay, hours, conditions and job security. The Industrial Revolution led to changes, and problems for workers in terms of productivity, hours of work, wages and unemployment. If you failed to produce, you lost your job. Hours worked increased to as many as 80 hours per week. Wages were low and the use of child labor was common.

    Unions today are focusing on job security and union recognition, just as the early crafts unions did. However, union negotiators today have also begun to address such issues as global competition, drug testing, benefits such as day care and elder care, violence in the workplace and employee stock ownership programs.

Learning Goal 2

2. | | | | | |
    |---|---|---|---|---|
    | a. | Taft-Hartley | f. | Taft-Hartley Act |
    | b. | Landrum-Griffin | g. | Landrum-Griffin |
    | c. | Wagner Act | h. | Wagner-Act |
    | d. | Norris-LaGuardia | i. | Fair Labor Standards Act |
    | e. | Wagner Act | | |

Learning Goal 3

3. | | | | | |
    |---|---|---|---|---|
    | a. | Agency shop | c. | Open shop |
    | b. | Closed shop | d. | Union shop |

4. There are three options available for resolving these disputes. The players union could have filed grievances against the owners before going on strike, in an attempt to resolve their differences without putting an end to the season. Either side could have brought in a mediator, before or during the strike. The mediator's job is to make suggestions for resolving the dispute. Lastly, arbitration could have been used. In arbitration, the parties agree to bring in a third party to make a binding decision, a decision that both parties must adhere to. The arbitrator must be acceptable to both parties. (In fact, in this case, an arbitrator was discussed between the players and the owners, but neither side could agree on the choice of an arbitrator!)

Learning Goal 4

5. | | | | | |
    |---|---|---|---|---|
    | a. | Primary boycott | e. | Picketing |
    | b. | Lockout | f. | Injunction |
    | c. | Strike | g. | Secondary boycott |
    | d. | Strikebreakers | | |

6. The role of unions is likely to be much different from that of the past. Union leadership is aware of the need to be competitive with foreign firms. Unions have taken a leadership role in introducing such concepts as continuous improvement, constant innovation and employee involvement programs. In the future, unions will help management in training, work design such as self-managed teams, and in recruiting and training foreign workers, unskilled workers and others.

Learning Goal 5

7. U.S. executives are responsible for billion dollar corporations. They often work 70 or more hours per week. Many can show stockholders that they have turned potential problems into profitable success. Further, many top performers in sports, movies and

entertainment are paid large sums, so is it therefore out of line that CEOs of major corporations should be compensated in the same way? Furthermore, there is not a plentiful supply of seasoned, skilled professionals to manage large corporations, especially through the difficult times we have experienced in the early 2000s.

8. The drawbacks of the high level of pay are most noticeable when an executive makes staggering sums, while the financial performance of the company may be lagging. Some question the compensation paid to a departing CEO whose performance forced them to resign their job involuntarily. Stakeholders could certainly question these practices in a business. In comparison to our global competitors, U.S. executives earn substantially more than their counterparts. In the U.S. the average CEO earns 160 times what the average hourly worker earns, while in Japan and Europe the CEOs of large corporations earn, comparatively, quite a bit less. American CEOs typically earn two to three times as much as executives in Europe and Canada.

9. A comparison of jobs traditionally held by men with jobs traditionally held by women would show that women earn about 80 percent of what men earn, thought the differences vary by profession, job experience and tenure and the person's level of education. In the past, disparities could be explained by the fact that women only worked 50 to 60 percent of their available years after they left school, whereas men worked all of those years. As fewer women left the work force for an extended period, this changed. Another explanation for the disparity may be that many women try to work as well as care for families, and thus do not move ahead in their careers as quickly as men. Others opt for lower paying jobs that are less demanding.

In today's knowledge based economy, it appears that women will compete with men, financially, in such areas as health care, telecommunications and knowledge technology.

10. The major question surrounding the issue of sexual harassment is the fact that while managers and workers may know that their company has a sexual harassment policy they don't know what it says. Conduct becomes illegal when: 1) an employee's submission to such conduct is made either explicitly or implicitly a term of employment, or an employee's submission to or rejection of such conduct is used as the basis of employment decisions affecting the worker's status or 2) the conduct interferes with a worker's job performance or creates an unhealthy atmosphere.

Companies are becoming more sensitive to comments and behavior of a sexual nature. Suggestions are more management training, mandatory sexual harassment workshops for all employees and a revamping of the human resource department if necessary to ensure compliance.

11. The issue of <u>child-care</u> will remain a concern in the 21st century. There are questions surrounding who should pay for child care, and around the cost of absences related to child care. The number of companies that offer child-care is growing, and some have begun to provide such benefits as discount arrangements with child-care chains, vouchers, referral services, on-site daycare and sick-child centers.

The <u>elder care</u> issue has arisen because the workforce of the U.S. is aging. Older workers are more likely to be concerned with finding care for elderly parents than with finding day care for children. Businesses do not seem to be responding to the need for elder care as quickly as they could, even though it is estimated that elder-care givers cost employers billions of dollars in lost output and replacement costs.

Companies feel that <u>alcohol and drug abuse</u> is a serious problem in the workplace because so many workers are involved. Drug testing is growing at a rapid pace.

<u>Violence in the workplace</u> is a growing trend. Still, many companies don't offer formal training for dealing with prevention of violence in the workplace, because managers feel the issue is overblown by the media.

PRACTICE TEST

MULTIPLE CHOICE

LG 1	# 1-2
LG 2	# 3-5
LG 3	# 6-9
LG 4	# 10-13
LG 5	# 14-20

TRUE-FALSE

LG 1	#1-3
LG 2	# 4-7
LG 3	# 8-11
LG 4	# 12-15
LG 5	# 16-20

1.	b	11.	d		1.	T	11.	T
2.	c	12.	c		2.	F	12.	T
3.	d	13.	c		3.	T	13.	F
4.	b	14.	a		4.	F	14.	T
5.	a	15.	b		5.	T	15.	F
6.	d	16.	d		6.	T	16.	F
7.	a	17.	b		7.	T	17.	T
8.	d	18.	d		8.	F	18.	F
9.	c	19.	a		9.	T	19.	T
10.	b	20.	b		10.	T	20.	T

CHAPTER 13 – MARKETING: BUILDING CUSTOMER RELATIONSHIPS

LEARNING GOALS

After you have read and studied this chapter, you should be able to:

1. Define marketing and explain how the marketing concept applies in both for profit and nonprofit organizations.
2. List and describe the four Ps of marketing.
3. Describe the marketing research process and how marketers use environmental scanning to learn about the changing marketing environment.
4. Explain now marketers meet the needs of the consumer market through market segmentation, relationship marketing, and the study of consumer behavior.
5. List ways in which the business-to-business market differs from the consumer market

LEARNING THE LANGUAGE

Listed below are important terms found in the chapter. Choose the correct term for the definition and write it in the space provided.

Benefit segmentation	Marketing	Product
Brand name	Marketing concept	Promotion
Business-to-business (B2B) market	Marketing mix	Psychographic segmentation
Consumer market	Marketing research	Relationship marketing
Customer relationship management (CRM)	Market segmentation	Secondary data
Demographic segmentation	Mass marketing	Target marketing
Environmental scanning	Niche marketing	Test marketing
Focus group	One-to-one marketing	Volume, or usage segmentation
Geographic segmentation	Primary data	

1. A word, letter or group of words or letters is a _____ that differentiates one seller's goods and services.

2. All the techniques sellers use to motivate people to buy products or services are called _____.

3. Dividing the marketing by geographic area is _____.

4. All individuals and organizations that want goods and services to use in producing other goods and services or to sell, rent or supply goods to others is known as the _____.

5. The process known as _____ is being used when an organization tests products among potential users.

6.   Information that has already been compiled by others and published in journals and books or made available online is called _____.

7.   A _____is any physical good, service or idea that satisfies a want or need plus anything that would enhance the product in the eyes of a consumer, such as a brand.

8.   The process of _____is dividing the market by age, income, and education level.

9.   A three-part business philosophy called the _____involves (1) a customer orientation, (2) a service orientation, and (3) a profit orientation.

10. A _____is a small group of people who meet under the direction of a discussion leader to communicate their opinions about an organization, its products, or other given issues.

11. The process known as _____calls for finding small, but profitable market segments and designing or finding products for them.

12. The ingredients that go into a marketing program are the _____ and include product, price, place, and promotion.

13. The process known as _____ is marketing toward those groups (market segments) an organization decides it can serve profitably.

14. The process called _____ is the analysis of markets to determine opportunities and challenges, and to find the information needed to make good decisions.

15. The process of _____means dividing the market by determining which benefits of the product to talk about.

16. The _____consists of all the individuals or households that want goods and services for personal consumption or use.

17. The process of_____ consists of planning and executing the conception, pricing, promotion, and distribution of goods and services to facilitate exchanges that satisfy individual and organizational objectives.

18. _____ calls for learning as much as possible about customers and doing everything you can to satisfy them with goods and services over time.

19. The process of dividing the total market into several groups whose members have similar characteristics is called _____.

20. Data referred to as _____, are data that you gather yourself, not from secondary sources such as books and magazines.

21. The marketing strategy known as _____ has the goal of keeping individual customers over time by offering them products that exactly meet their requirements.

22.   The process of _____ is identifying the factors that can affect marketing success.

23.   Dividing the market by using a group's values, attitudes and interests is _____.

24.   _____ is dividing market by usage (volume of use).

25.   Developing a unique mix of goods and services for each individual customer is called _____.

26.   _____ is the term used to describe developing products and promotions to please large groups of people.

ASSESSMENT CHECK

Learning Goal 1
What is Marketing?

1.   The four eras defined in the evolution of marketing are:

        a. _____

        b. _____

        c. _____

        d. _____

2.   Describe the general philosophy of business during the production era.

3.   How was the selling era different from the production era?

4.   Describe the three parts of the marketing concept.

        a. _____

        b. _____

        c. _____

5.   The idea of customer relationship management is to _____

_____

6.   Give some examples of how non-profit organizations use marketing.

Learning Goal 2
The Marketing Mix

7.   Managing the controllable parts of the marketing process involves:

a. _____

b. _____

c. _____

d. _____

8.   List the steps in the marketing process.

a. _____   f. _____

b. _____   g. _____

c. _____   h. _____

d. _____   i. _____

e. _____

9.   What is "concept testing"?

10.   What are prototypes?

11.   When does test marketing occur?

12.   Identify some of the factors involved in setting an appropriate price for a product.

13.   What are marketing intermediaries?

14.   List six promotion techniques.

        a. _____   d. _____

        b. _____   e. _____

        c. _____   f. _____

15. Relationship building with customers includes: _____

        _____

Learning Goal 3
Providing Marketers with Information

16.   What are three things which marketing research helps to determine?

        a. _____

        b. _____

        c. _____

17.   What are the four steps of the marketing research process?

        a. _____

        b. _____

        c. _____

        d. _____

18.   Distinguish between primary and secondary data.

19.	What are six general sources of secondary data?

a. _____   d. _____

b. _____   e. _____

c. _____   f. _____

20.	Which data should be gathered first, primary or secondary? Why?

21.	Why or when will a company use primary data?

22.	What are the sources of primary data?

a. _____   e. _____

b. _____   f. _____

c. _____   g. _____

d. _____

23.	The most common forms of surveys are:

a. _____   c. _____

b. _____   d. _____

24.	How can data collected in the research process be used?

25.	If the results of the actions taken based on market research are not as expected, what can the company do?

26.	What are the factors included in an environmental scan?

a. _____   d. _____

b. _____   e. _____

c. _____

27. What is the most dramatic global change in terms of marketing?

28. What are the most important technological changes in marketing? Why?

29. What are some social trends that marketers must monitor?

30. How has the Internet affected competition for "brick and mortar" companies?

31. How does marketing change with a change in the economy?

32. What determines if a product is a business-to-business product or a consumer product?

Learning Goal 4
The Consumer Market

33. Why do companies use market segmentation?

34. What kind of segmentation is being used when we:

    a. Segment by what qualities a customer prefers?   _____

    b. Segment by where people live?   _____

    c. Segment by age, income, or education?   _____

    d. Segment by a group's values, attitudes or interests? _____

    e. Segment by how much a customer uses?   _____

35.   What is the difference between niche marketing and one-to-one marketing?

36.   The mass marketer tries to sell products: _____

37.   The goal of relationship marketing is: _____

38.   How has technology aided in the development of relationship marketing?

39.   What are the steps in the consumer decision-making process?

       a.   _____

       b.   _____

       c.   _____

       d.   _____

       e.   _____

40.   Describe the four types of influences on the consumer decision-making process.

       a.   _____

       b.   _____

       c.   _____

       d.   _____

41. In the area of consumer behavior what are:

Learning: _____

_____

Reference group: _____

_____

Culture: _____

_____

Subculture: _____

_____

Cognitive dissonance:_____

_____

Learning Goal 5
The Business-To-Business Market (B2B)

42. What types of organizations are included in the B2B market?

43. Why do business-to-business marketing strategies differ from consumer marketing strategies?

44. What are six factors that make business-to-business marketing different from consumer marketing?

a. _____

b. _____

c. _____

d. _____

e. _____

CRITICAL THINKING EXERCISES

Learning Goal 1

1.   Todd Whitman was a full-time student at a community college in the St. Louis area. In addition to going to school, Todd also worked for a company out of Idaho (Todd's home state) that made ice cream. As Todd tells it "Alan Reed owns a potato farm in Idaho. He was looking for another market for his potatoes when he realized that the chemical make up of the potato was such that it could be used in making a tasty ice cream without using any sugar - i.e. a sugar free ice cream. He figured there had to be a market for that kind of product, one made without any artificial products to sweeten, so he made a few batches and tried it on his friends, without telling them it was made from potatoes." He called the ice cream Al and Reed's. This is where Todd came in. While in St. Louis, Todd's job was to attempt to get the product sold to St. Louisans. His employer shipped him a few gallons (as much as he could hold in his home freezer). Todd started trying to sell Al and Reed's to local grocery store chains, and ultimately got one of them to carry the ice cream in a couple of stores on a trial basis. He also brought some samples in to his Introduction to Business class, after persuading his teacher to allow a taste test. The product went over well, until the students found out it was made from potatoes!

   Todd continued his promotional efforts with grocery stores, calling on them whenever he could. He left promotional pamphlets that explained the concept and production of ice cream made from potatoes, and offered the stores discounts for buying in volume.

   a.   Did Todd and Alan Reed use the marketing concept? Did Alan learn about customer needs? Which of the eras described in the evolution of marketing do you think Todd and Alan exemplify?

   b.   What steps in the marketing process did Todd and Alan Reed take?

   c.   What potential problem might they encounter with this product? How could Todd and Alan use the last step of the marketing process to overcome the problem?

d.   Identify the product, promotion and place variables in this situation. What price do you think they should charge? Why?

2.   We read in earlier chapters about the "revolutionary" concepts of organizational design such as cross-functional, self managed teams, and such concepts as continuous improvement. What does all that have to do with marketing?

Learning Goals 2,3

3.   Sun-2-Shade is a revolutionary automotive product. Using technology available from the eyewear industry Eric, our entrepreneur, had created a car windshield that automatically darkens in the sun and lightens when in the shade or on a cloudy day. Now is the time to begin developing a marketing plan for our product.

a.   What need did Eric see when he came up with the idea of Sun-2-Shade?

b.   Who/what do you think should be Sun-2-Shade's customers?

c.   How could concept testing have helped Sun-2-Shade?

d.   Conduct an environmental scan for Sun-2-Shade.

e.   Could Sun-2-Shade make use of one-to-one marketing?

Learning Goal 3

4.   Marketing research is conducted to determine the needs of the market and the best ways to fill those needs.

Using the four steps outlined in your book, suggest a market research project that might be of use to Sun-2-Shade.

a. _____

b. _____

c. _____

d. _____

Learning Goal 4

5.   The major segmentation variables are:

Geographic   Psychographic   Volume
Demographic   Benefit

Listed below are various products. Identify a target market for each product, then list the segmentation variable that could be used to identify that target market. There could be more than one target market for some products.

Example:
Head and Shoulders Shampoo:
Target market: People with dandruff
Variables: Benefit, health

a. Toyota Yaris automobile

b. Nike footwear

c. McDonalds

d. Campbell's nacho cheese soup

6. Chad Allen turned on his CD player to listen to music while he was studying, and all he heard was a loud buzzing coming from his speakers. "Oh no! Now what?" thought Chad. Well Chad found the problem, and realized that the system was shot. "Well, we've got to have music for the party coming up in two weeks, so I'm going to have to get a new player" Chad said to his roommate on the way to class. He looked through the ads in the Sunday paper, and saw several sales at a couple of different stores. He spent part of the weekend, and part of a few days the following week researching different component pieces on the Internet, comparing each for price and sound quality and talking to sales people about which system was the best value. A couple of friends gave Chad their opinions of the brands, based on their experience with the specific brand Chad was looking at. Chad knew this brand was a good one, because his sister had purchased it last year. He bought the new system the following weekend, before the sale went off. He felt somewhat uneasy at how much he had spent, but when he saw an ad for that same system in an upscale magazine for $100 more, he felt better.

Identify the steps in the decision making process that Chad took, and what factors influenced his decision, using the figure in your text.

Learning Goals 4,5
7. Let's continue helping Sun-2-Shade to develop a marketing plan:

   a. Who would you choose as Sun-2-Shade's target market?

   b. If you were to choose the consumer market, what are some variables that you would want to consider?

   c. How would marketing your product to a business market differ from marketing the product to the consumer market?

8.   Would you classify Sun-2-Shade product as a consumer good or as a business good? What characteristics of the business-to-business market will affect Sun-2-Shade's marketing efforts, and how?

9.   Determine whether the following describes a consumer or a business-to-business product.

   a.   Monsanto buys apples to sell in its company cafeteria. _____

   b.   Jeff Walter buys a lawn mower for his lawn mowing business._____

   c.   Darlene Knott buys a lawn mower to mow her lawn. _____

   d.   Marti Galganski buys apples for her daughter's lunch. _____

PRACTICE TEST

MULTIPLE CHOICE – Circle the best answer

Learning Goal 1
1.   When Maritza Toros opened her Mexican restaurant in a fashionable suburb of Kansas City, she believed that the most important element of her success would be advertising. She made sure that a significant portion of her budget was devoted to advertising in local papers, sent out coupons and really focused on the promotional aspects of the restaurant. Which of the four eras of marketing does it seem that Maritza emphasized?
   a.   production era
   b.   sales era
   c.   marketing era
   d.   customer relationship management

2.   Which of the following would not be included in a discussion of the marketing concept?
   a.   A customer orientation
   b.   Service orientation
   c.   Profit orientation
   d.   A cost orientation

3.   Learning as much as possible about customers and doing everything you can to satisfy them and exceed their expectations is:
   a.   customer relationship management.
   b.   marketing management.
   c.   market segmentation.
   d.   Promotion

4.	Which of the following is not considered to be one of the marketing mix variables?
	a.	producing a want satisfying product
	b.	promoting the product
	c.	minimizing the cost of producing the product
	d.	setting a price for the product

5.	When McDonald's considered adding pizza to their menu, the company made pizza available in some of their typical markets, to determine customer reactions. That process is called:
	a.	promotion
	b.	test marketing
	c.	outsourcing
	d.	concept testing

6.	Intermediaries are:
	a.	consumers who are in the middle of the consumer decision making process.
	b.	advertising agencies responsible for developing the advertising campaign for a new product.
	c.	companies responsible for developing products to sell to businesses.
	d.	organizations that are in the middle of a series of organizations that distribute goods from producers to consumers.

Learning Goal 3
7	Marketing research helps determine all but which of the following?
	a.	how distribution needs will change
	b	what customers have purchased in the past
	c.	what changes have occurred to change what customers want
	d.	what customers are likely to want in the future

8.	What is the first step in the marketing research process?
	a.	analyze data
	b.	collect data
	c.	define the problem
	d.	develop potential solutions

9.	When Sun-2-Shade needed some information about the potential market for their product, the marketing team looked to the Internet to find industry trends, and to look at the market for eyewear products, which use the same technology that is used in their self-darkening windshield. The type of information the marketing team was using is:
	a.	secondary data
	b.	surveys
	c.	primary data
	d.	focus groups

10.	The factors included in an environmental scan include all of the following except:
	a.	technological factors
	b.	competitive factors
	c.	management factors
	d.	economic factors

11. The increase in the number of older Americans has created a growing demand for nursing homes, health care, continuing education and more. This is as a result of the changes in the _____ factors in the environment.
    a. sociocultural
    b. economic
    c. technological
    d. competitive

12. Which of the following products would be considered as the "business to business" market?
    a. classes at a university for a college freshman
    b. pens and pencils for that student
    c. books for the class
    d. a computer for the instructor to use while teaching the class

Learning Goal 4

13. Johnson and Johnson targets children with Sesame Street bandages, and GM targets women for their Chevy Blazer vehicle. These are examples of:
    a. benefit segmentation.
    b. volume segmentation.
    c. psychographic segmentation.
    d. demographic segmentation.

14. We FlyU Anywhere is a travel agency that specializes in creating exotic trips to unusual destinations for their clients. They will create a "designer" vacation just for you. The most accurate description for the kind of marketing this travel agency is using would be:
    a. Niche marketing
    b. One-to-one marketing
    c. Customer Relationship marketing
    d. Stakeholder marketing

15. The company that makes the Nautica brand licensed with the Stride-Rite company to make an athletic shoe to compete with Nike. The company wants the shoe to be used for athletics, not worn just for style. Nautica is making use of:
    a. market analysis
    b. market segmentation
    c. niche marketing
    d. one-to-one marketing

16. At one time, companies developed products and promotions to please large groups of people, and tried to sell as many products to as many people as possible. This is known as:
    a. relationship marketing.
    b. a consumer orientation.
    c. forming a community of buyers.
    d. mass marketing.

17. Kelly Butler is out looking for a new car. Kelly is an aspiring lawyer, and she is looking for a car that will help her to project that "lawyer "image. Kelly is influenced by:
    a. a cultural influence.
    b. a reference group.
    c. cognitive dissonance.
    d. the consumer market.

18. After Kelly bought her car, she realized just how much money she had spent! She spent some time wondering if she had made the right decision. Kelly seems to be suffering from:
   a. cognitive dissonance
   b. consumer behavior
   c. self-doubt
   d. psychological influences

Learning Goal 5
19. Which of the following is not descriptive of the business-to-business market?
   a. there are relatively few customers in the industrial market
   b. industrial customers are relatively large
   c. industrial buyers are generally more rational that consumer buyers
   d. industrial markets tend to be geographically scattered

20. Marketing strategies for the business-to-business market:
   a. differ from consumer marketing strategies because the nature of the buyers is different
   b. are basically similar to the consumer market, because business buyers are consumers
   c. are not concerned with relationship marketing techniques
   d. are concerned with the same types of influences as those in the consumer market.

TRUE-FALSE

Learning Goal 1
1. _____ The idea of customer relationship management is to enhance customer satisfaction and stimulate long-term customer loyalty.

2. _____ Non profits for the most part do not need to make use of marketing techniques.

Learning Goal 2
3. _____ Coupons rebates and cents-off deals are part of the promotion variable of the marketing mix.

4. _____ Test marketing refers to the development of an accurate description of your product and then testing it by asking people whether the idea appeals to them.

5. _____ Setting an appropriate price includes considering the cost involved in producing, promoting, and distributing the product.

Learning Goal 3
6. _____ To keep costs lower, it is best to use secondary data first, when possible, in the market research process.

7. _____ Socio-cultural factors such as population growth and changing demographics may affect some marketers, but are not important for most organizations.

8. _____ If the economy begins to fall on hard times, about the only thing marketers can do is to cut production and wait for better times.

9. _____ The process of dividing the total market into several groups is called target marketing.

10. _____ An example of psychographic segmentation is dividing the market by whether or not your customers live in cities or in suburban areas.

11. _____ The Big and Tall Men's stores, which cater to men who are of certain heights and weights, is an example of a company using niche marketing.

12. _____ Relationship marketing leads away from mass production toward more custom-made goods and services.

13. _____ When selling to the Chinese market, it is important to avoid demonstrating how your product makes the customer stand out from the crowd, because the Chinese relate better to a group identity. This is an example of a cultural influence.

Learning Goal 5

14. _____ The reason for distinguishing between consumer markets and the business to business market is because the strategies for reaching the market are different, because the buyers are different, and the B2B market is much smaller.

15. _____ The business-to-business market is smaller than the consumer market in terms of the number of buyers, but large, in terms of the size of the buyers.

16. _____ Business to business sales tend to be less direct than consumer sales, because business buyers use more middlemen.

You Can Find It on the Net

Rollerblade's Web site contains a lot of information about a variety of areas. Visit this site at www.rollerblade.com

Does Rollerblade's Web site help the company strengthen the relationship it has with its customers?

How does the site attempt to create new relationships with new customers?

How do the elements of Rollerblade's Web site reflect their target market? Be specific.

Does Rollerblade invite comments from visitors to its Web site? If so, how does this affect its attempt to build positive relationships with its customers?

ANSWERS

LEARNING THE LANGUAGE

1. Brand name	10. Focus group	19. Market segmentation
2. Promotion	11. Niche marketing	20. Primary data
3. Geographic segmentation	12. Marketing mix	21. Relationship marketing
4. Business-to-business market	13. Target marketing	22. Environmental scanning
5. Test marketing	14. Marketing research	23. Psychographic segmentation
6. Secondary data	15. Benefit segmentation	24. Volume segmentation
7. Product	16. Consumer market	25. One-to-one marketing
8. Demographic segmentation	17. Marketing	26. Mass marketing
9. Marketing concept	18. Customer relationship management	

ASSESSMENT CHECK

A Brief History of Marketing

1. The four eras defined in the evolution of marketing are:
    a. production era
    b. selling era
    c. marketing concept era
    d. customer relationship era

2. The business philosophy of the production era was "Produce as much as you can because there is a limitless market". This was due to the combined factors of limited production capability and vast demand for products. The goals of business centered on production because most goods were bought as soon as they became available so there was a need for greater and greater production.

3. The selling era came about because eventually businesses developed mass-production techniques, and production capacity often exceeded market demand. This is directly opposite from the production era. The business philosophy turned from an emphasis on production to an emphasis on selling, and most companies emphasized both selling and advertising.

4. The three parts of the marketing concept were:
    a. A customer orientation, which is to find out what customers want and provide it for them.
    b. A service orientation, making sure everyone in the organization has the same objective of customer satisfaction.
    c. A profit orientation, which is marketing the goods and services that will earn the firm a profit and enable it to survive and expand.

5. The idea of customer relationship management is to enhance customer satisfaction and stimulate long-term customer loyalty.

6. Marketing is used in many ways by non-profit organizations. Charities use marketing to raise funds or to obtain other resources. For example, the Red Cross uses promotion to encourage people to donate blood. Schools use marketing to attract new students and

churches use marketing to attract new members and raise funds. Politicians use marketing to get votes and states use marketing to attract businesses and tourists.

Learning Goal 2
The Marketing Mix

7 . Managing the controllable parts of the marketing process involves:
   a. designing a want satisfying <u>product.</u>
   b. setting a <u>price</u> for the product.
   c. placing the product in a <u>place</u> where people will buy it.
   d. <u>promoting</u> the product.

8. The steps in the marketing process are:
   a. Find opportunities
   b. Conduct research
   c. Identify a target market
   d. Design a product to meet the need, based upon research results
   e. Test the product
   f. Set a price
   g. Select a distribution system
   h. Design a promotional program
   i. Build a relationship with your customers

9. In concept testing, an accurate description of a product is developed, and then people are asked whether the concept appeals to them.

10. Prototypes are samples of the product that you take to consumers to test their reactions.

11. Test marketing occurs after a prototype is developed, and most likely before a company will proceed further to find investors and a location, for example.

12. Setting a price depends on a number of factors. In a competitive market, it is wise to set a price close to your competitors. The costs involved in producing, distributing, and promoting the product must also be considered. If you want to create an image of quality, you might price the product higher.

13. Marketing intermediaries are organizations that specialize in distributing products. They are called middlemen because they're in the middle of a series of organizations that distribute goods from producers to consumers.

14. Six promotion techniques are:
   a. advertising   d. publicity
   b. personal selling   e. word of mouth
   c. public relations   f. sales promotion

15. Relationship building with customers includes responding to suggestions from consumers and post purchase service.

16. Marketing research helps to determine:
    a. what customers have purchased in the past
    b. what situational changes have occurred to change what customers want
    c. what customers are likely to want in the future

17. The four steps of the marketing research process are:
    a. Define the question and determine the present situation
    b. Collect data
    c. Analyze the research data
    d. Choose the best solutions

18. Primary data are statistics and information not previously published that you gather on your own through observation, surveys, and personal interviews or focus groups. Secondary data are previously published reports and research from journals, trade associations, the government, information services and others.

19. General sources of secondary data are:
    a. Government Publications
    b. Commercial Publications
    c. Magazines
    d. Newspapers
    e. Internal sources
    f. General sources

20. Secondary data should be gathered first, because it is less expensive to obtain than primary data.

21. Secondary data may not provide all the information managers need to make decisions. Companies will use primary data when additional, in-depth information is needed.

22. Sources of primary data are:
    a. Interviews
    b. Surveys
    c. Observation
    d. Focus groups
    e. On-line surveys
    f. Questionnaires
    g. Customer comments

23. The most common methods of gathering survey information are:
    a. telephone surveys
    b. online surveys
    c. mail surveys
    d. personal interviews.

24. The data collected in the research process must be turned into useful information. Good interpretation of the data collected can help a company find useful alternatives to specific marketing challenges. After analyzing the data, market researchers determine alternative strategies and make recommendations as to which strategy may be best and why.

25. If the results of the actions taken based on market research are not as expected, the company can take corrective action and conduct new studies in the ongoing attempt to provide consumer satisfaction at the lowest cost.

26. The factors included in an environmental scan include:
   a. global   c. sociocultural   e. economic
   b. technological   d. competitive

27. The most dramatic global change in terms of marketing is the growth of the Internet.

28. The most important technological changes in marketing also involve the Internet and the growth of consumer databases. Using these, companies can develop products and services that more closely match the needs of consumers.

29. Marketers must monitor social trends such as population growth, and changing demographics such as the growing population of older people and the shifting ethnic nature of the American population.

30. Brick and mortar companies must be aware of new competition from the Internet. Consumers can now search literally all over the world for the best prices through the Internet so brick and mortar stores must adjust their prices accordingly.

31. When an economy is growing, there is a demand for expensive products. When the economy slows, marketers have to adapt by offering products that are less expensive or more tailored to to consumers with modest incomes.

32. The buyer's reason for buying and the end use of the product determine whether a product is considered a consumer product or an industrial product.

Learning Goal 4
The Consumer Market

33. Consumer groups differ in age, education level, income and taste, and a business can't usually fill the needs of every group. So the company must decide what groups to serve, and develop products and services specially tailored to meet their needs.

34. a. benefit
    b. geographic
    c. demographic
    d. psychographic
    e. volume

35. Niche marketing is the process of finding small but profitable market segments and designing or finding products for them. One-to-one marketing means developing a unique mix of goods and services for each individual customer.

36. The mass marketer tries to sell products to as many people as possible, using mass media, such TV, radio, and newspapers.

37. The goal of relationship marketing is to keep individual customers over time by offering them new products that exactly meet their requirements.

38. Technology enables sellers to work with individual buyers to determine their wants and needs and to develop goods and services specifically designed for them. Enterprise Resource Planning links firms so that suppliers can meet the needs of the manufacturer when producing want satisfying products.

39. The steps in the consumer decision-making process are:
    a. Problem recognition
    b. Information search
    c. Alternative evaluation
    d. Purchase decision
    e. Postpurchase decision (cognitive dissonance)

40. a. Marketing mix influences - product, price, promotion, place
    b. Sociocultural influences - Reference groups, family, social class, culture, subculture
    c. Situational influences - Type of purchase, social surroundings, physical surroundings, previous experience
    d. Psychological influences - Perception, attitudes, learning, motivation

41. a. Learning involves changes in an individual's behavior resulting from previous experiences and information
    b. A reference group is the group that an individual uses as a reference point in the formation of his or her beliefs, attitudes, values or behavior.
    c. Culture is the set of values, attitudes, and ways of doing things that are passed down from one generation to another in a society.
    d. Subculture is the set of values, attitudes and ways of doing things that result from belonging to a certain ethnic group, religious group, racial group or other group with which one identifies.
    e. Cognitive dissonance is a type of psychological conflict that can occur after a purchase, particularly a major purchase.

Learning Goal 5
The Business-To-Business Market (B2B)

42. The business to business (B2B) market includes manufacturers, intermediaries such as retailers, institutions and the government.

43. The strategies of business-to-business marketing differ from consumer marketing strategies because the nature of the buyers is different.

44. The factors that make business-to-business different from consumer marketing are:
    a. The number of customers in the B2B market is relatively few
    b. The size of business customers is relatively large
    c. B2B markets tend to be geographically concentrated
    d. Business buyers generally are more rational than ultimate consumers are
    e. B2B sales tend to be direct

CRITICAL THINKING EXERCISES

Learning Goal 1
1. a. From the story, it doesn't sound as if Al found an opportunity to fill a need for a sugar free ice cream and then found a way to develop it, which would be the first part of the marketing concept. There also doesn't appear to be a concern for customer satisfaction, other than to make sure the consumers liked the product. It sounds more like he had extra potatoes and needed to find a novel way to sell them! This exemplifies the production era when the main marketing concern was distribution and storages. The difference today in the business environment is the level of demand and the competition.

b. Alan recognized the need for a sugar free ice cream. At least he thought he did. We don't know how much research he did on the actual demand for a sugar free ice cream. He did test the concept by making small batches and testing it with his friends. He made the product in small batches at first. Todd did some research in his business class. You could say the concept testing was combined with the test marketing stage or that St. Louis served as a test market. The brand name stemmed from the originator's name, Alan Reed (Al and Reed's). The marketing middlemen are Todd, and then the grocery stores, which finally agreed to sell the product through Todd's efforts. Promotion was done primarily through pamphlets and personal selling by Todd. There is no mention made of any effort to build a relationship with the customer.

c. Probably the biggest potential problem is the negative reaction to the product. It could be that consumers will not be attracted to ice cream made from potatoes, and would wonder about the taste. (The students actually liked the taste of the ice cream until they found out it was made from potatoes!) By talking with consumers, grocery store managers (who are consumers, too, and must be convinced) Todd and Alan may have found ways to overcome the perception that ice cream made from potatoes must taste terrible.

d. Product – sugar free ice cream made from potatoes

Promotion – personal selling, such as Todd taking the ice cream to the grocery store. They also offered discounts to the grocers, which could be seen as a form of promotion.

Place – Todd's efforts were to place the product in the grocery store

Price – how much would you pay for this product? Would it be considered a premium product? Often sugar free versions of products are a little higher in price than the regular product. Would you pay $5 per gallon?

2. It has become clear that everyone in a firm has to work together to exceed customer's expectations. Companies have begun to see that employees will not provide first-class goods and services to customers unless they receive first-class treatment from their employer. Therefore, we have seen changes in organizational design, and a focus on the "internal" customer. Cross functional teams, discussed in previous chapters, are practicing continuous improvement and uniting employees in a joint effort to produce goods and services which will both please customers and assure a profit for the firm. Continuous improvement in processes are also focused on satisfying the customer while competing with speed, better higher quality products and lower prices.

3. a. This may be a situation where Eric is creating a need! Since the windshield would keep cars cooler on hot, sunny days, this kind of product could be popular in areas that are sunny for a good part of the year, like the Southwest, for example. However, it has potential for any area of the country.

b. There is a potential for two types of customers, the automotive manufacturers, for installation as an option in new cars, and the after-market dealers, like auto supply stores, for people who want the product to be installed later. There will still be a need for a retailer of some kind, to install the windshield. So another potential customer would be companies that repair damaged windshields.

c. Asking people if they need a product such as this would have given Eric a feel for what demand might have been. He would have to be sure to ask the right questions of the right people to get an accurate idea. He could have given prototypes to friends, or potential customers, for use, to "field test" or test market the product.

d. The <u>Social</u> environment consists of trends and population shifts. A trend toward higher end, more luxury-type cars, contributes to a positive outlook for Sun-2-Shade's product.

An aging population, with a stronger interest in health and comfort also makes for a positive outlook for the company.

Since this type of equipment could possibly be offered only in certain kinds of cars, <u>economic</u> factors such as disposable income, and unemployment, would affect demand for the cars, and thus for Sun-2-Shade'sproduct. The company may have to overcome a perception that this product is a prestige product, which could affect demand. In a slowing economy Sun-2-Shade will need to focus on the advantages their product offers, and be sure to downplay the fact that a self-darkening windshield will be more expensive. This also could have an impact globally, as foreign economies are slow. When economies are growing, Sun-2-Shade can take advantage of a prestige image, if that is what they want to create.

With a rapidly expanding <u>global </u>market, there may be possibilities outside the United States, as well as potential competition. Sun-2-Shade will have access to foreign manufacturers with manufacturing facilities here as well.

Right now, it doesn't seem that Sun-2-Shade appears to have much direct <u>competition,</u> so the company may have an advantage. There are no "brick and mortar" store selling this product.

<u>Technology</u> has affected Sun-2-Shade simply by virtue of the fact that the process for creating the windshield has only been in existence for a few years. Further, new high-tech production techniques will help Sun-2-Shade to produce more products with fewer people at a lower cost. Also, technology will enable Sun-2-Shade to reach global customers.

e. Can Sun-2-Shade adopt a one to one marketing strategy? Basically, the product must be made to suit many different models of car, with different windshield sizes and shapes. The product is "custom made" for "customized marketing." The possibility exists for allowing customers to choose the color of their windshield.

Learning Goal 3
4. a. Sun-2-Shade may want to determine what kind of demand there will be for their product in the next five years. They may want to find out if their primary market should be younger or older drivers, and relate that to the type of car being driven. They may also want to determine if there are other markets they could enter. For example, over-the-road truckers could make use of this product, but it may have to be of a different size and shape to fit onto a semi.

b. Collecting secondary data for the automotive market may be easily done to determine potential demand for autos and their product in the automotive market. Trade journals and government publications would provide sales forecasts for the type of cars Sun-2-Shade is targeting. The truck market may require some primary research, such as focus groups or some kind of survey, possibly distributed through the mail, or directly to truckers in some way.

c.   Analysis of the data may indicate there is a big market for the product for the truck market. Alternatively, it may indicate that sales are predicted to go flat for the kinds of cars Sun-2-Shade has targeted, or for the automotive industry in general. This would indicate that the company may want to target a different car segment, or another market altogether.

d.   Choosing the best solution would be to choose the market that will be the most profitable for Sun-2-Shade and still meet the needs of their stakeholders.

5.   Sample Answers:
        a. Ford Focus
           Target market - Young drivers, may be buying their first car
           Variables – Could be demographic, such as age, income, family life cycle could also
                        be benefit , since the Yaris is fuel efficient.
        b. Nike
           Target market – Teenagers, boys and girls, interested in sports
           Variables – Demographic – sex, age and Psychographic – interests, self image

        c. McDonalds
           Target market – Families with young children
           Variables – Demographic – family life cycle, age, income, and Psychographic –
                        lifestyle

        d. Campbell's nacho cheese soup
           Target market – Consumers in the west and southwest
           Variables – Geography – region Demographic - nationality, or Culture

6.   Problem recognition came when Chad realized his system couldn't be fixed. Chad searched for information through the newspaper ads, and also by going to the stores and talking to salespeople. He was evaluating the alternatives by comparing each component piece for value and sound. When he finally made his purchase, he felt "cognitive dissonance," uneasy as to how much he spent, until he saw an ad for the same brand at a more expensive price.

Along the way, several factors influenced Chad's decision. He spoke to friends, which could be considered a reference group. Family may have been an influence, as Chad's sister has the same brand. There was a cultural influence as well, just from the fact that Chad felt the importance of having a new c.d. system for his party, rather that using a less expensive alternative. The price variable of the marketing mix was an influence, as the system was on sale. You could consider the psychological influence of learning, as Chad's friends had learned that this was a good brand through experience, and passed that information along. You may have thought of other influences as well.

7. Keep in mind these are suggested answers, and you may come up with a totally different plan.

    a. We have mentioned two target markets for Sun-2-Shade- the original equipment automotive market, to be installed as cars are assembled, and a consumer market, through auto parts stores perhaps. A third market, which is complementary to the original automotive market, is car windshield installation and repair companies. You may have decided on another way to approach the market.

    b. If you chose the consumer market, variables could include: Income, because the owners who would be interested may own cars that are higher end. With research you may find out that age could be a consideration. This is where research can really come in handy.

    c. To market to the business-to-business market, Sun-2-Shade must focus on personal selling, in a very concentrated market. The automotive industry has few domestic producers, but there are several foreign manufacturers with production facilities here in the United States. You would have to focus on quality, be able to meet the volume required to sell to the business market, and meet delivery requirements that may include dealing with a just-in-time inventory control system. This would require a sophisticated production and delivery system on the part of Sun-2-Shade.

8. Sun-2-Shade's product could be classified as both a consumer product and a product for the business-to-business market. If Eric sells the windshield through after market auto equipment retailers, the product would be considered a consumer good, in general. In attempting to reach the automotive manufacturers, Eric is. developing a business-to-business marketing relationship.

    The characteristics of the business-to-business market listed in your book will affect Sun-2-Shade in a number of ways. First, the primary market is the automotive industry, so there will be relatively few customers compared to the consumer market. Those car manufacturers are very large corporations, among the largest in the world, each with significant buying power. The domestic car market, at least, is concentrated in one geographic area. If Eric were to try to appeal to buyers for foreign manufacturers, he would have to do some more traveling. These buyers will consider Eric's product based on the "total product offer," including how much more marketable Sun-2-Shade will make their product, in addition to factors such as quality and price. If the customer is the auto industry, Eric won't need to use wholesalers or retailers, marketing middlemen, he will sell directly to the car companies. For the consumer market, he will have to use at least a retail distribution center.

9.   a. Business   c. Consumer
      b. Business   d. Consumer

PRACTICE TEST

MULTIPLE CHOICE

LG 1   # 1-3
LG 2   # 4-6
LG 3   # 7-12
LG 4   # 13-18
LG 5   #19-20

TRUE-FALSE

LG 1   #1-2
LG 2   # 3-5
LG 3   #6-8
LG 4   #9-13
LG 5   # 14-16

1. b	11. a	1. T	9. F
2. d	12. d	2. F	10. F
3. a	13. d	3. T	11. T
4. c	14. b	4. F	12. T
5. b	15. b	5. T	13. T
6. d	16. d	6. T	14. F
7. a	17. b	7. F	15. T
8. c	18. a	8. F	16. F
9. a	19. d		
10. c	20. a		

CHAPTER 14 – DEVELOPING AND PRICING PRODUCTS AND SERVICES

LEARNING GOALS

After you have read and studied this chapter, you should be able to:

1. Explain the concept of a total product offer.
2. Describe the various kinds of consumer and industrial goods.
3. List and describe the functions of packaging.
4. Describe the differences among a brand, a brand name, and a trademark, and explain the concepts of brand equity and loyalty.
5. Explain the role of brand managers and the steps of the new-product development process.
6. Draw the product life cycle, describe each of its stages, and describe marketing strategies at each stage.
7. Explain various pricing objectives and strategies.
8. Explain why nonpricing strategies are growing in importance.

LEARNING THE LANGUAGE

Listed below are important terms found in the chapter. Choose the correct term for the definition and write it in the space provided.

Brand	Everyday low pricing (EDLP)	Product screening
Brand association	Generic goods	Psychological pricing
Brand awareness	High-low pricing strategy	Shopping goods and services
Brand equity	Industrial goods	Skimming price strategy
Brand loyalty	Knockoff brands	Specialty goods and services
Brand manager	Manufacturers' brand names	Target costing
Break-even analysis	Penetration strategy	Total fixed costs
Bundling	Price leadership	Total product offer
Commercialization	Product analysis	Trademark
Competition-based pricing	Product differentiation	Unsought goods and services
Concept testing	Product life cycle	Value
Convenience goods and services	Product line	Variable costs
Dealer (private) brands	Product mix	

1. The process used to determine profitability at various levels of sales is called _____.

2. The method of pricing known as a _____ is when a product is priced low to attract many customers and discourage competitors.

3. The strategy of _____ involves setting prices that are higher than EDLP stores, but having many special sales where the prices are lower than competitors.

4. A _____ consists of everything that consumers evaluate when deciding whether to buy something; also called a value package.

5.   The degree to which customers are satisfied, like the brand, and are committed to further purchases is called _____.

6.   A theoretical model called the _____ shows what happens to sales and profits for a product class over time.

7.   A strategy known as _____ is one in which a new product is priced high to make optimum profit while there is little competition.

8.   A brand that has been given exclusive legal protection for both the brand name and the pictorial design is called a _____.

9.   The linking of a brand to other favorable images is called _____.

10.   Products identified as _____ are used in the production of other products and are sometimes called business goods.

11.   Conducting a _____ involves making cost estimates and sales forecasts to get a feeling for the profitability of new product ideas.

12.   A _____ is a name, symbol, or design (or combination thereof) that identifies the goods or services of one seller or group of sellers and distinguishes them from those of competitors.

13.   The process of _____ calls for taking a product idea to consumers to test their reactions.

14.   Products called _____ are products that the consumer wants to purchase frequently with a minimum of effort.

15.   Grouping two or more products together and pricing them as a unit is known as _____.

16.   Products called _____ don't carry the manufacturer's name, but carry a distributor or retailer's name instead.

17.   Products with unique characteristics and brand equity are perceived as having no reasonable substitute. The consumer puts forth a special effort to purchase these products, called _____.

18.   How quickly or easily a given brand name comes to mind when a product category is mentioned is _____.

19.   A group of products known as the _____ are physically similar or are intended for a similar market.

20.   Nonbranded products called _____ usually sell at a sizable discount compared to national or private-label brands.

21.   Designing a product so that it satisfies customers and meets the profit margins desired by the firm is called _____.

22. Products known as _____ are products that consumers are unaware of, haven't necessarily thought of buying, or find that they need to solve an unexpected problem.

23. Consumers buy _____ only after comparing value, quality, and price from a variety of sellers.

24. A combination of factors called _____ includes awareness, loyalty, perceived quality, images and emotions people associate with a brand name.

25. The brand names of manufacturers that distribute a product nationally are called _____.

26. Costs known as _____ change according to the level of production.

27. Consumers want a good quality product at a fair price, so they calculate the _____ of a product by looking at the benefits, and subtracting the costs to see if benefits exceed the costs.

28. Illegal copies of national brand-names goods are known as _____.

29. A _____ has direct responsibility for one brand or one product line.

30. The process of _____ is designed to reduce the number of new-product ideas being worked on at any one time.

31. Known as _____ these are all the expenses that remain the same no matter how many products are sold.

32. Promoting a product to distributors and retailers to get wide distribution and developing strong advertising and sales campaigns to generate and maintain interest in the product among distributors and consumers is called _____.

33. The creation of real or perceived product differences is called _____.

34. The practice of _____ is setting prices lower than competitors and then not having any special sales.

35. The term _____ is used to describe the combination of product lines offered by a manufacturer.

36. The procedure of _____ is one by which one or more dominant firms set the pricing practices that all competitors in an industry follow.

37. A pricing strategy called _____ is based on what all the other competitors are doing.

38. Pricing goods and services at price points that make the product appear less expensive is known as _____

ASSESSMENT CHECK

Learning Goal 1
Product Development and the Total Product Offer

1. To satisfy consumers today marketers and managers must _____

    _____

2. What are the factors that make up the total product offer?

    a. _____   g. _____

    b. _____   h. _____

    c. _____   i. _____

    d. _____   j. _____

    e. _____   k. _____

    f. _____   l. _____

3. Why does a company develop a variety of total product offers?

4. What is the difference between a product line and a product mix?

Learning Goal 2
Product Differentiation

5. How does a marketer create a perception of product differentiation?

6. List the four different classes of consumer goods and services. Give an example of each
    kind.

    a. _____

    b. _____

    c. _____

    d. _____

7.   What are three variables important to marketers of convenience goods?

a. _____   c. _____

b. _____

8.   Describe the characteristics of shopping goods.

9.   Why will consumers put forth a special effort to purchase a specific brand name when purchasing specialty products? How are these goods marketed?

10.   What are the best appeals, or ways to promote:

Convenience goods:

Shopping goods:

Specialty goods:

Unsought goods:

11.   What determines into which class a product falls? Can one consumer good be classified in several ways?

12.   What distinguishes a consumer good from an industrial (or B2B) good? Can a good be classified as both? How would the marketing be different?

13.   In discussing industrial goods, describe:

Installations: _____

Capital items: _____

Accessory equipment: _____

14.   Classes of industrial goods/services include:

Learning Goal 3
Packaging Changes the Product

15.   What are three ways in which packaging can change a product?

a. _____

b. _____

c. _____

16.   Describe RFID in packaging.

17.   Why is packaging carrying more of the promotional burden today than in the past?

18.   Identify the functions of packaging.

a. _____

b. _____

c. _____

d. _____

e. _____

f. _____

Branding and Brand Equity

19.   What is the difference between a brand, brand name and a trademark?

20.   How does a brand name benefit buyers and sellers?

21.   How does a manufacturer's brand name become a generic brand?

22.   Describe the important components of brand equity.

23.   Why is perceived quality an important part of brand equity and what is the key to creating perceived quality?

24.   What are brand preference and brand insistence?

25.   What techniques can a company use to create brand associations?

26.   What are the responsibilities of a brand manager?

Learning Goal 5
The New Product Development Process

27.   What are four reasons for product failure?

a. _____   c. _____

b. _____   d. _____

28.   Identify the steps in the new product development process.

a. _____   d. _____

b. _____   e. _____

c. _____   f. _____

29.   What are important sources of new product ideas?

a. _____   c. _____

b. _____

30.   What are the criteria needed for product screening?

31.   In the product analysis step of the new product development process, what happens to products that don't meet established criteria?

32.   What are product concepts?

33.   What questions are answered by concept testing?

34.   What are two important elements of the marketing effort during commercialization?

a. _____

b. _____

Learning Goal 6
The Product Life Cycle

35.   What are the four stages of the product life cycle?

a. _____   c. _____

b. _____   d. _____

36. Why is the product life cycle important?

37. Identify the marketing strategies for the Marketing Mix variables in each stage of the Product Life Cycle by completing the following chart:

	Product	Price	Promotion	Place
Introduction				
Growth				
Maturity				
Decline				

38. What happens to sales, profits, and competitors during each of the stages in the Product Life Cycle?

	Sales	Profits	Competitors
Introduction			
Growth			
Maturity			
Decline			

Learning Goal 7
Competitive Pricing

39. What are five pricing objectives?

a._____ d._____

b._____ e._____

c._____

40. What objective is a firm using when it prices its products low, and why?

41. Pricing objectives should be influenced by:

42. Discuss the important considerations in cost-based pricing.

43. What are the important elements of target costing?

44. What is the major price consideration when evaluating competition based pricing?

45. Define the break-even point. What is the formula for determining a break-even point?

46. What are some of the expenses included in:

   fixed costs:

   variable costs:

47. What happens when sales go higher than the break-even point?

48. What are six pricing strategies other than competition based, cost based, and demand based?

   a. _____   d. _____

   b. _____   e._____

   c. _____   f _____

49.   What pricing strategy is being used when the company:

   a. _____   Sets prices high to make optimum profit when there is little competition?

   b. _____   Sets prices higher than those at stores, using EDLP, but has special sales?

   c. _____   Prices products at points that make them appear less expensive?

   d._____   Prices products low to attract customers and discourage competition?

   e. _____   Groups products together and prices them as a unit?

   f. _____   Sets prices lower than competitors and usually doesn't have sales.

50.   What is the main idea behind EDLP?

51.   What is the problem with a high-low pricing strategy?

52.   Describe demand oriented pricing.

53.   How is the Internet affecting pricing?

Learning Goal 8
Nonprice Competition

54.   In using non-price competition, what aspects of their products will firms tend to stress?

CRITICAL THINKING EXERCISES

Learning Goal 1

1. When people buy a product, they evaluate and compare on several dimensions: For each product below, identify some of the dimensions that may influence the buyer.

   a. Bicycle _____

   _____

   b. Toothpaste _____

   _____

   c. A new suit _____

   _____

2. Identify 3 product lines that General Motors sells, and a specific item in each line. What other products may make up their product mix?

   Product line _____ Item _____

   Product line _____ Item _____

   Product line _____ Item _____

Learning Goal 2

3. The two major product classifications are consumer goods and services and industrial goods and services.

   a. Classify the following products

   1. Milk _____

   2. Steel _____

   3. Tickets to the Olympics _____

   4. Dry cleaners _____

   5. Diesel engines _____

   6. Flashlight batteries _____

   7. Auto repair _____

   8. Heart surgeon _____

   9. Management consultant _____

   10. Winter coat _____

b. Consumer goods and services are further classified as either: convenience, shopping, specialty or unsought. Indicate the correct class for each of the **consumer** items you identified above.

1._____   5._____

2._____   6._____

3._____   7._____

4._____

4.   Marketing strategies will change depending upon the category of the product. Identify the most appropriate way to market:

a.   a new car model -

b.   a marketing consulting firm -

c.   banking services -

d.   a funeral home -

Learning Goal 3
5.   Packaging is carrying the promotional burden for products more than ever, and performs a number of functions: attract attention, describe contents, explain benefits, provide information, indicate price, value, and uses, and protect goods. Evaluate the importance of packaging, which function(s) may be the most important and how well the packaging performs those functions for the following:

a.   Lunch meat (like bologna) _____

_____

b.   Children's cereal (like Froot Loops) _____

_____

c.   Potato chips (like Pringles) _____

_____

6.   You are in conference with the marketing manager of Sun-2-Shade, and are still in the process of developing a marketing plan. Sun-2-Shade is a company that manufactures automobile windshields that self-darken in the same manner as some eyewear, automatically darkening in the sun, and going back to light in the shade, on a cloudy day or in the evening.

In evaluating the windshield to be produced by Sun-2-Shade, you want to know what dimensions customers might consider when purchasing Sun-2-Shade from an auto parts store or an after-market windshield installation and repair company. Are the same things going to be important if the main customers are the auto manufacturers? What additional or different dimensions might manufacturers consider?

Just before your meeting, you jotted down some other questions that you feel need to be answered in order to create an effective marketing plan:

a) What is the total product offer?

b) How can we differentiate the product?

c) How would Sun-2-Shade be classified?

d) Will packaging be an important consideration for Sun-2-Shade?

7.   a.   Are you a brand loyal consumer? What products can you name for which you will only purchase a certain brand? What level of brand loyalty would you consider your type of purchase pattern? What factors have influenced your decision to only buy that brand?

        b.   What is the first brand name that comes to mind when you think of?

             1.   digital camera   _____

             2.   milk   _____

             3.   DVD player   _____

4. a sports car   _____

5. soft drink   _____

Why do you think it was more likely that you could think of a national brand for some of these products, but not for others?

   c. Why is it a problem for a manufacturer when their brand name becomes generic?

8. You have just been named as a product manager for the new company formed by the merger of Nestle and Ralston-Purina, aptly named Nestle-Purina. Your manager has told you that your primary objective is to develop new products and bring them to market. This is your first day on the job! How will you accomplish the objectives your boss has given you?

9. The product life cycle is a model of what happens to classes of products over time. It consists of four stages. Draw and label the illustration outlined below.

10. There are different marketing strategies used in each stage of the product life cycle. Using your text, give a specific example of a marketing strategy from one of the four P's that could be used for the following products.

<u>MARKETING STRATEGY</u>

a. Introduction   Global Positioning Systems   _____

                                                 _____

                                                 _____

b. Growth   Digital cameras   _____

                                                   _____

                                                   _____

c. Maturity   Fast food   _____

                                                   _____

                                                   _____

d. Decline   VCRs   _____

                                                   _____

Learning Goal 7

11. Among the objectives that firms use in setting prices are:

Achieve a target profit	Increase sales
Build traffic	Create an image
Achieve greater market share	Social objectives

Match the correct pricing objective to each of the following statements.

a. _____   Kroger's advertises large eggs at 10 cents a dozen.

b. _____   Nestle Purina changes a price that gives them a 25% profit on dog food, higher than they need. Consumers are willing to pay the high price for this particular dog food.

c. _____   Farmers in Arkansas receive subsidies on their grain products, so they can keep their prices artificially low. This keeps prices on derivative products low enough for a larger market to purchase.

d. _____   Retailers, facing several dismal Christmas seasons in a row, slashed prices on a wide variety of merchandise several years in a row.

e. _____   Movado watches sell from $500 and up in the retail stores that carry the brand.

f. _____   If you go to Midas Muffler with a bid from a competitor, Midas will meet that price in order to keep your business.

12. a. How many units will Sun-2-Shade have to sell to break even if their fixed costs are $1,200, 000, the price (revenue from each unit) is $500 and the variable cost per unit is $100 per unit?

b. How much profit will Sun-2-Shade make if they sell 5,000 units?

c. What would the break-even point (the number of units which need to be sold in order to break even) be if Sun-2-Shade raised their price to $600? _____

d. The marketing department has said that at a price of $600, Sun-2-Shade would be able to sell about 2000 units. Should they raise their price? Why or why not?

13. After determining which pricing objectives fit with the firm's objectives, a business can use any of several different strategies.

Skimming   Bundling
Penetration   Psychological pricing
High-low pricing   Demand oriented pricing
Everyday low pricing (EDLP)

Match the correct pricing strategy to each of the following:

a. _____   Home theater systems can run as high as $100,000 or more and there are only a few companies offering the systems.

b. _____   Hotel and motel prices in Breckenridge Colorado are higher from October to May, times which Breckenridge would describe as their peak season.

c. _____   Larry Dietzel, a real estate agent, advised his clients to price their home at $199,900 when they listed with his agency.

d. _____   Carl Godwin is just starting out in the home remodeling and construction business. When he makes a bid, it is generally significantly lower than the bids of any of his competition, as Carl wants the business.

e. _____   Chad Stahr is a home do-it-yourself guy. He most often shops at Lowes, because although they usually don't run sales, he knows the store will be the lowest price around on the tools he needs.

f. _____ When the Mays family took a trip to Europe, they went to Uniglobe travel, where the travel agent worked out a trip for them that included airfare, hotels and some of the special tours that they were interested in taking, all for one price.

g. _____ A major retailer in St. Louis charges "full retail" for most of the clothing lines, but has regular "special holiday" sales, during which they lower their prices considerably.

14. Many companies will try to sell their products by promoting something other than price. Identify three types of products in the marketplace that are promoted using nonprice competition. What are the companies using to promote their products?

a. _____

b. _____

c. _____

PRACTICE TEST

MULTIPLE CHOICE – Circle the best answer

Learning Goal 1
1. Which of the following would <u>not</u> be included in the total product that consumers consider when they purchase a product?
   a. Price
   b. Image created by advertising
   c. Brand name
   d. Buyer's income

2. Ford Motor Company produces cars, trucks, and SUVs and provides financing. These products are part of Ford's
   a. product mix
   b. product depth
   c. product width
   d. product line

Learning Goal 2
3. Companies that distribute bottled water, like Evian or Aquafina, have the challenge of making a product that looks the same from one company to another appear to have qualities unique to that brand. Companies create these perceived differences using
   a. consumer goods classification.
   b. the product life cycle.
   c. the product mix.
   d. product differentiation.

4. Small businesses often have an advantage in product differentiation because
   a. they have fewer products, so they can spend more time working on them.
   b. they are more flexible in adapting to customer wants and needs.
   c. larger businesses aren't interested in getting close to the consumer.
   d. larger businesses don't have to differentiate their products.

5. Which of the following is not one of the classifications of consumer products?
   a. convenience goods and services
   b. unsought goods and services
   c. shopping goods and services
   d. desired goods and services

6. Which of the following would be considered a specialty good/service?
   a. toothpaste
   b. funeral services
   c. washing machine
   d. Rolex watch

7. The best way to promote products like clothes and shoes is to emphasize:
   a. location of stores.
   b. advertising in specialty magazines.
   c. price differences, quality differences or some combination of the two.
   d. a web site where customers can place orders.

8. When a manufacturer buys a laptop computer for employees use at work, the computer would be considered a:
   a. business good
   b. specialty good
   c. consumer good
   d. shopping good

9. The factory that Sun-2-Shade, a manufacturer of self-darkening windshields, is building on the outskirts of Denver is an example of a(n) _____ type of business good.
   a. installation
   b. accessory equipment
   c. production
   d. support

Learning Goal 3
10. Because products are often being sold in self-service outlets, rather than by salespersons:
   a. brand names have become less important.
   b. packaging has become more important, as a way to promote the product.
   c. the popularity of generic products has declined.
   d. packaging has become less important, because consumers want to see what they are buying.

11. Which of the following would <u>not</u> be found in a list of the functions of packaging?
   a. protect the goods inside
   b. attract the buyer's attention
   c. provide information
   d. cross label opportunities

12.   The Jolly Green Giant would be an example of a:
        a.   brand name
        b.   generic name
        c.   trademark
        d.   knockoff brand

13.   Rollerblade is working to make sure that when people refer to inline skating, they don't use the name Rollerblade to refer to the sport. Rollerblade is afraid that their brand name will become a:
        a.   generic good
        b.   knockoff brand
        c.   private brand
        d.   trademark

14.   Each time you purchase toothpaste, you will only buy Close 'n Brite, toothpaste guaranteed to give you fresh breath and whiter teeth. If the store is out of this brand you will make a point of going to a different store to buy that product. This is an example of :
        a.   brand equity
        b.   brand awareness
        c.   brand preference
        d.   brand insistence

Learning Goal 5
15.   The process of taking a product idea to consumers to test their reactions is known as:
        a.   test marketing
        b.   product screening
        c.   concept testing
        d.   business analysis

16.   The new product development process begins with:
        a.   product screening
        b.   product analysis
        c.   commercialization
        d.   idea generation

Learning Goal 6
17.   The importance of the product life cycle is that:
        a.   different stages in the product life cycle call for different marketing strategies.
        b.   most brands follow the same pattern in the product life cycle.
        c.   all products go through the product life cycle in the same length of time.
        d.   in the growth stage, marketers will differentiate their product from competitors.

18.   Sony, and makers of personal digital assistants, have made the prices of these products more competitive, have increased the number and kinds of stores in which they are available, have offered a variety of choices, but not a lot, and are advertising extensively. These products are in the _____ stage of the product life cycle.
        a.   introduction
        b.   growth
        c.   maturity
        d.   decline

19. Which of the following is not included in a list of pricing objectives?
   a. increasing sales
   b. increasing market share
   c. global sensitivities
   d. create an image

20. When Sony considers how to price a new product, they determine what price they think their customers will pay, and then identify what profit the company needs. From there they determine the features they can offer on this product. This method of determining price is known as:
   a. demand oriented pricing
   b. cost based pricing
   c. target costing
   d. value pricing

21. If fixed costs are $100,000, variable cost per unit is $40 and the selling price is $60, how many units must be sold for the firm to break even?
   a. 10,000
   b. 1,000
   c. 2500
   d. 5000

22. When the Japanese entered the DVD player market, they priced the product lower than the U.S. makers in order to capture a large share of the market quickly.
   This strategy is called a:
   a. penetration strategy
   b. EDLP
   c. high-low pricing strategy
   d. skimming strategy

23. Upscale retailers, such as Nordstrom's, feature customer service as their significant point of difference, and use that difference to compete with less expensive stores. This is known as:
   a. upscale competition
   b. nonprice competition
   c. market force competition
   d. service competition

TRUE-FALSE

1. _____ In today's market, marketers must learn to listen to consumers and adapt to a constantly changing market.

2. _____ To create an attractive value package an organization must always begin with a low price.

3. _____ It is often easier for larger companies to establish a close relationship with customers because they have representatives in most parts of the country.

Learning Goal 2

4. _____ An example of a convenience good would be a candy bar.

5. _____ Products can be classified as either a consumer or business product, but not as both.

Learning Goal 3

6. _____ One major function of packaging is to make sure a product fits well in all global markets.

7. _____ New technology is now enabling companies to track products through a radio signal attached to the product.

Learning Goal 4

8. _____ Brand loyalty means that your product comes to mind when a product category is mentioned.

9. _____ An example of a dealer, or private, brand would be Cherokee, sold exclusively in Target stores nationwide.

Learning Goal 5

10. _____ A brand manager, or product manager, has the responsibility for all the elements of the marketing mix for one brand or product line.

11. _____ An important source of new product ideas is company employees.

Learning Goal 6

12. _____ Sales of a product peak late in the growth stage of the product life cycle.

13. _____ One marketing strategy in the maturity stage is to differentiate your product so that it will appeal to more market segments.

Learning Goal 7

14. _____ A firm will pursue only one pricing strategy at a time.

15. _____ Pricing objectives generally will have no effect on the other marketing mix variables.

16. _____ The break-even point is the point where sales revenue is equal to profits.

17. _____ When movie theaters charge lower rates for children, and companies give discounts to senior citizens, they are using demand oriented pricing.

18. _____ Most pricing depends upon what the competition is charging.

19. _____ Marketers won't generally compete on product attributes other than price.

Learning Goal 8

20. _____ One way to avoid price wars is to establish friendly relationships with consumers.

You Can Find It On the Net

Tommy Hilfiger is a major manufacturer of clothing for, perhaps, people of all ages. What image do you have of the Tommy name? Who do you think wears their clothes?

Now, visit their web site at www.tommyhilfiger.com

How does the web site reinforce the Tommy Hilfiger brand name and image? Give examples to support your answer.

How does Tommy appear to differentiate their product from a major competitor, such as Abercrombie and Fitch. (**www.abercrombie.com**)

Compare the Abercrombie web site to Tommy's. Are they targeting the same market? Why or why not?

Where do you think Tommy Hilfiger is on the Product Life Cycle. What suggestions can you give to extend their product life cycle?

ANSWERS

LEARNING THE LANGUAGE

1. Break-even analysis	14. Convenience goods and services	27. Value
2. Penetration strategy	15. Bundling	28. Knockoff brands
3. High-low price strategy	16. Dealer (private) brands	29. Brand manager
4. Total product offer	17. Specialty goods and services	30. Product screening
5. Brand loyalty	18. Brand awareness	31. Total fixed costs
6. Product life cycle	19. Product line	32. Commercialization
7. Skimming price strategy	20. Generic goods	33. Product differentiation
8. Trademark	21. Target costing	34. Everyday low pricing (EDLP)
9. Brand association	22. Unsought goods and services	35. Product mix
10. Industrial goods	23. Shopping goods and services	36. Price leadership
11. Product analysis	24. Brand equity	37. Competition based pricing
12. Brand	25. Manufacturer's brand names	38. Psychological pricing
13. Concept testing	26. Variable costs	

ASSESSMENT CHECK

Learning Goal 1
Product Development and the Total Product Offer

1.   To satisfy consumers today marketers and managers must learn to listen and to adapt constantly to changing market demands.   The organization must constantly monitor changing consumer wants and needs, adapt products, policies, and services accordingly.

2.   a. Price
      b. Store surroundings
      c. Guarantee
      d. Brand name
      e. Service
      f. Speed of delivery
      g. Convenience
      h. Internet access
      i. Image created by advertising
      j. Package
      k. Buyer's past experience
      l. Reputation of producer

3.   A company develops a variety of product offers because different consumers want different total product offers.

4.   Product lines are groups of products that are similar or are intended for a similar market. A product mix is the combination of all product lines that a company has available for sale.

Learning Goal 2
Product Differentiation

5.   Marketers use a mix of pricing, advertising and packaging to create a unique attractive image to differentiate their products.

6. The four different classes of consumer goods and services are:
    a. Convenience - bread
    b. Shopping – appliances
    c. Specialty – expensive watches, such as a Rolex
    d. Unsought – emergency car towing

7. a. location   c. image
    b. brand awareness

8. Comparisons of shopping goods are based on the quality, price, and style from a variety of sellers. Shopping goods are sold largely through shopping centers so that consumers can shop around and compare. Because consumers compare, marketers can emphasize price differences, quality differences, or some combination of the two.

9. Specialty goods and services have a perceived value for the customer, have no reasonable substitute, and as a result, consumers will put forth a special effort to purchase a specific brand name.

    Specialty goods are often marketed through specialty magazines and through interactive Web sites.

10. The best appeals, or ways to promote:

    Convenience goods is to make them readily available and to create the proper image

    Shopping goods is to create an appeal based on a combination of price, quality and service.

    Specialty goods is to reach special market segments though advertising

    Unsought goods rely on personal selling and some kinds of advertising

11. Whether a good or service falls into a particular class depends on the individual consumer. For example, what is a shopping good for one consumer could be a specialty good for another. So any good can conceivably be classified into any of the categories.

12. Consumer goods are purchased for personal consumption, while industrial (or business) goods are products used in the production of other products. A product can be classified as both a consumer and/or an industrial good depending upon the end use of the product. If a computer, for example, is bought as a consumer good, it would be sold through a store, whereas if it was bought by a business for business uses, the computer would likely be sold through personal selling or the Internet. The marketing varies by how the good is classified.

13. Installations are major capital equipment such as new factories and heavy machinery.

    Capital items are products that last a long time and cost a lot of money.

    Accessory equipment consists of capital items that are not quite as long lasting or as expensive as installations.

14. Classes of industrial goods/services include:

Production goods, which includes raw materials, component parts and production materials.

Support goods, which includes installations such as buildings, equipment and capital items; accessory equipment, which include tools and office equipment; supplies, like paper clips and other office supplies; services like maintenance and repair.

Learning Goal 3
Packaging Changes the Product

15. Packaging changes the product by changing its,
    a. visibility   c. attractiveness
    b. usefulness

16. RFID stands for radio frequency identification chips. These chips are attached to products and send out signals telling a company where products are at all times. The advantages RFID has include the fact that more information can be carried in the chips, items don't have to be read one at a time, and items can be read at a distance.

17. Packaging is carrying more of the promotional burden than in the past because many products that were once sold by sales persons are now being sold in self service outlets, and the package has been given more sales responsibility.

18. The functions of packaging are:
    a. Protect the goods from damage, be tamperproof and yet be easy to open and use
    b. Attract the buyer's attention
    c. Describe the contents of the product
    d. Explain the benefits of the product
    e. Provide information on warranties and any warnings
    f. Give an indication of price, value, and uses

Learning Goal 4
Branding and Brand Equity

19. A brand is a name, symbol, or design, or a combination of those, that identifies the goods or services of one seller and distinguishes them from competitors. A brand name is the part of the brand that is a word, letter or group of words or letters comprising a name, and a trademark is a brand that has been given exclusive legal protection for the brand name and the pictorial design.

20. For the buyer, a brand name assures quality, reduces search time, and adds prestige to purchases.

For a seller, brand names facilitate new-product introductions, help promotions efforts, add to repeat purchases, and differentiate products so that prices can be set higher.

21. A brand name can become generic when a name becomes so popular, so identified with the product that it loses its brand status and become the name of the product category. Examples include aspirin, nylon, escalator, and zipper.

22.   The core of brand equity is brand loyalty. A loyal group of customers represents substantial value to a firm. Another part of brand equity is brand awareness. A third element is perceived quality.

23.   Perceived quality is an important part of brand equity because a product that is perceived as better quality than its competitors can be priced higher.

        The key to creating a perception of quality is to identify what consumers look for in a high-quality product and then to use that information in every message the company sends out. Factors influencing the perception of quality include price, appearance and reputation.

24.   Consumers develop brand preference when they prefer one brand over another. This happens when companies use effective promotion that focuses on quality, price, appearance and reputation. When consumers reach the point of brand insistence, the product becomes a specialty good, and consumers will go out of their way and pay a premium for that brand.

25.   Brand associations can be created by linking your brand to other product users, to a popular celebrity, to a particular geographic area, or to competitors.

26.   The responsibilities of a brand manager include all the elements of the marketing mix: product, price promotion and place.

Learning Goal 5
The New Product Development Process

27.   Reasons that products fail include:
        a. products that don't deliver what they promise
        b. poor positioning
        c. not enough differences from competitors
        d. poor packaging

28.   The steps in the new product development process are:
        a. Idea generation
        b. Screening
        c. Product analysis
        d. Development
        e. Testing
        f. Commercialization

29.   Three important sources of new product ideas are:
        a. employees
        b. research and development
        c. suppliers

30.   Criteria needed for screening include: whether the product fits in well with present products, profit potential, marketability and personnel requirements.

31.   Products that don't meet established criteria in the product analysis phase of the new product development process are withdrawn from consideration.

32.   Product concepts are alternative product offerings based on the same product idea that have different meanings and values to consumers.

33.   Questions answered by concept testing include: Do customers see the benefit of this product? How frequently would they buy it? At what price? What features do they like and dislike? What changes would they make? Different samples are tested using different packaging, branding, ingredients, and so forth until a product emerges that's desirable from both production and marketing standpoints.

34.   Two important elements for the marketing effort during commercialization are:
        a.   promoting the product to distributors and retailers to get wide distribution.
        b.   developing strong advertising and sales campaigns to generate and maintain interest.

Learning Goal 6
The Product Life Cycle

35.   The stages of the product life cycle include:
        a.   Introduction   c.   Maturity
        b.   Growth   d.   Decline

36.   The product life cycle is important because different stages in the product life cycle call for different marketing strategies.

37.

Life Cycle Stage	Product	Price	Place	Promotion
Introduction	Offer market-test product; keep product mix small	Skimming or penetration price strategy	Selective distribution; wholesalers	Advertising and sales promotion to stimulate primary demand
Growth	Improve product	Adjust price to meet competition	Increase distribution	Competitive advertising
Maturity	Product differentiation	Further price reductions	Intensify distribution	Emphasize brand name and product benefits and differences
Decline	Cut product mix	Consider price increases	Drop some outlets	Reduce advertising

38.

Life Cycle Stage	Sales	Profits	Competitors
Introduction	Low sales	Losses	Few
Growth	Rapidly rising sales	Profits peak	Growing number
Maturity	Peak sales	Declining profits	Stable number, then declining
Decline	Falling sales	Profits fall to losses	Numbers decline further

Learning Goal
Competitive Pricing

39. Five pricing objectives include:
   a. Achieve a target return on investment or profit
   b. Build traffic in a store or to a web site
   c. Achieve a greater market share
   d. Create an image
   e. Further social objectives

40. A firm may be attempting to further social objectives when pricing products low so that people with less money can afford the product.

41. Pricing objectives should be influenced by other marketing mix variable decisions, such as product design, packaging, branding, distribution and promotion.

42. Companies often develop cost accounting systems to measure production costs and come up with a price. The question is whether the price will be satisfactory to the market. In the long run, the market determines what the price of a product will be.

43. Target costing is demand based. This means that a product will be designed so that it satisfies customers and meets the firm's desired profit margins. To use target costing, the firm will estimate the selling price people would be willing to pay for a product and subtract the desired profit margin. The result is the target cost of production.

44. Competition based pricing is a strategy based on what the competition is charging. The price can be at, above or below the competition. It depends on customer loyalty, perceived differences in the product, and the competitive climate.

45. The break-even point is the point where revenues from sales equal all costs. The formula is:

$$\text{Break even point} = \frac{\text{Fixed costs}}{\text{Price per unit - variable cost per unit}}$$

46. <u>Fixed costs</u>: include rent and insurance which don't vary with the level of production.

<u>Variable costs</u> include expenses for materials and the direct cost of labor used in making goods. These costs vary with the level of production.

47.   When sales go above the break-even point, the firm makes a profit.

48.   Six pricing strategies other than competition-based, cost-based and demand based include:

a. skimming strategy
b. penetration strategy
c. everyday low pricing (EDLP)

d. high-low pricing
e. bundling
f. psychological pricing

49.
a. skimming
b. high-low
c. psychological
d. penetration
e. bundling
f. everyday low pricing

50.   The main idea behind everyday low pricing is to have consumers come to the store whenever they want a bargain, rather than wait until there is a sale.

51.   The problem with a high-low pricing strategy is that it teaches consumers to wait for sales, thus cutting into profits.

52.   Demand oriented pricing is used when price is set on the basis of consumer demand rather than cost or some other calculation. An example is movie theaters with low rates for children or companies offering discounts for senior citizens.

53.   Customers can now compare prices of many goods and services on the Internet, and can get lower prices on many items. Price competition is going to heat up with the Internet, as more customers have access to price information from around the world. As a result, nonprice competition will increase.

Learning Goal 8
Nonprice Competition

54.   Firms using nonprice competition will stress product images and consumer benefits such as comfort, style, convenience, and durability.

CRITICAL THINKING EXERCISES

Learning Goal 1

1.
a. In the purchase of a bicycle, a consumer may evaluate the product in terms of price, guarantee, reputation of the producer, brand name, past experience, and on the service the retailer may provide. Other considerations would be how the buyer will use the product (mountain biking vs street), the brand image and durability

b. In buying toothpaste, a purchaser may look at price, package, image created by advertising, brand name and the buyers' past experience.

c. For a new suit, the dimensions may be price, store surroundings, image of the store, brand name, guarantee, and past experience with that brand.

2. Suggested answers:
Product line - Chevrolet   Item - Cobolt
Product line - Pontiac   Item - Grand Am
Product line - Hummer   Item –H3

Other products may include financing, including credit cards.

3. a   1. Consumer   6. Consumer
2. Industrial   7. Consumer
3. Consumer   8. Consumer
4. Consumer   9. Industrial
5. Industrial   10. Consumer

b. 1. Milk - Convenience
2. Tickets to the Olympics - Specialty
3. Dry Cleaners - Probably convenience service but could be shopping service
4. Flashlight batteries- Convenience
5. Auto repair - Unsought
6. Heart Surgeon - Unsought
7. Winter coat - Shopping

4. a. A car is a shopping good, so the best way to market this product would be to ensure customers that they are getting a good quality product at a good price. A car dealer may want to promote the services they offer customers, such as extended hours for getting a car serviced, or free oil changes for the life of the car.

b. A marketing consulting firm sells a specialty service. This type of service would best be marketed through a business oriented magazine, or a newspaper such as the Wall Street Journal. A good website will also be important.

c. Banking services are considered to be convenience service. A bank will need to be conveniently located, near potential customers. It is important for the bank to make services available on the Internet while still ensuring privacy and safety for its customers.

d. A funeral home's services would be considered unsought goods. This type of product requires advertising, but locally, like in the newspaper and the Yellow Pages to bring people to the door. Once a family contacts the funeral home, effective personal selling is a must.

5. a. For lunchmeat like bologna, the primary consideration would be protecting the product from spoiling, and enabling the buyer to see what they are getting. The price or uses won't be listed on the package, but the package may need to attract the buyer's attention, as it is a crowded market. The main problem with the package is that once it is opened, most lunchmeat packages don't easily close, so the product gets stale quickly.

b. For a children's cereal, the most important variable would be attracting the children's attention! For the parent, nutrition information would be important to include on the package. Further, keeping the product fresh would be important. For the most part, most kids' cereals do a great job of attracting children's attention, and by law must provide nutrition information on each box. As with the lunchmeat, the problem with most of theses packages is that once they are opened, they are difficult to re-close, and the cereal can turn stale quickly.

c. One of the considerations for potato chips is protection from damage, as chips break easily. In fact, that consideration was one of the factors Proctor & Gamble looked at when they introduced Pringles. The package needs to attract attention, as it is a crowded market. Most companies have not found a good way of keeping chips from breaking, and the same old problem arises: once they are opened, the package doesn't close very well, and the product can get stale quickly.

Learning Goals 1, 2, 3

6. a. The total product offer for Sun-2-Shade could include convenience, image, and comfort while driving. An additional benefit is that the car interior stays cooler in the summer while parking in a sunny area. Customers will also consider price, service (what happens if the windshield gets scratched?) and the image Sun-2-Shade could create through effective advertising. These are just suggestions – you may have thought of several more possible answers.

b. Sun-2-Shade's product is unique. It is the only company to offer this type of product up to this point. It would likely be considered a luxury type product. You could differentiate the product by giving it an image of not only convenience, but of the "ultimate," the kind of auto accessory that everyone needs to have in today's image-conscious world. You could create the perception that this product isn't merely a luxury, but a <u>necessity</u>. Advertising could be aimed at the end consumer, with the idea of people asking for the product when they go to the dealership to buy the car.

The main consideration for an auto manufacturer will be price, how much it will add to the sticker price of the car, guarantee, and speed of delivery and reputation of Sun-2-Shade. The ease of installation is also important.

c. Sun-2-Shade's product would be classified as a consumer good, when we are aiming our marketing strategy at the end consumer, and as a B2B good when we are marketing toward the auto manufacturers. It could be positioned as either a shopping good or a specialty good for the consumer market.

d. Packaging won't be an important variable for Sun-2-Shade other than for shipping to the retailers for installation for the after-market.

7. a. Your answer to the first part of this question will be unique to you. Many consumers are brand loyal to personal care items such as deodorant or toothpaste, but that isn't always the case. You may only wear a certain brand of jeans because they fit you well or you like the style. The influences on brand loyalty for those products would be advertising, and knowing that the product meets their needs. Some people are loyal to certain car brands. Those influences could include advertising, perceived quality, price, reputation and product features.

b. You could come up with a ready answer for a digital camera (Kodak or Olympus), a sports car (Ford Mustang) and a soft drink (Pepsi or Coke) but not perhaps for milk or DVD players. The reasons for this come from brand awareness and advertising, for example, the manufacturers of these products have done. Some manufacturers simply dominate the market, like Ford and the sports car market, or Kodak for digital cameras. Other markets are so competitive and there are so many brand names and price points that it is difficult to develop a high level of brand awareness, let alone brand insistence. The markets for some products like milk and dairy products may be dominated by private or local brands.

c. The problem with a brand name becoming generic is that the producer must then come up with a new brand name, and begin the process of developing brand awareness and brand loyalty all over again.

8. As a new product manager, I will need to start with generating ideas from many different sources. I would investigate my competitors, and try to generate ideas from our own company personnel.

Once enough ideas have been generated, I would then have to screen them for profitability and potential. Any product ideas not meeting the criteria we have set will be dropped from further analysis.

The next step will be to develop a product concept. If we develop a new premium pet food for example, as a concept, then we need to create a prototype to test with consumers and their pets. During that step we would make sure pets like the product, determine how much people might be willing to pay for a premium pet food, how people will view this product, and what flavors the pet prefers.

If the product tests well, we would take it to market through our traditional retailers, or perhaps through the Internet. We may choose to offer the product through pet stores rather than the grocery stores, to reinforce the idea of a premium product.

9.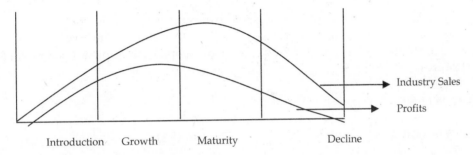

Introduction   Growth   Maturity   Decline

10. Possible answers
   a. High price; Promote as a necessity for driving safety in upscale publications; stress need and uses for product

   b. Change advertising to change product image; Add distribution outlets; Decrease price, or give price "deals."

   c. Add new menu items, such as healthier versions of standard items; Look for new target markets; price deals

   d. Reduce advertising; Limit the product variations; eventually consolidate distribution outlets

11. a. Build traffic   d. Increase sales
    b. Achieve a target profit   e. Create an image
    c. Social objectives   f. Achieve a greater market share

12. a. The number of units Sun-2-Shade would have to sell to break even is 3,000.
         $$\frac{1,200,000}{\$500-\$100} = 3,000 \text{ units}$$

b. The break-even point is 3,000 units, so any unit sold beyond 3,000 will generate profits. If the company sells 5,000 units, profits will be generated by 2,000 of those units.

$$\begin{array}{ll} \text{Price per unit} & = \$500 \\ \underline{\text{Variable cost per unit}} & = \underline{\$100} \\ \text{Profit per unit} & = \$400 \end{array}$$

400 x 2000 = $800,000 profit

c. If Sun-2-Shade raised their price to $600, the break-even point would be 2,400 units.

$$\frac{\$1,200,000}{\$600-\$100} \quad = \quad 2,400 \text{ units}$$

d. No, they should not raise their price to $600. If they will break even at 2,400 but can only sell 2,000 units at that price, they will be losing money.

13.
a. Skimming pricing
b. Demand pricing
c. Psychological pricing
d. Penetration pricing

e. Everyday low pricing (EDLP)
f. Bundling
g. High-low pricing

14.   There are multiple answers. Some examples would be:

Cosmetics -   Promoted by showing how the product enhances looks
Food items -   Promoted by emphasizing flavor, freshness, convenience
High Definition televisions-   Promoted by emphasizing picture quality and other features.

PRACTICE TEST

MULTIPLE CHOICE
LG 1   #1-2
LG 2   # 3-9
LG 3   # 10-11
LG 4   # 12-14
LG 5   # 15-16
LG 6   # 17-18
LG 7   # 19-22
LG 8   # 23

TRUE-FALSE
LG 1   # 1-3
LG 2   # 4-5
LG 3   # 6-7
LG 4   # 8-9
LG 5   #10-11
LG 6   # 12-13
LG 7   # 14-19
LG 8   #20

1.	d	12.	c
2.	a	13.	a
3.	d	14.	d
4.	b	15.	c
5.	d	16.	d
6.	d	17.	a
7.	c	18.	b
8.	a	19.	c
9.	a	20.	c
10.	b	21.	d
11.	d	22.	a
		23.	d

1.	T	11.	T
2.	F	12.	F
3.	F	13.	T
4.	T	14.	F
5.	F	15.	F
6.	F	16.	F
7.	T	17.	T
8.	F	18.	F
9.	T	19.	F
10.	T	20.	T

CHAPTER 15 – DISTRIBUTING PRODUCTS QUICKLY AND EFFICIENTLY

LEARNING GOALS

After you have read and studied this chapter, you should be able to:

1. Explain the concept of marketing channels and the value of marketing intermediaries.
2. Give examples of how intermediaries perform the six marketing utilities.
3. Describe the various wholesale intermediaries in the distribution system.
4. Explain the distribution strategies retailers use.
5. Explain the various kinds of nonstore retailing.
6. Explain the various ways to build cooperation in channel systems.
7. Describe the emergence of logistics.
8. Outline how intermediaries move goods from producers to consumers through the use of various transportation modes and storage functions.

LEARNING THE LANGUAGE

Listed below are important terms found in the chapter. Choose the correct term for the definition and write it in the space provided.

Administered distribution system	Inbound logistics	Rack jobbers
Agents/brokers	Information utility	Retailer
Cash-and-carry wholesaler	Intensive distribution	Reverse logistics
Channel of distribution	Intermodal shipping	Selective distribution
Contractual distribution system	Logistics	Service utility
Corporate distribution system	Marketing intermediaries	Supply chain (or value chain)
Direct marketing	Materials handling	Supply-chain management
Direct selling	Merchant wholesalers	Telemarketing
Drop shippers	Outbound logistics	Time utility
Electronic retailing	Place utility	Utility
Exclusive distribution	Possession utility	Wholesaler
Freight forwarder		

1. The process of _____ brings raw materials, packaging, other goods and services, and information from suppliers to producers.

2. The economic term _____ refers to the want-satisfying ability or value that's added to goods or services by organizations when the products are made more useful or accessible to consumers than they were before.

3. A marketing intermediary known as a _____ sells to other organizations.

4. A(n) _____ is a distribution system in which producers manage all the marketing functions at the retail level.

5. The movement of goods within a warehouse, from warehouses to the factory floor, and from the factory floor to various workstations is _____.

6. The function of _____ involves planning, implementing, and controlling the physical flow of materials, final goods, and related information from points of origin to the point of consumption to meet customer requirements at a profit.

7. The distribution strategy known as _____ puts products into as many retail outlets as possible.

8. The sale of goods and services by telephone is called _____.

9. A firm adds value to products through _____ by having them where people want them.

10. The use of _____ includes using multiple modes of transportation to complete a single long distance movement of freight.

11. The process of managing the movement of raw materials, parts, work in progress, finished goods, and related information through all the organizations involved in the supply chain; managing the return of such goods, if necessary; and recycling materials when appropriate is called _____.

12. The distribution strategy known as _____ sends products to only one retail outlet in a given geographic area.

13. Providing fast, friendly service during and after the sale and teaching customers how to best use products over time is considered to be _____.

14. The whole set of marketing intermediaries in the _____ includes wholesalers and retailers that join together to transport and store goods in their path from producers to consumers.

15. A _____ is an organization that sells to ultimate consumers.

16. A distribution system called a _____ is one in which all the organizations in the channel of distribution are owned by one firm.

17. A distribution strategy that sends products to only a preferred group of retailers in an area is called _____.

18. An organization adds value called _____ to products by opening two-way flows of information between marketing participants.

19. Organizations called _____ assist in moving goods and services from producers to industrial and consumer users.

20. Wholesalers known as a _____ furnish racks or shelves full of merchandise to retailers, display products, and sell on consignment.

21. A _____ is an organization that puts many small shipments together to create a single large shipment that can be transported more cost-effectively to the final destination.

22. Wholesalers called _____ solicit orders from retailers and other wholesalers and have the merchandise shipped directly from a producer to a buyer.

23. Wholesalers that serve mostly smaller retailers with a limited assortment of products are _____.

24. Marketing intermediaries called _____ bring buyers and sellers together and assist in negotiating an exchange but don't take title to the goods.

25. Adding value to products by making them available when they're needed is called _____.

26. The concept of _____ is doing whatever is necessary to transfer ownership from one party to another, including providing credit, delivery, installation, guarantees, and follow-up service.

27. The function of _____ refers to managing the flow of finished products and information to business buyers and ultimate consumers.

28. In a _____ members are bound to cooperate through contractual agreements.

29. Independently owned firms called _____ take title to the goods they handle.

30. Selling to consumers in their homes or where they work is called _____.

31. Selling goods and services to ultimate consumers over the Internet is known as _____.

32. The _____ consists of the sequence of linked activities that must be performed by various organizations to move goods from the sources of raw materials to ultimate consumers.

33. Any activity known as _____ directly links manufacturers or intermediaries with the ultimate consumer.

34. Bringing goods back to the manufacturers because of defects or for recycling materials is called _____.

ASSESSMENT CHECK

Learning Goal 1
The Emergence of Marketing Intermediaries

1. Channels of distribution ensure: _____

_____

2.   Why do we need marketing intermediaries?

3.   Describe how marketing intermediaries create exchange efficiency in the distribution system.

4.   Discuss the "value versus the cost" of intermediaries. In other words, is it cheaper to avoid intermediaries?

5.   What are three basic points to remember about middlemen?

      a. _____

      b. _____

      c. _____

Learning Goal 2
Utilities Created by Intermediaries

6.   List six utilities created by intermediaries.

      a._____   d. _____

      b._____   e. _____

      c._____   f. _____

7.   Who creates form utility? How is it created?

8.   How does an intermediary add time utility?

9.   How do intermediaries add place utility?

420

10. How do intermediaries provide possession utility? What activities are involved?

11. How do intermediaries add information utility?

12. Which of the utilities is becoming the most important utility for retailers? Why?

Learning Goal 3
Wholesale Intermediaries

13. What is the difference between a "retail sale" and a "wholesale sale"?

14. Distinguish between these merchant wholesalers:

   a. full-service wholesalers:

   b. limited-function wholesalers:

15. Identify the functions a full service wholesaler will perform

   a. _____

   b. _____

   c. _____

   d. _____

   e. _____

   f. _____

   g. _____

   h. _____

16. Describe how rack jobbers operate.

17. How does a cash and carry wholesaler function?

18. How does a drop shipper operate?

19. How are agents and brokers different from merchant wholesalers?

20. What is the difference between and agent and a broker?

21. Describe the difference between manufacturer's agents and sales agents.

22. Describe the role of a broker.

Retail Intermediaries

23.   Distinguish between the various types of retailers.

a. _____

b. _____

c. _____

d. _____

e. _____

f. _____

g. _____

h. _____

24.   Describe the three retail distribution strategies:

a. Intensive distribution:

b. Selective distribution:

c. Exclusive distribution:

Learning Goal 5
Nonstore Retailing

25.   What are six types of non-store retailing?

a. _____   d. _____

b. _____   e. _____

c. _____   f. _____

26.   What are the "battles", or challenges, of e-tailing?

27.   What kinds of customer service problems have electronic retailers experienced? How are they trying to improve the customer service problems?

28.   How are brick and mortar stores using electronic retailing? What will be needed in the future?

29.   Traditional retailers have learned that selling on the Internet calls for: _____
_____

30.   How have companies used telemarketing? What is likely to happen to telemarketing in the future?

31.   The benefits of vending machines are: _____
_____

The benefits of kiosks and carts are: _____
_____

32.   What kinds of products are sold using direct selling? How is direct selling changing?

33.   Describe multilevel marketing.

34.   What are two attractions of multilevel marketing for employees?

a. _____

b. _____

35.   What are some forms of direct marketing?

a. _____   c. _____

b. _____   d. _____

36. Why has direct marketing become so popular?

37. What has been the impact of interactive video and interactive websites on direct marketing?

Learning Goal 6
Building Cooperation in Channel Systems

38. What is the benefit to a manufacturer of a corporate distribution system?

39. Identify the characteristics of the three types of contractual distribution systems.

   a. Franchise systems:

   b. Wholesaler sponsored chains:

   c. Retail cooperatives:

40. What functions does the producer take on in an administered distribution system? Why do retailers cooperate?

41. How does a supply chain compare to a channel of distribution?

42. How do supply chain systems "pay for themselves"?

43.   What is a "value chain"?

Learning Goal 7
The Emergence of Logistics

44.   Discuss the problems and complexities of shipping from one country to another.

45.   What solutions are companies turning to in order to manage the customs problems?

46.   What are "factory processes"?

47.   Logistics is as much about *information* as about the movement of goods because: _____
       _____

48.   What is meant by the term "third party logistics"?

Learning Goal 8
Getting Goods from Producer to Consumer Efficiently

49.   Name six criteria used to evaluate transportation modes.

       a._____   d._____

       b._____   e._____

       c._____   f._____

50.   List five transportation modes used to transport products, in order of volume.

       a._____   d._____

       b._____   e._____

       c._____

426

51.   What does the term "piggyback" mean in shipping?

52.   When would a company use a freight forwarder? Other than combining shipments, what functions may a freight forwarder offer?

53.   What is the benefit of using trucks for shipping?

54.   The least expensive way to ship is: _____

       The drawback to this form of shipping is _____

55.   What are "fishyback" and "birdyback" forms of distribution?

56.   What kinds of products are primarily shipped using pipelines?

57.   The fastest way of shipping is: _____

       The drawback to this form of shipping is: _____

58.   What is an intermodal marketing company?

59.   What do the costs of storage include?

60.   Distinguish between:

storage warehouses:

distribution warehouses:

61.   Describe RFID technology.

CRITICAL THINKING EXERCISES

Learning Goal 1
1.   How would you describe the relationship between the first two "P's" in the marketing mix, product and price, and the third "P", place, or distribution?

2.   What do you think is the channel of distribution for:
        a. cars   b. soft drinks   c. business forms (like blank invoices)

3. Joe Dell and his friend Woody were complaining as they were shopping for suits about how expensive they seemed to be. "Man" said Joe, "if we just had one of those outlet malls where we could avoid the "middleman "we'd be better off. That outlet store down at the Lake of the Ozarks is always advertising about how much lower their prices are because they get shipments direct from the manufacturer. Wouldn't it be a better deal if we just didn't have to deal with these expensive stores?" Woody replied: "Well Joe, I understand what you mean, but in my marketing class we've talked about marketing intermediaries, or middlemen, and they're not as bad as you think! Besides, if you go to an outlet store, you're still using a middleman!" What did Woody mean?

Learning Goal 2

4.   Marketing intermediaries add value to products by creating six utilities:

Form   Possession
Time   Information
Place   Service

Match the correct response to each example:

a. _____   St. Lukes's Hospital sponsors a "pediatric party" every Saturday for its young patients to show what will happen while they are in the hospital for surgery.

b. _____   Although it is a division of a larger retailing company, Macy's, a large department store, offers its own credit card.

c. _____   Many colleges are offering classes in the late afternoon, and on weekends to meet the needs of a diverse student body.

d. _____   McDonald's restaurants can be found in some Wal-Mart superstores, where you can order your meal from the Wal-Mart check-out counter.

e. _____   St. Louis Community College offers classes on three different campuses, as well as on the Internet, to provide convenience for their students.

f. _____   At Dierbergs, a grocery chain, the butcher will cut steaks to your specifications from their meat display.

Learning Goals 1,2,3

5.   Sun-2-Shade manufactures self-darkening windshields for automobiles. Their main customers are likely to be the automobile manufacturing companies. (For more information on this company, look at previous chapters.) The company is looking at its distribution function, and you and the marketing manager must make a proposal soon. In general, what kind of marketing intermediaries should the company consider? How does the classification of Sun-2-Shade as a shopping good, a specialty good, or a business good affect the answer to this question? What will the channel of distribution look like? Is there a need for a marketing intermediary if the company targets primarily the automotive manufacturers? What kind of utilities will our customers find most important?

6.   There are several types of wholesalers:

Full-service

Limited Service (Function) , which includes: *Rack jobbers, Cash and carry wholesalers and Drop shippers*

Agents and Brokers, which include: *manufacturer's agents and sales agents*

Identify the correct type of wholesaler with the following:

a. _____   These wholesalers have begun selling to the public in larger stores, and have begun to allow their customers to use credit cards, although traditionally customers were required to pay cash.

b. _____   Jim Stoeppler represents a number of companies that manufacture various components of certain kinds of uniform, such as a hat manufacturer and a shirt maker.

c. _____   L'Eggs are displayed in the store on a rack. When the product is sold, the company shares the profit with the retailer.

d. _____   Homedics is a wholesaler that stores thousands of different products for their customers. They offer credit and will ship products within 24 hours of receiving an order. They often offer deals to their customers, and have recently expanded their sales and marketing force to include some market research function.

e. _____   Peabody Coal will sell their product to this wholesaler, who will then make arrangements for the coal to be shipped from the mine to an AmerenUE facility in southern Missouri.

f. _____   Larry Jackson owns a commercial real estate company in suburban Seattle. His company will connect potential buyers with sellers and negotiate the contracts. After the deal is done, Larry is no longer involved with either party.

g. _____   Maria Alvarez loves being self-employed. She sells for a small textile company that is based in North Carolina, and acts as their sales force for the entire East Coast and the Midwest. However, she is not an employee of the textile company.

Learning Goal 4

7. The three types of retail distribution strategies are:

Intensive distribution
Selective distribution
Exclusive distribution

Which strategy would likely be used for:

a. Chewing gum _____   d. Tickets to the Olympics _____

b. Athletic shoes _____   e. Designer snow skis _____

c. Potato chips _____   f. Winter coats _____

Learning goal 5

8. There are several types of nonstore retailing:

Electronic retailing   Direct selling
Telemarketing   Multilevel marketing
Vending machines, kiosks and carts   Direct marketing

Determine which is being described in each of the following:

a. _____ Catalogs, telemarketing, and on-line shopping all help to make this form of retailing very convenient for consumers.

b. _____ In Japan, everything from bandages and face cloths to salads and seafood are sold in machines located in airports, movie theaters and other public places.

c. _____ Lingerie, artwork, baskets, jewelry and plastic bowls are sold at "parties" held at a customer's home or work place.

d. _____ Companies "reach out and touch someone" using this form of marketing, to supplement or replace in-store selling and supplement online retailing.

e. _____ Retailers like this form of retailing, as it lends an outdoor marketplace atmosphere to the mall in which they are located.

f. _____ Using this form of retailing, a new salesperson's job is to sell the products provided by the company and to recruit several people who will use the product and recruit others to sell and use the product.

g. _____ Traditional "brick and mortar" stores are beginning to use this type of non-store retailing.

Learning Goal 6

9.   A further look at Sun-2-Shade's distribution system shows the need to consider the kind
         of cooperation necessary for us to create an efficient system.

         In what kind of distribution system (corporate, contractual or administered) will Sun-2-
         Shade take part? Can you describe what their supply chain might look like? What are
         the important aspects of Sun-2-Shade's supply chain management?

Learning Goal 7

10.   Think back to what we have learned in previous chapters about marketing and meeting the
         needs of our customers, as well as what we have learned in this chapter. What forces have
         created the change over the years to return the focus of marketing to the area of logistics?

11.   Five basic modes of transportation are:

         Railroad   Ship (water)
         Truck   Airplane
         Pipeline

         A. Using the figure in your text, determine which mode of transportation would likely
             be used in the following situations when:

         1. _____   Speed of delivery is the most important criterion, and cost is not a
                              essential element.

         2. _____   There is a need to serve multiple locations fairly quickly.

         3. _____   Products are bulky, cost is a major consideration and speed of
                              delivery is not an essential element.

         4. _____   There is a need for constant or steady delivery to a minimal number
                              of locations; speed of delivery is not important.

         5. _____   There are multiple locations, bulky products, and cost and speed of
                              delivery are of equal but moderate importance.

B. Which do you think would be the best choice of transportation mode for Sun-2-Shade? Why?

PRACTICE TEST

MULTIPLE CHOICE – Circle the best answer

Learning Goal 1

1. Which of the following is an activity that would not be considered a distribution function?
   a. storage
   b. transportation
   c. inventory
   d. production

2. Which of the following statements is accurate regarding marketing intermediaries?
   a. Intermediaries add cost to products, but not value.
   b. Intermediaries perform some functions cheaper and faster than manufacturers.
   c. The functions performed by marketing intermediaries are easily eliminated.
   d. Intermediaries have never performed their job efficiently, that's why they are being eliminated.

Learning Goal 2

3. In some areas of the country, Wal-Mart stays open 24 hours a day, most days of the year. This is an example of:
   a. service utility
   b. place utility
   c. time utility
   d. possession utility

4. _____ utility is rapidly becoming the most important utility for many retailers as they face competition from direct marketing form s of retailing, such as the Internet or catalogs.
   a. Place
   b. Form
   c. Time
   d. Service

Learning Goal 3

5. The major difference between wholesalers and retailers is that:
   a. retailers sell only in certain parts of the country, while wholesalers are nationwide.
   b. wholesale organizations are generally more profitable than retail organizations.
   c. retailers sell goods to consumers for their personal use, and wholesalers sell to businesses for their use.
   d. retailers sell to final consumers, while wholesalers sell to another member of the channel of distribution, not final consumers.

6. Sam's Club sells to retailers, but doesn't offer transportation. Sam's will also allow a final consumer to shop, but charges an annual fee, and they have begun to allow customers to use credit, but the store will not deliver. Sam's is an example of a:
    a. rack jobber.
    b. freight forwarder.
    c. drop shipper.
    d. cash and carry wholesaler.

7. Cindy Murphy wants to get into fashion merchandising. Because of the risks involved in high fashion, and how quickly fashions go out of date, Cindy doesn't want to start a company in which she has title to the clothing. Cindy will have to rule out which of the following in her choice of business?
    a. broker
    b. agents
    c. merchant wholesaler
    d. manufacturer's agent

Learning Goal 4
8. Borders, Lowe's Hardware and Office Max are stores that offer wide selections of a product category at competitive prices. These stores can be so price competitive that they will drive out smaller businesses. These stores are known as:
    a. discount stores
    b. supermarkets
    c. supercenters
    d. category killers

9. After a few years of relying on the Internet to market their product, management at The Flying Noodle, a pasta company, has decided that it is time to get their product into the supermarket. This kind of basic pasta product will do best with:
    a. selective distribution
    b. intensive distribution
    c. exclusive distribution
    d. nonstore retailing distribution

Learning Goal 5
10. Which of the following is not true regarding retailing over the Internet?
    a. Most retailers can get away without going online.
    b. The Internet has helped to boost sales for many small retailers.
    c. Electronic retailers have had some problems with handling customer complaints.
    d. Brick and mortar stores are going online so that customers can pick and choose which shopping technique suits them best.

11. One of the fastest growing aspects of retailing is:
    a. vending machines
    b. telemarketing
    c. direct marketing
    d. multilevel marketing

12. Which of the following would not be an example of direct marketing?
    a. Ordering a book from Amazon.com
    b. Providing consumers with information via CDs and web sites.
    c. Sending in an order form from an advertising supplement in the newspaper
    d. Buying a soda from the vending machine at school

Learning Goal 6
13.　Midas Muffler, Baskin-Robbins, and other franchisors are examples of a:
   a.　corporate distribution system.
   b.　contractual distribution system .
   c.　retail cooperative.
   d.　administered distribution system.

14.　Compared to a channel of distribution, a supply chain:
   a.　is longer, because it includes links from suppliers.
   b.　is shorter, because it doesn't include the manufacturer.
   c.　is similar to a channel of distribution, but includes totally different members.
   d.　is considered another form of wholesaling.

15.　Which of the following is <u>not</u> included in a list of the benefits of supply chain management systems?
   a.　They allow companies to save on inventory.
   b.　They provide for customer service improvement.
   c.　The can help to make a company more responsive to market changes.
   d.　They create a more efficient method of production.

Learning Goal 7
16.　Logistics is:
   a.　the moving of goods within the warehouse, and within a factory.
   b.　the process of changing raw materials and parts and other inputs into finished goods.
   c.　planning, implementing, and controlling the physical flow of materials, final goods, and related information from points of origin to points of consumption.
   d.　an effort to make sure that all of the organizations in a channel of distribution are owned by one firm.

17.　Third party logistics refers to:
   a.　bringing goods back to the manufacturers because of defects or to recycle.
   b.　the use of outside firms to help move goods.
   c.　managing the flow of finished products to business buyers and ultimate consumers.
   d.　the movement of goods within a warehouse, from warehouses to the factory floor and from the factory floor to various workstations.

18.　Dave Klein is a produce farmer in northern California. His major customers are grocery stores in the Midwest. Dave's product will only last for about 2 weeks after it has been picked, so Dave is concerned with getting his product to his customers quickly, but also needs to be aware of the cost of shipping, as produce is a perishable item. He ships almost daily when his produce is in season. Which form of shipping is Dave MOST likely to use?
   a.　trucks
   b.　ships
   c.　air
   d.　rail

19.   When Hans Kaupfmann bought his car while on a trip to Germany, he wasn't sure how it would be shipped. The dealer assured him that many people buy cars and have them shipped to overseas destinations. The dealer explained that it's a smooth transition from land to sea and back to land, by trucking the car to the port, loading the entire truck trailer on to the ship, then trucking again to the destination. This process is known as:
   a. piggyback
   b. fishyback
   c. bi-modal transportation
   d. transatlantic transportation

20.   A _____ gathers, then redistributes products.
   a. distribution warehouse
   b. storage warehouse
   c. full-service wholesaler
   d. drop shipper wholesaler

TRUE-FALSE

Learning Goal 1

1. _____   A channel of distribution consists of marketing intermediaries who join together to store and transport goods in their path from producer to consumer.

2. _____   Generally, it is much less expensive and much faster when we can avoid the use of a marketing intermediary and go straight to the producer.

3. _____   Marketing intermediaries can be eliminated but their activities can't.

Learning Goal 2

4. _____   Form utility is typically provided by producers rather than intermediaries.

5. _____   When Lowe's makes arrangements for a refrigerator to be delivered to the buyer's home, they are providing time utility.

Learning Goal 3

6. _____   Merchant wholesalers do not buy what they sell; they primarily match buyers with sellers.

7. _____   A sales agent, or manufacturer's agent, can represent several companies.

Learning Goal 4

8. _____   Exclusive distribution would be used by a producer of a product such as skydiving equipment.

9. _____   An example of a category killer would be Office Depot or Borders Books.

Learning Goal 5

10. _____   One of the challenges of electronic retailing is providing service and keeping customers.

11. _____   The benefit of vending machines is their convenient location.

12. _____   Multilevel marketing is not a good way to make money, because it costs too much to get into.

Learning Goal 6

13. _____ In a corporate distribution system, a retailer signs a contract to cooperate with a manufacturer.

14. _____ The primary concern of supply chain managers is keeping costs down, regardless of anything else.

15. _____ Supply chain management enables companies to carry lower levels of inventory and improve customer service.

Learning Goal 7

16. _____ Today, logistics is as much about the movement of information as it is about the movement of goods.

17. _____ A major issue in marketing in the future will be how to ship goods to other countries in the fastest way possible and still keep costs low.

Learning Goal 8

18. _____ A smaller manufacturer may make use of a freight forwarder because they don't ship enough product to fill a railcar or truck.

19. _____ Intermodal shipping uses multiple modes of transportation to complete a single long-distance movement of freight.

20. _____ A distribution warehouse hold products for a relatively long time, until they can be distributed to the appropriate retailer or customer.

You Can Find It on the Net

Compare shopping on the Internet to shopping in a store. Visit www.cdnow.com or www.amazon.com and check out the prices of three of your favorite c.d.s

How do the prices compare to the price you pay in the store? (You may have to actually visit the store to determine this!)

How much does shipping add to the price of the c.d.'s?

How does the web site encourage you to buy the product?

What problems do you see with shopping for music over the Internet?

How does the web site overcome those problems?

Which type of shopping do you prefer, Internet or store? Why?

ANSWERS

LEARNING THE LANGUAGE

1. Inbound logistics	13. Service utility	24. Agents/brokers
2. Utility	14. Channel of distribution	25. Time utility
3. Wholesaler	15. Retailer	26. Possession utility
4. Administered distribution system	16. Corporate distribution system	27. Outbound logistics
5. Materials handling	17. Selective distribution	28. Contractual distribution system
6. Logistics	18. Information utility	29. Merchant wholesalers
7. Intensive distribution	19. Marketing intermediaries	30. Direct selling
8. Telemarketing	20. Rack jobbers	31. Electronic retailing
9. Place utility	21. Freight forwarder	32. Supply chain (or value chain)
10. Intermodal shipping	22. Drop shippers	33. Direct marketing
11. Supply chain management	23. Cash and carry wholesaler	34. Reverse logistics
12. Exclusive distribution		

ASSESSMENT CHECK

Learning Goal 1
The Emergence of Marketing Intermediaries

1.   Channels of distribution ensure communication flows and the flow of money and title to goods. They also help ensure that the right quantity and assortment of goods will be available when and where needed.

2.   Marketing intermediaries perform marketing tasks like transporting, storing, selling, advertising, and relationship building faster and cheaper than most manufacturers could.

3. Marketing intermediaries create exchange efficiency in the distribution system by reducing the number of transactions necessary to get the product to the buyer. Marketing intermediaries are better at performing their functions than a manufacturer would be.

4. Some people believe that if they could get rid of the intermediary they could reduce the cost of what they buy. However, if we got rid of a retailer, for example, we may be able to buy a product for a little less, but we would still have to drive further and spend more time looking for the product. The value of intermediaries is that they make products available to us at times and places that are convenient for us. That often outweighs the cost they add to the product.

5. Three basic points to remember about middlemen include:
    a. Marketing intermediaries can be eliminated, but their activities cannot.
    b. Intermediaries have survived because they have performed functions faster and cheaper than others.
    c. Intermediaries add cost, but the cost is usually offset by the value they create.

Learning Goal 2
Utilities Created by Intermediaries

6. The six utilities created by intermediaries are:
    a. Form   d. Possession
    b. Time   e. Information
    c. Place   f. Service

7. Form utility is created mostly by producers. Form utility is created by taking raw materials and changing their form so that they become useful products.

8. Intermediaries add time utility to products by making them available when they're needed, like a retailer which is open 24 hours a day.

9. Place utility is added to products by having them where people want them, in a convenient place.

10. Possession utility is added by doing whatever is necessary to transfer ownership from one party to another, including providing credit. Activities include delivery, installation, guarantees, and follow-up service.

11. Intermediaries add information utility by opening two-way flows of information between marketing participants. Newspapers, sales people, libraries, web sites, and government publications are all information sources made available by intermediaries.

12. Service utility is becoming the most important utility for retailers, because without personal service they could lose business to electronic marketing or direct marketing.

Learning Goal 3
Wholesale Intermediaries

13. A *retail sale* is a sale of goods and services to <u>consumers</u> for their own use. A *wholesale sale* is the sale of goods and services to <u>businesses and institutions</u> for use in the business or for resale.

14. a. Full-service wholesalers perform all distribution functions.
    b. Limited function wholesalers perform only selected functions.

15. The functions a full service wholesaler will perform include:
    a. Provide a sales force
    b. Communicate manufacturer's advertising deals and plans
    c. Maintain inventory for producer
    d. Arrange or undertake transportation
    e. Provide capital by paying cash or quick payment
    f. Provide suppliers with marketing information
    g. Granting credit to customers
    h. Assume risk by taking title

16. Rack jobbers are limited function wholesalers. They furnish racks or shelves full of merchandise to retailers, display products and sell on consignment. They keep title to goods until they are sold and share the profits with the retailers.

17. A cash-and-carry wholesaler is a limited function wholesaler that serves mostly smaller retailers with a limited assortment of products. Traditionally, retailers went to such wholesalers, paid cash, and carried the goods back to their stores. Today, some stores allow retailers and others to use credit cards for purchases.

18. A drop shipper solicits orders from retailers and other wholesalers and have the merchandise shipped directly from a producer to a buyer. They own the merchandise but don't handle, stock or deliver it. That is handled by the producer.

19. Agents and brokers never own the products they distribute. Usually they do not carry inventory, provide credit, or assume risks. While merchant wholesalers earn a profit from the sale of goods, agents and brokers earn commissions or fees based upon a percentage of the sales revenue.

20. An agent maintains long-term relationships with the people they represent, whereas a broker is usually hired on a temporary basis. Once a broker negotiates a contract between a buyer and a seller, the relationship ends.

21. A manufacturer's agent may represent one or several manufacturers in a specific territory, as long as the suppliers are not competitors. A sales agent represents a single producer in a larger territory.

22. A broker has no continuous relationship with a buyer or seller. Once the broker negotiates a contract between a buyer and a seller, their relationship ends.

Learning Goal 4
Retail Intermediaries

23. The various types of retailers are:
    a. Department stores – sell a wide variety of products in separate departments
    b. Discount stores – sell many different products at prices below department stores
    c. Supermarkets - sell mostly food with other nonfood items like paper products
    d. Warehouse clubs – sell food and general merchandise in very large facilities; may require membership
    e. Convenience stores – sell food and other often needed items at convenient locations

f. Category killers – sell a huge variety of one type of product; dominates a category of goods

g. Outlet stores – sell general merchandise directly from the manufacturer at a discount

h. Specialty stores – sell a wide selection of goods in one category

24. a. Intensive distribution - puts products into as many outlets as possible. Products that need intensive distribution include convenience goods.

b. Selective distribution – the use of only a preferred group of the available retailers in an area. Manufacturers of shopping goods use this type of distribution.

c. Exclusive distribution – the use of only one retail outlet in a given geographic area. Auto makers and producers of specialty goods use this.

Learning Goal 5
Nonstore Retailing

25. Six types of nonstore retailing are:
   a. Electronic retailing
   b. Telemarketing
   c. Vending machines, kiosks and carts
   d. Direct selling
   e. Multilevel marketing
   f. Direct marketing

26. The major challenges, or battles, of e-tailing are getting customers and delivering the goods, providing helpful service, and keeping customers.

27. Electronic retailers have had problems with handling complaints, taking back goods that customers don't like, and providing personal help. Some sites are trying to improve customer service by adding help buttons that you can click on to get almost instant assistance from a real person.

28. Traditional retailers are going online, so that now customers can pick and choose which shopping form they prefer. Companies that want to compete in the future will probably need both a store presence and an online presence to provide consumers with all the options they want.

29. Traditional retailers have learned that selling on the Internet calls for a new kind of distribution system. Both traditional retailers and Internet retailers have to develop new distribution systems to meet the demands of today's Internet-savvy shoppers.

30. Telemarketing has been used by companies to supplement or replace in-store selling and to complement online selling. The National Do Not Call Registry is expected to eliminate 80% of telemarketing calls.

31. The benefit of vending machines is their location in areas where people want convenience items, such as airports, office buildings, schools and service stations.

The benefits of kiosks and carts are that they have lower costs than stores. Therefore they can offer lower prices on items such as T-shirts and umbrellas. Mall owners often like them because they are colorful and create a marketplace atmosphere. Customers enjoy interactive kiosks because they dispense coupons and provide information when buying products.

32. Major users of direct selling include cosmetics, and vacuum cleaner manufacturers. Other businesses are using direct selling for lingerie, artwork, plants and other goods. Because so many buyers work outside the home during the day, many of the sellers are sponsoring parties at workplaces or in the evenings and on weekends.

33. Multilevel marketing sales people work as independent contractors. They earn commissions on their own sales and create commissions for the "upliners" who recruited them. In multilevel marketing, an "upliner" is an individual who has recruited others to sell for them. The "downliners" are the people who have been recruited to sell.

34. The main attractions of multilevel marketing for employees are:
a. great potential for making money
b. low cost of entry

35. Direct marketing includes:
a. direct mail
b. catalog sales
c. telemarketing
d. on-line marketing

36. Direct marketing has become popular because shopping from home or work is more convenient for consumers than going to the store. Consumers can shop in catalogs and free-standing advertising supplements in the newspaper and then buy by phone, by mail, or by computer.

37. Direct marketing changed when consumers became more involved with interactive video. Producers now provide information on a c.d. or on websites that consumers can access. Companies that use these tools have become major competitors for those who market using paper catalogs.

Learning Goal 6
Building Cooperation in Channel Systems

38. A corporate distribution system is one in which all of the organizations in the channel of distribution are owned by one firm. If the manufacturer owns the retail firm it can maintain control over its operations.

39. Franchise systems - the franchisee agrees to all of the rules, regulations, and procedures established by the franchisor. This results in consistent quality and level of service.

Wholesaler-sponsored chains - each store signs an agreement to use the same name, participate in chain promotions and cooperate as a unified system of stores, even though each store is independently owned and managed.

Retail cooperatives - the arrangement is much like a wholesaler-sponsored chain except it's initiated by the retailers. The same cooperation is agreed to, and the stores remain independent.

40. In an administered distribution system the producer manages all of the marketing functions at the retail level. This includes display, inventory control, pricing, and promotion. Retailers cooperate with producers in administered distribution systems because they get so much help for free.

41. A supply chain is longer than a channel of distribution because it includes suppliers to manufacturers whereas the channel of distribution begins with manufacturers. Channels of distribution are part of the supply chain.

42. A supply chain pays for itself from inventory savings, customer service improvement and responsiveness to market changes.

43. The term "value chain" is just another word for a supply chain. This term may be used because such systems are so effective and efficient.

Learning Goal 7
The Emergence of Logistics

44. When shipping from country to country the major questions are how to ship goods in the fastest way possible and still keep costs low. This is especially challenging when shipping bulky merchandise such as cars. It is sometimes impossible to use trucks or trains because the goods have to travel over water. Shipping by air is often prohibitively expensive. The last source is by ship. The questions are how to get goods to the ship and from ship to buyer, as well as handling trade duties and taxes.

45. To better manage customs problems, many companies are turning to Web-based trade compliance systems. ClearCross and Xporta are systems that determine what paperwork is needed by cross-checking their databases for information about foreign trade duties and taxes, U.S. labor law restrictions, and federal regulations.

46. Factory processes change raw materials and parts and other inputs into outputs, such as finished goods.

47. Logistics is as much about the movement of information as it is about the movement of goods because customer wants and needs must flow through the system all the way to suppliers and must do so in real time. Information must also flow down through the system.

48. Third party logistics is the term used to describe the use of outside firms to help move goods from here to there. It is part of a larger trend toward outsourcing.

Learning Goal 8
Getting Goods from Producer to Consumer Efficiently

49. Six criteria used to evaluate transportation modes are:
    a. Cost
    b. Speed
    c. On-time dependability
    d. Flexibility in handling products
    e. Frequency of shipments
    f. Reach

50. Five transportation modes used in transporting products, listed by volume are:
    a. Railroad
    b. Trucks
    c. Pipeline
    d. Water transportation
    e. Air

51. A piggyback system means that a truck trailer is detached from the cab of a truck, loaded onto a railroad flatcar and taken to a destination where is will be offloaded, attached to a truck and driven to customers' plants.

52.   A company would use a freight forwarder when it doesn't ship enough goods to fill a railcar or truck. The freight forwarder can combine many small shipments to create a single large shipment that can be transported cost-effectively, by either truck or train. Other than shipping, a freight forwarder may offer warehousing, customer assistance, and other services along with pickup and delivery.

53.   A benefit of using trucks for shipping is that trucks are able to reach more destinations than other forms of transportation because a truck can deliver door to door.

54.   The least expensive way to ship is water transportation. The drawback is that water transportation is so slow.

55.   Fishyback and birdyback forms of distribution are similar to piggyback. In fishyback, the truck trailer is loaded onto ship, and re-connected to the truck cab at the destination. With birdyback, the trailer is loaded onto an airplane.

56.   Pipelines are used primarily to transport water, petroleum and petroleum products.

57.   The fast way of shipping is by air.

        The drawback of shipping by air is that it is very expensive.

58.   Services that specialize in intermodal shipping are known as intermodal marketing companies.

59.   The costs of storage include the cost of the storage warehouse (distribution facility) and its operation plus movement of goods within the warehouse.

60.   Storage warehouses - store products for a relatively long time, such as seasonal goods, like snow shovels and lawnmowers.

        Distribution warehouses - are facilities used to gather and redistribute products.

61.   RFID technology tags merchandise so that it can be tracked from the time it's loaded off the supplier's docks to when the customer buys the product. This is the latest in tracking technology.

CRITICAL THINKING EXERCISES

Learning Goal 1
1.   The type of product will determine what kind of transportation and storage will be called for, and what kinds of stores (retailers) will carry the product. The type of transportation mode and the kind of storage will be a part of the final price of the product, as well as the kind of store - i.e. the image of the store where it's sold and its pricing policies.

2. The channel of distribution for

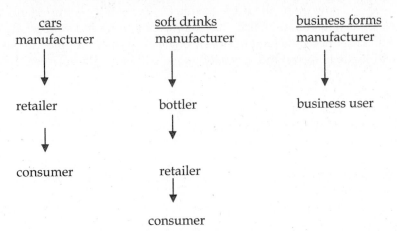

cars	soft drinks	business forms
manufacturer	manufacturer	manufacturer
↓	↓	↓
retailer	bottler	business user
↓	↓	
consumer	retailer	
	↓	
	consumer	

3. What Woody was trying to tell Joe is that, first, the outlet store is a type of middleman, called a retailer. Further, retailers and the other type of middlemen, wholesalers, add many things to a product that would be difficult to replace. In the first place, Joe would have to drive to wherever the suit he chose was manufactured, if he were to really avoid a middleman. That could be as far away as the Far East! The retailer is much closer. Secondly, if he decided to have the manufacturer ship the suit to him, he would have to pay for shipping the suit to his home, which could be expensive. He would have to contact the manufacturer during working hours, which for a manufacturer would probably be Monday - Friday, between 8a.m. and 5 p.m. Then he would have to try it on, and figure out any alterations, perhaps ship the suit back to be altered, or find someone to alter it for him. Further, Joe would not be able to see the suit before it was sent, or would have to spend hours looking through the manufacturer's warehouse looking through hundreds of suits (that is after having traveled to the Far East in the first place...)

In short, middlemen provide value through adding convenience such as transportation and storage, and enable us to shop for and find exactly what we want, at times convenient for us with far less effort. Therefore, while middleman organizations can be eliminated, their functions cannot.

Learning Goal 2

4. a. Information   d. Place and possession
   b. Possession   e. Place
   c. Time   f. Form

5. If Sun-2-Shade targets primarily the auto industry, the company will not necessarily need a wholesaling middleman, unless it uses some kind of a broker in lieu of employing a sales force. The channel of distribution will look like one of these two suggestions:

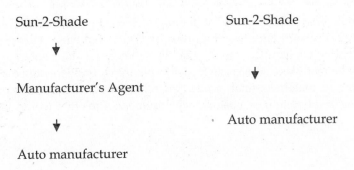

Sun-2-Shade	Sun-2-Shade
↓	
Manufacturer's Agent	↓
↓	Auto manufacturer
Auto manufacturer	

The most important utility for the end consumer may be information utility, as the consumer may need to know more about the product. Place utility is important, but is affected by our classification of Sun-2-Shade as either a shopping good or specialty good or a business good. This affects the kind of store we will choose, as shopping goods may be found in several kinds of stores and specialty goods will be found in fewer, different kinds of stores.

For the auto manufacturers, time and place utility will be important, as they will need the product delivered when they need it, where they need it.

Learning Goal 3

6.   a. Limited service: cash and carry   e. Limited service: drop shipper
      b. Manufacturer's agent   f. Broker
      c. Limited service: rack jobber   g. Sales agent
      d. Full service

Learning Goal 4

7.   a. Intensive   d. Exclusive
      b. Selective   e. Exclusive
      c. Intensive   f. Selective

Learning Goal 5

8.   a. Direct marketing   e. Kiosks, carts
      b. Vending machines   f. Multilevel marketing
      c. Direct selling   g. E-tailing
      d. Telemarketing

9.   Sun-2-Shade will be an integral part of an automaker's supply chain, and will want to be linked electronically to their customers. Sun-2-Shade's supply chain will include suppliers of raw materials as well as the auto manufacturers. The critical element of their supply chain management system will be to coordinate the receipt of the raw materials needed to make the windshield and the process of manufacturing, with the orders coming in from customers. This process is known as outbound logistics.

Sun-2-Shade won't be using retailers right away, since the company will most likely be focusing on the automakers at first. When it does begin to sell to retailers, it will become part of yet a different supply chain.

10.   As we have learned in earlier chapters the focus today is on meeting the needs of our customers in every way possible. But the idea of meeting customer needs goes beyond developing need-satisfying products, and today extends to meeting our customers demands for quick delivery at reasonable prices. This includes our global as well as domestic customers. We can meet customer demands for high quality, reasonably price products, delivered when we want them, by focusing on logistics and supply chain management. Focusing on these important areas of marketing will ensure that products are stored, delivered, handled and shipped in the most cost efficient manner. As customer demands have increased, so has the focus on planning, implementing, and controlling the physical flow of materials, final goods and related information from points of origin to points of consumption to meet customer requirements – in other words, logistics.

11.   A.
      1. Air   4. Pipeline
      2. Truck   5. Railroad
      3. Water

      B.   The best transportation mode for Sun-2-Shade would probably be by truck to
           both the auto manufacturers and the retailers. For auto manufacturers, which
           are located a considerable distance from Sun-2-Shade's production facility, a
           combination of rail and truck could be used for flexibility, number of deliveries,
           and speed. The major problem with trucks is the cost, but it serves the other
           needs best.

PRACTICE TEST

MULTIPLE CHOICE   **TRUE-FALSE**
LG 1   # 1-2   LG 1   # 1-3
LG 2   # 3-4   LG 2   # 4-5
LG 3   # 5-7   LG 3   # 6-7
LG 4   # 8-9   LG 4   # 8-9
LG 5   # 10-12   LG 5   # 10-12
LG 6   # 13-15   LG 6   # 13-15
LG 7   #16-17   LG 7   # 16-17
LG 8   # 18-20   LG 8   # 18-20

1. d   11. c   1. T   11. T
2. b   12. d   2. F   12. F
3. c   13. b   3. T   13. F
4. d   14. a   4. T   14. F
5. d   15. d   5. F   15. T
6. d   16. c   6. F   16. T
7. c   17. b   7. T   17. T
8. d   18. a   8. T   18. T
9. b   19. b   9. T   19. T
10. a   20. a   10. T   20. F

CHAPTER 16 – USING EFFECTIVE PROMOTIONAL TECHNIQUES

LEARNING GOALS

After you have read and studied this chapter, you should be able to:

1.   Define promotion and list the four traditional tools that make up the promotion mix.
2.   Define advertising and describe the advantages and disadvantages of various advertising media, including the Internet.
3.   Illustrate the steps of B2B and B2C selling processes.
4.   Describe the role of the public relations department and how publicity fits in that role.
5.   Explain the importance of various forms of sales promotion including sampling.
6.   Give examples of word of mouth, viral marketing, blogging, and podcasting.

LEARNING THE LANGUAGE

Listed below are important terms found in the chapter. Choose the correct term for each definition and write it in the space provided.

Advertising	Promotion	Push strategy
Blog	Promotion mix	Qualifying
Infomercial	Prospect	Sales promotion
Integrated marketing communication (IMC)	Prospecting	Sampling
Interactive promotion	Publicity	Trial close
Personal selling	Public relations (PR)	Viral marketing
Podcasting	Pull strategy	Word-of-mouth promotion
Product placement		

1.   The promotional tool known as _____ stimulates consumer purchasing and dealer interest by means of short-term activities.

2.   Paid, nonpersonal communication, or _____, goes through various media by organizations and individuals who are in some way identified in the advertising message.

3.   The management function of _____ evaluates public attitudes, changes policies and procedures in response to the public's requests, and executes a program of action and information to earn public understanding and acceptance.

4.   A _____ is a promotional strategy in which heavy advertising and sales promotion efforts are directed toward consumers so that they will request products from retailers.

5.   The step in the selling process referred to as the _____ consists of a question or statement that moves the selling process toward the actual close.

6.   The _____ is the combination of promotion tools that an organization uses.

7. A promotional tool that involves people talking about products they have purchased is called _____.

8. In the selling process _____is making sure that people have a need for the product, the authority to buy and the willingness to listen to a sales message.

9. Researching potential buyers and choosing those most likely to buy is called _____.

10. A technique known as _____ combines all the promotional tools into one comprehensive, unified promotional strategy.

11. An online diary is known as a _____; it looks like a web page but is easier to create and update by posting text, photos, or links to other sites.

12. The form of promotion known as _____is any information about an individual, product, or organization that's distributed to the public through the media and that's not paid for, or controlled by, the seller.

13. A _____is the promotional strategy in which the producer uses advertising, personal selling, sales promotion and all other promotional tools to convince wholesalers and retailers to stock and sell merchandise.

14. A full-length TV program devoted exclusively to promoting goods and services is known as a(n) _____.

15. The promotion tool of _____ is the face-to-face presentation and promotion of products and services.

16. The process of _____is an effort by marketers to inform and remind people in the target market about products and to persuade them to participate in an exchange.

17. Putting products into TV shows and movies where they will be seen is called _____.

18. A tool named _____allows marketers to go beyond a monologue, where sellers tried to persuade buyers to buy things, to a dialogue where buyers and sellers can work together to create mutually beneficial exchange relationships.

19. The term _____is used to describe everything from paying people to say positive things on the Internet to setting up multilevel selling schemes whereby consumers get commissions for directing friends to specific Web sites.

20. A person with the means to buy a product, or _____also has the authority to buy, and the willingness to listen to a sales message.

21. A promotional tool in which a company lets consumers have a small sample of the product for no charge is called _____.

22. A means of distributing audio and video programs via the Internet is called _____ and it lets users subscribe to a number of files, also known as feeds, and then hear or view the material at the time they choose.

ASSESSMENT CHECK

Learning Goal 1
Promotion and the Promotion Mix

1.   What are the tools of the promotion mix?

a._____   c._____

b._____   d._____

2.   What is the idea behind Integrated Marketing communication?

Learning Goal 2
Advertising: Fighting to Keep Consumer Interest

3.   List the various categories of advertising

a. _____   f. _____

b. _____   g. _____

c. _____   h. _____

d. _____   i. _____

e. _____

4.   What is the difference between propaganda and advertising?

5.   How does the public benefit from advertising?

a. _____

b. _____

c. _____

6.   List some of the advantages and disadvantages of each form of advertising media.

	Advantages	Disadvantages
a. Newspapers	_____	_____
	_____	_____
	_____	_____
	_____	_____
b. Television	_____	_____
	_____	_____
	_____	_____
	_____	_____
c. Radio	_____	_____
	_____	_____
	_____	_____
d. Magazines	_____	_____
	_____	_____
	_____	_____
	_____	_____
e. Outdoor	_____	_____
	_____	_____
	_____	_____
f. Direct mail	_____	_____
	_____	_____
	_____	_____

g. Yellow pages   _____   _____

_____   _____

_____   _____

_____   _____

h. Internet   _____   _____

_____   _____

_____   _____

_____   _____

7.   Why are infomercials so successful in selling products?

8.   Describe the benefits to corporations of Internet advertising.

9.   How is the Internet changing the approach to customers?

10.   What are the two approaches to advertising in the global market?

a. _____

b. _____

11.   Evidence supports the theory that the most effective global promotional strategies are:

_____

12.   Distinguish between "globalism" and "regionalism" in advertising.

Learning Goal 3
Personal Selling: Providing Personal Attention

13. Describe "effective selling." How does technology help the salesperson to be effective?

14. What are the seven steps in the personal selling process?

a._____   e. _____

b._____   f. _____

c._____   g. _____

d. _____

15. In personal selling, what is the difference between prospecting and qualifying?

16. Where do sales people find prospects?

17. What activities occur in the preapproach?

18. What is the idea during the first sales call during the approach stage?

19. What is the main idea when making the presentation?

20. What should the salesperson do in answering objections?

21. What activities are involved in closing a sale?

22.   Identify the activities involved in the follow up.

23.   According to the text, what are the two goals of a salesperson?

24.   How does the role of the salesperson in the B2C (Business to Consumer) sales process differ from that in the B2B (Business to Business) sales process?

25.   What does the salesperson do during the presentation in the B2C sales process?

26.   During the trial close in B2C selling, the salesperson must be aware that: _____

        _____

27.   Why is follow-up important in B2C selling?

Learning Goal 4
Public Relations: Building Relationships

28.   Identify the three steps in creating a good public relations campaign.

        a. _____

        b. _____

        c. _____

29.   It is the responsibility of a public relations department to: _____

        _____

30.   What are the advantages of publicity over other promotional tools?

        a. _____

        b. _____

        c. _____

31. What are three drawbacks of publicity?

   a. _____

   b. _____

   c. _____

32. One way to see that publicity is handled well by the media is to: _____

   _____

Learning Goal 5
Sales Promotion: Getting a Good Deal

33. List 5 types of B2B sales promotions.

   a. _____   d. _____

   b. _____   e. _____

   c. _____

34. List the various consumer sales promotion techniques.

   a. _____   g. _____

   b. _____   h. _____

   c. _____   i. _____

   d. _____   j. _____

   e. _____   k. _____

   f. _____   l. _____

35. Sales promotion programs are designed to: _____

   _____

36. The most important *internal* sales promotion efforts are directed at: _____

   _____

37. List the internal sales promotion efforts

   a. _____

   b. _____

   c. _____

456

38.   What is a virtual trade show, and what is the benefit for dealers and distributors?

39.   Identify the main targets for developing sales promotion efforts, in order.

    a. _____

    b. _____

    c. _____

40.   What is the benefit of sampling as a sales promotion tool?

41.   Define event marketing.

Learning Goal 6
How New Technologies are Affecting Promotion

42.   What is the idea behind word of mouth promotion?

43.   What are some ways that companies are creating word of mouth promotion?

44.   What is one of the best ways to reduce negative word of mouth?

45.   How important will blogging be in the future of marketing?

46.   What does podcasting allow for?

47. How are new technologies affecting promotion?

48. Because so much information about consumers is now available, companies are tending to use the traditional promotional tools: _____

_____

49. According to the text, what is the best way to reach:

a. large homogenous groups of consumers _____

b. large organizations _____

51. What is the idea behind a push strategy?

52. What should happen when a pull strategy is successful?

53. Describe a total systems approach to marketing.

CRITICAL THINKING EXERCISES

Learning Goal 1
1. Sun-2-Shade is a company that makes self-darkening windshields for automobiles. (We have worked on this company in previous chapters.) While we haven't yet decided on a promotion mix for Sun-2-Shade, discuss the steps we will we take to create our promotion campaign, as specifically as possible to this point.

Learning Goal 2

2.   There is a variety of media available to use for advertising. Using the chart in your text, determine what might be the most appropriate form of advertising media for: (there may be more than one answer for each)

a. _____   A rock concert at an outdoor theater

b. _____   Sales at the local mall

c. _____   Products aimed specifically at women

d. _____   A local news television show

e. _____   Long distance telephone service

f. _____   Credit cards

g. _____   Computer software

h. _____   A self-darkening windshield for a car/truck

3.   No matter what the specific promotion mix will be for Sun-2-Shade, a company that manufactures self darkening windshields for vehicles, there is no doubt that the Internet and technology will play an important role. How would you incorporate the use of the Internet into the promotion mix for Sun-2-Shade?

Learning Goal 3

4.   We're continuing to work on a promotion mix for Sun-2-Shade (see question 1). We know it will include some form of personal selling. Using the seven steps in your text, prepare an outline for a sales presentation to your automotive manufacturing customers.

Learning Goal 4

5.   The Fox affiliate in large midwestern city added a news broadcast to its lineup. In order to compete with the larger affiliates, the Fox affiliate (Channel 30) decided to air their program at 9:00 p.m. Before the news broadcast went on the air, the station surveyed viewers regarding their likes and dislikes about the current local news broadcasts. Shortly before the new show was to premiere, the station began promoting the show, the news anchors, and how this show was going to be different from current shows.

One of the changes the new show made was to avoid, as much as possible, the real "bad news" stories as leads to the broadcast, leaving them until later in the show. They made a point of finding "good news" stories about the city and its inhabitants. They did this because that's what viewers said they wanted. During the broadcast, just before a commercial break, a screen will show with the exact show times of each of the upcoming stories, in response to customer complaints that other stations will use upcoming stories as "hooks" but actually not air the story until much later in the broadcast. In promoting the show, and during the news broadcast, mention is made of the way the station is responding to viewer requests. Further, during the broadcast, the station's telephone number was flashed, and viewers were encouraged to call with complaints, requests, or suggestions.

How do these actions by the television station demonstrate a "good" public relations program?

Learning Goal 5

6.   Identify three main groups that are the main focus of sales promotion efforts, and a technique used to reach each group.

Group   Technique

a. _____   _____

b. _____   _____

c. _____   _____

7.   Continuing with developing the promotion mix for Sun-2-Shade, identify some sales promotion techniques you would use for employees, the B2B market and the B2C market.

8.   How do the other elements of the promotion mix affect word of mouth promotion?

Product _____

Sales promotion _____

Advertising _____

Publicity _____

Personal selling _____

Learning Goals 1-6

9.   Now that we have covered the promotion mix variables, you are an expert in designing an effective promotion campaign. What do you think would be the most effective promotion mix for Sun-2-Shade to use? Will it be more important to use a push or a pull strategy, a combination, or a "total systems" approach? How will you use new tools such as podcasting, blogging and viral marketing?

PRACTICE TEST

MULTIPLE CHOICE – Circle the best answer

Learning Goal 1

1.   Promotion is an effort by marketers to:
   a.   help retailers sell products.
   b.   inform, remind, and persuade people to buy.
   c.   segment markets to reach them more effectively.
   d.   search for new prospects.

2.   Sun-2-Shade is a company that makes self-darkening windshields for cars and trucks. Which of the following would not be included as part of Sun-2-Shade's promotion mix?
   a.   Designing an interactive Web site for customers to ask questions and order products.
   b.   Sponsoring a NASCAR race.
   c.   Hiring a sales force to call on automotive customers.
   d.   Expanding the product line to include sunglasses custom made to match the customer's windshield colors.

3.   Technology and the Internet have:
   a.   had little impact on the area of advertising.
   b.   affected other areas of business more than advertising.
   c.   had a tremendous impact on promotion.
   d.   increased the need for personal selling.

Learning Goal 2

4.   Which of the following would not be included in a discussion of the benefits of advertising, according to the text?
   a.   Advertising creates a lot of job security.
   b.   Advertisements are informative.
   c.   Advertising pays for the production cost of television and radio.
   d.   Some kinds of advertising, such as direct mail, allow a company to target very specific markets.

5.   Product placement refers to:
   a.   paying to put products into TV shows and movies where they will be seen.
   b.   the location of products on a grocery store shelf.
   c.   the image the product has in the mind of the consumer.
   d.   the location of the product at any given point in the channel of distribution.

6.   Which media would be best if you are interested in targeting a specific audience, need flexibility, have a local market and don't have a lot of money to spend?
   a.   The Internet
   b.   Television
   c.   Outdoor
   d.   Radio

7.   Which of the following would not be included in a discussion of the benefits of advertising using infomercials?
   a.   They can show the product in great detail.
   b.   Infomercials are low in cost.
   c.   It is the equivalent of sending your best salesperson into the home.
   d.   Infomercials provide the opportunity to show the public how a product works.

8.   In personal selling, the relationship must continue for a long time, as the salesperson responds to new requests for information from current customers. This is an important part of the _____step in personal selling.
   a.   prospecting
   b.   closing
   c.   follow-up
   d.   presentation

9.   What is the first step in the B2B personal selling process?
   a.   Approach
   b.   Make presentation
   c.   Prospect and Qualify
   d.   Preapproach

10.   Which of the following is true regarding personal selling today?
   a.   Automation has had a big impact on personal selling with the use of high-tech hardware and software.
   b.   The objective of an initial sales call is to make a sale immediately.
   c.   Big customers should always be treated with more care than small ones.
   d.   It is more difficult to find customers in the business-to-business market than in the consumer market.

11.   The first formal step in the B2C personal selling process is:
   a.   Approach
   b.   Make presentation
   c.   Prospect and qualify
   d.   Preapproach

12.   Which of the following is not a part of developing a good public relations program?
   a.   Listen to the public
   b.   Inform people of the fact you're being responsive
   c.   Develop policies and procedures in the public interest
   d.   Advertise in a way that promotes positive word of mouth.

13.   It is the responsibility of the public relations department to:
   a.   work closely with marketing to develop an appropriate advertising campaign.
   b.   have a presence at trade shows and conventions.
   c.   maintain close ties with the media, community leaders, government officials and other corporate stakeholders.
   d.   develop an effective sales presentation format.

14.   Which of the following is not considered to be a benefit of publicity?
   a.   Publicity may reach people who wouldn't read an advertisement.
   b.   Publicity may be placed on the front page of a newspaper.
   c.   You can control when the publicity release will be used.
   d.   Publicity is more believable than other forms of promotion.

15. When Mary Lynn went to the grocery store last week, she took with her several coupons she had received in the mail that week. While at the store, Mary Lynn was offered samples of several food items and she actually bought a few of those, using the in-store coupons. She also bought a particular brand of toothpaste, because the tube came with a free toothbrush. Mary Lynn is taking advantage of:
    a. viral marketing
    b. sales promotion
    c. advertising
    d. publicity

16. Which of the following is <u>not</u> true regarding sales promotion efforts?
    a. Sales promotion efforts are aimed first at employees, then dealers, then at the end consumer.
    b. Sales promotion can be done both internally and externally.
    c. Sales promotion programs are designed to supplement other promotion efforts.
    d. Sales promotion efforts are designed to create long-term relationships.

17. One of the best ways to reduce negative word of mouth is to:
    a. mount an aggressive publicity campaign to refute any bad events surrounding your product.
    b. take care of consumer complaints quickly and effectively.
    c. run continuous positive advertising campaigns.
    d. motivate your sales force and give them information to overcome bad publicity.

18. Viral marketing is
    a. An Internet based form of notification of a potential computer virus.
    b. A term used to describe promotional efforts such as paying people to say positive things about your product on the Internet.
    c. A system in which consumer can access company information on their own and supply information about themselves in an ongoing dialogue.
    d. A function that evaluates public attitudes and executes a program of action and information to earn public understanding.

19. Podcasting refers to:
    a. a means of distributing audio and video programs via the Internet that lets users subscribe to a number of files and then hear or view the material at the time they choose.
    b. an online diary that looks like a web page.
    c. a promotional tool that involves people telling other people about products they have purchased.
    d. putting products into television shows and movies where they will be seen.

20. The city of San Antonio has made an effort to develop promotional materials for travel agents and bus tour companies that are within a 300-mile radius of the city. City officials are hopeful that these efforts will encourage tourism in the area when agents suggest the city to their clients. San Antonio is making use of a:
    a. push strategy
    b. pull strategy
    c. segmentation strategy
    d. targeting strategy

TRUE-FALSE

Learning Goal 1
1. _____ Integrated marketing communication combines all the promotional tools into a comprehensive and unified promotional strategy.

2. _____ The first step in developing a promotion campaign is to identify the target market.

Learning Goal 2
3. _____ One of the benefits of Internet advertising is that marketers can reach the people they most want to reach, which are consumers researching products in which they are interested.

4. _____ In global advertising, the evidence supports the theory that promotional strategies can be implemented worldwide with few changes.

5. _____ The current trend in promotion is to build relationships with customers over time.

Learning Goal 3
6. _____ The follow up step in personal selling is the least important .

7. _____ The objective during an initial sales call is to make a sale, or get a commitment to a sale.

8. _____ In today's environment, B2B sales personnel will need to learn how to add value to the product they are selling through providing all the information a potential customer needs.

Learning Goal 4
9. _____ One of the advantages of publicity is that the company has control over how the media will use the story.

10. _____ One of the problems with publicity is that it is not believable.

Learning Goal 5
11. _____ Sales promotion can be used as an attempt to keep salespeople enthusiastic about the company and the product.

12. _____ Event marketing means sponsoring events such as rock concerts or being at various events to promote your products.

Learning Goal 6
13. _____ Companies are tending to use the traditional promotional tools less today because so much information about consumers is now available.

14. _____ When using a pull strategy, advertising and sales promotion efforts are directed at consumers.

15. _____ When designing a promotion mix, one should keep in mind that large, homogenous groups of consumers are usually most efficiently reached through advertising.

16. _____ Blogging is expected to have a huge impact on marketing in the future.

You Can Find It On the Net

You can visit virtually any web site to observe how companies implement the techniques we have discussed in this chapter. Here are a few suggestions.

Visit www.gap.com

Do they attempt to create a dialogue with the customer? How?

How do they attempt to develop a relationship with you, the customer?

Visit www.cdnow.com

What sales promotion techniques does cd now use?

How does cd now make their website "user friendly"?

How does cd now promote to their buyers, or create a dialogue with their users?

Track the sites you visit over a few days. Can you remember the advertising you saw?

Think back to the ads you may have seen while visiting various Internet sites. How many do you remember? What products were they selling? How effective do you think Internet advertising is?

ANSWERS

LEARNING THE LANGUAGE

1. Sales promotion	9. Prospecting	16. Promotion
2. Advertising	10. Integrated marketing communication (IMC)	17. Product placement
3. Public relations (PR)	11. Blog	18. Interactive promotion
4. Pull strategy	12. Publicity	19. Viral marketing
5. Trial close	13. Push strategy	20. Prospect
6. Promotion mix	14. Infomercial	21. Sampling
7. Word-of-mouth promotion	15. Personal selling	22. Podcasting
8. Qualifying		

ASSESSMENT CHECK

Learning Goal 1
The Importance of Marketing Communication and Promotion

1.   The tools of the promotion mix are:
   a. Personal selling   c. Sales promotion
   b. Advertising   d. Public relations

2.   The idea of integrated marketing communication is to use all the promotional tools and company resources to create a positive brand image and to meet the strategic marketing and promotional goals of the firm.

Learning Goal 2
Advertising: Fighting to Keep Consumer Interest

3.   The various categories of advertising are:
   a. Retail advertising
   b. Trade advertising
   c. Business- to-business advertising
   d. Institutional advertising
   e. Product advertising

   f. Advocacy advertising
   g. Comparison advertising
   h. Interactive advertising
   i. Online advertising

4.   Advertising and propaganda are both nonpersonal communication, but in the case of advertising, organizations and individuals are in some way identified in the message. Propaganda does not have an identified sponsor.

5.   The public benefits from advertising because
   a. ads are informative.
   b. it provides us with free TV and radio because advertisers pay for the production costs.
   c. advertising also covers the major costs of producing newspapers and magazines.

467

6. The advantages and disadvantages of each form of advertising media are:

a.	Newspapers	Good local coverage ads placed quickly high acceptance; ad can be clipped and saved	Ads compete with other features; poor color; ads get thrown away
b.	Television	Sight, sound, motion reaches all audiences; high attention with no competition	High cost; short exposure time; takes time to prepare ads
c.	Radio	Low cost; can target specific audiences; flexible; good for local marketing	People may not listen; short exposure time; audience can't keep ad
d.	Magazines	Target specific audiences; good use of color; long life ad can be clipped and saved	Inflexible; ads must be placed weeks before publication; cost is relatively high
e.	Outdoor	High visibility and repeat exposures; low cost; local market focus	Limited message, low selectivity of audience
f.	Direct mail	Best for targeting specific markets; very flexible; ad can be saved	High cost; consumer rejection as junk mail; must conform to postal regulations
g.	Yellow pages	Great coverage of local markets; widely used by consumers; available at point of purchase	Competition with other ads; cost may be too high for very small businesses
h.	Internet	Inexpensive global coverage; available at any time; interactive	Relatively low readership

7. Infomercials allow the seller to show the product in detail, which helps the product to sell itself. They allow for testimonials and for showing the customer how the product actually works, and allow for the use of drama, demonstration, graphics, and other advertising tools.

8. When marketers advertise on sites such as Yahoo they can reach the people they most want to reach. The goal is to get customers and potential customers to a Web site where they can learn more about the company and its products. When customers go to the web site, the company can provide information and interact with the customer, so Internet advertising becomes a means to bring customers and companies together..

9. The Internet is changing the approach in advertising from "promoting to" to "working with" customers. The trend is to build relationships with customers over time. That means carefully listening to what consumers want, tracking their purchases, providing them with better service, and giving them access to more information.

10. The two approaches to advertising in the global market are:
   a. to develop a promotional strategy that can be implemented worldwide
   b. to design promotions that are targeted at specific countries and or regions

11. Evidence supports the theory that the most effective global promotional strategies are those that are specifically designed for individual countries.

12. Globalism is the idea of producing one ad for everyone in the world, and regionalism is to develop specific ads for each country and /or for specific groups within a country.

Learning Goal 3
Personal Selling: Providing Personal Attention

13. Effective selling is a matter of helping others to satisfy their wants and needs. Sales people can use the Internet, portable computers, pagers, and other technology to help customers search the Internet, design custom-made products, look over prices, and generally do everything it takes to complete the order.

14. The steps in the personal selling process are:
   a. Prospect and qualify   e. Answer objections
   b. Preapproach   f. Close sale
   c. Approach   g. Follow-up
   d. Make presentation

15. Prospecting involves researching potential buyers and choosing those most likely to buy. To qualify people means to make sure that they have a need for the product, the authority to buy, and the willingness to listen to a sales message. People who meet these criteria are called prospects.

16. Sales people find prospects at trade shows, the company website, and people at companies who were recommended to you by others who use your company's product.

17. Before making a sales call, the sales representative must do further research, which is done during the preapproach. As much as possible should be learned about customer's wants and needs. All that information should be stored in a database.

18. The objective of an initial sales call is to give an impression of professionalism, create rapport, build credibility, and to start a relationship.

19. During the sales presentation, the idea is for the sale representative to match the benefits of his or her value package to the client's needs. The presentation can be tailored to the customer's needs.

20. A sales person must anticipate objections the prospect may raise and determine proper responses. Think of questions as opportunities for creating better relationships. You are there to resolve the doubts the customer has.

21. Closing techniques include a trial close, which helps finalize the sales. The final step is asking for the order and showing the client where to sign.

22. The follow-up includes handling customer complaints, making sure that the customer's questions are answered, and supplying what the customer wants.

23. The goals of a salesperson are to help the buyer buy, and to make sure the buyer is satisfied after the sale.

24. In both B2B and B2C sales, knowing the product comes first. However, in retail sales the salesperson does not have to do much prospecting or qualifying. Also, retail salespeople don't usually have to go through a preapproach step.

    The first formal step in the B2C sales process then is the approach. The idea is to show the customer that you are there to help and that you are friendly, and knowledgeable. You also need to discover what the customer wants.

25. During the presentation in the B2C selling process you show customers how the products you have meet their needs. You answer questions that help the customer choose the right product for them.

26. During the trial close in B2C selling the salesperson must be aware that a customer needs to spend some time thinking about the purchase. It is important not to be too pushy, and to know how far to go.

27. After- sale follow-up is an important but often neglected step in B2C sales. If the product is supposed to be delivered, the salesperson should follow up to be sure it is delivered on time. The same is true if the product has to be installed.

Learning Goal 4
Public Relations: Building Relationships

28. The three steps in creating a good public relations campaign are:
    a. Listen to the public
    b. Change policies and procedures
    c. Inform people that you're being responsive to their needs

29. It is the responsibility of the public relations department to maintain close relationships with the media, community leaders, government officials, and other corporate stakeholders.

30. The advantages of publicity over other promotional tools are:
    a. stories are published for free.
    b. it may reach people who would not read an advertisement.
    c. it's more believable than advertising.

31. Three drawbacks of publicity are:
    a. The company has no control over how or when the media will use the story.
    b. The story may be altered, and could end up not as positive as the original.
    c. Once a story has run, it won't be repeated.

32. One way to see that publicity is handled well by the media is to establish a friendly relationship with media representatives, being open with them when they seek information.

Learning Goal 5
Sales Promotion: Getting a Good Deal

33.   Five types of B2B sales promotion are:
a.   Trade shows   d   Catalogs
b.   Portfolios for salespeople   e.   Conventions
c.   Deals (price reductions)

34.   The various consumer sales promotion techniques are:
a.   Coupons   g.   Bonuses (Buy one, get one free)
b.   Cents-off promotions   h.   Catalogs
c.   Sampling   i.   Demonstrations
d.   Premiums   j.   Special events
e.   Sweepstakes   k.   Lotteries
f.   Contests   l.   In-store displays

35.   Sales promotion programs are designed to supplement the other promotion mix variables by creating enthusiasm for the overall promotional program.

36.   The most important internal sales promotion efforts are directed at salespeople and other customer-contact people.

37.   Internal sales promotion efforts include:
a.   sales training
b.   development of sales aids like flip charts, audiovisual displays and videotapes
c.   participation in trade shows where sales people can get leads

38.   A virtual trade show is a trade show on the Internet. This allows customers to see many products without leaving the office, and the information is available 24 hours a day.

39.   The main targets for developing the sales promotion efforts in order are:
a.   company' employees to generate enthusiasm internally
b.   distributors and dealers so that they are eager to help promote the product.
c.   final consumers using samples, coupons, cents-off deals, displays, store demonstrations, premiums, and other incentives like contests, trading stamps and rebates.

40.   Sampling is a quick effective way of demonstrating a product's superiority at the time when consumers are making a purchase decision.

41.   Event marketing means sponsoring events such as rock concerts or other events to promote products.

Learning Goal 6
How New Technologies are Affecting Promotion

42.   The idea behind word of mouth promotion is to get people talking about your products and your brand name so they remember them when they go shopping.

43.   Companies are using clever commercials, and stores are using clowns, banners, music, fairs and other attention getting devices to create word of mouth. Companies have begun to create word of mouth by paying people to go into Internet chat rooms and talk

favorably about various products and services. The term for this and other forms of Internet word of mouth promotion is <u>viral marketing</u>. Companies are creating word of mouth through sending testimonials, and paying commissions for sending people to specific Web sites.

44.   One of the best ways to reduce the effects of negative word of mouth is to take care of consumer complaints quickly and effectively.

45.   Clearly blogging is a phenomenon of the future. Bloggers can spread the word about products very quickly, and it is expected that business information will be revolutionized by bloggers.

46.   Podcasting allows you to become your own newscaster, and gives broadcast radio and television programs a new distribution method.

47.   As people purchase goods and services on the Internet, companies keep track of those purchases and gather other facts and figures about those consumers. They can use the information to design catalogs and brochures specifically designed to meet the wants and needs of individual consumers as demonstrated by their purchasing behavior.

48.   Because of the availability of so much information, companies are tending to use traditional promotional tools less and are putting more money into direct mail and other forms of direct marketing, including catalogs and the Internet.

49.   According to the text, the best way to reach:
    a.   large homogeneous groups of consumers are most efficiently reached through advertising
    b.   large organizations - are best reached through personal selling

51.   The idea of a push strategy is to push the product through the distribution system to the stores.

52.   In a pull strategy, heavy advertising and sales promotion efforts are directed toward consumers so they'll request the products from retailers. If it works, consumers will go to the store and order the products. Seeing demand, the storeowner will then order them from the wholesaler. The wholesaler in turn will order from the producer. The idea is to pull products down through the distribution system.

53.   A total systems approach to marketing is when promotion is a part of supply chain management. In such cases retailers would work with producers and distributors to make the supply chain as efficient as possible. Then a promotional plan would be developed for the whole system. The idea would be to develop a value package that would appeal to everyone.

CRITICAL THINKING EXERCISES

Learning Goal 1
1.   a.   The first step in developing a promotion campaign is to <u>identify a target market</u>. We have discussed several possibilities in previous chapters: specifically the automotive manufacturers and the after market, which could consist of windshield installation and repair companies.

b. The second step is to <u>define the objectives for each element of the marketing mix</u>. The overall goal will be to create awareness of the product, and to inform both the target market, the automotive industry, and ultimate consumers. The company may depend on consumers to go to the dealers to ask for the product. Here are some examples:

Personal selling – this form of promotion will be an important tool, because this product will require that some detailed information be provided to the buyer. This will be focused on the main target market – the automotive industry.

Advertising - This may be important for the consumer market to create awareness and to inform them of the benefits. Since there are no competitors at this point, Sun-2-Shade will not have to focus on brand awareness quite yet. The company could also create awareness by using product placement in movies, to illustrate the product's qualities. How about James Bond?

Public relations – The company can make use of public relations to enhance the goal of creating awareness. The company could sponsor any number of activities designed to introduce automakers to the product.

Sales promotion – This form of promotion may be more important to focus on later in the promotion campaign. But for right now, again to create awareness, Sun-2-Shade could give away sunglasses which use the technology the company is using for the windshields, along with information indicating that with their product, there is no need to take sunglasses on and off all the time.

c. The third step is to <u>determine a promotional budget</u>. This will determine how much can be spent on each method of promotion. The amount we can spend on promotion will depend on how much revenue we have, or anticipate that we will have, generated.

d. The fourth step is to <u>develop a unifying message.</u> The message in the campaign could be one of luxury and convenience, along with other benefits you may have identified.

e. The fifth step, <u>implement the plan,</u> will coordinate all the elements of the promotion effort. This means making sure that all of our promotional efforts will send the same message.

f. Lastly, <u>evaluate effectiveness</u> is to measure the results, which depends upon clearly written objectives.

Learning Goal 2

2. a. Radio, newspaper
   b. Newspaper, radio
   c. Magazines, Internet sites aimed at women
   d. Outdoor, local TV, radio
   e. TV, Direct mail
   f. Direct mail, TV
   g. Magazines
   h. Newspaper, direct mail, Web site

3. The Internet is changing organizations' approach to customers, creating an environment in which a company will work with, rather than promote to, their customers. Sun-2-Shade will need to create a relationship with customers by listening to what they want in terms of product and service, and giving them access to information. This will require the web site to be interactive so customers can talk to the company, and even to each other, ask questions and get as much information as possible. Links to the auto manufacturers that offer our product could be incorporated as well.

4.   A sales presentation for Sun-2-Shade will have to begin with prospecting. Which carmakers are you going to target? Are you going to go after just one carmaker, or several? Initially, you will probably be wise to begin with just one. The question then becomes which maker to go after. After research, you may be able to make that decision more easily.

Then, the preapproach will call for learning as much as possible about the products your customer sells. Which models will be the best suited for Sun-2-Shade? What's the production volume on those models? What's the competition doing? How could Sun-2-Shade benefit your customer?

Making the approach will involve making an appointment with the <u>right person</u>, the decision-maker. You will need to look professional, and have a prototype of the product with you; in other words, drive one of their car models equipped with your windshield to the sales call. Come prepared with questions geared to help you find out what they may be looking for.

During the presentation, you will have to show the carmaker how Sun-2-Shade will make their cars better than the competition. You could discuss the benefits of convenience, luxury, having something the competition doesn't have. You could come prepared with visuals demonstrating how Sun-2-Shade works on any model. This can be done with a computer graphics program, or with Power Point presentations.

You will also want to know something about who your customer's customers are, in order to be able to demonstrate how Sun-2-Shade will appeal to them. Objections will have to be overcome by showing how easily Sun-2-Shade works with their cars, again by driving a car (one of their models of course) with Sun-2-Shade installed, and taking the customer for a ride to demonstrate the Sun-2-Shade luxury.

Eventually you will have to close the sale, by asking to make Sun-2-Shade an available option, or asking your customer to put Sun-2-Shade in some of their cars. Finally, always be available for questions, "hand-holding," and problems that may arise. Keep in mind that this process will take a lot of time, and won't be accomplished in one sales call.

Learning Goal 4

5.   It sounds like the station really wanted to know what people thought of their programming, and what people wanted in a news program. The first step of a good public relations program is to do research to evaluate public attitudes, which is exactly what the station did, by researching the market before the premier, and by publishing the station's phone numbers and encouraging viewers to call. The station also seems to have responded by avoiding, as much as possible, the "bad news" stories as lead ins, which is in the public interest, especially as the broadcast is at 9:00 p.m. when it is possible that older children could be watching. They also seem to have avoided the scandalous stories upon which many TV news programs seem to have thrived. This is also illustrated by the fact that they tell the viewers exactly when a news story will air, allowing viewers to change the channel if children are likely to be watching a story that parents don't want them to see, for example. Lastly, during the broadcast and in their advertising they are mentioning the specific ways in which they have responded to viewer requests, which is the third step in a good public relations program.

Learning Goal 5

6. Suggested answers:

Group	Technique
a. Salespeople	Sales training, conventions, trade shows
b. Dealers	Catalogues, trade shows, "deals"
c. Customers	Coupons, sweepstakes, displays, samples

7. Sales promotion is the tool that stimulates interest by means of short-term activities. Sales promotion can take place both internally and externally. The most important internal sales promotion efforts are directed at sales people, and other customer contact people.

For sales people: The sales force needs to be fully informed about the process used to make these windshields. This will help in overcoming any objectives the customers will have. To aid in the presentations to the automakers, it will be extremely important to have product samples, even a car with the windshield installed, as mentioned earlier. The sales force could allow a company decision maker to drive the car for 24 hours to demonstrate how well the process works.

Dealers/Intermediaries: The intermediaries that are important to win over in this case are car dealerships. They will be an extremely important group because they will basically serve as the sales force to the ultimate consumer. They can reach dealers at trade shows, but it will be vital also for Sun-2-Shade to have an interactive website for car dealers to visit. Sun-2-Shade could sponsor contests for dealers. For example, if a dealer sells a certain number of cars with the windshield installed, the dealer wins a prize like a trip to the Caribbean. Each dealership sales person would also be eligible to win cash prizes, for example, if they sell a certain number of cars with the windshield.

Consumers: The goal is to make the ultimate consumer aware of this product, both in terms of what its benefits are, and what car models can be equipped with it. If they go to a dealership that has ordered cars with the windshield installed, they will be able to "sample" the product. But how do we make them aware enough to ask to see the windshield in the first place? For one thing, Sun-2-Shade must be installed in cars that are shown at consumer tradeshows, the annual auto shows held in major cities each year. Demonstrations at car shows and in the dealership will be important. Advertising will drive this effort so the customer is aware of the product in the first place. Some time later, Sun-2-Shade could offer a coupon for 50% off an after market installation of a windshield when the customer buys an installed windshield.

Learning Goal 6

8. Product - A good product will generate positive word of mouth because customers will be happy with the product and pass the word along.
    Sales promotion - Techniques such as special events and contests often create positive word of mouth promotion
    Advertising - When an advertisement is easily remembered or funny it will often create positive word of mouth. A good technique is to advertise to people who already use your product.
    Publicity - A news story can create word of mouth by stimulating the public's interest in the product.
    Personal selling - A good sales person can help the customer to develop a positive image of the product, thus creating positive word of mouth.

9.   Your response to this question will really depend upon whom you have selected as you primary target market. Assuming you have decided to go after the automotive manufacturers as your primary market, then most likely your promotion mix will include lots of personal selling, some advertising in the form of brochures, perhaps, aimed at the car dealerships who will be selling the cars with your product installed. It should also include a well-designed web site, with interactive features. If your research has been done, and a need for this kind of product has been established, you could design a public relations campaign <u>for the auto manufacturer,</u> indicating that the company listened to your need for a product like Sun-2-Shade, then made the product in response.

However, reaching the consumer will also be important, as you want the customer to be familiar with your product, and to ask for the product at the dealership. As mentioned earlier, you should have your own web site, with attractive graphics and interactive sales techniques. You may be able to advertise on-line, on Web sites that appeal to an affluent market, for example, which may be more likely to purchase your product for their car. You may also consider direct marketing, such as order forms in upscale magazines.

An important part of your advertising strategy may be to place your product on cars that are shown in feature movies. With this kind of promotion, the customer will see the product "in action".

By sponsoring strategically selected newscasts, podcasting may work to expose consumers to your product who may then go to their dealer and request your product. You could use viral marketing by finding current customers and paying them to go into automotive chat rooms to make positive remarks about Sun-2-Shade's products. These same consumers could be involved in creating their own blog and talking about the benefits they have gained by using your product.

Most likely you will use a combination of a push and pull strategy for the product. You will be using primarily a push strategy if you are aiming primarily at the automotive manufacturers. A combination will be most effective if you are aiming at the consumer market. Probably the best approach, once you are an established company, will be to work with your customers, retailers and develop a value package that will appeal to everyone, the manufacturers, retailers and consumers.

PRACTICE TEST

MULTIPLE CHOICE

LG 1   *# 1-3*
LG 2   *# 4-7*
LG 3   *# 8-11*
LG 4   *# 12-14*
LG 5   *#15-16*
LG 6   *# 17-20*

1. b
2. d
3. c
4. a
5. a
6. d
7. b
8. c
9. c
10. a
11. a
12. d
13. c
14. c
15. b
16. a
17. b
18. b
19. a
20. b

TRUE-FALSE

LG 1   *# 1-2*
LG 2   *# 3-5*
LG 3   *# 6-8*
LG 4   *# 9-10*
LG 5   *# 11-12*
LG 6   *# 13-16*

1. T
2. T
3. T
4. F
5. T
6. F
7. F
8. T
9. F
10. F
11. T
12. T
13. T
14. T
15. F
16. T

CHAPTER 17 – UNDERSTANDING FINANCIAL INFORMATION AND ACCOUNTING

LEARNING GOALS

After you have read and studied this chapter, you should be able to:

1. Understand the importance of financial information and accounting.
2. Define and explain the different areas of the accounting profession.
3. List the steps in the accounting cycle, distinguish between accounting and bookkeeping. and explain how computers are used in accounting.
4. Explain how the major financial statements differ.
5. Explain the importance of ratio analysis in reporting financial information.

LEARNING THE LANGUAGE

Listed below are important terms found in the chapter. Choose the correct term for the definition and write it in the space provided.

Accounting	Depreciation	Liquidity
Accounting cycle	Double-entry bookkeeping	Managerial accounting
Accounts payable	Financial accounting	Net income or net loss
Annual report	Financial statement	Notes payable
Assets	Fixed assets	Operating expenses
Auditing	Fundamental accounting equation	Owner's equity
Balance sheet	Government and not-for-profit accounting	Private accountant
Bonds payable	Gross profit (gross margin)	Public accountant
Bookkeeping	Income statement	Ratio analysis
Cash flow	Independent audit	Retained earnings
Certified internal auditor (CIA)	Intangible assets	Revenue
Certified management accountant (CMA)	Journal	Statement of cash flows
Certified public accountant (CPA)	Ledger	Tax accountant
Cost of goods sold (cost of goods manufactured)	Liabilities	Trial balance
Current assets		

1. A yearly statement called the _____ states the financial condition, progress, and expectations of an organization.

2. A company's _____ is the difference between cash coming in and cash going out of a business.

3. Items known as _____ can or will be converted into cash within one year.

4. An accounting system called _____ is used for organizations whose purpose is not generating a profit but serving ratepayers, taxpayers, and others according to a duly approved budget.

5. Assets that are relatively permanent, or _____ include items such as land, buildings and equipment.

6. A_____ is the book where accounting data are first entered.

7. Long term liabilities that represent money lent to the firm that must be paid back are _____.

8. The amount of the business that belongs to the owners minus any liabilities owed by the business is the formula for _____.

9. A _____ is a summary of all the data in the account ledgers to show whether the figures are correct and balanced.

10. An accountant known as a(n) _____ is trained in tax law and is responsible for preparing tax returns or developing tax strategies.

11. How fast an asset can be converted into cash is its _____.

12. A(n) _____ is an evaluation and unbiased opinion about the accuracy of a company 's financial statements.

13. Accounting used to provide information and analyses to managers within the organization to assist them in decision-making is called _____.

14. A concept called _____ is a system of writing every business transaction in two places.

15. An accountant called a _____ passes a series of examinations established by the American Institute of Certified Public Accountants

16. The economic resources, or things of value, owned by the firm are called _____.

17. _____ are current liabilities involving money owed to others for merchandise or services purchased on credit but not yet paid for.

18. A firm's _____ is how much the firm earned by buying, or making, and selling merchandise.

19. Accounting information and analyses prepared for people outside the organization is _____.

20. _____ is revenue left over after all costs and expenses, including taxes, are paid.

21. The financial statement called a _____ reports the financial condition of a firm at a specific time.

22. An accountant who works for a single firm, government agency, or nonprofit organization is called a(n) _____,

23. The recording, classifying, summarizing and interpreting of financial events and transactions, called _____ provides management and other interested parties the information they need to make good decisions.

24. A company's _____ is the value of what is received from goods sold, services rendered and other financial sources.

25. The job of reviewing and evaluating the records used to prepare the company's financial statements is called _____.

26. A _____ is the summary of all transactions that have occurred over a particular period.

27. The six-step procedure called the _____ results in the preparation and analysis of the major financial statements.

28. A type of expense called the _____ is a measure of the cost of merchandise sold or cost of raw materials and supplies used for producing items for resale.

29. A _____ is one who provides accounting services to individuals or businesses on a fee basis.

30. Accounts known as _____ indicate what the business owes to others (debts).

31. A specialized accounting book known as a _____ is one in which information from accounting journals is accumulated into specific categories and posted so managers can find all the information about one account in the same place.

32. A _____ is a professional accountant who has met certain educational and experience requirements, passed a qualifying exam in the field, and been certified by the Institute of Certified Management Accountants.

33. The recording of business transactions is called _____

34. The _____ shows a firm's profit after costs, expenses and taxes; it summarizes all of the resources that have come into the firm, all the resources that have left the firm and the resulting net income.

35. _____ is the systematic write-off of the cost of a tangible asset over its estimated useful life.

36. Long-term assets that are relatively permanent are known as _____ and include patents, and copyrights that have no real physical form but do have value.

37. The financial statement called a _____ reports cash receipts and disbursements related to a firm's three major activities: operations, investment, and financing.

38. A _____ is an accountant who has a bachelor's degree 2 years of internal auditing experience, and has passed an exam administered by the Institute of Internal Auditors.

39. Assets equal liabilities plus owner's equity is the _____ and is the basis for the balance sheet.

40. Costs involved in operating a business, such as rent, utilities, and salaries are called _____.

41. The assessment of a firm's financial condition and performance, or _____is done through calculations and interpretations of financial ratios developed from the firm's financial statements.

42. The accumulated earnings from a firm's profitable operations that were kept in the business and not paid out to stockholders in dividends are _____.

43. Short-term or long-term liabilities, or _____, are those that a business promises to repay by a certain date.

ASSESSMENT CHECK

Learning Goal 1
The Importance of Accounting Information

1. Why is it important to know something about accounting?

2. Financial transactions can include:

3. What are two purposes of accounting?

    a. _____

    b. _____

4. Who are the users of accounting information?

    a. _____

    b. _____

c. _____

d. _____

Learning Goal 2
Areas of Accounting

5.   List the five key working areas of accounting.

a. _____

b. _____

c. _____

d. _____

e. _____

6.   Identify the areas with which managerial accounting is concerned.

a. _____

b. _____

c. _____

d. _____

7.   How does financial accounting differ from managerial accounting?

8.   In what document can you find the information derived from financial accounting?

9.   What are some of the things a public accountant might do?

a. _____

b. _____

c. _____

10. What does it mean when financial reports are prepared in accordance with GAAP?

11.	Describe the Sarbanes-Oxley Act.

12.	Describe internal audits.

13.	The responsibilities of the tax accountant are:

a. _____

b. _____

14.	Who are the primary users of government and not-for-profit accounting information? What do the users of this information want to ensure?

Learning Goal 3
Accounting versus Bookkeeping

15.	How do accountants differ from bookkeepers?

16.	What are the six steps in the accounting cycle?

a. _____

b. _____

c. _____

d. _____

e. _____

f. _____

17.	What is the benefit of double-entry bookkeeping?

18.   What is the difference between a journal and a ledger?

19.   List the benefits provided by using computers in accounting.

a. _____

b. _____

c. _____

d. _____

e. _____

Learning Goal 4
Understanding Key Financial Statements

20.   Describe the three key financial statements

a. _____

b. _____

c. _____

21.   The difference between the financial statements can be summarized this way:

22.   The fundamental accounting equation is:

_____ = _____ + _____

23.   How would you calculate your net worth?

24.   What kinds of things are considered assets?

25. In what order are assets listed on a balance sheet?

26. Describe the three categories of assets on a balance sheet.

 a. _____

 b. _____

 c. _____

27. What is the difference between current liabilities and long-term liabilities?

28. Describe:

 a. Accounts payable:

 b. Notes payable

 c. Bonds payable

29. How is "equity" calculated? What is shareholder's equity?

30. What is the use of a capital account?

31. An income statement

 a. summarizes: _____

 _____

 b. reports the firm's operations over _____

 _____

32.   What is the formula for developing an income statement, according to GAAP?

33.   What is the difference between:

      a.   revenue and sales?

      b.   between gross sales and net sales?

34.   Costs that make up cost of goods sold include:

35.   How does gross margin differ between a service firm and a manufacturing firm?

36.   Describe the two categories of expenses.

37.   What is the "bottom line"?

38.   Describe the three major activities for which cash receipts and disbursements are reported on a statement of cash flows.

      a.   _____

      b.   _____

      c.   _____

39.   How would you describe a poor, or negative, cash flow?

40.   What questions may be answered by a statement of cash flows?

a. _____

b. _____

c. _____

d. _____

41.   How do cash flow problems start?

42.   A path to preventing cash flow problems that often develop is for a business to maintain:

_____

Learning Goal 5
Analyzing Financial Statements: Ratio Analysis

43.   Financial ratios provide key insights into how a firm compares to other firms in the same industry in what key areas?

a. _____   b. _____

b. _____   c. _____

44.   What do liquidity ratios measure?

45.   Two key liquidity ratios are:

a. _____

b. _____

46.   The formula for the current ratio is as follows:

47.   The current ratio is compared to:

a. _____

b. _____

48.   The formula for the acid test ratio is:

49.   To what kinds of firms is the acid test ratio important?

50.   What do leverage ratios measure?

51.   What is the formula for the debt to equity ratio, and what does it measure?

52.   What does it mean if a firm has a debt to equity ratio above 100%?

53.   What do profitability ratios measure?

54.   What are three profitability ratios?

        a.   _____

        b.   _____

        c.   _____

55.   What is the difference between Basic EPS and diluted EPS?

56.   What is the formula for determining Basic Earnings Per Share?

57.   What is the formula for return on sales and for what do firms use this ratio?

58. What is the formula for return on equity? What does it measure?

59. What do activity ratios measure?

60. What is the formula for inventory turnover? What does it measure?

61. What is meant by inventory turnover ratios that are:

    a. lower than average?

    b. higher than average?

CRITICAL THINKING EXERCISES

Learning Goals 1,2

1. Match the following terms with the descriptions below. Some of these terms are describing general areas of accounting, others are similar but more specific, so use your text to help you to differentiate the terms!

Annual report	Tax accountant
Auditing	Independent audit
Certified internal auditor	Managerial accounting
Certified management accountant (CMA)	Private accountant
Certified public accountant (CPA)	Public accountant
Financial accounting	

a. _____ Markus Larsen works for a mid-sized, publicly held company. He is responsible for the preparation and analysis of financial information for people and organizations outside the firm.

b. _____ Jim Hopson has his own small accounting firm. He provides business assistance to his clients in a number of ways. Most recently he helped a small business by designing an accounting system for the firm, and helped them select the correct software to use to get them started.

c. _____ Bob Glenn is majoring in accounting, but plans to specialize in this area, as he enjoys preparing budgets and checking to determine if costs for departments are within the budget. Bob also feels that with growing emphasis on global competition, outsourcing , and organizational cost cutting the job market for this area of accounting may be very strong.

d. _____ Harry Winston prepares tax returns for his company, and develops strategies to minimize the company's tax burden.

e. _____ Nancy Hoffman works for Monsanto on a full time basis to help the company keep accurate financial information.

f. _____ Hector Perez's job is to guarantee that proper accounting procedures and financial reporting are being carried on within the company. For this job Hector not only examines the financial health of a company but looks into organizational efficiencies and effectiveness.

g. _____ Kimberly Chung recently passed a series of examinations to meet the state's requirement for education and experience, and she can now work as a private or public accountant in this type of position in accounting.

h. _____ Irena Manovich is involved with this type of accounting, which is concerned with measuring and reporting costs of production, marketing and other functions, preparing budgets, checking to see that units are staying within budgets and designing strategies to minimize taxes.

i. _____ In his job as a public accountant for a major accounting firm, Ryan Deiker performs this job, which is to determine if a firm has prepared its financial statements according to accepted accounting principles.

j. _____ As a stockholder in Microsoft, Gary Ford receives this document each year. Gary has noticed that more information is going into this yearly report, as pressure builds from stakeholders.

k. _____ Because internal financial controls are very important for firms, Eric Minette, who is a private accountant, ensures that proper accounting procedures and financial reporting are being carried out within the company for which he works.

Learning Goal 3

2. Sun-2-Shade is a new company that manufactures self-darkening windshields for automobiles. The company is doing very well! They need a bookkeeper to help them with their paperwork, and an accountant. You have been given the task of writing a brief job description for each job. How would you write the job description for each?

Bookkeeper –

Accountant –

3. The Accounting Cycle is as follows:

1) analyze documents
2) record transactions in journals
3) post to ledgers
4) trial balance
5) prepare financial statements
6) analyze financial statements

Identify which of the following activity is being described in each statement.

a. _____ Joan Perez has finished analyzing and categorizing original documents, and is getting ready for the next step in the accounting cycle, which will be this activity.

b. _____ Joan is summarizing all the data, to check that all the information is correct

c. _____ The accountant for Joan's company is getting ready to evaluate the financial condition of the firm from the financial statements.

d. _____ Joan is just beginning the bookkeeping process, and is in the process of dividing the firms transactions onto categories such as sales documents, purchasing receipts and shipping documents.

e. _____ While Joan has prepared the journals, this step is often done by computer.

f. _____ Once the summary statements show that all the information is correct, then the accountant will do this, in accordance with generally accepted accounting principals, so that she can analyze them.

Learning Goal 4
4. a. Two key financial statements are the balance sheet and the income statement.
    Indicate whether each of the following accounts would be found on a balance sheet or an income statement.

1. _____ Cash

2. _____ Retained earnings

3. _____ Accounts payable

4. _____ Interest expense

5. _____ Rent expense

6. _____ Property

11. _____ Notes payable

12. _____ Accounts receivable

13. _____ Equipment

14. _____ Advertising expense

15. _____ Wages expense

16. _____ Supplies expense

7.	_____	Commission revenue	17.	_____ Utilities expense
8.	_____	Gross sales	18.	_____ Cost of goods sold
9.	_____	Common stock	19.	_____ Inventories
10.	_____	Supplies expense	20.	_____ Gross Profit

b. Identify the current assets and list them in order of their liquidity.

1. _____

2. _____

3. _____

5. The balance sheet reports the financial condition of a firm at a specific time. The basic formula for a balance sheet is:

Assets = Liabilities + Owner's Equity

<u>Total assets</u> consist of current, fixed and intangible assets

<u>Total liabilities</u> consist of current and long-term liabilities

<u>Owner's Equity</u> consists of various types of stock and retained earnings

Using the following list of accounts, construct an accurate balance sheet for Sun-2-Shade, Inc.

BE CAREFUL! Not all of the accounts listed will be used for the balance sheet.

SUN-2-SHADE, INC.
List of accounts

Accounts payable	$25,000	Utilities	$12,000
Net sales	$600,000	Supplies	$3700
Accounts receivable	$110,000	Investments	$45,000
Depreciation expense	$4000	Rent	$35,000
Inventories	$62,000	Long-term debt	$60,000
Advertising	$28,000	Common stock	$130,000
Wages and salaries	$125,000		
Notes payable (current)	$15,000		
Rental revenue	$3000		
Cost of goods sold	$313,000		
Property, plant, equipment	$200,000		
Cash	$18,000		
Retained earnings	$165,000		
Accrued taxes	$40,000		

SUN-2-SHADE, INC.
BALANCE SHEET
Year ending December 31, 20__

6. The income statement reports all the revenues and expenses of a firm for a specific period of time. The basic formula for an income statement is:

Revenue - Cost of goods sold = Gross profit (gross margin)
Gross profit - operating expenses = Net income (loss) before taxes
Net income before taxes - taxes = Net income (loss)

Using the previous list of accounts construct an accurate income statement for Sun-2-Shade. For purposes of illustration, assume a 28% tax rate on income.
Be careful! Not all the accounts listed will appear on an Income Statement!

SUN-2-SHADE, INC.
INCOME STATEMENT
Year ending December 31, 200_

7.   Cash flow problems arise when a firm has debt obligations that must be met before cash from sales is received.

Prepare a personal cash flow statement for two weeks. Include all projected income and all projected cash disbursements (payments) Do you have a cash flow problem?

Cash flow forecast	Week one	Week two
Projected income (Include all sources of income)	_____	_____
Projected "outgo" (Include all expenses)	_____	_____
Surplus (Deficit)	_____	_____

Learning Goal 5

8.   Liquidity ratios measure a firm's ability to pay short-term debt. *Using the balance sheet and income statement you calculated earlier :*

a.   Calculate the current ratio for Sun-2-Shade

b.   Calculate the acid-test ratio for Sun-2-Shade

c.   What shape does Sun-2-Shade appear to be in?

9.   Leverage ratios refer to the degree to which a firm relies on borrowed money for its operations.

a.   Calculate the Debt to owner's equity ratio for Sun-2-Shade

b.   If the industry average is .75, how does Sun-2-Shade compare?

10.   Profitability ratios measure how effectively the firm is using its resources.

a.   If Sun-2-Shade has approximately 30,000 shares of common stock outstanding, what is their Basic Earnings per share?

b.   Calculate their Return on sales.

c.   What is Return on Equity?

11.   Activity ratios measure the effectiveness of the firm in using the available assets.

a.   If the average inventory for Sun-2-Shade is 70,000, what is the inventory turnover rate?

b.   If the industry average is 3.5, what does that indicate for Sun-2-Shade?

PRACTICE TEST

MULTIPLE CHOICE – Circle the best answer

Learning Goal 1
1. Which of the following is not one of the activities associated with accounting?
    a. recording
    b. summarizing
    c. classifying
    d. promoting

2. The purpose of accounting is to:
    a. allow for government tracking of business activities.
    b. make sure a business is paying its taxes.
    c. help managers evaluate the financial condition of the firm .
    d. provide a method of spending money wisely.

Learning Goal 2
3. The type of accounting that is concerned with providing information and analyses to managers within the organization is called:
    a. financial accounting
    b. managerial accounting
    c. auditing
    d. tax accounting

4. Jim Hopson is an accountant who works for a number of businesses as a "consultant." He has helped to design an accounting system, provides accounting services, and has analyzed the financial strength of many of his clients. Jim is working as a:
    a. private accountant.
    b. certified management accountant.
    c. certified internal auditor.
    d. public accountant.

5. This legislation created new government reporting standards for publicly traded companies.
    a. The Public Company Oversight Act
    b. The Robinson-Patman Act
    c. The Sarbanes-Oxley Act
    d. The Clayton Act

Learning Goal 3
6. If you were a bookkeeper, the first thing you would do is:
    a. record transactions into a ledger.
    b. develop a trial balance sheet.
    c. prepare an income statement.
    d. divide transactions into meaningful categories.

7. A specialized accounting book in which information is accumulated into specific categories and posted so managers can find all information about one account in the same place is a:
    a. ledger
    b. journal
    c. trial balance sheet
    d. double entry book

8. Which of the following is true of the use of computers in accounting?
    a. Computerized accounting systems are primarily used only in large corporations.
    b. Computers have been programmed to make financial decisions on their own.
    c. Computers can free up accountants to do important tasks, such as financial analysis.
    d. Computerized accounting systems have actually made the accounting process slightly more complicated because of the need to understand the software.

Learning Goal 4
9. The _____reports the firm's financial condition on a specific day.
    a. income statement
    b. cash flow statement
    c. statement of stockholder's equity
    d. balance sheet

10. Which of the following would be considered a current asset?
    a. accounts payable
    b. accounts receivable
    c. copyrights
    d. buildings

Use the information below to answer questions 11 and 12:
Net sales	$30,000
Total Assets	16,000
Taxes	2,300
Cost of goods sold	12,500
Total Liabilities	8,000
Operating expenses	3,200

11. Net income is:
    a. 14,000
    b. 17,500
    c. 14,300
    d. 12,000

12. Equity is:
    a. 16,000
    b. 24,000
    c. 8,000
    d. can't determine from information given.

13. Which of the following assets would be considered to be the most liquid assets?
    a. current assets
    b. fixed assets
    c. intangible assets
    d. long-term assets

14. Gross profit (gross margin) is equal to:
    a. Gross sales minus net sales.
    b. Operating expenses minus taxes.
    c. Revenue minus cost of goods sold.
    d. Cost of goods sold minus operating expenses.

15. Which of the following would not be shown on a statement of cash flows?
    a. cash from operations
    b. cash paid for long term debt obligations
    c. cash raised from new debt or equity
    d. cash paid in donations

Learning Goal 5
16. Financial ratios
    a. are used to calculate profits from one year to the next
    b. are a poor indicator of a company's financial condition
    c. are only used by independent auditors
    d. are helpful to use in analyzing the actual performance of a company

17. The calculation for the current ratio is:
    a. net income divided by net sales.
    b. net income after taxes divided by number of common shares outstanding.
    c. cost of goods sold divided by average inventory.
    d. current assets divided by current liabilities.

18. Which kind of ratio is used to determine the ability of a firm to pay its short-term debts?
    a. activity ratios
    b. profitability
    c. debt
    d. liquidity

19. A debt to equity ratio of over 100% would mean:
    a. the company has more debt than equity.
    b. the company has more equity than debt.
    c. by comparison with other firms, the company is probably in good shape.
    d. the company is in too much debt, and should restructure.

20. Earnings per share, return on sales and return on equity are all :
    a. activity ratios
    b. profitability ratios
    c. liquidity ratios
    d. debt ratios

TRUE-FALSE

Learning Goal 1
1. _____ It is not necessarily important know something about accounting if you want to understand business.

2. _____ Financial transactions include buying and selling goods, acquiring insurance and using supplies.

Learning Goal 2
3. _____ Financial accounting is used to provide information and analyses to managers within the firm to assist in decision making.

4. _____ A private accountant is an individual who works for a private firm that provides accounting services to individuals or businesses on a fee basis.

5. _____ An annual report is a yearly statement of the financial condition, progress and expectations of the firm.

6. _____ A tax accountant will perform the internal audits for a firm in order to determine what a firm's tax liability will be.

7. _____ The primary users of government accounting information are individuals and groups that want to ensure that the government is fulfilling its obligations.

Learning Goal 3
8. _____ In double entry bookkeeping two entries in the journal and the ledgers are required for each transaction.

9. _____ Trial balances are derived from information contained in ledgers.

10. _____ Computerized accounting systems assist in making financial information readily available whenever the organization needs it.

Learning Goal 4
11. _____ The fundamental accounting equation is assets = liabilities - owner's equity

12. _____ The "bottom line" is shown in the balance sheet.

13. _____ Cash flow is generally not a problem for companies that are growing quickly.

14. _____ Revenue is considered to be the same as sales.

15. _____ Retained earnings are accumulated earnings from the firms profitable operations that were kept in the business.

Learning Goal 5
16. _____ The four types of financial ratios include liquidity, debt, profitability and activity ratios.

17. _____ The higher the risk involved in an industry, the lower the return investors expect on their investment.

18. _____ There are two forms of earning per share, basic and diluted.

You Can Find It on the Net

Do you know what your personal balance sheet looks like? For a way to find out, visit the web site at www.betheboss.com. Click on the Resources link, and go to the worksheets. Use this worksheet to develop your own personal financial statements. Any surprises? What's your net worth? Would you be a good risk for a business loan, or to get involved in franchising, as the web site describes? Why or why not?

ANSWERS

LEARNING THE LANGUAGE

1. Annual report	16. Assets	30. Liabilities
2. Cash flow	17. Accounts payable	31. Ledger
3. Current assets	18. Gross margin (gross profit)	32. Certified Management Accountant (CMA)
4. Government and not-for-profit accounting	19. Financial accounting	33. Bookkeeping
5. Fixed assets	20. Net income or net loss	34. Income statement
6. Journal	21. Balance sheet	35. Depreciation
7. Bonds payable	22. Private accountant	36. Intangible assets
8. Owner's equity	23. Accounting	37. Statement of cash flows
9. Trial balance	24. Revenue	38. Certified Internal Auditor (CIA)
10. Tax accountant	25. Auditing	39. Fundamental accounting equation
11. Liquidity	26. Financial statement	40. Operating expenses
12. Independent audit	27. Accounting cycle	41. Ratio analysis
13. Managerial accounting	28. Cost of goods sold (cost of goods manufactured)	42. Retained earnings
14. Double entry bookkeeping	29. Public accountant	43. Notes payable
15. Certified Public Accountant (CPA)		

ASSESSMENT CHECK

Learning Goal 1
The Importance of Accounting Information

1. You have to know something about accounting if you want to succeed in business, and learning some basic accounting terms is mandatory. It's almost impossible to run a business without being able to read, understand, and analyze accounting reports and financial statements.

2. Financial transactions can include specifics like buying and selling goods and services, acquiring insurance, paying employees, and using supplies.

3. Two purposes of accounting are:
   a. to help managers evaluate the financial condition and operating performance of the firm
   b. to report financial information to people outside the firm such as owners, creditors, suppliers, employees, investors, and the government.

4. Users of accounting information include:
   a. government agencies, such as the IRS
   b. other regulatory agencies
   c. stockholders, creditors, financial analysts and suppliers
   d. managers of the firm

5.   The five key working areas of accounting are:
   a.   Managerial accounting
   b.   Financial accounting
   c.   Auditing
   d.   Tax accounting
   e.   Government and not-for-profit accounting

6.   Managerial accounting is concerned with:
   a.   measuring and reporting costs of production, marketing, and other functions
   b.   preparing budgets(planning)
   c.   checking whether or not units are staying within their budgets (controlling)
   d.   designing strategies to minimize taxes.

7.   Financial accounting differs from managerial accounting because the information and analyses are for people outside the organization.

8.   Much of the information derived from financial accounting is contained in the company's annual report.

9.   A public accountant might:
   a.   provide business assistance by designing an accounting system for a firm
   b.   help to select the correct computer and software to run the system
   c.   analyze the financial strength of an organization .

10.   The independent Financial Accounting Standards Board defines what are *generally accepted accounting principles* that accountants must follow. If financial reports are prepared "in accordance with GAAP", users know the information is reported according to standards agreed on by accounting professionals.

11.   The Sarbanes-Oxley Act created new government reporting standards for publicly traded companies, following the scandals involving companies such as WorldCom, Enron and Tyco.
   The act also created the Public Company Accounting Oversight Board (PCAOB) which is charged with overseeing the American Institute of Certified Public Accountants.

12.   Internal audits are performed by private accountants to ensure that proper accounting procedures and financial reporting are being carried on within the company. Public accountants will conduct independent audits of accounting records. Financial auditors examine the financial health of an organization and additionally look into operational efficiencies and effectiveness.

13.   A tax accountant is responsible for:
   a.   preparing tax returns
   b.   developing tax strategies.

14.   The primary users of government accounting information are citizens, special interest groups, legislative bodies, and creditors. These users want to ensure that government is fulfilling its obligations and making the proper use of taxpayers' money.

Learning Goal 3
Accounting versus Bookkeeping

15.   Accountants classify and summarize the data provided by bookkeepers. They interpret the data and report them to management. They also suggest strategies for improving the financial condition and progress of the firm. Accountants are especially important in financial analysis and income tax preparation.

16.   The steps in the accounting cycle are:
   a.   Analyze source documents, such as sales documents, purchasing receipts and shipping documents.
   b.   Record transactions into journals
   c.   Post journal entries into ledgers
   d.   Prepare a trial balance
   e.   Prepare financial statements: income statement, balance sheet, and statement of cash flows
   f.   Analyze financial statements

17.   It is possible that a bookkeeper could make a mistake when recording financial transactions.
   In double entry bookkeeping, two entries in the journal and the ledgers are required for each company transaction. The entries can be double checked to make sure that there have been no mistakes.

18.   A *ledger* is a specialized accounting book in which information from accounting *journals* is accumulated into specific categories and posted so managers can find all the information about one account in the same place.

19.   Most companies find that computers
   a.   simplify the mechanical tasks involved in accounting, which lets managers and other users get financial reports when and how they want them.
   b.   free up accountants to do more important tasks such as financial analysis.
   c.   can handle large amounts of financial information.
   d.   allows for continuous auditing which helps managers prevent cash flow problems and other financial difficulties by allowing them to spot trouble early.
   e.   Computers can also help make accounting work less monotonous.

Understanding Key Financial Statements

20.   a.   Balance sheets report the firm's financial condition on a specific date.
   b.   Income statements summarizes revenues, cost of goods, and expenses, for a specific period of time, and highlights the total profit or loss the firm experienced during that period.
   c.   The Statement of cash flows provides a summary of money coming into and out of the firm that tracks a company's cash receipts and cash payments.

21.   The difference between the financial statements can be summarized this way: The balance sheet details what the company owns and owes on a certain day. The income statement indicates what a firm sells its products for and what its selling costs are over a specific period of time. The statement of cash flows highlights the difference between cash coming in and cash going out of a business.

22. The fundamental accounting equation is: <u>Assets</u> = <u>Liabilities</u> + <u>Owner's equity</u>

23. To calculate your net worth, you would add up everything you own – cash, property, money owed to you; in other words, all your assets. From that you would subtract the money you owe to others, your liabilities, such as credit card debt, IOUs, current car loan, and student loans, for example. That figure tells you your net worth, or equity.

24. Assets include productive, tangible items such as equipment, buildings, land, furniture, fixtures, and motor vehicles that help generate income, as well as intangibles of value such as patents or copyrights.

25. Assets on a balance sheet are listed in order of their liquidity, which refers to how fast an asset can be converted into cash.

26. a. Current assets are items that can or will be converted into cash within one year. Current assets include cash, accounts receivable, and inventory.
    b. Fixed assets are long-term assets that are relatively permanent such as land buildings and equipment. They are often referred to as property, plant and equipment on a balance sheet.
    c. Intangible assets are long-term assets that have no physical form but have value. Examples include patents, trademarks, copyrights, and goodwill.

27. Liabilities are what the business owes to others. Current liabilities are payments due in one year or less; long-term liabilities are payments not due for one year or longer.

28. a. Accounts payable is money owed to others for merchandise and/or services purchased on credit but yet not paid. If you have a bill you haven't paid, you have an account payable.
    b. Notes payable are short-term or long-term loans that have a promise for future payment
    c. Bonds payable are money loaned to the firm that it must pay back.

29. The value of things you own, <u>assets</u>, minus the amount of money you owe others, <u>liabilities</u>, is called <u>equity</u>. The value of what stockholders own in a firm minus liabilities is called stockholders equity.

30. Businesses that are not incorporated identify the investment of the sole proprietor or partner(s) through a capital account. For them, owner's equity means the value of everything owned by the business less any liabilities of the owners, such as bank loans.

31. The income statement
    a. summarizes all of the resources, called revenue, that have come into the firm from operating activities, money resources used, expenses incurred, and resources left after covering expenses.
    b. reports the firm's financial operations over a particular period of time, usually a year, a quarter of a year or a month.

32. The formula for an income statement is:
   Revenue
   <u>- Cost of Goods Sold</u>
   Gross Margin
   <u>-Operating Expenses</u>
   Net Income before Taxes
   <u>-Taxes</u>
   = Net income (or loss)

33.   a.   Revenue is the value of what is received for goods sold, services rendered, and other financial sources. Most revenue comes from sales, but there could be other sources of revenue such as rents received, money paid to the firm for use of its patents, interest earned, and so forth.

       b.   Gross sales are the total of all sales the firm completed. Net sales refer to sales minus returns, discounts, and allowances.

34. The cost of goods sold includes the purchase price plus any freight charges paid to transport goods plus any costs associated with storing the goods. In other words, all the costs of buying and keeping merchandise for sale are included in the cost of goods sold.

35. It's possible in a service firm that there may be no cost of goods sold; therefore, net revenue could equal gross margin. In a manufacturing firm, it is necessary to estimate the cost of goods manufactured.

36. Two categories of expenses are selling and general expenses. Selling expenses are related to the marketing and distribution of the firm's goods or services, such as salaries for salespeople, advertising and supplies. General expenses are administrative expenses of the firm, such as office salaries, depreciation, insurance and rent.

37. The "bottom line" is the net income or net loss the firm incurred from operations.

38. The three major activities for which cash receipts and disbursements are reported on a statement of cash flows include:
       a.   Operations – cash transactions associated with running the business
       b.   Investments – cash used in or provided by the firm's investment activities
       c.   Financing – cash raised from new debt or new equity capital, or cash used to pay expenses, debts or dividends

39. A poor, or negative, cash flow indicates that more money is going out of the business than is coming in from sales or other sources of revenue.

40. Questions answered by a statement of cash flows may be:
       a.   how much cash came into the business from current operations, in other words, from buying and selling goods and services?
       b.   Was cash used to buy stocks, bonds or other investments?
       c.   Were some investments sold that brought in cash?
       d.   How much money came into the firm from issuing stock?

41. Cash flow problems start when, in order to meet the demands of customers, more and more goods are bought on credit. Similarly, more and more goods are sold on credit. This can go on until the firm uses up all the credit it has with banks that lend it money. When

the firm requests money from the bank to pay a crucial bill the bank refuses the loan because the credit limit has been reached. All other credit sources may refuse a loan as well. The company needs to pay its bills or else its creditors could force it into bankruptcy.

42. A path to preventing cash flow problems that often develop is for a business to maintain a working relationship with a bank.

Learning Goal 5
Analyzing Financial Statements: Ratio Analysis

43. Firms provide key insights into how a firm compares to other firms in the same industry in the key areas of:
   a. liquidity
   b. debt
   c. profitability
   d. overall business activity

44. Liquidity ratios measure the company's ability to pay its short-term debts. Short-term debts are expected to be repaid within one year and are of importance to the firm's creditors who expect to be paid on time.

45. Two key liquidity ratios are:
   a. current ratio
   b. quick ratio

46. Current ratio = $\dfrac{\text{Current assets}}{\text{Current liabilities}}$

47. The current ratio is compared to
   a. competing firms within the industry to measure how the company sizes up to its main competitors.
   b. the previous year to note any significant changes.

48. Acid test ratio = $\dfrac{\text{Cash + marketable securities + receivables}}{\text{Current liabilities}}$

49. This ratio is important to firms with difficulty converting inventory into quick cash.

50. Leverage ratios measure the degree to which a firm relies on borrowed funds in its operations.

51. Debt to equity ratio = $\dfrac{\text{Total liabilities}}{\text{Owner's equity}}$

   This ratio measures the degree to which the company is financed by borrowed funds that must be repaid.

52. A debt to equity ratio of above 100% would show that a firm actually has more debt than equity. It's possible that this firm could be perceived as a risk to both lenders and investors. It's always important to compare ratios to other firms in the same industry because debt financing is more acceptable in some industries.

53. Profitability ratios measure how effectively the firm is using its various resources to achieve profits.

54.   Three profitability ratios are:
        a.   Earnings per share
        b.   Return on sales
        c.   Return on equity

55.   Basic earnings per share measures the amount of profit earned by a company for each share of outstanding common stock. Diluted EPS measures the amount of profit earned by a company for each share of outstanding common stock, but takes into consideration stock options, warrants, preferred stock and convertible debt securities that can be converted into common stock.

56.   Basic earnings per share = $\dfrac{\text{Net Income}}{\text{Number of Common shares outstanding}}$

57.   Return on sales   = $\dfrac{\text{Net Income}}{\text{Net Sales}}$

        Firms use this ratio to see if they are doing as well as the companies they compete against in generating income on sales they achieve.

58.   Return on equity   = $\dfrac{\text{Net Income}}{\text{Total Owner's Equity}}$

        Return on equity measures how much was earned for each dollar invested by owners.

59.   Activity ratios measure the effectiveness of the firm's management in using assets that are available.

60.   Inventory turnover   = $\dfrac{\text{Cost of Goods Sold}}{\text{Average Inventory}}$

        The inventory turnover ratio measures the speed of inventory moving through the firm and its conversion into sales. Inventory sitting by idly in a business costs money.

61.   a.   A lower than average inventory turnover ratio often indicates obsolete merchandise on hand or poor buying practices.
        b.   A higher than average ratio may signal lost sales because of inadequate stock. An acceptable turnover ratio is generally determined on an industry-by-industry basis.

CRITICAL THINKING EXERCISES

Learning Goals 1,2

1. a.   Financial accounting
    b.   Public accountant
    c.   Certified management accountant (CMA)
    d.   Tax accountant
    e.   Private accountant
    f.   Auditing
    g.   Certified public accountant (CPA)
    h.   Managerial accounting
    i.   Independent audit
    j.   Annual report
    k.   Certified internal auditor (CIA)

2.   BOOKKEEPING JOB DESCRIPTION - The bookkeeper for Sun-2-Shade will be responsible for collecting all original transaction documents, and dividing them into meaningful categories (sales, purchasing, shipping, and so on). The information will be recorded into journals on a daily basis, using the double-entry method. The bookkeeper will also be responsible for recording the information from the journals into ledgers. Must be familiar with computer accounting applications.

ACCOUNTANT JOB DESCRIPTION - The accountant for Sun-2-Shade will be responsible for classifying and summarizing the data provided by the bookkeeper. He/she will interpret the data, report to management, and suggest strategies for improving the financial condition and progress of the firm. Must be able to suggest tax strategies and be skilled in financial analysis. Must be a Certified Management Accountant.

3.   a.   Record in journals   d.   Analyze source documents
       b.   Take a trial balance   e.   Post to ledgers
       c.   Analyze financial statements   f.   Prepare financial statements

Learning Goal 4

4.   a   1. Balance sheet   11. Balance sheet
           2. Balance sheet   12. Balance sheet
           3. Balance sheet   13. Balance sheet
           4. Income statement   14. Income statement
           5. Income statement   15. Income statement
           6. Balance sheet   16. Income statement
           7. Income statement   17. Income statement
           8. Income statement   18. Income statement
           9. Balance sheet   19. Balance sheet
           10. Income statement   20. Income statement

       b. 1. Cash
           2. Accounts receivable
           3. Inventories

5.

BALANCE SHEET

SUN-2-SHADE

Year ending December 31, 200 _

Assets
Current assets

Cash	$ 18,000	
Investments	45,000	
Accounts receivable	110,000	
Inventory	62,000	
Total current assets		**$235,000**
Property, plant and equipment		
(Less accumulated depreciation)		200,000
Total Assets		**$435,000**

Liabilities and Stockholder's equity
Liabilities

Current liabilities		
Accounts payable	$25,000	
Notes payable (current)	15,000	
Accrued taxes	40,000	
Total current liabilities		**$80,000**
Long-term Debt		60,000
Total liabilities		**$140,000**

Stockholder's equity

Common stock	$130,000	
Retained earnings	165,000	
Total stockholders equity		**$295,000**
Total liabilities and stockholder's equity		**$435,000**

6.

SUN-2-SHADE, INC.
INCOME STATEMENT
Year ending December 31, 200 _

Revenues
Net sales	$600,000	
Rental revenue	3,000	
Total revenues		**$603,000**
Cost of goods sold		313,000
Gross profit		**$290,000**
Operating Expenses		
Wages and salaries	$125,000	
Rent	35,000	
Advertising	28,000	
Depreciation	4,000	
Utilities	12,000	
Supplies	3,700	
Total Operating Expenses		**$207,700**
Net Income Before Taxes		$ 82,300
Less Income Taxes		23,044
Net Income After Taxes		**$ 59,256**

7.　　Everyone's answer will vary, obviously. The things to look at include your wages for the next two weeks, and any other income you will be receiving within the next two weeks (not including that $10 your friend owes you unless you <u>know</u> they're going to pay you!), and any expenses that will be due within the next two weeks, such as car payments, insurance, rent, groceries, utility bills, cell phone bills, credit card payments, tuition, books, and so on.

Learning Goal 5

8.　　a.　Current ratio: $\dfrac{\$235,000}{\$80,000} = 2.9$

　　　b.　Acid-test ratio: $\dfrac{\$173,000}{\$80,000} = 2.16$

　　　c. It seems that Sun-2-Shade is financially sound from the liquidity perspective, as their ratios are above the benchmark of the 2:1 ratio.

9.　　a.　Debt/Owner's equity ratio: $\dfrac{\$140,000}{\$295,000} = .47$

　　　b.　Sun-2-Shade seems to be in very good shape, and could actually afford to take on slightly more debt, according to the industry average.

10.　　a.　Earnings per share: $\dfrac{\$59,256}{30,000} = \$1.98$ share

　　　b.　Return on sales: $\dfrac{\$59,256}{\$600,000} = 10\%$ approximately

　　　c.　Return on equity: $\dfrac{\$59,256}{\$295,000} = 20.1\%$

11.   a. Inventory turnover: $\dfrac{313,000}{70,000}$ = 4.47 times

     b. Sun-2-Shade's turnover is high, compared to the industry average. This could indicate that they are running the risk of lost sales from inadequate stock.

PRACTICE TEST

MULTIPLE CHOICE
LG 1 # 1-2
LG 2 # 3-5
LG 3 # 6-8
LG 4 # 9-15
LG 5 # 16-20

1.	d	11.	d
2.	c	12.	c
3.	b	13.	a
4.	d	14.	c
5.	c	15.	d
6.	d	16.	d
7.	a	17.	d
8.	c	18.	d
9.	d	19.	a
10.	b	20.	b

TRUE-FALSE
LG 1 # 1-2
LG 2 # 3-7
LG 3 # 8-10
LG 4 # 11-15
LG 5 #16-18

1.	F	10.	T
2.	T	11.	F
3.	F	12.	F
4.	F	13.	F
5.	T	14.	F
6.	F	15.	T
7.	T	16.	T
8.	T	17.	F
9.	T	18.	T

CHAPTER 18 – FINANCIAL MANAGEMENT

LEARNING GOALS

After you have read and studied this chapter, you should be able to:

1. Describe the importance of finance and financial management to an organization and explain the responsibilities of financial managers.
2. Outline the financial planning process and explain the three key budgets in the financial plan.
3. Explain the major reasons why firms need operating funds and identify various types of financing that can be used to obtain these funds.
4. Identify and describe different sources of short-term financing.
5. Identify and describe different sources of long-term financing

LEARNING THE LANGUAGE

Listed below are important terms found in the chapter. Choose the correct term for the definition and write it in the space provided.

Budget	Finance	Revolving credit agreement
Capital budget	Financial control	Risk/return trade-off
Capital expenditures	Financial managers	Secured bond
Cash budget	Financial management	Secured loan
Cash flow forecast	Indenture terms	Short-term financing
Commercial finance companies	Leverage	Short-term forecast
Commercial paper	Line of credit	Term-loan agreement
Cost of capital	Long-term financing	Trade credit
Debt financing	Long-term forecast	Unsecured bond
Equity financing	Operating (master) budget	Unsecured loan
Factoring	Promissory note	Venture capital

1. Organizations called _____ make short-term loans to borrowers who offer tangible assets as collateral.

2. In a process known as _____ a firm periodically compares its actual revenues, costs and expenses with projected ones.

3. Borrowed capital that will be repaid over a specific time period longer than one year is called _____

4. A line of credit called a _____ is guaranteed by the bank.

5. A _____ is a promissory note that requires the borrower to repay the loan in specified installments.

6. An _____ is a loan that is not backed by any specific assets.

7. Managers called _____ make recommendations to top executives regarding strategies for improving the financial strength of a firm.

511

8. Funds known as _____ are raised from operations within the firm or through the sale of ownership in the firm.

9. The _____ is the rate of return a company must earn in order to meet the demands of its lenders and expectations of its equity holders.

10. A written contract or _____ is a promise to pay a supplier a specific sum of money at a definite time.

11. A _____ is a prediction of revenues, costs, and expenses for a period of one year or less.

12. Funds raised through various forms of borrowing that must be repaid are called _____.

13. A(n) _____ is the budget that ties together all of a firm's other budgets; it is a projection of dollar allocations to various costs and expenses needed to run or operate the business given projected revenue.

14. A _____ is a loan backed by something valuable, such as property.

15. A forecast called a _____ predicts cash inflows and outflows in future periods, usually months or quarters.

16. A given amount of unsecured short-term funds or a _____ is what a bank will lend to a business, provided funds are readily available.

17. A bond backed only by the reputation of the issuer is known as a debenture bond, or a (n) _____.

18. Raising needed funds through borrowing to increase a firm's rate of return is called _____.

19. _____ is used to describe the process of selling accounts receivable for cash.

20. A _____ highlights a firm's spending plans for major asset purchases that often require large sums of money.

21. A financial plan that sets forth management's expectations called a(n) _____ allocates the use of specific resources throughout the firm.

22. A _____ is a prediction of revenues, costs and expenses for a period longer than one year, sometimes extending 5 or 10 years into the future.

23. Unsecured promissory notes of $100,000 and up are known as _____ and mature in 270 days or less.

24. The practice of _____ is buying goods and services today and paying for them later.

25. The term _____ refers to borrowed capital that will be repaid within one year.

512

26. The function in a business called _____ is acquiring funds for the firm and managing funds within the firm.

27. The principle of _____ means the greater the risk a lender takes in making a loan, the higher the interest rate required.

28. A bond issued with some form of collateral is a _____.

29. The terms of the agreement in a bond issue are known as _____.

30. The _____ estimates a firm's projected cash inflows and outflows that the firm can use to plan for any cash shortages or surpluses during a given period.

31. The job of managing the firm's resources so it can meet its goals and objectives is _____.

32. Major investments, or _____, are for long-term assets such as land, buildings, equipment, or intangible assets such as patents, trademarks, and copyrights.

33. Money that is invested in new or emerging companies that are perceived as having great profit potential is known as _____.

ASSESSMENT CHECK

Learning Goal 1
The Role of Finance and Financial Managers

1. What is the difference between an accountant and a financial manager?

2. Two key responsibilities of a financial manager's task are to:

   a. _____

   b. _____

3. Controlling funds includes managing:

   a. _____

   b. _____

   c. _____

4. Businesses of what size need to be involved in financial management?

5.   Describe three of the most common ways for any firm to fail financially.

      a._____

      b._____

      c._____

6.   For what activities are financial managers responsible?

Learning Goal 2
Financial Planning

7.   What is the overall objective of financial planning?

8.   What are the three steps involved in financial planning?

      a. _____

      b. _____

      c. _____

9.   What is the basis for projecting sales and various costs and expenses?

10.   Identify three types of budgets

      a._____

      b._____

      c._____

11.   What is the primary concern in a capital budget?

12.   How do cash budgets help managers? When is a cash budget prepared?

13.   What is the function of an operating budget?

14.   How do financial control procedures help managers?

       a.   _____

       b.   _____

       c.   _____

Learning Goal 3
The Need for Operating Funds

15.   What are four key areas for which businesses need operating funds?

       a._____

       b._____

       c._____

       d._____

16.   The challenge of sound financial management is to see that: _____

       _____

17.   Describe the time value of money. What is the importance of the time value of money?

18.   Why do financial managers try to keep cash expenditures to a minimum?

19.   Why do financial managers want to make credit available?

       a.   _____

       b.   _____

       c.   _____

20.   What is a problem with offering credit?

21.   What does inventory control have to do with finance?

22.   What job does a financial manager have with regard to capital expenditures?

23.   A firm can seek to raise needed capital through

        a.   _____

        b.   _____

        c.   _____

Learning Goal 4
Obtaining Short-Term Financing

24.   Why do firms need to borrow short-term funds?

        a.   _____

        b.   _____

        c.   _____

25.   What are seven sources of short-term financing?

        a.   _____   e.   _____

        b.   _____   f.   _____

        c.   _____   g.   _____

        d.   _____

26.   Which of these forms is the most widely used source of short term financing? Why?

27.   Describe the invoice terms of 2/10 net 30, when using trade credit.

28.   Why might a supplier require a promissory note?

29.   What steps are recommended when borrowing from family or friends?

        a. _____

        b. _____

        c. _____

30.   Why is it important for a businessperson to keep a close relationship with a banker?

31.   Describe four types of bank loans.

        a. _____

           _____

        b. _____

           _____

        c. _____

           _____

        d. _____

           _____

32.   Describe the process of pledging.

33.   Discuss a firm's use of commercial finance companies.

34. Describe the process of factoring.

35. How is factoring different from taking out a loan?

36. What kinds of companies sell commercial paper? What are the benefits of commercial paper?

37. What are the drawbacks of using credit cards as a source of short term funds?

Learning Goal 5
Obtaining Long-Term Financing

38. What are three questions financial managers ask when setting long-term financing objectives?

    a. _____

    b. _____

    c. _____

39. What is long-term capital used for?

40. What are the two major sources of initial long-term financing?

    a. _____ b. _____

41. Firms can borrow long-term funds by either:

    a. _____

    b. _____

42.	What is the tax advantage of a term-loan agreement?

43.	What are some drawbacks to a long-term loan?

   a.	_____

   b.	_____

   c.	_____

44.	What is the risk/return trade-off?

45.	What types of organizations can issue bonds?

   a.	_____

   b.	_____

   c.	_____

   d.	_____

46.	To put it simply a bond is: _____

   _____

47.	What does a potential investor measure when deciding whether or not to buy a bond?

48.	What is another name for a debenture bond?

49.	What are the sources of equity financing?

   a.	_____

   b.	_____

   c.	_____

50.   The purchasers of stock become: _____

       The number of shares of stock available for purchase is determined by: _____.

51.   What is the term for the first time a company offers to sell its stock to the general public?

52.   What is the most favored source of long-term capital? Why?

53.   Why is it that many businesses can't rely on retained earnings as a source of funding?

54.   Why is it important to be careful when choosing a venture capital firm??

55.   What are the two key jobs of the finance manager, or CFO?

       a.   _____

       b.   _____

56.   How can a firm use leverage to get a higher rate of return for stockholders, compared to equity funding?

CRITICAL THINKING EXERCISES

Learning Goal 1

1.   Among the functions a finance manager performs are:

Planning	Collecting funds (credit management)
Auditing	Controlling funds
Managing taxes	Obtaining funds
Advising top management	Budgeting

Match the correct function to each statement below.

a. _____   Before Sun-2-Shade sends out quarterly financial statements, Debbie Breeze does her job, which is to ensure that no mistakes have been made, and that all transactions have been treated in accordance with established accounting rules and procedures.

b. _____   Joe Saumby determined that his firm's accounts receivable were too high, and developed a more effective collection system.

c. _____   Ann Bizer decided to include money for a new bank of computers in the operating budget.

d. _____   In an effort to generate capital, Gerald McMillian decided that his company should "go public" and make a stock offering.

e. _____   A major automotive company developed a long-range objective of automating its production facilities, which would cost millions of dollars.

f. _____   In order to monitor expense account spending, many companies require employees to submit a receipt for any expenditure over $25.

g. _____   During a period of high inflation, the Kroger Company changed some of their accounting practices to reduce the company's tax liability.

h. _____   In a report to the CEO and other top managers in his company, Joe Kelley outlined the effect of newly proposed pollution control requirements on the company's long-range profit forecasts.

Learning Goal 2

2.   The text identifies three kinds of budgets

Operating (master) budget	Cash budget
Capital budget	

Determine which type of budget is being described in each of the following:

a. _____   St. Louis Community College District projects that $350,000 will be spent for attendance and participation in conferences and seminars.

b. _____ Kevin Nelson, the finance manager for TNG Enterprises, has just finished work on the budget that will enable him to determine how much money the firm will have to borrow for the next year.

c. _____ At Whitfield School, a fund raising activity helped the school add money to the funds allocated to purchasing computer equipment for student and faculty use.

d. _____ Phillip Knott is the comptroller for a major electronics firm. At their annual finance meeting, he presented a summary of all the budgets for board approval.

3. Planning is a critical element in the management process. What is the relationship between strategic planning and long-term financial planning and forecasting?

Learning Goal 3
4. Eric is the owner/founder of Sun-2-Shade, a company that manufactures self-darkening windshields for the automotive industry, and Eric is upset! He has just stormed into Sun-2-Shade's finance manager's office "What's going on? I just looked at our inventory levels, and they're lower than what I think we ought to see. Don't we have the money to buy inventory? How are we going to make our orders? And what's the idea of all these credit sales? Visa? MasterCard? And another thing! Why are we always paying our bills at the last minute? Are we that short of cash? " "Hold on" said Bill Whittier, the new finance manager, " things look pretty good to me. We're actually in great shape!" " What? I don't understand!" replied Eric. "You know, I want to look into building a new plant within the next 2 years. Sales are going to continue to go way up. I need to know whether or not we're going to be able to afford it. Right now, it looks as if we are too short of cash. Explain!"

Learning Goal 4
5. There are several sources of short-term funds:

Trade credit	Factoring
Promissory notes	Commercial paper
Family and friends	Credit Cards
Commercial bank loans	

Match the correct type of short-term financing to each of the following:

a. _____ A major Midwestern retailer often sells its accounts receivable for cash.

b. _____ Lou Fusz auto network finances its inventories, using the vehicles themselves as collateral for the loans.

c. _____ During a recent recession, Van Nuys Enterprises had some problems paying their bills on time. Afterwards, Van Nuys' suppliers required them to sign a written contract in order for them to buy with credit.

d. _____ Echo Enterprises recently raised some "quick cash" through selling $100,000 promissory notes. Echo agreed to pay the principle plus interest within 90 days of the sale. Monterrey Bay Co. bought Echo's promissory notes as an investment for their extra cash.

e. _____ Kellwood bills its retail customers on a 2/10 net 30 basis.

f. _____ To pay an unexpectedly high liability insurance premium, the owner of a small chemical company borrowed money from his best friend.

g. _____ Dave Flynn has just opened a small business in a suburb of his home town of Atlanta. To promote the business Dave created some color brochures, and determined that it would be cheaper for him to print the brochures himself rather than have the job done at a printer so he purchased a color laser printer with his personal credit card, and charged the business later.

6. There are several kinds of loans:

Unsecured loans
Secured loans (including pledging)
Inventory financing

Line of credit
Revolving credit agreement
Commercial finance companies

Match each type to the following examples:

a. _____ Ternier Steel Company is using their most recent shipment of coal as collateral for a short-term loan.

b. _____ In their commodities brokerage business, Bartholomew Enterprises needs guaranteed loans without having to apply for the loan each time it is needed. They are willing to pay a fee for the guarantee.

c. _____ Rivertown Insurance is having some short-term cash problems. They have substantial accounts receivable which they intend to use as collateral for a loan.

d. _____ Danny Noble Enterprises has been in business for a fairly long time and has a great financial record. When they needed money they went to their banker and applied for the loan without needing to put up collateral.

e. _____ Because they often have a need for short term funds with short notice, Binny and Jones Manufacturing applied to their bank for a "continual" sort of unsecured loan. The bank lends Binny a given amount without Binny having to re-apply each time. While not a guaranteed loan, the funds will be available if Binny's credit limit is not exceeded and the bank has the money available.

f. _____ Because they were considered a credit risk, PPI, Inc. had to pay a higher rate of interest, and pledge their inventory as collateral for the loan. They went to General Electric Capital Services because they couldn't obtain funding from a commercial bank.

7.   There are 2 general sources of long-term funds

        Debt capital - loans and bonds
        Equity capital - stock, retained earnings, venture capital

        Match the correct type of financing to each of the following statements:

a. _____   The unsecured form of these are commonly referred to as "debentures."

b. _____   If a firm cannot obtain a long-term loan or can't sell bonds it will turn to this type of financing.

c. _____   Generally the most favored source of long-term capital.

d. _____   These can be either secured or unsecured.

e. _____   For this, a business must sign a term-loan agreement because of the long repayment period.

f. _____   The key word here is "ownership."

g. _____   This source of funds can involve a high degree of risk for companies choosing it and firms providing this type of funding may hold companies to strict standards before investing their capital.

h. _____   Using this source saves the company interest payments, dividends and any underwriting fees, and won't dilute ownership.

i. _____   The terms of agreement are called indenture terms.

j. _____   Good sources of start up capital for new companies, they often want a stake in the ownership of the business.

k. _____   When using this form of financing, a company has a legal obligation to pay interest.

8.   Eric and his finance manager, Joel, are in disagreement over how to finance the future growth of Sun-2-Shade. "I just want to stay out of debt if I can" says Eric, "so I think the best idea is to sell stock, go public." "Well, I understand your perspective Eric, but I'm not sure you have thought of all the consequences of selling stock. Do you like being your own boss?" asks Joel. "Yeah, sure!" replies Eric," but what the heck does that have to do with wanting to sell stock in the company?" What does Joel mean, and what are the other arguments for and against each type of funding?

9. If leverage means raising money through debt, what do you suppose is meant by a "leveraged buyout"?

PRACTICE TEST

MULTIPLE CHOICE – Circle the best answer

Learning Goal 1
1. Which of the following is not included in a list of reasons why businesses fail financially?
    a. Inadequate expense control
    b. Poor control over cash flow
    c. Undercapitalization
    d. Stock is undervalued

2. Jackie Jones is a finance manager for Pokey Poseys, a wholesale florist. As finance manager, which of the following would not be one of Jackie's responsibilities?
    a. preparing financial statements
    b. preparing budgets
    c. paying bills on time
    d. planning for spending funds on long-term assets, such as plant and equipment

3. Internal audits are important because:
    a. the firm needs to keep a constant look out for employees who may be committing fraud.
    b. internal audits help to make accounting statements more reliable.
    c. they aid in the development of financial statements.
    d. the firm uses the audits to determine desired profits for the following year.

Learning Goal 2
4. Which of the following is <u>not</u> one of the steps involved in financial planning?
    a. Develop financial statements for outside investors.
    b. Forecast short and long-term financial needs.
    c. Establish financial controls.
    d. Develop budgets to meet financial needs.

5. A _____ forecast predicts revenues, costs, and expenses for a period longer than one year.
    a. short-term
    b. long-term
    c. cash flow
    d. revenue

6. Guillermo Reta-Martinez is currently in the process of projecting how much his firm will have to spend on supplies, travel, rent, advertising, and salaries for the coming financial year. Guillermo is working on the _____.
    a. operating (master) budget
    b. capital budget
    c. cash budget
    d. advertising budget

7.   Financial controls are designed to help managers to:
        a.   develop the appropriate budgets.
        b.   predict cash inflows in future periods.
        c.   manage the day to day cash needs of a business.
        d.   identify variances from the financial plan and take corrective actions.

Learning Goal 3
8.   The time value of money means that
        a.   the value of money will fall over time.
        b.   it is better to make purchases now, rather than wait until later.
        c.   a monetary system will devalue it's money over time.
        d.   it is better to have money now, than later.

9.   What is the major problem with selling on credit?
        a.   A sizeable portion of a firm's assets could be tied up in accounts receivable.
        b.   You can't control when customers will pay their bills.
        c.   It makes production scheduling more difficult.
        d.   Customers who aren't allowed to buy on credit become unhappy.

10.   Companies must maintain a sizable investment in inventories in order to:
        a.   be able of accept credit cards.
        b.   satisfy customers.
        c.   increase demand for their products.
        d.   reduce the need for long-term funds.

11.   Debt financing:
        a.   refers to funds raised through various forms of borrowing.
        b.   is always more expensive than selling stocks.
        c.   refers to funds raised through selling ownership in the firm.
        d.   requires that the firm pay interest from after tax profits.

Learning Goal 4
12.   Which of the following is a source of short-term funds?
        a.   The sale of bonds
        b.   The use of trade credit
        c.   Venture capital
        d.   The use of retained earnings

13.   The credit terms 2/10 net 30 means:
        a.   The full amount of a bill is due within 2-10 days
        b.   Customers will receive a 10 percent discount if they pay in 30 days
        c.   A 2 percent discount will be given if customers pay within 30 days
        d.   Customers will receive a 2 percent discount if they pay within 10 days

14.   Factoring is a term that means:
        a.   determining the credit terms for a trade credit agreement.
        b.   selling accounts receivable as a way to raise cash
        c.   determining whether to use debt or equity financing to raise funds
        d.   using a continual line of credit.

15. Commercial finance companies accept more risk than banks, and the interest rates they charge are usually _____ than commercial banks.
    a. higher
    b. about the same as
    c. lower
    d. more variable

Learning Goal 5
16. Using equity financing includes _____ as a source of funds
    a. the sale of bonds
    b. the sale of stock
    c. the sale of inventory
    d. the sale of accounts receivable

17. One of the benefits of selling bonds, over selling stock, as a source of long-term funds is that
    a. bonds don't have to be paid back.
    b. the company isn't required to pay interest.
    c. bondholders do not have a say in running the business.
    d. interest is paid after taxes are paid.

18. When a corporation takes out a long-term loan, the company must:
    a. calculate a risk/return tradeoff.
    b. sign a term-loan agreement.
    c. agree to indenture terms.
    d. sell its commercial paper.

19. The most favored source of meeting long-term capital needs is:
    a. selling stock.
    b. venture capital.
    c. selling bonds.
    d. retained earnings.

20. When a major automotive firm decided to purchase one of it's competitors, the firm borrowed a significant portion of the funds it needed to make the purchase. This is known as using:
    a. venture capital.
    b. leverage.
    c. retained earnings.
    d. equity capital.

TRUE-FALSE

Learning Goal 1
1. _____ Financial managers examine the financial data prepared by accountants and make recommendations to top executives about strategies for improving the financial strength of a firm.

2. _____ Financial understanding is important primarily for anyone wanting to major in accounting, but not necessary for others involved in business.

3. _____ Because taxes represent a cash outflow, financial managers are involved in planning tax strategies, and in tax management.

Learning Goal 2

4. _____ The cash budget is often the first budget that is prepared.

5. _____ Financial control means that the actual revenues, costs, and expenses are reviewed and compared with projections.

6. _____ The short-term forecast is the foundation for most other financial plans.

Learning Goal 3

7. _____ Finance managers will sometimes pay bills as late as possible as a way of managing cash for daily operations.

8. _____ One way to decrease the expense of collecting accounts receivable is to accept bank credit cards.

9. _____ Firms may use innovations such as just-in-time inventory control to help reduce the amount of funds tied up in inventory.

Learning Goal 4

10. _____ When suppliers are hesitant to give trade credit to organizations with a poor credit rating, or which have no credit history, they may ask for the customer to sign a promissory note as a condition for obtaining credit.

11. _____ One benefit of borrowing from friends or family is that you don't have to draw up formal papers like you do with a bank loan.

12. _____ It is important for a businessperson to keep close relations with a banker because the banker may be able to spot cash flow problems early and point out problems.

13. _____ A line of credit guarantees a business a given amount of unsecured short-term funds, if funds are available.

Learning Goal 5

14. _____ Long-term capital is generally used to pay for supplies, rent, and travel.

15. _____ Only the federal government can issue bonds.

16. _____ Potential investors in bonds measure the risk involved in purchasing a bond with the return the bond promises to pay.

You Can Find It On the Net

What are some of the financial considerations of starting and managing your own small business? Visit www.smallbusiness.com , and click on the Financial Management link.

What are the primary steps in developing a financial management system?

What are the ways to manage cash shortages?

What are the various charts of accounts when developing a budgeting system?

What are the various considerations when developing the funding request in a business plan?

ANSWERS

LEARNING THE LANGUAGE

1. Commercial finance companies	12. Debt financing	23. Commercial paper
2. Financial control	13. Operating budget	24. Trade credit
3. Long-term financing	14. Secured loan	25. Short-term financing
4. Revolving credit agreement	15. Cash flow forecast	26. Finance
5. Term-loan agreement	16. Line of credit	27. Risk/return tradeoff
6. Unsecured loan	17. Unsecured bond	28. Secured bond
7. Financial managers	18. Leverage	29. Indenture terms
8. Equity financing	19. Factoring	30. Cash budget
9. Cost of capital	20. Capital budget	31. Financial management
10. Promissory note	21. Budget	32. Capital expenditures
11. Short-term forecast	22. Long-term forecast	33. Venture capital

ASSESSMENT CHECK
Learning Goal 1
The Role of Finance and Financial Managers

1. Financial managers use the data prepared by accountants and make recommendations to top management regarding strategies for improving the health of the firm. It is the equivalent of a lab technician who takes the measures of a person's health (the accountant) and the doctor who interprets the reports (the finance manager).

2. Two key responsibilities of a financial manager's task are to:
   a. obtain funds.
   b. control the use of those funds effectively.

3. Controlling funds includes managing:
   a. the firm's cash.
   b. credit accounts.
   c. inventory

4. Finance is important no matter what the size of the organization, and is a challenge that all businesses must face throughout their existence.

5. The three most common ways for any firm to fail financially are:
   a. Undercaptitalization - not enough funds to start with
   b. Poor control over cash flow
   c. Inadequate expense control

6. Financial managers are responsible for seeing that the company pays its bills at the appropriate time and for collecting overdue payments to make sure that the company does not lose too much money to bad debts. They are also involved in tax management and internal audits.

Learning Goal 2
Financial Planning

7. Financial planning involves analyzing short-term and long-term money flows to and from the firm. The overall objective of financial planning is to optimize the firm's profitability and make the best use of its money.

8. Financial planning involves:
    a. Forecasting both short-term and long-term financial needs
    b. Developing budgets to meet those needs
    c. Establishing financial controls

9. The basis for projecting expected sales and various costs and expenses is often a company's past financial statements.

10. Three types of budgets are:
    a. Operating (master) budgets
    b. Capital budgets
    c. Cash budgets

11. The capital budget primarily concerns itself with the purchase of such assets as property, plant, and equipment

12. Cash budgets are important guidelines that assist managers in anticipating borrowing, repaying debt, operating expenses, and short-term investments. The cash budget is prepared after other budgets have been prepared.

13. The operating, or master, budget ties together all the firm's other budgets and summarizes a company's proposed financial statements. It is in this budget that the firm determines how much the company will spend on supplies, travel, rent, advertising, salaries and so forth. It is the most detailed budget.

14 Control procedures help managers
    a. identify variances to the financial plan.
    b. take corrective action if necessary.
    c. provide feedback to help identify which accounts, departments and people are varying from the financial plan.

Learning Goal 3
The Need for Operating Funds

15. Four basic financial needs affecting both small and large businesses are:
    a. Managing day-by-day needs of the business   c.   Acquiring needed inventory
    b. Controlling credit operations   d.   Making capital expenditures

16. The challenge of sound financial management is to see that funds are available to meet daily cash needs without compromising the firm's investment potential.

17. Money has a time value, which means that if someone offered to give you money today or one year from today, you would benefit by taking the money today. You could start collecting interest or invest the money you receive today, and over time, your money would grow. For a firm, the interest earned on investments is important in maximizing the profit the company will gain.

18.   Financial managers often try to keep cash expenditures at a minimum to free funds for investment in interest-bearing accounts. It is not unusual for finance managers to suggest the firm pay bills as late as possible and collect what is owed as fast as possible.

19.   Financial mangers know that making credit available helps
       a.   keep current customers happy
       b.   attract new customers.
       c.   reduce the time and expense involved in collecting accounts receivable, by accepting credit cards.

20.   The major problem with selling on credit is that as much as 25 percent or more of the business's assets could be tied up in its accounts receivable so the firm has to use some of its available cash to pay for the goods or services already given to customers who bought on credit. As a result financial managers must develop efficient collection procedures.

21.   To satisfy customers, businesses must maintain inventories that often involve a sizable expenditure of funds. A carefully constructed inventory policy assists in managing the use of the firm's available funds and maximizing profitability.

22.   Financial managers and analysts evaluate the appropriateness of capital purchases. It is critical that companies weigh all the possible options before committing what may be a large portion of its available resources.

23.   A firm can seek to raise needed capital through:
       a.   borrowing money – debt capital
       b.   selling ownership – equity capital
       c.   earning profits – retained earnings

Learning Goal 4
Obtaining Short-Term Financing

24.   Firms need to borrow short-term funds for:
       a.   purchasing additional inventory.
       b.   for meeting bills that come due unexpectedly.
       c.   to obtain short-term funds when the firm's cash reserves are low.

25.   Seven sources of short-term financing are:
       a.   Trade credit   e.   Factoring accounts receivable
       b.   Promissory note   f.   Commercial paper
       c.   Family and friends   g.   Credit cards
       d.   Commercial bank loans

26.   The most widely used source of short-term funding is trade credit, because it is the least expensive and most convenient form of short-term financing.

27.   Terms of 2/10 net 30 means that the buyer can take a 2 percent discount for paying within 10 days. The total bill is due (net) in 30 days if the purchaser does not take advantage of the discount. If the buyer does not take advantage of that discount, the annual interest adds up to 36 percent per year.

28. Some suppliers hesitate to give trade credit to organizations with a poor credit rating, no credit history, or a history of slow payment. In such cases, the supplier may insist that the customer sign a promissory note as a condition for obtaining credit.

29. When borrowing from family or friends:
    a. Agree on specific terms.
    b. Write an agreement.
    c. Pay them back the same way you would a bank loan.

30. It is important for a businessperson to keep friendly and close relations with a banker, because the banker may spot cash flow problems early and point out danger areas. Additionally, the banker may be more willing to lend money in a crisis if the businessperson has established a strong, friendly relationship build on openness and trust.

31. Four types of bank loans are:
    a. <u>Secured loans</u> are backed by something of value, which is known as collateral. If the buyer fails to make payment on the loan, the lender may take possession of the collateral.
    b. <u>Unsecured loans</u> don't require the lender to offer collateral. These loans are usually only offered to long standing customers or customers who are financially stable.
    c. <u>A line of credit is</u> a short term unsecured loan that the bank will lend to the business provided the bank has funds available. It is designed to speed up the borrowing process so that the firm doesn't have to apply for a new loan every time it needs funds.
    d. A <u>revolving credit agreement</u> is a line of credit that is guaranteed.

32. In the process of pledging, some percentage of the value of accounts receivables pledged is advanced to the borrowing firm. As customers pay off their accounts, the funds received are forwarded to the lender to repay the funds that were advanced. Inventory is often pledged as collateral, as well as buildings, machinery, and company owned stocks and bonds.

33. Commercial finance companies are used by businesses when the business can't obtain a short term loan from a bank. The commercial finance company will make short-term loans to borrowers with tangible assets such as property, plant and equipment, and will charge higher interest rates than commercial banks, because the commercial credit companies are willing to accept higher degrees of risk.

34. In the process of factoring, a firm sells many of its products on credit to consumers and businesses, creating accounts receivable. Some of these buyers may be slow in paying their bills, causing the company to have a large amount of money due in accounts receivable. A factor is a market intermediary that agrees to <u>buy</u> the accounts receivable from the firm at a discount for cash. It is expensive, but many small businesses, as well as some large businesses use factoring as a source of cash.

35. Factoring is the <u>sale of an asset</u>, not taking out a loan.

36. Commercial paper is unsecured, so only financially stable firms, mainly large corporations, are able to sell it. Commercial paper is a way to get short-term funds quickly and for less than bank interest rates. It is also an investment opportunity for buyers who can afford to put up cash for short periods to earn some interest.

37.   The drawbacks of using credit cards as a short term source of funds is that their use can be very risky and costly. Interest rates can be very high, and users must pay penalties if they fail to make payments on time. Credit cards are best used as a last resort.

Learning Goal 5
Obtaining Long-Term Financing

38.   Three questions financial managers ask when setting long-term financing objectives are:
a.   What are the long-term goals and objectives of the firm?
b.   What are the financial requirements needed to achieve these goals and objectives?
c.   What sources of long-term capital are available, and which will fit our needs?

39.   In business, long–term capital is used to buy fixed assets such as plant and equipment and to finance expansion of the organization.

40.   a.   debt financing which must be repaid   b.   equity financing

41.   Firms can borrow funds by either:
a.   getting a loan from a lending institution
b.   issuing bonds

42.   A major tax advantage of a term-loan agreement is that the interest paid on the long-term debt is tax deductible.

43.   Drawbacks to long term loans include:
a.   long-term loans are often more expensive to the firm than short-term loans, because larger amounts of capital are borrowed.
b.   since the repayment period could be as long as twenty years, the lenders are not assured their capital will be repaid in full so most long-term loans require some form of collateral.
c.   lenders may require certain restrictions on a firm's operations to force the firm to use responsible business practices.

44.   The risk/return trade-off is the idea that the greater the risk a lender takes in making a loan, the higher the rate of interest it requires.

45.   The types of organizations that can issue bonds are:
a.   federal, state, and local governments
b.   federal government agencies
c.   corporations
d.   foreign governments and corporations.

46.   To put it simply, a bond is like a company IOU with a promise to repay on a certain date. It is a binding contract through which an organization agrees to specific terms with investors in return for investors lending money to the company.

47.   Potential investors in bonds measure the risk involved in purchasing a bond with the return, or interest, the bond promises to pay and the company's ability to repay the bond when promised.

48.   Another name for a debenture bond is an unsecured bond, backed only by the reputation of the issuer.

49. Sources of equity financing are:
    a. selling ownership in the firm in the form of stock.
    b. using retained earnings the firm has accumulated and kept to reinvest in the business.
    c. venture capital.

50. The purchasers of stock become owners in an organization.

    The number of shares of stock available for purchase is determined by the organization's board of directors.

51. The first time a company offers to sell its stock to the general public is called an initial public offering, or an IPO.

52. Retained earnings are usually the most favored source of meeting long-term capital needs, since the company saves interest payments, dividends, and any possible underwriting fees. There is also no dilution of ownership in the firm, which occurs with selling stock.

53. Many organizations do not have sufficient retained earnings on hand to finance extensive capital improvements or business expansion.

54. It's important to be careful when choosing a venture capital firm because the venture capital firm generally wants a stake in the ownership of the business. Venture capitalists also expect a very high return on their investment and competent management performance.

55. Two key jobs of the finance manager or CFO are:
    a. to forecast the need for borrowed funds
    b. to manage borrowed funds.

56. If a firm's earns more than the interest payments on borrowed funds, then the business owners are realizing a higher rate of return than if they used equity financing.

CRITICAL THINKING EXERCISES

Learning Goal 1
1. a. Auditing
    b. Collecting funds
    c. Budgeting
    d. Obtaining funds
    e. Planning
    f. Controlling funds
    g. Managing taxes
    h. Advising top management

Learning Goal 2
2. a. Operating(master) budget
    b. Cash budget
    c. Capital budget
    d. Operating (master) budget

3. Strategic planning helps the firm to determine what businesses it should be in within the next 5-10 years. Decisions about which direction a company should take could not be made without some knowledge of the expense of entering certain markets, as well as the profit potential of those same markets. Long-term forecasts give top management some sense of the income or profit potential with different strategic plans.

Learning Goal 3

4.   Eric doesn't understand some basic ideas about financial management. Bill needs to explain the financial needs of all businesses: managing daily operations, managing accounts receivable, obtaining needed inventory (including inventory management) and major capital expenditures, and how a finance manager deals with each area.

One of the first things a finance manager will do is to see that funds are available to meet daily cash needs, without using too much cash and not being able to take advantage of other investments. So, bills are paid at the latest date possible to allow the firm to take advantage of interest-bearing accounts. Sun-2-Shade allows for credit purchases because it helps to keep their customers happy and helps to attract new customers. With effective collection procedures, selling on credit can be a benefit to the firm. It's important to keep inventories at a level necessary to fill orders, but too high an inventory level will tie up funds that could be used elsewhere for investment. Programs like just-in-time inventory help to reduce the amount of funds a firm must tie up in inventory.

There is no way to tell if the firm can afford to build a new plant in two years, but the finance manager will be able to evaluate the various alternatives, such as buying a facility, expanding on a current facility or building their own building.

Learning Goal 4

5.   a.   Factoring
             b.   Bank loan (inventory financing)
             c.   Promissory note
             d.   Commercial paper
             e.   Trade credit
             f.   Family and friends
             g.   credit card

6.   a.   Inventory financing
             b.   Revolving credit agreement
             c.   Secured loan
             d.   Unsecured loan
             e.   Line of credit
             f.   Commercial credit company

Learning Goal 5

7.   a.   Debt financing - bonds   g.   Equity financing - venture capital
             b.   Equity financing   h.   Equity financing - retained earnings
             c.   Equity financing - retained earnings   i.   Debt financing - bonds
             d.   Debt financing – loans, bonds   j.   Equity financing – venture capital
             e.   Debt financing - loans   k.   Debt financing – loans, bonds
             f.   Equity financing - stock

8.   Joel's point to Eric is that when you sell stock to the public, the common stockholders get voting rights, and management must answer to the stockholders because stockholders are owners, and they have voting rights. Creditors, such as lending institutions or bondholders generally have no say in running the business. The plus side of the equity financing is that there is no repayment obligation, as there is with debt financing, and the firm is not legally liable to pay dividends to the stockholders. Interest on debt is a legal obligation. However, the interest is tax deductible, whereas dividends are paid out of after-tax profits, and so are not deductible.

9. Leveraged buyouts occur when one firm purchases the assets of another using funds that were borrowed, either through selling bonds or obtaining loans, or a combination of both.

PRACTICE TEST

MULTIPLE CHOICE

LG 1 # 1-3
LG 2 # 4-7
LG 3 # 8-11
LG 4 # 12-15
LG 5 # 16-20

1.	d	11.	a
2.	a	12.	b
3.	b	13.	d
4.	a	14.	b
5.	b	15.	a
6.	a	16.	b
7.	d	17.	c
8.	d	18.	b
9.	a	19.	d
10.	b	20.	b

TRUE-FALSE

LG 1 # 1-3
LG 2 # 4-6
LG 3 #7-9
LG 4 #10-13
LG 5 #14-16

1.	T	9.	T
2.	F	10.	T
3.	T	11.	F
4.	F	12.	T
5.	T	13.	T
6.	T	14.	F
7.	T	15.	F
8.	T	16.	T

CHAPTER 19 – SECURITIES MARKETS: FINANCING AND INVESTING OPPORTUNTIES

LEARNING GOALS:

After you have read and studied this chapter you should be able to:

1. Identify and explain the functions of securities markets and discuss the role of investment bankers in securities markets.
2. Compare the advantages and disadvantages of debt financing by issuing bonds and identify the classes and features of bonds.
3. Compare the advantages and disadvantages of equity financing by issuing stock, and explain the differences between common and preferred stock.
4. Describe the various stock exchanges where securities are traded.
5. Explain how to invest in securities markets and various investment objectives such as long-term growth, income, cash, and protection from inflation.
6. Analyze the opportunities bonds offer as investments
7. Explain the opportunities stocks offer as investments.
8. Explain the opportunities in mutual funds and exchange-traded funds (ETFs) as investments, and the benefits of diversifying investments.
9. Discuss specific high-risk investments, including junk bonds, buying stock on margin, and commodity trading.
10. Explain securities quotations listed in the financial section of a newspaper and describe how stock market indicators like the Dow Jones Industrial Average affect the market.

LEARNING THE LANGUAGE

Listed below are important terms found in the chapter. Choose the correct term for the definition and write it in the space provided.

Bond	Futures markets	Preferred stock
Buying stock on margin	Initial public offering (IPO)	Program trading
Capital gains	Institutional investors	Prospectus
Commodity exchange	Interest	Securities and Exchange Commission (SEC)
Common stock	Investment bankers	Sinking fund
Debenture bond	Junk bonds	Stockbroker
Diversification	Maturity date	Stock certificate
Dividends	Mutual fund	Stock exchange
Dow Jones Industrial Average (the Dow)	(NASDAQ)	stocks
Exchange traded funds (ETFs)	Over-the-counter market (OTC)	Stock splits

1. _____ are commodities markets that involve the purchase and sale of goods for delivery sometime in the future.

2. Large investors known as _____ are organizations such as pension funds, mutual funds, insurance companies, and banks that invest their own funds or the funds of others.

3.	The _____is an exchange that provides a means to trade stocks not listed on national exchanges.

4.	Evidence of stock ownership called a _____ specifies the name of the company, the number of shares it represents, and the type of stock being issued.

5.	Trading known as _____ means giving instructions to computers to automatically sell if the price of stock dips to a certain point to avoid potential losses.

6.	The most basic form of ownership in a firm is _____, which confers voting rights and the right to share in the firm's profits through dividends, if offered by the firm's board of directors.

7.	A _____ is a reserve account in which the issuer of a bond periodically retires, some part of the bond principal prior to maturity so that enough capital will be accumulated by the maturity date to pay off the bond.

8.	A registered representative who works as a market intermediary known as a _____, buys and sells securities for clients.

9.	An organization that is known as a _____ is one whose members can buy and sell securities for companies and investors.

10.	The exact date the issuer of a bond must pay the principal to the bondholder is known as the _____.

11.	Stock called _____ gives its owner's preference in the payment of dividends and an earlier claim on assets than common stockholders if the business is forced out of business and its assets sold.

12.	Specialists called _____ assist in the issue and sale of new securities.

13.	The payment the issuer of a bond makes to the bondholders to pay for the use of borrowed money is called _____.

14.	A _____is a bond that is unsecured (i.e. not backed by any collateral.)

15.	The process of _____is the purchase of stocks by borrowing some of the purchase cost from the brokerage firm.

16.	The part of a firm's profits that may be distributed to stockholders as either cash payments or additional shares of stock are called _____.

17.	A _____is an action by a company that gives stockholders two or more shares of stock for each one they own.

18.	The technique of _____means buying several different investment alternatives to spread the risk of investing.

19.	Shares of ownership in a company are called _____.

20.   A _____ is an organization that buys stocks and bonds and then sells shares in those securities to the public.

21.   A corporate certificate called a _____ indicates that a person has lent money to a firm.

22.   The average cost of 30 selected industrial stocks called the _____ is used to give an indication of the direction of the stock market over time.

23.   A securities exchange called a _____ specializes in the buying and selling of precious metals and minerals and agricultural goods.

24.   The _____ is the federal agency that has the responsibility for regulating the various exchanges.

25.   A condensed version of economic and financial information called a _____ must be filed with the SEC before issuing stock; it must be sent to potential purchasers of the firm's stock.

26.   The _____ is a nationwide electronic system that communicates over-the-counter trades to brokers.

27.   _____ are the positive differences between the purchase price of a stock and its sale price.

28.   A (n) _____ is the first public offering of a corporation's stock.

29.   High-risk, high-interest bonds are called _____.

30.   Collections of stocks that are traded on exchanges are called _____, and are traded more like individual stocks than like mutual funds.

ASSESSMENT CHECK

Learning Goal 1
The Function of Securities Markets

1.   Describe the two major functions of securities markets.

     a.   _____

     b.   _____

2.   Explain the difference between the primary and the secondary markets

3. What functions do investment bankers perform for companies?

    a. _____

    b. _____

4. What are some examples of institutional investors?

Learning Goal 2
Debt Financing By Selling Bonds

5. What legal obligation does a company have when selling bonds?

6. What is meant by the term "coupon rate" with regard to bonds?

7. What factors affect the interest rate of a bond? Can the rate of interest change, once it has been set?

8. What is meant by the terms:

    a. denomination: _____

    _____

    b. principal: _____

    _____

9. If a $1,000 bond has an interest rate of 10% and a maturity date of 2020, what does that mean to a bondholder?

10. List the advantages of raising long-term capital by selling bonds.

 a. _____

 b. _____

 c. _____

 d. _____

11. What are the disadvantages?

 a. _____

 b. _____

 c. _____

12. Describe the two classes of corporate bonds.

13. Why are sinking funds attractive to firms and investors?

 a. _____

 b. _____

 c. _____

14. What the characteristics of a callable bond, and what is the benefit to a company?

15. What are the features of a convertible bond, and why would an investor convert a bond to common stock?

Learning Goal 3
Equity Financing By Selling Stock

16. What is meant by a stock's par value?

17. Describe the important elements of dividends. How are dividends different from interest paid on bonds?

18. List the advantages of raising funds through the sale of stock.

    a._____

    b._____

    c._____

19. Describe the disadvantages of issuing stock.

    a._____

    b._____

    c._____

20. What are the benefits of owning preferred stock?

    a._____

    b._____

21. Why is preferred stock referred to as a "hybrid investment"?

22. Describe how preferred stock dividends differ from common stock dividends.

    a._____

    b._____

    c._____

23. How is preferred stock like a bond?

24. How do preferred stock and bonds differ?

25. The special features of preferred stock are that it can be:

    a. _____

    b. _____

    c. _____

26. What are three rights of holders of common stock?

    a. _____

    b. _____

    c. _____

Learning Goal 4
Stock Exchanges

27. What are the two major national exchanges? Which one is referred to as the "Big Board"?

28. What does it mean when it is said that the NYSE and AMEX are "floor based exchanges."? How does this differ from the NASDAQ and over-the-counter trading?

29. What are regional exchanges?

30. Which exchange has the largest number of listings?

31. How does the Securities Act of 1933 protect investors?

32.   Discuss the provisions of the Securities and Exchange Act of 1934.

        a. _____

        b. _____

        c. _____

33.   Insider trading involves: _____

        _____

        The term "insider" includes: _____

        _____

34.   How is it possible for Americans to purchase stocks in foreign companies, and for
        foreigners to purchase stock in American companies?

Learning Goal 5
How to Invest in Securities

35.   How does a stockbroker trade securities?

36.   What is the benefit of trading on-line?

37.   What kind of customers use online trading?

38.   The first step in any investment program is to: _____

        _____

39.   Describe the five criteria to use when selecting an investment option.

   a. _____

   b. _____

   c. _____

   d. _____

   e. _____

Learning Goal 6
Investing in Bonds

40.   What are the best investments for those who desire low risk and guaranteed income?

41.   What are two questions first time bond investors may ask? What are the answers to the questions?

42.   What does it mean to sell a bond:

   at a discount? _____

   at a premium? _____

43.   As interest rates go up bond prices: _____

44.   In terms of interest rates, the higher the market risk of a bond, compared to other bonds:

   _____

   Investors will invest in a bond considered risky only if: _____

Learning Goal 7
Investing in Stocks

45.   According to investment analysts, what determines the market price of a stock?

46.   In the stock market, describe:

Bulls: _____

_____

Bears: _____

_____

47.   Describe:

a. Growth stocks: _____

_____

b. Income stocks: _____

_____

c. Blue chip stocks: _____

_____

d. Penny stocks: _____

_____

48.   What is the difference between a limit order and a market order?

49.   What is the difference between a round lot and an odd lot?

50.   Why would a company declare a stock split? How does a stock split work? How does a stock split benefit an investor?

Learning Goal 8
Investing in Mutual Funds and Exchange-Traded Funds

51.   What benefit does a mutual fund offer to an investor?

52.   What are the various types of mutual funds?

53.   Describe an index fund.

54.   What is the difference between a no-load and a load fund?

55.   What is the difference between an open-end fund and a closed-end fund?

56.   Discuss the primary characteristics of ETFs.

57.   Describe the type of investment strategy known as a portfolio strategy, or allocation model.

Learning Goal 9
Investing in High Risk Investments

58.   Why are junk bonds considered "junk"?

59.   What is a "margin"? What does a 50% margin rate mean?

60.   What is the downside of buying on margin?

61.   What kinds of items are traded on a commodity exchange?

62.   What kind of an investment are commodities, for most investors?

Learning Goal 10
Understanding Information from Securities Markets

63.   How is the price of a bond quoted?

64.   What information is included in a bond quote?

65.   What information is contained in a stock quote?

        a. _____

        b. _____

        c. _____

        d. _____

        e. _____

        f. _____

        g. _____

        h. _____

        i. _____

66. What information is contained in a mutual fund quote?

a. _____

b. _____

c. _____

d. _____

e. _____

f. _____

67. What is the net asset value, or NAV and how is it calculated?

68. What is a criticism of the Dow Jones Industrial Average? What do many investors prefer to follow instead of the Dow?

69. What happens in a stock market "crash" and how often has it happened?

70. What happened to stock market during the period 2000-2002? What do analysts many feel was the cause?

71 What are curbs and when are they put into effect?

72. What are circuit breakers and when are they put into effect?

73.   What investing challenges and changes do we face in the 21st century?

a. _____

b. _____

c. _____

d. _____

e. _____

f. _____

74.   What lessons can be learned from the stock market crashes in the past?

CRITICAL THINKING EXERCISES

Learning Goal 1

1.   Sun-2-Shade is a young company that makes self-darkening windshields for the automotive industry. The financial manager of Sun-2-Shade has convinced management that new capital is needed for future growth. He hasn't yet decided on whether or not to issue stocks or bonds, but he knows that he wants to avoid the difficulty of looking for and marketing to potential investors himself, and prefers to let "experts" perform those functions. How should he go about pursuing this issue?

Learning Goal 2

2.   In discussing bonds, there are several terms with which you need to be familiar:

Bond	Secured bonds
Interest	Sinking fund
Principal	Callable bond
Maturity date	Convertible bond
Unsecured bonds (debentures)	

Match the correct term to each of the following descriptions:

a. _____   Gerry Hoffman will receive this on the date her bond becomes due in the year 2010.

b. _____   Beth Galganski will receive the principle value of her bond on this date.

c. _____ Tom Huff is in finance with Sun-2-Shade. Each quarter Sun-2-Shade puts money in this fund to pay off previously issued bonds, and Tom checks the amount of money the company has in the fund to be sure the company can pay off their bond issue on the maturity date.

d. _____ Because it has declared bankruptcy in the past, and the future is uncertain, Bridge Financial Systems would probably not be able to issue this type of bond.

e. _____ Bonnie Andersen receives $100 per year from her bond because this is a 10% bond.

f. _____ Mobil Oil issued an unsecured one at 14.4 percent due in 2020.

g. _____ TNG Enterprises issued this kind of bond, because they forecasted a decline in interest rates in a few years, and wanted the flexibility of being able to pay off the bond early.

h. _____ Bill Paterson bought this type of bond because he anticipated exchanging it for common stock in the firm later.

i. _____ Caldwell Industries used real estate holdings as collateral for their bonds.

Learning Goals 2,3
3. As the finance manager of Sun-2-Shade, Eric the owner has come to you for advice about whether or not to issue stock, or bonds to raise new capital. What would you tell him about the advantages and disadvantages of each type of security?

4. In discussing stocks, there are several terms with which you need to be familiar:

    Stock   Pre-emptive right
    Stock certificate   Cumulative preferred stock
    Dividends   Common stock
    Preferred stock

    Match the correct term to each of the following:

    a. _____ Carmen Arauz was considering buying this type of stock, but was somewhat concerned about the risk when she learned that as a stockholder of this type, if the firm closed, she would be the last to share in the firm's assets.

    b. _____ When her grandson was born, Judi Burton bought 100 shares of her favorite stock, and gave his parents this, as evidence of his ownership, which showed the number of shares owned, the name of the company, and the type of stock.

    c. _____ As Judi's grandson Burke grew he received these periodic payments from his stock, which his parents invested for college.

    d. _____ When Judi was deciding which kind of stock to purchase, she decided upon this type, because the dividends are fixed and must be paid before other dividends are paid. Further, there are no voting rights with this type of stock.

    e. _____ What Burke doesn't have is this, which is the right of the stockholder to purchase new shares when the firm makes a new issue, so that his proportionate ownership in the company is maintained.

    f. _____ One of the advantages of Burke's stock is that if the company misses his dividend, the company must pay it before it pays any other, and the missed dividends accumulate.

    g. _____ Either common or preferred, this represents ownership in a firm.

5. Why do you think Judi Burton decided to buy her grandson Burke preferred stock instead of common stock?

Learning Goal 4

6. The three major stock exchanges in the United States are:

NYSE
AMEX
NASDAQ
OTC

Match the correct answer to each of the following statements.

a. _____ The largest stock exchange in the United States.

b. _____ Provides companies and investors with a means to trade stocks not listed on the national exchanges.

c. _____ Some large companies, like Microsoft are traded on this exchange as well as federal, state and city government bonds.

d. _____ Referred to as the Big Board.

e. _____ The second largest floor based exchange.

f. _____ Lists approximately 3,300 companies, including many technology companies.

g. _____ Recently merged with Archipelago, a securities trading company that specializes in electronic trading. This merger made this exchange a publicly traded company.

h. _____ A network of several thousand brokers, who maintain contact with each other and buy and sell securities through a nationwide electronic system.

Learning Goal 5

7. Five criteria to use when selecting a specific investment strategy are

Investment risk   Liquidity
Yield   Tax consequences
Duration

Read the following situations and evaluate the criteria in terms of the needs of the potential investors.

a. A young couple wants to invest money to begin a college tuition fund for their 5-year-old child. Since the child has no income, they are going to put the account in his name to avoid taxes.

b. A two-career couple; both anticipate retirement within the next five years.

c. A single person, just graduating from college; just starting a high paying job and wants to build capital. Not concerned about losing money at first.

Learning Goal 6

8. The managers of Sun-2-Shade are considering whether or not to issue stocks or bonds. Naturally, if the company issues bonds it wants to make sure that the bond is attractive for investors. What are the considerations that the managers need to look at to attract potential investors in their bonds? What will potential investors consider?

Learning Goals 7,8

9. As a potential investor in stocks, there are several terms used in securities trading with which you should be familiar:

Stockbroker	Stock splits
Growth stocks	Round lots
Income stocks	Margin calls
Blue chip stocks	Mutual funds
Penny stocks	ETFs
Market order	Diversification
Limit order	Bulls
Bears	Prospectus
Capital gains	Index fund
Buying on margin	

Match the term that would apply to the following descriptions:

a. _____ In 2006 Monsanto gave its stockholders one additional share of stock for every share they owned. This reduced the price from $80 per share to around $40 per share.

b. _____ Evelyn Minervi likes to dabble in the stock market. Last year she bought a number of stocks of this type, which each sold for $1.45 cents per share, but which were considered fairly risky.

c. _____ Joe Contino works in this job for a major brokerage firm, buying and selling stocks and bonds for his clients.

d. _____ Ron Stahl recently purchased this amount, exactly 100 shares, of Navistar stock.

e. _____ Dexter Inholt wanted to buy 500 shares of Ford at $40, each, but he only had $12,000 to invest, so he borrowed the $8,000 he still needed from his brokerage firm.

f. _____ The stock of Citigroup, which pays regular dividends and has had fairly consistent growth in its stock price, is considered this type of stock.

g. _____ Marina Vasquez called her broker and asked him to buy Pepsico stock at the best price he could get, under this type of order.

h. _____ Hong Le believed the stock market was going to take a big jump after the most recent national elections, and purchased the stocks she wanted in anticipation of stock price increases.

i. _____ Lee Kornfeld, a prosperous doctor, has a lot of money invested in the market. He recently called his broker and told her to buy the stock of several firms after the price went down to a certain level under this type of order.

j. _____ Dexter Inholt bought Pfizer stock on margin a few weeks ago. When Pfizer's stock took a slight dip in price, Dexter Inholt got worried that his broker would issue this and would ask him to come up with some money to cover the losses the stock suffered.

k. _____ LaTonya Adams is a first time investor, unfamiliar with the market. She wants to get into the market, but diversify her risk, and invest in lots of firms. Her brother advised her to get into one of these, because then an expert does the research and manages the fund.

l. _____ Because he is investing money for his son's college education, Tim Martin decided to invest in several public utilities, because they offer a high dividend yield for the investment and usually keep up with inflation.

m. _____ The Chesterfield Investment Club always sends for this document, which discloses the financial information of the firms in which the club is interested in investing.

n. _____ Monte McHewie sold many of the stocks he was holding after he heard some economic news that led him to believe prices in the stock market were going to decline soon, indicating this type of market.

o. _____ Lindsey Schopp has a portfolio that consists of 10 percent high-risk growth stocks, 40 percent mutual funds, 30 percent government bonds, and 20 percent commodities. Lindsey has focused on this in creating her portfolio.

p. _____ Casey Argetsinger bought several shares of a relatively new company, for $7.50 per share. The stock paid no dividend, but was in the biotechnology field, and was predicted to grow by 20 percent per year over the next 10 years.

q. _____ When Ben and Casey Miller decided to buy a house, they sold a number of the stocks they had been holding. They found that there was a significant difference between what they paid for the stock, and the price at which they were able to sell it. So much so, that they were able to make a substantial down payment on their new house. This difference in selling prices was called their _____.

r. _____ Chad Mueller is 21 years old, and working at his first job out of college. He knows the value of saving money early, and wants to start investing now in mutual funds. He has decided on this type of fund, one that focuses on certain kinds of stock which covers the whole stock market.

s. _____ Samantha Glenn is a new investor who has decided to try a new way to diversify. Samantha is focusing on this kind of investment, which is a collection of stocks that unlike a mutual fund can be trading throughout the entire trading day, offering Samantha more flexibility than a mutual fund.

Learning Goal 9
10. Whereas the stock exchanges trade securities, commodities exchanges specialize in buying and selling goods such as grains, livestock, metals, natural resources and foreign currency. Jordan Reish has a large farm in the Midwest. His primary crop is corn. Jordan usually sells the crop he will plant in the spring and harvest in the summer, in the fall before the crop is even planted. General Mills is always happy to see Jordan and others like him selling their unplanted crops, and spends a good deal of time buying these futures contracts. What are Jordan and General Mills doing, and why?

11.　The financial section of the Wall Street Journal contains stock and bond quotes, the Dow Jones Index and mutual fund quotes. Complete the following exercises, using the Wall Street Journal, or your local newspaper , or online, at a variety of sites, such as www.excite.com , www.yahoo.com www.motleyfool.com or, for mutual funds, at www.morningstar.com .

a.　Get the stock quotes for a company of your choice and get the following information.

1.　What was the actual price of the stock at the close of the day?　＿＿＿＿＿＿＿＿＿

2.　What was the net change in dollars?　＿＿＿＿＿＿＿＿＿

3.　What was the highest price the stock traded for in the previous year?＿＿＿＿＿＿＿

4.　How many shares were traded that day?　＿＿＿＿＿＿＿＿＿

5.　What is the company's earnings per share?　＿＿＿＿＿＿＿＿＿

6.　What is the P/E ratio for this company?　＿＿＿＿＿＿＿＿＿
Click on Key Statistics for this company.

7.　What was the last dividend paid and when was it paid?　＿＿＿＿＿＿＿＿＿

8.　When was the last stock split, and what was the split factor?　＿＿＿＿＿＿＿＿＿

b.　Go to www.yahoo.com and click on finance. Click on mutual funds.
Choose a mutual fund and answer the following questions:

1. What is the net asset value?　＿＿＿＿＿＿＿＿＿

2. Is this a "no load" fund?　＿＿＿＿＿＿＿＿＿

3. What is the fund family?　＿＿＿＿＿＿＿＿＿

4. What is the year to date return?　＿＿＿＿＿＿＿＿＿

5. What is the Morningstar rating?　＿＿＿＿＿＿＿＿＿

6. What is the minimum investment?　＿＿＿＿＿＿＿＿＿

d.　Look at the Dow Jones Industrial Average during the time your class is studying this chapter. Answer the following questions:

1. Have stock prices trended up or down over the last 6 months?

2. What was the highest Dow Jones Industrial Average in the last 6 months?

3. What was the lowest?

PRACTICE TEST

MULTIPLE CHOICE – Circle the best answer

Learning Goal 1

1.   One of the major functions of the securities markets is to:
    a.   advertise the sale of stocks and bonds of major corporations.
    b.   provide long term funding for corporations.
    c.   assist businesses in finding long-term funding to finance business expansion or buying major goods and services.
    d.   provide investors with information regarding the value of stock and bond issues offered by major corporations.

2.   Which of the following statements is not true?
    a.   The only time a corporation receives the money from the sale of stock is after the IPO.
    b.   The IPO is handled in the secondary market.
    c.   The first public offering of a corporation's stock is called an IPO.
    d.   Investors buy and sell stocks in the secondary market.

3.   An investment-banking firm underwrites a new issue of stocks and bonds by:
    a.   buying the entire bond or stock issue a company wants to sell at an agreed discount.
    b.   guaranteeing a minimum price in the market for a stock or bond.
    c.   selling the entire bond issue for the issuing firm in global markets.
    d.   putting up collateral for long term loans, such as bonds.

Learning Goal 2

4.   Which of the following is not considered an advantage of selling bonds?
    a.   The debt is eventually eliminated when the bonds are paid off.
    b.   Interest on the bonds is not a legal obligation.
    c.   Bondholders have no say in running the firm.
    d.   interest is tax deductible.

5.   Issuing a _____ permits a bond issuer to pay off the bond's principal prior to its maturity date.
    a.   sinking fund
    b.   convertible bond
    c.   callable bond
    d.   maturity date

6.   On the maturity date of a bond, the issuing company will pay:
    a.   the bondholder the bond principal in full.
    b.   the investment banking firm the sinking fund.
    c.   the bondholder the interest accrued for the duration of the bond.
    d.   a dividend to the institutional investors.

Learning Goal 3

7.   One of the disadvantages of issuing stock is that:
    a.   the company is legally obligated to pay dividends.
    b.   stockholders have the right to vote for the board of directors.
    c.   selling stock hurts the condition of the balance sheet since it creates debt.
    d.   Stockholder investments must be repaid.

8. Daddy Warbucks bought his daughter Annie some stock for her birthday. The type of stock Daddy bought has a fixed dividend, and if the dividend isn't paid when it is due, the missed dividend will accumulate and be paid later. Daddy bought Annie
    a. common stock
    b. preferred stock
    c. convertible stock
    d. preemptive right stock

9. Dividends are paid:
    a. based on the prevailing market price of the stock.
    b. before a firm pays interest to bondholders.
    c. as determined by the stockholders.
    d. from a firm's profits.

Learning Goal 4
10. Which stock exchange is a network of several thousand brokers who maintain contact with one another and buy and sell securities though an electronic system of communication?
    a. NASDAQ
    b. NYSE
    c. AMEX
    d. Chicago exchange

11. The largest exchange in the United States is the:
    a. NASDAQ
    b. NYSE
    c. AMEX
    d. Chicago exchange

12. When the International Ladies Investment Club is deciding on which stock to purchase, the Club will often request a _____ before making that decision.
    a. insider report
    b. income statement
    c. prospectus
    d. disclosure statement

Learning Goal 5
13. One of the benefits of trading on-line is that:
    a. investing on-line is more accurate.
    b. when you invest on-line you are more likely to make a good decision.
    c. on-line trading services is less expensive than regular stockbroker commissions.
    d. insider trading is less likely on-line.

14. Linda Hutton is considering investing in the stock market. Linda wants to be sure to be able to get her money back whenever she wants. Linda is concerned with:
    a. growth
    b. yield
    c. tax consequences
    d. liquidity

Learning Goal 6
15.   The best type of bond for an investor who wants low risk is:
        a. a premium bond.
        b. a U.S. government bond.
        c. a discount bond.
        d. a callable bond.

16.   A bond that sells for more than face value is called a
        a. premium bond
        b. U.S. government bond
        c. discount bond
        d. callable bond

Learning Goal 7
17.   Maria Chadwick is interested in investing in the stock of a corporation that pays regular
        dividends and generates consistent growth in the price of a share. Maria is interested in
        purchasing
        a. growth stocks
        b. income stocks
        c. blue chip stocks
        d. penny stocks

18.   When the price of a share of U.S. On Line went up to $150 per share, the company
        declared a 3 for 1 stock split. The price of a share of U.S. On Line stock is now
        approximately:
        a. $100 per share
        b. $75 per share
        c. $50 per share
        d. $25 per share

19.   Irena Dadiavich bought several shares of Google stock a couple of years ago for around
        $100. When Irena saw that Google was selling for over $400 a share she decided to sell
        all of her shares and take the profits to buy a new car. The difference between the price
        at which Irena bought the stock and the price at which she sold it is called:
        a. a market order
        b. capital gains
        c. a bear market
        d. premium

Learning Goal 8
20.   The benefit of a mutual fund for investors is that
        a. mutual funds help investors to diversify and invest in many different companies.
        b. an investor doesn't have to do as much research.
        c. mutual funds are less expensive than most individual shares of stock.
        d. mutual funds don't charge a commission or up-front fee.

21.   An index fund is a mutual fund that:
        a. guarantees dividends
        b. offers a minimum return
        c. only invests in stocks listed on the Dow Jones Industrial Average
        d. invests only in certain kinds of stock.

Learning Goal 9

22. Adam Culbreath wanted to invest in the stock market, but didn't have the entire $10,000 he needed to buy the shares of the company he wanted. Adam does have $7,000, so he decided to borrow the remainder in order to be able to buy the stock he wanted. Adam:
    a. is investing in junk bonds.
    b. is buying on margin.
    c. is completely safe as he can always count on the price of his stock to go up.
    d. is interested in diversification.

Learning Goal 10

23. If the paper reports the corporate bond price as 89 ½, the price an investor would have to pay is:
    a. $890.50
    b. $8950
    c. $895
    d. $89.50

24. Which of the following is not included in a stock quote?
    a. The last dividend paid per share.
    b. The P/E ratio.
    c. The average price for the last year
    d. The highest and lowest price the stock has sold for over the past 52 weeks.

25. The Dow Jones Industrial Average:
    a. identifies recessions from the last 30 years.
    b. gives an indication of the ups and downs of the stock market over time.
    c. compiles average stock prices of all stocks on the NYSE.
    d. shows the average stock price of 20 stocks for the last year.

TRUE-FALSE

Learning Goal 1

1. _____ In the securities markets, the secondary markets handle the sale of previously issued securities between investors.

2. _____ An institutional investor is a large investor who buys the entire bond or stock issues a company wants to sell.

Learning Goal 2

3. _____ A company is legally bound to pay the interest on a bond, but not the principal amount.

4. _____ A sinking fund is a provision allowing for a company to pay off a bond prior to its maturity date.

5. _____ Bonds are almost always issued on denominations of $1,000

Learning Goal 3

6. _____ Dividends are declared by a company's board of directors.

7. _____ Common stock normally does not include voting rights.

8. _____ Preferred stock can be convertible to shares of common stock.

Learning Goal 4

9. _____ The Securities and Exchange Commission is responsible for regulating activities in the various exchanges.

10. _____ Insider trading involves the use of knowledge or information that individuals gain through their position that allows them to benefit unfairly from fluctuations in security prices.

11. _____ Investors in the United States are unable to invest in foreign companies, and vice versa.

Learning Goal 5

12. _____ A stockbroker is a registered representative who acts as an intermediary to buy and sell stocks for clients

13. _____ A young person saving for retirement can afford to invest in higher risk stocks than a person who is nearing retirement age.

14. _____ One of the major criteria to consider when investing is duration, which is the amount of time your money is committed to that investment.

Learning Goal 6

15. _____ In general, as interest rates go up, bond rates will also rise.

16. _____ The higher the market risk of a bond, compared to other bonds, the higher the interest rate the issuer of the bond may offer to investors.

Learning Goal 7

17. _____ "Bulls" are investors who believe that stock prices are going to rise, so they buy in anticipation of the increase.

18. _____ Companies may offer a stock split when the price of their stock is too high and the company wants to stock to be more desirable in the market.

19. _____ A market order tells a broker to buy or sell a particular stock at a specific price.

Learning Goal 8

20. _____ Mutual funds are probably the best way for smaller investors to get started.

21. _____ The portfolio strategy, or allocation model refers to a strategy of diversified investment.

Learning Goal 9

22. _____ Buying stock on margin means borrowing stock from a stockbroker, selling it, then buying the stock back at a lower price than what you paid.

Learning Goal 10

23. _____ One of the items found in a stock quote will be the highest price paid in the last 52 weeks.

24. ____ Many investors believe the Dow is not an accurate measure of stock prices, and prefer to follow a stock index such as Standard and Poors 500.

You Can Find It On The Net

How much would you have made, or lost, if you had invested in the stock market a year ago? Go to **www.yahoo.com** , and click on Finance/Quotes. Go down to historical quotes, and follow the instructions. Alternatively, do a search of the yahoo site for historical stock price quotes. This should get you to the correct page.

If you had purchased $1000 of a blue chip stock, such as Coca-Cola, General Electric or IBM exactly one year ago, what would your capital gain, or loss, be as of today?

Calculate the same information for a technology related company, such as Cisco, Microsoft or Yahoo.com Would you have a capital gain? How much?

Now, visit an online broker such as www.etrade.com or www.ameritrade.com How do their fees compare to trading online with a discount broker such as Charles Schwab – www.charlesschwab.com, or a traditional broker such as A.G. Edwards www.agedwards.com

ANSWERS

LEARNING THE LANGUAGE

1. Futures market	11. Preferred stock	21. Bond
2. Institutional investors	12. Investment bankers	22. Dow Jones Industrial Average
3. Over the counter market (OTC)	13. Interest	23. Commodity Exchange
4. Stock certificate	14. Debenture bond	24. Securities and Exchange Commission (SEC)
5. Program trading	15. Buying stock on margin	25. Prospectus
6. Common stock	16. Dividends	26. (NASDAQ)
7. Sinking fund	17. Stock split	27. Capital gains
8. Stockbroker	18. Diversification	28. Initial Public Offering (IPO)
9. Stock exchange	19. Stocks	29. Junk bonds
10. Maturity date	20. Mutual fund	30. Exchange-traded funds (ETFs)

ASSESSMENT CHECK

Learning Goal 1
The Functions of Securities Markets

1. Two major functions of securities markets are:
   a. to assist businesses in finding long-term funding they need to finance operations, expand their businesses, or buy goods and services.
   b. to give investors a place to buy and sell investments such as stocks and bonds to help build their financial future.

2. The primary market handles the sale of new securities. This is the only time corporations make money on the sale of securities. After the corporation has made its money, the secondary market handles the trading of securities between investors. The proceeds of sales in the secondary market go to the investor selling the stock, not to the corporation whose stock is sold.

3. Investment bankers
   a. help companies prepare the extensive financial analyses necessary to gain SEC approval for stock or bond issues.
   b. underwrite new issues, which means that the investment banker will buy the entire bond or stock issue a company wants to sell at an agreed upon discount and then sell the issue to private or institutional investors at full price.

4. Institutional investors are mutual funds, pension funds, insurance companies and banks. Because they have such large buying power, they are a powerful force in the securities markets.

Learning Goal 2
Debt Financing By Selling Bonds

5. A company that issues bonds has a legal obligation to pay regular interest payments to investors and repay the entire bond principal amount at a prescribed time, called the maturity date.

6.	The interest rate paid on bonds is also called the bond's coupon rate.

7.	The interest rate paid on a bond varies according to factors such as the state of the economy, the reputation of the company issuing the bond, and the going interest rate being paid by U.S. government bonds or bonds of similar companies. Once an interest rate is set it can't be changed.

8.	a.	Denomination is the amount of debt represented by one bond. Bonds are almost always issued in multiples of $1,000

	b.	Principal is the face value of a bond. The issuer of a bond is legally required to repay the bond principal to the bondholder in full on the maturity date.

9.	A 10% bond with a maturity date of 2020 means that the bondholder will receive $100 in interest per year until the year 2020, when the full principal, most likely $1000, must be repaid. Interest is usually paid in two installments each year.

10.	a.	Bondholders are not owners of a firm so they have no vote on corporate matters.
	b.	The interest paid on bonds is tax deductible for the firm.
	c.	Bonds are a temporary source of funding. They are eventually repaid, and the debt is eliminated.
	d.	Bonds can be repaid before the maturity date if they contain a call provision, and can also be convertible to common stock.

11.	a.	Bonds are an increase in debt and could adversely affect the firm.
	b.	Interest on bonds is a legal obligation. If interest isn't paid, bondholders can take legal action.
	c.	The face value of bonds must be repaid at maturity, which could cause cash flow problems.

12.	Unsecured bonds, called debentures, are not supported by any collateral. Generally only firms with excellent credit ratings can issue debentures. The other class of bonds, secured bonds, is backed by some tangible asset, or collateral, that is pledged to the bondholder if bond interest isn't paid.

13.	Sinking funds are attractive to firms and investors because:
	a.	They provide for an orderly retirement of a bond issue.
	b.	They reduce the risk of not being repaid, and so make the bond more attractive as an investment.
	c.	They can support the market price of a bond because of reduced risk.

14.	A callable bond permits the bond issuer to pay off the bond's principal before its maturity date. Callable bonds give companies some discretion in long-term forecasting. The company can benefit if they call in a bond issue that pays a high rate of interest, and re-issue new bonds at a lower rate of interest.

15.	A convertible bond is a bond that can be converted into shares of common stock in the issuing company. If the value of the firm's common stock grew in value over time, bondholders can compare the value of the bond's interest with the possibility of a sizable profit by converting to a specified number of common shares.

16. A stock's par value is a dollar amount assigned to each share of stock by the corporation's charter. Some states use par value as a basis for calculating the state's incorporation charges and fees. Today most companies issue "no-par" stock.

17. Dividends are a part of a firm's profits that <u>may</u> be distributed to shareholders. Dividends are declared by a corporation's board of directors and are generally paid quarterly. Unlike bond interest, which is a legal obligation, companies are not required to pay dividends.

18. The advantages of raising funds through the sale of stock are:
    a. Because stockholders are owners, they never have to be repaid.
    b. There is no legal obligation to pay dividends.
    c. Selling stock can improve the condition of the balance sheet because it creates no debt.

19. The disadvantages of issuing stock are:
    a. As owners, stockholders can alter the direction of the firm, through voting for the board of directors.
    b. Dividends are paid out of after tax profits.
    c. Management decision-making can be hampered by the need to keep the stockholders happy.

20. Owners of preferred stock:
    a. have a preference in the payment of dividends.
    b. have a prior claim on company assets if the firm goes out of business.

21. Preferred stock is referred to as a hybrid investment because it has characteristics of both bonds and stocks. For example, preferred stock does not normally include voting rights in the firm.

22. Preferred stock dividends differ from common stock dividends in several ways.
    a. Preferred stock is generally issued with a par value that becomes the base for the dividend the firm is willing to pay.
    b. The owner is assured that the dividends on preferred stock must be paid in full before any common stock dividends can be distributed.
    c. Common stock dividends are declared by the board of directors, and may or may not be declared in any given quarter.

23. Both preferred stock and bonds have a face (or par) value and both have a fixed rate of return. Preferred stocks are rated by Standard and Poors and Moody's Investment Service just like bonds.

24. As debt, companies are legally bound to pay bond interest and must repay the face value of the bond on its maturity date. Even though preferred stock dividends are generally fixed, they do not legally have to be paid, and stock never has to be repurchased. Though both bonds and stock can increase in market value, the price of stock generally increases at a higher percentage than a bond.

25. The special features of preferred stock are that it can be:
   a. Callable, like bonds. This means a company could require preferred stockholders to sell back their shares.
   b. Convertible to common stock.
   c. Cumulative. If one or more dividends are not paid when due, the missed dividends of cumulative preferred stock will accumulate and be paid later.

26. Three rights of common stockholders are:
   a. the right to vote for the board of directors and important issues affecting the company.
   b. to share in the firm's profits though dividends declared by the board of directors.
   c. preemptive right, which is the first right to purchase any new shares of common stock the firm decides to issue. This right allows common stockholders to maintain a proportional share of ownership in the company.

Learning Goal 4
Stock Exchanges

27. The two major national exchanges are the New York Stock Exchange (NYSE) and the American Stock Exchange (AMEX). The New York Stock Exchange is the largest, and is referred to as the Big Board. These are referred to as national exchanges because they handle stocks from all over the country.

28. A floor based exchange means that trades take place on the floor of the stock exchange. The OTC and NASDAQ markets make trades though a telecommunications network which links dealers so that they can trade securities electronically rather than in person.

29. Regional exchanges deal mostly with firms in their own areas and handle the stock of many large corporations listed on the New York exchange. They are often used by institutional investors since transaction costs are less than those of large exchanges.

30. The New York Stock Exchange lists the largest companies, while the NASDAQ has the largest number of listings.

31. The Securities Act of 1933 protects investors by requiring full disclosure of financial information by firms selling new stocks or bonds. Congress passed this act to deal with the "free-for-all" atmosphere that existed during the Roaring Twenties.

32. The Securities and Exchange Act of 1934:
   a. created the Securities and Exchange Commission, which has the responsibility at the federal level for regulating activities in the various exchanges.
   b. companies trading on the national exchange must register with the SEC and provide annual updates.
   c. established guidelines companies must follow when issuing stock, and guidelines to prevent insiders from taking advantage of privileged information.

33. Insider trading involves the use of knowledge or information that individuals gain through their position that allows them to benefit unfairly from fluctuations in security prices.

   The term "insider" includes just about anyone with securities information that is not available to the general public.

34. Stock exchanges operate all over the world, and expanded communications and the relaxation of legal barriers enable investors to buy securities from companies almost anywhere in the world. A significant number of foreign companies are listed on the NYSE. Foreign investors can easily invest in U.S. securities because exchanges in foreign countries trade large amounts of U.S. securities. The number of U.S. companies that are listed on foreign stock exchanges is growing.

Learning Goal 5
How to Invest in Securities

35. Stockbrokers place an order with a stock exchange member who goes to the place at the exchange where the bond or stock is traded and negotiates a price. When the transaction is completed, the trade is reported to your broker who notifies you to confirm your purchase. The same procedures are followed if you sell stocks or bonds.

36. On-line trading services are less expensive than regular stockbroker commissions.

37. Customers interested in online trading services are primarily those who are willing to do their own research and make their own investment decisions without the assistance of a broker. The leading online brokerage services provide market information but no advice.

38. The first step in any investment program is to analyze such factors as desired income, cash requirements, growth prospects, level of risk, and hedging against inflation.

39. The five criteria to use when selecting an investment option are:
    a. Investment risk – the chance that your investment could go down in value in the future.
    b. Yield - the rate of return.
    c. Duration – the length of time for which you are committing your assets.
    d. Liquidity – how quickly you can get back your money if you need to.
    e. Tax consequences – how the investment affects your tax situation.

Learning Goal 6
Investing in Bonds

40. For those who desire low risk and guaranteed income, U.S. Government bonds are a secure investment backed by the full faith and credit of the federal government. Municipal bonds are also secure, and are offered by local governments, and often have advantages such as tax free interest.

41. Two questions first time bond investors have are
    a. "If I purchase a bond, do I have to hold it to the maturity date?" The answer is no. However if you decide to sell your bond before its maturity date, you are not guaranteed to get the face value of the bond.
    b. " How do I know how risky a particular bond issue is as an investment?" Standard and Poor's and Moody's Investor Service rate the level of risk of many corporate and government bonds.

42. A discount is a price less than face value. If your bond does not have features that make it attractive to other investors, you may have to sell your bond at a discount.
    A premium is a price above face value. If the bond is highly valued, you may be able to sell it at a premium.

43. As interest rates go up, bond prices fall, and as interest rates go down, bond prices go up.

44. In terms of interest rates, the higher the market risk of a bond, compared to other bonds, the higher the interest rate the issuer of the bond must offer to investors.

   Investors will invest in bonds considered risky only if the potential return to them is high enough.

Learning Goal 7
Investing in Stocks

45. According to investment analysts, the market price of a common stock is dependent upon the overall performance of the corporation in meeting its business objectives.

46. Stock investors are called bulls when they believe that stock prices are going to rise, so they buy stock in anticipation of the increase. When overall stock prices are rising, it is called a bull market.

   Bears are investors who believe that stock prices are going to decline. These investors sell their stocks before they expect prices to fall. When the prices of stocks decline steadily, it is referred to as a bear market.

47. a. Growth stocks are stocks of corporations whose earnings are expected to grow at a rate faster than other stocks. They are often considered risky, but they offer investors the potential for high returns.
   b. Income stocks offer investors a high dividend yield on their investment.
   c. Blue chip stocks are the stock of high quality companies. They pay regular dividends and generate consistent growth in the company stock price.
   d. Penny stocks sell for less than $2. These stocks are considered very risky investments.

48. A market order tells a broker to buy or to sell a stock immediately at the best price available. A limit order tells the broker to buy or to sell a particular stock at a specific price if that price becomes available.

49. Companies and brokers prefer to have stock purchases conducted in *round lots*, which are purchases of 100 shares at a time. Investors often buy stock in *odd lots* which are purchases of less than 100 shares at a time.

50. When investors cannot afford to buy shares of stock in companies selling for a high price, the company may choose to declare a stock split; that is, they issue two or more shares for every share of stock currently outstanding. This has the effect of dropping the price of a share, proportionately. For example, if a stock was selling for $150 and you had one share, after a two for one stock split, you would have two shares, and each share would be valued at about $75. This may increase demand for the stock, which may cause the price to go up in the near future.

Learning Goal 8
Investing in Mutual Funds and Exchange-Traded Funds

51. The benefit of a mutual fund to an investor is they can buy shares of the mutual fund and share in the ownership of many different companies they could not afford to invest in individually. Thus mutual funds help investors diversify.

52. Mutual funds range from very conservative funds that invest only in government securities or secure corporate bonds to others that specialize in emerging high-tech firms, Internet companies, foreign companies, precious metals, and other investments with greater risk. Some mutual funds even invest only in socially responsible companies.

53. An index fund is a fund that invests in a certain kind of stock. The most recommended is an index fund that covers the whole stock market.

54. A no-load fund is one that charges no commission to either buy or sell its shares. A load fund would charge a commission to investors.

55. An open-end fund will accept the investment of any interested investors. Closed-end funds offer a specific number of shares for investment. Once the fund reaches its target number, no new investors are admitted into the fund.

56. ETFs are similar to mutual funds in that they are collections of stocks that are traded on exchanges. Unlike mutual funds, ETFs can be traded throughout the entire trading day, like individual stocks. Advantages include more flexibility, and lower fees than mutual funds.

Learning Goal 9
57. A portfolio strategy, or allocation model involves a strategy of buying several different investment alternatives to spread the risk of investing. The term for this is diversification. By diversifying investments, the investor decreases the chance of losing everything.

Learning Goal 9
Investing in High Risk Investments

58. Standard & Poor's Investment Advisory Service and Moody's Investor Service consider junk bonds as non-investment grade bonds because of their high-risk and high default rates. Junk bonds rely on the firm's ability to pay investors interest, and strong cash flow. If the company can't pay off the bond, the investor is left with a bond that isn't worth more than the paper it's written on.

59. The margin is the amount of money an investor must invest in a stock purchase. If a margin rate is 50 percent, an investor may borrow 50 percent of the stock's purchase price from a broker.

60. The downside of buying on margin is that investors must repay the credit extended by the broker, plus interest. If an investor's account goes down in market value, the broker will issue a margin call, requiring the investor to come up with more money to cover the losses the stock has suffered. If the investor is unable to make the margin call, the broker can legally sell shares of the investor's stock to reduce the broker's chance of loss.

61. Items such as coffee, wheat, pork bellies, petroleum, and other commodities that are scheduled for delivery at a given date in time are traded on the commodities market. A commodity exchange specializes in the buying and selling of precious metals and minerals, and agricultural goods. Other commodities include corn, plywood, silver, gold, U.S. Treasury bonds, potatoes, cattle, and various foreign currencies.

62. Commodities markets are high risk investments, and trading in commodities is not for the novice investor.

Learning Goal 10
Understanding Information From Securities Markets

63. A bond price is quoted as a percentage of $1000.

64. A bond quote in the paper contains the name of the company issuing the bond, the interest rate, whether or not this is a convertible bond, the maturity date, the price of the bond, the volume of bonds sold that day, and the current yield.

65. A stock quote will contain the following information:
    a. The percent of change in the stock's price for the year to date
    b. The highest and lowest price over the past 52 weeks
    c. The company name and stock symbol
    d. Last dividend per share
    e. The dividend yield
    f. The price/earnings (P/E) ratio
    g. The number of shares traded that day
    h. The closing price for the day
    i. The net change of the stock price from the previous day

66. The information contained in a mutual fund quote includes:
    a. Name of the fund family
    b. Price at which a fund's share can be purchased or sold, called the Net Asset Value (NAV)
    c. Name of the specific fund
    d. Rate of percentage return of the fund year to date
    e. Change from the previous day's NAV
    f. Rate of percentage return of the fund for the past three years

67. The Net Asset Value, NAV, is the market value of the mutual fund's portfolio divided by the number of shares it has outstanding. The NAV is the price per share of the mutual fund.

68. Critics of the Dow Jones Average argue that if the purpose of the Dow is to give an indication of the direction of the broader market over time, the 30-company sample is too small to get a good statistical representation. Many investors and market analysts prefer to follow stock indexes like the Standard and Poor's 500 that tracks the performance of many more companies. Investors also closely follow the NASDAQ.

69. A stock market crash occurs when the stock market loses a significant part of its value in a single day. The largest crashes occurred in 1929, 1987, and 1997.

70. The Dow, S&P and NASDAQ declined significantly during the early 2000s, although there wasn't a significant one-day crash. Investors lost trillions of dollars in market value from 2000-2002.

There are many different opinions as to what caused the crashes of 1929, 1987, 1997 and the decline during the 2000-2002 period. Many analysts believe that program trading was a big cause of the stock market drop in 1987. In program trading, investors give computers instructions to automatically sell if the price of their stock dips to a certain price to avoid potential losses.

71. Program trading curbs are put into effect when the Dow moves up or down more than a certain number of points (2 percent of the previous quarter's average value.) Basically this means a key computer is turned off so program trading must be done by hand, rather than automatically by computer.

72. Circuit breakers are more drastic restrictions than curbs, and are triggered when the Dow falls 10, 20, or 30 percent in one day. Depending upon the rate of decline and the time of day the circuit breakers will halt trading between a half hour and two hours to give traders a chance to assess the situation. If the Dow drops 30 percent trading closes for the entire day.

73. The challenges that investors face in the 21st century include
   a. the possibility of terrorist attacks.
   b. closely linked global economies.
   c. Investor confidence and trust in corporations and the stock market have eroded.
   d. mistrust of investment analysts who were overly optimistic in company evaluations.
   e. there is intense competition between the NYSE and the NASDAQ.
   f. traditional brokers are changing the way they do business due to challenges from online brokers.

74. Lessons to be learned are the importance of diversifying your investments and understanding the risks of investing with borrowed money that may have to be repaid quickly when prices fall. It is also wise to take a long-term perspective. It's important to do research, keep up with the news, and make use of investment resources such as newspapers, magazines, newsletters, the Internet, and TV programs.

CRITICAL THINKING EXERCISES

1. The finance manager of Sun-2-Shade has the opportunity to avoid the difficulties of a new issue by making use of specialists in the securities markets such as investment bankers. These companies will underwrite the new issue, by purchasing the entire issue for a discount. The investment banker will then sell the issue on the open market to either private or institutional investors, such as pension funds, mutual funds, insurance companies, or banks.

Learning Goal 2
2. a. Principal
    b. Maturity date
    c. Sinking fund
    d. Unsecured bond (debenture)
    e. Interest

   f. Bond
   g. Callable bond
   h. Convertible bond
   i. Secured bond

3. As we learned in previous chapters, one of the jobs of a finance manager is to determine the best way for a firm to raise long-term capital. When deciding which form of long-term funding is best a finance manager will weigh the options of both equity and debt funding.

You will probably tell Eric that bonds offer several long term financing advantages. Perhaps one of the most important to Eric will be that bondholders are not owners of the firm, so they won't have a vote on corporate matters. So, Eric and his management team will maintain control over the firm. Other benefits include the fact that bond interest is tax deductible, and that eventually the debt will be repaid. If interest rates are high when the bonds are issued, they can be called and re-issued when rates have lowered.

Conversely, when the firm goes into debt by issuing bonds, there could be an adverse affect on the market's perception of the firm. If for some reason a cash flow problem develops, interest is a legal obligation, and the firm would still have to pay interest, even with a negative cash flow, and provisions have to be made for when the face value has to be paid off. This could also negatively affect cash flow.

Stocks offer the opportunity for a firm to stay out of debt, and there is no legal obligation to pay dividends. Selling stock can also improve the look of the balance sheet.

The downside of stock issues is that the structures of ownership changes and stockholders have the right to vote on the board of directors, and sometimes decisions have to be made with the primary goal of keeping stockholders happy. Eric may not want to give up his ownership control. Another downside is that dividends, if paid, are not tax deductible.

Learning Goal 3
4. a. Common stock
   b. Stock certificate
   c. Dividends
   d. Preferred stock
   e. Pre-emptive right
   f. Cumulative preferred
   g. Stock

5. While both forms of stock represent ownership, there are several differences between preferred and common stock. First, an owner of common stock has the right to vote, and so can influence corporate policy. Judi probably did not consider this to be important, as Burke was a baby, and wouldn't really be concerned about such things! Further, common stock is considered to be more risky than preferred, because if a company closes, common stockholders share in assets only <u>after</u> bondholders and preferred stockholders. Also, while preferred dividends are fixed, and sometimes accumulate, common stock dividends will only be paid after both bondholders and preferred stockholders receive their interest and dividends. If Judi was interested in starting a "college fund" for Burke, then the preferred stock was a better match for her needs.

Learning Goal 4
6. a. NYSE
   b. OTC
   c. NASDAQ
   d. NYSE
   e. AMEX
   f. NASDAQ
   g. NYSE
   h. OTC

7. a. This couple would probably want a low to moderate risk investment, which will increase their principal over time. Tax consequences will be minimal, at least at first, as the child will have little income in the early years. (If they opt for an interest or dividend bearing type of account, the child will be earning income, and tax consequences may become a more important consideration). They will choose an investment that will yield a high return over the long run, and liquidity isn't important for now.

    b. Since this investment may be for retirement, this couple will probably want a low risk investment, with as high an after-tax yield as they can earn. It will be of short duration, since they plan to retire in five years, and they may want to keep it fairly liquid in case they retire in less than five years. A big factor will be the tax consequences, as they are a two-income family, and are probably in a high tax bracket with few deductions.

    c. A young, single person will choose a higher risk investment than the others, because they probably are not concerned with long-term considerations such as retirement. Since they want to build capital, the yield will be important for the short term. This individual may want to keep investments of short duration to make a large return in a few years, when they may want the money as a down payment for a house, for example, and they may want them fairly liquid. Tax consequences will be important, as there are few deductions, and they may be in a relatively high bracket

Learning Goal 6

8. Managers at Sun-2-Shade will have to determine the market's perceived rate of risk for this bond. If the bond is considered risky, as determined by Standard & Poors and Moody's Investors Service, then the interest rate will have to be higher than if it were considered to be a safer investment. Investors will invest in a bond that is considered risky only if the potential return to them is high enough.

    Sun-2-Shade will be offering corporate bonds and the face value will most likely be $1,000. Investors will consider how soon the bond matures, the interest rate, and whether or not it has other features that will allow the investor to sell either at a premium or a discount.

Learning Goals 7,8

9. a. Stock split
    b. Penny stocks
    c. Stockbroker
    d. Round lot
    e. Buying on margin
    f. Blue chip
    g. Market order
    h. Bull
    i. Limit order
    j. Margin call
    k. Mutual fund
    l. Income stock
    m. Prospectus
    n. Bear
    o. Diversification
    p. Growth stock
    q. Capital gains
    r. Index fund
    s. ETFs

Learning Goal 9

10. In the commodities market, buying or selling goods for delivery sometime in the future, is known as the futures market. This allows farmers, like Jordan, to fix a price for their crops, and aids in planning, and allows buyers, like General Mills, to fix a price so that they may also plan. It prevents the risk of being caught by a price increase, and gives

businesses a form of price insurance that enables them to continue business without worrying about fluctuations in commodity prices.

Learning Goal 10

11.   Your answers for each section will vary according to which companies you choose to study, and when you are studying this chapter. As for the Dow Jones Industrial Averages, stock prices trended upward in the mid-1990s and the average broke 9000 for the first time in early 1998. Stock prices quickly recovered from the drop in October 1997. By late 1999, the Dow Jones Industrial Average hit over 11,000. During the early 2000s the Average varied, and in early 2001, the Dow Jones fell rapidly, plunging to below 10,000. It started a very slow recovery in mid- 2003.

PRACTICE TEST

MULTIPLE CHOICE

LG 1	*#1-3*
LG 2	*# 4-6*
LG 3	*#7-9*
LG 4	*#10-12*
LG 5	*#13-14*
LG 6	*#15-16*
LG 7	*#17-19*
LG 8	*# 20-21*
LG 9	*#22*
LG 10	*#23-24*

1.	c	13.	c
2.	b	14.	d
3.	a	15.	b
4.	b	16.	a
5.	c	17.	c
6.	a	18.	c
7.	b	19.	b
8.	b	20.	a
9.	d	21.	d
10.	a	22.	b
11.	b	23.	c
12.	c	24.	c
		25.	b

TRUE-FALSE

LG 1	*#1-2*
LG 2	*#3-5*
LG 3	*#6-8*
LG 4	*#9-11*
LG 5	*#12-14*
LG 6	*#15-16*
LG 7	*#17-19*
LG 8	*#20-21*
LG 9	*#22*
LG 10	*#23-24*

1.	T	13.	T
2.	F	14.	T
3.	F	15.	F
4.	F	16.	T
5.	T	17.	T
6.	T	18.	T
7.	F	19.	T
8.	T	20.	T
9.	T	21.	T
10.	T	22.	F
11.	F	23.	T
12.	T	24.	T

CHAPTER 20 – UNDERSTANDING MONEY, FINANCIAL INSTITUTIONS, AND THE FEDERAL RESERVE

LEARNING GOALS

After you have read and studied this chapter, you should be able to:

1. Explain what money is and how its value is determined.
2. Describe how the Federal Reserve controls the money supply.
3. Trace the history of banking and the Federal Reserve System.
4. Classify the various institutions in the American banking system.
5. Explain the importance of the Federal Deposit Insurance Corporation and other organizations that guarantee funds.
6. Discuss the future of the U.S. banking system.
7. Evaluate the role and importance of international banking and the role of the World Bank and the International Monetary Fund.

LEARNING THE LANGUAGE

Listed below are important terms found in the chapter. Choose the correct term for the definition and write it in the space provided.

Banker's acceptance	Electronic funds transfer (EFT) system	Open-market operations
Barter	Federal Deposit Insurance corporation (FDIC)	Pension funds
Certificate of deposit (CD)	International Monetary Fund (IMF)	Reserve requirement
Commercial bank	Letter of credit	Savings and loan association (S&L)
Credit unions	M-1	Savings Association Insurance Fund (SAIF)
Debit card	M-2	Smart card
Demand deposit	Money	Time deposit
Discount rate	Money supply	World Bank
Electronic check conversion (ECC)	Nonbanks	

1. Nonprofit, member-owned financial cooperatives called_____ offer the full variety of banking services to their members.

2. An electronic funds transfer tool called _____converts a traditional paper check into an electronic transaction at the cash register and processes it through the Federal Reserve's Automated Clearing House.

3. The _____is a percentage of commercial banks' checking and savings accounts that must be physically kept in the bank.

4. The technical name for a savings account is a _____, for which the bank can require prior notice before the owner withdraws money.

5. A _____ is a promise that the bank will pay some specified amount at a particular time.

6. _____ is anything that people generally accept as payment for goods and services.

7. The interest rate the Fed charges for loans to member banks is the _____.

8. Financial organizations known as _____ accept no deposits, but offer many of the services provided by regular banks including pension funds, insurance companies, commercial finance companies, consumer finance companies and brokerage houses.

9. A time deposit (savings) account called a _____ earns interest to be delivered at the end of the certificate's maturity date.

10. A computerized system known as _____ electronically performs financial transactions such as making purchases, paying bills, and receiving paychecks.

11. The part of the FDIC that insures holders of accounts in savings and loan associations is called the _____.

12. An electronic funds transfer tool known as a _____ serves the same function as checks, in that it withdraws funds from a checking account.

13. The activity called _____ is to trade goods and services for other goods and services.

14. A financial institution called a _____ accepts both savings and checking deposits and provides home mortgage loans.

15. The _____ is the amount of money the Federal Reserve Bank makes available to buy goods and services.

16. A _____ is a promise by a bank to pay the seller a given amount if certain conditions are met.

17. _____ are amounts of money put aside by corporations, nonprofit organizations, or unions to cover part of the financial needs of members when they retire.

18. A profit-seeking organization that receives deposits from individuals and corporations in the form of checking and savings accounts and then uses some of these funds to make loans is called a _____.

19. The _____ is an independent agency of the U.S. government that insures bank deposits.

20. The buying and selling of U.S. government bonds by the Fed is called _____ and has the goal of regulating the money supply.

21. The _____ includes everything in M-1 plus money that may take a little more time to obtain, such as savings accounts, money market accounts, mutual funds, and certificates of deposit.

22. The technical name for a checking account is a(n) _____, from which money can be withdrawn anytime on demand by the depositor.

23. The _____ assists the smooth flow of money among nations.

24. The _____, also known as the International Bank for Reconstruction and Development, is primarily responsible for financing economic development.

25. Money that can be accessed quickly and easily, such as currency, checks, traveler's checks, is called the _____ money supply.

26. A _____ is an electronic funds transfer tool that is a combination credit card, debit card, phone card, driver's license card and more.

ASSESSMENT CHECK

Learning Goal 1
Why Money Is Important

1. Describe five characteristics of a "useful" form of money.

   a. _____

   b. _____

   c. _____

   d. _____

   e. _____

2. What is e-cash and how can you use it?

3. What is the difference between M-1 and M-2? Which is the most commonly used definition?

4. What would happen if the Fed were to make too much money available in the economy?

5.   What would happen if the Fed took money out of the economy? What would happen if too much money were taken out of the economy?

6.   Why does the money supply need to be controlled?

7.   What does a "falling dollar" mean? What does a rising dollar mean? What does this mean for the prices of European goods?

8.   What makes our dollar "weak" or "strong"?

9.   When the economy is strong the demand for dollars: _____

      When the economy is weak the demand for dollars: _____

      So the value of the dollar depends upon: _____

Learning Goal 2
Control of the Money Supply

10.   What organization is in charge of monetary policy?

11.   What are the five major parts of the Federal Reserve System?

      a. _____

      b. _____

      c. _____

      d. _____

      e. _____

12.   What is the primary function of the board of governors?

25.   Why were land banks established?

26.   Describe the evolution of the central bank.

27.   Describe the state of banking by the time of the Civil War.

28.   Describe the formation of the Federal Reserve System.

29.   What led to the bank failures of the 1930's?

30.   Why did the government start the federal deposit insurance program?

Learning Goal 4
The American Banking System

31.   Identify four types of banking institutions.

a.   _____

b.   _____

c.   _____

d.   _____

32. What kinds of institutions are included in a list of nonbanks?

   a. _____

   b. _____

   c. _____

   d. _____

   e. _____

33. What are two types of customers for commercial banks?

   a. _____

   b. _____

34. How does a commercial bank make a profit?

35. Describe NOW and Super NOW accounts.

36. Describe the characteristics of a certificate of deposit (CD).

37. Identify the services offered by commercial banks in addition to checking (demand deposits) and savings accounts (time deposits):

   a. _____   g. _____

   b. _____   h. _____

   c. _____   i. _____

   d. _____   j. _____

   e. _____   k. _____

   f. _____   l. _____

38. What services are being offered through ATMs?

39.   What is another name for savings and loans institutions, and why are they known as such?

40.   Why did so many S&Ls fail between 1979 and 1983?

41.   To improve the financial power of S&Ls, the federal government: _____

_____

42.   What services do credit unions offer their members?

43.   What has been the result of competition between nonbanks and banks?

44.   What financial services are offered by:

       a.   Life insurance companies _____

            _____

       b.   Pension funds _____

            _____

       c.   Brokerage firms _____

            _____

       d.   Commercial and consumer finance companies_____

            _____

Learning Goal 5
How the Government Protects Your Funds

45.   List the three major sources of financial protection

        a. _____

        b. _____

        c. _____

46.   In the case of a bank failure the FDIC : _____

_____

_____

47.   Why were the FDIC and the FSLIC created?

48.   How was SAIF formed?

49.   What does the NCUA provide for?

Learning Goal 6
The Future of Banking

50.   What does the Gramm-Leach–Bliley Act provide for? How will this benefit consumers?

51.   What banking services are available to customers through online banking?

52.   Benefits online banks can offer to customers include: _____

_____

53.   How have customers responded to Internet banks? Why?

54.   The benefit of electronic funds transfer is that: _____

_____

55.   What are the electronic funds transfer (EFT) tools?

    a.   _____   d.   _____

    b.   _____   e.   _____

    c.   _____

56.   Describe electronic check conversion (ECC).

57.   How is a debit card different from a credit card?

58.   How are smart cards different from other cards?

59.   What is:

    a.   direct deposit? _____

           _____

    b.   direct payment? _____

           _____

Learning Goal 7
International Banking and Banking Services

60.   What three services are offered to banks to help businesses conduct business overseas?

    a.   _____

    b.   _____

    c.   _____

61.   What could be the international impact of the Federal Reserve System changing interest rates?

62.   The net result of international banking and finance has been: _____

_____

_____

63.   The World Bank is primarily responsible for: _____

64.   What criticisms have been aimed at the World Bank?

65.   What is required by the International Monetary fund?

        a. _____

        b. _____

        c. _____

66.   What is the IMF designed to oversee? What is the goal of the IMF?

67.   Why the IMF been in the news in recent years?

68.   Debt relief advocates want the World Bank and the IMF to forgive the debts of poor countries because: _____

_____

CRITICAL THINKING EXERCISES

Learning Goals 1,2

1.   Using what you have learned in this chapter as well as in other chapters about economics, answer this question: What is the importance of the stability of the value of money, and controlling the money supply in the international marketplace today?

2   Sun-2-Shade is a company that makes self-darkening windshields for the automotive industry. Sun-2-Shade has made it big! The company has done so well here in the U.S. that management is seriously considering expanding into overseas markets. It is your job to research the idea, and you want to begin by helping other top managers understand some of the considerations of "going global." Within the context of the "value" of money compared to other currencies, what are some of the issues you will want to bring up to your managers?

Learning Goal 2

3.   The Fed uses three major tools to control the money supply
         Reserve requirement
         Open market operations
         Discount rate

a.   Complete the following chart illustrating how each tool is used, and its effect on the money supply and the economy:

TOOL	ACTION	EFFECT ON MONEY SUPPLY	EFFECT ON ECONOMY
Reserve requirement	Increase reserve requirement	_____	_____
	Decrease reserve requirement	_____	_____
Open market Operations	Buy government securities	_____	_____
	Sell government securities	_____	_____
Discount rate	Increase discount rate	_____	_____
	Decrease discount rate	_____	_____

b.   Identify whether the Federal Reserve would increase or decrease the money supply in the following situations, and what the effect would be .

         1. High unemployment   _____

         2. High rates of inflation _____

4.   When the Fed regulates the money supply using one of the three tools just mentioned, what happens to interest rates overall?

Learning Goal 3

5.   The American banking system has a long history. List the major events that led up to the establishment of the Federal Reserve System, and subsequent events that have affected the American banking system.

a. _____

b. _____

c. _____

d. _____

e. _____

f. _____

g. _____

h. _____

i. _____

j. _____

k. _____

l. _____

Learning Goal 4

6. The American banking system consists of three types of organizations:
    Commercial banks
    Savings and loans
    Credit unions

    Match each of the following descriptions to the correct type of institution:

    a. _____   Offers interest-bearing checking accounts called share draft accounts at relatively high rates.

    b. _____   Also known as thrift institutions.

    c. _____   Offer a wide variety of services, to depositors and borrowers, including ATMs, credit cards, short and long term loans, financial counseling, automatic payment of telephone bills, safe deposit boxes, tax deferred individual retirement accounts, overdraft checking account privileges.

    d. _____   Have been able to offer NOW and Super NOW accounts since 1981.

    e. _____   Since they are member owned and non-profit, they are exempt from federal income taxes.

7. What are three kinds of checking accounts, and what is the difference between them?

    a. _____

    b. _____

    c. _____

8. How are credit unions different from commercial banks and S&Ls?

9. Describe how nonbanks are becoming an important financial force, and how they compete with traditional banking institutions.

10. What is the difference between FDIC, SAIF, and NCUA? Why were the FDIC and the predecessor to SAIF, (known as the FSLIC) created?

11. In your opinion, with today's economic conditions, and the competitive banking industry, is it still important to have organizations such as the FDIC, SAIF and the NCUA?

Learning Goal 6
12. Compare what you have learned in earlier chapters about the trends in businesses to become more efficient and competitive to the trends in the U.S. banking industry.

Learning Goal 7
13. In previous chapters, we have discussed the global nature of the marketplace, and the need for U.S. businesses to become and stay more competitive. How does what we have learned in those chapters about U.S. business, relate to international banking, and the U.S. banking industry?

PRACTICE TEST

MULTIPLE CHOICE – Circle the best answer

Learning Goal 1
1. In referring to the money supply, which of the following is money that can be accessed quickly and easily, and includes coins and paper money as well as checks?
    a. M-1
    b. M-2
    c. M-3
    d. money supply

2. Which of the following would <u>not</u> be included in a list of characteristics of money?
    a. Portability
    b. Divisibility
    c. Stability
    d. Usability

3. The term _____ is used to describe the situation of "too much money chasing too few goods."
    a. recession
    b. inflation
    c. deflation
    d. monetary policy

4. When the price of a European coffee maker becomes less expensive to buy here in the United States, you could say that we are experiencing a
    a. falling dollar.
    b. inflated dollar.
    c. rising dollar.
    d. stable dollar.

Learning Goal 2
5. Which of the following is <u>not</u> one of the functions of the Federal Reserve?
    a. buying and selling foreign currency
    b. supervising banks
    c. lending money to member banks
    d. setting tax rates

6. When the Fed increases the reserve requirement,
    a. interest rates will go down.
    b. banks will have more money to lend.
    c. inflation could go up.
    d. banks have less money to lend.

7. The discount rate is:
    a. the amount of money member banks must keep on hand at the Fed.
    b. the interest rate Fed charges for loans to member banks .
    c. the rate the Fed charges for selling bonds.
    d. the interest rate banks charge other banks.

8.   The bank failures of 1907 and the resulting cash shortage problems led to the creation of
        a.   the Federal Reserve System.
        b.   the gold standard.
        c.   monetary policy.
        d.   the money supply.

9.   After the stock market crash of 1929, and the resulting bank failures of that time, Congress passed legislation creating:
        a.   laws which prevented banks from failing.
        b.   the Federal Reserve System.
        c.   federal deposit insurance.
        d.   nonbanks.

10.   The technical name for a savings account is a:
        a.   demand deposit.
        b.   time deposit.
        c.   certificate of deposit.
        d.   deposit insurance.

11.   Which of the following organizations would be considered a nonbank institution?
        a.   the Missouri Public School Retirement System
        b.   the Educational Employees Credit Union
        c.   Heartland Bank
        d.   Southwest Savings

12.   The difference between a NOW account and a savings account is that:
        a.   a NOW account doesn't pay interest, and a savings account does.
        b.   a NOW account has a maturity date, but a savings account does not.
        c.   you can't withdraw money from a NOW account until the maturity date, but you can withdraw from a savings account any time.
        d.   you can write checks on a NOW account, but not on a savings account.

13.   Which of the following services would not be offered to customers by commercial banks?
        a.   credit cards
        b.   inexpensive brokerage services
        c.   pension funds
        d.   traveler's checks

14.   Competition between banks and nonbanks, such as insurance companies and pension funds, has
        a.   decreased with the deregulation of the banking industry.
        b.   not changed in 50 years, since the creation of the Federal Reserve System.
        c.   increased significantly as nonbanks offer many of the services provided by regular banks.
        d.   stabilized with the bull stock market of the late 1990s.

15.   The Federal Deposit Insurance Corporation insures accounts up to:
     a. $10,000.
     b. $50,000.
     c. $100,000.
     d. $500,000.

16.   Funds in savings and loan institutions are protected by:
     a. Federal Deposit Insurance Corporation (FDIC).
     b. National Credit Union Association (NCUA).
     c. Federal Savings and Loan Insurance Corporation (FSLIC).
     d. Savings Association Insurance Fund (SAIF).

Learning Goal 6

17.   Smart cards
     a. are a new credit card offered by nonbanks.
     b. combine the functions of credit cards, debit cards, phone cards and other types of cards.
     c. are a form of direct deposit.
     d. allow employers to make direct payments to your creditors.

18.   Internet Banking:
     a. are few in number and not expected to grow.
     b. allows customers to do all financial transactions from home.
     c. have higher expenses because they have to hire administrators of the online systems and software designers.
     d. will most likely continue in organizations that offer traditional banking facilities as well as online services.

Learning Goal 7

19.   Which of the following is <u>not</u> a way banks help businesses conduct business overseas?
     a. guarantee a certain exchange rate
     b. offer letters of credit
     c. bankers acceptance
     d. money exchange

20.   The organization which is responsible for financing economic development is the:
     a. Federal Reserve Bank.
     b. International Monetary Fund.
     c. World Bank.
     d. Bank of the Americas.

21.   The World Bank:
     a. Makes loans only to countries that can afford to make payments of the loans.
     b. Has come under criticism from environmentalists.
     c. Has been praised in developing nations by AIDs activists.
     d. Works with countries to eliminate sweatshops.

TRUE-FALSE

Learning Goal 1

1. _____ The banking system is becoming simpler as the flow of money from one country to another becomes freer.

2. _____ Bartering is still used by buyers and sellers, online as well as in some developing nations.

3. _____ In order to make money more difficult to counterfeit, the U.S. has changed the look of some of the denominations of its paper currency.

4. _____ If there is too much money in the economy, prices will go up because people will bid up the prices of goods and services, causing inflation.

Learning Goal 2

5. _____ There are 15 Federal Reserve Banks.

6. _____ An increase in the reserve requirement would encourage businesses to borrow money and thus stimulate the economy.

7. _____ The most commonly used tool used by the Fed is open market operations.

Learning Goal 3

8. _____ Continental currency, the first paper money printed in the United States, became very valuable over the years as the first form of money used in the U.S.

9. _____ Stagflation is a situation of slow economic growth combined with inflation.

Learning Goal 4

10. _____ Commercial banks have two types of customers – borrowers and lenders.

11. _____ Unlike a NOW account, a certificate of deposit has a maturity date, and that is when interest is paid.

12. _____ Commercial banks are offering a wider variety of services, such as brokerage services, financial counseling, automatic payment of bills, and IRAs.

13. _____ Nonbanks are becoming more competitive with other financial organizations and are offering many of the same services

Learning Goal 5

14. _____ The only type of institution in which funds are protected by the U.S. government is a commercial bank.

15. _____ The SAIF is part of the FDIC and was originally known as the FSLIC.

Learning Goal 6

16. _____ Bankers are encouraging transactions that utilize an electronic funds transfer system, as EFT reduces costs.

17. _____ Debit cards are the same as smart cards and offer the same functions.

18. ____   Direct deposit is a preauthorized electronic payment into a merchant's account.

19. ____   The result of international banking has been to link the economies of the world into one interrelated system with no regulatory control.

20. ____   The International Monetary Fund has the responsibility of assisting the smooth flow of money among nations.

You Can Find It On The Net

How many U.S. dollars will buy a British pound? We can find out at **www.xe.com/ucc**
Check out this site and find out!

How many U.S. dollars does it take to buy a euro?

How many U.S. dollars will it take to buy a Japanese yen?

How much did your tuition cost in Canadian dollars?

If you are traveling in France, and your hotel costs 600 euros per night, are you staying at the French equivalent of the penthouse at the Ritz, or at a youth hostel?

ANSWERS

LEARNING THE LANGUAGE

1. Credit unions	10. Electronic Funds Transfer System (EFT)	19. Federal Deposit Insurance Corporation (FDIC)
2. Electronic check conversion (ECC)	11. Savings Association Insurance Fund (SAIF)	20. Open-market operations
3. Reserve requirement	12. Debit card	21. M-2
4. Time deposit	13. Barter	22. Demand deposit
5. Banker's acceptance	14. Savings and Loan Association (S&L)	23. International Monetary Fund (IMF)
6. Money	15. Money supply	24. World Bank
7. Discount rate	16. Letter of credit	25. M-1
8. Nonbanks	17. Pension funds	26. Smart card
9. Certificates of deposit (CD)	18. Commercial bank	

ASSESSMENT CHECK

Learning Goal 1
Why Money Is Important

1. Five characteristics of a "useful" form of money are:
    a. Portability – money needs to be easy to carry around
    b. Divisibility – different sized coins are made to represent different values
    c. Stability – the value of money is more stable (unlike the value, or prices, of bartered goods)
    d. Durability – Coins last for a long time
    e. Difficult to counterfeit – money must be hard to copy, so it must be elaborately designed

2. Electronic, or e-cash is the latest form of money. You can e-mail e-cash to anyone using websites, and make online bill payments.

3. These terms stand for different definitions of the money supply. M-1 includes coins and paper bills, money that is available by writing checks and money that is held in traveler's checks or money that is easily available to pay for goods and services. M-2 includes all of that, but adds in money held in savings accounts and other forms of savings that is not as readily available. M-2 is the most commonly used definition of money.

4. If the Fed made too much money available, prices would go up, assuming that the same amount of goods and services were available. People would bid up prices to get what they want, causing inflation. This could be called "too much money chasing too few goods."

5. If money were taken out of the economy prices would go down because there would be an oversupply of goods and services compared to the money available to buy them. If too much money is taken out of the economy, a recession could occur. People would lose jobs and the economy would stop growing.

6. The money supply needs to be controlled because this allows us to manage the prices of goods and services. Also, controlling the money supply affects employment and economic growth or decline.

7. A falling dollar means that the amount of goods and services you can buy with a dollar goes down. A rising dollar means that the amount of goods and services you can buy with a dollar goes up. Thus the prices you pay for a European good would be lower if the American dollar was strong relative to the euro. When the euro gains strength and rises in value against the dollar, the cost of European goods goes up.

8. What makes a dollar weak or strong (falling or rising dollar) is the position of the U.S. economy relative to other economies.

9. When the economy is strong, the demand for dollars is high, and the value of the dollar rises. When the economy is weak, the demand for dollars declines, and the value of the dollar falls.

   So, the value of a dollar depends upon a strong economy.

Learning Goal 2
Control of the Money Supply

10. The Federal Reserve System (the Fed) is in charge of monetary policy.

11. The Federal Reserve System consists of
    a. The board of governors
    b. The Federal Open Market Operations
    c. 12 Federal Reserve Banks
    d. Three advisory councils
    e. The member banks of the system

12. The board of governors administers and supervises the 12 Federal Reserve System banks. The primary function of the board of governors is to set monetary policy.

13. The Federal Open Market Committee has 12 voting members and is the policy-making body. The committee is made up of the seven members of the Board of Governors plus the president of the New York Reserve Bank. Four others rotate in from the other Reserve Banks. The advisory councils offer suggestions to the board and the FOMC. The councils represent the various banking districts, consumers, and member institutions, including banks, savings and loans, and credit unions.

14. The Federal Reserve
    a. buys and sells foreign currencies.
    b. regulates various types of credit.
    c. supervises banks.
    d. collects data on the money supply and other economic activity.
    e. determines the level of reserves that must be held by financial institutions.
    f. lends money to member banks.
    g. sets the rate charged for such loans, the discount rate.
    h. buys and sells government securities.

15.   a.   The most commonly used tool to manage the money supply is open market operations.

           b.   The most powerful tool the Fed uses is the reserve requirement.

16.   When the Fed increases the reserve requirement banks have less money to loan, and money becomes scarce. In the long run, this tends to reduce inflation. It is so powerful because of the amount of money affected when the reserve is changed.

A decrease in the reserve requirement increases the funds available to banks for loans, so banks make more loans, and money becomes more readily available. An increase in the money supply stimulates the economy to achieve higher growth rates but can also create inflationary pressures.

17.   a.   To decrease the money supply, the federal government sells U.S. government securities to the public. The money it gets as payment is taken out of circulation, decreasing the money supply.

           b.   If the Fed wants to increase the money supply, it buys government securities from individuals, corporations, or organizations that are willing to sell.

18.   One reason the Fed is called the banker's bank is that member banks can borrow money from the Fed and then pass it on to their customers as loans. The discount rate is the interest rate that the Fed charges for loans to member banks.

19.   An increase in the discount rate by the Fed discourages banks from borrowing and consequently reduces the number of available loans, resulting in a decrease in the money supply.

A decrease in the discount rate encourages member bank borrowing and increases the funds available for loans, which increases the money supply.

20.   The federal funds rate is the rate that banks charge each other.

21.   When you write a check to a local retailer, the retailer takes the check to its bank. If your account is at the same bank, your account is simply reduced by the amount of the check. It is a simple process.

22.   When you write a check from out of state, the process becomes more complex. From the retailer, our check goes to the retailer's bank, which then deposits your check for credit in the closest Federal Reserve Bank. That bank will send the check to your local Federal Reserve Bank for collection. The check is then sent to your bank and the amount of the check will be deducted from your account. Your bank will authorize the Federal Reserve Bank in your area to deduct the amount of the check. That bank will pay the Federal Reserve Bank that began the process in the first place. It will then credit the deposit account in the bank where the retailer has its account. This is a costly process, so banks encourage the use of credit card, debit cards and other forms of electronic transfers.

The History of Banking and the Need for the Fed

23.   Strict laws in Europe limited the number of coins that could be brought to the New World by colonists, and besides, there were no banks in the colonies. So, colonists were forced to barter for goods.

24.   Massachusetts issued its own paper money in 1690 because the demand for money was so great. This money was called continental currency, and it became worthless after a few years because people didn't trust its value.

25.   Land banks were established to lend money to farmers.

26.   In 1781, Alexander Hamilton persuaded Congress to form a central bank, a bank where banks could keep their funds and borrow funds if needed. It was the first version of a federal bank, but closed in 1811. It was replaced in 1816 because state chartered banks couldn't support the War of 1812.

27.   By the time of the Civil War, banking was a mess. Different banks issued different currencies. During the war, coins were hoarded because they were worth more as gold and silver than as coins. The problems with the banking system continued after the Civil War and climaxed in 1907 when people got so nervous about the safety of banks that they withdrew their funds, creating a "run on the banks." Many banks failed and there was a cash shortage.

28.   The cash shortage problems of 1907 led to the formation of an organization that could lend money to banks – the Federal Reserve System. It was to be a" lender of last resort" during emergencies, such as the cash shortage. Under the Federal Reserve Act of 1913, all federally chartered banks had to join the Federal Reserve. State banks could also join. The Federal Reserve became the banker's bank.

29.   The stock market crash of 1929 led to bank failures in the early 1930s. The stock market began tumbling, and people ran to the bank to get their money out. In spite of the Federal Reserve, banks ran out of money, and states were forced to close banks.

30.   In 1933 and 1935 Congress passed legislation to strengthen the banking system, to further protect us from bank failures. The most important move was to establish federal deposit insurance.

Learning Goal 4
The American Banking System

31.   a. Commercial banks
       b. Savings and loan associations
       c. Credit unions
       d. Mutual savings banks

32.   Institutions included in a list of nonbanks are:
       a. Life insurance companies
       b. Pension funds
       c. Brokerage firms
       d. Commercial finance companies
       e. Corporate financial services

33.   a.   Depositors
        b.   Borrowers

34.   A commercial bank uses customer deposits as inputs, on which it pays interest, and invests that money in interest-bearing loans to other customers, mostly businesses. Commercial banks make a profit if the revenue generated by loans exceeds the interest paid to depositors plus all other operating expenses.

35.   A NOW account typically pays an annual interest rate but usually requires depositors always to maintain a certain minimum balance in the account, and may restrict the number of checks that depositors can write each month. A Super NOW account pays a higher interest to attract larger deposits. However Super NOW accounts require a larger minimum balance. They sometimes offer free, unlimited check-writing privileges.

36.   Certificates of deposit deliver interest at the end of the maturity date. They are available for periods of three months up to many years; the longer the CD is to be held, the higher the interest. Interest rates depend on economic conditions and the prime rate at the time of the deposit.

37.   Services offered by commercial banks in addition to checking accounts (demand deposits) and savings accounts (time deposits) include:

        a.   Credit cards   g.   Tax-deferred IRAs
        b.   Life insurance   h.   Traveler's checks
        c.   Brokerage services   i.   Trust departments
        d.   Financial counseling   j.   Overdraft checking account privileges
        e.   Automatic bill paying   k.   ATMs
        f.   Safe-deposit boxes   l.   Loans

38.   Automated teller machines, or ATMs, give customers the convenience of 24 hour banking at a variety of outlets, such as supermarkets, department stores and so on, in addition to the bank's regular branches. Depositors can do much of their banking at their own discretion using an ATM card. New ATMs can dispense maps and directions, phone cards, and postage stamps. They can sell tickets to movies, concerts, sporting events and more. They can show movie trailers, news tickers, and video ads. Some can take orders for flowers and DVDs, and download music and games.

39.   S&L's are often known as thrift institutions since their original purpose was to promote consumer thrift, or saving, and home ownership.

40.   Between 1979 and 1983 many savings and loan institutions failed for a variety of reasons. The biggest reason may be the fact that capital gains taxes were raised, making investments in real estate less attractive. Investors walked away from their real estate loans, and left S&Ls with property that was worth less than the money the S&L had loaned to the investors. When the property was sold, the S&Ls lost money.

41.   To improve the financial power of S&Ls, the government permitted them to offer NOW and Super NOW accounts, to allocate up to 10 percent of their funds to commercial loans, and to offer mortgage loans with adjustable interest rates. Further, savings and loans were allowed to offer banking services such as financial counseling to small businesses, and credit cards.

42. Credit unions offer their members interest-bearing checking accounts at relatively high rates, short-term loans at relatively low rates, financial counseling, life insurance and a limited number of home mortgage loans.

43. The diversity of financial serves and investment alternatives offered by nonbanks has led banks to expand the services that they offer. As competition between banks and nonbanks has increased, the dividing line between them has become less apparent. In fact, banks today are merging with brokerage firms to offer full-service financial assistance.

44. a. Life insurance companies provide financial protection for their policyholders. They invest the funds they receive from policy holders in corporate and government bonds. Recently more insurance companies have begun to provide long-term financing for real estate development companies.

    b. Pension funds are amounts of money put aside by organizations to cover part of the financial needs of members when they retire. A member may begin to collect a monthly draw on the fund upon reaching a certain age. To generate additional income, pension funds invest in low return, but safe corporate stocks or in other conservative investments.

    c. Brokerage firms have traditionally offered services related to investments in various stock exchanges. They have now made inroads into regular banks' domain by offering high-yield combination savings and checking accounts. In addition firms offer checking privileges on accounts. Investors can also get loans from their broker.

    d. Commercial and consumer finance companies offer short-term loans to businesses or individuals who either cannot meet other credit requirements or who have exceeded their credit limit and need more funds. These finance companies' interest rates are higher than those of regular banks.

Learning Goal 5
How the Government Protects Your Funds

45. a. Federal Deposit Insurance Corporation (FDIC)
    b. Savings Association Insurance Fund (SAIF)
    c. National Credit Union Administration (NCUA)

46. If a bank were to fail, the FDIC would arrange to have its accounts transferred to another bank or pay off depositors up to a certain amount. If one of the top ten banks in the United States would fail, the FDIC has a contingency plan to nationalize the bank so that it wouldn't fail.

47. The FDIC and the FSLIC were started during the Great Depression. Many banks and thrifts failed during those years, and people were losing confidence in them. The FDIC and FSLIC were designed to create more confidence in banking institutions.

48. The government placed the FSLIC under the FDIC, in order to get more control over the banking system. When they did that, they gave it a new name, the Savings Association Insurance Fund, or SAIF

49. The NCUA provides up to $100,000 coverage per individual depositor per institution. The coverage includes all accounts, and additional protection can be obtained by holding accounts jointly or in trust.

Learning Goal 6
The Future of Banking

50. The Bramm-Leach-Bliley Act allows banks, insurers, and securities firms to combine and sell each other services. This allows banking consumers to have one-stop shopping for all their financial needs. As companies compete for business, the total cost of banking and other financial services is likely to go down. This may also make it easier to calculate taxes, and in fact, the financial firm may do it for you.

51. Online banking services include transferring funds, paying your bills, and checking on account balances. You can apply for a car loan or mortgage online and get a response immediately. You can also buy and sell stocks online.

52. Benefits online banks can offer include better interest rates and lower fees because they do not have the cost of physical overhead that brick and mortar banks have.

53. Many consumers are pleased with the savings and convenience, but not all consumers are happy with the service they receive from Internet banks. Many are nervous about the security of banking online. People fear putting their financial information into cyberspace where others may see it. Also, consumers often want to talk to a knowledgeable person when they have banking problems. Overall it seems that Internet banking customers miss the one-on-one help, and the security of local banks.

54. The benefit of EFT is that funds can be transferred more quickly and more economically than with paper checks.

55. EFT tools include:
    a. electronic check conversion   d. direct deposit
    b. debit cards,   e. direct payments
    c. smart cards

56. ECC saves both time and money in check clearing. When a customer makes a payment with a check, it is run through a check reader where the information is captured electronically. The check is verified against a database for acceptance. The transaction is electronically transferred, and funds are debited from the customer's account and deposited automatically into the merchant's account. With electronic check clearing there are no trips to the bank, and the risk of lost or stolen checks is reduced.

57. A debit card serves the same function as a check, in that it withdraws money directly from a checking account. Debit cards look like credit cards but they function differently. The difference is that you can spend no more than is in your checking account. To make a purchase, you swipe the debit card in a point of sale terminal at the retailer. When the sale is recorded, an electronic signal is sent to the bank, and funds are automatically transferred from your account to the retailer's account. A record of the transaction appears immediately.

58. Smart cards are a combination of credit cards, debit cards, phone cards, and more. The magnetic strip found on other cards is replaced on a smart card with a microprocessor.

The card can then store information, including a bank balance. Each merchant can use the information to check the card's validity and spending limits, and the transaction can debit the amount on the card. Some smart cards are used to allow entrance into buildings and secure areas, such as university dorms, to buy items, and serve as ATM cards. Parents can use smart cards to monitor children's transactions.

59.   a.   Direct deposit is a credit made directly to a checking or savings account.

        b.   A direct payment is a preauthorized electronic payment. A customer signs a form when he or she wants automatic payment to a certain company, and the designated company is authorized to collect funds for the amount of the bill from the customer's account.

Learning Goal 7
International Banking and Banking Services

60.   Banks help businesses conduct business overseas by providing:
      a.   letters of credit
      b.   banker's acceptances
      c.   money exchange

61.   If the Federal Reserve decides to lower interest rates, foreign investors can withdraw their money from the United States and put it in countries with higher rates. The opposite is also true, so that when the Fed raises interest rates, money could come into the U.S. just as quickly.

62.   The net result of international banking and finance has been to link the economies of the world into one interrelated system with no regulatory control. American firms must compete for funds with firms all over the world. What has evolved is a world economy financed by international banks.

63.   The World Bank is primarily responsible for financing economic development.

64.   Environmentalists charge that the World Bank finances projects that damage the ecosystem. Human rights activists argue that the bank supports countries that restrict religious freedoms and tolerate sweatshops. AIDS activists complain that the bank does not do enough to get low-cost drugs to developing nations.

65.   The International Monetary fund was established to assist the smooth flow of money among nations. It requires:
      a.   members to allow their currency to be exchanged for foreign currencies freely
      b.   members to keep the IMF informed about changes in monetary policy
      c.   nations to modify those policies on the advice of the IMF to accommodate the needs of the entire membership.

66.   The IMF is an overseer of member countries' monetary and exchange rate policies. The IMF's goal is to maintain a global monetary system that works best for all nations.

67.   The IMF was frequently in the news because it was lending money to nations whose currencies had fallen dramatically and whose banks were failing, as was happening in Asian countries, Latin America, and Russia. IMF failures have taken place in several countries.

68. Debt relief advocates want the World Bank and the IMF to forgive the debts of poor countries because many of them cannot afford to feed their people, much less pay back huge loans.

CRITICAL THINKING EXERCISES

Learning Goals 1,2

1. The stability of the value of money in the global marketplace is important because if the value of money is not stable, other countries will not accept that money in trade. In other words, if the marketplace believes your money will not be valuable to use, the market will not accept your money as payment for what you want to buy.

   The money supply needs to be controlled in order to control prices, and in part, the American economy. If there is too much money in the economy, prices of goods and services will increase, because demand will be greater than supply. If there is less money, people will not be spending at the same rate, demand correspondingly goes down, and prices will go down. That could result in an oversupply of goods and services, and possibly a recession. What makes a dollar weak or strong is the position of the U.S. economy relative to other economies. When the economy is strong, people want to buy dollars and the value of the dollar rises. The value of the dollar depends on a strong economy.

2. Some of the "money" issues Sun-2-Shade will need to research relate to how strong the American dollar is compared to the currency of the countries in which Sun-2-Shade is interested. If our dollar is weak, or falling, in comparison to the euro, the British pound, the Japanese yen, or others, Sun-2-Shade could be very affordable for their target market. If the American dollar is strong, or rising, the price of Sun-2-Shade's product could be too high for some.

   Further, we would want to know what the forecast might be for the future of the U.S. economy. Is our economy expected to be strong? What are the forecasts for recession, inflation, income growth, both here, and in our target countries?

Learning Goal 2

3. a.

Tool	Action	Effect on Money supply	Effect on Economy
Reserve Requirement	Increase	Decrease	Slows down
	Decrease	Increase	Stimulated
Open market operations	Buy securities	Increase	Stimulated
	Sell securities	Decrease	Slows down
Discount rate	Increase	Decrease	Slows down
	Decrease	Increase	Stimulated

   b. 1. In a situation of high unemployment, the Federal Reserve may increase the money supply, which would have the effect of reducing interest rates. This would be a tool to stimulate the economy and encourage businesses to borrow, which could create jobs.

2. With high rates of inflation, the Fed may choose to decrease the money supply. This would have the effect of raising interest rates, which may cool the economy and fight inflation.

4.   When the Fed takes action to increase the money supply, (either by decreasing the reserve rate, decreasing the discount rate or buying government bonds) interest rates will go down. Think of _interest_ as the _price_ of money. When the supply goes up, the price will generally go down. Correspondingly, if interest rates have declined, demand for goods and services could go up, the economy begins to grow, and inflation may begin to heat up. The opposite effect occurs when the Fed reduces the money supply. Interest rates will rise, which will slow demand for goods and services, which slows economic growth. Inflation will also then slow down, as supply begins to be equal to or exceed demand, and prices will stabilize.

Learning Goal 3

5.   a. Paper money established in 1690.
   b. Land banks established to lend money to farmers.
   c. Central bank established in 1781.
   d. Central bank closed in 1811.
   e. Second central bank established to support War of 1812.
   f. Division between state banks and central bank.
   g. Central bank closed in 1836.
   h. Civil War - banks issuing their own currency.
   i. Cash shortage problems in 1907; banks began to fail.
   j. Federal Reserve System established in 1907 to lend money to banks.
   k. Stock market crash of 1929 and subsequent bank failures in 1930s.
   l. Legislation passed to strengthen banking system, establishing federal deposit insurance in 1933 and 1935.

Learning Goal 4

6.   a. Credit unions
   b. Savings and loan
   c. Commercial banks
   d. Savings and loan
   e. Credit union

7.   1. Non-interest bearing checking accounts
   2. NOW accounts, which pay an annual interest rate and require depositors to maintain a minimum balance at all times. The number of checks that can be written is restricted.
   3. A Super NOW account pays higher interest than a NOW account. They require a larger minimum balance than regular NOW accounts, and typically offer free and unlimited check-writing privileges.

8.   Credit unions offer services similar to banks and S&Ls, but differ in their ownership structure. Credit unions are financial cooperatives, owned by members, while banks and savings and loans are often publicly held corporations. Credit unions are also not for profit institutions, while banks and credit unions are profit-making organizations.

9.   Nonbanks are financial institutions that accept no deposits but offer many of the services offered by regular banks. Nonbanks include life insurance companies, pension funds, brokerage firms, commercial finance companies, and corporate financial services. The diversity of financial services and investment alternatives offered by nonbanks has

caused banks to expand the services they offer. For example, life insurance companies invest the funds they receive from policyholders in corporate and government bonds. In recent years, more insurance companies have begun to provide long-term financing for real estate development projects. In fact, banks today are merging with brokerage firms to offer full service financial assistance. Pension funds typically invest in corporate stocks and bonds, and government securities. Some large pension funds lend money directly to corporations. Brokerage houses have made serious inroads into regular banks' domain by offering high-yield combination savings and checking accounts. In addition, investors can get loans from their broker.

Learning Goal 5
10.   The FDIC is a government agency that protects bank deposits of up to $100,000. In the case of a bank failure, the FDIC would arrange to have your accounts at that bank transferred to another bank, or pay you off up to $100,000. The FDIC covers about 13,000 institutions, which are mostly commercial banks. SAIF insures the accounts of depositors in thrift institutions, or savings and loans. It is part of the FDIC. SAIF was originally called the Federal Savings and Loan Insurance Corporation. NCUA is the agency that protects depositors in credit unions.

Both the FDIC and the FSLIC were established to protect the deposits of customers, and to create more confidence in the banking industry at a time when many institutions were failing. This was during the Great Depression, and hundreds of banks were failing. To get more control over the banking system, the government placed the FSLIC under the FDIC and gave it the name of The Savings Association Insurance Fund, SAIF.

11.   Answers will vary. Economic conditions to consider would be the American economy – are we is a period of growth? Heading toward a recession? A period of inflation? Other factors to consider are the competitive factors in the banking industry. With nonbanks performing significantly more banking functions, how are banks competing? How does this affect the banks' profitability? If banks are struggling to stay in business, then insurance on our funds remains an important security.

Learning Goal 6
12.   Trends in the banking industry have paralleled changes we have seen in other industries. We have studied how companies have begun putting the customer first, and have streamlined their operations to better satisfy customer's needs at lower costs. Banks have begun to look at customer needs, and have made "one-stop shopping" available for all a customer's financial needs. One company can provide you with credit cards, mortgages, all kinds of insurance, and brokerage services. As the competition increases, costs will go down, benefiting consumers. Further, the Internet has made online banking available, in the same way that the Internet has made the purchase of all kinds of products available from Internet stores. The online banking industry has suffered from customer service problems, just like online stores have done, and so, like other retail businesses, we will likely have a combination of online and brick and mortar financial institutions.

Learning Goal 7
13.   The U.S. banking system is directly tied to the success of banking and businesses throughout the world. American firms must compete for funds with firms all over the world. If a firm in another country is more efficient than one here in the United States, the more efficient firm will have better access to international funds. Therefore, U.S. businesses must compete not only in the marketplace, but in the financial arena as well.

Further, today's money markets form a global system, and international bankers will not be nationalistic in their dealings. They will send money to those countries where they can get the best return on their money with an acceptable risk. When the Federal Reserve System makes a move to lower interest rates in the U.S., foreign investors may withdraw their money from the U.S. and put it in countries with higher rates. To be an effective player in the international marketplace and financial worlds, the U.S. must stay financially secure and businesses must stay competitive in world markets.

PRACTICE TEST

MULTIPLE CHOICE		TRUE-FALSE	
LG 1	# 1-4	LG 1	#1-4
LG 2	# 5-7	LG 2	#5-7
LG 3	# 8-9	LG 3	#8-9
LG 4	#10-14	LG 4	#10-13
LG 5	# 15-16	LG 5	#14-15
LG 6	#17-18	LG 6	#16-18
LG 7	#19-20	LG 7	#19-20

1.	a	11.	a	1.	F	11.	F
2.	d	12.	d	2.	T	12.	T
3.	b	13.	c	3.	T	13.	T
4.	c	14.	c	4.	T	14.	F
5.	d	15.	c	5.	F	15.	T
6.	d	16.	d	6.	F	16.	T
7.	b	17.	b	7.	T	17.	F
8.	a	18.	d	8.	F	18.	F
9.	c	19.	a	9.	F	19.	T
10.	b	20.	c	10.	F	20.	T
		21.	b				

CHAPTER A- WORKING WITHIN THE LEGAL ENVIRONMENT OF BUSINESS

LEARNING GOALS

After you have read and studied this chapter, you should be able to:

1. Define business law, and distinguish between statutory and common law, and explain the role of administrative agencies.
2. Define tort law and explain the role of product liability in tort law.
3. Identify the purposes and conditions of patents, copyrights, and trademarks.
4. Describe warranties and negotiable instruments as covered in the Uniform Commercial Code.
5. List and describe the conditions necessary to make a legally enforceable contract, and describe the possible consequences if such a contract is violated.
6. Summarize several laws that regulate competition and protect consumers in the United States.
7. Explain the role of tax laws in generating income for the government and as a method of discouraging or encouraging certain behaviors among taxpayers.
8. Distinguish among the various types of bankruptcy as outlined by the Bankruptcy Code.
9. Explain the role of deregulation as a tool to encourage competition.

LEARNING THE LANGUAGE

Listed here are important terms found in this chapter. Choose the correct term for each definition below and write it in the space provided.

Administrative agencies	Copyright	Patent
Bankruptcy	Damages	Precedent
Breach of contract	Deregulation	Product liability
Business law	Express warranties	Statutory law
Common law	Implied warranties	Strict product liability
Consideration	Involuntary bankruptcy	Taxes
Consumerism	Judiciary	Tort
Contract	Negligence	Uniform Commercial Code (UCC)
Contract law	Negotiable instruments	Voluntary bankruptcy

1. Something of value, one of the requirements of a legal contract, is called _____.

2. _____ refers to government withdrawal of certain laws and regulations that seem to hinder competition.

3. Forms of commercial paper (such as checks) known as _____ are transferable among businesses and individuals and represent a promise to pay a specified amount.

4. Rules, statutes, codes, and regulations called _____ are established to provide a legal framework within which business may be conducted and that are enforceable by court action.

5. The _____ is a comprehensive commercial law, adopted by every state in the United States that covers sales laws and other commercial law.

6. Specific representations by the seller that buyers rely on regarding the goods they purchase are called _____.

7. A _____ is a wrongful act that causes injury to another person's body, property, or reputation.

8. The legal process of _____ is one by which a person, business, or government entity unable to meet financial obligations is relieved of those obligations by a court that divides any assets among creditors, allowing creditors to get at least part of their money and freeing the debt or to begin anew.

9. A _____ is a document that protects an individual's rights to materials such as books, articles, photos, and cartoons.

10. State and federal constitutions, legislative enactment, treaties of the federal government, and ordinances (written laws) are known as _____.

11. _____ are guarantees legally imposed on the seller.

12. A social movement known as _____ seeks to increase and strengthen the rights and powers of buyers in relation to sellers.

13. A _____ occurs when one party fails to follow the terms of a contract.

14. A legally enforceable agreement between two or more parties is a _____.

15. A document called a _____ gives inventors exclusive right to their inventions for 20 years.

16. The body of law known as _____ comes from decisions handed down by judges and is also known as "unwritten law."

17. A set of laws called _____ specify what constitutes a legally enforceable agreement.

18. Legal procedures called _____ are initiated by a debtor.

19. The part of tort law known as _____ holds businesses liable for harm that results from the production, design, sale, or use of products they market.

20. Federal or state institutions and other organizations created by Congress or state legislatures with delegated power to pass rules and regulations within their mandated area of authority are known as _____.

21. The branch of the government called the _____ oversees the legal system through the court system.

22. Bankruptcy procedures filed by a debtor's creditors are a(n) _____.

23. Federal, state and local governments raise money through _____.

24. The monetary settlement awarded to a person who is injured by a breach of contract is known as _____.

25. Decisions judges have made in earlier cases, or _____, guide the handling of new cases.

26. In tort law, behavior is called _____ when it causes unintentional harm or injury.

27. Legal responsibility for harm or injury caused by a product regardless of fault is known as _____.

ASSSESSMENT CHECK

Learning Goal 1
The Need for Laws

1. What is the difference between criminal law and civil law?

2. Discuss the difference between statutory and common law.

3. Why is common law often referred to as unwritten law? How does precedent relate to common law?

4. What do we mean when we say that administrative agencies hold quasi-legislative, quasi-executive and quasi-judicial powers?

Learning Goal 2
Tort Law

5. What is the difference between an intentional tort and negligence?

6.   How is it that a company can be held liable for damages from a defective product even if the company didn't know of the defect?

7.   What impact has the rule of strict liability had on businesses?

Learning Goal 3
Laws Protecting Ideas: Patents, Copyrights, and Trademarks

8.   In order to file for a patent an inventor must (or should):

      a.   _____

      b.   _____

      c.   _____

9.   What are your chances of receiving a patent? How much will you spend in fees over the life of a patent? How long will it take to get your patent?

10.   What is required by the American Inventor's Protection Act? Why was this act passed?

11.   What is a business-method patent?

12.   How long does a patent last compared to a copyright?

13.   What are the provisions of the Copyright Act of 1978?

14.   What are the rights of the holder of a copyright? What happens if a work is created by an employee in the course of a job?

15.   What is the definition of a trademark? How long does a trademark last?

Learning Goal 4
Sales Law: The Uniform Commercial Code

16.   What are the areas covered by the Uniform Commercial Code?

a. _____   f. _____

b. _____   g. _____

c. _____   h. _____

d. _____   i. _____

e. _____

17.   Describe the difference between express and implied warranties.

18.   Describe the difference between a full and a limited warranty.

19.   What are four conditions that must be met by a negotiable instrument?

a. _____

b. _____

c. _____

d. _____

20.   What is considered an "endorsement" with regard to negotiable instruments?

21.   A contract is legally binding if:

      a. _____

      b. _____

      c. _____

      d. _____

      e. _____

      f. _____

22.   An offer becomes legally binding only when: _____

23.   The principle of mutual acceptance means that: _____

_____

24.   How is a person determined to be competent to enter a contract?

25.   When does a contract become illegal and not enforceable?

26.   What kind of contracts must be put in writing?

27.   Describe three results of a breach of contract.

      a. _____

      b. _____

      c. _____

28.   Identify three elements that must be present in a contract.

   a. _____

   b. _____

   c. _____

Learning Goal 6
Laws to Promote Fair and Competitive Practices

29.   What are four important pieces of pro-competitive federal legislation?

   a. _____

   b. _____

   c. _____

   d. _____

30.   What two things does the Sherman Act forbid?

   a. _____

   b. _____

31.   The Clayton Act prohibits:

   a. _____   c. _____

   b. _____   d. _____

32.   Describe:

   a. exclusive dealing

   b. a tying contract

   c. an interlocking directorate

33.   Discuss the major elements of the Federal Trade Commission Act.

34. What areas does the FTC cover?

35. The Robinson Patman Act prohibits: _____

The Robinson-Patman Act applies to: _____

_____

The act specifically outlaws: _____

_____

36. What is required of CEOs by the Sarbanes/Oxley Act?

37. List four basic rights of consumers proposed by John F. Kennedy.

a. _____   c. _____

b. _____   d. _____

Learning Goal 7
Tax Laws

38. How are taxes used?

39. What is the purpose of a sin tax?

40. A tax credit is: _____

41. What are three basic areas from which taxes are levied?

a. _____

b. _____

c. _____

42. The federal government receives its largest share of taxes from: _____

States and local governments make extensive use of : _____

School districts general depend upon: _____

43. A key tax issue currently revolves around: _____

Learning Goal 8
Bankruptcy Laws

44. Identify the two major amendments to the bankruptcy code. What do they say?

a. _____

_____

b. _____

_____

45. What are the provisions of a Chapter 7 bankruptcy?

46. In what order are assets distributed among creditors in a Chapter 7 bankruptcy?

First: _____

Then:

a. _____

b. _____

c. _____

d. _____

e. _____

f. _____

47. What does Chapter 11 bankruptcy allow?

48. What does a Chapter 13 bankruptcy permit? How does this compare to a Chapter 7? How does a Chapter 13 proceed?

49.   The move toward deregulation began because: _____

_____

50.   How has deregulation affected these industries?

Airlines:

Telecommunications:

Utilities:

51.   As a result of corporate scandals many have called for: _____

_____

CRITICAL THINKING EXERCISES

Learning Goal 1

1.   Determine if statutory or common law is being described in the following examples.

a. _____   Joe sued Susan because he was injured while using end tables Susan had given him to prop up his car while working on the muffler. The judge in the case ruled in Susan's favor based upon past cases of implied warranties

b. _____   The CEO of a major firm in the electronics industry has refused to sign off on the financial statements for his company because they don't meet his criteria. He is afraid of being held liable for those statements under the Sarbanes-Oxley Act.

c. _____   Lane Halverson filed bankruptcy under Chapter 13 in October, 2006

d. _____   A farmer in the Midwest was sued by his neighbors because his farm animals were so smelly that the neighbors were getting sick. The neighbors sued and the judge ruled in favor of the neighbors after considerable research on similar cases.

Learning Goal 2

2. How has the definition of product liability changed, and how has that affected manufacturers?

Learning Goal 3

3. Eric has developed a new formula for the product his company manufactures, a self-darkening windshield for vehicles. Eric would like to protect this formula because he has just learned that a competitor has recently been using Eric's process. Eric is very busy right now, and feels like he just doesn't have time to deal with anything complicated right now and that he will probably wait for a while before he decides to do anything about this new formula. What would you advise him about protecting his new product?

Learning Goal 4

4. Determine if the issue described below refers to an express warranty or an implied warranty.

    a. _____ Shirley Glenn got severe food poisoning after eating at a restaurant near her home and sued the restaurant for her medical expenses.

    b. _____ Geraldo Santino bought a drill that worked for 6 months and then quit. The paperwork that came with the drill said that the manufacturer would repair any problems the drill had for 5 years after the purchase, so Geraldo sent the drill to the manufacturer, and received it back within 7 days, fully repaired.

Learning Goal 5

5. A contract will be legally binding if it meets the following conditions:

    An offer is made   Both parties are competent
    There is voluntary acceptance of the offer   The contract is legal
    Both parties give consideration   The contract is in proper form

    Given the information below, determine whether each contract is legally binding (assuming other conditions are met) and why or why not.

    a. A resident of Tennessee signs an IOU to a casino in Las Vegas.

b. You see a newspaper ad for a used car, and after looking the car over, you agree to pay the owner $800 on the spot, with an oral contract.

c. A 17-year-old puts a down payment on a new motorcycle.

d. A student offers to buy your well-used Understanding Business textbook for $10, and you agree.

6. Three actions that can be taken when a breach of contract occurs are:
   Specific performance
   Payment of damages
   Discharge of obligation

Indicate which action might be taken in each of the following breach of contract situations.

a. An actor fails to show up for a scheduled theater performance, without prior warning.

b. A typist working for an author finds that she doesn't have time to finish the manuscript, and quits.

c. An art dealer fails to deliver a piece of sculpture when promised for an art show.

Learning Goal 6
7. Which of the following major pieces of federal legislation would be associated with each of the situations below?

Sherman Act   Robinson--Patman Act
Clayton Act   Federal Trade Commission Act

a. _____ Prohibits conspiracies in restraint of trade and attempts to monopolize.

b. _____ A greeting card company unsuccessfully attempted to coerce its independently owned distributors into carrying only the products it manufactures.

c. _____ The agency created by this act has conducted three times as many investigations and brought twice as many cases in the 1990s as it did in the 1980s. The legislation prohibits unfair methods of competition in commerce.

d. _____ Prohibits several forms of price discrimination and applies to buyers as well as sellers.

8. Using the list of consumer protection laws in Figure A-4 in your text, identify the law associated with each of the following statements.

a. _____ A coat label indicates that the coat is made from "various" wool products.

b. _____ Baby cribs are required to have slats close enough together to prevent an infant's head from getting caught between the slats.

c. _____ Fisher-Price was forced to recall a toy that had caused several injuries to young infants.

d. _____ A car has a sticker price of $16,999.

e. _____ The FDA has "food filth" allowances for such products as peanut butter and chocolate.

f. _____ "Surgeon General's Warning: Cigarette Smoke Contains Carbon Monoxide.

g. _____ Hot dogs are labeled as "all meat" or "all beef," but must contain only meat products.

h. _____ The monthly statement on a Shell credit card indicates a periodic rate per month of 1.5% and an annual percentage rate of 18%.

i. _____ The warranty for a Fisher-Price camera discloses that there is a three-year express warranty, and describes the conditions.

j. _____ A bankruptcy filed several years ago will not show up on a credit report needed for a loan approval.

k. _____ A tee-shirt label indicates that the shirt is 50% cotton and 50% polyester, and provides care instructions.

l. _____ Marti Gilchrist purchases a fur coat that is part rabbit and part pine martin.

m. _____ Apple Jacks cereal contains sugar, corn, wheat and oat flour, salt, dried apples, apple juice concentrate, and cinnamon. These ingredients must be accurately labeled.

n. _____ A toy with a mechanical arm is packaged with a warning that it is intended only for children 8 years and older.

o. _____ Indicates that flammable fabrics and wearing apparel can't be transported interstate.

p. _____ Anheuser-Busch brought out Michelob Ultra in 2002. The cans and bottles had to have a warning label in a visible place on the container. This is especially important as women are one of the target markets.

q. _____ When Judith Durham buys a box of Snack-Wells cookies, she knows exactly what ingredients are in the cookies and how much fat they contain.

Learning Goal 7

9. As you read in this chapter, the federal government gets most of its revenue from taxes paid on income received by businesses and individuals. Review what you learned about economics in Chapter 2. Why would the government <u>lower</u> taxes during a period of economic difficulties, as was done in the early 2000s? Wouldn't that action tend to reduce government revenues? Why or why not?

Learning Goal 8

10. When persons or businesses file for bankruptcy, they are relieved of their financial obligations by the courts.

Most bankruptcies are filed under one of the following three sections of the act:
         Chapter 7   Chapter 11   Chapter 13

Which section of the bankruptcy law is being invoked in each of the following situations?

a. _____ LTV Corporation filed for reorganization, and continued operations after declaring bankruptcy.

b. _____ When the fast-food restaurant Jim S. owned failed, he filed for bankruptcy and sold all the assets to pay off his creditors, including his SBA loan.

c. _____ Because of recent revisions in the bankruptcy law, a small dry cleaner was enabled to declare bankruptcy and set up a three year schedule for repayment to his creditors.

Learning Goals 2, 3,4,5,8,9

11. The types of laws governing business are varied. They include:

Contract law	Bankruptcy law
Sales law (Uniform Commercial Code)	Tort law
Patent law	Deregulation

Match the correct type of business law to each of the following situations.

a. _____ Firestone is being sued by the families of individuals injured by accidents caused by alleged defects in the Firestone tires.

b. _____ A Sears Kenmore washer comes with a 12-month warranty.

c. _____ United Airlines declared itself unable to meet its debt obligations, and filed for Chapter 11 reorganization.

d. _____ The formula for a woman's facial moisturizer is advertised as being protected from duplication until the year 2010.

e. _____ Bob and Dee Slone sued for damages when their building contractor failed to complete the building of their new home.

f. _____ Southwest Airlines was able to take advantage of the opportunities presented when the government stepped away from governing the routes airlines could fly.

Learning Goal 9

12. In the last two decades as your text indicates, several industries have been deregulated, including the telecommunications industry. In the early 1980s in an effort to stimulate competition and give consumers more choices, ATT was forced to divide into several smaller companies, then called the "Baby Bells" which were allowed to compete for phone service with ATT. Since that time the "Baby Bells" have grown up, and are now large corporations. With the deregulation of the telecommunications industry in 1996, many options have been opened for phone service. How do you think you as a consumer have benefited from that deregulation?

PRACTICE TEST

MULTIPLE CHOICE – Circle the best answer

Learning Goal 1

1. In Missouri, a law was passed to allow riverboat gambling. The law has been challenged in the legislature several times by different groups. This kind of law is an example of:
   a. common law.
   b. statutory law.
   c. tort law.
   d. liability law.

Learning Goal 2

2. The fact that a company can be held liable for damages or injuries caused by a product with a defect even if the company did not know of the defect at the time of the sale is referred to as:
    a.   business law
    b.   negligence
    c.   strict product liability
    d.   implied warranty

Learning Goal 3

3. A _____ is a document that gives inventors exclusive rights to their inventions for 20 years.
    a.   trademark
    b.   copyright
    c.   express warranty
    d.   patent

Learning Goal 4

4. The Uniform Commercial Code covers:
    a.   sales law
    b.   bankruptcy law
    c.   product negligence
    d.   contract law

Learning Goal 5

5. Which of the following is <u>not</u> a requirement for a contract to be legally enforceable?
    a.   Both parties must be competent
    b.   An offer must be made
    c.   There must be voluntary acceptance
    d.   Both parties must receive money

6. When John Pegg decided he wanted to buy a car, he went looking in the used car ads, and found one in his price range, $3000, from a private seller. John, who is 16, drove the car, and decided he wanted to buy it. What needs to happen to make John's purchase an enforceable contract?
    a.   The contract needs to be written up
    b.   John needs to find a person older than he, like a parent, to make the contract for him
    c.   The seller must wait for 3 days before he can sell it to John
    d.   All of the above

7. Billy Joel and Elton John had to cancel a booking for their joint concert in St. Louis because Billy Joel fell ill. If they had not made arrangements to re-book the concert, the cancellation could be considered a breach of contract, and the results could be:
    a.   Specific performance.
    b.   Payment of damages.
    c.   Discharge of obligation.
    d.   Could be all of the above.

8.   The _____prohibits exclusive dealing, tying contracts and interlocking directorates.
    a.   Clayton Act
    b.   Federal Trade Commission Act
    c.   Robinson-Patman Act
    d.   Interstate Commerce Act

9.   Which of the following is not one of the rights of consumers outlined by President John F. Kennedy?
    a.   the right to safety
    b.   the right to be informed
    c.   the right to be heard
    d.   the right to fair prices

Learning Goal 7

10.   The federal government receives most of its revenues from:
    a.   individual and corporate income taxes.
    b.   sales taxes.
    c.   property taxes.
    d.   sin taxes.

Learning Goal 8

11.   Chapter ____ of the bankruptcy code allows businesses to continue operations while paying a limited portion of their debts.
    a.   7
    b.   11
    c.   13
    d.   22

Learning Goal 9

12.   How has deregulation affected business in the U.S.?
    a.   Some industries have become more competitive.
    b.   Some companies must follow a stricter code of ethics.
    c.   Many businesses are raising prices because the government is not controlling them anymore.
    d.   Companies are becoming less ethical.

TRUE-FALSE

Learning Goal 1

1. _____   It isn't necessary for business people to know laws governing business, as long as their lawyers understand them.

2. _____   Common law is often referred to as unwritten law.

3. _____   Administrative agencies are allowed to pass rules and regulations in their areas of authority, but cannot take action if they feel a rule or regulation has been violated.

Learning Goal 2

4. _____   A company can be held liable for injuries resulting from use of their product even if the company had no prior knowledge that the product could be harmful.

5. _____ Negligence is a willful act that results in injury – in other words, the act is intentional.

Learning Goal 3
6. _____ A submarine patent is one that has not yet been granted and is subject to court review.

7. _____ A copyright lasts for the lifetime of the creator of the work, but ends after their death.

Learning Goal 4

8. _____ An express warranty is a specific representation by the seller that is relied upon by the buyer regarding the goods.

9. _____ An endorsement is the signature of the payee on the back of a negotiable instrument, such as a check.

Learning Goal 5
10. _____ Any contract for the sale of real property, such as land, must be written.

11. _____ If a breach of contract occurs, the individual who breached the contract will always be required to live up to the contract eventually.

Learning Goal 6
12. _____ The Sherman Act prohibits price discrimination.

13. _____ Exclusive dealing refers to the selling of goods with the condition that the buyer will not buy goods from a competitor.

Learning Goal 7
14. _____ A major tax issue in the future will the that of charging tax on Internet purchases.

Learning Goal 8
15. _____ In a bankruptcy case, the first thing to be paid will be federal and state taxes.

Learning Goal 9
16. _____ Deregulation has affected most businesses in a positive way, and no businesses have suffered.

You Can Find It On The Net

After learning so much about business, are you interested in starting your own company? Click on http://www.business.gov/index.html

Select Business Laws. What areas does this site indicate are of importance to you as a small business owner? Can you see why it is important that as a business person you are familiar with business law?!

ANSWERS

LEARNING THE LANGUAGE

1. Consideration	10. Statutory law	19. Product liability
2. Deregulation	11. Implied warranties	20. Administrative agencies
3. Negotiable Instruments	12. Consumerism	21. Judiciary
4. Business law	13. Breach of contract	22. Involuntary bankruptcy
5. Uniform Commercial Code (UCC)	14. Contract	23. Taxes
6. Express warranties	15. Patent	24. Damages
7. Tort	16. Common law	25. Precedent
8. Bankruptcy	17. Contract law	26. Negligence
9. Copyright	18. Voluntary bankruptcy	27. Strict product liability

ASSESSMENT CHECK

Learning Goal 1
The Need for Laws

1. Criminal law defines crimes, establishes punishments, and regulates the investigation and prosecution of people accused of committing crimes. Civil law involves legal proceedings that do not involve criminal acts. It includes laws regulating areas such as marriage, payment for personal injury and so on.

2. Statutory law is written law, and includes state and federal constitutions, legislative enactments and so forth. Common law is the body of law that comes from decisions handed down by judges.

3. Common law is referred to as unwritten law because it does not appear in any legislative enactment, treaty, or other such document. Under common law principles, what judges have decided in previous cases is important in deciding current cases. These decisions are called precedent, and they guide judges in handing new cases.

4. Some administrative agencies hold quasi-legislative, quasi-executive and quasi-judicial powers. This means an agency is allowed to pass rules and regulations within its area of authority, conduct investigations in cases of suspected rules violations, and hold hearings when it feels the rules and regulations have been violated. Administrative agencies issue more rulings affecting business and settle more business disputes than courts do.

Learning Goal 2
Tort Law

5. An intentional tort is a willful act that results in injury. Negligence deals with *unintentional* behavior that causes harm or injury.

6. The rule of "strict liability" refers to product liability. It is the idea that a company can be liable for damages caused by placing a product on the market with a defect even if the company did not know of the defect at the time of the sale.

7.   The rule of strict product liability has caused serious problems for businesses. A number of companies have been forced into bankruptcy due to asbestos litigation, for example. Several other industries, such as the chemical and paint industries, are at risk in the area of product liability. The gun industry, for example, has been accused of damages under the rules of strict product liability, and lawsuits have been filed on behalf of individuals affected by gun violence. Businesses and insurance companies have called for legal relief from huge losses that are often awarded in strict product liability suits.

Learning Goal 3
Laws Protecting Ideas: Patents, Copyrights, and Trademarks

8.   In order to file a patent an inventor must, or should:
      a.   file forms
      b.   make sure the product is truly unique.
      c.   The advice of a lawyer is usually recommended.

9.   Close to 70 percent of patent applications are approved. The minimum cost to an inventor is $6,600 in fees over the life of the patent. It can take up to 2 years to get a patent approved, and approval time is expected to increase to 45 months by 2008 if more patent examiners are not hired.

10.   The American Inventor's Protection Act requires patent applications to be made public after 18 months regardless of whether a patent has been granted. This law was passed in part to address critics that argued some inventors would intentionally delay or drag out a patent application because they expected others to develop similar products or technology. When someone else filed for a similar patent, the inventor would claim the patent, which is referred to as a submarine patent and demand large fees for its use.

11.   A business-method patent involves different business applications using the Internet.

12.   A patent lasts for 20 years. A copyright protects an individual's right to materials for the lifetime of the author or artist plus 70 years and can be passed on to the creator's heirs.

13.   The Copyright Act of 1978 gives a special term of 75 years from publication to works published before January 1, 1978 whose copyrights had not expired by that date.

14.   The holder of an exclusive copyright may charge a fee to anyone who wishes to use the copyrighted material. If a work is created by an employee in the normal course of a job, the copyright belongs to the employer and lasts 95 years from publication or 120 years from creation, whichever comes first.

15.   A trademark is a legally protected name, symbol, or design, or combination of those, that identifies the goods or services of one seller and distinguishes them from those of the competition. A trademark belongs to the owner forever, so long as it is properly registered and renewed every 10 years.

Sales Law: The Uniform Commercial Code

16.   The areas covered by the Uniform Commercial Code are:
    a. Sales   f. Warehouse receipts
    b. Commercial paper   g. Bills of lading
    c. Bank deposits and collections   h. Investment securities
    d. Letters of credit   i. Secured transactions
    e. Bulk transfers

17.   An express warranty is often enclosed with the product when purchased. It spells out the
       seller's warranty agreement. An implied warranty is legally imposed on the seller. It is
       implied that the product will conform to the customary standards of the trade or industry
       in which it competes.

18.   A full warranty requires a seller to replace or repair a product at no charge if the product is
       defective. Limited warranties typically limit the defects or mechanical problems that are covered.

19.   Negotiable instruments must be:
       a.   Signed by the maker
       b.   Made payable on demand at a certain time
       c.   Made payable to the bearer or to order
       d.   Contain an unconditional promise to pay a specific amount of money

20.   An endorsement in the area of negotiable instruments is the signature of the payee on the
       back of the negotiable instrument, such as a check.

Learning Goal 5
Contract Law

21.   A contract is legally binding if:
       a.   An offer is made
       b.   There is voluntary acceptance of the offer
       c.   Both parties give consideration
       d.   Both parties are competent
       e.   The contract is legal (for a legal act)
       f.   The contract is in proper form

22.   An offer is legally binding only when all other conditions of a contract have been met.

23.   The principle of mutual acceptance means that both parties to a contract must agree on the
       terms of the contract.

24.   In order to be judged competent to enter into a contract, a person must not be under the
       influence of drugs or alcohol, be of sound mind and be of legal age.

25.   A contract covering an illegal act is illegal and not enforceable.

26.   An agreement for the sale of goods worth $500 or more must be in writing. Contracts that cannot
       be fulfilled within one year and contracts regarding real property must also be in writing.

27.   a.   Specific performance i.e. the person may be required to live up to the agreement
      b.   Payment of damages
      c.   Discharge of obligation, which means to drop the matter

28.   A contract does not have to be complicated, but should have the following three elements.
      a.   It should be in writing.
      b.   mutual consideration is specified.
      c.   there is a clear offer and agreement.

Learning Goal 6
Laws to Promote Fair and Competitive Practices

29.   a.   Sherman Act (1890)
      b.   Clayton Act (1914)
      c.   Federal Trade Commission Act (1914)
      d.   Robinson—Patman Act (1936)

30.   The Sherman Act forbids
      a.   contracts, combinations or conspiracies in restraint of trade,
      b.   actual monopolies or attempts to monopolize any part of trade or commerce.

31.   The Clayton Act prohibits exclusive dealing, tying contracts, interlocking directorates and buying large amounts of stock in competing corporations.

32.   a.   Exclusive dealing is selling goods with the condition that the buyer will not buy goods from a competitor.
      b.   A tying contract requires a buyer to purchase unwanted items in order to purchase the desired items.
      c.   An interlocking directorate occurs when a board of directors includes members of the board of competing corporations.

33.   The Federal Trade Commission Act prohibits unfair methods of competition in commerce. This act set up the Federal Trade Commission (FTC). The FTC deals with a wide array of issues.

34.   The FTC covers competitive issues in a number of different areas, from misleading claims, telemarketer's practices and funeral pricing. The FTC's is now responsible for overseeing mergers and acquisitions in the healthcare, energy, computer hardware, automotive and biotechnology industries.

35.   The Robinson-Patman Act prohibits price discrimination.

      It applies to both sellers and buyers who knowingly induce or receive an unlawful discrimination in price. It also stipulates that certain types of price cutting are criminal offenses.

      It specifically outlaws price differences that substantially weaken competition unless the differences can be justified by lower selling costs. It also prohibits advertising and promotional allowances unless they are offered to all retailers.

36. The Sarbanes/Oxley Act requires CEOs to verify the accuracy of their firms' financial statements to the SEC.

37. a. The right to safety   c. The right to choose
    b. The right to be informed d. The right to be heard

Learning Goal 7
Tax Laws

38. Taxes have traditionally been used as a source of funding for government operations and programs. They have also been used as a method of encouraging or discouraging certain behaviors among taxpayers.

39. The purpose of a sin tax is to reduce the use of certain types of products. This is what has happened in the cigarette and alcohol industry.

40. A tax credit is an amount that can be deducted from a tax bill.

41. Taxes are levied from a variety of sources, including:
    a. income taxes
    b. property taxes
    c. sales taxes

42. The federal government receives its largest share of taxes from income tax.
    State and local governments make extensive use of sales taxes.
    School districts general depend upon property taxes.

43. A key tax issue currently revolves around Internet taxation, especially Internet transactions.

Learning Goal 8
Bankruptcy Laws

44. Two major amendments to the bankruptcy code include
    a: The Bankruptcy Amendments and Federal Judgeships Act of 1984. This legislation allows a person who is bankrupt to keep part of the ownership in a house, $1,200 in a car, and some other personal property.

    b. The Bankruptcy Reform Act of 1994 amends more than 45 sections of the bankruptcy code and creates reforms that speed up and simplify the process.

45. Chapter 7 calls for straight bankruptcy, which requires the sale of nonexempt assets. Under federal exemption statutes, a debtor may be able to retain up to $7,500 of equity in a home, up to $1,200 of equity in an automobile, up to $4,000 in household furnishings, and up to $500 in jewelry. When the sale of assets is over, the resulting cash is divided among creditors.

46. First, creditors with secured claims receive the collateral for their claims, or repossess the claimed asset. Then, unsecured claims are paid in this order
    a. Costs involved in the bankruptcy case
    b. Any business costs incurred after bankruptcy was filed
    c. Wages, salaries, or commissions
    d. Employee benefit plan contributions
    e. Refunds to consumers who paid for undelivered products
    f. Federal and state taxes

47. Chapter 11 allows a company to reorganize operations while paying only a limited portion of its debts. A company continues to operate, but has court protection against creditors' lawsuits while it tries to work out a plan for paying off its debts. Under certain conditions, the company can sell assets, borrow money, and change officers to strengthen its market position. A company will continue to operate but has court protection against creditor's lawsuits while it tries to work out a reorganization plan.

48. Chapter 13 bankruptcy permits individuals and small business owners to pay back creditors over a period of three to five years. Chapter 13 proceedings are less complicated and less expensive than Chapter 7 proceedings. The debtor files a proposed plan for paying off debts to the court. If the plan is approved, the debtor pays a court appointed trustee in monthly installments, and the trustee pays each creditor.

Learning Goal 9
Deregulation

49. The move toward deregulation began because there was a concern that there were too many laws and regulations governing business and that these laws and regulations were costing the public money.

50. The most publicized examples of deregulation have been in the airlines and the telecommunications industry.
    a. Airlines: When restrictions were lifted in the airline industry, the airlines began competing for different routes and charging lower prices. New airlines were created to take advantage of new opportunities.
    b. Telecommunications: Deregulation gave consumers many more options in the telephone service market.
    c. Utilities: California was the first state to deregulate the electric power industry. Since then, the state has had significant problems with the deregulation of the electric power industry. Many states have halted the deregulation process.

51. As a result of corporate scandals in 2002, many in government and society called for even more government regulation and control of business operations to protect investors and workers.

CRITICAL THINKING EXERCISES

Learning Goal 1
1. a. Common law
    b. Statutory law
    c. Statutory law
    d. Common law
Learning Goal 2
2. At one time, the legal standard for measuring product liability was if a producer knowingly placed a hazardous product on the market. Today, many states have extended product liability to the level of strict liability. Legally this means without regard to fault. Therefore, a company could be liable for damages caused by placing a product on the market with a defect even if the company did not know of the defect at the time of the sale. This has subjected manufacturers to expensive lawsuits.

Learning Goal 3

3. You will probably advise Eric to apply for a patent as soon as possible. A patent will give Eric protection for his new formula for 20 years from the date of the application, which means that his competitor will not be able to copy this new formula anytime soon. You should also let Eric know that once his patent application has been filed he has to make it public within 18 months regardless of whether the patent has been granted.

Learning Goal 4

4. a.   implied warranty
   b.   express warranty

Learning Goal 5

5. a   Yes, this is a binding contract. Although the signer is a resident of Tennessee, he is in Nevada, where gambling is legal.
   b.   No, this is not binding. Oral contracts are binding only when the value of the goods is less than $500. It's usually best to get a written contract for the protection of both parties.
   c.   No, this is not a binding contract because a minor isn't legally competent to make a contract.
   d.   Yes this is a binding contract. The offer was voluntary, so was the acceptance and both parties received consideration.

6. a.   Payment of damages
   b.   Discharge of obligation
   c.   Specific performance

Learning Goal 6

7. a.   Sherman Act (1890)
   b.   Clayton Act (1914)
   c.   Federal Trade Commission Act (1914)
   d.   Robinson-Patman Act (1936)

8. a.   Wool Products Labeling Act
   b.   Consumer Product Safety Act
   c.   Child Protection Act
   d.   Automobile Information Disclosure Act
   e.   Food, Drug and Cosmetic Act
   f.   Cigarette Labeling Act
   g.   Pure Food and Drug Act
   h.   Truth-in-Lending Act
   i.   Magnuson-Moss Warranty-Federal Trade Commission Improvement Act
   j.   Fair Credit Reporting Act
   k.   Textile Fiber Products Identification Act
   l.   Fur Products Labeling Act
   m.   Fair Packaging and Labeling Act
   n.   Child Protection and Toy Safety Act
   o.   Flammable Fabrics Act (1953)
   p.   Alcohol Labeling Legislation
   q.   Nutrition Labeling and Education Act

Learning Goal 7

9. Your answers will vary. Here are some suggestions to keep you thinking. When the government lowers the tax rate, it should mean that people have more money in their

pockets to spend. If the theory holds true, then when people buy goods and services with that extra cash, they increase demand for goods and services, and that should actually increase jobs as companies try to keep up with that demand. When people have jobs they pay taxes, so the reduction in the tax *rate* is made up for by the increase in the number of people working and paying taxes, as well as from companies which experience higher profits. The idea is to create jobs and put people to work so that they will have more money to spend. This will keep tax revenues coming in.

Learning Goal 8
10.   a. Chapter 11
        b. Chapter 7
        c. Chapter 13
Learning Goals 2,3,4,5,,8,9

11.   a.   Tort law   d.   Patent law
        b.   Sales law (UCC)   e.   Contract law
        c.   Bankruptcy law   f.   Deregulation

Learning Goal 9

12.   Answers will vary, but you may have mentioned such devices as cellular phone service, more options on your land lines, lower prices for example.

PRACTICE TEST

MULTIPLE CHOICE   **TRUE-FALSE**
LG 1   #1   *LG 1   # 1-3*
LG 2   #2   *LG 2   # 4-5*
LG 3   #3   *LG 3   #6-7*
LG 4   #4   *LG 4   #8-9*
LG 5   #5-7   *LG 5   # 10-11*
LG 6   #8-9   *LG 6   #12-13*
LG 7   #10   *LG 7   #14*
LG 8   #11   *LG 8   #15*
LG 9   #12   *LG 9   #16*

1.	b	7.	d
2.	c	8.	a
3.	d	9.	d
4.	a	10.	a
5.	d	11.	b
6.	b	12.	a

1.	F	9.	T
2.	T	10.	T
3.	F	11.	F
4.	T	12.	F
5.	F	13.	T
6.	F	14.	T
7.	F	15.	F
8.	T	16.	F

CHAPTER B –USING TECHNOLOGY TO MANAGE INFORMATION

LEARNING GOALS

After you have read and studied this chapter, you should be able to:

1. Outline the changing role of business technology.
2. List the types of business information, identify the characteristics of useful information, and discuss how data is stored and mined.
3. Compare the scope of the Internet, intranets, extranets, and virtual private networks as tools in managing information.
4. Review the hardware most frequently used in business and outline the benefits of the move toward computer networks.
5. Classify the computer software most frequently used in business.
6. Evaluate the human resource, security, privacy and stability issues in management that are affected by information technology.

LEARNING THE LANGUAGE

Listed below are important terms found in the chapter. Choose the correct term for the definition and write it in the space provided

Broadband technology	Information systems (IS)	Public domain software (freeware)
Business Intelligence	Information technology (IT)	Shareware
Cookies	Internet2	Virtual private network (VPN)
Data processing (DP)	Intranet	Virtualization
Extranet	Network computing systems (Client/server computing)	Virus

1. The name for business technology in the 1970s was_____ and included technology that supported an existing business, and was used primarily to improve the flow of financial information.

2. A private data network called a _____ creates secure connections or "tunnels" over regular Internet lines.

3. The private Internet system known as the _____links government supercomputer centers and a select group of universities; it runs 22,000 times faster than today's public infrastructure and supports heavy-duty applications.

4. Accessibility through technology, or _____ , allows business to be conducted independent of location.

5. A semiprivate network known as a(n) _____ uses Internet technology and allows more than one company to access the same information or allows people on different servers to collaborate.

6. Software that is copyrighted but distributed to potential customers free of charge is called _____.

7. A piece of programming code known as a _____ is inserted into other programming to cause some unexpected and, for the victim, usually undesirable event.

8. Technology called _____ helps companies to do business; includes such tools as automated teller machines (ATMs) and voice mail.

9. Technology known as _____ offers users a continuous connection to the Internet and allows them to send and receive mammoth files that include voice, video, and data much faster than ever before.

10. Computer systems that allow personal computers (clients) to obtain needed information from huge databases in a central computer (the server) are called _____.

11. Technology called _____ helps companies to change business by allowing them to use new methods.

12. Software that is free for the taking is _____.

13. Pieces of information such as registration information or user preferences, known as _____ are sent by a Web site over the Internet to a Web browser that the browser software is expected to save and to send back to the server whenever the user returns to that web site.

14. A company wide network called an _____ is closed to public access, and uses Internet-type technology.

15. _____ is any variety of software applications that takes out useful insights from an analysis of an organization's raw data.

ASSESSMENT CHECK

Learning Goal 1
The Role of Information Technology

1. What was the primary role and use of data processing?

2. How did Information Systems differ from data processing?

3. What is the role of the CIO in business today?

4. How does IT break use time and place to better serve customers?

5. Describe a virtual office and a virtual community.

6. What is knowledge technology and how is it different from IT?

7. Knowledge technology changes the flow of information in that: _____

_____

8. How do KT and BI help business people in doing their jobs?

Learning Goal 2
Types of Information

9. Describe five types of information.

a. _____

b. _____

c. _____

d. _____

e. _____

10. "Infoglut" is _____

11. Referring to information overload, the most important step toward gaining perspective is to:

_____

_____

12. Describe four characteristics of useful information.

a._____

b._____

c._____

d._____

13. The goals in managing information are:

a. _____

b. _____

c. _____

14. What is a data warehouse, and what is its purpose?

15. What is data mining and what does it do?

16. What must be done to make data mining successful?

Learning Goal 3
The Road to Knowledge: The Internet, Intranets, Extranets, and Virtual Private Networks

17. To manage knowledge, a company needs to learn how to: _____

_____

_____

18. How can a company prevent competitors from getting into their intranets?

19. What are some applications of an intranet? How does this benefit the company?

20.   How is an intranet different from an extranet? How can an extranet be used?

21.   Since the extranet is a semiprivate network, what is a potential problem?

22.   One way to increase the probability of total privacy (of an extranet) is to use: _____

      Two problems with this method are: _____

      _____

23.   Describe how a virtual private network solves the problems involved with the use of an
      extranet, and the benefits of the VPN.

24.   How do enterprise portals function?

25.   How does broadband technology solve the problems of traffic jams on the Internet?

26.   What applications does the Internet2 support?

      a.   _____

      b.   _____

      c.   _____

      d.   _____

      e.   _____

27.   What is a vBNS?

The Enabling Technology: Hardware

28.   What are some hardware components?

a. _____   e. _____

b. _____   f. _____

c. _____   g. _____

d. _____

29.   Identify some examples of wireless information appliances.

30.   What is meant by the term "wi-fi"?

31.   Describe the major benefits of computer network systems

a. _____

b. _____

c. _____

32.   Describe the drawbacks of networks.

33.   What have some companies looked into to avoid the drawbacks of computer networking systems?

34.   What is the benefit of this thin client network?

35.   What is another option for companies looking to avoid problems with networks, besides thin client networks? What is the benefit?

Learning Goal 5
Software

36. What are six major business uses of software?

a._____   d._____

b._____   e._____

c._____   f. _____

37. Identify the major elements of each of the following types of software

Word Processing	Desktop Publishing	Spreadsheets	Database	PIMs	Graphics/ Presentation
Communications	Message Center	Accounting / Finance	Integrated Programs	Groupware	

Learning Goal 6
Effects of Information Technology on Management

38. Identify the major issues arising out of the growing reliance on information technology:

a. _____   c. _____

b. _____   d. _____

39. What impact has technology had on organizational structures?

40.   One of the major challenge technology poses for human resource managers is:

_____

To address these concerns: _____

41.   What are the benefits of telecommuting for companies?

    a. _____

    b. _____

    c. _____

42.   What are the benefits of telecommuting for employees?

43.   What are some drawbacks to telecommuting?

    a. _____

    b. _____

    c. _____

44.   How are companies attempting to alleviate the problems of telecommuting?

45.   By whom is information typically stolen?

    a. _____

    b. _____

    c. _____

46.   How are computer viruses spread?

47.   Describe "phishing."

48.   Identify the legal issues that have arisen from direct, real-time communication.

49.   Since September 11, security officials are most worried about: _____

50.   What could be the impact of cyber terrorists?

51.   What is the function of the Critical Infrastructure Protection Board?

52.   What is the purpose of the Critical Infrastructure Information Act of 2002?

53.   What are some of the privacy issues that arise from the use of technology?

54.   What information does a cookie contain, and what does it do?

55.   What is spyware?

56.   To prevent your computer from receiving cookies you can: _____

_____

57.   What is causing computer glitches?

a. _____

b. _____

c. _____

d. _____

e. _____

f. _____

CRITICAL THINKING EXERCISES

Learning Goal 1

1.   Trace the development of business technology from the 1970's to the 1980's to the present.

2.   We have read in previous chapters of the need to meet increasing global competition, and of the movement toward customized products and marketing. How does information technology change business to make those jobs possible?

3.   Review Figure B.1 in your text. How has information technology changed your school, or your place of employment in each of these areas?

4.   What is one of the biggest problems with the age of information technology in terms of managing the information? How can business people overcome this problem? How have you, as a student, experienced the problem?

5.   Help! You are swamped by the data, reports, facts, figures, and tons of paper and E-mail being sent to you! It's your job as a low level sales employee to manage the dissemination of all this "stuff" and make sure it makes sense to everyone who gets it- in other words; your job is to manage all that information! What can you do to make this information useful?

6.   Compare Intranets and Extranets. Do you know a company that has an intranet? How is it used? What are the applications in this company?

7.   Are you "evolved"? What kinds of computer hardware do you use? What kinds of hardware do your friends use? How do you keep up with your friends? What kind of computerized instruction do you have in your classes?

Learning Goal 5

8.   Five major uses for software include:

Writing (word processing)   Presenting   information   visually
(Graphics)
Manipulating numbers (spreadsheets)   Communicating
Filing and retrieving data (databases)   Accounting

Match the application being used to the following examples:

a. _____   Richard Bolt uses this software to record his students' grades, average the grades and totals the grades at the end of the semester. It's easy to change scores if an error is made, because the computer will automatically recalculate averages and totals when the new score is recorded.

b. _____   Ray Smith uses Outlook Express to send and retrieve messages from work.

c. _____   Steve Nicholson is a marketing manager who uses this type of software to keep track of all his sales people. He has all the information regarding territories, sales quotas, expenses, sales calls and more right at his fingertips.

d. _____   Ryan Charles used this software to create a more interesting report for his science project. After he had finished writing the report, he created a pie chart and a bar chart to illustrate the findings of his research.

e. _____   Lin Brinkman works in a law office. Whenever there is a need for a certain kind of document for a specific case, all Lin has to do is pull the document up on her screen and insert the relevant information.

f. _____   Elizabeth Dean creates the financial statements for her small business each month with Peachtree, a software which makes the process much easier.

Learning Goal 6

9.   What has happened to organizational structures and methods of work as a result of the increased use of technology?

10.   What are some of the security and privacy issues that are important to recognize with the increasing use of information technology?

PRACTICE TEST

MULTIPLE CHOICE – Circle the best answer

Learning Goal 1

1. In the 1990's, business technology changed from doing business, to changing business and technology came to be known as _____.
   a. data processing
   b. information technology
   c. information systems
   d. knowledge technology

2. Using _____ a new employee can sit at a workstation and let the system take over doing everything from laying out a checklist of each thing required on a shift to answering questions and offering insights that once would have taken up a supervisor's time.
   a. data processing
   b. information technology
   c. knowledge technology
   d. virtualization

Learning Goal 2

3. A problem managers have with the rapid advance of information technology has been:
   a. the skyrocketing cost of information.
   b. the hardware and software products available can't keep up with the expansion of information.
   c. the increased layers of management.
   d. information overload, with the huge amount of information available.

4. The most important step toward gaining perspective in dealing with infoglut is to:
   a. identify your key goals then eliminate information that doesn't relate to the goals.
   b. get as much information as you can, then sift through it.
   c. limit the information you retrieve by limiting your search to only certain websites.
   d. look for a system which will handle the information more readily.

5. Which of the following is not included in a list of characteristics of useful information?
   a. Timeliness
   b. Quality
   c. Completeness
   d. Accessibility

Learning Goal 3

6. At MEMC Electronics, employees can update their addresses; submit requisitions, timesheets and payroll forms online. The company's system is closed to public access, but all employees have access. MEMC is using an _____
   a. intranet
   b. extranet
   c. internet
   d. electronic data interchange system

7.   A(n) _____ is a private data network that creates secure connections or "tunnels" over regular Internet lines.
        a.   enterprise portal
        b.   virtual private network
        c.   broadband
        d.   wireless information appliance

8.   A system that runs 22,000 times faster than a traditional modem and supports heavy-duty applications is known as:
        a.   broadband technology
        b.   the Internet
        c.   an extranet
        d.   Internet 2

Learning Goal 4

9.   _____includes pagers, cellular phones, printers and scanners and personal digital assistants.
        a.   Software
        b.   Multimedia
        c.   Extranets
        d.   Hardware

10.   In recent years, businesses have moved from:
        a.   network computing systems to mainframe systems.
        b.   client/server computing to network computing systems.
        c.   database systems to information processing.
        d.   mainframe systems to network computing systems.

11.   Which of the following is a benefit of networks?
        a.   unnecessary information is deleted from the system
        b.   saves time and money
        c.   customers can access information more quickly
        d.   companies can see their products more clearly

Learning Goal 5

12.   Which of the following projects would be best suited to a spreadsheet program?
        a.   Personalizing a standardized letter to clients.
        b.   Recording the sales figures from several different stores, and calculating profits.
        c.   Updating lists and schedules, keeping track of inventory.
        d.   Making a presentation more appealing with sound clips, video clips, and clip art .

13.   A major difference between groupware and other types of software is that groupware
        a.   is less expensive than other forms of software because it is distributed free.
        b.   can replace more management functions than others.
        c.   allows computers to talk to one another.
        d.   runs on a network and allows several users to work on the same project at the same time.

14.   Wi-Fi stands for:
        a.   wired firewall
        b.   windows friction
        c.   wireless fidelity
        d.   wonderful fiction

15.   For workers, perhaps the most revolutionary effect of computers and increased use of the Internet is:
   a.   the amount of information which has been made available to managers.
   b.   the ability to allow employees to work from home.
   c.   the spread of viruses.
   d.   the amount of personal information available and people who can access it.

16.   Which of the following is <u>not</u> considered a benefit of telecommuting?
   a.   It saves money by retaining valuable employees during long leaves.
   b.   It involves less travel time and cost.
   c.   It can increase productivity.
   d.   It avoids isolation of workers.

17.   In the movie *The Matrix - Reloaded,* a rebel group breaks into government computers and accesses some very sensitive information. The term to describe this group would be:
   a.   hackers
   b.   viruses
   c.   cookies
   d.   computer illiterates

18.   One of the problems with today's direct, real-time communication is:
   a.   existing laws do not address the legal issues.
   b.   public information is more difficult to obtain.
   c.   communication is not face to face.
   d.   having to be careful to constantly update antivirus programs.

19.   Today, corporate and government security officials are most worried about:
   a.   inoculating computers from viruses.
   b.   cyber terrorism.
   c.   privacy issues.
   d.   consumers' fears of using credit cards on the Internet.

20.   Which of the following is <u>untrue</u> regarding concerns about privacy issues and the Internet?
   a.   Hackers can easily trap and read your messages.
   b.   Companies can track employee emails.
   c.   The Internet makes personal information very easy to retrieve.
   d.   Cookies allow you to protect your computer from hackers using spyware.

True-False

Learning Goal 1

1. _____   The role of information technology has changed as technology has evolved.

2. _____   Information technology creates organizations and services that are independent of location.

3. _____   A virtual office would include cellular phones, pagers, laptop computers and personal digital assistants

4. _____ With the increased use of the Internet, information has become easier to manage

5. _____ One type of information available to businesses today is data that indicate the personal preferences of customers.

6. _____ Data mining is looking for hidden patterns in a data warehouse.

Learning Goal 3

7. _____ An extranet is a company wide network which is closed to everyone outside the specific company using the intranet.

8. _____ Broadband technology offers users a continuous connection to the Internet.

9. _____ The Internet 2 will support heavy-duty applications, such as videoconferencing, research, distance education and other sophisticated applications.

Learning Goal 4

10. _____ Personal digital assistants are actually word processing programs.

11. _____ A computer network will help a company file, store and access data more easily.

12. _____ A thin client network is a hybrid of mainframe and network computing.

Learning Goal 5

13. _____ Business people most frequently use software for such things as word processing and manipulating numbers, among other uses.

14. _____ Database programs are basically the electronic equivalent of an accountant's worksheet plus features such as math functions, statistical data analysis and charts.

Learning Goal 6

15. _____ Computers have allowed organizations to eliminate middle management functions and flatten organizational structures.

16. _____ Computer security has gotten simpler today with new security programs.

You Can Find It On the Net

As we have discussed in this chapter, there is a lot of information on the web for just about any topic you can imagine. Let's find out what some of the employment statistics are for computer related occupations.

Visit the Bureau of Labor Statistics at **www.bls.gov**. (Talk about Information Overload!)

Go to the Occupations link, and then to the Wages by Area and Occupation link. Look at the classification of 800 occupations by the SOC system.

What is the employment total for Computer and Mathematical occupations?

What is the mean salary?

Return to the main page, and look in the Occupational Outlook Handbook A-Z Index for computer related jobs and investigate some of the jobs listed.

Which did you find that are declining? Why?

Which are expected to grow? Why?

ANSWERS

LEARNING THE LANGUAGE

1. Data processing	6. Shareware	11. Information technology
2. Virtual private network	7. Virus	12. Public domain software
3. Internet2	8. Information systems	13. Cookies
4. Virtualization	9. Broadband technology	14. Intranet
5. Extranet	10. Network computing systems (client/server computing)	15. Business intelligence

ASSESSMENT CHECK

Learning Goal 1
The Role of Information Technology

1.   The primary role of data processing was to support existing business by improving the flow of financial information.

2.   Information Systems went from supporting business to actually doing business. Customers began to interact with the business through such means as ATMs and voice mail.

3.   The role of the CIO is to help the business use technology to communicate better with others while offering better services and lower costs.

4.   Information technology uses time and location to bring products to the customer in the most convenient way. IT allows businesses to deliver goods and services whenever and wherever it is convenient for the customer. IT creates organizations and services that are independent of location. Being independent of location brings work to people and allows businesses to conduct business around the globe 24 hours a day.

5.   A virtual office includes cellular phones, pagers, laptop computers, and personal digital assistants. This technology allows you to access people and information as if you were in an actual office. Virtual communities are formed when people who would otherwise not have met communicate with each other through computer networks.

6.   Knowledge technology is information charged with enough intelligence to make it relevant and useful. It adds a layer of intelligence to filter appropriate information and deliver it when it is needed. Information technology makes information available, as long as you know how to use it and where to find it.

7.   Knowledge technology changes the traditional flow of information in that instead of an individual going to the database, the database comes to the individual

8.   KT will "think" about individual needs and reduce the amount of time finding and getting information. As KT became more sophisticated it became known as business intelligence. Businesspeople who use BI can focus on deciding how to react to problems and opportunities.

Learning Goal 2
Types of Information

9.   Five types of information are:

   a.   Business process information – all transaction data gathered from business transactions.
   b.   Physical-world observations – result form the use of which has to do with where people and items are located.
   c.   Biological data – identification from physical scans such as fingerprinting, and use of biometric devices.
   d.   Public data – free data available from people using the internet email and instant messaging.
   e.   Data indicating preferences or intentions – left by Internet shoppers.

10.   Infoglut refers to information overload resulting from a deluge of information from a variety of sources.

11.   The most important step toward gaining perspective on information overload is to identify the four or five key goals you wish to reach, then eliminating the information that is not related to those priorities.

12.   Four characteristics of useful information include:
   a.   Quality - information is accurate and reliable.
   b.   Completeness – enough information to allow you to make a decision but not so much as to confuse the issue
   c.   Timeliness – information must reach managers quickly
   d.   Relevance – different managers have different needs

13.   The goals in managing information are
   a.   storing
   b.   sorting
   c.   getting useful information to the right people at the right time.

14.   A data warehouse is storage of data on a single subject over a specific period of time. The purpose of a data warehouse is to get data out so that it is useful information.

15.   Data mining is software that looks for hidden patterns in a data warehouse. It discovers previously unknown relationships among the data.

16.   The success of data mining depends upon access to data to mine in the first place. Multiple data storage systems must be integrated in some way before the data can be connected.

Learning Goal 3
The Road to Knowledge: The Internet, Intranets Extranets and Virtual Private Networks

17.   To manage knowledge, a company needs to learn how to share information throughout the organization and to implement systems for creating new knowledge. This need is leading to new technologies that support the exchange of information among staff, suppliers, and customers.

18.   Companies can construct a firewall between themselves and the outside world to protect corporate information. A firewall can be software, hardware or both and allows only authorized users access to the intranet.

19.   Intranet applications can include allowing employees to update their addresses or submit company forms such as requisitions, timesheets, or payroll forms online. This benefits the company by saving money or generating increased revenues because these applications eliminate paper handling and enable decision making.

20.   An intranet operates only within a company. An extranet is a semiprivate network that uses Internet technology so that more than one company can access the same information or so people on different servers can collaborate. A common use is to allow access to outside customers to share data and process orders, specifications, invoices and payments.

21.   One of the potential problems with an extranet is that it can be accessed by outsiders with enough knowledge to break into the system.

22.   One way to increase the probability of total privacy of an extranet is to use a dedicated line.

        Two problems with this method are that a dedicated line is expensive and limits use to computers directly linked to that line.

23.   A virtual private network solves the problem of extranet privacy by creating secure connections, or "tunnels," over regular Internet lines. The idea is to give the company the same capabilities as dedicated lines at a much lower cost. Companies can use public lines securely. This allows for on-demand networking, and an authorized user can join the network for any desired function at any time, for any length of time, while keeping the corporate network secure.

24.   Portals serve as entry points to resources such as e-mail, financial records, schedules, and employment and benefits files. Portals identify users and allow them access to areas of the intranet based upon their roles as customers, suppliers, employees, etc. They make information available in one place so users don't have to deal with several different Web interfaces.

25.   Broadband technology solves the Internet traffic jam problem by offering users a continuous connection to the Internet, and allowing them to send and receive large files faster than before.

26.   The Internet 2 supports heavy-duty applications such as:
        a. videoconferencing
        b. collaborative research
        c. distance education
        d. digital libraries
        e. full-body simulation environments known as tele-immersion.

27.   vBNS, or very high speed Backbone Network Service links government supercomputer centers and a select group of universities.

Learning Goal 4
The Enabling Technology: Hardware

28. Hardware components include
    a. computers,
    b. pagers
    c. cellular phones
    d. printers
    e. fax machines
    f. scanners
    g. personal digital assistants

29. Wireless information appliances include PDAs, smart phones, two-way paging devices and in-dash computers for cars.

30. Wi-fi refers to the term wireless fidelity, which allows users to access the internet virtually anywhere they can tap into a wireless network. People can basically take the internet with them.

31. A computer network system:
    a. Saves time and money
    b. Provides easy links to other areas of the company and makes it easy to find someone who can offer solutions to a problem.
    c. Allows employees to see complete information

32. Maintaining a large number of desktop computers can be expensive. When computers are down or being updated with new software, or training people to use new software there is a cost in lost productivity. Adding new software often causes problems with PC's, as it often conflicts, or even disables, existing software.

33. Some companies have looked at a hybrid of mainframe and network computing systems. In this model, applications and data reside on a server, which handles the processing needs for all the client machines on the network. The PCs lack the possessing power to handle applications on their own. This is called a thin-client network.

34. With a thin client network, software changes and upgrades only need to be made on the server, so the cost is lower.

35. Another option to networks is to rent software and hardware access by way of the Internet on an as-needed basis. For example, IBM offers pay-as-you-go computing, involving all types of information technology. The benefit to this solution is cost savings.

Learning Goal 5
Software

36. The six major business uses of software are:
    a. Writing - word processing
    b. Manipulating numbers - spreadsheets
    c. Filing and retrieving data - databases
    d. Presenting information visually – graphics
    e. Communicating - email and instant messaging
    f. Accounting

37. **Word Processing**: can personalize letters, update documents, revise forms to customer needs
Desktop Publishing: Combines word processing with graphics to produce designs
Spreadsheets: allows for quick calculations, is the electronic equivalent of an accountants worksheet, combined with other features
Database: allows users to work with information normally kept in lists. Can create customized reports
PIMs: specialized database allowing users to track business contacts
Graphics/Presentation programs: allows visual summary of spreadsheet data
Communications programs: allows computers to exchange files with other computers, retrieve database information and send and receive mail
Message Center Software: more powerful than traditional communications packages. Allows for more efficient way of delivering messages from phone, fax or e-mail
Accounting/Finance: helps users record financial transactions and generate financial reports
Integrated Programs: offer two or more applications in one package
Groupware: allows people to collaborate and share ideas by working on the same project at the same time

Learning Goal 6
Effects of Information Technology on Management

38. The major issues arising out of the growing reliance on information technology are:
    a. human resource changes   c. privacy concerns
    b. security threats   d. stability

39. Technology has made the work process more efficient as it replaces many bureaucratic functions. Computers often eliminate middle management functions and flatten organizational structures.

40. One of the major challenges technology poses for human resource management is the need to recruit and/or train employees proficient in technology applications.

    To address these concerns managers often hire consultants, and outsource the technology training.

41. The benefits of telecommuting include:
    a. saving money with smaller less expensive office space.
    b. retaining valuable employees while they are on leave.
    c. taking advantage of the experience offered by retired employees costs.

42. Workers with disabilities will be able to be gainfully employed, and men and women with small children will be able to stay home. Employees can work extra hours at home rather than at work, and this may help to improve morale and reduce stress.

43. Some of the drawbacks could include:
    a. consistent long-distance work gives workers a feeling of being left out of the office loop.
    b. loss of the energy people can get through social interaction.
    c. the intrusion that working at home makes into the personal life.

44. Companies are using telecommuting as a part-time alternative to alleviate some of the problems and complaints of this kind of work schedule.

45. Information typically is stolen by:
    a. hackers who break into computers
    b. employees who steal the information
    c. companies which lose it through incompetence, poor gatekeeping or bad procedures

46. Computer viruses are spread by downloading infected programming over the Internet or by sharing an infected disk.

47. Phishing is an online security threat. A scammer will embellish an email with a stolen logo from a well-known brand, which makes a message look authentic. Messages will often state "account activation required" or "Your account will be canceled if you do not verify". When victims click the link they are sent to a phony Web site that takes personal data which is used to commit fraud.
    The best way to avoid the problem is to open a new window and go to a web site directly, rather than accessing the account through email.

48. Existing laws do not address the problems of real-time communication. Copyright and pornography laws are coming into the virtual world, and legal questions involving intellectual property and contract disputes, online sexual and racial harassment, and the use of electronic communication to promote crooked sales schemes are being raised. Cyber-crimes cost billions of dollars every year.

49. Since September 11, corporate and government security officials are most worried about cyberterrorism.

50. Cyber terrorists could shut down the entire communications, money supply, electricity and transportation systems. E-mail and Web browsing across many parts of the Internet could be disrupted.

51. The Critical Infrastructure Protection Board is a part of the Office of Homeland Defense. It was created to devise a plan for improving the security of America's infrastructure. In order to do this, the agency needs the cooperation of businesses across the country.

52. The Critical Infrastructure Information Act of 2002 provides that critical infrastructure information which is voluntarily submitted a covered federal agency is exempt from disclosure under the Freedom of Information Act. This was necessary because while the participation of businesses is critical to success of anti-terrorism efforts, businesses are hesitant to provide information because they are afraid that customers will lose faith in the business if they are aware of breaches in security.

53. The increase of technology creates major concerns about privacy. E-mail can easily be "snooped", and companies routinely monitor their employees' use of e-mail. As more personal information is stored in computers, Web surfers have access to all sorts of personal information about individuals.

54. A cookie contains your name and password that the Web site recognizes the next time you visit the site so that you don't have to re-enter the same information every time you visit. Other cookies track your movements around the Web and then blend that information with their databases and tailor the ads you receive accordingly.

55. Spyware can be installed on your computer without your knowledge which can infect your system with viruses and track your online behavior.

56. To prevent your computer from receiving cookies you can use P3 to set up your browser to communicate only with Web sites that meet certain criteria.

57. Experts say that computer glitches are combinations of
   a. human error
   b. computer error
   c. malfunctioning software
   d. overly complex equipment
   e. bugs in systems
   f. naïve executives who won't challenge consultants or in-house specialists.

CRITICAL THINKING EXERCISES

Learning Goal 1

1. In the 1970's, business technology was known as data processing. It was used primarily to <u>support</u> the existing business, to improve the flow of financial information. In the 1980's, the name changed to information systems, and the role changed from supporting business to <u>doing</u> business. Customers interacted with the technology in a variety of ways. In the 1990's, businesses have shifted to using new technology on new methods of doing business, and the role of information technology has become to <u>change</u> business.

   Information technology has evolved into knowledge technology, which brings data to the individual, instead of requiring the individual to go to the database.

2. "In the old days" customers had to go to a business during business hours to meet their needs for consumer products, and employees had to "go to the office" to work. We went to the bank for a loan. Businesses decided *when* and *where* we did business with them. Information technology has changed all that. Information technology allows businesses to deliver products and services whenever and wherever it is convenient for the customer. Companies can go global much more easily, and can open global markets more quickly.

   Even further, IT has enabled businesses to become better and faster at serving customer needs by reducing product development times, getting customer feedback quickly, allowing companies to make changes in products easily and quickly, allowing companies to solve customer problems instantly by using databases, reducing defects, cutting expensive product waste. This has allowed businesses to become more customer oriented and thus more competitive in a global marketplace.

3. These are just some examples of how Information technology has changed many schools. You may have lots of other examples:
   <u>Organization:</u> Students can get grades over the net, find out school schedules, find out who is teaching certain courses, e-mail assignments to teacher, get syllabi and other course information. Teachers can enter grades online.
   <u>Operations:</u> Students can register online, and order books online.
   <u>Staffing:</u> With online registration and payments, the need for office personnel may be reduced.
   <u>New products:</u> Online courses are offered at many schools in many different academic areas.

<u>Customer relations:</u> Students can communicate with instructors, and vice versa via e-mail with questions and problems.

<u>New markets:</u> With online courses, schools can reach students who wouldn't ordinarily attend a particular school, or who may not attend at all, without the online access.

Learning Goal 2

4.　　One of the biggest problems of information technology and the information highway is the overwhelming amount of information available. Today business people are deluged with information from voice mail, the Internet, fax machines, and e-mail. Businesspeople refer to this information overload as "infoglut."

As a student you may note several areas where information overload could be a problem. For example, in searching for a college you had a base of thousands of schools from which to choose. Most likely all, or most, of these schools have websites full of information about their programs, campus and so on. You made your selection based upon your goals, or criteria, such as geography, finances, programs, entrance requirements and many other possibilities.

5.　　The first thing you need to do is to improve the quality of the information by combining the facts and figures and so on into something that is meaningful. Put sales reports together and summarize weekly or monthly figures. Note any trends in sales over a given period, and double check for accuracy in all the information you use. (Quality)

Secondly, you will need to make sure that you are using the latest sales reports, and double-check your figures. Since you will be sending this information to various sales managers, check to be sure that you have included all the data needed to give the managers an accurate picture of how sales are going and why. You don't need to include anything that may not be relevant, such as reports from committees or other areas that don't pertain to sales. (Completeness)

In addition, you need to work fast! If a sales person is not meeting quotas, a few weeks is too long to wait to find out why. With E-mail, your reports can be sent out almost as soon as they're finished. (Timeliness)

Lastly, be sure that the sales reports you are sending are appropriate to the management level at which they'll be received. Lower level managers will need inventory information perhaps, but not industry trends. Middle level managers may want your sales forecasts based upon past trends, but not vacation schedules for various salespeople. (Relevance)

Learning Goal 3

6.　　An intranet is a company-wide network closed to public access, which uses internet-type technology. An extranet is a semiprivate network that uses Internet technology so more than one company can access the same information, or so people on different servers can collaborate. One of the most common uses of extranets is to extend an intranet to outside customers.

You may find any number of examples of how this operates where you work or go to school, from filing forms online to email.

Learning Goal 4

7.　　You may be surprised at how much, or how little, computer hardware impacts your life, without realizing it. Many students of traditional college age have given up "traditional" phone calls in favor of text messaging on their mobile phones, or instant messaging on their computers. You may be in classes with an instructor using a wireless laptop to aid in instruction, and keep track of your assignments using a PDA on which you have stored your friend's phone numbers and e-mail addresses. You may have an

MP3 player with video capability to download your favorite movies, or you may listen to podcasts. The possibilities are endless.

Learning Goal 5

8.   a.   Spread sheet - to store and manipulate numbers
     b.   Communicating - to send and retrieve messages
     c.   Database - to store and organize information
     d.   Graphics- to make a pictorial presentation
     e.   Word processing for writing
     f.   Accounting

Learning Goal 6

9.   Computers have often enabled businesses to eliminate middle management functions, and thus flatten organization structures. Perhaps the most revolutionary effect of computers and the increased use of the Internet and intranets may be the ability to allow employees to stay home and do their work from there, or telecommute. Using computers linked to the company's network, workers can transmit their work to the office and back easily, either from home, or from their virtual office.

10. One problem today is hackers, who break into computer systems for illegal purposes. Today, computers not only make all areas of the company accessible, but also allow access to other companies with which the firm does business. Another security issue involves the spread of computer viruses over the Internet. Viruses are spread by downloading infected programming over the Internet or by sharing an infected disk. A major concern is a problem with privacy as more and more personal information is stored in computers and people are able to access all sorts of information about you. One of the key issues in the privacy debate is: isn't this personal information already public anyway?

PRACTICE TEST

MULTIPLE CHOICE		TRUE-FALSE	
LG 1	# 1-2	*LG 1*	#1-3
LG 2	#3-5	*LG 2*	#4-6
LG 3	#6-8	*LG 3*	# 7-9
LG 4	#9-11	*LG 4*	#10-12
LG 5	#12-14	*LG 5*	#13-14
LG 6	#15-20	*LG 6*	#15-16

1.	b	11.	b	1.	T	9.	T
2.	c	12.	b	2.	T	10.	F
3.	d	13.	d	3.	T	11.	T
4.	a	14.	c	4.	F	12.	T
5.	d	15.	b	5.	T	13.	T
6.	a	16.	d	6.	T	14.	F
7.	b	17.	a	7.	F	15.	T
8.	d	18.	a	8.	T	16.	F
9.	d	19.	b				
10.	d	20.	d				

CHAPTER C – MANAGING RISK

LEARNING GOALS
After you have read and studied this chapter, you should be able to:

1. Discuss the environmental changes that have made risk management more important.
2. Explain the four ways of managing risk
3. Distinguish between insurable and uninsurable risk.
4. Explain the rule of indemnity.
5. Discuss the various types of insurance that businesses may buy.
6. Explain why businesses must carry workers' compensation insurance.
7. Tell others why businesses cannot manage environmental damage on their own.

LEARNING THE LANGUAGE

Listed here are important terms found in this chapter. Choose the correct term for each definition below and write it in the space provided.

Health maintenance organizations (HMOs)	Mutual insurance company	Rule of indemnity
Insurable interest	Preferred provider organizations (PPOs)	Self-insurance
Insurable risk	Premium	Speculative risk
Insurance policy	Pure risk	Stock insurance company
Law of large numbers	Risk	Uninsurable risk
Medical savings accounts (MSAs)		

1. A _____ is a type of insurance company owned by stockholders.

2. A written contract known as a(n) _____ is between the insured and an insurance company that promises to pay for all or part of a loss.

3. The _____ says that an insured person or organization cannot collect more than the actual loss from an insurable risk.

4. The threat of loss with no chance of profit is called _____.

5. The _____ is a principle which states that if a large number of people are exposed to the same risk, a predictable number of losses will occur during a given period of time.

6. A chance of either profit or loss is called _____.

7. The chance of loss, the degree of probability of loss, and the amount of possible loss is called _____.

8. A _____ is a type of insurance company owned by its policyholders.

9. Health care organizations known as _____ require members to choose from a restricted list of doctors.

10. The fee charged by an insurance company for an insurance policy is a _____.

11. A(n) _____ is one that no insurance company will cover.

12. The practice of setting aside money to cover routine claims and buying only "catastrophe" policies to cover big losses is called _____.

13. A(n) _____ is a risk that the typical insurance company will cover.

14. Health care organizations similar to HMOs except that they allow members to choose their own physicians for a fee are called _____.

15. The possibility of the policyholder to suffer a loss is called _____.

16. Tax-deferred accounts known as _____ allow people to save money for medical expenses.

ASSESSMENT CHECK

Learning Goal 1
The Increasing Challenge of Risk Management

1. What is an ERM, and what are the goals of an ERM

2. Why is risk management getting more attention from today's businesses?

Learning Goa 2
Managing Risk

3. Describe the two kinds of risk.

a. _____

_____

b. _____

_____

4. The kind of risk of most concern to business people is: _____

5.   List four methods businesses use to manage pure risk.

   a. _____   c. _____

   b. _____   d. _____

6.   What are of examples of how can a firm reduce risk?

   a. _____

   b. _____

   c. _____

   d. _____

7.   How do some companies avoid risk?

8.   Why are some firms turning to self-insurance? What is the benefit for firms choosing to self-insure?

9.   Self-insurance is most appropriate when: _____

10.   What does it mean for a company to "go bare" with self-insurance, and what is the risk?

Learning Goal 3
Buying Insurance to Cover Risk

11. What is a BOP?

12 Describe four kinds of uninsurable risk.

   a. _____

   b. _____

   c. _____

   d. _____

13. Identify the guidelines used to evaluate whether or not a risk is insurable.

a. _____

b. _____

c. _____

d. _____

e. _____

f. _____

Learning Goal 4
Understanding Insurance Policies

14. What makes the acceptance of risk possible for insurance companies is: _____

_____

15. How are appropriate premiums for each policy determined?

16. Can a person purchase more than one policy to cover the same risk? Explain.

Learning Goals 5,6
Types of Insurance

17. What are three types of insurance to cover losses?

a. _____

b. _____

c. _____

18. Property losses result from: _____

Liability losses result from: _____

19. What are four major options for health insurance?

a. _____   c. _____

b. _____   d. _____

20. What are the features of an HMO?

21. What are some complaints about HMOs?

22. What are some characteristics of a PPO?

23. Why do most businesses and individuals choose to join an HMO or a PPO?

24. Describe the features of a medical savings account.

25. Describe disability insurance.

26. Who provides worker's compensation and what does it guarantee?

27. Who does professional liability insurance cover? What is another name for this type of insurance?

28. What is product liability insurance?

29. What should you do about insurance coverage if you have a home-based business?

Learning Goal 7
The Risk of Damaging the Environment

30.   What are the issues involved in risk management and the environment?

CRITICAL THINKING EXERCISES

Learning Goal 1

1.   The "environment" changes so rapidly that it is difficult to identify all the changes that could affect a business in terms of risk management. Evaluate the company for which you work, or a company with which you are familiar. What is happening today in the environment (you remember this from chapter 1 - the economic and legal, technological, competitive, social, global business environments)? How do the changes you have identified increase the necessity for risk management for this firm? What actions can the firm take to minimize the risk of loss from these changes?

Learning Goal 2

2.   Businesses have four options to avoid losses stemming from pure risk situations.

Reduce the risk   Buy insurance to cover the risk
    Avoid the risk   Self-insure against the risk

Read the following situations, and determine which option the firm is choosing in each case. Use each option only once.

a. _____   The president of an asbestos removal firm in Merriam, Kansas closed his firm for four months.

b. _____   A group of 27 accounting firms formed its own insurance company to insure themselves.

c. _____   Workers and visitors on construction sites are required to wear hard hats.

d. _____   Senoret Chemical Company experienced a 1600% increase in its liability coverage premium.

Learning Goal 3

3.   Many variables determine which risks are insurable. Using your text, determine which of the following situations would constitute an insurable risk.

a. _____   TNG Enterprises would like to buy insurance to cover loss of computer equipment from power surges and possible spills.

b. _____ Gilmores, Inc. a retail store in Kalamazoo, wanted to insure against losses occurring when a competitor, Hudsons, implemented an aggressive marketing campaign.

c. _____ Daimler-Chrysler wants to buy insurance to cover losses created by a breakdown of their robotic and computer driven manufacturing systems.

d. _____ PPI, a small manufacturing firm, wants to insure themselves against losses created by damage from a fire set accidentally.

e. _____ Residents in Morgan City, Louisiana, East Lansing, Michigan and Valley Park, Missouri want to buy flood insurance.

f. _____ Residents of Morgan City, Louisiana, however, face a high risk of flooding, because the Mississippi River is cutting a new tributary through that city, and floods regularly.

g. _____ Boeing has extensive contracts with the government to build fighter planes. The company wants insurance to cover losses that may occur if Congress cuts the defense budget by over 20%.

Learning Goal 4
4.   Eric owns a company that makes self-darkening windshields for vehicles, Sun-2-Shade. He is aware of the risks of owning a business, and is considering various insurance plans. Eric would like to make sure that he won't incur any losses, and so is thinking about buying policies from two different companies just to make sure that not only will he be covered, but could make money while the company was down. Eric figures that he will be able to make claims on both policies if something happens, and even make money when both companies pay on the claim. As Eric's advisor, what would you tell him about this plan?

Learning Goals 5,6
5.   You are a small business owner, currently working out of your home and you are concerned about the kinds of insurance that you should carry for your business. Currently, your business consists of yourself, and 3 employees. You have turned to a small business consultant to advise you. What do you think the consultant will say about the need for insurance?

Learning Goal 7

6. Discuss the issues that companies need to be aware of in the area of risk management and environmental damage.

PRACTICE TEST

MULTIPLE CHOICE – Circle the best answer

Learning Goal 1
1. Risk management has become an important concern for businesses today because:
    a. rapid environmental changes are becoming a major source of risk for companies.
    b. insurance companies have done such a good job of marketing their products.
    c. companies want to insure themselves against potential losses.
    d. lawyers have made insurance claims a part of a company's legal strategic plan.

Learning Goal 2
2. Which of the following is not one of the options a firm has available to manage risk?
    a. reduce the risk
    b. avoid the risk
    c. buy insurance against the risk
    d. find another company to take the risk

3. When Macy's orders inventory for the Christmas season, the company has to predict what their customers will want to buy that season. The kind of risk being described is
    a. speculative risk.
    b. pure risk.
    c. insurable risk.
    d. self-insurance

4. It is when a company has several widely distributed facilities that _____ is the most appropriate.
    a. reducing the risk
    b. avoiding the risk
    c. self-insurance
    d. finding another company to take the risk

Learning Goal 3
5. An insurable risk is one in which:
    a. the loss is a specific amount.
    b. the loss is not accidental.
    c. the risk is dispersed.
    d. the policyholder has no insurable interest.

6. The law of large numbers states that:
    a. a large number of people must make claims before an insurance company will begin to pay out.
    b. if a large number of people are exposed to the same risk, a predictable number of losses will occur during a given period of time.
    c. items that will be covered by an insurance policy must not be above a certain amount, i.e. the large number which is set by actuaries.
    d. if losses from an occurrence are large enough, and insurance company will turn the policies over to a reinsurance company.

7. The idea that an insured person or organization cannot collect more than the actual loss from an insurable risk is called the:
    a. law of large numbers.
    b. rule of indemnity.
    c. disability insurance
    d. insurable interest.

Learning Goal 5
8. A type of insurance that requires members to choose from a restricted list of doctors is called a:
    a. health maintenance organization.
    b. preferred provider organization.
    c. disability insurance.
    d. medical savings account.

9. Disability insurance
    a. replaces all your income if you become disabled.
    b. starts immediately after your disability.
    c. is required from employers.
    d. replaces a portion of your income.

10. If a person is injured when using a product and sues the manufacturer, the company is covered by
    a. workers compensation.
    b. disability insurance.
    c. product liability insurance.
    d. business interruption insurance.

Learning Goal 6
11. Which of the following is <u>not</u> true of worker's compensation insurance?
    a. It guarantees payment of wages, medical care, and rehabilitation services for employees who are injured on the job.
    b. Only employers in right to work states are required to provide worker's compensation insurance.
    c. The insurance provides benefits to the survivors of workers who die as a result of work-related injuries.
    d. The cost of insurance varies by the company's safety record, payroll and types of hazards faced by workers.

12.   Business concern about damage to the environment:

    a. is primarily restricted to companies in the United States.

    b. is declining as companies add more insurance coverage as part of their strategic plans.

    c. has become a global issue because of concerns over issues such as global warming and safety in power plants.

    d. is primarily a concern of companies in the European Union and Eastern Europe.

TRUE-FALSE

Learning Goal 1

1. _____   An enterprise risk management system includes defining what risks a company will manage.

2. _____   Environmental risks to businesses stem primarily from natural disasters such as floods or hurricanes.

Learning Goal 2

3. _____   A firm can reduce risk by establishing loss prevention programs such as fire drills, health education and accident prevention programs.

4. _____   Pure risk is the threat of loss with no chance for profit.

5. _____   When a company "goes bare" in terms of insurance, the company is getting the bare minimum insurance coverage from its insurance provider.

Learning Goal 3

6. _____   One type of risk that cannot be covered is loss from accidental injury.

Learning Goal 4

7. _____   The rule of indemnity states that you can have two insurance policies to cover the same risk of loss.

Learning Goal 5

8. _____   One of the complaints about an HMO is that members can't choose their own doctors.

9. _____   PPOs are less expensive than HMOs because you can choose your own doctor

10. _____   Medical savings accounts are tax-deferred accounts that allow you to save money for future medical expenses.

11. _____   Many professionals other than doctors and lawyers are buying malpractice insurance which is also known as professional liability insurance.

12. _____   Most homeowner's insurance policies have adequate protection for a home based business.

13. ____ Workers' compensation insurance guarantees payment of wages for employees injured on the job, but will not cover medical expenses, as those should be covered by medical insurance programs.

14. ____ Concerns about the environment stem from issues such as global warming and hazards from nuclear power plants.

You Can Find It on the Net

Visit the website **http://www.rmmag.com/** which is the website for Risk Management magazine.

What are the major concerns addressed in the current issue of the magazine? How do those concerns reflect what we have discussed in this chapter?

What is the RIMS?

Visit the home page of the insurance company you currently use for car, homeowners, or other insurance policies. What types of products does this company offer? Use this company's website to determine if you have adequate insurance to cover your needs.

Can this company insure your small business? What kinds of business insurance do they offer for your small business?

ANSWERS

LEARNING THE LANGUAGE

1. Stock insurance company	7. Risk	13. Insurable risk
2. Insurance policy	8. Mutual insurance company	14. Preferred Provider Organization (PPO)
3. Rule of indemnity	9. Health maintenance organizations (HMOs)	15. Insurable interest
4. Pure risk	10. Premium	16. Medical savings accounts (MSAs)
5. Law of large numbers	11. Uninsurable risk	
6. Speculative risk	12. Self insurance	

ASSESSMENT CHECK

Learning Goal 1
The Increasing Challenge of Risk Management

1. An ERM is an enterprise risk program, designed by executives for their companies. The goals of an ERM can include:
   a. defining which risks the program will manage.
   b. what risk management processes, technologies, and investments will be required.
   c. how these efforts will be coordinated across the firm.

2. Occurrences such as 9/11, wars in the Middle East, corporate and government scandals, major natural disasters, social unrest, and the threat of terrorism and disease have made risk management more complex and gotten the attention of business leaders around the world. Further risks stem from the threat of security failures from hackers and viruses.

Learning Goal 2
Managing Risk

3. a. Speculative risk involves a chance of either profit or loss. It includes the chance the firm takes to make extra money by buying new machinery, acquiring more inventory and making other decisions in which the probability of loss may be relatively low and the amount of loss is known. An entrepreneur takes speculative risk on the chance of making a profit.
   b. Pure risk is the threat of loss with no chance for profit. It involves the threat of fire, accident or loss. If such events occur, a company loses money, but if the events do not occur, the company gains nothing.

4. The kind of risk of most concern to business-people is pure risk.

5. Firms can manage risk by
   a. Reducing the risk
   b. Avoiding the risk
   c. Self-insure against the risk
   d. Buy insurance against the risk

6. Examples of reducing risk include:
    a. A firm can reduce risk by establishing loss-prevention programs such as fire drills, health education, safety inspections, equipment maintenance, and accident prevention programs.
    b. Retail stores use mirrors, video cameras, and other devices to prevent shoplifting.
    c. Manufacturers have safety devices to protect workers from injury.
    d. Product recalls are used to prevent customer injuries.

7. Companies avoid risk by not accepting hazardous jobs and by outsourcing shipping and other functions. For example, the threat of lawsuits has driven away some drug companies from manufacturing vaccines, and some consulting engineers refuse to work on hazardous sites. Some companies are losing outside members of their boards of directors for lack of liability coverage.

8. Many companies and municipalities have turned to self-insurance because they either can't find or can't afford conventional policies. Self-insurance lowers the cost of insurance by allowing companies to take out insurance only for large losses.

9. Self insurance is most appropriate when a firm has several widely distributed facilities.

10. When a company "goes bare" the company is paying claims straight out of its budget. This is a very risky strategy for a company. The risk is that the whole firm could go bankrupt over one claim if the damages are high enough.

Learning Goal 3
Buying Insurance to Cover Risk

11. A BOP is a business ownership policy. This is a package that includes property and liability insurance, and reduces the cost of insurance.

12. Four kinds of uninsurable risk include:
    a. Market risks (from price changes, style changes, new products)
    b. Political risks (from war or government restrictions)
    c. Personal risks (from loss of job)
    d. Risks of operation (strikes or inefficient machinery)

13. An insurable risk is evaluated using the following criteria
    a. The policyholder must have an insurable interest.
    b. The loss should be measurable.
    c. The chance of loss should be measurable.
    d. The loss should be accidental.
    e. The risk should be dispersed
    f. The insurance company can set standards for accepting risk.

Learning Goal 4
Understanding Insurance Policies

14. What makes the acceptance of risk possible for insurance companies is the law of large numbers.

15. Appropriate premiums for insurance policies are determined by using the law of large numbers. This states that if a large number of people or organizations are exposed to the same risk, a predictable number of losses will occur. The premium is supposed to be high enough to cover expected losses and still earn a profit for the firm. Today, however, higher premiums are being charged to cover higher anticipated court costs and damage awards.

16. The rule of indemnity says that an insured person or organization cannot collect more than the actual loss from an insurable risk. So, for example, a person can't buy two insurance policies and collect from both for the same loss.

Learning Goals 5,6
Types of Insurance

17.   Three types of insurance include:
        a.   property and liability
        b.   health
        c.   life insurance

18.   Property losses result from fires, accidents, theft, or other perils.

Liability losses result from property damage or injuries suffered by others for which the policyholder is held responsible.

19. Four major options for health insurance are:
        a.   health care providers, such as Blue Cross/Blue Shield,
        b.   health maintenance organizations (HMOs)
        c.   preferred provider organizations (PPOs)
        d.   medical savings accounts (MSAs)

20. HMOs offer a full range of health care benefits. Emphasis is on helping members stay healthy instead of on treating illnesses. Members do not receive bills and do not have to fill out claim forms for routine service. HMOs employ or contract with doctors, hospitals and other systems of health care and members must use those providers. HMOs are less expensive than comprehensive health insurance providers.

21. Members complain about not being able to choose doctors or to get the care they want or need. Some physicians complain that they lose some freedom to do what is needed to make people well and that they often receive less compensation than they feel is appropriate for the services they provide.

22. Preferred provider organizations contract with hospitals and doctors, but do not require members to choose only from those physicians but members have to pay more if they don't use a doctor on the preferred list. Members pay a deductible before the PPO will pay any bills. When the plan does pay, members usually have to pay part of the bill. This payment is called co-insurance.

23. Most individuals and businesses choose to join a PPO or an HMO because they can cost as much as 80 percent less than comprehensive individual health insurance policies.

24. With a medical savings account, you or your employer put part of the money currently spent on health insurance into an account. This would be used to buy a catastrophic insurance policy that covers major medical expenses, less a deductible. This allows you to go to almost any doctor, get the services you need and pay for them with the funds in your MSA. The assumption is that you will go to the doctor less than with other plans and that you will bargain for a good price.

25. Disability insurance replaces part of your income if you become disabled and unable to work. Usually, before you can begin collecting there is a period of time you must be disabled. The premiums for such insurance vary depending on your age, occupation, and income.

26. Workers compensation insurance guarantees payment of wages, medical care, and rehabilitation services for employees who are injured on the job. Employers in all 50 states are required to provide this type of insurance. This insurance also provides benefits to the survivors of workers who die as a result of work-related injuries.

27. Professional liability insurance covers people who may be found liable for professional negligence, such as lawyers, doctors, dentists, mortgage brokers, and real estate appraisers. This is also known as malpractice insurance.

28. Product liability insurance provides coverage against liability arising out of products sold.

29. Homeowner's policies usually don't have adequate protection for a home-based business, so you may need to add an endorsement, or rider, to increase the coverage. If clients visit your office and or if you receive deliveries regularly, you may need home-office insurance, which protects you from slip and fall lawsuits and other risks associated with visitors. More elaborate businesses may need other kinds of insurance.

Learning Goal 7
The Risk of Damaging the Environment

30. It is clear that risk management goes beyond the protection of individuals and businesses from known risk. Risk management has become an international issue. The process means evaluating the worldwide risks and prioritizing these risks so that international funds can be spent where they will do the most good.

CRITICAL THINKING EXERCISES

Learning Goal 1
1. Your answers to this question will vary. However, some suggestions as to how to minimize risk may include developing an enterprise risk management program for the company, to determine what risks pose the greatest danger to the company, and how to manage those risks.

Learning Goal 2
2.   a. Avoid risk
        b. Self-insure against the risk
        c.   Reduce the risk
        d. Buy insurance to cover the risk.

Learning Goal 3

3.   a.   Yes, companies can buy insurance against the loss of computer equipment.

       b.   No, this would be an uninsurable risk.

       c.   No, a company cannot insure against inefficient machinery or machinery that breaks down or doesn't work.

       d.   Yes you can insure against fire damage.

       e.   Yes, probably, unless the occurrence of loss has been too high.

       f.   No, most likely because the probability of flooding in Morgan City is too high.

       g.   No this would be a "political risk" and is uninsurable.

Learning Goal 4

4.   While it is understandable that Eric would be concerned about taking care of losses his business may experience, the rule of indemnity will prevent Eric from filing claims with two different insurance companies for the same incident. The rule of indemnity states that an insured person or organization can't collect more than the actual loss from an insurable risk. If a company carries two policies, the two insurance companies would calculate any loss and divide the reimbursement.

Leaning Goals 5,6

5. As a small business owner located in your home, you will need to have a regular homeowner's policy, but there will be additional coverage that you should consider.

You may need a rider to cover business equipment, and if customers or clients call on you, you may need home office insurance. If you manufacture items at your home business, you should consider a business owner policy. Depending upon the type of business you own, you may want to consider professional liability insurance or product liability insurance.

Since you have employees, you may want to check into offering other insurance coverage for them. Employers often offer life insurance, disability insurance, retirement plans, and health insurance.

You will probably be required to offer worker's compensation insurance. The cost of worker's compensation insurance will be determined by your company's safety record, its payroll and the types of hazards faced by your workers.

Learning Goal 7

6.   The risk of environmental harm is international in proportion. Nuclear power plants have been shut down because of violations in safety standards, but coal fired plants cause environmental damage also. Other fuel sources haven't been fully developed and nuclear power plants are still considered to be a necessity. So, making nuclear power plants safer will be an issue for years to come.

Some U.S. businesses are doing what they can to protect the environment from damage due to greenhouse gases, but many feel there is a need for more careful evaluation of environmental risks. Businesses around the world must be aware of the consequences of risks from global warming. Prioritizing those risks will be an important part of a risk management program for global businesses in the coming years.

PRACTICE TEST

MULTIPLE CHOICE

LG 1	*#1*
LG 2	*#2-4*
LG 3	*#5*
LG 4	*#6-7*
LG 5	*8-10*
LG 6	*#11*
LG 7	*#12*

1.	a	7.	b
2.	d	8.	a
3.	a	9.	d
4.	c	10.	c
5.	c	11.	b
6.	b	12.	c

TRUE-FALSE

LG 1	*# 1-2*
LG 2	*# 3-5*
LG 3	*#5*
LG 4	*#7*
LG 5	*#8-12*
LG 6	*# 13*
LG 7	*#14*

1.	T	8.	T
2.	F	9.	F
3.	T	10.	T
4.	T	11.	T
5.	F	12.	F
6.	F	13.	F
7.	F	14.	T

CHAPTER D- MANAGING PERSONAL FINANCES

LEARNING GOALS

After you have read and studied this chapter, you should be able to:

1. Describe the six steps of learning to control your assets
2. Explain ways to build a financial base including investing in real estate, saving money, and managing credit.
3. Explain how buying the appropriate insurance can protect your financial base.
4. Outline a strategy for retiring with enough money to last a lifetime.

LEARNING THE LANGUAGE

Listed below are important terms found in this chapter. Choose the correct term for the definition and write it in the space provided.

401(k) plan	Individual Retirement Account (IRA)	Umbrella policy
Annuity	Roth IRA	Variable life insurance
Contrarian approach	Social Security	Whole life insurance
Executor	Tax deferred contributions	Will
Disability insurance	Term insurance	

1. Pure insurance protection for a given number of years is _____.

2. A (n) _____ is a tax-deferred investment plan that enables you and your spouse to save part of your income for retirement. A traditional one allows people who qualify to deduct from their reported income the money they put into an account.

3. A contract to make regular payments to a person for life or for a fixed period is a(n) _____.

4. The term _____ is used to describe the Old-Age, Survivors, and Disability Insurance Program established in 1935.

5. Whole life insurance, or _____, invests the cash value of the policy in stocks or other high yielding securities.

6. Life insurance that stays in effect until age 100 is known as _____.

7. Buying stock when everyone else is selling, or vice versa is called the _____.

8. A document referred to as a(n) _____ names the guardian for your children, states how you want your assets distributed, and names the executor for your estate.

9. A savings plan called a _____ is one that allows you to deposit pretax dollars and whose earnings compound tax free until withdrawal, when the money is taxed at ordinary income tax rates.

10. A broadly based insurance policy called a (n) _____ saves you money because you buy all your insurance from one company.

11. Insurance that pays part of the cost of a long-term sickness or an accident is _____.

12. A(n) _____ is a person who assembles and values your estate, files income and other taxes, and distributes assets.

13. A(n) _____ is one where you don't get up-front deductions on your taxes, but the earnings grow tax fee and are also tax free when they are withdrawn.

14. _____ are retirement account deposits for which you pay no current taxes, but the earnings gained are taxed as regular income when they are withdrawn at retirement.

ASSESSMENT CHECK

Learning Goal 1
The Need for Personal Financial Planning

1. How do the lifetime earnings of a typical full-time worker with a college degree compare to the earnings of an individual with a high school diploma?

2. What are six steps you can take today to get control of your finances?

   a. _____

   b. _____

   c. _____

   d. _____

   e. _____

   f. _____

3. What is the process for developing a personal balance sheet?

4. What are the steps in developing a personal income statement?

5.   What's the best way to keep track of expenses?

6.   What items are important to include in a household budget?

a. _____   f. _____

b. _____   g. _____

c. _____   h. _____

d. _____   i. _____

e. _____

7.   How is running a household's finances like running a small business?

8.   The first thing to do with the money remaining after you pay your monthly expenses is:

_____

This is true because: _____

_____

9.   What's a good way to plan for large purchases, such as a car?

10. What is the best way to save money in general?

11. For what types of things should you borrow money?

12.   How can you accumulate capital?

13.   What are the investment benefits of buying a home?

        a. _____

        b. _____

        c. _____

14.   What are the tax benefits of home ownership?

15.   The key element to getting an optimum return on a home is: _____.

16.   One of the worst places to keep long-term investments is: _____

        This is because: _____

17.   One of the best places to invest over time has been: _____

18.   When is the best time to buy stocks? What is the term used to describe this kind of
        investing?

19.   If you finance a purchase using a credit card, what will it do to the total cost of your
        purchase, when compared to paying cash?

20.   What are three reasons why credit cards are an important element in a personal financial system?

a._____

b._____

c._____

21.   Should you carry a balance on a credit card? Why or why not?

22.   The danger of a credit card is: _____

_____

Learning Goal 3
Protecting Your Financial Base: Buying Insurance

23.   People or businesses should buy life insurance to: _____

_____

24.   How much insurance does a family need?

25.   Multiyear level-premium insurance is: _____

_____

26.   Explain whole life insurance. What is a universal life policy?

27.   What is the difference between a fixed and a variable annuity?

28.   What is the danger of not having health and disability insurance?

29. What is meant by guaranteed replacement cost when referring to homeowners insurance?

30. What is an insurance rider?

Learning Goal 4
Planning Your Retirement

31. Describe the problems surrounding the Social Security system.

32. Why is a traditional IRA a good deal for an investor?

33. The earlier you start saving: _____

   _____

34. What is the basic difference between a Roth IRA and a traditional IRA? Which is the best type of IRA for younger people?

35. A key point to remember about taking money out of an IRA is: _____

   _____

36. What are some investment choices for IRAs? Can you switch from one type to another?

37. Describe a simple IRA.

38. What are the benefits of 401(k) plans?

    a. _____

    b. _____

    c. _____

39. Describe the characteristics of 401(k) plans.

40. Who is a Keogh plan for?

41. What is the advantage of a Keogh plan?

42. How is a Keogh plan like an IRA?

43. A financial planner is: _____

    _____

    A CFP is: _____

    _____

44. What is a "financial supermarket"?

45. What are the areas a financial planner will cover?

46.   Discuss the steps involved in estate planning.

a. _____

b. _____

c. _____

47.   Describe a durable power of attorney.

CRITICAL THINKING EXERCISES

Learning Goal 1

1.   What is the benefit of investing in an education?

2.   The six steps to get control of your finances are:

Take an inventory of you financial assets
Keep track of all of your expenses
Prepare a budget
Pay off your debts
Start a savings plan
Only borrow money to buy assets that have the potential to increase in value

Do as many of these steps as possible in the time frame of a week. Use a separate sheet of paper so you're not limited by the space provided in this book:

Inventory of assets: Do you own a car? house? appliances? stocks? savings account? checking account? collectibles?

Expenses: What do you spend in a day on food? newspapers? travel? supplies? What do you spend in a month on food? housing? car payments? utilities? Are you spending more than you are earning? Keep a small notebook handy to record all your spending for each day for a week.

Budget: Listing all your sources of revenue, determine how much you can spend in a month. Set up accounts for money you are going to pay to yourself, for savings, and for major purchases you will want to make sometime in the future as well as for items which may not be paid every month, but will come due eventually, like car or life insurance. Can you spend less than you are making?

Pay off your debts: Can you pay off your credit cards, if you have them? Are there any other debts that can be paid off now?

Start a savings plan: In your budget, did you pay yourself first?

Identify those loans that were for articles which will *depreciate* in value (educational loans don't count! Your education will help you accumulate capital in the long run!)
It's not easy, is it?!

Learning Goal 2
3.   "The principle is simple: To accumulate capital, you have to earn more than you spend."

A. Take a few minutes to think about the way you spend money (beyond money for tuition, books and other school related items.) Using your text for suggestions, list some ways in which you could begin to accumulate capital for the future:

1. _____

2. _____

3. _____

4. _____

B. Investigate the real estate market in your area. Determine the amount by which home prices in your area have appreciated (or depreciated) in the last 5 years. You can probably find a source for this information in your campus library or on the Internet.

C. Let's assume you have found a house in your area for $110,000. What are the mortgage interest rates in your area for a 30-year, fixed rate mortgage? With a $10,000 down payment, what will your monthly mortgage payments be? To get this information, go to http://financialplan.about.com and click on the mortgage link. Scroll until you find the mortgage calculator.

    If, over time, inflation averages 3 percent, how long will it take for the value of your house to double? (Hint: remember the rule of 72, in chapter 2) You can also use the web site listed above to determine the impact of inflation on the prices of goods and services you may be interested in.

D. Interest on mortgage payments is tax deductible. Assume that you are in the 28% tax bracket and that the payments on your house are $1,200 per month. What is your real cost?

4.   Credit cards are a helpful tool to the financially careful buyer. If you have credit cards, you are probably aware of the advantages:

Useful for identification
Helpful to keep track of purchases
Convenient, in place of cash

You may also be aware of the disadvantages, primarily high interest rates and the convenience of purchasing something you cannot afford.

A. If you have credit cards, figure the amount you spent last month using each card, and for what purchases. What is the interest rate on your cards? Did you make purchases you would not have made without the card?

B. Look at the budget you developed earlier. Do you have an account for credit card payments? Did you budget to pay the entire amount, or only a portion of the bill?

C. Look at your recent credit card statements. How much did you pay in interest on credit card accounts over the last six months? The last year? That is the amount by which you could have increased your capital account.

Learning Goal 3

5. Consider your lifestyle today and evaluate the kind of insurance needs you have. Are you single or married? Do you have children? If you are married does your spouse work? Are you both, or either one, covered by health insurance? Do you rent an apartment or a house, or do you have a mortgage? If you are married, what would happen to your financial situation if one of you was unable to work?

Learning Goal 4

6. A. Why should you invest in an IRA as a young person?

B. Again, using the rule of 72, if you invest $1,000 in something that earns 10 percent interest, how long would it take to double the amount?

C. How much would your $1000 be worth in 15 years, if you are earning 10 percent?

7. Compare and contrast a Keogh, 401(k) and an IRA.

PRACTICE TEST

MULTIPLE CHOICE – Circle the best answer

Learning Goal 1

1. When planning for the future, an investment in a college education will:
   a. provide you with new ideas.
   b. give you a chance to learn about different ways of life.
   c. improve your earning potential.
   d. guarantee a certain type of job.

2. Jerry and Jane are having a discussion about their finances. They are wondering what to do about the amount of money they are spending, how to control their financial situation as well as how to reach their financial goals. One technique to help them would be to:
   a. prepare a budget.
   b. do an asset inventory.
   c. develop an income statement.
   d. quit spending money on anything but the bare basics.

3. The first step in taking control of your finances should be:
   a. keep track of all your expenses.
   b. prepare a budget.
   c. pay off your debts.
   d. take an inventory of your assets.

4. When developing a personal balance sheet, which of the following would not be on a list of personal assets?
   a. a bicycle
   b. car
   c. savings account
   d. mortgage

5. The <u>first</u> thing you should do when you have extra money is:
   a. pay cash for a car.
   b. start a savings plan.
   c. pay off your debts.
   d. put a down payment on a house

6. In terms of borrowing money, the advice is to:
   a. borrow money to buy a car to take advantage of interest tax deductions.
   b. borrow money to invest in the stock market because historically the stock market pays the best returns.
   c. borrow money to pay off credit cards because the interest will be lower on a loan than on the credit cards.
   d. borrow money only to buy assets that have the potential to increase in value or generate income

7. To accumulate capital you have to:
    a. get the highest paying job you can find.
    b. live frugally and invest the money you accumulate.
    c. borrow money and invest.
    d. buy assets which appreciate in value.

8. One of the best investments a person can make is in:
    a. a home
    b. cars
    c. credit cards
    d   an apartment

9. From a financial standpoint it is best to buy:
    a. a large home in a neighborhood where homes are less expensive.
    b. a small home in a great neighborhood.
    c. the smallest home in the least expensive neighborhood.
    d. the largest home in the most expensive neighborhood you can afford.

10. One of the worst places for a young person to keep their investments is in:
    a. a bank or savings and loan.
    b. a stock market mutual fund.
    c. the stock market in general.
    d. home ownership.

11. The contrarian approach to investing is:
    a. to stay out of the market no matter what the experts are saying.
    b. to buy when others are selling.
    c. to only buy mutual funds, contrary to the belief that the money to be made is in individual stocks.
    d. to invest predominantly in the bond market when others are investing in the stock market.

12. One of the dangers of a credit card is that:
    a. it is difficult to keep track of purchases.
    b. it can be an inconvenience carrying too many credit cards around.
    c. merchants won't accept credit cards as a form of identification.
    d. consumers may buy goods they wouldn't normally buy if they had to pay cash.

Learning Goal 3
13. _____ life insurance is the type in which some part of the money you pay goes toward pure insurance and another part toward savings.
    a. A fixed annuity
    b. Whole
    c. Variable
    d. Term

14. Guaranteed replacement cost in homeowners insurance means that:
    a. the insurance company guarantees they will replace the lost items for you.
    b. the insurance company guarantees they will pay the current value of a lost item.
    c. the insurance company will pay you what it costs to replace the items.
    d. the insurance company will pay you something for lost items, but the amount can't be determined, so they guarantee an average of market value.

Learning Goal 4
15. Which of the following is <u>not</u> likely to happen with the social security system in the future?
    a. serious cuts in benefits
    b. reduced cost of living adjustments
    c. later retirement age to collect
    d. lower social security taxes

16. Which of the following is considered the best type of retirement investment for a younger person?
    a. Traditional IRA
    b. Roth IRA
    c. savings accounts
    d. Keogh accounts

17. The invested money in a traditional IRA account:
    a. is taxed as you go along.
    b. is not taxed.
    c. is subject to double taxation.
    d. is not taxed until it is withdrawn.

18. One of the benefits of a Roth IRA is that
    a. contributions aren't taxed.
    b. earnings grow tax free.
    c. you can take the money out before the age of 59 ½ without penalty.
    d. you can invest up to $12,000 a year.

19. A tax sheltered retirement program designed to encourage small-business owners and self-employed people to invest for retirement is called a(n):
    a. Keogh Plan
    b. 401(k) plan
    c. Roth IRA
    d. Simple IRA

20. Which of the following is not included as a step in the financial planning process?
    a. Select a guardian for minor children.
    b. Prepare a durable power of attorney.
    c. Develop an investment plan.
    d. Prepare a will.

TRUE-FALSE

Learning Goal 1
1. _____ In developing an income statement for yourself, your pay check would be considered as revenue.

2. _____ One of the best ways to keep track of your expenses is to carry a notepad with you everywhere you go and record what you spend as you go through the day.

3. _____ It could be said that running a household is similar to running a small business.

4. _____ The statistics indicate that a majority of the population in the U.S. has accumulated enough money by retirement to live comfortably.

5. _____ The first steps to accumulating capital are finding employment and living frugally.

6. _____ It's not necessary to save for large purchases such as a car or home, since the purchase price will be so high that you will have to borrow money anyway.

Learning Goal 2

7. _____ One of the investment benefits of owning a home is that it is a way of forced savings.

8. _____ While it is a good investment, home ownership generally provides no tax advantages.

9. _____ The bank is probably the best place to keep savings, because it is a safe investment.

10. _____ Over a long period of time, the stock market has proved to be one of the best investments.

11. _____ Credit card limits prevent people from spending too much with a credit card.

Learning Goal 3

12. _____ Other than life insurance, you should also carry health, disability, and auto insurance policies.

13. _____ The reason to carry life insurance is for protection from the risks of loss of income.

Learning Goal 4

14. _____ One of the benefits of a 401(k) plan is that employers often match part of your deposit.

15. _____ A tax deferred investment means that taxes on your money are deferred until you can afford to pay them.

16. _____ One step in estate planning is to prepare a will.

You Can Find It On The Net

There are two things a college student would like to have more of: Time and Money! Well, we all have the same amount of time, but we vary in how much money we have. All of us can find ways to use and spend our money more effectively.

To learn more about this, go to the site **http://financialplan.about.com** . Using the search function, search the site for "budgets for college students". You should come up with a budget worksheet for college students. This budget worksheet can be printed out and completed. Did you find any surprises?

To get further advice from this site, click on the "Money by Stage or Life age" link, and then on whichever age grouping applies to you. What advice did you find? How many of this site's suggestions are you already following?

ANSWERS

LEARNING THE LANGUAGE

1. Term insurance	6. Whole life insurance	11. Disability insurance
2. Individual Retirement Account (IRA)	7. Contrarian approach	12. Executor
3. Annuity	8. Will	13. Roth IRA
4. Social Security	9. 401(k) plan	14. Tax deferred contributions
5. Variable life insurance	10. Umbrella policy	

ASSESSMENT CHECK

Learning Goal 1
The Need for Personal Financial Planning

1. The lifetime of a full time worker with a bachelor's degree earns 62% more than an individual with a high-school diploma.

2. Six steps you can take to get control of your finances are:
   a. Take an inventory of your financial assets
   b. Keep track of all your expenses
   c. Prepare a budget
   d. Pay off your debts
   e. Start a savings plan
   f. If you have to borrow money, only borrow it to buy assets that have the potential to increase in value.

3. The process for developing a personal balance sheet begins with the fundamental accounting equation – assets = liabilities + owner's equity. This process starts with listing your assets, such things as a TV, DVD, computer, and so on. Your assets are evaluated on their current value, not the purchase price. If you have debts list them. Subtract debts from your assets to get your net worth.

4. In developing a personal income statement, begin with revenue, which is everything you take in from your job, investments and so on. You subtract all your costs and expenses to get net income or profit.

5. The best way to keep track of expenses is to carry a notepad with you wherever you go and record what you spend as you go through the day. At the end of the week, record your journal entries into a record book. Develop certain categories, or accounts, to make the task easier and more informative. Be sure to keep a *detailed* record.

6. Items that are important to include in a household budget are:
   a. mortgage or rent
   b. utilities
   c. food
   d. clothing
   e. vehicles
   f. furniture
   g. life insurance
   h. car insurance
   i. medical care

7. Running a household takes the same careful record keeping, the same budgeting process and forecasting, the same control procedures and the same need to periodically borrow funds to run a household's finances as it does to run a small business.

8. The first thing to do with the money remaining after you pay your monthly expenses is to pay off your debts.

   This is true because it is better to pay off a debt that costs 16 percent than to put the money in a bank account that earns a very low rate of interest.

9. A good way to plan for large purchases such as a car is to save some money each month in a separate account. Then when it comes time to make the purchase, you'll be able to make a significant down payment so that you can reduce finance charges.

10. The best way to save money is to pay yourself first. That is, take your paycheck, take out money for savings, and then plan what to do with the rest.

11. You should only borrow money to buy assets that have the potential to increase in value or generate income, or to cover the most unexpected expenses.

Learning Goal 2
Building Your Financial Base

12. To accumulate capital, you have to live frugally and earn more than you spend. The necessary lifestyle is one of sacrifice, not luxury.

13. The investment benefits of buying a home include:
    a. A home is an investment you can live in
    b. Payments are relatively fixed, and as your income rises, payments get easier to make
    c. It is a good way to force yourself to save

14. Interest on mortgage payments and real estate taxes are tax deductible. During the first few years, almost all the mortgage payments go for interest on the loan so almost all the early payments are tax deductible.

15. The key element to getting the optimum return on a home is a good location. A home in the "best part of town", near schools, shopping and work is usually a sound financial investment.

16. One of the worst places for young people to keep long-term investments is in a bank or savings and loan. This is because interest paid on savings accounts is relatively low compared to other investment choices, such as the stock market.

17. One of the best places to invest over time has been the stock market. The stock market has historically paid a higher rate of return than other investment choices.

18. The best time to buy stocks is when stock prices are low. This is called a contrarian approach.

19. If you finance a large purchase with a credit card, you may end up spending more than if you pay with cash, because of the finance charges on a credit card.

20. Three reasons why credit cards are an important element in a personal financial system are:
   a. Credit cards are needed as a form of identification
   b. They are a way to keep track of purchases
   c. Credit cards are convenient

21. If you use a credit card, you should pay the balance in full during the period when no interest is charged. Not having to pay 14 percent interest is as good as earning 14 percent tax-free.

22. The danger of a credit card is that too often, consumers are tempted to make purchases they would not make if they had to pay cash or write a check, and pile up debt as a result.

Learning Goal 3
Protecting Your Financial Base: Buying Insurance

23. A couple or business should buy life insurance to provide protection from risks of a sudden drop in income from the loss of a spouse or business partner.

24. Newsweek magazine suggests that a family should have 7 times the family income plus $100,000 for college.

25. Multiyear level-premium insurance is a term insurance policy that guarantees you'll pay the same premium for the life of the policy.

26. With whole life insurance some part of the money you pay for the insurance goes toward pure insurance and another part goes toward savings, so you are buying both insurance and a savings plan. A universal life policy is a form of whole life insurance that lets you choose how much of your payment should go to insurance and how much to investments.

27. An annuity is a contract to make payments to a person for life or for a fixed period. A fixed annuity is an investment that pays the policy holder a specified interest rate. A variable annuity provides investment choices identical to mutual funds.

28. Hospital costs are too high to risk financial ruin by going uninsured. It is a good idea to supplement health insurance policies with disability insurance that pays part of the cost of a long-term sickness or an accident. Your chances of becoming disabled at an early age are much higher than your chances of dying from an accident.

29. Guaranteed replacement cost means that the insurance company will give you whatever it costs to buy all of the items you have insured, rather than the depreciated cost of the items.

30. A rider on an insurance policy will cover expensive items that may not be covered under a regular homeowners or renter's policy.

Planning Your Retirement

31. The problems surrounding the Social Security system stem from the fact that the number of workers paying into social security is declining, but the number of people retiring and living longer is increasing dramatically. The result is likely to be serious cuts in benefits, a much later retirement age, reduced cost of living adjustments and/or much higher social security taxes. Young people will not be able to count on Social Security to provide them with enough money to retire on.

32. A traditional IRA is a good deal for people who qualify because the invested money isn't taxed when the money is invested. That means fast and good returns.

33. The earlier you start saving the better because your money has a chance to double and double again. For example if you save $4000 a year for 35 years in an IRA and earn 11 percent a year, you will accumulate savings of more than $1.5 million.

34. People who invest in a Roth IRA don't get up-front deductions on their taxes like they would with a traditional IRA, but earnings grow tax free and are tax free when they are withdrawn.

    So, traditional IRAs offer tax savings when they are deposited and Roth IRAs offer tax savings when they are withdrawn. The best type of IRA for younger people is the Roth IRA.

35. A key point to remember with IRAs is that you can't take the money out of either type of IRA until you are 59 ½ years old without paying a 10 percent penalty and paying taxes on the income.

36. Some investment choices for IRAs include a local bank, savings and loan or credit union. Insurance companies also offer IRAs. You can also put funds into stocks, bonds, mutual funds, or precious metals. You can switch from fund to fund or from investment to investment with your IRA funds.

37. A simple IRA can be offered by companies with fewer than 100 employees. Employees of these companies can contribute up to $10,000 of their income annually compared with the $4,000-$5,000 limit of regular IRAs. This makes for a good employee benefit for smaller companies.

38. The benefits of 401(k) plans are
    a. The money you put in reduces your present taxable income
    b. Tax is deferred on the earnings
    c. Employers often match part of your deposit

39. With a 401(k) plan you can usually select how the money in the plan is invested: stocks, bonds, and in some cases real estate. The money invested in a 401k should be diversified, and not put into only one company.

40. A Keogh plan is for small business people who don't have the benefit of a corporate retirement system. This can be an alternative for doctors, lawyers, real estate agents, artists, writers and other self-employed people.

41. The advantage of Keogh plans is that participants can invest up to $40,000 per year.

42. A Keogh plan is like an IRA because funds aren't taxed until they are withdrawn, nor are the returns they earn. As with an IRA account, there is a 10 percent penalty for early withdrawal. Also, funds may be withdrawn in a lump sum or spread out over the years like an IRA.

43. A financial planner is an individual who assists in developing a comprehensive program that covers investments, taxes, insurance, and other financial matters. A CFP is a certified financial planner. This person will have completed a curriculum on 106 financial topics and a 10-hour exam.

44. A financial supermarket provides a wide variety of financial services ranging from banking services to mutual funds, insurance, tax assistance, stocks, bonds, and real estate.

45. Most financial planners begin with life insurance, and explore health and disability insurance. Financial planning covers all aspects of investing all the way to retirement and death. A financial planner can steer you into the proper mix of IRA investments, stocks, bonds, precious metals, real estate and so on.

46. The steps involved in estate planning include:
   a. Select a guardian for your minor children
   b. Prepare a will
   c. Prepare a durable power of attorney

47. A durable power of attorney gives an individual you name the power to take over your finances if you become incapacitated. A similar document for health care delegates power to a person named to make health decisions for you if you are unable to make such decisions yourself.

CRITICAL THINKING EXERCISES

Learning Goal 1

1. History has shown that an investment in education has paid off regardless of the state of the economy. We have studied in previous chapters about the need for constant updating. This includes education! Statistics show that a person with an undergraduate degree earns about twice as much as someone with only a high school diploma.

2. Obviously, everyone will have different answers. This is primarily to get you started on the road to good personal financial planning. It is important to take a look at how you spend your money, what areas need to be curtailed, what kinds of assets you have been able to accumulate, whether or not you are spending less than you earn, your debts and credit card bills, and so on.

Learning Goal 2

3.   A. This is another section where each individual will have varied answers. Some suggestions may include: living at home while going to school, buying used books, keep clothing allowances to a minimum, walking or riding a bike when you can, eating at home, or if you are in a house or apartment, making meals at home. For students returning to school after being out for a while, the methods of accumulating capital will be different - and you may already have discovered ways of your own!

          B. Prices in different parts of the country vary widely. Some areas that have been hit by unemployment may have seen a decline in the price of homes. Other areas may have seen above average increases.

          C. Using the rule of 72 you can calculate how long it will take for the value of any asset to double. In this case, the rate of inflation is 3 percent. 72 divided by 3 = 24. So the value of a $110,000 house will double to $220,000 in 24 years. If you have a 30-year mortgage, your house will be almost paid off, and you will have a $220,000 asset. (If you put money in a savings account in a bank and earn 3% interest, it will take 24 years for the savings to double, if you don't make any additional deposits. That's how the rule of 72 works.)

          D. In this example, with a house payment of $1200, and a 28% tax bracket, you can calculate your real cost by multiplying $1200 x .28, which equals $336. Subtract $336 from $1200 and your real cost will be $864 with an interest deduction.

4.   Your answers will vary. If you have no credit cards yet, use this information to make good decisions about whether to apply for a credit card, and how to use it.

Learning Goal 3

5.   Your answers to this exercise will be determined by what your situation is. If you are married and have children your insurance needs will be different from someone who is younger and/or unmarried.

Learning Goal 4

6.   A. An IRA is a good deal for a young investor, because the invested money is not taxed. When you put money into an IRA you save in taxes. If you continue to invest in an IRA, you will have a significant amount of money by the time you retire. The earlier you start, the better. For example if you start putting $2,000 a year in an IRA between the ages of 23-28 at 12% interest, you would have *invested* only $12,000, but even if you never add another penny by the time you are 65 you will have almost $900,000, because of compounded interest. If you continued nonstop from age 23 until age 65, you would have almost $2 million.

          B. 72 divided by 10 = 7.2 years. Your $1,000 would double to $2,000 in 7.2 years.

          C. If your money doubles every 7.2 years, in approximately 15 years your money will have doubled twice, to $4,000.

7.   The money invested in an IRA is not taxed. Earnings are not taxed until you take them
out when you retire, presumably when you are at a lower tax rate. The money cannot be
taken out until the age of 59 1/2 without paying a penalty. An IRA is for workers to use
as a supplement to a company-sponsored retirement plan and Social Security. It is not
connected with your employer. A 401(K) plan is offered by employers, who will often
match your contribution. Further, you can borrow the funds from a 401(K), whereas that
isn't an option in an IRA.

The Keogh plan is for small business people who do not have the benefit of a corporate
retirement system, whereas the 401(K) is a company sponsored program. The benefit
over an IRA is that the maximum amount that can be invested is much greater.

A Keogh is like an IRA and the 401(K) in that the funds are not taxed, nor are the
earnings, and there is a penalty for early withdrawal. All these plans are designed to
protect people from the decline in the value of the Social Security system.

PRACTICE TEST

MULTIPLE CHOICE   **True-False**

LG 1   # 1-6   LG 1   #1-6
LG 2   # 7-12   LG 2   # 7-11
LG 3   # 13-14   LG 3   # 12-13
LG 4   # 15-29   LG 4   #14-16

1. c   11. b   1. T   9. F
2. a   12. d   2. T   10. T
3. d   13. b   3. T   11. F
4. d   14. c   4. F   12. T
5. c   15. d   5. T   13. T
6. d   16. b   6. F   14. T
7. b   17. d   7. T   15. F
8. a   18. b   8. F   16. T
9. b   19. a
10. a   20. c